A.K.A. Michael

The Story Behind the Headlines

By Michael Garramone

For more information about Michael Garramone
akamichael.com
akamichaelbook@outlook.com

Acknowledgements

To my mother, Alma, for birthing me, and forcing me to grow up overnight. I'll always love you, in my own odd way.

To Mary Schirmer, for helping me to edit my manuscript/montage. Mjschirmer@yahoo.com

Contents

Queens Woman Linked to Thefts

By JOSEPH B. TREASTER

A 42-year-old woman who had been released from Creedmoor State Hospital in 1977, two years after being acquitted by reason of insanity of murdering her husband, was accused yesterday of possession of goods that the police said a gang of youths had taken in burglaries in Manhattan, Queens and Long Island.

The police said the woman, identified as Alma Garramone of 34-20 150th Street, Flushing, Queens, had been arrested at her home, along with her 17-year-old son Michael. Both were charged with possession of stolen property. She was being held in $50,000 bond.

Among the stolen goods, the police said, were 20 Lucite cases filled with models of the sets of Broadway plays that had been kept in storage by the Museum of the City of New York, thousands of dollars' worth of mechanics' tools, cases of liquor, television sets and a number of uniforms of a military academy.

The police said they believed that as many as half a dozen youths had worked together in the burglaries.

A spokesman for Thomas J. Santucci, the Queens District Attorney, said their procedure was to steal a van, drive around until they found a likely burglary target, empty the goods from the home or warehouse into the van and drive back to Mrs. Garramone's home.

Detective Paul Lizio said it was not clear how Mrs. Garramone may have been involved in the robberies, beyond receiving some of the stolen property. He estimated that the youths had carried out at least 75 burglaries in the last six months. Others said that some of the property recovered in Mrs. Garramone's home had been missing for a year.

A spokesman for the State Office of Mental Health said that in her two years at Creedmoor, Mrs. Garramone had been a "model patient." In 1977, he said, she was found by several review groups at the hospital to be "no longer a danger to herself or others." A six-member Civil Court jury agreed, the spokesman said, and Mrs. Garramone was released.

The New York Times

Published: March 12, 1980

Copyright © The New York Times

vii

PROLOGUE

After school one day, I decided to stop at Marcus Capeeto's house on the way home to see if he was there. Marcus and I had gone to school when we were younger but now I was going to private school and I was in the sixth grade. It was 1975. A couple of the other kids in the neighborhood thought he was a little crazy. He wasn't a little crazy, he was nuts, but he was still my best friend. When I got there I noticed him working on his bike in his driveway.

"Hey, Marcus."
"Hey, Mike."
"What's up? What are you doing?"
"I had to fix my bike. Why? What's up?"
"Nothing. You want to go for a ride to Bowne Park or something?"
"Yeah. All right."
"Okay, so ride me over to my house so I can change my clothes. Then we'll go."

After we got to my house and walked into the kitchen, Marcus asked me if I had a soda.
"Yeah, there's probably something in the fridge."

Marcus walked over to the refrigerator stopped and said, "Holy shit... what's that?"
"What?"
"That!" he said as he pointed up at the refrigerator.

I looked on top of the fridge and saw a handgun. I wasn't really surprised to see a handgun in my house because I knew my parents owned one or two for the stores, but I had never seen either of them leave one out like this.

"Shit, I guess one of my parents left it out," I said.
"Wow," Marcus exclaimed. "Let me look at it."

Before Marcus would think of grabbing it, I shoved a chair over and picked it up. The first thing I noticed was that it was loaded because it was a revolver. After I got off the chair, Marcus kept insisting for me to let him see it.

"If I let you see it, you've got to be real careful with it. Ya' know, we could kill each other with this thing."

"I know, Mike. I won't fuck around. I've just never held a handgun before."

I let him hold it but even as I handed it to him, I wondered a little bit about his "crazy" spells.

"Wow, cool!" he said as he pointed it towards the doorway.

After that we both fooled around with it for a few minutes, and then I put it in the dining room. When my mother got home a little while later, I told her what we had found in the house.

"Where was it?" she said.
"On top of the refrigerator," Marcus answered.
"How did it get here?"
"I don't know." I answered.
"Well where is it now?"
"It's in the dining room, I put it there after Marcus and I checked it out."
"Son of a bitch," she said.

Obviously she was mad, but luckily it wasn't with me, I thought. After Marcus left that night, I did my homework, watched some TV, and then went to bed. The next morning my mother woke me up at 5:00.

"Why are you waking me up so early? It's still dark out. I've got school today. I can't go to the country."
"I know. We're not going to the country. We're going over to the store to talk to your father."
"What the hell do I have to talk to him for?"
"You don't. You just have to come with me to talk to him, that's all."

Man, I knew I shouldn't have done that thing with the mortgage money. Now I've got to be the middle man every time my mother needs money from my father. Besides that, why does my mother have to ask my father for money? He should just give it to her. She's worked just as hard as my father has over the years to buy the luncheonette.

We got there at about 5:30 and sat in the car waiting for my father. Luckily my mother had taken some pillows and a blanket for me, so I could go back to sleep. After a little while I heard my mother start up the car, so I asked her what was going on. "Nothing. We're leaving. Your father had his employee open the store."

When we got home, I went back to bed for a little while. Then I woke up, ate some breakfast, and went to school.

The next morning we went through the same routine, but my father didn't show up to open that morning either. During the ride back home, I wondered why my mother couldn't call my father on the phone for money, but I guess she had her reasons. After we got home and I had a little more sleep then I got up, ate breakfast, and went to school.

The next morning my mother really had her hands full trying to get me out of bed.

"Come on, Ma. He wasn't there for two days. He's probably not going to be there today either," I reasoned.

"Come on, Michael. You've got to come with me. Don't argue."

I could tell that she was serious, but I still really didn't feel like going, and I actually started to get pissed at my father for making my mother and now me go through this every morning. I obviously had fallen asleep on the ride over there, because the next thing I heard was my mother say, "Come on, Michael, get up. Your father's here."

"I'm too tired, Mom. Let me stay here and sleep."

"All right, go to sleep. I'll be right out."

A minute or two later I heard my mother and father start arguing. Man, why the hell do I have to be here for this? I can't understand why they couldn't argue on the phone or something. I guess because it was something new they had started doing they needed some time to work out the guidelines.

After thinking for a second or two more, I wondered if I should go in and say my peace about the whole situation. Na, I thought. It'll be fine. Besides, Nicky looked like he knew what he was talking about the day he warned me about getting involved. I can go back to sleep anyhow. Just before I dozed off, I heard someone blow off firecrackers, and I thought to myself, That's funny. It's March, it's not even close to the fourth of July.

A few minutes later my mother opened the car door and got in. Good, I thought, now I can go home and get some sleep. After a few minutes I hadn't heard the car start yet, so I opened my eyes and said, "Come on, Ma. Let's go home... I'm tired."

After a few seconds my mother said, "Michael... get up. Get up, Michael."

I could tell from the tone of her voice that she was serious, so I sat up. My mother turned around in the car seat to face me, and I don't know why but when I first looked into her face it scared me for a second. Then my mother looked into my eyes and said, "Michael... no matter what happens, Mommy loves you okay?"

"What...What are you talking about...? What happened...?"

"Nothing, Michael. Just come here and give me a hug."

As I hugged her, she squeezed me tightly for a few seconds and then started to cry.

"Mom...! What's wrong?!?"

"Nothing, Michael. Nothing." Then she started the car, and we drove off.

I asked her one more time during the ride home if everything was all right and she gave me the same answer, being that my mother had never lied to me before, I figured everything was okay. I lay back down, even though something didn't seem right. I woke up a little while later and asked my mother if we were home yet.

"No, Michael, we're not home yet."
"Well, ya' know, I've got school today."
"Don't worry, Michael. You might not have to go to school today."

Cool! I thought as I shut up quickly and went back to sleep.

When we got home, my mother told me to go back to bed.

"Why should I? I'm only going to get a little sleep."
"Don't worry. I'll let you sleep longer."
"Yeah, but then I'll be late."
"I'll give you a note. Now go to bed."

About an hour later my mother woke me up, made me breakfast, and then sent me to school with my note.

At the end of the day on the way home, Neil asked me if I wanted to do my homework at his house. I thought about it for a second or two, and then I decided to go home. As I walked up to the corner of my block, I saw three cop cars and two unfamiliar cars parked on my lawn. I walked over to a parked car across the street and sat on the hood, wondering why there were cop cars at my house.

I wondered if my mother had a problem with one of the boarders at my house. Or maybe they were there because of this morning with my father. Na, stop dreaming. Nothing happened last night.

Instead of going inside, I decided to wait and see what happened from outside for now. Because there were never any police cars in my neighborhood, a big crowd had gathered. They all stared towards my house. A whole range of thoughts, and emotions ran through my head. Just as I was about to decide whether or not to go inside, they brought my mother out in handcuffs.

They put my mother into the cop car, and I watched them drive down my street. I sat out there with them trying to overhear any type of information I could, and then I heard Debbie, Marcus's mother say, "Oh, my God, Michael. Come here," as she started walking towards me.

"Debbie... what's going on at my house?"
"Oh nothing. Nothing."
"Should I go over there?"
"Well, no. Let's go to my house, and we'll call from there, okay?" she said.

After we got there, Debbie got me some cookies and milk and sat me down with some cartoons on TV. Debbie walked back into the room a little while later and told me to wait for my Aunt Marie to come over.

I sat at Marcus's house for about an hour and figured that something had to be wrong. After a while, I decided to lie down to rest and prepare myself for the blow that seemed to be coming. When my Aunt Marie got there, she woke me up and took me over to my house. We got inside, and she told Ronnie and Russell, my cousins, that they could go out and play. I sat there with Marie for about an hour, and she wouldn't or couldn't tell me what had happened. Then finally my cousin Ronnie burst through the door yelling, "Look! Look! It's in the newspaper! 'Wife shoots and kills husband!' "

Well... I guess those weren't firecrackers last night, I thought.

"Ronnie, you little bastard. Get out of here with that newspaper," my aunt screamed.

I jumped up and grabbed the newspaper from Ronnie. There it was plain as day: my mother's name, my father's name, my name, and my address.
"I guess I'm fucked..." I said.
"Oh, my God, Michael. I didn't know how to tell you. Ronnie, get outside," Marie yelled.

Tears were running down Marie's cheeks as she held out her arms for me to hug her. I hugged Marie for her sake; I didn't need to be consoled at that moment while my soul was tearing in half. It was too painful for me right then to comprehend. I was numb. Marie was sitting down, and I held her as she sobbed for herself, my father, her sister and me.

"There, there, Marie... it'll be all right. It'll be okay," I told her as I rubbed her back.
"?!...Wait a minute... I'm supposed to be consoling you, Michael."
"Don't worry, Marie. I'm fine... except for a splitting headache."
"Oh, Michael, I'm so sorry," she said.
"For what, Marie? It wasn't your fault. But now it's over... it's done... there's no changing it."
"I can't believe you're taking it this way, Michael. You do realize what happened, don't you?"
"Yeah... I realize."

Later that night there was some talk about where I was going to sleep.

"Marie, listen. I'm sleeping in my house in my bed tonight. Now if George wants to beat the shit out of me like I've seen him beat the shit out of Ronnie and Russell over the years that's fine. But he better kill me tonight because I'm not going anywhere."

I could see that George wanted to slap me, but he was holding back his temper. This one time I wish he would have, because I would have definitely ended Ronnie and Russell's misery with him on this night somehow.

That night I cried for an hour then I forced myself to cry for another half hour. After that, I swore I would never cry about anything, because nothing could ever make me this sad, or hurt this bad. Then I got pissed. I got pissed at myself for not going into the store with my mother. I got pissed at the world for letting everybody own a gun, and finally I got pissed at God.

So what's the deal, God? I was a bad kid because I didn't go to church last Sunday? I go to Catholic school. I go to confession, I made my communion. What the fuck for? What the fuck could I have possibly done in my twelve years on this Earth that was so bad that I should deserve this fate? Fine, I thought, you know what? Fuck this. Nothing is the truth any more, nothing is believable, and nothing lasts forever from here on in. I'll have to jot this one down as a major fucking lesson, too. But that's it. I don't give a fuck about rules, fuck regulations, fuck conversations, fuck me, and fuck you, God. Fuck everything. I was blowing circuits left and right. I blew circuits I didn't even know I had.

After I got over that trip, I started to think about what was going to happen to my own little world.

Oh shit, Mike. Where the fuck are you going to live? What are you going to do with yourself? How are you going to eat? You didn't even eat dinner tonight. What about tomorrow? What's going to happen to the house? Fuck it, I'll quit school and get a job. Oh, shit, what about the business?!? I'll go to work there. I can run that place. I've done it before. We can't lose the business. I know where to get the supplies for the store. I'll use my mother's car. I've been driving for years now with her.

Wait a minute- I wonder where my father's car is. I saw it parked in front of the luncheonette last night. Maybe I can go to the police department and get the keys to it. Then I'll sneak back and drive it home. Shit, what about the keys to the store? I wonder if it's locked up. What if people are walking out with everything?? No, wait, Mike, the cops must've locked it up. They probably found my father's keys. Okay... now as far as cooking and selling shit in there, I've got that covered. The newspaper guys get paid on Sundays. The food, ice cream and soda guys get paid at the end of each month for last month's load. Fuck, it's the end of the month already. Okay... I've got about two hundred bucks in the bank. I know my mother bought me some U.S. saving bonds. Maybe I can sell them or sell some stuff around the house. Yeah, I'll sell the fucking lawn mower I hate cutting the grass anyhow. If that doesn't add up, I'll save the newspaper article from tonight and ask the bill collectors to cut me a break for a month or two. Then I've got the rent, electric, and garbage pick-up to worry about soon. Okay, I know that the electric company won't shut off the electric for a little while. That leaves the rent and the garbage; well, these guys have got to cut me some slack also. Shit, I can probably make most of this money in two weeks. I've gone in there at 6:00 in the morning, and the place is packed with all the people catching the train to Manhattan. Man, I'm bad in the mornings. Fuck it. I'll have to sleep there. Maybe I won't open on Sundays for a while after I make a little money. The house is making money with the boarders my mother's renting too. Maybe, I could use some of that money. But then I've got to pay the mortgage, and bills here. Well, wait a minute... my grandfather can help me with some bill's, he's got some money, but what if he can't live here anymore...fuck...

I juggled all of these thoughts in my mind until it short-circuited again and it shut me down, and I fell asleep.

"Michael... no matter what happens, mommy loves you okay."

These words are branded into my soul forever, and they were the epitaph for my childhood... my innocence... and my wonderful, bright eyed point of view about life. I didn't know it then, but something deep inside me died with my father that morning, like a candle, snuffed out. Being that I didn't have any siblings, I suddenly felt very alone, and detached from the outside world, and nobody, could console this pain. Trial by fire, my rite to manhood.

So how did this happen... it's the same question I asked myself. We were a good, hard-working family, was it fate... my destiny written in some ancient scrolls somewhere, or just a tragic mistake that never should have happened.

My father's death was just the beginning of the events in my life, unbeknownst to me. They just kept coming in like waves thrashing me about. At times I thought I would surely drown, but I didn't, I persevered, and I lived through them all. Occasionally I'll see an old friend and he'll look at me, shake his head and say "Mike... you've been through it all man" It makes the badge I wear on my chest shine a little brighter, but sometimes, I'll ask myself why I was so lucky.

At times I'll look at all of the tragic events that took place in my life after my father's death. My life would be on an unfamiliar road, and changed forever each time, and I've wondered whom I would have become if I would have been able to stay on that temporary road for long. I've come to assume that life just has a way of smacking you upside your head when you're not looking, the trick is learning when to duck.

Maybe my story will allow you to see the mistakes I made in my life so you can avoid them, maybe some of you will feel that your life is not so bad after all. Maybe you'll laugh... maybe you'll cry, or maybe you'll just enjoy my story... well... enjoy.

CHAPTER 1

BRIGHT EYED AND BUSHY TAILED

The first memories I have about myself are of being 5 years old, in 1968. Man, I was handsome and strong, I thought; just look at these muscles. I lived in Astoria, Queens, N.Y., with my grandfather, Baisilo Giannini, and my parents, John and Alma Garramone. We lived in a one-bedroom apartment. My grandfather, or Basil as my mother would call her father, would always tell me never to forget that I was second generation Italian. After a little talk about my moral character, like how smart I was, he'd joke with me and say in his Italian accent, "Buta you face, it'sa looka like a little monkey."

My grandfather would always babysit me while my parents were out working, they both had two jobs because they wanted to get a piece of the better life. As for me, I thought life was pretty good. The only thing I thought might be better was if my parents were around more often instead of getting a piece of that better life. But being with my grandfather had its advantages. My grandfather let me get away with more things.

By the time I was 6 my grandfather and I would talk for hours about stories from when he was in Italy. He explained to me that he had started to work for a restaurant owner when he was 13 part-time. By the time he was 17 the owner, who had no heirs, had died and left both restaurants to my grandfather.

"Really, Grandpa? If you had two restaurants, then why did you leave?"
"Why!?! Becausa my brother, he'sa get killed ina war and then one week'a later they tell'a me I gotta go to war!" He'd say, as he'd slap his knee.
"So what did you do, Grandpa?" I asked.
"So what I do!?! I jumpa ona boat and come over here to America."

He went on to tell me how he started to work in construction for Barnaby Construction Company. Two of the proudest jobs he did with them were working on Astoria Pool and the biggest building in the world, the Empire State Building.

"And'a you know who'sa the last concrete man to get laid off!?" he'd say proudly.
"No... who, Grandpa?"
"Me! Baisilo Giannini, I'ma do the whole 72nd floor by myselfa. Buta you no gonna do

1

construction. You gonna be a doctore' or a lawyer."

"Really, Grandpa, I can be a doctor?"

"Sure... you can'a be anything you wanna, Michael."

But by the time he'd try to teach me to speak Italian, I'd insist that I had to watch cartoons.

I really didn't remember my father's parents too much because they lived in New Jersey, and my parents never seemed to have the time to drive out to their house. They were too busy. For a little while, my cousin Dino came to live with us, he was my first cousin. It was nice to have him there because I had no brothers or sisters.

Dino was about 6 month's older than me, but I was a little bigger than him. The nice thing about him living with me was having a playmate around all the time, day and night. One of the things we loved to do was to take our big metal Tonka trucks downstairs to play in the dirt.

In a neighborhood with six-story buildings, the only piece of dirt available was a missing block of sidewalk that had a four-inch wide tree in the middle of it. But we were kids, and kids adapt. To us it was as big as a city park. Once we got past the scheduling of whose turn it was to kick, or pick up the shit the city dogs had left on our dirt since the last time, we were fine. Before long, Dino and I were inseparable. Then for some reason, Dino left before Christmas, and I felt kinda bad opening presents without him, especially since I got an electric train set.

The best part about that Christmas, though, was when my father got an idea to lower the dead Christmas tree out of our fifth floor apartment on a rope. The fun part was when it crashed through someone's window, and my father looked back inside wide-eyed and said, "Oh, shit!"

I thought it was funny and started laughing until my mother looked at me and said, "Oh yeah, it's real funny, especially since I told your father not to do it!"Which made me quiet.

"Now go downstairs and see if everything is all right, John," my mother said to my father.

When my father came back up a few minutes later, he was smiling.

"What are you smiling about?" my mother said.

"Well, I went downstairs and nobody was there; so I asked a neighbor if they knew the people who lived there, and they told me that the people had gone away."

"So what's so funny?" my mother asked.

"Can you imagine this poor bastard coming home and seeing a Christmas tree crashed through his apartment window? He's gonna think an elf was pissed at him or something."

I felt like busting out with laughter, but I decided to try to hold it in. I did this long enough until I saw my mother smile, and then we all busted out with laughter. After we all calmed down, my father called the super of the building and then went to fix the window with him.

A few days after that, even though my mother told me to wait for my father to come home, I decided to set up my electric trains. I really loved my train set, and I could watch them for hours. I got it all pieced together, but after I plugged it in, it still didn't work, so I checked the entire track set-up. The only possible explanation was that whatever came out of the wall wasn't working, so I stuck my finger in the wall socket and felt it. "Zaaaaaap!" My fingertip was throbbing, and my head felt like someone had slapped it really hard. I sat there and experienced my first migraine headache from the pain, and then screamed out my disapproval.

"What's the matter, Michael? Come in here, and let mommy see," my mother said.

Boy, I thought, if she can kiss this and make it go away she must really be magic. I walked inside and held up my finger while I was crying.

"But there's nothing there, Michael."
"Ahh, he'sa tired," my grandfather said.

Tired...! I've never been more awake in my life, I thought.

"Here, let me kiss it and put you to bed then," my mother said.

Yeah, if you don't believe that this is serious, than going to sleep doesn't sound like a bad idea right now, I said to myself.

After my mother put me to bed, I wondered how something I liked so much could hurt me so bad.

The only other strong memory I have of living in Astoria before we moved was the time my neighbor's dog got a hold of my arm and started to shake me around like a rag doll. These neighbors were friends of ours and, after taking a nap, I woke up and didn't see my mother around. I figured that she must be next door.

I walked into their apartment, and after the door closed behind me, I started to call out for my mother. The only thing I heard was a low growl in response. The neighbor's apartment was set up differently than mine. Luckily for me they had two doors that led into their kitchen, one through the hallway, and one through the living room. I ran in circles through those doors screaming with the dog chasing me until I was dizzy, but I dare not stop.

Their dog was the biggest, meanest, German shepherd I had ever seen. When the neighbors took him for a walk they used to have to put a muzzle on him. He knocked me down and tried to bite me even with his muzzle on one time. Now I had walked right into the lion's den. I didn't know where my mother was, but after she heard my screams, I heard her yelling out in the hallway. As I was running in circles I screamed, "In here! In here!"

To which my mother replied, "Where?!?"

I decided to try to make a grab for the door handle and looked over my shoulder to see him come flying around the corner for the umpteenth time with a dizzy look on his face. He tackled me into the front door, and managed to grab my arm in his mouth. After hearing the noise of me being tackled my mother realized where I was, but now she couldn't get the door open because the dog, and I, were dancing behind it.

My mother forced her way into their apartment, grabbed a big metal frying pan, and cracked it over the dog's head several time's until he let go. By then it didn't matter to me because I had "decided" to pass out.

I awoke in time to see a doctor try to cauterize my arm. It's a process where they use electricity to burn your wound closed. It's a very "shocking" experience for a six-year-old, pun intended. Needless to say, I volunteered my little kid "freaking" dance, but I did go through the whole procedure very un-optimistic about the outcome, although it did look a lot better when he was done. Once it healed I could only see where his canine teeth had bit me.

A couple of weeks after that, my mother came home one day and told me that we were going to move into a nice big house we bought. Not wanting to move from our house, I said, "Why? We live in a nice house now."
"No, Michael, this is a little house. We're going to move into a big house with a big yard."
"Really...? A big yard?"
"Yes, a real big yard where you can play."
"Well, I'd like to take a look at the yard then, I guess."

A few days later, my mother and I went to Flushing to look at our new house.

"Well, Michael, come out of the car and take a look at this place."

It was strange. I had never thought I would or could live in anything so huge in my life. The house was actually three stories tall. When we went inside and walked around for a minute or two, I thought for sure we would get lost if we went any farther. After we walked through the basement and all eleven rooms, I told my mother that we didn't have enough people in our family to live in all these rooms. She explained to me that I shouldn't worry about it too much, because a lot of people lived this way. The outside was just as mind-boggling as the inside. We walked around the front yard and into the backyard. When we got back there, I saw a little house there.

"Wow, what's that?" I asked.
"It's a garage, Michael."
"Is it ours too?" I asked.
"Yes, it goes with the house," she said.
"Cool! I want to live in there by myself."
"Well, we'll talk about it once we move in," my mother assured.
"What about the grass? Can I play on it?" I asked.
"Yes, Michael. This is going to be our house. You can play anywhere you want to."
"Even the front yard?"
"Yes, Michael, anywhere in the yard you want to."

My mother and I sat on the grass together, and we started talking about how nice it would be to live there. I couldn't put my finger on it, but even though it seemed like a good idea, something about this house scared me deep inside. I told my mother how I felt, and she just shrugged it off and reassured me that everything would be fine.

The next couple of days we shuttled between Astoria and Flushing. My father and some friends helped us move on a hot summer day in 1969. By the time we got all of our belongings there, they barely filled three rooms of our new home. We set up a bedroom in the living room for the first week or so until my mother decided who would get which room. The one thing I really liked about the living room was that we could make a fire in our new fireplace. There wasn't a day that went by that I didn't ask my mother if I could put the fireplace to good use, but she would tell me that we didn't need to light a fire because it was still warm out, as if I cared about the weather.

My grandfather also moved in with us, but Dino still wasn't back. I asked my mother why he wasn't with us anymore, and she told me that he went home to live with his mother again. It's too bad, because I know he would have enjoyed it there. After we got a little more settled, my mother asked me which room I thought I would like, so I told her I still wanted to live in the garage. She looked at me like I was nuts and said "You can't live in the garage."

"Well, why not? It doesn't seem like anyone else wants to live in there."
"Well, there's no bathroom out there."
"Well... I could come inside when I have to go to the bathroom," I reasoned.
"What about at night when you have to go?"
"I'll come inside then, too," I said.
"Michael, the door will be locked."
"Why, are you going to lock me out? Is it because you don't want me to live out back?" I asked.
"No, it's not to lock you out. It's to lock out any burglars," she explained.
"Why? Do we have burglars here? We didn't have any back home."
"Yes, we did," she said.
"We did?"
"Well... no, we didn't. I mean yes, we did. What I mean is.... Listen, I bought this house because of all the rooms it has. Now there are six bedrooms inside, so pick one because you are not living in the garage."

I thought I put up a good fight, but you know how stubborn mothers can get.

I still thought the upstairs was a little spooky, so I decided to take a small room off the kitchen next to the back porch which was a corner room. It wasn't really a bedroom it was more of a pantry, or a breakfast room, but it was pretty large. I figured it was the best location because I had my own door to the back yard, and I could make a quick exit just in case there was a boogieman living in our house. Another door led into the kitchen, where there was a bathroom and a side door to the driveway. There were two doors that went into the dining room, one of them was a swinging door, which I thought was odd.

Before I moved in, my mother decided that we should paint my room. I wanted to paint it purple, but my mother was being stubborn again, so we stuck with white. I thought it was a cool idea because I never painted a room before. My job as it turned out was to paint from the floor as high as I could reach, but as hard as I tried I couldn't get my mother to let me paint from the ladder. After a couple of hours, my job was done, so I asked my mother if I could paint my fire engine with some red paint that I found in the garage.

"Well, I don't think you could do any harm, and it'll keep you busy, so let's go. I'll open the can for you."

She set me up with the can of red paint and a brush. My fire engine was a metal one that I could sit in and pedal, so it took me a little while to paint it. One thing I did notice was this paint smelled different than the other paint we were using, but I figured it smelled that way because it was old and spoiled.

When I got done with my fire engine, I looked into the can and saw that I had a bunch of paint left, so I looked around and decided that my wooden sandbox would look nice if it was red. After I painted that and a bunch of sand, I figured that now the tree next to my sandbox would have to be red also. While I was painting the tree, I started to feel a little dizzy, but I thought nothing of it as I started on the fence and garage. After I painted a few strokes on the garage, I realized that I didn't have enough paint for the whole garage, so I figured since I had so much paint on myself anyhow, I would look pretty cool if I was red. I got undressed down to my underwear and used up the rest of the paint. If I had to admit it, I did look pretty good in red.

When I was finished painting myself, I decided to take a little cruise and show myself off. As I started down the driveway, I saw Mrs. Courtard's daughter, Virginia. They were our new neighbors. Mrs. Courtard looked older than my grandfather, who was about seventy, so Virginia had to be about fifty years old.

"Michael... does your mother know that you're red?" she said sweetly.
"Oh, yeah. She told me I could paint," I reassured her.
"Well, it's getting a little late. Why don't we ask her if you should take your little drive now?" she said.

I pedaled over to the side door as Virginia walked over and rang the bell. My mother opened the door and took a look at me. "Michael! What did you do!?"
"Well, I painted... you said I could," I explained.

My mother asked me to stand up so she could take a look at me, and then she said, "Oh, my God, look at you. You're covered in it."

Then my mother thanked Virginia and asked her where she had found me.

"He was just about to make a left turn out of the driveway. You know, Alma, it smells like enamel paint. You're probably going to have to use some turpentine or kerosene to get it off. So if you don't have any, come over because I'm sure we have some. Good luck."

My mother told me to ride around back, and she would meet me there. As I was pedaling towards the back, I heard my mother say, "Oh, my God, wait until your father sees this," which stopped me dead in my tracks. I thought for a moment that maybe I should haul ass out of the driveway, but then realized I had nowhere I could go. Besides, my father is a guy; he'll probably like my paint job anyway.

My mother tried using turpentine, but I yelled like an alley cat and tried to get away because it burned. My mother didn't know what to use, so she called my father who was at the cab company where he worked.

The conversation went something like this, "John, your son painted himself with red enamel paint... No, just about completely. I'm trying to use turpentine, but he keeps yelling that it burns. What else can I try? Huh? Well, yeah... I guess it's kinda funny, but I've got to get this paint off of him. He's covered from head to toe. No, John, I'm not going to take any pictures of him. Besides, if I made this into a funny matter, he might try blue next time. Oh, you still think it's funny, huh? Well, wait until you see what he painted for you. No, you'll probably see when you get home. Just go into the backyard. It'll be waiting for you there... Gas? Are you sure that'll work? All right, if I don't call you back, then that means it worked. Bye."

Well, for the most part the gasoline worked, but my eyebrows and hair were red for a few more days. After my father came home and saw what I had done, he advised me that I had better check with him before I decided to paint anything else around the house, and this is the short version.

My mother had a priest come over to bless the house. I had been to Church before, and the priests were always dressed in white. I was a little leery of him because he was dressed in what looked like a long black dress, and he seemed a little too serious about what he was there for. This didn't seem like it was unfolding the way my mother had explained it to me, he seemed more serious, then friendly. He sat down with my mother and father and explained to them what he would be doing. Then he asked the whole family to follow him through each of the rooms as he went along. He sprinkled a little water in each room, and I thought it was a little odd because I couldn't understand a word he was saying. I asked my mother if she understood what he was saying, and she told me that he was speaking in Latin.

"Latin?" I said, "How are we supposed to understand him if he's speaking in Latin? Why doesn't he speak in English so we can understand him?"

My mother gave me a look and said, "Be quiet... I'll tell you later."

We headed upstairs to the bedrooms after we got done with the first floor. We had to wait for my Grandfather because he couldn't make the stairs so well. After we got done with the three smaller rooms on the second floor, the priest started on the master bedroom. I was pretty bored by then, so I was glad that there were only the two rooms in the attic after this one. The priest started talking his funny Latin again, when all of a sudden, the biggest black raven I had ever seen flew right through the screen window. I got scared for a second and then remembered that I was standing there with a priest. I looked up at him to reassure myself and saw him standing there with his eyes wide open along with his mouth, so I decided to get scared again.

My father started to chase the bird around the bedroom, while my mother shouted, "John, don't touch the bird! Just leave it alone, and open the other window!"

My father looked at my mother as he was trying to catch it and said, "Alma, it's just a bird."

As my mother said, "John, please don't touch the bird" again, my father caught it.

He looked at it and then showed it to my mother. "It's just a bird," He said as he pushed it back out the window and let it go.

My mother looked at the priest who was still standing there with the same look on his face and said, "Father... do you think everything is okay?" The priest said, "I don't know. Nothing like this has ever happened to me before."

"Do you want to bless this room again?" my mother asked.
"No, I'm going back to St. Andrew's and talk to the other priests and see what they think," he explained.

I looked at him and waited for him to smile again like he did downstairs, but he never did.

After he left, in a hurry, we all went back to the kitchen. My mother was a little upset and asked my father to wash his hands.

"Alma," my father said. "Come on, it was a God-damned bird! Forget about it." And they left the conversation at that.

My grandfather was taking care of me while my parents were still working two jobs each. My mother was working at La Guardia airport during the day and at White Castle on Bell Boulevard and Northern Boulevard in Bayside at night. They made great little hamburgers there. My father would work at the office in a cab service during the day and then at night at a place called Bruno and Delayo, which was some kind of paper mill in New Jersey. My father would leave the cab place in Astoria and come home at about 4 in the afternoon, do some chores and go to sleep. He'd wake up about 12 in the morning, and then he would drive out to Hackensack, New Jersey. When he got there, he'd get the truck he drove and go to Manhattan to do his route. He would get done about 7 a.m. and then drive back to Jersey, get his car, drive home, take a shower and go to work at the cab business. I'd get to see my mother a little more during the day, because she had shorter hours, and then I'd get to see my father during the weekends while he was doing house chores. I guess they had a reason for working so much, but sometimes I would miss them.

On one weekend my father told me that I was going to have to start doing some chores around the house to help out. I didn't like the idea until he told me that I would get paid to do them, which sounded better. Oh, well, I guess it was only a matter of time before I was going to have to go to work around here anyway, I thought.

The money had sounded good, but since it was such a big house and having no brothers or sisters to help out, it was a pretty big job. I had to take out all the garbage in the house from the kitchen, bathrooms, and bedrooms to the big garbage cans outside, and then take them to the curb. I had to cut the grass once a week, with a push-mower, trim the bushes every two weeks, with scissors clipper's, and sweep out all three floors of the hallway once a week. My mother and father took a bedroom for themselves, but not the master bedroom. She didn't want to sleep in that room after what took place with the priest. All the other rooms were empty. Because I didn't get to see my father much, he would put a note under my door that would lead me to three, four or five other notes which would all get me closer to my money until I would find where he hid it that week.

I was out playing in the front yard one day and, while I was out there, this funny little blond girl kept yelling, "Hey... Hey you..."

I figured she'd stop in a little while if I didn't answer her, but she didn't. She kept it up for about another ten minutes until I yelled, "What! What do you want?"
"What's your name?" she asked.
"You mean to tell me that you called for fifteen minutes just to find out my name?"
"Yeah, but you weren't answering so I kept calling you," she added.

After I told her my name, I thought that would be the end of it, but it wasn't. "Do you live here now? How old are you? Do you have a dog or a cat? Brothers or sisters?"

Awwww jeez, I knew I shouldn't have answered her, I thought. After about two minutes of answering her questions, I lied, and told her I had to go inside now.

"Okay, I'll see you tomorrow," she answered. Not if I can help it, I thought.

One day I was in the basement, and I found a bunch of kid books like "Huck Finn" and "The Wizard of Oz." I asked my mother if she could read them to me, and she said, "Do you like these books? Well, here's what I'm going to do. I'm going to get you a dictionary instead, and you're going to read them yourself."

That night my mother showed me how to look up words in the dictionary and how to look up the meanings of words I couldn't understand. After a few days, it was almost like I was in a trance. I could hardly put the books down.

A few days later my mother said, "Michael, you need to go outside and get some fresh air. Why do you think we bought this big house with the yard and all?"
"Yeah, I know but I'm enjoying myself," I insisted.
"I know you are, but you need to go outside also," she explained.
"Well, all right. Whatever," I answered.
"Hey... where are you going with the books?!"
"Outside."
"Where?!"
"To read."

"Michael, leave the books inside!"

I put the books down, shrugged my shoulders, and went outside to play.

My mother took in a tenant; his name was James Doig. She told me that he came from the Midwest, wherever that was. I asked her where he was going to live, and she said that he was going to take the master bedroom with its own bath on the second floor. I gasped and said, "The raven room?"

My mother looked at me and said, "Don't you dare tell him that story. Besides, I already had another priest come back and bless this house again."
"Where was I? I didn't see him." I asked.
"I don't know. You were probably outside playing," she said.
"Yeah, but Ma, the first priest was even scared of that room."
"The priest was not scared of that room, there's no boogie man in there, and don't tell him that story, okay!"

I agreed, but I couldn't help looking at Jim like I might not see him again for a long time each time I saw him.

The summer was just about over, and I was seven years old by now. My mother mentioned that I would have to start school soon, so I asked her what school was.

"Well, it's a place you go during the day, and they teach you things, and you do school work."
"Work? What do you mean? Like you and dad?" I said.
"Yes, kinda," she answered.

At first I didn't like the idea, but then thought to ask, "Well, what are they going to pay me?"
"They're not going to pay you anything, Michael."
"Oh, so I have to work for free?"
"No, it's not that kind of work. It's like when we read together, and you'll do some adding and subtracting like I showed you. Then sometimes they'll give you homework."
"Homework... Jeez, don't I do enough work around here?"
"Not that kind of homework. Don't worry, you'll like it."
"Well, that's okay... I don't think I want to go."
"You have to go."
"Well, who's gonna make me?"
"I am," she said.
"But I thought you loved me. Why are you going to make me go to a place like that?"
"I do love you. You'll like it. Now go outside and play."

I went outside and thought to myself, boy, I didn't think my mother was going to send me to work at another job already. I thought I would get to be a kid for a while.

My father started to do some work around the house in his spare time, as if he had any. The first project was to put up paneling on the hallway walls. I decided to watch him, but after I sat there for about ten minutes my father said, "What'a ya' doing?"

"I'm watching."

"Huh? Watching your ass. Get over here and help me."

"I'm going to go to work?" I asked.

"Yeah," he answered.

"Well, what'a ya' going to pay me?"

"Oh, you want to get paid, huh? Okay, what do you want to be, a helper or a carpenter?"

"A carpenter makes more money, right?" I asked.

"Yeah, he does. So I guess you want to be a carpenter then right?"

"Okay," I said.

"All right wise guy, go get the tape measure and that pencil. Now mark the piece of paneling where we're going to cut out a piece for around the window. I need 3 1/2 feet up and 2 1/2 in, then 4 feet up and then 2 1/2 back out to the edge."

When I looked at the tape measure and saw all these little lines on it, I turned to my father and said, "What are all these little lines in between the numbers?"

He stopped what he was doing, walked over to me, pointed at the little lines on the tape measure, and said, "Well, these are eights and these are sixteenths."

I sat there for a moment and wondered if I should bluff my way out of it because I was sure that carpenters made more than helpers, but decided that I didn't want to mess up the paneling. So I said I didn't know what he was talking about.

"Well, you know what just happened, don't ya? You just got demoted. You're now a helper, and helpers make two dollars a day."

Boy, I thought, that's a bummer. I almost had a good paying job.

We finished up the hallway in a couple of weekends. My job didn't turn out to be so bad, though. All I had to do was hold the paneling while he cut it, and then help my father hold it against the wall while he nailed it. By the time we had finished the hallway, my father had showed me how to use the little lines on the tape measure, and he even helped me to cut a piece of paneling or two. I was pretty proud of myself. My grandfather would say, "That'sa good. You learna construction. Makea you strong likea bull."

Yeah, I would think, I do feel pretty good. I get two dollars a day working with my father, and I get my five-dollar allowance for doing my chores. That's almost ten dollars a weekend.

Sometimes I would walk to the toy store with my father. Once there I would walk up and down the aisles and decide which toy I wanted to buy for myself. I would walk up and down the aisles at Eisenstat's Toy and Hardware store for almost an hour trying to make a decision. It really felt good to know that I could buy almost any toy on the shelf with the money I had saved up in my pocket. Especially when I saw another kid my age come in with his parent, yipping and yapping like a little puppy waiting to get a table scrap. Now it felt good. I was actually standing there like a man, deciding what I wanted to buy and how much of my money I wanted to spend. After I bought what I wanted, I would start walking back home with my new toy and I guess I figured out why my parents worked so hard themselves.

Mom took me shopping; she bought me a bunch of nice dress clothes. She said that they were to be school clothes and that I couldn't wear them to play in. I was to change my clothes after school. She told me that I had a week left before I had to go to work in that school thing. My mother got another tenant; he was a pretty young guy, it seemed. I thought he was pretty cool, because he had on Army pants and boots. He told me that he had come from Vietnam. I asked my mom where Vietnam was, and she said that it was a long ways away from here.

On the last weekend before school, my mother took me over to the stone pool, on 20th Avenue by the Whitestone Expressway. We called it the stone pool because it was made out of concrete that hadn't been painted. The stone pool wasn't very deep and wouldn't become a pool until the big kids would stop up the drains with their shirts. Until that, it only had six big sprinklers that would shoot up into the air. That day I was over there, and for some reason I started to spin myself around in circles with my arms stretched out and my head looking straight up in the air, looking at the sky. I started to get dizzy, so naturally I kept doing it. I mean, hey, I'm a kid, and I was supposed to do these things. My mother yelled over to me that I had better stop because I was going to get dizzy, and I yelled back, "I know. That's what I'm trying to do." When I stopped, I started stumbling around in circles, looking for myself, and then I fell down, hit my head, and blacked out.

When I woke up and opened my eyes, I was looking at a small white ceiling. My mouth felt a little numb, and so did my knee. I looked down and saw the backs of people with white coats on and my mother standing there with her girlfriend MaryAnn from Whitestone facing me. Then it felt like my knee was being tickled, so I sat up and placed my head between the shoulders of the two people with white jackets on. I looked at my knee and saw these people working on me with a needle and thread. They were sewing up my leg like my mother would do to my old pants!

"Whoa! What the hell are you doing?!?" I yelled as I tried to yank my leg away from them.

My mother tried to console me by saying, you'll be all right, don't worry, which of course made me worry.

MaryAnn on the other hand started saying, "Now you've got a real man's cut. You're one of the boys now," which was a step in the right direction and calmed me down a little bit. But the problem was when the doctor went to stitch me again, I would see my mother close her eyes and make a bad face, which made me think about what was about to happen. Now each time the doctor would touch that area of my knee, I would rehearse my specialized little kid freak. I did this until Maryann, who had babysat me a few times said, "Michael, calm down. Why are you freaking out? You already got some stitches in your lip, and you weren't yelling then."

"I did...? I wasn't...? Where...? Right here?" I said pointing to my numb lip as I asked.
"Yes, right there. You got four of them," she answered.
"Wow, let me have a mirror. I want to see," I said.

Maryann said, "If I give you a mirror, will you let the doctor finish his work?" I was so intrigued by the stitches in my lip that I didn't have time to worry about my knee now, so I said yes.

The doctor finished his work, and then we went outside and left.

My father was home when I got there. "So," he said, "I hear you're a big tough guy now. I guess I've got to get you a job on the docks now."

I smiled, even though it hurt, and said, "Yeah, I guess."
"Come here, and let me take a look at the job you did on yourself,"

I walked over to my father, and he lifted up my lip. "Hmmm, not bad. I guess you get to have a small glass of wine, with soda, at dinner, champ."

That night when I went to bed, I decided that maybe too much of a good thing is not so good after all.

School started, Because my mother had taught me at home, instead of sending me to kindergarten, I would be starting out in the first grade. I got to go to the first day of school with a stitched-up lip and knee. I got to talk to a whole bunch of kids who wanted to see them. The school was named P.S. 21 on 149th Street by the big fields where I had flown kites. A few teachers came out in a little while and called out names to get us in order. As the teachers were doing this, mothers and fathers walked their kids in a line that was forming and said their goodbyes. This would start a howling, which made a few other kids howl, until there was more and more howling. It seemed like most of the kids in the whole yard were crying. It really made me wonder exactly what I was getting involved in and if I should make a run for it before I was trapped inside.

They finally herded us into classrooms where we could take off our jackets. It got much calmer once we got in there.

For the most part it seemed like this school thing would be okay, but I was still wondering what kind of work they wanted me to do for them.

After half of the first day went by, we went into a big room in the school that they called the lunchroom. I guess now I know why my mother gave me a sandwich. I just wondered if I should save some for dinner. We went outside after lunch and got to run around and play for a while until some lady came out with a small loudspeaker and screamed, "Everybody freeze!"

Half of the kids stopped dead in their tracks from fear; the other half slowed down until they stopped, and about ten or fifteen kids kept right on playing and shouting. The lady walked over to them and yelled into the speaker two feet from their heads, "Do you know what freeze means!?"

I looked over at an older kid who was laughing and asked, "What the hell is going on?"
"Don't worry about it," he said. "That's the way they get us ready to line up so we can go back

inside."

The lady, who was a teacher, made us go through this four or five times until she thought we had it down well enough. While we were practicing how to freeze, I noticed that there were kids whom I had seen in my neighborhood who also went to this school. The funny thing about this situation was that there were so many kids here. I mean, there had to be at least seventy-five kids in this big school yard.

When we got back inside my new teacher had put five spelling words up on the board: cat, sat, dog, run and fun. She explained that she wanted us to know how to spell these words by the end of the week, and the way we would do this was by writing them five times each and putting each one of them into a sentence. I looked around the room and was pretty surprised when I saw a few kids with their mouths open and their eyes the size of owls. Not only could I spell these words but I also figured that I could save time and put all the words into one sentence. The DOG and me had FUN when we went for a RUN while the CAT SAT down and watched.

The end of the school day came sooner than I expected, and I was glad that we got to leave before dinner time. But just in case, I went and asked the teacher if we would be able to leave every day at this time, just to be sure. She smiled and told me that we would get to leave at this time every day. "Whew," I thought. I wouldn't want to have to carry these new books they gave us with my lunch and maybe a dinner to every day.

My mother picked me up after school and told me that, from now on, she would drive me to the school bus stop in the morning and then pick me up from there later in the afternoon when I got home. She asked me how my day went, and I told her it was real easy and that the teacher had given us some words to write a few times. "You see? That's what I meant by homework," she said.

The school week went by pretty fast, and my mother said that we were going to pick up Dino and take a ride out to the country on the weekend. Dino now lived in Corona with his mother and father, Linda and Richie. He also had three sisters, Donna the oldest, then Dino, then Tina, and then Brenda. The cool thing was that my Aunt Marie lived right downstairs with her two sons, Ronnie and Russell, and George, her husband. They shared one big house together.

We went over there Friday night and picked up Dino. My mother wanted to get an early start in the morning, which could mean anything from one o'clock in the morning until 6 a.m. with my mother and her planned trips. At first I used to ask her where we were going, but I never knew where that place was after she would tell me, so I stopped asking. On the ride over to my house, I asked Dino if he took all his stuff with him. He said that he took everything that he thought he would need, with a blink of his eye. Good, we agreed. Maybe he would be staying here forever this time.

My mother got us up at about 5 in the morning. By the time she got us dressed and fed, it was about 5:30. Dino and I decided to go right back to sleep once we got in the car. When we woke up, we were in Wurtsboro, N.Y. My mother got us a motel room and then went and got a few newspapers. After a little breakfast, we set out for some country roads, and I asked my mother to show me where we were on a map. It's funny, but it seems like we went farther away from home each time. I couldn't believe we were so far away, and there were still people and things out here. My father was always working, so he seldom got the chance to come with us.

We drove around for a while until we found a big stream. My mother went to check the water out and then told Dino and me that we could go swimming if we wanted. We thought it was a great idea, but then asked about what we were going to wear. My mother said, "Well, don't worry. There's nobody around. You can go skinny dipping."

After we got undressed, we eased into the water and started swimming out to the middle of the stream. By the time we got out there, the water was getting colder as it got deeper but it was still warm enough to enjoy it. After we swam for about half an hour, Dino told me that he was getting cold and wanted to get out. He was a little bit smaller than I was, so I guess the cold got to him sooner. Being that I still wanted to swim, I turned to him and said, "Yeah, but if you go back to the car now, I'll have to go back, too. Why don't you stay out for a little while longer?"

"Well, okay, Michael," he said through chattering teeth. "I'll stay out a little bit longer."

After about fifteen minutes I heard my mother yell, "Michael, move!"
"Why?" I asked.

She pointed at Dino and said, "Because Dino is peeing on you!"

I looked over towards Dino and saw that he was standing up on a rock holding the sides of his arms while his teeth were chattering like a monkey. Then I saw he was peeing straight up in the air with no hands because he had on a little boner. I yelled back to my mother that he wasn't peeing on me; he was peeing into the water. She yelled back, "You're right, Michael. He's not peeing on you; he's peeing in the water that is traveling downstream right to where you're playing."

Then I looked down and noticed that his little bubbles were dancing around my body. "Argggg," I yelled as I dove underwater. I swam back around towards Dino, and when I came up from the water, I yelled, "What the hell are you doing?!"

He turned towards me while he was still peeing, and I said, "Cool! Dino, your lips are blue." He looked back at me and said through chattering teeth, "I'm freeeezing."

After he said that, I helped him off the rock and got him back to the car. When I got there, my mother said, "Oh, my God, Dino. Your lips are blue!"
I looked at my mother and said, "I know. It's cool."

My mother looked back at me while she started drying Dino off and said, "No, it's not cool. He could get very sick from this. He's smaller than you so he gets colder quicker."

Dino looked at my mother with worried eyes and said, "I tttold him I I I was cccold."

My mother wrapped Dino in a blanket and held him close to her, while she said to me, "Don't ever let this happen again. If he tells you he's cold, or you see that his lips are blue, take him out of the water."

As my mother held him close to her, Dino put a stupid look on his face and slowly stuck his tongue out at me. I looked at him and said, "Don't forget. I still get to pee on you."

He looked back at me and said, "No, you don't. We're even for you letting me fffreeze."

We drove around for a while until my mother found a few garage sales. We hated when she found these things because she would always take forever, even when we were back home. When we got back near the motel, we went out and ate dinner at a restaurant. After dinner we went back to the motel. We watched TV for a while, and then Dino and I started to have a pillow fight until my mother said, "Okay, that's enough, hold on." Then she got up went over to the suitcase and got out the Super 8-video camera. She sat down in the corner of the room, turned on the camera, and said, "Okay, kill yourselves but watch the lamps. I don't want to have to pay for them." By the time we got done killing ourselves, my mother had gone through three rolls of film. We fell asleep shortly after that.

The next morning, after breakfast, my mother told us that we were going to an auction. After she explained to us what an auction was, I said, "Oh... it's like a big garage sale, right?"
"Well, kinda," she answered.
"Well, we'd like to do something else. Can you take us back to the stream? I'll watch Dino's lips," I asked.
"No, I don't think so. But they sell a lot of animals there so you two can enjoy yourselves," she answered.

It was about a half-hour ride through farmland to the auction house. The place had two buildings; one was a huge barn, and the other one looked like a big airplane hangar. My mother told me that's where they kept the animals, so Dino and I hightailed it over there. My mother caught up to us and told us to meet her in a half hour and not to split up, to stay together even if we had to go to the bathroom. While we stood there looking around, we couldn't believe all the different farm animals that were there, and the weird smell. I overheard a man telling his son who was about my age, "Well, if we get those rabbits, you're gonna take care of them."

I looked into one of the boxes where somebody was displaying them and saw that there were about seven baby rabbits. I went over and asked this kid how much he thought he'd have to pay for them, and he said about fifteen bucks. I couldn't believe my ears, a whole box of baby rabbits for fifteen bucks. I looked around and saw that there were a few other boxes with rabbits in them and then asked this other kid how I could get some, being that I had about twenty dollars in allowance saved up at home. He said to me, "Well, when they bring out the rabbits for sale and the man starts hollerin' out prices, just put your hand up in the air and point at him." I looked at Dino and said, "All right! We're going to buy some rabbits, Dino." Dino looked at me and said, "Cool."

We walked around and looked at some of the other animals, and then we figured it was about time to go meet my mother. After we met her, she took us over to the other building just in time for the auction to start. We thought they would bring the animals out first, but instead they brought out all kinds of junk that my mother liked to get. Then they brought out all different kinds of food. My mother told me that the people there would grow the stuff on their farms and then bring it to auction to sell. By this time, Dino and I were getting a little bit antsy, so we asked my mother if we could walk around for a little while. She said that would be fine, but that we had to stay in this building and stay together. We got up and started to walk around for a little bit, and then we heard the man on the speaker say that they were going to start auctioning the animals, so we ran back.

When we got over there, I saw the kid I had been talking to. We went over to where he was standing, by the fence where they would walk the animals around. First, the big animals came out: The horses, bulls and cows. Then the smaller ones like pigs, sheep and goats. Then finally they brought out the chickens, ducks and rabbits. When they got to the rabbits, I watched how this other kid bid on his rabbits and figured, Boy, this is a cinch. He got his box for twenty dollars, and I hoped that I would get the box that I wanted for less.

After two more boxes of rabbits came out, I saw that my box was next.
"I'm gonna do it Dino."
"Yeah, do it... let's get some rabbits," he answered.

Once the bidding started, we saw that there was one older lady who was bidding against us. When the bid hit twenty-two dollars, I looked at her, turned to Dino, and said, "What should I do?"
"Bid, bid, bid! We'll get the money! We gotta get the rabbits, Mike!"

I glanced over in my mother's direction, saw her, and yelled out, "Yup! Right here!" like some of the other people did.

The older lady waved her hand at me in order to show me that she wasn't going to raise the bid, so I knew that we had won. Just as Dino and I looked at each other, cheering, I heard my mother say, "Michael, what did you just do?!?"
"Well, I bought some rabbits. I'm only short two dollars, though. Could you lend it to me? Please?" I asked.
"And what... do you think... you're going to do with all those rabbits?" she asked.
"Oh, well, I was going to feed, water and take care of them at home."
"Oh, so I guess you were going to ask me if you can have some rabbits," my mother said.
"Oh, Aunt Alma, please can we have the rabbits?" Dino pleaded.
"You stay out of this," she told him.
"Okay, Aunt Alma."

I gave Dino a look as if to say, Thanks for helping, sarcastically, and he looked back at me as if to say, Sorry, you're on your own now.

"Well... I'll take care of them. Can I have them?" I asked.
"I don't think it's a good idea, Michael. Maybe one or two, but not seven. I'm going to see if I can give some of them back."

As my mother went to talk to someone who worked there, I turned to Dino and said, "Gee, good thing I had you here with me, tough guy."

When my mother came back, she seemed a little angry, and she said, "I can't believe that after all the money I spent here, they can't take back a little box of rabbits. The guy pointed to a sign and said, "Sorry, Ma'am. All sales are final."

Dino and I looked at each other and realized that we were both trying to hold back a smile.

As my mother paid for everything, along with the rabbit food, Dino and I ran off to play with some of the animals before we left. My mother decided that, since we were leaving in the morning, she would take the scenic route back to the motel, which took about two hours so we could see the countryside.

Dino got dropped off at home early the next morning, unfortunately.

A couple of weeks into the school year, my mother and father bought into the taxi cab business that my father worked for. My father told me that he was partners with somebody and that they had about ten cars.

"Wow, cool," I said. "Do I get to drive one?"
"Well, not yet, but maybe if we're short one guy some day, you'll have to take a cab out."
"Cool. Do I get to keep the money?"
"Sure, sure, of course you do."

Monday Morning, time for some Elvis...

Ugh... morning, time for school. I've always disliked getting up in the mornings, but Mondays are definitely the worst. My mother had come up with a new system for waking me up in the mornings now. She would walk into my room with a portable record player and put on Elvis' records full blast until I'd get up and turn it off. I swore if I ever ran into this Elvis guy, he'd be real sorry he made records. I've got to say, though, throughout all my complaining it was still a lot better than my grandfather's system for getting me up. Gramps would come in and call me to get up. Then after a few minutes he'd come back and call me again. By the third time, he would pour a glass of water on my head. This had a knack for waking me up pretty fast.

This school thing wasn't turning out to be so bad after all. That's not to say that I wouldn't rather be at home playing outside. We did a little bit of school work, ate some lunch, and then played or painted. The schoolwork was pretty easy, I thought, and one day I asked a girl in my class if she thought the work was easy.

"No, it's not," she answered.
"Well, it's all spelling words, and I think they're easy to spell."
"I think they're hard. If you think they're easy, let me see you close your eyes and spell the new ones that are up on the blackboard now."

After I did this, she told me to spell some other words around the room, which I did also quickly, to which she replied, "Wow, I'm going to tell the teacher you're smart."

"No, wait a minute. If you do that, I might get some harder work," I said.

"No, you won't," she answered as she ran over to the teacher.

The teacher came over a few minutes after that and told me to spell a few words that she spoke, and then she asked me to come over to her desk. When I got there she pulled out a gray covered schoolbook, the same one that my mother had made me study. It had different words for different grades. She called out some of the words and said, "Oh, my God, you're almost spelling up into the third grade words."

I spent the next couple of days at school leaving the classroom and going to some small room on the second floor where some older kids were. They gave me a bunch of different tests to do for a while and then sent me back to my class. I thought to myself, Boy, this is something. While everyone is painting, I've got to do more work than they do now.

I saw the little girl who told on me, and I said to her, "Gee, thanks. Now they put me in a little room by myself, and I've got to do work the whole time I'm there."

"I'm sorry," she answered. "I didn't know they would do that to you."

That week went by pretty slowly, and I was more than happy to see Friday come along. When the end of the school day did come around, my teacher called me over to her desk. She had a letter for me to give to my mother. As I walked out to the school bus, I just knew it had something to do with the tests I had been taking, and I wondered if I should eat the evidence like they did on TV. But I decided to give it to my mother instead when I got off the bus.

When we got home from the bus stop, she opened the letter, read it, and said, "Oh, Michael, this is great. This says that they had you tested, and they feel that you are smart enough to go into the second grade, and they're wondering if that would be all right with me if they skipped you up a grade."

I knew that letter had something to do with those tests, and now I really thought I should have eaten it.

"Yeah, but that means that I have to do more work now, right?" I asked.

"Well, yeah, but it also means that you'll get finished with school a lot faster now," she answered.

Whoa... I think I like the sound of that, I thought. "Okay, I'll do it."

After I changed into my play clothes, I went out back to play with the rabbits. My grandfather had built them a small house to live in and put up some chicken wire so they could have a yard. As I played with them, I wondered if I should study that whole book my mother gave me, get tested, and then be finished with school once and for all. When I asked her at dinnertime, she said that she didn't think it was possible, but I could try anyhow.

"But your father is going to be proud when he hears this," she said.

"Are you going to tell him?" I asked.

"No, I'll do a better one. I'll put it on his pillow in his room, and he'll see it when he comes home from work."

After dinner my mother told me to finish up my homework as she got ready for work. By the time I got done, she came in my room, kissed me good night, and told me to wash my face and brush my teeth before I went to bed, and not to stay up too late reading comic books. Aside from her waitress uniform, she looked pretty. She had bright green eyes, but her long black hair was up into something she called a beehive, whatever that meant. My mother hardly had any time off any more, and I didn't get to see her much during the week so it was nice when we did see each other. That night I watched some TV with Gramps and stayed up late reading comic books.

It's nice not having to get up early on Saturdays, but according to my grandfather, 9:30 was too late, so I'd get up. I ate breakfast and got my dose of Saturday morning cartoons. After that I went outside and finished my chores.

My father hadn't come home the last few nights because he stayed out at his parent's house in New Jersey. So he didn't get to see my letter from school yet. Their house was closer to his second job, and then I would guess he drove straight over to the taxi business from there. Oh well, maybe he'll see the letter from school tonight when he gets home from New Jersey, I thought.

I decided to do all of my house chores that day instead of splitting them up between Saturday and Sunday, so I could have more time to play on Sunday. By the time I got done with everything but cutting the grass, it was dinnertime and I was pretty tired, so I didn't do much that night but watch TV.

The next morning my father came and woke me up. "Well, I see you did good at school," he said.

I sat up with one eye open and said, "Yeah, I guess I did."

"Well, that calls for a little bonus for your allowance."

Then he whipped out a twenty and held it in front of my face, which made both of my sleepy eyes shoot open wide.

"Get dressed, and I'll take you to the toy store and buy you something also," he added.

"All right!" I yelled as I jumped up and grabbed my pants.

"Hold on, hold on. Get washed up, eat some breakfast, and put on some clean clothes first," he said.

I looked around and I thought, Man, I got up pretty fast. I'd like to get up like this every morning.

After breakfast we went over to Eisenstat's, and I picked out some toys. I got a G.I. Joe jeep, and a bunch of Hot Wheel cars. When we got back home, my father told me that he wasn't going to put up any paneling. Instead, he would help me mow the grass with the new motorized lawn mower we had gotten. I opened up the new toys on the back porch as my father went into the garage and got the lawn mower.

"Hey, Dad!" I yelled.
"Yeah, what do you want?" he shouted over the sound of the lawn mower.
"Can you make me a bathroom in the garage so I can live there?" I asked.
"What...? You want to live in the garage...? What are you nuts?" he asked.
"Yeah, can I?"
"Ask your mother," he said.

Oh well, it was a good day, so I figured I should try my luck.

I got so involved with the toys I didn't even notice that my father had finished cutting all the grass until I saw him push the lawn mower back from the front yard. After he put away the lawn mower, he told me he was going to take a shower, and then we would go food shopping and have a barbecue. He told me to go tell my mother before she started to cook anything, as he hosed down the lawn mower. It was great when my father would have a barbecue, because he always cooked steak and baked potatoes. We ate out on the back porch like real men instead of inside at the table. When I got done, my mother told me to bring my toys in and get washed up. "Remember, tomorrow's a school day," she reminded.

"You ain't nothing but a hound dog, crying all the time...."

Morning, time for Elvis...

After an hour or two at school, a teacher came in and asked me to go with her. She took me over to a new classroom and introduced me to the teacher.

"Hello, Michael, welcome to the second grade," I was told. I looked around the classroom and noticed a few kids from my neighborhood who rode on the school bus with me.

The teacher gave me a seat next to the windows, which I thought was pretty cool. He told me not to worry about anything, that I could just listen to what was going on for now. After about an hour or two, I realized that I wasn't in that kiddy class any more. All of a sudden the classroom door swung open, and this kid ran into the class and starts yelling, "Aaaaaah, help! He's going to kill me!"

Then he jumped on the first desk and started hopping from desk to desk, heading straight for me. I was sitting there a little scared, thinking, Oh shit, what did I get myself into with those tests? When he got on top of my desk, he started scratching at the window trying to get out. By now all the other kids were yelling, "Go, Marcus, go!"

The principal ran in and shouted, "Somebody grab him!"

Marcus looked left and then right wildly. As he went to hop off my desk he stepped on my right hand. I reached over and grabbed his leg and yelled, "Get off my hand!" As I knocked him off balance and got him off my hand, he grabbed me and said, "Let go. They're going to get me!"

I looked into his crazed eyes for a second, and then I let him go. He ran straight at the principal and, just as he got to the principal he slid under his legs, popped up, and then ran down the hall. The principal stepped out of the classroom, looked down the hall, and shook his head. After a moment or two, he walked back in and told the class to settle down. When it got quiet, he said he was sorry to the teacher and left. I looked over at one of the other kids and said, "Does this happen all of the time?"

"Naa, not all the time. That's just crazy Capeeto."

"Boy, I'm glad he's not in this class," I said.

"He is," the kid answered.

"Then I want out of here. I'm not staying in this class if he goes here," I said.

"Don't worry, he's never here, and when he is he usually runs out after an hour or so. Hey, my name is Keith Brawly. What's yours?"

I told him my name, and then he said, "Don't worry too much. This class is pretty easy."

When I got home that day, my mother asked me how my day went. I looked at her and said, "Oh, not too bad, except for that kid who jumped up on my desk and stepped on my hand."

"What do you mean somebody jumped on your desk and stepped on your hand?" she asked.

After I explained the whole story to her, I added that I wasn't too sure I wanted to stay in that class. She answered, "I don't blame you. I'm going to talk to the principal about it."

Over the next few days I got to know some of the other kids in my class. One of the kids was named Danny Barbuto; another was Tony Morealass. Some of the other kids nicknamed Tony "Crybaby William" because sometimes he would get so mad that he would start crying.

Thursday morning when I went into class that crazy Capeeto kid was there. I kept an eye on him for most of the day, waiting for him to bug out, but he didn't. By the end of the school day, he came over to me and said, "Hey, thanks for letting go of me, and I'm sorry for stepping on your hand."

"Well, I guess it's okay, but why was the principal chasing you?"

"I don't remember, but I wasn't going to let him catch me," he answered.

After I saw that he wasn't so bad, I figured it might be good to know this guy in case anyone tried to bother me at school. I asked him where he lived, and he told me his street. I said, "That's funny, I live over by that street myself. Maybe we live close to each other."

"Yeah, I think we do," he said.

After school I heard that little girl from across the street at exactly 4 o'clock. She kept yelling my name over and over until she made me nuts. I ran out to the front yard and yelled, "What do you want?!?"

"What'a ya' doing?" she asked.

"Nothing. Why? What do you want?"

"Can you cross the street and come play yet?" she asked.

"No, I can't. I'm not allowed," I answered.

"When do you think you'll be able to?"

I could see that this was going to be a long one, so I figured I'd make an excuse so I could leave. "I'm not sure. I've got to go do my homework now," I said.

As I walked away I thought, Gee, what a funny girl.

At school the next day a teacher came into class and asked me to get my things and go with her. I asked her where I was going, and she said, "Just right down the hall," so I got my coat and books and followed her.

When we got to the new class, she said hello to the teacher, and then she looked at me and said, "This is your new teacher, Mrs. Dwarf."

Mrs. Dwarf looked at the class and said, "Class, this is Michael. Everybody say hello to him."

It felt nice to be introduced but also a little embarrassing at the same time. The teacher took me over to a desk, and told me that this was my new desk now. I put my books in my desk and observed the rest of the class that day.

When I got home, I told my mother about my day, and she said, "I know. I spoke with the teachers about having you moved to another class."

That Saturday after my dose of cartoons, I went out and did my chores early. It was pretty hot out, so I decided to fill up my rubber-lined wading pool with water. After I got done filling it, I figured that by the time I got done with the lawn, the hose water in the pool would be warmer. After I finished lunch and mowing I decided that the water would be warm enough to put my goldfish in with my toys also. So I went in and got a pot to put my goldfish into it. Then I went back outside and slowly poured them into the rubber pool. Then I went and hosed off and jumped in with them. Now it really made my toy boats seem like they were in an ocean.

I was in there having a grand old time when this really big kid, who looked like a teenager, walked over to me and said, "Hey, how you doing?"
"Fine," I answered, "Who are you?"
"My name is Willie. I'm the kid that lives in back of you," he told me.
"Oh, my name's Michael."

I thought it was a little strange that he had just walked into my yard especially since there was a wooden fence and garage that separated our yards. He asked me if I had any brothers or sisters, and then after I answered him, he said, "Well, I just wanted to let you know that I run this block, and everybody does what I say."
"Well, I don't have to listen to you. I can just tell you to get out of my yard," I suggested.
"Well... if you don't want me to get mean then you'll listen to what I say," he warned.

I looked at him and, even though he was twice my size, I said, "Ya know what? I think you should get out of my yard now." After I said this, he pulled out a little pen knife and opened it. So I asked him what was he going to do, stab me?

"No, something better," he answered as he reached down and sliced open the pool. I watched helplessly as my fish and my toys poured out of the pool onto the ground. As I was yelling and screaming at him, he said, "Ya see? Now you'll listen to me."

Then I started yelling at him and for my grandfather until he left my yard. I tried to grab a pot and rescue some of my fish, and I couldn't believe someone could do something like that to someone else. I was still pretty upset about it when my mother got home and told her all about it. She and my father ended up going to Willie's house that night. I don't know much about what was said there that night, but I did end up getting some new fish.

"I'm all shook up..."

Monday morning, time for Elvis. I dragged myself out of bed and stumbled over to the turntable. I was running a little late, so my mother drove me over to the other school bus stop that was two blocks away from my house instead of the one I usually went to in the opposite direction.

It was funny, but all the kids who were in my first second grade class were at this bus stop. Because I hadn't seen them since I was escorted out of class, most of them asked me where I went. I explained to them that I was sent to another classroom down the hall. Keith Brawly introduced me to his little brother, Brian. Anthony Spinelli was there with his little brother, too.

The one thing I liked about my new class was that it was much quieter there than in my old class. A girl came over to me and asked me if I was the boy who had gotten stitches on the first day of school. I told her that I was the one who was showing off the stitches in the school yard, and then she looked at me and said, "Wow, do you want to be my boyfriend?"

"Well, that depends. What is a boyfriend? What do I have to do?" I asked.
"Well, nothing really. You just have to sit by me and hold my hand a lot," she answered.

I really didn't want to do it, but I didn't want to hurt her feelings. She looked like she really wanted me to hold her hand or something.

"Well, okay," I answered meekly. "I'll try it for a little while."

I did it until about lunchtime, but I started getting bored with it. It must've shown because she was holding someone else's hand by the end of lunchtime. Oh, well, I guess it wasn't meant to be. The rest of the week went by pretty quickly. The schoolwork was a little bit harder than the first class I was in, but that was okay because I was getting used to it.

My mother woke me up on Saturday. She told me to get dressed and eat something because we were going to my cousin's house in Corona. I would always have fun with all my cousins over there. Ronnie and Russell were older, and they would always have either cool or dangerous things we could do. One of the games we used to play was barrel rolling. I don't mean just rolling around a barrel in the yard. We would get these big four-foot barrels from the warehouse across the street from their house and then roll it over to the corner where there was our "Dead Man's Hill."

The hill ran along the wall built for the Long Island Railroad on one side and this huge warehouse that ran down past three quarters of a city block on the other side. At the bottom of the hill, there was a stop sign and a pretty busy street. We would find long sticks so that we could push the barrel from behind as we would follow it. We had two tricks for stopping it. The first trick was to beat, shove and jab it either into the train wall or the factory wall with our sticks. The second trick we had was to position ourselves along the hill, and then we would throw old tires, branches, or anything else we could find in front of it. Sometimes these two tricks had to be used together in order to stop the barrel. But even with all these tricks, we still managed to lose control of my cousin Russell one day.

We had pushed him so hard that he was bouncing two feet over the junk we were throwing in front of him. I ran alongside the barrel and yelled to Russell that we couldn't stop him. He was yelling, "Aaaaaaaaaaa" as he rolled along. I told him not to worry because Dino and I were going to run down to the bottom of the hill and try to stop the cars for him.

Dino and I took off like rockets, and when we got down there, the cars weren't even slowing down as we were yelling for them to stop. Russell was getting closer, and it looked like there was one more car for him to beat. I prayed, but it didn't look too good. Russell was still yelling at the top of his lungs, "Aaaaaaaaaaaaa, somebody stop me!" He flew right into the intersection just as the car passed in front of him by a second. Then he smashed into a parked car across the street.

We ran over to the barrel, but Russell wasn't making a sound. I called out, "Russell, are you okay?"

There were no sounds coming from the barrel for a moment, and then we heard, "Whoaa, help me out of this. I'm dizzy."

As we were helping him out of the barrel, a guy came out of the house and yelled, "Hey, you kids'a, what'a you do to my car?"

We looked at each other and said, "Oh, shit, run."

Russell looked up at Dino and said, "I can't run. I'm too dizzy." Dino looked back at him and said, "Well, if you don't, I think we're going to get beat up."
"Really?" Russell asked.
"Really!" Dino answered.

By now the guy made it over to our side and said, "You sonama bitcha, looka what you did to my car."

With that we all bolted. I figured I was okay because all I had to do was beat Russell back up the hill. It looked pretty funny, because Russell was still bouncing off the walls while he ran because he was dizzy. Well, so much for barrel racing down Dead Man's Hill for a while.

On Sunday I was talking to the new tenant at the top of the stairs. I liked him because he had some

G.I. Joe dolls with some cool uniforms, and he also had a Japanese one. He would make them fight in his bed. I asked him where he had gotten them, and he told me that he had gotten them at the toy store. After that I did some chores and then went to play with the rabbits.

"It's now or never, come hold me tight, kiss me my darling, be mine tonight." Ugh... that's Elvis on the record player. It must be morning.

School went by pretty smoothly, except for a fight I saw in the schoolyard. It was a kid who was in my first 2nd grade class, Danny Barbuto, fighting with this other kid, Tommy Faye, who lived down the corner from me. I had never seen a school yard fight before, and I was very amazed when I saw Danny bouncing Tommy's face off the concrete while he had him on the floor. He did it four or five times until Tommy stopped moving. I thought he must've killed Tommy but Tommy got up on one knee after Danny got off him and then rolled over onto his back. Danny stood there for a minute before some teachers grabbed him. I walked over to Tommy and looked at the huge bumps he had on his forehead. The teachers called for an ambulance, but he was still lying there by the time we went in for lunch.

My mother told me she planned for us to have another trip this weekend. She said that she was going to take all the cousins this time. I could hardly wait for the weekend that week in school. On Friday night my mother went to Corona and picked up all of my cousins. We stayed up late and played until my mother put us to bed. When my mother woke us back up, it was still dark out, and she got us dressed, fed and into the car where she had put a bunch of pillows for us to go back to sleep. I woke up some time later to the sounds of "The bear went over the mountain, the bear went over the mountain." We all joined in and kept singing and singing. Finally my mother said, "Okay, kids, that's enough now. You've been singing that song for over an hour."

We ended up in a small town where my mother had an old girlfriend. My mother went and got us a room in some big old hotel and then called her girlfriend. After her girlfriend came over, they talked for about an hour. We all complained that we were bored, and we wanted to go outside and play. My mother asked her girlfriend how safe it was with cars and all, and her friend said it would be fine for us to play outside. So we went out and played downstairs for a while. After about a half-hour Russell came back over and said, "Hey, there's a graveyard down at the bottom of the hill; let's see if it's spooky."

We looked at each other, and I said, "Well, why not? There's a bunch of us so we'll be all right."

We went down the hill to the graveyard and started running around like ghosts were chasing us, and then we found a huge pile of flowers. They looked as though someone was throwing them out, so we decided to take out the good ones and put them onto the graves that didn't have any. We did this for about an hour until we heard my mother say, "Michael! Dino! Russell! Ronnie! Donna! Where the hell are you?!" This was not her usual tone in calling us, so we knew we were in trouble. I yelled back, "We're down here, Ma!"

After a minute or two I saw her coming over the top of the hill with a wooden spoon in her hand. We looked at each other and said, "Uh oh, somebody's going to get it."

"You little bastards, get over here right now. I've got the whole town yelling at me for you kids running around on top of their relatives."

"Yeah, but if we come over there you're going to hit us," I said.

"I'm not going to hit you. Just run back to the hotel room, and I'm going to pretend that I'm hitting you guys in the room."

We all looked at each other and then back at her and said, "You promise?"

"Yes, I promise, you little bastards. Now get moving before I change my mind," she answered.

Then we all ran back to the hotel room.

When my mother got there, she grabbed a pillow and said, "Every time I hit the pillow one of you scream like I'm hitting you."

It took a few times, but we finally got down a system of yelling one at a time instead of all of us yelling each time she hit the pillow. After my mother went out to apologize to the hotel owners, she told us that we would have to stay in the room for a while and pretend like we were being punished. A little while later she came back upstairs and said, "Okay, everybody go downstairs quietly and pile into the car." We left and were singing about the bear that went over the mountain in no time.

After driving for a little bit, my mother passed what looked to be a big historical marker. I pleaded with her until she finally turned around for us to see it. When we got back to it and got out of the car, my mother said, "This is not a historical marker; it's an old overgrown crypt."

We asked her what that was, and she explained to us that people go there after they die to be buried. "Cool," I said, "Can we go inside and see the bodies?" I asked.

"No, you can't go see the bodies. Anyhow there's probably a door on this place, so you can't get in," she answered.

"Where? Where's the door?" I asked.

"It's got to be on one of these four sides," she answered.

On that note I jumped out of the car and took off like a rocket, scampering through the bushes to find the doorway.

Most of the bushes around the crypt were taller than I was so my mother kept calling out, "Michael, where are you?"

I yelled back, "Over here. I'm okay."

I turned the last corner, and found the doorway, which was open. As I slowly walked over to the doorway, my cousin Dino caught up to me. I took half a step inside as Dino grabbed my arm. I looked around after my eyes adjusted to the different light and saw three coffins. Two of them were lying across some pipes that were about four feet off the ground. The funny thing about them was that they were shaped like teardrops. I looked over at the third coffin as my mother called my name again, and I realized that the lid was off and there was a skeleton in it!

"Wow, Ma, the door is open and there's a skeleton inside. Can I keep it?" I said.

"Oh sure, Michael. The doors open. Yeah, I guess you can keep the skeleton," she answered.

"All right!" I answered. "But you're going to have to help me carry it to the car," I added.

My mother turned the last corner, and after she walked down the overgrown steps, she said, "Oh, my God, the door's open." Then she took a few more steps down the overgrown steps and said, "Michael, there's a skeleton! Get the hell out of there!"

"I know. You said I could have it."

"Get the hell out of there!!" she yelled.

I could tell by the tone of her voice that I should move, so I ran outside and up the stairs. When I ran back out, I had run up onto the wrought iron fence that had fallen down into the stairwell some time ago. Just as I got to my end of it, the other end, which was by my mother's and Dino's feet, started to rise. The fence had been lying there for so long that you weren't able to tell it was a fence because it had sticks and leaves on it. My mother glanced down at the ground that was rising and yelled, "Dino! The ground!"

My cousin Dino, and my mother, gave out one big scream. Dino was gone, he ran up the steps, through the bushes, and dove into the back window of the station wagon with my other cousins.

My mother wasn't as fast as Dino, and as she was slipping up the steps I yelled, "Mom, it's only me, look." I stood back up and bounced the fence again.

"You little bastard. You scared the shit out of me. Come on, let's go," she said.

"Yeah, but you said I could keep the skeleton," I pleaded.

"Get in the car before I make you a little skeleton," she answered.

I walked back to the car mumbling something about her not letting me do anything. After this my mother found a place where we could go swimming. We stayed there until our lips were just about blue, and then we left.

My mother wanted some time to go to some garage sales and antique shops. Whenever it was one or two of us, sometimes my mother would take us into the shop. But when the whole gang was there, we'd have to wait in the car for her. It wasn't too bad that day since she only made us suffer for a total of two hours. We went to a diner after that and then back to the hotel. After playing a few games and a pillow fight or two, we went to bed.

The next day my mother told us that we were going to have a picnic. We all went to the grocery store, and she let us each pick out what we wanted to eat and what each of us wanted for dessert. Then she drove around for a while to find a good spot. Along the way, we drove past what seemed like a little town on the right side of the road. There were about fifteen houses and a big warehouse behind it. My mother pulled off the road and backed up to it. We could see that the place had been deserted for some time by all the broken windows. As soon as the car stopped, my cousins and I piled out of the car, and we ran towards the houses. My mother ran after us and yelled for us to come back. We all dragged our feet and butts on the way back and asked her if we could go play there. She walked towards the first house as she was explaining to us that, if she did let us play there, we would have to be very careful. Then she walked up two steps of an old house and said, "If I let you play here, none of you can go inside any of these houses. If one of you goes inside, then we all leave. I don't even want you walking on any of the porches," she warned.

"Can we break some windows?" I asked.
"Well, okay, but only on these houses because they're falling down anyhow," she answered.

On that note we took off to gather up some rocks. After a little while, I don't remember who it was, but someone came up with the idea of going up on the front porch of one of these houses so we could break the small windows on the front door. As my cousin Donna, who was in the back of the bunch, stepped onto the porch, we heard my mother yell, "I thought I told you not to go into the houses!"

We started making up stories about how we weren't really in the houses as my mother stormed towards us.
Crash!

I couldn't believe it, my mother fell through the porch. Luckily for her, she only fell through up to her thigh, with her other leg still on top of the porch. We all looked at each other like the "Little Rascals" on TV after something bad had happen, with our mouths, and eyes wide open.

My mother said in a low growl, "Didn't I tell you not to play on these houses? I'm going to kill you when I get my hands on you." We knew she was hurt, and we also knew that we were in trouble. "Now get over here and help me out of this hole!" she yelled.

We all just stood there looking to see who was brave enough to make the first move towards helping her. She looked right at me and screamed, "Why aren't you helping me!"

I looked back at her and said, "Because you're going to kill us."
"Don't worry. I'm not going to kill you."
"Do you swear to God?" we asked.
"Yes!"
"You promise?"
"Yes, I promise. Now get over here and get me out of this fucking hole before I fall through again," she yelled.
"But if we come over there, maybe there will be more weight over there, and we'll all fall through," I explained.
"Maybe we could start the car and go get help." Russell suggested.
"No," Ronnie said, "we could start the car, get a rope, and pull her out of the hole."
"Nobody is going to start the car, and you're not going to pull me out of here using a rope. Now get the fuck over here and pull me out of this hole before I break my promise and kill everyone of you little bastards," she threatened.

We looked at each other one last time, and then we all ran to help her. It was tough because she wasn't budging. But with one final heave, we pulled her out. My mother gave out a shriek of pain when we did, but at last we got her out. She got up and limped back towards the car, and I couldn't believe it, my mother actually had tears coming down her cheeks.

When we got to the car, my mother said, "I think I have a cut on the back of my leg."

My mother pulled her pants down and then asked Donna to look at the back of her leg. We could see from the front that her leg was bruised and had large scratches on it. Donna walked around the back of her and winced. Then she wrinkled her face and said, "It looks bad, Aunt Alma."

She asked me to look at it as Ronnie, Russell, and Dino leaned over to look. My mother had a scrape with a big splinter in it. She looked back in the direction of the scrape and then hobbled into the car. While she was sitting there, she lifted her knee up to her chest, looked at it, and said, "I've got to pull this out," as we all squealed. We all had a different contorted look on his or her faces as she slowly pulled out the long splinter. By this time my cousin Donna was crying and saying, "We're sorry, Aunt Alma. We won't go on the porch anymore."

After she put her pants back on, we drove over to a town drugstore. Then I went in and got her some Band-Aids and stuff. My cousins and I tried to be overly nice to my mother for the rest of the night on the drive home after she patched herself up, and we ended up having a picnic in front of the hotel.

It was still light out after we dropped off my cousins and got home, light enough for me to see that the same rabbit got out of the cage again. At least he stayed close to the cage. Oh well, I'll catch him later, I thought.

"We're caught in a trap... I can't get out... because I love you too much, baby."

"Grumph..." Time to turn off the record player.

I got to go to the nurse's station today at school. A colored kid dared me to put my finger in the doorway, and then he deliberately slammed the door on it when I took him up on his dare before lunch. It stung like hell but nothing was broken, so I got to stay there for most of the day before they got in touch with my mother. I left school that day with a bandage on my finger. After I showed my mother my finger, I went out to play.

The funny blond girl from across the street started calling me again once I got out there. Then she asked me if I could cross the street yet. I figured what the hell; I could cross streets in the country, why can't I do it here? It's not like I've asked and my mother she said no or anything. Besides I had a good reason. I could show off my bandage to this funny little blond girl. She was pretty impressed after I got over there.

After she told me her name, Barbara asked me what happened to my finger, so I told her. Then she asked me why I was so stupid, to which I didn't have a real answer. As she started to tell me about some of the other kids who lived on the street, my mother walked down the driveway towards her car. She looked across the street and said, "Michael, what are you doing across the street?"

"I don't know," I lied as I ran back across, which seemed to make my mother even angrier.

"Don't you know you could get run over crossing the street like that!?!"

"Yeah, but I cross the street when we're upstate," I answered.

"But this is not upstate. You could get run over by a car or a bus here," she scolded.

We worked it out after a little while of talking where, as long as the light was red on the corner and there were no other cars coming, I could cross, which was fine with me.

I saw my father one day this week. He told me that we were going to spend the weekend at my grandparent's house. I hadn't really seen them since they moved to a new house in New Jersey. That weekend we left early Friday night because my grandmother was cooking us dinner. It was a pretty long drive, and I asked him where his parents lived.

"Upper Saddle River, New Jersey." he answered.

"Well, how long till we get to this place?" I asked.

"Why? You gotta go to the bathroom?" he asked.

"No."

"Then hold your horses. We'll be there in a little bit."

When we got there I hardly remembered them, but they both gave me a big hug and a kiss. My grandparent's lived in a large split-level ranch house with two fireplaces. Their yard was only about three times the size of mine, and my yard was big. My grandfather still had his old Cadillac. He bought it in 1952, and my father told me they used it only to go to church on Sundays. He used his new Caddy for everyday driving. When we walked into my grandmother's house, the smell of Italian food cooking was incredible. After I kissed my grandmother, I asked her what smelled so good. She said it was fresh meat sauce with meatballs, pork and brajole (Italian ham). I walked over to my father and asked him what "brajole" was. He said, "It's meat; there's some sliced on the table with the cheese."

After I walked over to the table, my father told me to eat the breadstick, cheese and brajole together, then I should eat a few grapes. Man, it was good.

After my father showed me where the bathroom was, we sat down for dinner. My father's mother was the type who would say, "C'mon, eat! What's the matter? You sick?" if there was still a lot of food on the table. My grandfather poured me a little wine with dinner as he told my father "He's big enough."

Boy, I thought, I had never had a glass of wine without some soda in it, and I don't care what it tastes like because my grandfather thinks I'm big enough so I'll make sure I drink it all. Besides that, I know he makes it himself so I wouldn't dare make him think I didn't like it.

By the time I got finished at dinner, I was afraid of leaving the table for fear of bursting. After watching some TV, my father told me that we were going over to Uncle Mike's house the next day, so I could meet him and his kids.

"You'll like it there. He's got nine kids, and he one of his boys is named Michael too," he told me.

Wow, nine cousins, I could hardly wait to meet them.

The next day we got there about noontime. Their house was right next to an apple orchard, and there was a huge boulder in their front lawn. It had to be fifteen feet tall, and at least that round. The first person I got to meet was Steven; he seemed a little bit older than I was. Then I met his brother Robert. My father took me upstairs to the kitchen, and I met my Aunt Joanne and Uncle Mike. I asked Joanne where all the other kids were, and she explained that they weren't all there, but she would tell me all their names anyhow.

"First, there's David."
"Where is he?" I interrupted.
"Well, he's at a place called Vietnam now, where he flies jets."
"Where is that place?" I asked.
"Well, it's a long ways away from here." I was told. This was the same thing my mother had said about our boarder, so I still didn't know.

"Then there's Susan who's away at school, and then there's Elizabeth who's still at home along with Michael, Robert, Steven, Joany, Pattie and Thomas, who are still running around somewhere today," Uncle Mike added.

I was told to go downstairs where Robert and Steven were watching TV. After talking for a few minutes, we realized that playing with little Army men and trains was something we all enjoyed doing. Steven and Robert took me down to the basement to where they had a huge piece of plywood set up with a train set. It was much smaller than the Lionel trains my father had packed away, but it was still a pretty big set. They had the same little plastic Army men that I had at home, so we ended up down there playing on the papier-mâché' mountain and little plastic town figurine train set-up.

Long after dinner and past midnight, my Aunt Joanne came down and said it was time for bed. Then she told me I was sleeping over and that Steven would lend me pajamas, which I thought was great because now we would get an earlier start at playing Army.

After I washed up the next morning, my aunt gave me back my clothes to wear after she washed them, which I thought was nice. I went down to the kitchen with Steven, and he asked me what kind of cereal I wanted to eat. I asked him what kind he had, and he said it would be easier if I told him what I liked. "Why is that?" I asked him. He slid open the bottom cupboard doors and said, "This is why."

I don't think I ever saw so much cereal in one house in my life. There must have been twelve to fifteen different boxes of cereal, so I decided to mix three or four of them together.

As we were eating breakfast, my Aunt Joanne asked Steven and me what we planned to do. After telling her that we planned to go back to the basement, she firmly suggested we grab some bikes and go ride in the apple orchard to get some fresh air. The apple orchard was huge, and we rode around for hours. I swore that Steven could never get lost after he got us out of the apple orchard. After lunch we played a game of football on the lawn. Most of the kids were home, so it was neat that we didn't have to get anyone else to come over and play. It almost made me think that I would like to have a brother or sister. At the very least I could split up my chores. My father came back in the early afternoon and told me that we would have to leave soon. He explained that he had to drive me home and then drive back out to Jersey to go to work that night, so I said my goodbye's, and we left shortly after that.

Over the next few months I helped my father finish off paneling in four bedrooms. We also had the floors re-sanded and put some new rugs in the house. It was starting to look pretty nice.

I was talking to the young guy who lived at the top of the stairs in room #1 one day. I liked him because he started telling me a bunch of funny stories about being in Viet Nam. I asked where Viet Nam was and he told me it was the asshole of the world.

"The world has an asshole??"
"Yeah, and that place is it."
"Well, I hope I don't have to go there."
"I hope so to kid," he answered.

After talking to him for a while, I walked into his room with him, which was much messier than when he first moved in. The first thing I noticed was that he had put up burlap bags on the walls and windows. The burlap bags didn't seem to bother him, so I asked him why he had done it. He said, "It's so the gooks can't see in at night."
"What the hell are gooks?!?" I said, as strange ideas of new boogiemen that I had never heard of that could get me at night came into mind, not that his explanation of gooks changed my thoughts on that.

"They're slimy, slanted-eyed yellow bastards" he said as my face contorted in horror.
"What kind of monster is that? Where do they come from?" I figured if this big guy was putting up burlap bags on his windows, I might want to know all about these things and put something on my windows.

"No, no, they're not those kind of monsters. Don't you know nuttin'?" he asked.
"No... but tell me more," I said.

Then he went on to explain that he had been at war and what gooks were. I told him that my grandfather was telling me that he had a big war in his country.

"NO... not back then, boy. We're having a war right now while you and I are talking."
"You mean right now there's a war going on?" I asked.
"Right now as we're talking, guys my age are dying for nothing. We're not gonna win over there."
"Why are we there fighting then," I questioned.

There was a long silence, and then he said, "I don't know why. I think you should leave now... I'm busy." As I left I thought, Man, that sounded like a funny war to be in.

A few days later I told my mother about the "gooks" and burlap bags. A few days after that, two big guys in white jackets came over to visit the young guy at the top of the stairs. My mother told me they were his friends, but the guy in #1 didn't seem like he wanted to go with them. They ended up going into his room to talk for a while. When they left, I saw that they had given my friend a white jacket like theirs, but it looked like he had it on backwards. After a few days I asked my mother why my friend wasn't back, and she told me that he wasn't coming back. I asked her if it have anything to do with me telling her about the burlap bags. Then she said to me, "Michael, you don't understand. He didn't come from his parents' house; he came from a hospital, a VA Hospital. He was in a war, you see, and his best friend was killed standing right next to him. So he had some trouble understanding what had happened to his friend."

"That's why he was in a hospital?" I asked.
"Yes"
"But you go to the hospital when you're sick. He didn't look sick to me?" I asked.
"It's not that kind of hospital. It's the kind of hospital you go to when you're a little confused about things, and they help you figure things out." she answered.
"Yeah, but this is his room now."
"Well, we'll check on him in a little while and see when he can come back," she answered.

I didn't really like the sound of that, and I was kinda mad at myself for telling my mother about the "gooks."

I went to Corona this weekend. My crazy cousins had a new game they made up. First, you had to walk around and collect as many rocks as you could find and put them into a big pile. Then we would give out the rocks according to each person's strength. Then we'd face the 10-foot high wall for the elevated train track and start throwing rocks over to the other side of the tracks. The fun would start when the kids on that side would throw things back over at us.

It was nuts; everything from bicycle handlebars to bottles would be crashing all around. Sometimes it made me wonder how big these other kids were by the size of the things they were throwing. This skirmish only lasted fifteen minutes, but my cousin Russell told me that the week before they had a battle for almost an hour. Man, I thought, I'm amazed that I didn't get hit with anything after this short time. Imagine what would happen if I had to dodge this stuff for an hour, I thought.

My mother and father had some storm windows put on the house. I heard my father tell my mother that they would pay for themselves in no time with the heating bills. It cost a lot to cover thirty-three windows, he complained. All I cared about was that they were on the house none too soon; it was getting cold outside.

Now I would pity the poor kids who had to walk to school on these cold mornings, not realizing that I would be walking too some day. Some mornings my mother would yell at my grandfather for giving me a few sips of his coffee with Italian liquor in it. She'd say, "Daddy, you can't give him any liquor before he goes to school. He'll be bouncing off the walls." I liked it though; it woke me up.

I didn't mind when it got cold this time of year because it meant that Christmas was right around the corner. My father decided to have a barbecue one day out of the blue. He made his usual stuff: a big salad, steaks, and baked potatoes. I didn't believe him until I saw him put on his jacket and go brush the snow off the gas grill. I got my jacket on and rushed out also. Then I walked over to him and said, "Dad, you're crazy! Look at the thermometer. It's 30 degrees."

"I know, son," he answered. "The perfect temperature for a barbecue." I guess he must've been right because those steaks tasted great.

Christmastime was here; we set up our first tree at that house. The tree was her job, she said. My father and I got outdoor Christmas lights and, best of all, we got a big statue of Santa Claus and one of Frosty the Snowman. When we got back to the house my mother said to us, "I sent the two of you out for Christmas decorations and you bring back this? Where are you going to put them now?"

"We'll put them up on top of the front porch roof," my father explained.

After we finally got them up there, my father put some bricks inside of them so they wouldn't blow away. Then we lit them up as we hung up Christmas lights. It was the best thing I ever saw. When we got inside my mother had hung a bunch of decorations on the tree and all kinds of candy, from candy canes to chocolate.

On Christmas Eve, my father had another one of his barbecues while it snowed, and my mother prepared a big goose for dinner the next day. I was amazed at its size and thought, Boy, I'm glad I didn't have to kill this big chicken. After dinner and some TV that night, I put out some snacks for Santa and Rudolph. I made a peanut butter and jelly sandwich for Santa, and cut up some vegetables for Rudolph. I'm sure it would be a long night for them and they would get hungry.

On Christmas Day I finally got to eat anything I wanted to off the Christmas tree. I'll tell you, there is one good thing about not having any brothers or sisters. I mean, even though I would like someone to help me with the chores, I made up for it with all the presents on Christmas. After we had dinner, my mother said, "Michael, you know that your cousins are coming over in a little while. Maybe you want to put away some of your toys. Don't forget that they're going to have some toys out here, too, once they open up their presents."

"No, that's okay. I want them to play with my toys, too," I answered.

"Well, okay," she said, "just remember I told you."

When my cousins came, we had a great time. We had a nice fire in the fireplace, and my mother let us throw all the Christmas wrapping paper in there to burn. My cousins stayed pretty late, and we had a great time even though half my toys were broken after they left.

New Year's Day and my birthday came around in January. It was kind of nice having my birthday so close to Christmas because I could ask for a gift that I didn't get at Christmas. Boy, my first Christmas, New Year and birthday in my new house. I guess this was not turning out so bad moving here and all, I thought.

Aside from school, the next couple of months were spent indoors, which got pretty boring. It was too cold to go out for very long. I'd wander out and go plop myself down in a snow bank or throw snowballs at cans. Then I'd go back in and figure out some new way to keep myself amused.

One day, out of boredom, I decided to take a hammer to some of my cars and make them look banged up a bit. I figured that because I had more Hot Wheel cars, I'd bang up a couple of Johnny Lighting cars instead of them.

After about ten minutes of my banging, my mother came down into the basement and asked me what all that banging was. I told her that my cars were getting into accidents as I gave another one a whack.

"What the hell are you doing to your cars!" my mother yelled.

"I'm just denting them a bit," I said.

"Well, I go out and buy them for you, not so you can smash them and throw them away," she explained.

"Jeez, I'm still going to keep them. I like them smashed up a little bit, that's all," I said.

"I think what you have is cabin fever," she said.

"I don't have a fever. I feel fine," I answered. "Well, do you have anything else I can break?"

"Well," she thought, "maybe I could give you something you can break."

"Cool! How about the small TV in the kitchen?" I asked.

"No, not the TV. Here, you can smash up that old typewriter over there, okay?"

That weekend we got hit with a blizzard. My cousin Dino happened to be there for that, and we wanted to go out to play in the snow. My mother bundled us up in so many winter clothes that Dino and I made a deal: If either of us fell on his back, the other guy would have to help him up, and we shook hands on it. We had a great time that day out in the snow and for that whole weekend, so we were both pretty sad when he left Sunday night.

Winter drifted into spring and then into summer. My mother told me that she and my father were going to sell their part of the taxi business, and I asked her if we were going to have to move. She told me that we didn't have to move just because they were selling that business. "Your father is actually looking at a new business, one that I'm sure you're going to like."

As thoughts of toy stores danced through my head, she said, "It's a pizzeria."

Pop went my thought.

"A pizzeria? What do we know about pizza?" I asked.

"What's there to know? A little dough, a little sauce and a little cheese," she answered.

"Yeah, but does Dad know how to cook pizza? I thought he only knew how to barbecue steaks."

"Don't worry, we'll send Grandpa over to keep an eye on him. What do you think, Daddy? You want to go to work and make some pizza and Italian food?" she joked.

"What? You think'a I'ma not know how to cook. I tella you I hada three restaurants ina Italy. I hada leavea because'a the war. I'ma leave everything and come to this country. Sure'a, I show Johnny how to cook."

Wow, I thought, if we sold my grandfather's cooking we'd be rich in no time, he cooks great.

That Sunday I asked my father to take me over to the pizzeria. When we got there, I got out of the car, looked at the place, and said, "Dad, there's nothing here - just blocks and blocks of houses and an empty store."

"Well, that's just it, Mike. There's nothing around for blocks. If someone around here wants to get any food, they have to drive all the way over to Northern Boulevard for something and eight blocks in this direction is La Guardia Airport, and all the people work on this end of the airport," he explained.

"But, Dad there's nothing in this place? How are you going to make pizza?" I tried to tell him. "Michael, I'm buying all the stuff for this place. The oven will be delivered on Wednesday. Then a carpenter is going to build all the counters. Then the tables and chairs are going to be delivered. Oh, yeah, I'm also getting two pinball machines."

That was all he had to say, pinball machines. I knew this place was going to make it now.

School was letting out in a couple of weeks, time for summer vacation. Barbara, that funny little girl from across the street, had introduced me to all the kids on her block. First, there was Ingra Leadera next to Barbara's house, then next to Ingra's house there were three boys, George who was a little younger than I was, Phil who was about a year and a half older, and then Uhdest Lemanis. I had never seen a big kid like Uhdest before; he was huge. He was 17 years old, and they told me that he was almost 6'3."

It was pretty cool playing with Phil and George. Since Phil was older, he had some cool toys. We would spend hours playing with Hot Wheel cars and G.I. Joes. When Barbara would come over and ask me why I was always playing over there instead of with her at her house, I would try to tell her that it was because she didn't like climbing trees and smashing models, but she wouldn't understand.

"Well, I knew you first, so you should come play over at my house, too," she would say.
"All right, I will," I said.
"When?"
"I don't know... soon."
"You promise?"
"Well, yeah. I promise."
"Okay." she said before she left.
"Ohhhh, Michael's going over to Barbara's to play house and have a tea party," Phil kidded.
"No, I'm not."
"What'a ya' think she wants to do? Climb trees or have a water balloon fight?" Phil asked me.
"No! I won't play."
"Oh really? She makes us all play sometimes. Doesn't she, George," he said.

When George looked at me and gave me a half smile, I knew I was doomed.

Willie, the kid who lived behind me, called me over to the fence that separated our properties. He started talking like he hoped all was forgiven, so I believed him. After talking for a few minutes, he asked me if I wanted to go over and play in his yard. I asked him if he had any good toys to play with, and he said, "Yeah, plenty. Do you like G.I. Joes? Come on. Come into my yard, and we'll play over here."

When I got there, I asked him where his G.I. Joes were and he said, "Right here." Then POW! he punched me square in the face.

I looked at him and said, "What'a ya' crazy!" before he punched me several more times in the face.

While I was struggling to get away from the beating I was receiving, I noticed his mother was washing dishes, and she glanced at me occasionally. I fought my way over to her at the window in the hopes that she did recognize what she was seeing. I banged on the window and asked her to help me as Willie punched me in the head. She looked at me and said, "Go away. Go play in your own yard."

I knew then that I was on my own. I lunged at Willie, first swinging wildly as I repeated every curse I had ever heard. Willie started back pedaling as some of my punches started to land. Then, as I was hitting him, he made his way out of his gate that was a few feet from the kitchen window and slammed it behind himself. I ran and kicked it as he held it shut. Then from nowhere I heard Willie's mother yell, "Don't you dare kick my fence!"

"Oh...! Now you can fucking see!" I shrieked. "What did you do - put your fucking glasses on? You were blind when your son was trying to beat the shit out of me, but now you see everything?"
"Hey!" Willie yelled. "You can't talk that way to my mother!"
"Fuck you! You motherfucker! I'll fucking kill you if you come inside this gate," I screamed.
"Get out! Get out of my yard!" Willie's mother screamed as she banged on the window.

I told Willie that he better never come near me again, and then I ran home.

When I ran into the kitchen, my grandfather was cooking dinner. He looked at me and said, "What happen to you? You looka like you get beat up."
"I did, Grandpa. Is it bad?" I asked.
"C'mere, letta me see. Eh, it'sa nota so bad. Go washa your face," he said.

My mother and father thought it was bad, though. Bad enough to go over there with the cops that night. After about an hour, my parents came back home. My mother asked me why I had cursed at Willie and his mother, and I said, "Well, yeah, I guess I did some cursing after I realized that I was dying, you know."
"Well, I know. It's okay, Michael," she answered.
"Now," my father said, "anyone ever tries to beat you up like that again, I don't care what you have to do. Pick up a stick or whatever, and you beat their ass. Don't ever take a beating like that again."
"Yeah, but he's twice my size," I added.
"Exactly the reason why I'm telling you to pick up a stick and hit him with it."
"John, you can't tell him to beat someone up with a stick."

My father walked over to me, pointed at my face and said, "He has a black eye, and a fat lip, that kid is twice his size, and my son is not going to stand there and get the shit beat out of him! Next time, you pick up a stick and hit him if you have too."

Well, it kinda all made sense to me. I certainly was getting a beating and if I had a stick, I probably would have made him stop a lot sooner. Sounded like a plan to me.

One day I was across the street playing tag with a bunch of other kids from our block. We decided that we could use the whole block, but we couldn't step into the street; otherwise, you'd be out of bounds. While Phil and I were up on the next corner, I stopped and saw this kid playing in his yard across the street.

"Do you know him?" Phil asked me.
"Yeah," I said. "That's that Capeeto kid."

Just then, Marcus turned and saw me looking at him.

"Run!" I shouted. "He's going to step on my fingers."

Marcus yelled, "Hey, I told you I was sorry."
"I know, I was just joking," I said.
"Exactly where do you live?" he asked.

I pointed down the block.

"Well, I live over here. I guess we can be friends."
"I guess."
"Well, see you around," he said as he ran off.
"Where do you know that kid from?" Phil asked.
"Oh, he was running across the top of the desk's at school, and stepped on my hand. That's how I met him."
"And you want to be friends now?"
"Well, the principal was chasing him, but he said he was sorry."
"Oh, I guess that explains it," Phil said.

My mother, Grandfather, and I went to the grand opening of the pizzeria. I wasn't sure what to expect considering that I had never been to a grand opening before. Somewhere in the back of my head I wondered if there would be a parade, fireworks, or a ribbon cutting, but alas, there was nothing of the sort. When we pulled up I said, "Well at least it looks like a pizzeria now, I just hope Dad knows how to make pizza or we're doomed."

We went inside, and the place looked really good. The big oven was there along with the new countertop, soda machines, a jukebox, and a pinball machine. My father said, "Well, it's going to be our first day of business so I made the first pie for us. Eat it, and tell me how it is."

I couldn't believe it, the pizza actually tasted good. There weren't too many people who showed up that day but my father said he wasn't worried, and boy, was he right. After a while he had to quit his night job because it got too busy.

My father would bring home the extra slices and pies he had left over from that night. It was great for a while always having pizza around, but then it was like, Oh no, not more pizza. I started to give it away to my friends, which made me pretty popular with them.

During that week my mother kinda started a new job. She would go out during the day and try to sell these bowls and cups that were made out of plastic to people in the neighborhood. The name of the stuff was Tupperware; my mother explained to me that in no time everybody would be using it. The only item that interested me was this big plastic ice tray thing that let you make ice Popsicles. All you had to do was pour in some Kool-Aid or juice, cover it with the handles, and put it in the freezer. That I liked; the rest of it just looked like junk to me.

After a few weeks of this, my mother told me that she enjoyed selling the Tupperware because she was able to meet a bunch of people who lived in the neighborhood. She told me that she met this one Italian lady named Chickie, which I thought was a funny name for a lady. She said that Chickie had three kids and was divorced. There was Angie, who was about a year older than I was, than Tina who was older than Angie, and then Anthony who was the oldest. She said that she had spoken to Chickie, and she said that Tina did some babysitting and that she could watch me sometimes.

My mother took me over to the "slide." The slide was a huge slide that was about four stories high. When you got there, you would buy some tokens and then grab a burlap bag and start climbing the stairs. It felt like it took forever to get to the top, but it was worth it.

My mother let me stay there until I worked up a good sweat and then took me over to the "stone pool" on the other side of the expressway. "Remember, Michael," she warned. "No more spinning in circles. You know what happened last time."

We stayed there for an hour or two, and then my mother bought us some hot dogs from a hot dog stand. After she got them, we went and sat in the car under the shade with doors open. While we were eating, this huge German shepherd jumped into the back seat with me, and lay down. My mother and I looked at each other wide-eyed. Then I looked over at the dog and said, "Ma, he's staring at my hot dog."
"I know," she said. "Here, let me give him a piece of mine."

She handed him a big piece, and he took one chew and swallowed it.

We looked at each other, and then my mother said, "He must be hungry. I'll give him the rest of it," and he swallowed that, too.

Then I handed him mine, and in one gulp it was gone. I asked my mother if we could keep him, and she said no because she believed he belonged to someone.

"Here, look. He's got dog tags on. This is what we'll do. We'll take some money and go buy some more hot dogs, and then as I drive us home, you keep giving him little pieces. When we get home, I'll call the owner."

I went and got the hot dogs, and we started the ride home. But a few blocks away from the house I said, "Ma, hurry up. I'm running out of hot dogs."

"We're almost home, Michael. Save the last piece for when we get there."

When we got in the driveway, I closed some of the car windows as my mother took down the phone number on his tags. Then I gave him the last piece of hot dog and closed the door. My mother went inside to call the owner. I stayed outside and watched the dog as he watched me.

My mother came out a few minutes later and said, "Well, I spoke with the owner, and he said that he doesn't want the dog."

"What do you mean?" I asked. "Who wouldn't want a dog like this?"

"Well, the guy said that he paid about four-hundred dollars for him, and then he sent him to guard dog school so he could watch his business. But the dog kept biting everyone who worked there. The last straw came when the dog bit him, so he opened the gate and let him go."

"What now, if he doesn't want him back?"

"Well, actually he said that if we wanted him, I could go over there and pick up all the dog's papers."

"All right! Can we keep him, mom? Please? Pretty please?"

"I don't know, Michael. You already have Peewee and Seewee, and this dog looks like he could eat more than you, and a dog and cat" she said.

"Well, let's see if he listens to you, Ma. If he doesn't, then we won't keep him. Okay?" I asked. "Well, I'll try. The guy said that his name is Duke. Open the door, and let's see."

I opened the door and stood back as my mother said in a firm voice, "Duke, come here." And he did. "Duke, sit down," and he did. "Duke, lay down," and he did. "Wow," my mother said. "That's the first time a big dog ever listened to me."

After that we decided to put him in the basement until my father came home to see what he thought about it.

When he got home we all went to the basement, and my father said, "Whoa! That's a big dog."

"What do you think, Dad... should we keep him?"

"Well, if he listens to your mother, sure. Why not? We could use a big dog around here." So we ended up keeping him.

We bought him a big doghouse and got him a long chain for the backyard. But after a little while, we all realized that he only listened to my mother for the most part. Feeding him became one of my new chores though. He ate a big bowl of dry food during the day and then eight cans of dog food at night.

One day my mother asked me if I would like to go to work with my father on Saturday at the pizzeria.

"All day?" I asked.

"Yes."

"Will I get paid?"

"Yes, Michael, your father will pay you," she answered.

"Okay, cool."

Working in the pizzeria wasn't so bad; one of my jobs was to shred the cheese for the pizza using the shredding machine. Then sometimes I'd go with the delivery boy and deliver pizzas with him. The first time I went with him we delivered the pizza, and he got paid and then handed me fifty cents.

"What's that for?" I asked. "My father already pays me."

"Really? Well, this is a tip. It's from the people we just delivered the pizza to," he explained. "Cool! I like your job a lot better than mine. Nobody tips me for shredding mozzarella cheese."

"Well, when you get a little older you'll probably get this job. You've still got some time before you can carry pies by yourself," he explained.

In between working, I'd talk to some of the customers. Otherwise, I'd play the jukebox or the pinball machine. By now my father knew how to throw the pizza dough up in the air and catch it. I asked him to show me how to do it. But I dropped three of them on the floor, and my father said, "Okay, go take a break, champ. I've got to make some pies."

For dinner my father told me to run down the block and go to the butcher shop. "He's got a big bag full of steaks for us. Go there, and come right back. Understand?"

When I got back, my father took two of the metal baking dishes and put the steaks in them. Then he filled them with peppers, onions, mushrooms and olives. Then he made some garlic bread and made me a wine and soda for dinner. I couldn't believe how fast the steaks were cooked. But this oven was five times the size of the one we had at home.

After dinner it was time for work again. We worked until 9:00 at night. It was a long day but I didn't mind. Besides, I got to keep my father company all day, I figured.

I was playing in the backyard one morning. I had this game I would play with this big old seeder we had. It was about four feet long and looked like a long wheel. It had nails sticking out of it, and they would make little holes in the ground as you rolled it along. What I would do is build these little towns with some of my toys and then run them over with it. I would get a big kick out of it. While I was doing it this day, I heard someone say, "Hey, you having fun?" I turned to look, and Willie the kid from behind my house was standing next to my garage.

"You better get out of here, Willie," I said. "You're not allowed over here anymore."

"Well, I'm not in your yard," he said as he pointed down to the curb that ran down the length of my driveway out to the street.

"Yeah, but you better get out of here anyway. Besides, those neighbors are friends of mine, and if I don't like you, neither do they," I told him.

On that note, he walked over, stood in front of me and the seeder, put one foot on top of it, and said, "Oh yeah, you little shit, what are you going to do about it? Maybe it's time for me to whip your ass again."

Well, I knew what time it was, and it wasn't time for an ass whipping. Gee, this is too easy, I thought, as I ran his foot over with the seeder.

He screamed out like a baby. "Maaaaaa!" which sounded like music to me.

Willie pulled his foot off the seeder and ran screaming back to his house. My mother came from upstairs and asked me what all the yelling and screaming was about. I told her what had happened, and she said, "Michael, you didn't really hurt him, did you?"

"Well, I hope so because he really hurt me that day he beat me up," I answered. "Besides, didn't you tell me that Willie's mother told you to keep me out of their yard? Well, that's just what I told him before he came into mine."

That night Willie's mother and father came over to my house with the police. After a few minutes my mother called me outside where everybody was arguing. "This little kid ran over your kid with the seeder?" the cop said.

"Yeah," I said before anyone got a chance to speak, "And I told him to stay out of my yard and he didn't. Then he came over and stood in front of me and told me that maybe he should beat me up again, and I wasn't going to let him beat me up like he did last time."

"All right, all right. From now on, your kid doesn't go into their yard, and make sure you keep this little guy over here. Okay, that's it, nobody goes in nobody's yard, got it," the cop said as he pointed at me and Willy.

When we got inside, my father turned to me and said, "What happened? He came over here and acted like a wiseass again?"

"Yep," I answered.

"I knew he was a wiseass from the day I went over to talk to his parents, the time he beat you up. He was leaning against the wall smiling at me," my father explained.

"Yup, and I remembered what you told me, so I did it," I added.

"Well, look, Michael, don't really hurt him bad, okay? Just hit him in the leg if he's ever dumb enough to come back after this. All right?" he asked.

"All right," I answered.

One of our neighbors from the building next door let their dog come into our yard to poop and Duke broke his chain and killed the other dog. My mother was very upset about it and asked my father if we should get rid of him. My father told her Duke was just guarding his house. Man, I knew Duke was big, but I didn't think he could kill another dog. A few days after that, I did what my mother always told me not to do. I took Duke for a walk by myself. I think I got the idea from seeing Barbara sitting on her front steps with Ronnie, her sister, and I wanted to act like a tough guy. So I got Duke's leash, unchained him, and took him for a walk past Barbara's house.

"Wow! I can't believe you're walking that big dog all by yourself!" Barbara yelled across to me.

Then her sister, Ronnie, said, "Does your mother let you walk that dog?"
"Oh yeah, I walk him all the time," I lied confidently.

I got to the corner, turned left and Duke saw our cat Seewee. Then he growled and started to run towards the cat. I took one, two, three steps with him and lift off. He almost lifted me out of my sneakers. I flew about six feet through the air before I landed. The first thought that went through my head as he dragged me down the sidewalk was, Oh, man, if I let go of this leash I'm dead. My mother will kill me for taking him for a walk. But after being dragged for another couple of feet, I figured I'd have a better chance with my mother at this rate, so I let go of Duke's leash.

As I watched Duke try to catch up to my cat, I figured that it was a good thing that I gave Seewee some time to get away by holding onto the leash. I had been wearing shorts and a tank top, so I had scrapes and scratches just about from head to toe. I even had scratches on my nose from hanging on to the leash while I tumbled and spun around. I got back around the corner, and Ronnie said, "Michael, where's your dog?"
"He's probably in Mexico by now," I answered.
"Oh, my God, are you all right? You look like you're hurt bad," Ronnie asked.

I had a lot of blood on me and then I said, "I don't know. I can't see all of me yet. Besides, now my mother is going to kill me," I added.
"Well, come here. You can cross the street now," Ronnie said as she looked both ways.

Ronnie was Barbara's older sister; she was about two years older than I was. When I got there, Ronnie told me that I did a pretty good job on myself as she took me into their house. Ronnie stood me up on a chair and grabbed some tissues. She wet them down and started dabbing water on my cuts. Barbara walked around me and said, 'Boy, you've got scratches all over you."
"Well, Barb, don't just stand there gawking. Grab some tissues and help me," Ronnie said.

After a few minutes their mother, Fran, walked in. "What's going on here?" she said.
"This is the boy from across the street. He fell down, and we're helping him," Barbara answered.
"Fell down? He looks like he got run over by a truck."

After I explained to Fran what had happened, she said she would call my mother to let her know I was all right. I stayed at Barbara's house while I got patched up for about a half hour, and then I went home. When I got home, Duke was lying down by the front door. He had come home by himself.

"Look what you did to me, you son of a bitch!" I yelled.
Duke, who was much bigger than I was, sat up and looked at me as if I wasn't there until I opened the front door and he trotted inside. "Ma," I yelled. "Duke's home."
"Come in here, and let me look at you," she said.

I went inside, and she started to explain to me all over again why I shouldn't walk the dog all by myself. I had to stand there with egg on my face, with bandages all over, and listen to the whole reason all over again.

My mother grounded me, which meant I had to stay in my yard for two days that time. On the second day of my punishment, I was playing over by the garage with the seeder again when I heard, "Hey, you little motherfucker. I'm gonna kick your fucking ass when my foot gets better, so watch out!" It was Willie, and he was in my yard again.

"Oh," I said as I glanced around the yard for a stick, "You're gonna kick my ass as soon as your foot gets better?"

"Yeah, you little fuck. Worse than the first time." Willie said.

"I think you better get out of my yard, Willie," I warned.

"What...! Who the fuck do you think you are, you little fuck, to tell me to get out of your yard?" he replied.

As I bolted towards a pitchfork, Willie tried to hobble away as he yelled, "Whoa." Willie was half a hobble out of my yard when I closed my eyes and threw the pitchfork.

"Yeeeeeowwwww!" Willie screamed as he crumpled to the floor. I had gotten him right in his bandaged foot.

"Maaaaaaaa! Maaaaaaa!" Willie screamed.

While Willie was lying on the ground I asked him if I should go get another pitchfork to remind him not to come in my yard. "No! No! I'll remember, I'll remember. Maaaaaa!" he screamed.

Just then Willie's mother ran up.

"Oh, my God!" she yelled. "What happened? What happened?" Willie pointed at me and screamed, "He did it! He did it!"

"You little bastard!" she shrieked at me.

"Oh, now you can hear fine, but when I'm screaming for help standing right in front of you, you can't hear fucking shit, right?!" I screamed at her.

At the moment I was so angry I wanted to stick her with the pitchfork. My mother had run out by now and yelled, "Michael! What did you do?!?"

"He wouldn't get out of my yard so I threw the pitchfork at him," I answered.

"Oh my God, oh my God, should I call 911?" my mother yelled from the porch.

"No! I took it out of his foot," Willie's mother yelled. "But your son is an animal!"

I watched Willie's mother try to pick him up, but he was too big, so she helped him to his good foot, and they hobbled away. Then I looked over at my mother who was standing there with her mouth wide open.

"What...?... Well, I told him to get out of my yard!" I said.

"What... did you do!?"

"Well, Dad said to hit him with a stick," I explained.

"Michael... a pitchfork is not a stick," she answered. "Go to your room!"

My father came into my room when he came home from work that night.

"What are you, fucking nuts!" my father said. "You stab him with a pitchfork? I tell you to hit him with a stick, and you stab him with a pitchfork."

Oh, shit, I thought, here comes that beating I never wanted to get from my father. Think fast, think fast, Mike.

"Wait a minute," I stammered. "Do you remember the beating he gave me? I couldn't open my eye for a week."

My father stood there for a second, closed his eyes, and said, "I know... but, Michael, you can kill someone like that."

"Yeah, but I threw it at his legs," I suggested.

"Michael, do not throw anything sharp at anyone. Understand?"

"Yes."

"Do you know what a stick looks like?" he said sarcastically.

"Yes."

"If you have to, you find some sticks tomorrow, unless your mother punishes you."

"Well, you just said I didn't have to be punished," I reminded him.

"Shut up and listen. If you have to, you find some sticks and you hide them wherever you think Willie will come into the yard. And if you have to, you only hit him with a stick. Understand?"

"Yes"

"Okay now get washed and get ready for bed," he said.

That night while I was in bed I thought about what had happened. I couldn't believe how angry I had gotten at Willie's mother. I guess it just shocked me when I saw that she was able to give sympathy to her son when she wasn't able to find any for me the day Willie beat the crap out of me while she watched. But for Willie, I had no sympathy. I was actually glad I skewed him.

Wow, you know, maybe I could have killed him today, I thought. Maybe I ought to watch it when I get that mad. But I've got to say, Mike, you did some fast thinking when Dad was going to whip your butt. Maybe I should ask God to forgive me on this one. Wow, what a day.

My mother told me that school would be starting soon. Please don't remind me, I told her. Then she told me that there was a chance that I would be going to a new school.

"Well, what's wrong with my school?" I asked.

"This one is a little better. It's a Catholic school," she answered.

"Catholic school? What does that mean? I've got to stay in church all day?" I asked.

"No," she answered, "but I'm pretty sure that the nuns are the teachers, so you better be good."

"The nuns are teachers?" I asked.

"Yes."

"But do you mean I have to be good or I have to be a saint?"

"No, you'll just have to be as good as you are," she said as she smiled. "You'll also have to wear a uniform."

"Oh, like they wear in jail, huh? You're sending me there because of what I did to Willie, right?"

"No, I'm not sending you to jail, but that wasn't a good thing that you did to Willie," she answered. "Do you know it cost your father and I two-hundred dollars to get Willie's foot stitched up again?" she added.

"Two hundred dollars...? Well, I wouldn't have paid it."

"Don't be a smart ass. Now go outside and play," she told me.

"Yeah, but I don't want to change schools," I moaned.

"Well, Michael, sometimes life is unfair. Now go outside and play before you end up spending the whole day in your room!" She scolded.

Grumble, grumble, grumble, I thought as I walked outside. I knew I had to go to this school because of Willie, so I better not see him today or I might just try out one of my new sticks on him, I thought.

The young guy who delivered pizza for us didn't show up while I was working at the store. That meant I got to do all the deliveries that were close to the store. My father would send me out with a hand drawn map with phone numbers on it in case I got lost. For the ones that were more than a block or two, he would wait until he had two or three of them and then he would do them in his car. Before he left he'd say, "Okay, Michael, you know how to work the cash register, right? You know how to serve a slice, soda or Italian ice. If anyone asks you for a sandwich, you tell them you have to wait until your father comes out of the basement, all right?"

"All right," I answered.

After he left, about five customers came into the store. By the time he came back, four of them were still seated and eating.

"So how'd you make out?" he asked.

"Fine. As a matter of fact, if you show me how to make the sandwiches and a pizza pie, you could make deliveries and I could work behind the counter," I boasted.

"That's okay, tough guy. If you were to fall into that oven and cook yourself like a pork chop, your mother would kill me," he answered.

"Oh before I forget, someone called for a pie. I took their phone number and address like you do," I explained.

It got real busy around dinnertime as usual, so my father showed me how to make a bunch of different sandwiches, but I still couldn't put them in the oven. At least they were ready by the time he got back. I was pretty tired by the end of the day, but I was glad that I helped my father at the store. Before we closed that night, my father said, "Hey, Michael, you worked hard today so I'm going to give you twenty-five dollars for today along with your five-dollar allowance. So that'll make it thirty, All right?"

"Holy cow! Thirty bucks. I made about twenty bucks in tips today. That makes like fifty bucks I made today. Cool!"

"Really? You made that much in tips?" he asked. "Well, I guess you did all right for yourself then," he added.

"Hey, Dad," I said. "I don't mind working this hard if I can get paid like this each Saturday. As a matter of fact, I'd rather work with you all week long than go to school," I suggested.

"Well, we'll see what happens, champ."

My head was swimming all the way home with the thoughts of which toys I wanted to buy. But I knew that somehow I had to convince my mother to let me go to work in the pizzeria instead of going to Catholic school.

CHAPTER 2

IT'S JUST A BAD DREAM

I still had most of the rabbits my mother had bought me, but now they were big. Not only had they gotten big, but they had also gotten much smarter, so smart that now a bunch of them knew how to get out of their large cage. I had to chase the rabbits around the yard and catch them every night before I went to bed. A few of them had already got out and got away. I couldn't figure out how they kept getting out, so one day I decided to watch them for an hour or two and see how they did it. They always seemed to get out early so I got up early to see what was happening.

About an hour later, I saw the gray rabbit, the one that always got out, climb up the chicken wire just like it was a ladder and then hop off the top of the wire. I couldn't believe it when I saw it. He stayed outside the wire until one or two of the other ones climbed out. Then they'd just walk around eating grass. After seeing that, I decided that if they wanted to get out that badly, I wouldn't bother to catch the ones who were able to do this trick. But I did create a way for these guys to get back in by making some steps so they could hop back in at night to go to sleep. It all made sense when I realized that there wasn't much of a fight to catch them late at night. They seemed to let me catch them. It worked out pretty well until they would teach a new one to get out, and I would have to show that one how to get back in with the steps I made for them.

Chickie's daughter Tina from around the corner was coming over to babysit me these days. She ended up taking me to Whitestone Pool, over by the Whitestone Bridge one day. We went with two of her girlfriends who were sisters; their names were Liz and Eve. I had seen them coming and going from one of the buildings next to my house so I kinda knew them from the neighborhood. They were all a little older than I was which I thought was pretty cool. By this time I had run across a copy or two of Playboy and didn't mind going with a bunch of girls at all, although there did come a time that day when I became a little uncomfortable.

It was after we had been swimming for a while, and I didn't see that Tina had given back the key to the locker room after I had changed back into my clothes. So I got the idea that I wanted to go swimming again. Tina said, "Well, what we'll do is we'll hold up the big beach towel, and you can get changed behind it, Okay?"

I figured it would be all right, so I went along with it and started to change. After I had taken off my underwear, I looked up and saw Tina with the same funny look that I had on my face when she had taken me into the changing booth with her earlier that day. I turned in the other direction and said to her, "Hey! What'a you lookin' at?!"

"Oooooo, look at his little pee pee," Eve said.

Now she and her sister both had that silly look on their faces.

"Hey, it gets bigger, you know," I threatened.

"Ooooooo, let me see it again," Liz said.

I stood there, and shook my hips, putting on a little show, and Tina said, "Michael, turn around, you little flirt, and put on your bathing suit. I won't look."

After that we went swimming again. It made me glad that I was smart enough to know how to swim in the deep pool because the kiddie pool always had a strange degree of warmness to it. At the end of the day, we took the number 15 bus back into Flushing. The nice thing about the bus was that it stopped on my block. When I got home, my grandfather had cooked some chicken for dinner, so I asked Tina if she'd like to have dinner with me and my grandfather, which she did. After dinner she told my grandfather that he was the best cook in town, which made my grandfather smile.

After a while, Tina would come over even if she didn't have to baby sit me. She'd just pick me up and I'd spend the whole day with her and her friends. I thought it was kinda neat to hang out with older kids. She had another girlfriend named Sandra Mossberg. Sandra had a big family with a bunch of kids. She also had two little brothers, Todd, who was a little older than I was, and Jeff, who was a little younger. Todd was quiet like me and kept to himself. Jeff was the total opposite. He had a big mouth and was always talking. He always wanted to wrestle or fight- come rain or shine. Sandra also had a brother named Sammy, who was huge with long hair. He hung out with a kid who lived next to him, Jimmy Marnell. Jimmy had a younger brother, Bobby, who would come over and play with Jeff and Todd and me whenever Tina would take me there. We would have fun playing for hours, but somehow Jeff would always manage to turn it into a wrestling match.

Sometimes Tina took me over to Bench Park, which was two blocks away from my house. There were some older guys who would hang out on one side of the park, and sometimes Sammy and Jimmy would stay with the older guys while I would stay with Tina and her friends. I always had fun hanging out with Tina.

My mother took all my cousins to an Italian restaurant for Dino's birthday. She asked Dino what he wanted to eat, and he said he wanted pizza. "Pizza? I could have taken us to our pizzeria if you wanted pizza," my mother told him.

"Yeah, we all want pizza," all of my cousins and I yelled.

"Fine, pizza it is," she said. "But we'll get a special one with everything on it, okay?"

When the pizza came out it was huge. My mother gave us each a slice, and we all tried different ways of getting it into our mouths. My cousin Russell yelled, "Let's see who can eat their pizza the fastest. On the count of three: One, two, three."

We each started to gobble up our slice. After a few moments Russell and I looked like we were going to be tied for first place, so I started to eat faster. But the only way it seemed like I could beat him was if I chewed my food less than I was doing, so that's what I did. Then I took one big gulp from my mouthful, and it got stuck. I tried to drink some water, but it wouldn't go down. Then I tried to spit it out, but nothing happened. Then I started doing an Indian rain dance to try and attract some attention to the fact that I was choking. I heard my cousin Dino say, "Look at Michael. He's acting funny."

"Funny! Oh, my God, he's choking!" my mother yelled.

She leaped over to my side of the table and did what any mother would do, I guess. She stuck her hand down my throat and grabbed for the pizza. It almost made me throw up, but she got her hand and the pizza out of there before I did throw up.

When she got finished and I was still trying to catch my breath, my cousins were yelling, "That was funny, Aunt Alma. Do it again."

No, once was enough for this act, I thought, as I gasped for air.

My mother started to slice everybody's pizza into smaller pieces as she said, "Okay, no more races. Now everyone just eat their pizza".

Once I was able to start eating again, I chewed every square inch of my pizza at least five times.

My mother took me shopping for school clothes. I told her she didn't have to buy me any clothes if she would let me go to work with my father instead of school, but she wasn't able to see my point of view for some reason. Oh well, if she was buying school clothes like these, at least I wasn't going to that Catholic school that we had talked about.

When school finally did start, I was in the third grade. We couldn't talk during class any more, and the school books seemed like they were harder. On the bus ride home, I saw that Capeeto kid. I went over and talked with him. I asked him what class he was in, and he told me it didn't matter because he didn't think he was going to be here that long. Then he asked me if I wanted to come over to his house this weekend to play. I told him that I had to work on Saturday at the pizzeria, and then I had to do some chores on Sunday morning, but I would be able to come over Sunday afternoon if that was okay. He said it would be good in the afternoon. "Oh, yeah," he added. "If you have any Hot Wheels or G.I. Joe's, bring them too."

After work that Saturday, my father told me that I didn't have to come in on Saturdays any more. I asked him why, and he said because I wouldn't have any time to be a kid now that school had started. I didn't like the idea because that meant I wouldn't get the same amount of money I was making, so I said, "Dad, I don't mind working on Saturdays."

"Yeah, I know, but the business is doing better and I've got some full-time people now. So there's not a lot of things for you to do to keep you busy now. But we'll see what happens, okay?" he explained.

That day went by very slowly and I could hardly keep myself amused. I didn't get to make any money on tips because the new delivery boy wouldn't take me with him. That night on the ride home I figured that maybe I wouldn't mind staying home on Saturdays more often, especially since I really didn't have to do anything but hang out all day.

I found my dog Peewee having puppies one morning. I didn't really know what was happening to her at first, so I yelled for my mother.

"It's all right, Michael. She's just having her puppies," my mother reassured me.

"Like that!" I remarked, "I thought she was dying."

Peewee was a little dog, so her puppies looked like big gerbils to me. There were eight of them altogether, and they were crawling around making little yapping sounds with their eyes closed.

That afternoon I loaded up my wagon and headed over to Marcus Capeeto's house. After I knocked on the front door he came outside and said, "Cool. What did you bring?"

"Some G.I. Joes and Hot Wheel cars," I answered.

"I got a bunch of G.I. Joe stuff, too. Some of it was my brother Freddy's stuff," he explained.

We went into his garage to get his toys. It was huge, two stories and almost the size of a small house. After he rummaged around for a little bit, he dragged out a big box. It was loaded with G.I. Joe stuff.

We had a great time all afternoon. At dinnertime Marcus's mother called him to eat.

"Oh, who is this, Marcus? You made a new friend?" she asked.

"Yeah. Mike, this is my mom. Debbie's her name," he said, "And Mom, this is Mike. He lives down the block. I met him at school."

I looked at Marcus and smiled, not knowing if she knew about Marcus running across desks. Marcus smiled back as if she didn't, so I didn't say anything.

"Well, it's probably time for you to go home and eat dinner, Michael. So you guys pack up for tonight, okay?" she said as she walked back inside.

As we were packing up I said, "You know, Marcus, I had a fun time today. Some of the other kids told me that I shouldn't play with you because you're crazy."

"Yeah, I know they all say that."

"Well, Marcus, you did step on my hand while you were running around on top of the desks, you know," I explained.

"Well, I don't know what happened. On that day the principal had grabbed me in a bear hug because he said I was acting up again. The next thing I know, he's carrying me out of the classroom, and I couldn't breathe, so I got away from him and ran," he told me.

"Well, if you can, next time give me a signal that you're going to get nuts so I can run away, okay?" I asked.

"Yeah, I'll try," he said. "Well, to be honest, they say I'm hyperactive"

"What does that mean?" I asked with a raised eyebrow.

"They say I make decisions to fast without thinking."

"Well, that's weird, my mother says I take too long to make a decision sometimes?"

"Hmmm... that is weird."

"Well, maybe I'll see you at school tomorrow. See ya'," I said as I walked off with my wagon full of stuff.

I got home, and my grandfather said, "Aye, what'sa matter for you? I'ma cook over an hour ago. Now it'sa cold," my grandfather explained. "Go washa you hands and'a face. I'ma heating it up," he added.

When my father got home that night, he told us that he had just heard that one of the owners at Bruno and Delayo's had been shot and killed and a driver was wounded.

"Gee, Dad, I guess you're lucky you quit that job huh?" I told him.

"Hmm, you don't know how lucky I was. That would've happened on my shift. That driver would have been me," he explained.

One Saturday my mother told me we were driving over to my Aunt Linda's house. I complained that I didn't want to drive over to Corona see them because I wanted to get some of my chores done. My mother explained that it was a different Aunt Linda, and she lived twenty minutes away from us.

"I have another Aunt Linda?"

"Yes, and she has a son, named Jackie, and a daughter named Dawn. Aunt Marie, and Aunt Linda will be there with their kids. We're going to have a barbeque."

"Why would I have two aunts named Linda?"

"It's a long story, I'll tell you some other time. And, your cousin Shery, is staying with her."

"How many other relatives do I have that I don't know about?" I asked.

"This is it, there aren't any other ones."

When we went to go meet my new aunt it was nice seeing all my cousins. Then, I got to meet my new cousin Jackie, his sister Dawn, and Shery. I also got to meet my new uncle, and oddly enough, his name was Richie also. Boy, I thought, I had nice muscles, but my new Uncle Richie had real muscles, he even had big veins popping out of them. My Aunt Linda was very pretty, she had blonde hair, and was very thin compared to my other Aunt Linda.

My cousin Jackie was my age, which was cool, and my cousin Dawn was a baby, like a couple of months old. Shery, was a little older then us, and she was beautiful. My cousins and I swooned over every word she said.

Shery would babysit us from time to time, whenever the family would get together. It was funny, because babysitters would never last watching us, we'd burn them up. But we all loved Shery, if she told us to jump out of a five story window, we would do it with a smile on our faces for her. Then, one day, she was gone. My cousins, and I, were told that she moved. We sat there screaming and crying, 'Nooooo, it's not fair. Where is she? She can stay in my room. I'll sleep on the couch.'

For weeks, and weeks we'd complain, but, it never brought her back. The world just swallowed her up, and we never even got to say goodbye.

About a month into my new school year, my mother informed me that I was switching schools.

"Well, what's wrong with my old school?"
"This one's a little better, and I told you that there was a chance that you would be going there."
"I'll also have to get you some uniforms," she added.
"Yeah, but you already bought me new clothes," I argued.
"Well, first, we have to see if they'll accept you at that school," she answered.
"What do you mean? They might not want me? Why not? I'm a pretty good kid, but if they don't want me, that's fine too. I'd rather not go anyway."
"Well, you have to take a little test to see if you could keep up with the other kids in your class," she answered.
"Ma, if they don't want me there, that's fine with me. I'm happy where I'm at," I restated.
"No, I think it's a better school so you're going to go," she told me. "We'll be going there tomorrow, so wear something nice," she added.

Well, Michael, I thought, if there's a test to get in maybe I could accidentally fail the test and not have to go.

The next day we went up to the school to talk with a nun who was in charge of something. I didn't like the idea of going to this place, and seeing all these kids wearing the same uniforms didn't change that idea. We walked into the nun's office, and she told us her name was Sister Ann. Then she said she was the vice principal and asked me what my name was. For a second or two I wondered if I should jump on her desk and step on her hand, but I decided to tell her my name instead. I took a little written test in her office and passed, and after a while it started making me a little sick to hear how well the two of them were getting along, I mean really sick. Being that she had a small sink in her office I asked her if I could go throw up, hoping that she would decide that there really wasn't any room in her school for a little boy who thinks it's okay to throw up in people's sinks. But instead she pulled her chair in front of me and said, "What's the matter, Michael? Are you feeling a little nervous?" To which I replied, "BARF" all over her habit.

As I wiped the drool away from my mouth, I figured, Cool, I'm outta here. But I forgot she was a nun. She told me that everything would be okay now, which was not what I wanted to hear. I thought it was pretty cool, though, that she had another uniform in her closet. Then she told my mother to cover my eyes while she cleaned up and changed. I had never heard my mother say she was sorry so many times for something she didn't do.

"Well," Sister Ann said after she cleaned up, "We got off to a little messy start, but I think Michael will do fine here."

Ugh, I thought.

When we got outside my mother said, "I can't believe what you did in there. I've never been so embarrassed in my life."

"I asked her if I could use her sink; I didn't ask her to sit in front of me. She must've known I was sick. It was her fault too." I told my mother.

"Sick! Not only did you get sick on her, but I saw a nun in her underwear. God is going to kill me for that," she explained.

We left the school and drove a few blocks away to a place called Murray's. It was where all the other kids went to get their uniforms. I wondered for a second if I should try to throw up on someone there as a last resort. After I got fitted the tailor told my mother the clothes would be ready in a few days so she could pick them up then.

"Oh, that's good," my mother said. "That means you can get your uniforms right away."
"Yeah, just great," I answered.

I went to my old school the next day and said goodbye to a bunch of the kids I had met there and to get my things. Then the following day I went to my new school with no uniform. The first thing I noticed was that it was quiet in this school. I mean real quiet. They also did something that I thought was a little funny. Whenever it was time to teach a new subject at a certain hour, the teacher would leave and another teacher would come in with her books and teach something else.

When I went to the lunchroom that day, I really stuck out like a sore thumb. All these kids were running around in uniforms, and there I was in street clothes. I felt like an alien. I sat by myself and checked out the other kids who were there. After a little while this blond-headed kid came over and said, "Hi, my name's Neil McGrorey. What's yours?" I told him my name, and he asked, "How come you don't have a uniform on?"

As I began to explain, I noticed that a fight was starting. One of the kids was pretty big; the other one was about my size. Then all of a sudden, the smaller guy pops the big guy right in the nose. The big guy started bleeding and ran for the bathroom, followed by the little guy, me, Neil and a bunch of other guys. When we got in the bathroom, the big kid looked in the mirror and cried, "You broke my nose."
"Nah, it's not broke," the smaller kid said.

The rest of us kinda took turns looking at it, and we all came to the same conclusion.
"Yeah, you broke his nose," I said.
"Really? Gee, I'm sorry. I didn't mean to break your nose," the smaller kid said to the bigger one.
"Hey, Neil, does this kinda stuff go on all the time?" I asked as I hoped it didn't.
"Naaa, not really, why? I bet you think you're in some kind of crazy school now, huh?" he said.
"Well, yeah, I was kinda thinking that," I told him. "Hey, do you know this guy?" I asked.
"Who? This guy?" he said as he pointed to the smaller kid.
"Yeah," I answered.
"That's Donde. I've known him for years. He's an Italian kid that lives on my block," he explained.

Hmmm, I thought, maybe I might want to be on friendly terms with this guy. "Well, I'd like to meet him," I asked Neil.
"Yeah, I guess. Why not? Hey, Donde, this is my new friend. Hey, what's your name?"

"Mike."

"Oh yeah, Mike. He wanted to meet you," Neil said.

When I looked at Donde he said, with the look of someone who wasn't sure if they were going to be in big trouble in a few minutes on his face, "Huh? Uhm... yeah... hi."

I walked over to him, shook his hand, and said, "You've got some punch there, buddy."

"Yeah, maybe too good," he answered.

"Well, it was nice to meet you. Maybe I'll see you later," I answered.

"You mean if he only gets suspended," Neil added as we walked back into the lunchroom.

When I got home after school, I told my mother about what a great school she had put me in and explained to her what had happened that day. Needless to say my mother freaked. I didn't spare any details when I explained it again, hoping that there was still time not to pick up my uniforms.

The next day my mother let me stay home from school, but she went instead. She told me that she wanted to speak to Sister Ann again before I went back. But as luck would have it, I went back the next day, stupid uniform and all. Another thing I noticed was that the schoolwork was a little harder now, so I was real happy after I got past my first week.

That Saturday I went over to my cousin's house in Corona. When I got there I ran upstairs to get Dino, but my aunt Linda told me that he was being punished. Dino knelt down on the other side of the door and yelled, "Hey, Michael, over here, under the door."

I ran over to the door, shoved my hand under it as if I was a kitten, and said, "Hey Dino! What's up? What did you do now?"

"Awwww, I don't know, but it was something that got my mother mad at me," he said as he grabbed my fingers.

"Linda, can I go in and see him?" I said as I looked up at her.

"No, Michael. He's being punished. Didn't I tell you that's what happens when people get punished, Dino? They don't get to do the things they want." she said.

"Can I go in for a little while? I'll be quiet. Please?" I asked her.

"Well, for a little while," she answered.

After she opened the door, I ran in and tackled Dino onto his bed. We wrestled for a little bit, and then we talked about the rabbits and Grandpa. Before you knew it, my Aunt Linda opened the door and told me I had to leave now. I hugged him, and then I left.

As I walked down the stairs I couldn't imagine what Dino could have possibly done so bad that Aunt Linda was mad enough not to let me spend some time with him on the few occasions we got to see each other now.

When I got downstairs, my Aunt Marie told me that Ronnie and Russell were playing over in the lot. The lot was next to my cousin's house. It had just been a huge empty lot until they built a big warehouse there. The warehouse was one story tall, but the garage doors were big enough to let in tractor-trailers. But one day after completing the whole building except for the dirt floor inside, they just stopped working on it. At first the older kids used to play there, but then we also went there after a while. The older kids used to drive cars in there and take them apart. The first few times we would sit there and watch how fast they would do it. Then after they didn't come back for them, we knew that we could go play with the cars.

Playing turned into breaking some of them, and for my cousin Russell they made nice fireplaces. He would tell everybody to go and collect paper and wood and bring it over to the car. Then he would carefully stuff the paper under the dashboard, and then he'd light the stuff on fire. He would keep bigger pieces of wood outside the car until the fire got bigger and then feed the wood into the fire. I kinda knew that maybe we shouldn't be doing this, but it was a lot better looking than burning one of my toy cars. Another reason why I knew it was not a good thing to do was that, whenever the fires would get big enough, the fire fighters on the other side of the block would open up their windows at the back of the firehouse and yell and curse at us. At that point my cousin Russell would make us wait until the fire truck was at the end of the block, and then he would yell, "Run!"

Then we'd run up the corner to the house. The first time I was there, I was pretty scared when the firemen started yelling at us, but after a couple of times it was no big deal. I always ended up doing something crazy whenever I went over my cousin's house, but this definitely took the cake, so to speak.

The following week one day after school my mother told me that she was taking me to meet her mother. It kinda surprised me because, aside from ever asking my mother if her mother was alive, I never thought she lived close enough to visit. My mother said that I would also get to meet her mother's new husband, Al Adamo. She really surprised me when she said that I would meet her half-brother and half-sister who were my age, too. I had to ask my mother twice whether or not they would be considered my aunt and uncle and she told me they would be.

"Wow, pretty cool," I said.

After I got there I felt that something was a little strange. After all the places we drove upstate, and how far it would take to visit my other relatives, it was odd to see that my grandmother lived six blocks away. My "uncle's" name was Billy; he looked just like Jerry Lewis did in his black and white movies with Dean Martin. My "aunt's" name was Frances, but everyone called her Franny and she looked a little like my mother.

After my mother talked with Mary, her mother, she decided to let me stay there a while and left. Franny, Billy, and I played together inside for about an hour. Then my Aunt Franny said that she was going to go outside and asked me if I wanted to go with her or stay inside with Billy. "Why don't we all go outside?" I said.
"I can't. I'm punished," Billy answered.

I figured I'd have more fun with Billy instead of waiting for my Aunt Franny to ask me to play jump rope or something with her, so I stayed inside. It turned out that I was glad that I decided to stay in with Billy because he had a cool game he would play whenever he was punished. He went into the kitchen and came back to the bedroom with a pot of water and a roll of toilet paper. He put the water next to the window in his room and then dunked a bit of toilet paper into the water. "Okay" he said, "Here comes one. Watch."

I peered out the window and saw some guy walking down the block towards us.
"Stand back, stand back," Billy exclaimed.

As soon as the guy got even with the window, swoosh, "swap" went the wet toilet paper. "What the fuck!" the guy yelled. "Who the fuck threw that?"

I almost peed in my pants as I tried to muffle my laughter into a pillow. After I watched him do it a few times, I decided to give it a whack myself. My target ended up being a young kid who was about my age. I lined him up and then let it rip. Whoosh, shwop! I got a direct hit on my first try. "Hey?!?" he yelled as he wiped the toilet paper from his neck. Then he looked up into the trees and said, "Ugh! Bird shit!" as he ran off. I don't know what kind of birds he was used to seeing, but I probably would have run off too if I thought that a bird that size just shit on me.

After about a half hour of this, I couldn't believe that the people couldn't see all the toilet paper, or bombs as we called them, all over the sidewalk, but they didn't. We decided to quit after some guy we had gotten ran into the small building my uncle lived in and rang the bell for a few minutes. Whew, that was close, I thought.

My mother picked me up after my grandmother had given us dinner, and I told my uncle I'd see him again soon. When we got in the car, my mother asked me if I had fun while I was there. "Oh, I had a great time there. I'd like to go back real soon, too." I told her.

My father said that he was taking me to my Uncle Mike's house this weekend to go crab fishing. He explained to me that it was a family tradition and that they hadn't done it together for some time.
"What do we use? Fishing poles?" I asked.
"No, you use crab cages, or you can use a kili line," he said.
"What's a kili line?" I asked him.
"Well, it's not much really. It's a string that you put either a fish head or a piece of chicken on, and you drop it over the side of the boat. After a little while you slowly pull the line up while someone waits with the fish net. If you have a crab on the end of the line, the other guy scoops it up with the net and throws it into the crab bucket," he explained.
"Where do we get the cages and stuff?" I asked.
"Your Uncle Mike's got all that stuff at his house, and whatever he doesn't have we can rent when we get the boat," he said. "So what we're going to do is this. We've got to leave here Sunday at about 4:00 in the morning, and then we'll meet everybody at the boat. After we go crabbing for a few hours, we'll go back to Mike's house, cook up all the crabs, and eat like kings, all right? Sounds good?" he added.

"Yeah, sounds great," I said.

I could hardly wait for school to end that week so I could go crabbing with my cousins but unfortunately I had to. My homeroom teacher's name was Sister Cleopher, which made the other kids shudder with fear by the very whisper of her name. I didn't understand why everyone was afraid of her but they all warned, You'll see why one day. That day had come a little sooner than I thought it would.

I was in our homeroom class one morning talking with this kid who lived in my neighborhood, when all of a sudden Sister Cleopher said, "Michael, Joseph, the two of you come up here right now!"

We had been doing a math assignment, and I figured she wanted us to do something on the blackboard. When we got up there, she screeched, "Joseph, put your hands out!" Joseph started crying as he raised his hands into position while the nun slid her ruler out of her desk. No... this can't possibly be happening, could it? I thought.

Joseph raised his hands waist high with his palms turned down and "Whack."

"Owwww," Joseph cried as the ruler slapped his hand. By now my jaw was waist high. Holy shit, I thought. "Smack" the ruler came down again. By the time she stopped smacking each hand three times Joseph had tears running down his face.

"Michael!" she snapped. "Put your hands out!"
"Uh uh, I'm not going to put my hands out there," I suggested.
"What do you mean? Put your hands out," she demanded.
"Look, Sister, you can send me home, throw me out or suspend me, but I'm not going to put my hands out," I said as I heard the whole classroom gasp as if I had just sent myself to the guillotine.
"Put your hand out now!" she demanded for a third time.
"No, I'm going to leave, Sister," I explained as I walked to get my coat. I might not have been the smartest kid in the whole school, but I wasn't that stupid to put my hands out for her.

The nun didn't say a word as I was leaving and, for an instance, I thought I saw her jaw drop.

As I walked home the route that my mother would drive me, I thought, Cool, maybe there's still some way for you to get yourself out of this school. When I got home, my mother said, "What happened? The school called."

After I got done explaining my story to her she said, "Hmmm, I don't think I'd put my hands out either. But listen, Michael, this is a good school and you can learn a lot, so be good when you go there. I'll make it up to you, okay?"

My mother had never really explained something to me that sincerely, so I decided that I would try to do my best.

Going crab fishing with my uncle and cousins that weekend was great. We really had a good time, and we started to do it every few weekends during the crab season. It almost started to get a little weird but, every time we'd go out crabbing, I always caught the first crab out of all of us. One time I even caught the first one without any bait in my cage.

Peewee's puppies were pretty big by now. We had given some of them away, and I had kept one of them for myself. One day I had been running around playing in the back yard with my puppy when I decided to get us something to drink. When I came back out with the water, I couldn't see Spanky anywhere. I glanced around the yard real quick and then ran out the driveway into the front to see if the puppy was in the street. I started calling and searching from the front yard and the sidewalk. Then I made my way towards the backyard.

After that I searched Mrs. Courtyard's yard because we didn't have a fence between us. By the time I got done with her yard, I was getting frantic. I ran out into the street and yelled Spanky's name over and over. Then I searched both sides of the street and halfway around each block. He was nowhere to be found. Then I decided to go back home and check my yard again.

When I got there, I sat down and mentally retraced my steps. Then as I sat there I looked for all the possible places that the puppy could have run in the amount of time that it took me to get some water inside. Maybe I was looking in the wrong direction, I thought. The cement wall of the two story-parking garage from the building next door enclosed the left side of my yard. Then there was the fence in the back yard that separated my yard from Willie's yard. On the right was where my garage was and the start of Mrs. Courtyard's yard. The only possible spot, I reasoned, was at the back yard fence. I walked over to the fence and climbed on it to look over it, and there he was, hanging from Willie's tree, with a string around his neck, next to Willie's tree house.

"Noooo, Willie! You motherfucker! I'm going to kill you!" I screamed.

I knew Spanky was dead because he wasn't moving and his little tongue was sticking out of his mouth. I ran inside and called my father at work.

"Dad, Willie killed my dog. He hanged him!" I cried.
"What? What the hell are you talking about?" he shouted.

After I explained to him what had happened I said, "Dad, I'm gonna kill him. I swear I'm gonna kill him. I'm gonna grab the pitchfork and stab him."
"Hold on, hold on! Don't be grabbing no pitchfork and go running into Willie's yard," he said. "You just go inside or go over to one of your friend's house, and I'll straighten this out when I get home. Do you hear me? Or I'll kick your fucking ass when I get home," he threatened.
"Fine. I won't," I said.
"I'm serious, Michael. He might be setting you up in a trap to get you to come into his yard so he could hurt you really bad, all right...?"
"All right," I answered.

I was so mad at Willie that I spent the next half hour hiding sticks and things in my yard, Mrs. Courtyard's yard, and up and down the side of the house. When I was done, I grabbed a baseball bat and sat on my back porch.

"Willie, come on out and play. I got another puppy over here, you motherfucker!" I yelled.

I sat out there for a half hour and pleaded for him out loud to come over to play, even though I didn't see any sign of him. When my mother came home from the supermarket, I explained to her what had happened. She didn't believe me at first, so I told her to go look over the fence into Willie's tree. She walked over to the fence looked over and said, "Michael, there's nothing there."

I ran over, hopped up on the fence, and pointed. "Look, there." I said.

I couldn't believe it, but when I looked over there nothing was there. For a moment I prayed that I was dreaming, but when I looked closer I could see the rope that had been cut. "There! Look at the rope. That's where he was hanging," I told her.

"Michael, it's just a rope. There's nothing there."
"Ma, what do you think, I looked in Willie's yard until I found a piece of rope tied in his tree, so I could make up a story about him hanging my dog?"
"Well, no, Michael. Come on, are you sure you really searched for your puppy?" she asked. "Let's look around the yard, and if we don't find it, then we'll drive around in the car, okay?" she explained.
"Ma, you can look around but I know what I saw, okay? Besides, Dad said he was going to go talk to Willie's parents, and he'd better tell them that I'm going to kill him if he comes into my yard," I yelled towards Willie's house again.

My father went over to Willie's house after he got home from work. It was quiet for a few minutes and then I heard my father yelling, "Playing! He was playing with the fucking puppy, and accidentally hanged it!"

He came back after few minutes and said, "If that sick little bastard ever comes in this yard you crack his fucking head open."
"John! What are you saying? He'll do it," my mother yelled.
"Oh, you're right... What I mean, Michael, is this: If he comes in this yard, you hit him with a stick. No pitchforks, no shovels. If you hit him in the shins that'll scare him off," my father corrected.
"Okay dad," I lied.

As far as I was concerned, his head was already cracked the next time I saw him. A short time after this my father enrolled me in karate classes.

School was going along pretty well now, and I finally caught up on everything. My mother would let me walk to and from school by now with all of the other kids, which was pretty cool. One day while I was walking home with Neil and Donde, Neil asked me if I wanted to come over to his house, which was up the block. I figured I'd go for a little while, so I said yes. When we got about halfway up the block, there were these two kids playing on the lawn of some big house. The younger one, who was about my age, put his hands on his hips, and said, "Oooo, you look so cute in uniforms."

"Awww, shut up, Ricky," Donde said.
"Who's that?" I asked.
"That's just Ricky and Bobby Dale," Neil said.

"Boy, they both have long hair," I said.

"Yeah, they do," Neil answered.

"What school do they go to?" I asked.

"They go to a different school whenever they're living here; otherwise, they go to school out in Long Island whenever they live with their father," Donde answered.

"How did the younger one break both his arms?"

"That's Ricky, he broke them riding his dirt bike."

"Yeah, a week apart," Neil added.

"What do you mean a week apart? He broke one, and then broke the other one a week later doing the same thing?" I asked.

"Yep. Tried jumping a ramp like Evel Knievel," Donde answered.

"Boy, he certainly doesn't learn his lesson the first time," I said.

When we came to Adelchie's house on the same block, he said he was going to go inside and change, and then he would meet us at Neil's house. Neil's mother and father were still working when we got there, but his older brother and sister were there.

They both went to St. Andrew's also, but I never saw them there. Neil ran upstairs, got changed, and then came back down.

"You hungry?" he asked.

"Well, yeah," I answered.

He made us each a peanut butter and jelly sandwich and two big glasses of chocolate milk. Neil ate his sandwich pretty funny, I thought. He would dunk them into his chocolate milk before each bite. When we got done, we went outside, and he introduced me to some of his friends who were outside playing. Donde came up the block on his chopper bicycle a few minutes after that.

"Hey, we've got enough guys here. Why don't we go play two-hand touch football over at Bowne Park?" Neil's friend Greg said.

"Well, I can't play in my school clothes. Besides, where is Bowne Park?"

"It's right down the block. Come on, I'll give you some play clothes to wear," Neil answered.

I went in with Neil, changed my clothes, and then called my mother and told her I'd be home at dinnertime.

When I got up to Bowne Park, there was a bunch of other kids from Neil's neighborhood willing to join in a game of football, so I got to meet another group of Neil's friends. We all ended up having such a good time up there playing football that we didn't realize that we played until way after dinnertime. I got yelled at by the time I got home for not calling home, to say I would be late, but it was almost, kinda worth it.

Life was pretty good for me now. A few years had past, and I had started the sixth grade. I was doing very well with my schoolwork. On the home front my parents had finished a lot of renovations to our house, and my mother had stopped working some time ago. We had even had a big pool installed in our back yard now. My parents had decided to put the pizzeria up for sale because they had bought a luncheonette much closer to the house. The luncheonette was over on 192nd Street and Station Road, right next to a train stop on the Long Island Railroad. It was right around the Flushing, Bayside border. One day, as we were getting the store ready to open, my father asked me what name we should give the new place. I didn't waste a second and blurted out, "Mike's Corner."

"Mike's Corner? Why not John's Corner or Alma's Corner?"
"Because Mike's Corner sounds cool Dad," I pleaded.
"Well, all right, you do this. You write down a few names on a piece of paper and think about it for a few days, okay?"

By the end of the next day I told my father my choices but insisted that I liked "Mike's Corner" the best.

"All right, fine," he said. "You like Mike's Corner the best. Then that's what we'll name it."

Man, I couldn't believe it. He actually said yes. Just think, Mike's Corner.

When the new store finally opened, I also worked there from time to time. Occasionally my friend Marcus and I would ride our bikes over to the store, and sometimes we would get a little kick out of playing a trick on some of the other kids who were there buying candy. Marcus and I would walk in, and I'd walk over to the candy and start stuffing it into my mouth without saying a word. I'd usually have a weird face on, and I'd start mumbling, "Mmmmm, candy." While some of the kids would stare at me with their mouths wide open, Marcus would say, "Don't stand too close to him. He's a little crazy." It was funny watching all the different reactions that the other kids would have. Some would run out of the store, or they'd stand there in disbelief waiting to see what I would grab next. Sometimes a kid would run over to my father and tell him that some crazy kid was eating all his candy, which would usually stop my performance by my father yelling at me to knock it off.

After a little while I learned how to serve customers cheeseburgers, ice cream sundaes, and egg creams. I also worked the register for ringing up sales on other things. It's kinda funny, but I didn't really look at it as work. It was more like fun for me, especially at the end of the day when I did get paid.

My mother's little trips to the country had also grown. Unfortunately she had a station wagon now, and it would be jammed packed every time we left to come home from one of these trips.

It was the same old story once we got home. We'd unpack the car, and my mother would start sorting through the stuff to determine which things she would sell, which things she would use, and which things would be packed away behind the attic walls or some other place in the house.

By now both of my Aunts had moved out of the house they were sharing in Corona. My Aunt Marie moved to another apartment in Corona, and Aunt Linda bought a house out in Hempstead, Long Island. It was weird going out there because every time we'd come to visit, my cousin Dino was always punished for something. The worst part about it is that even after I had traveled all the way out there, she still wouldn't let him out of his room at times. It got to a point where I wouldn't even bother to ask where Dino was. I'd just go and sneak upstairs and check his room. Nine times out of ten he would be lying on the bottom bunk with his hands behind his head staring up into the ceiling. Sometimes I'd walk into his room, and he wouldn't say a word or even bother to see who was there. He'd just stare straight up in the air.

"Dean. Dino, it's me, Mike." I'd say after I'd walk in.

"Hey, Mike, how are you?"

"I'm all right. How about you?"

"Oh, you know. Punished again."

"For what this time?"

"Who knows? Who the fuck cares?" But I'm telling you, Mike, as soon as I'm old enough or if I get some money I'm fucking gone."

"I wish I could help you, Dino."

"I know, Mike. Believe me, I wish you could too. You know, I'm like a plant. All I do is sit here, sometimes for a day, sometimes for a week, or sometimes for two weeks. Meanwhile Donna, Tina and Brenda, my sisters, get to play in our pool or run around the house with friends and play tag while I have to sit here and listen to them having fun. You know, sometimes I get punished for so long, friends of mine think I moved away. I'm telling you, Mike, she's sick. My mother's sick in the fucking head."

"Well, I don't know if it will work, Dino, but I'll ask my mother to ask your mother if you can come live with us again. Maybe my mother will have some luck."

"I hope so. I'm telling you, Mike, I'd rather be in jail than be here. As a matter of fact, I'd rather be anywhere."

I'd usually just end up sitting in his room with him for hours until my mother would come back to pick me up. Each time I'd leave, I'd hate the fact that I couldn't take him with me.

I didn't really know what was going on between my parents, but I did have a slight idea something wasn't right.

Lately my father wasn't spending a lot of time at home, and my mother no longer worked in the store with him. I can remember one day when my mother and I came home and my father's car was parked out front. After we went in, my mother told me to go upstairs and ask my father for the mortgage money. Being that I had never been asked to do this before, I thought it was a little strange.

"Dad."

"Yeah?"

"Mom told me to come up here and ask you for the mortgage money."

"She asked you to ask me?"

"Yeah."

My father pulled a roll of cash out of his pocket, whipped off a bunch of bills, and handed it to me. Boy, my eyes lit up. I don't think I'd ever held this much money before in my life. As I turned and walked down the stairs, I fantasized about sneaking off to the toy store and buying everything I ever wanted. I got down to the kitchen and handed my mother the money. Then I started to make myself a snack as she started to count it.

"Michael, take this money back upstairs and tell your father to shove it up his ass!"

"Um, I don't think I want to do that, Mom."

"Did you hear what I said!? Do it now!" she scolded.

Then she got up, pushed the money into my hand, and said, "Go! Before he leaves."

As I walked up the stairs I thought to myself, I don't want to be involved in whatever this is. Why should I have to tell him to stick it up his ass? Besides, he'll probably kill me for saying it.

Knock! Knock!

"Dad," I said hoping that he had left.

"Yeah?"

I walked into his room and said, "Listen, I don't really want to say this, but Mom told me I had to, so promise you won't kill me."

"Huh?" he said. "Yeah, I won't kill you. What did your mother say?"

"Well...," I said as I placed the money on the bed and stepped backwards, "she told me to tell you to stick it up your ass."

"What...? She told you to tell me that?"

"Yeah."

My father shook his head and then counted off a few more bills and placed them on the bed.

"If I come get the money, you're not going to whack me, are you?"

"No, Michael. I'm not going to whack you."

After I took the money and started back down the steps, I thought, Great, now any time my mother wants money from my father she'll make me get it.

One day I walked home from St. Andrew's with my friend Nicky Cardone from school. Nicky was an Italian kid, who lived in one of the buildings next to my house. We had decided to go to my house and help each other with schoolwork. When we got to my front walkway we heard my mother and father screaming at each other. To be honest, I don't know who looked more shocked, Nicky or me. I had never heard my parents yell at each other like this before. After a minute or two, I looked at Nicky and said, "Do you think I should go inside and see what's up?"

Nicky looked at me like I was crazy and said, "Hell, no! I wouldn't go in there if I was you. I tried getting in between my parents one time when they were arguing, and they ended up accidentally knocking the crap out of me. I was fighting for my life."

They ended up yelling at each other for another fifteen minutes. Then it got quiet, but it still sounded like they were fighting. About a minute later my father walked out limping.

"Dad? Are you and mom okay?"

"Your mother's fine, but she's fucking crazy, she stabbed me in my ass," he said as he walked past me and sped off in his car.

I didn't really know what was going on between my parents, but I did have a slight idea something wasn't right.

A couple of days after this last incident, my mother told me that my father wasn't going to be living at home any more.

"Why not?" I asked.

"Because we got into a fight, that's why."

"Yeah, but I get into fights with Marcus all the time, and we're still friends. Why can't you and Dad do the same?"

"Because we can't."

"Well, do I get to have a choice where I can live?"

"Why?"

"Because I'd rather go live with Dad because at least you'll have Grandpa. He won't have anybody."

"No, you can't. You'll be living here."

And that was the end of that in her mind.

A couple of weeks later, after school one day I decided to stop at Marcus's house on the way home to see if he was there. After I got up the driveway, I noticed him working on his bike.

"Hey, Marcus."

"Hey, Mike," he answered.

"What's up? What are you doing?"

"I had to fix my bike. Why? What's up?"

"Nothing. You want to go for a ride to Bowne Park or something?"

"Yeah, all right."

"Okay, so ride me over to my house so I can change my clothes. Then we'll go."

After we got to my house and walked into the kitchen, Marcus asked me if I had a soda.

"Yeah, there's probably something in the fridge."

Marcus walked over to the refrigerator stopped and said, "Holy shit, what's that?"

"What?"

"That!" he said as he pointed up at the refrigerator.

I looked on top of the fridge and saw a handgun. I wasn't really surprised to see a handgun in my house because I knew my parents owned one or two for the stores, but I had never seen either of them leave one out like this.

"Shit, I guess one of my parents left it out," I said.

"Wow," Marcus exclaimed. "Let me look at it."

Before Marcus would think of grabbing it, I shoved a chair over and picked it up. The first thing I noticed was that it was loaded because it was a revolver. After I got off the chair, Marcus kept insisting for me to let him see it.

"If I let you see it, you've got to be real careful with it, Marcus. Ya' know, we could kill each other with this thing."

"I know, Mike. I won't fuck around. I've just never held a handgun before."

I let him hold it. But even as I handed it to him, I wondered a little bit about his "crazy" spells.

"Wow, cool!" he said as he pointed it towards the doorway.

After that we both fooled around with it for a few minutes, and then I put it in the dining room. When my mother got home a little while later, I told her what we had found in the house.

"Where was it?" she said.

"On top of the refrigerator," Marcus answered.

"How did it get here?"

"I don't know."

"Where is it now?"

"I put it the dining room after Marcus and I checked it out."

"Son of a bitch," she said.

Obviously she was mad, but luckily it wasn't with me, I thought. After Marcus left that night, I did my homework, watched some TV, and then went to bed. The next morning my mother woke me up at 5:00.

"Why are you waking me up so early? It's still dark out." I said. "I've got school today. I can't go to the country."

"I know. We're not going to the country. We're going over to the store to talk to your father."

"What the hell do I have to talk to him for?"

"You don't. You just have to come with me to talk to him, that's all."

Man, I knew I shouldn't have done that thing with the mortgage money. Now I've got to be the middle man every time my mother needs money or wants to fight with my father. Besides that, why does my mother have to ask my father for money? He should just give it to her. She's worked just as hard as my father has over the years to buy the luncheonette.

We got there at about 5:30 and sat in the car waiting for my father. Luckily my mother had taken some pillows and a blanket for me, so I could go back to sleep. After a little while I heard my mother start up the car, so I asked her what was going on. "Nothing. We're leaving. Your father had his employee open the store."

When we got home, I went back to bed for a little while. Then I woke up, ate some breakfast, and went to school.

The next morning we went through the same routine, but my father didn't show up to open that morning either. During the ride back home, I wondered why my mother couldn't call my father on the phone for money, but I guess she had her reasons. After we got home and I had a little more sleep, I got up, ate breakfast, and went to school.

The next morning my mother really had her hands full trying to get me out of bed.

"Come on, Ma. He wasn't there for two days. He's probably not going to be there today either."
"Come on, Michael. You've got to come with me. Don't argue."

I could tell that she was serious, but I still really didn't feel like going, and I actually started to get pissed at my father for making my mother and now me go through this every morning. I obviously had fallen asleep on the ride over there, because the next thing I heard was my mother say, "Come on, Michael, get up. Your father's here."
"I'm too tired, Mom. Let me stay here and sleep."

My mother asked me again, and after I repeated myself she said, "All right, Michael. Go to sleep. I'll be right out."

A minute or two later I heard my mother and father start arguing. Man, why the hell do I have to be here for this? I can't understand why they couldn't argue on the phone or something.

After thinking for a second or two more, I wondered if I should go in and say my peace about the whole situation. Na, I thought. It'll be fine. Besides, Nicky looked like he knew what he was talking about the day he warned me about getting involved. I can go back to sleep anyhow. Just before I dozed off, I heard someone blow off firecrackers, and I thought to myself, That's funny. It's not even close to the Fourth of July.

A few minutes later my mother opened the car door and got in. Good, I thought, now I can go home and get some sleep. After a few minutes I hadn't heard the car start yet, so I opened my eyes and said, "Come on, Ma. Let's go home. I'm tired."

She didn't say anything, so I repeated myself again. After a few more moments of silence my mother said, "Michael..., get up. Get up Michael."

I could tell from the tone of her voice that she was serious, so I sat up. My mother turned around in the car seat to face me, and I don't know why but when I first looked into her face it scared me for a second because her eyes pierced right through me. Then my mother focused, looked into my eyes and said, "Michael, no matter what happens, Mommy loves you okay?"
"What are you talking about...? What happened...?"
"Nothing, Michael... just come here and give me a hug."

As I hugged her, she squeezed me tightly for a few seconds and then started to cry.

"Mom! What's wrong?!?"

"Nothing, Michael. Nothing." Then she started the car, and we drove off.

After I asked her one more time during the ride home and she gave me the same answer, I figured everything was okay and I lay back down. I woke up a little while later and asked my mother if we were home yet. "No, Michael, we're not home yet."

"Well, ya' know, I've got school today."

"Don't worry Michael. You might not have to go to school today."

Cool! I thought as I shut up quickly and went back to sleep.

When we got home, my mother told me to go back to bed.

"Why should I? I'm only going to get a little sleep."

"Don't worry. I'll let you sleep longer."

"Yeah, but then I'll be late."

"I'll give you a note. Now go to bed."

About an hour later my mother woke me up, made me breakfast, and then sent me to school with my note.

At the end of the day on the way home, Neil asked me if I wanted to do my homework at his house. I thought about it for a second or two, and then I decided to go home. As I walked up to the corner of my block, I saw three cop cars and two unfamiliar cars parked on my lawn. I walked over to a parked car across the street and sat on the hood, wondering why there were cop cars at my house.

I wondered if my mother had a problem with one of the boarders at my house. Or maybe they were there because of this morning with my father. Na, stop dreaming. Nothing happened last night.

Instead of going inside, I decided to wait and see what happened from outside for now. By now little pockets of people started to form on the corner of my block as they stared towards my house. A whole range of thoughts and emotions ran through my head, and just as I was about to decide whether or not to go inside, they brought my mother out in handcuffs.

They put my mother into the cop car, and I watched them drive down my street. I sat there thinking, and afraid, to ask anybody what was happening. I suppose for fear of finding out that it might be something I wouldn't be very happy with. Then I heard Debbie, Marcus's mother say, "Oh, my God, Michael. Come here," as she started walking towards me.

"Dolly, what's going on at my house?"

"Oh nothing. Nothing."

"Should I go over there?"

"Well, no. Let's go to my house, and we'll call from there, okay?" she said.

After we got there, Debbie got me some cookies and milk and sat me down with some cartoons on TV. Debbie walked back into the room a little while later and told me to wait for my Aunt Marie to come over.

I sat at Marcus's house for about an hour. I knew if I felt like it, I could just leave and go home and talk to my grandfather. But I was also sharp enough to know that what had happened last night wasn't normal. It was safer for me to sit here and avoid reality, because the other side of the coin meant that something had to be terribly wrong. After a while, I decided to lie down to rest and prepare myself for this blow that seemed to be coming. When my Aunt Marie got there, she woke me up and took me over to my house. We got inside, and she told Ronnie and Russell that they could go out and play. I sat there with Marie for about an hour, and she wouldn't or couldn't tell me what had happened. Then finally my cousin Ronnie burst through the door yelling, "Look! Look! It's in the newspaper! 'Wife shoots and kills husband!'"

Well, I guess those weren't firecrackers last night, I thought.

"Ronnie, you little bastard. Get out of here with that newspaper," my aunt screamed.

I jumped up and grabbed the newspaper from Ronnie. There it was plain as day: my mother's name, my father's name, my name, and my address.
"I guess I'm fucked," I said.
"Oh, my God, Michael. I didn't know how to tell you. Ronnie, get outside," Marie said.

Tears were running down Marie's cheeks as she held out her arms for me to hug her. I hugged Marie for her sake; I didn't need to be consoled at that moment while my soul was tearing in half. It was too painful for me right then to comprehend. Marie was sitting down, and I held her as she cried for herself, my father, her sister and me.

"There, there, Marie. It'll be all right. It'll be okay," I told her as I rubbed her back.
"Wait a minute. I'm supposed to be consoling you, Michael."
"Don't worry, Marie. I'm fine except for a splitting headache."
"Oh, Michael, I'm so sorry," she said.
"For what, Marie? It wasn't your fault. But now it's over. It's done. There's no changing it."
"I can't believe you're taking it this way, Michael. You do realize what happened, don't you?"
"Yeah... I realize."

That night there was some talk about where I was going to sleep.

"Marie, listen. I'm sleeping in my house in my bed tonight. Now if George wants to beat the shit out of me like I've seen him beat the shit out of Ronnie and Russell over the years for not going, that's fine. But he better kill me tonight because I'm not going anywhere."

I could see that George wanted to give me a slap, but he was holding back his temper. This one time I wish he would have, because I would have definitely ended Ronnie and Russell's misery with him on this night somehow.

That night I cried for an hour. Then I forced myself to cry for another half hour. There was a method to my madness because, after that, I swore I would never cry about anything, because nothing could ever make me this sad or hurt this bad again. Then I got pissed. I got pissed at myself for not going into the store with my mother. I got pissed at the world for letting everybody own a gun, and finally I got pissed at God.

So what's the deal, God? I was a bad kid because I didn't go to church last Sunday? I go to Catholic school. I go to confession, and I made my communion. What the fuck for? What the fuck could I have possibly done in my twelve years on this fucking Earth that was so bad that I should deserve this fate? Fine, I thought, you know what? Fuck this. Nothing is the truth any more, nothing is believable, and nothing lasts forever from here on in. I'll have to jot this one down as a major fucking lesson, too. But that's it. I don't give a fuck about rules, fuck regulations, fuck conversations, fuck me; and fuck you, God. Fuck everything. I was blowing circuits left and right. I blew circuits I didn't even know I had.

After I got over that trip, I started to think about what was going to happen to my own little world.

Oh shit, Mike. Where the fuck are you going to live? What are you going to do with yourself? How are you going to eat? You didn't even eat dinner tonight. What about tomorrow? What's going to happen to the house? Fuck it, I'll quit school and get a job. Oh, shit, what about the business?!? I'll go to work there. I can run that place. I've done it before. We can't lose the business. I know where to get the supplies for the store. I'll use my mother's car. I've been driving for years now with her.

Wait a minute- I wonder where my father's car is. I saw it parked in front of the luncheonette last night. Maybe I can go to the police department and get the keys to it. Then I'll sneak back and drive it home. Shit, what about the keys to the store? I wonder if it's locked up. What if people are walking out with everything? No, wait, Mike, the cops must've locked it up. They probably found my father's keys. Okay... now as far as cooking and selling shit in there, I've got that covered. The newspaper guys get paid on Sundays. The food, ice cream and soda guys get paid at the end of each month for last month's load. Fuck, it's the end of the month already. Okay, I've got about three hundred bucks in the bank. I know my mother bought me some U.S. saving bonds. Maybe I can sell them or sell some stuff around the house. Yeah, I'll sell the fucking lawn mower. I hate cutting the grass anyhow. If that doesn't add up, I'll save the newspaper article from tonight and ask the bill collectors to cut me a break for a month or two. Then I've got the rent, electric, and garbage pick-up to worry about soon. Okay, I know that the electric company won't shut off the electric for a little while. That leaves the rent and the garbage; well, these guys have got to cut me some slack also. Shit, I can probably make most of this money in two weeks. I've gone in there at 6:00 in the morning, and the place is packed with all the people catching the train to Manhattan. Man, I'm bad in the mornings. Fuck it. I'll have to sleep there. Maybe I won't open on Sundays for a while after I make a little money, I thought.

I juggled all of these thoughts in my mind until it short-circuited again and it shut me down, and I fell asleep.

The next day my Aunt Marie came over.

"Marie, I need the keys to the store," I said.

Marie asked me why I wanted the keys, so I explained it to her, and I probably made a mistake by telling her.

"Well, we'll see, Michael. I don't know where the keys are right now, and it's very hard to talk to your mother. She doesn't even have a lawyer yet. But we'll see, okay."
"Well, see if you can do it soon, Marie. You know the food is going to go bad, and after a while, all my father's customers might go somewhere else," I explained.

"What about my father's funeral? When is it being held?"
"Michael... you're not going to be able to go to John's funeral."
"Why? I didn't shoot him."
"I know, but John's family is a little hurt, and confused right now."
"Really? Well I'm a little hurt, and confused myself, Marie, but that doesn't mean I don't want to say goodbye to my father."
"I know, Michael, I'll ask, but you're probably not going to be able to go."
"That's fucking great. What are my cousins going to think, I don't care about my father? They'll never forgive me for that."
"We'll see what happens, Michael."

After a few days, with no response, I decided to call the police station myself. I was told that my father's car and keys were now part of evidence.

"Well, okay, forget about the car but I need the keys to the store."
"Sorry. They're part of evidence," I was told.
"Listen, the keys had nothing to do with my father getting shot, okay? But I need them for the store and for the house."
"I'm sorry. Why don't you see if your mother has a set?" the cop said.

Feeling frustrated from not getting an answer, I said, "Who... my mother... the murderer?"

After a long pause the cop said, "I'm really sorry, kid, but I can't help you. See if you can talk to your mother's lawyer, okay? I gotta go now."

The first time I spoke to my mother was about two weeks after the incident; it was the third time she called. I figured it wouldn't be very nice if a son didn't want to talk to his mother when she was in jail, so I talked to her.

"Michael."
"Yeah."
"I'm sorry you had to go through this."
"Yeah, so am I. I can't believe you did that, Ma," I added.

"Well, I can't believe I did it either, okay?"

"So what's going to happen to you now?"

"I'm not sure. I just got a lawyer."

"You could go to jail for a long time, couldn't you?"

"Yes, Michael, that's possible."

"Well, all right then. That's even more reason why I need the store keys."

"Oh, no, Michael. You can't go there."

"Why, Ma? Are you afraid I'm going to see a little blood on the floor? Look, John's dead, okay? I already did my crying for two hours, and let's not even mention that I wasn't able to go to his funeral. The business is all we have now. Besides, you and John broke your ass for years to get it, and I do not want to lose it because of this."

"No, Michael. I can't."

"I wish you could have said that the night you shot John, but you couldn't okay? Now give me the keys, Ma! I didn't ask you for an explanation about what happened. I haven't asked you for anything, but now I'm asking you for the keys. I can run the store, I know how to drive, and I can get the supplies, cook the food, and work the register. Anything I can't figure out, I'll call and ask you."

"Michael, you're too young."

"Well, what about the guy that worked for John? Maybe he still wants to work for us."

"I don't know if you can understand this, Michael, but your father had a suitcase with twenty thousand dollars in it that night. He was going to go into business with his brothers. They were going to buy a garbage route in Manhattan, and they were going to pay someone twenty thousand dollars for the route. From what I was told, the suitcase is gone, and I think your father's employee took it."

"Oh, great. That means we could have had another business. Listen, Ma, I don't want to lose this business, too, all right? I can run the store. Let me have the keys."

"What if someone tries to rob you, Michael?"

"I'll give them the money, make them a hamburger, and ask them to leave."

"No, I can't."

"I think you owe me the fucking keys, Ma. It's my store, too!"

"Don't talk to me like that."

"I don't think you're in a position to tell me how to talk to you. Will you give me the fucking keys?"

"No."

"Goodbye, Ma. Thanks... for everything."

Click.

A little while after that phone call, I walked past my grandfather's room, and he motioned for me to come over to him.

"Well, Gramps, I guess it's me and you again, just like the old times."

"Come'ere. You know I lika you, right?"

"I know, Gramps. I lika you, too."

"Here, you takea some money."

"Gramps, this is fifty bucks."

"It's okay. You take it. You're a younga man now, anda younga man needs some money ina his pocket, you understanda me?"

"Yeah, Grandpa. I understand you. Thanks."

My grandfather and I hugged each other for several moments, and then I left.

My mother ended up being placed in Creedmoor Psychiatric Hospital. I remember the first time I saw her, about two months later. I was with Marcus, and this black nurse had a big skeleton key to open up this big metal door and told us to go inside. We stepped into a visiting room about 10 x 15 feet, and at the end of this room was the long day room which had to be about 50 x 75 feet long. It was filled with crazy people, and my mother was nowhere in sight. We both looked at each other wide eyed and turned towards the nurse as she was closing this door. I'll never forget how she smiled at us; like she was feeding us to the lions. On a lighter note Marcus, who was an extremely hyperactive kid, turned towards me with this crazed look on his face, not unlike some of the individuals standing around us, and said to me in a low whispering growl, "I gotta get outta here."

I knew he had popped his cork, and on that note he turned towards the door and started punching, kicking, and scratching at the door. Then he started yelling, "They're gonna kill me. Help! Let me out."

It's a good thing my mother walked in and calmed him down real fast by telling him that he really didn't want to be acting like that in a place like this, because they might want to keep him there. At which point Marcus said very calmly, and wide eyed, "Hmm, maybe you're right, Alma."

The three of us had a little laugh about it, which was a good way to break the ice. We all talked about frivolous things for about an hour. One part of me wanted to ask her what happened that night, but I figured that this might not be the best of settings to ask, so I didn't. We ended up talking for about two hours, and my mother introduced us to a few of her new crazy friends, which was very interesting at the very least. Marcus and I left a short time later.

Over the last few weeks I'd ride my bicycle over to the store every couple of days late at night, and I'd try to get the front gates open. Each time I'd go there I'd take some different type of tool that I was sure would assist me in opening the padlocks, and each time it was in vain. I also realized that somebody else was getting into the store, because each time I'd go there I noticed that more and more things were thrown about the floor. As long as the electric was still on, it gave me a false hope that I could still get in there and save the "family business." I felt that way until the lights were shut off about a month later. The difference between my father's demise and the store's death was that my father's took minutes. The store took over a month to lurch up, roll over, and die. I sat there and knew that I was watching my future die. It was extremely painful knowing how hard my parents had worked to get where they were in life. It was almost like a second death in the family.

Back on the home front, I was still living at home but I had no desire to go to school. Nonetheless, my grandfather would fight to get me up for school every morning. If only he knew that every night I was watching the late show and the late, late show until five in the morning, he might have let me sleep. We used to have some times in the mornings. First, he started out with the cup of water on my head and then a tea pot, but one morning he got me real good.

He started with a cup of water on my head, so I turned the pillow over and spun the blanket around. Then he came in with a pot of water and poured it on me. I wasn't giving up, so I moved to the foot of the bed, rearranged the pillow and blankets, and went back to sleep. The third time he came in, he said nice and calmly, "Michael, are you gonna get upa?"

I said no, and he started pouring and pouring and pouring. It was either get up or drown. I thought he had brought in the hose, but when I sat up and opened my eyes, I saw why it had taken him a few minutes to come back the third time. He had filled up a big spaghetti pot and was standing at the foot of the bed pouring it on my head. It seemed like he won the battle but not the war. I jumped out of the bed, grabbed a new pillow and blanket, and told him I was taking a shower. Then I locked myself in the bathroom and went to sleep in the tub.

He came up in a little while and started banging on the door. I thought he was going to knock it down, and now I was too scared to come out. After he left, I thought up a new plan. What I would do is wake up in the morning, get dressed, walk out the front door, and then climb into one of the basement windows. I figured I could make a little rat's nest under the basement stairs and go back to sleep there. My nest soon turned into a little studio apartment. I had food, comic books and a flashlight. There was even a bathroom in the basement, so now everything was cool.

One morning a few weeks later, I don't know how, but he caught me. Maybe he saw me climb in the window. Anyhow it was going to get tough because now, when I left in the mornings, he would wait a while and then start checking the house. I didn't know where to sneak in because I didn't know where he was in the house. On top of that, he started locking the windows and doors when I left. I slept in the garage quite a few times, but it was always too hot in there because it was getting too close to summer. There were only two or three months of school left, but I was determined not to go and he was determined to make me go. This should give you somewhat of an idea on how set I was. I slept in the hall closet, in the linen closet, under my bed, under his bed, and inside the kitchen cabinets. This went on until school ended and summer vacation started.

It turned out to be a very interesting summer, because I started hanging out with Jimmy Marnell a lot more, mainly because he was a few years older than I was and I figured I needed someone to teach me the ropes. My work was to figure out the good lessons from the bad...

During that summer they started knocking down some old houses in my neighborhood. Marcus and I loved to volunteer our services for free after the workers had left. We figured they'd be happy the next day when they saw that someone was trying to help. After I told my mother about this, she would tell me to take the crystal doorknobs off all the doors.

One time Marcus and I were trying to get the whole fireplace mantle. The only problem was that we didn't know that it was marble and that someone had painted over it. It came crashing down on top of us, almost crushing us both. Another time Nicky Cardone and I dared Marcus to ride his bike off the second story of a new building that was being built and land into a sand pile. The little nut did it, when he hit the big sand pile he knocked the wind out of himself. We all thought he was dying for a while, but then it was cool. I mean, after all, we had grown up watching Evel Knievel, so taking our bikes, making ramps, and jumping over things was one of our hobbies.

The biggest ramp we ever made had to be the one we built with a full sheet of plywood which is eight feet long, in my backyard. We had the exit end up at about three and a half feet high. Then we would go across the street to George, and Phil's house, and being that their driveway was on an upward slant, you could really build up speed. This one time in my backyard Marcus was trying to show off in front of a bunch of our friends, and he jumped over the ramp going at top speed. We used to fly about eight to nine feet high, and this time Marcus flew well over that and landed right in the mud by my grandfather garden he had been watering. Everyone started laughing, and Marcus stood up, went home, took a shower, came back, and flew down the walkway. He landed splat, right in the mud again. It was a great show.

These days it was odd if Marcus and I weren't together. But like I mentioned earlier, Marcus was hyper as a kid. He even had to take some medication for a little while to calm himself down, but every now and then he'd, like, snap and he'd get this crazy look in his eyes. Then he'd go wild. One time he whacked me with a bike chain; another time he whacked me with a two by four. I got a scar from the nail that was in it. What I used to have to do was kinda like bum rush him, grab him in a headlock, and cut off just enough oxygen while I kept saying "Marcus, calm down."

Sometimes though I'd let him go too soon, and he'd try to whack me with something else, so I had to add to our routine. I'd have to hold him for a while longer, ask him if he was calm yet, and wait for him to stop trying to get away, or go limp. I mean, like all things, it still had a few kinks in the system, but overall, it worked pretty well.

The Fourth of July had come and gone by now. I'd say that out of all the holidays this one bothered me the most. In the past, my father always spent that day with me. He would always have at least two boxes of fireworks. One box he would give me to blow off around the store, and then at night he'd break out the big stuff. We used to start out under the Whitestone Bridge. Then we would go over to his friend's house in Corona. His friend's name was Vito, and he looked and dressed like a real gentleman. Vito would have his friends shoot off fireworks and huge mortars for hours. Because I had an idea of what the smaller fireworks had cost, I asked my father if his friend was rich. He'd tell me, I wouldn't worry about it, Michael. He's got plenty of money. My father would let me stay out with him way past midnight when we went out for the Fourth of July together, and I'd always have a great time with him.

By the end of that summer it was decided that my Aunt Marie would move into my house with her sons, Ronnie and Russell, and her husband, George. Russell, and I, shared one of the big rooms in the attic, Ronnie got his own room, and so did Marie and George.

It was decided that I would go to a new school. I liked the sound of that because I really didn't want to face my old classmates after what had happened with my family. I had already finished the 5th grade, and part of 6th in Catholic school, now they were putting me back in public school, into the 5th grade after I had stopped going to school. My new teacher's name was Mrs. Klavis. She sat me next to three other kids with whom I would become very good friends. Their names were Bobby Ortiz,

Michael De' Lovic and Arianna Santamaria. She would become my first steady girlfriend. Of course, the first assignment that day was to do a report about what you had done over the summer, which I thought would be an interesting assignment, considering I was staying up to all hours of the night, and hanging out with the older crowd.

Aside from Russell showing me how to cut school from the school we were now both attending, and the slow disappearance of my father's personal things, that school year was uneventful. By the beginning of the next summer, my Aunt Marie and her family moved out. Now it was just Grandpa, and me again.

During the course of the summer, my cousin Dino had run away from home a few times to come and stay with me. It made my Aunt Linda so happy that she decided to sign him away to the State. Now that he was the property of the State, he was placed in a home for boys for his own good.

We kept in contact the best we could over time, and then one day I got one of Dino's phone calls. He explained to me that the place he was in was a hell hole, and that he was getting into a lot of fist fights. Then he added that he needed to break out of there somehow before he had to hang up the phone.

It bothered me to think of Dino in a place like that. I knew Dino could fight, but he wasn't really a big kid, and I'm sure some of the bigger kids were messing with him. It's times like this that I didn't understand why Dino and I couldn't just live at my house with our grandfather, but aside from that, I wondered if he was better off locked up there or locked up in his bedroom by himself while his sisters were playing outside. At least where he was, he might be able to have a little fun now instead of sitting in his room all day long.

Dino did eventually run away from the home he was in, and he hitchhiked all the way back to Queens from Long Island. Food wasn't much of a problem for us because my grandfather would cook for us. I'm sure he knew about Dino's situation, but he never said anything about it, although I did find out from my Aunt Linda that Grandpa had told her that he would see Dino from time to time at the house and that he was okay.

My Aunt Marie and my cousins moved up to 169th Street, which was about 15 blocks away. They lived in a nice two-bedroom apartment with their mother and George. Their life was pretty good, except for when George would get a little heavy handed with them at times after he had been drinking.

Every now and then I'd ride over on my bike to hang out with them. My cousins were a little older than I was so they played nuttier games than I did. One time I was with Russell, and he went to see if any of his friends were hanging out in the alleyway. When we got there, this big biker dude was hanging out, and he yelled out, "Hey! You got any beer money?"

I knew my cousins drank a beer or two every now and then. I had even drunk a few with them, but who the hell was this guy to ask my cousin for beer money, I thought.

"Who's that?" I asked.

"That fat fuck... any time we get a couple of beers, he comes over and steals them from us," Russell answered.

"What's his name?"

"Big Al. You watch, though. I'm gonna get him this time."

Russell walked towards him and said, "Yeah, Al. Ronnie's coming by with some beers in a few minutes. He's with Vinny Wenzel. I guess they'll give you a few beers. We're going to meet them over by the back alley."

"Shit, you mean, I'll take their beers and then give them one or two," he said.

"Come on. I'm gonna get him," Russell whispered to me as we walked away.

Russell walked over to a garbage can and grabbed a clear wrapper that newspaper boys put newspapers in. Then we went to the roof of the building. When we got up there, Russell started to pee into the bag. When he was done he turned to me and said, "Here, I'll hold it open and you pee in it."

I had already gotten an idea as to what Russell had in mind for "Big Al" so I said to him, "Russell, I don't know. That guy's pretty big!"

"Come on, he's not gonna know whose pee it is. Besides, I'm the one who's gonna drop it on him."

After I got done peeing we walked over to the edge of the roof. Big Al was sitting on the wall down there. My cousin lined up his bomb and then let it go.

"Splat!"

It missed him by an inch, but obviously splashed all over him. Big Al smelled his hands and looked left, right and then up in the air at us.

"Russell! I'm gonna kill you!" he yelled as he took off running.

We both knew we were probably a little faster than he was and that he'd still have to run around the building in order to get to the front door, so we took off running. As we ran towards the roof door, my cousin warned me not to take the elevator because we'd be trapped in there. I don't think I ever ran down a flight of stairs so fast in my life. Being that we were on the roof when we started, it now made it seem like a seven-story building instead of a five-story one. As we were running down the stairs my cousin yelled out that if we didn't make it to the door we'd probably have to jump out of the hallway window. Just great, I thought. I heard Big Al slam through the front door of the building. I ran so fast I'd bet that my feet weren't even touching the stairs any more. By the time we got to the second floor, Russell slammed into the wall to stop and then flung open the window while Big Al got closer and closer.

"Fuck, Russell. What are we going to do?" I said.

"Mike, jump or die!" he answered as he looked out the open window.

On that note, we both climbed out the large window and jumped. After we hit the ground, Big Al stuck his head out that window and yelled out, "You little fucks!" Then he pulled his head back in the window, and we heard him start running down the stairs. When we had hit the ground my cousin yelled out in agony. I asked what was wrong, and he said that he thought he broke his foot. Just about when he got done saying this, Big Al turned the corner and growled, "Russell, I'm gonna kill you!" Russell looked at me and yelled at me to run, and then he took off. I ran like a jack rabbit in the opposite direction.

That night when I got home, my Aunt Marie called me and asked me how Russell had broken his ankle. I told her that we were playing tag, and we jumped out of a window. After that, I spoke to Russell, on the phone, and asked him how he was able to run on a broken ankle.

"Are you kidding me? He would have killed us. I figured the pain in my ankle was nothing compared to the pain I would have felt if he had caught me. I ran like a motherfucker, with tears running down my face from the pain."

It made me laugh to think that he had gotten away from Big Al, broken ankle and all.

Mike Sargent came back into town. He had lived in the apartment building next to my house when I was about nine; he was the stepson of the super next door. My mother had met Pat, his wife, Fran, and their young daughter, Valerie, some time ago. My mother used to invite him over to my house when I was younger, and even though he was about four years older than I was we'd make toy models and hang out together. I had overheard that Pat would beat him, which is why Mike had run away. The first thing I asked him when I saw him was where he had gone all these years.

"I've been around, Mike," he answered.
"Mike... what happened to your teeth? How did you lose them?"
"Well, I was on the shit for a while but now I'm clean," he said.
"What shit, Mike?"
"You know, smack... horse... heroin."
"Wow really? And it makes you lose your teeth?"
"Well, kinda ... sorta," he answered.

Mike was about 20 years old, but now, aside from his teeth, he looked like he was 30.

"Mike, I was sorry to hear about your dad. He was a real nice guy. I remember when he would bring us some of the car models from the store to build. So how you doing? You look okay," he asked.
"I'm fine, I guess."
"Well, you're a tough kid, Mike. I knew that from when we would wrestle on the lawn and you wouldn't give up. Where is your mother, if you don't mind me asking?"
"Naaaa, that's all right. They got her over in the nuthouse. You know, Creedmoor."
"How long does she have to stay there?" he asked.
"I'm not sure, Mike... I have no idea."
"Do you guys still talk?"
"Yeah, we still talk. She's my fucking mother. What am I supposed to do?" I answered.
"Shit, Mike. That's a rough one to take. It must've been tough. Sorry I wasn't around for you."
"Ah, that's all right, Mike. So where you living now?"
"Well, I was thinking of moving back to this area for a while. I was living in the Bronx for too

long, need a change of pace, ya' know," he explained.

"Well, shit, I'll ask my mother if you could live here if you want."

"Really? That would be cool," he said.

"You just have to wait until I go up to visit her because she doesn't call every day."

A few days after that, I saw my mother, and she told me to tell Mike to visit her before he moved in. A couple of days after his visit, Mike moved in. My mother had told him that, if he expected to stay there, he'd have to get a job in a little while to pitch in on the bills. One of the first things Mike asked me about after he moved in was whether or not I knew any older girls in the neighborhood. I figured that one of the older girls I knew was Tina, my old babysitter, so one day I went over to Tina's house to see if she wanted a boyfriend. Tina laughed when I asked her and explained to me that she had a steady boyfriend now. She told me that he had two new cars and money, and he was gorgeous, as if I cared.

"I've been with him for about three months now. He's definitely a keeper," she went on.

"Well, I'm happy for you, Tina. I'd really like to see you with a man instead of some of the boys I've seen you with," I answered.

"I know, tell me about it. So… how's your mother? Tell her I said hi, okay?"

"She's fine, I guess, and I'll tell her you said hello." Tina and I talked a little bit longer, and then I left.

When I got back home I explained to Mike that Tina was already taken and that I was going to have to try somebody else for him. I took him down to Bench Park after that to see if he would like to meet some of my older friends. He hit it off pretty well with them, which I thought was nice because now he could hang out with me at Bench Park. One thing that was pretty cool was that, while Mike was away, he had learned some Judo, and it wasn't long before he let everyone know that he was there for me if I needed it, kinda like a big brother.

One day out of the blue I felt like going to Manhattan by myself. I hadn't been there in a long time, and I always enjoyed the hustle and bustle of the city. I had a little change in my pocket so I knew I'd be all right once I got there. I got on the #7 train pretty early so I was with some of the morning rush hour. While I was riding along, I caught myself observing people on the train. I would look into their faces and try to decide what kind of life they lived or which life they should or could be living.

After the incident with my parents, I looked at the world a lot differently. I didn't even look at myself the same way any more. I felt like an adult trapped in a kid's body with no money or power to change the direction of my life. It was a very frustrating feeling to have at age twelve, but I knew that there wasn't a damn thing I could do about it. I wanted to quit school at ten years old and keep working at the pizzeria but then, like now, I was told, "Oh no, you can't get a job. You need to go to school." Then I'd look at how hard and long my parents had worked to get what they had. Aside from the house it was all gone in about two months. So how secure was it after all? Just to make this theory more interesting, it took a split second for the life that I knew to be over, and I didn't even have a hand in it. So if that second was so crucial in my life, why wouldn't every second in my life be that crucial, or is every second that crucial in my life?

I took the train to 42nd, down to the seedy end. As I walked through the crowd, I gazed at the pushers, junkies and whores mixed in with working and visiting people. Then I turned around at Penn Station and headed towards the skyscrapers into the white-collar neighborhood.

So, Michael, Where do you fit into this scheme now? I thought to myself. What are you going to be? A junkie... passive, or a pusher... aggressor? A doctor? A lawyer? What about school? Do I have the time to spend there? I am still a kid. I should have time to have some fun, right? It's funny, but growing up with my grandfather I sometimes missed not having parents around but then again, I didn't really see them much when they were around, because they were always working. So why should it be all that different now?

I contemplated my questions and answers for a little while, and I headed towards Central Park after a slice or two of pizza. No trip to the city is complete without a stop there. It took me a little while to get there because I wasn't really in any big hurry. The first thing I did on my list was to get the squirrels some nuts. Then I headed over to some wooden squirrel condominiums known as trees, and sat down. In no time I had a bunch of them climbing all over me for nuts. After getting them two more bags, I headed over to the zoo. One of the funniest things I saw while walking through the maze of caged animals was some kids whining and crying to their parents about doing or not doing something that they wanted to do.

I stayed in Central Park past nightfall..., after the squirrels had gone to bed. Well, Mike, this is supposed to be a scary place at night, right? So let's see what happens, I thought. What better way to check your balls, huh? I stayed in the park and sometime after midnight I passed a bum while I was walking.

"Hey, kid."
"Yeah... what do you want?!?"
"Don't be stupid... Go home. It ain't worse than this life, trust me."

I guess somehow he was telling me to get out of the rain. Besides, I was starting to get tired.

On the train ride home I observed the array of people on the train, which was a little bit of a different scene at that hour. On the morning train everybody looks fresh, and ready for the day. At this hour, aside from the riff raff at night, everyone looks tired and beat from working.

One day I came home, and my grandfather told me that two guys ran into the yard and grabbed Dino. He said that, when he ran out there to see what was going on, the guys told him that they were from the home that Dino had run away from, and then they took him away. Shit, that sucks, I thought. It really bothered me that they came and got Dino. He was family, you know.

About a week after this I went home, and two of my mother's old friends, Big Joe and Little Joe, were at the house. They were sitting out by the front door talking when I walked up.

Oh, shit, what now? I thought.

Big Joe and Little Joe told me that everything was all right, and then they walked me over to the driveway in front of something covered with a blanket.

"Your mother told me to tell you that she didn't know what to get you, and she hopes you really like it," Little Joe said.

What was there not to like, I thought. It's big enough to have to put a blanket on it, after all. I pulled the blanket off this lump and saw a brand new 5 1/2-horsepower mini-bike.

"Whoa! Too cool!" I exclaimed.
"You like it," Big Joe said gruffly.
"Yeah, it's great."
"Here, let me give you a kiss from your mother," Little Joe said.

This was a bit of a joke Little Joe made with me, because he knew I had realized that he and Big Joe were lovers for some time now.

"Ohhhh, that's okay, Joe... thanks anyway though." I said as I smiled at him.

Big Joe handed me a helmet and then said, "Your mother said you know how to ride this."
"Yeah, I know how to ride it."

After I got it started, I hopped on and took a ride. Man, I couldn't believe it. How the hell did my mother manage to get me a mini bike from in there? Shit, she's something. This is cool, I thought.

I whipped around the corner a few times, and then Little Joe waved me over to the house and told me they had to leave. I gave each one of them a hug, and then they left. Then I went back in the house to get warmer clothes on to go for a bigger ride. By the time I got ready to leave, Mike Sargent came home.
"Hey, Mike, check this out!" I yelled.
"Wow, brand new. Where did you get it?"
"My mother got it for me. Come on, let me take you for a ride."
"Wait a minute. Are you sure you know to ride?"
"Yeah, I swear it. I've been riding Jimmy Marnell's mini-bike for a long time."
"All right then, look, I'm gonna be going back down to 34th Avenue after I take a shower to see Michael's sister."
"Oh, you mean Winkie Dink."
"Huh?"
"Dondi."
"What?"
"Well, that's what Jimmy Marnell calls him."
"Yeah, well, sometimes Marnell's a wiseass," Mike said.
"You've been seeing a lot of her."
"I know. We were both talking about maybe moving in together. She wants to get out of her parents house. Besides, she's nineteen, a year younger than me, and even though she's never had a real

steady job, we both think we can work something out on our own."

"That's cool, Mike. I'm really glad to hear that. Just think if you didn't stop by my house you might have never met her."

"Yeah, imagine that."

When Mike went in to take a shower, I thought about how cool it had been having him around lately. When I was about nine, Mike was like a big brother to me. We were pretty close, and it was nice to see that, after his stepfather had abused him, he ran away from the home he was placed in and lived on the streets for a while, he really seemed happy. Mike came out a few minutes later smelling like a weird flower and said, "Let's go."

Instead of taking Mike straight there, I took him for a little blast. After we rode around for a little bit he tapped me on the shoulder and told me to take him over to 34th Avenue, so I turned onto Murray Lane and headed there.

As we were driving over there, I spotted Jimmy Marnell and Jimmy (Peck) Schlishman walking towards Bench Park. Peck lived around the corner from me, and Tina, my old babysitter, was a friend of his older sisters, which is how I had met him years ago. Peck was my age.

"Hey, dudes, what's up?" I yelled.
"Whoa, cool, a new mini-bike! Whose is it?" Marnell asked.
"It's mine," I boasted.
"No way," Peck said.
"Mike, tell them."
"Yep, it's his. My man's gonna get a piece of ass for sure now."
"Let me go for a ride," Peck said.
"Yeah, me, too," Jimmy added.
"Hold on. First, he's got to take me over to Laura's house."
"Meet us up at Bench Park later then."
"All right, I will."

I took off and headed down the block, and I guess to try to be a showoff I decided to blow the stop sign on 33rd Ave. As I got to the corner, Mike started slapping my shoulder and telling me to stop, so I punched it. As we flew through the intersection, I saw a van heading right at us as we flew right past his front bumper in the nick of time. I don't know what hurt more, my ego or my ribs from Mike squeezing them.

As I kept riding, I heard Mike yelling, "You crazy little fuck. My life just gets good and you almost end it!"

When I dropped Mike off at the laundry mat, I apologized for almost killing him.

"Yeah, Mike, thanks. But listen, you can't drive around on your mini bike like that because you will get killed. You hear me?"
"Yeah, Mike, I hear you. I learned my lesson."

I went to visit my mother at the state hospital a few days later. After I thanked her for the mini bike, I told her about Dino, and she explained that she was sorry to hear about it.

"Too bad I wasn't home," she said.
"Yeah, too bad," I said. "Well, you look a lot better Mom."
"That's because I stopped taking my medicine."

Oh shit, I thought, "Well, what do you mean? The Doctor stopped giving it to you?"
"No, ya' see, they give you all this medication so you can't walk, talk or think, and then they can prop you up in the corner like you're a lamp or something," she explained.
"Well, are you going to be all right if you don't take it?" I asked.
"What do you mean... all right?"
"Well, you don't feel like killing anybody, do you?"
"That's real fucking funny, Michael!"
"I'm sorry, but I'm kinda not joking when I ask you."
"No, Michael. I don't feel like killing anyone."

Visits with my mother weren't always enjoyable, but at the very least they were always interesting.

I went and spent the weekend at my Aunt Maries house. The funny thing about my cousin Russell was that he hated eating vegetables, so he would come up with a bunch of different ways of making them disappear. He would drown them in butter and then try to feed them to the dog, or he'd make any kind of deal with me or his brother for us to eat them when I was there. Then he came up with stuffing spoonfuls into his pockets. But the best one I thought was when he'd sit close enough to the window so he could flick spoonfuls out the open window. This worked well for about a month until one day George and I were walking into the building and George stopped, looked down at the ground at a huge assortment of vegetables, then looked up four flights to their kitchen window, and said, "That little bastard."

Needless to say when Russell came home, George slapped him around a little bit and then made him go downstairs and sweep up a month's worth of dinner vegetables.

As strange as it may sound, one of the latest crazes down at Bench Park was setting each other on fire. It was something Jimmy Marnell came up with, and we all started doing it to each other. What you would do was to get a can of lighter fluid and squeeze some on someone's pants, and then light them up without them knowing about it. So one day Bobby, Jimmy's younger brother, was hanging out and, while Marcus was talking to him, "Peck" and I were putting lighter fluid on the back of his pants legs. After we lit him on fire, Bobby started running around like the scarecrow from the Wizard of Oz, yelling, "Waaaa, I'm on fire!"

Unfortunately Bobby wasn't aware of this new game, and we might have put a little too much lighter fluid on him.

While he was running around for the first few seconds, we were calmly telling him to cool out because it was only fire, not that he understood our dry humor. But then after the fluid didn't burn itself out, we realized Bobby was in a little trouble. So now, as Bobby was running around yelling, we were beating the shit out of him with our shirts and jackets trying to put him out. By the time Bobby jumped onto the ground and pulled his pants halfway down, we put the fire out.

"What are you guys, fucking crazy!" he screeched. "You fucking set me on fire!"

"Sorry, Bobby. We do it to each other all the time. I guess we just put a little too much lighter fluid on you this time," I said.

"Well, you know what? Keep me out of this sick fucking game from now on. If you guys want to barbecue each other, that's fine, but count me out, all right!"

"All right, fine, Bobby. Don't have a shit fit about it," Marcus said, "The fire's out now, and we get the message."

After that Marcus and I took one more blast around the neighborhood on my mini-bike, and then we went home for the night.

When I got home that night, I ran into Mike Sargent.

"Hey, Mike, I've got some good news," he said.

"What's up?"

"Well, two things, number one is that I got a better paying job with an apartment as a custodian."

"Yeah? Cool."

"Oh, yeah, and I'm gonna get married."

"What? Really, Mike? No?"

"Yup."

"Really? Married? Well, you know what's best for you, I guess. Congratulations. Where's the apartment?"

"Well, it's in Coney Island."

"What...? Get the fuck out of here...? Coney Island...? Why all the way out there? Why can't you find something around here?"

"Well, I tried, and it's not as easy to find work like that around here. I know some people out there also, so we'll be all right."

"Well, it's not all good news, Mike. I think you should stay around here instead. Fuck that job out there. Get married and move in here with me. You can find work over here."

"Don't worry. We'll come around and visit everyone."

"Yeah, I bet," I said obviously unhappy about the whole situation.

Mike got married and moved away right after school started for me.

At this point, being with my grandfather was almost better than being with my parents because it was a different degree of a relationship. Because of that, I would listen more to his advice with an open mind. My grandfather would always soften my pocket with a five or ten now and then. One day I had come home, and my grandfather called out to me.

"Yeah, what do you want, Gramps?"

"Come ere."

"Yeah, what's up?" I said as I walked over to him.

He grabbed my hand and said, "You know, Michael. I likea you."

I smiled, hugged him, kissed the top of his head, and said, "I know, Grandpa. I likea you too."

As it turned out with my mother, she used the spousal abuse defense, and she won. The only problem was that since she said something about being out of her mind, the court decided to keep her at Creedmore State Hospital, indefinitely.

I had gone up to visit her again, and the place wasn't a pretty sight at any age. The patients would always wander into the visiting room and try to talk crazy talk to me. My mother would tell me to pretend I was talking back to some of them, because a few of them never got visitors.

After a couple of visits it actually wasn't that bad trying to talk to some of them. It almost got to be fun, but I still didn't think I'd like to live with them like my mother had to. Aside from the place being awkward, the conversations I'd have with my mother were too, kinda like nothing happened, and she was on some vacation type of thing.

After a few weeks at school, an interesting thing started to go on. About three times a week for about two hours a day, Michael De'Lovic, Bobby Ortiz, and I were taken out of our class and down the hall to a small office that was made over to be a little classroom. While we were there, we were given different grade school books for pre-algebra, where I had left off in Catholic school. Michael and Bobby had done some of this other work also, and some of it was pretty easy for them, too. We liked the special treatment, and I guess it kept our minds busy. Our regular class was still bouncing around with fractions, something the three of us had learned a long time ago.

By now I had started to date Arianna Santamaria, my first steady girlfriend, who was in my class. One thing cool about dating her was that she lived three blocks away from me. I'd walk her home, hang out till dinnertime, and then sometimes come back and hang out with her at night. Arianna's brother, Peter, took martial arts lessons, and sometimes when I'd see him leaving for class, I'd feel like going back to taking lessons myself like when I was younger. But I couldn't come up with any money now.

After I dated her for two months, one day out of the blue, Arianna told me she thought it would be good if we didn't see each other any more. Aside from living so close together, I thought it was really strange because we sat together in class.

"So what do you want me to do? Hide when I see you?"

Having never broken up with a person, I didn't really know what she meant, so I asked her to clarify.

"That's not what I meant, Michael. We can still be friends and all. I just don't want to be tied down to one person."

Even after her brother took me aside and explained it to me in a nice way, I was still a little perplexed. Ah, to be young.

The next day I rode my mini-bike down to 34th Avenue, and I ran into Jimmy Marnell, Peck, Joe DeSilvio and Moose.

"Hey, Mike. I'm sorry to hear about Mike," Jimmy said.
"What are you talking about? Mike who?"
"Mike Sargent. Why? Didn't you hear?"
"Hear what?"
"I'm sorry to tell you, man, but he's dead."
"No way... Get the fuck out of here."
"I'm serious. We just heard from Dondi, Mike's brother in-law."
"No, you're lying to me."
"I don't think he is, Mike. I was there too when Dondi told us," Peck said.
"No. No way," I said as I started up my mini-bike and rode over to Mike's in-law's house.

After I got there, I rang the doorbell a few times until Michael, Mike's brother in-law, opened the door. He looked at me and then at the ground and said, "I'm sorry, Mike. It's true."

I felt like someone punched me square in the stomach as Mike started to explain what he knew to me. As it turned out, as far as he could tell, Mike had a few words with some of the local guys and threatened to kick their ass one by one or all together at once. After nobody challenged him, he and his wife went home. Then about two days later while Mike was taking the trash to the trash room in the building, somebody stabbed him in the heart, and he bled to death.

I was shocked and felt very sick about it. I swore it had to be a mistake. I felt that way all the way up to his funeral day over at Gleason's funeral hall. Mike didn't really have any family, so I wasn't too surprised when I stopped by the funeral parlor and nobody was there.

As I walked over to the coffin, I just hoped it wasn't going to be him. That is until I got there and sure enough, it was him. He had just turned twenty-one a month ago and now his run was over. As I sat there and cried, I realized that it was the first time I had been to the funeral of someone I really cared about, so it really choked me up.

I didn't feel like going to school the next day. Then I just stopped going for a while until the weather started getting colder. A few weeks later I ran into Marcus, and he handed me a little card.
"What the hell is this?"
"It's a card from my sister, Jenny. She's inviting you to her birthday on October 15th. I think she has a crush on you."
"Yeah, screw you."
"No, I think you can talk to Jenny about that. She's the one who likes you."

By the time the 15th came around, I had wondered that whole day if I should go to Jenny's party. I mean, even though I was friends with her brother and family, I wondered if I did go maybe she'd think I wanted to be her boyfriend or something. I was still undecided when I got home, and I thought it was a little odd when I saw my Aunt Linda's car in my driveway. I walked into the kitchen, and my mother was there with Linda. I realized that my mother would only take a chance of sneaking out of the hospital if it was important or if she had a bone to pick with me, like she had done once before. I tried to play it off like nothing was wrong to figure out what was going on.

"Hey, what's up?"
"What the hell is this?" my mother asked as she held up a letter from school.
"I don't know," I answered.
"Well, it's a cut card from school, and it says that you missed a total of two weeks from school!"

Oh... I don't think you want to be around for this, Mike, I thought, so think fast.
"Hold on, I've got to go to the bathroom," I said as I walked into the bathroom next to the kitchen, closed the door, and then hopped out the window. I knew my mother would have to go back to the hospital soon that day, so I'd just wait it out until she left.

I started walking down the driveway, and I saw Barbara, the funny little blond girl from across the street, sitting on her porch in her front yard. I decided to go over and talk to her for a minute or two before I took off. I hadn't really seen much of Barbara and her family ever since my father died. We said hello and started talking for a minute or two when her oldest sister, Connie, walked out the front door to leave. This happened at the same time that my mother ran down the driveway, shouting my name. Connie stopped, looked at my mother, then at me, and yelled, "He's over here, Alma."

I couldn't really blame Connie; she was raised in a time when the neighborhood still raised a child. After I looked over my shoulder and saw my mother rushing across the street, I decided that this might be a good time to leave, and I took off running.

My mother and Connie started to chase me, but this rabbit was a little quick for that game. After I had run for a few blocks I slowed down, until I saw that they hadn't given up yet, so I turned on the turbo charge and got out of Dodge City. After I had lost them, I crossed Northern and walked down to 154th Street. Now I was down the block from Jimmy and Bobby Marnell's house. I figured that I'd stop by there and see if they were home, so I could lay low until my mother had to sneak back into Creedmore. Just before I went to cross the street, I saw my friend Ricky Dale riding on his skateboard, so I yelled out to him. He didn't hear me, so I looked to my left before crossing the street and saw this huge thing coming towards me. When I focused in on this thing, I saw a bunch of people in it with their hands on their cheeks with their mouths opened wide, like when you're shocked to see someone. Then two answers slammed into my brain immediately. Number one was that this is a city bus, and number two was the city bus. The only other thought I was able to squeeze out was, Oh shit...!

Wham!

The bus hit me square in the face. For a few seconds I felt myself flying through the air towards heaven, and I thought I was dead. Then "Bam," I hit the road face first. Well, I certainly ain't going to heaven, I thought.

After lying on the Street for a few moments, I felt myself starting to get wet so I tried to pick myself up. "No!" some people shouted. "Stay down, don't get up!"

Even after hearing them, I did somewhat of a push up, to try and get up. When I opened my eyes, I saw a huge puddle of blood, and I realized that it was mine. After I spit out a few pieces of my teeth, I decided to lie back down into the warm pool of blood.

Well... that's it. I'm gonna lie here and bleed to death just like my father did. I guess it's fitting, I thought.

I passed out for a little while, and then I realized that I was being put into an ambulance. After sitting in the ambulance for a few seconds, I felt myself start to float out of my body. It was amazing. I had gotten about ten to fifteen feet above the ambulance, and I was looking at the whole scene unfolding. Then I heard someone start shouting, "Michael...! Michael...! Don't you die on me! Michael!!"

Oh shit, I can't die in front of my mother; she'll really go crazy, I thought.

The next thing I knew I was back in my body in the ambulance, and I started saying, "Just leave me alone, Ma. Just leave me alone. I'm all right now."
"Michael, what do you mean? It's me, Debbie, Marcus's mother."
"Debbie? Where the hell did you come from?"

As Debbie was explaining to me how she ended up in the ambulance, and why my mother couldn't be there without getting in trouble, I decided to pass out. I briefly woke up in the emergency room to complain about them pulling my clothes off, of all things. Aside from that it was smooth sailing for five days because I was out like a light.

On the sixth day I woke up to the sound of my mother's voice. For a minute I thought that maybe the last two years of my life were just a bad dream, until I asked my mother who the stranger was who was sitting next to her. She explained to me that it was a guard from Creedmore. Well, so much for a dream.

After we talked for a little while, I asked her how badly I was hurt, aside from realizing that I had lost some teeth.

"Well, you got twelve stitches on your forehead, you broke your nose and fractured your top jaw, and you got 133 stitches in your mouth."
"Really? A hundred and thirty three stitches in my mouth?"
"Yes," she answered.
"Wow."
"Now listen, the bus company offered us fifty-thousand dollars to settle this case..."

"Cool! Fifty-thousand?" I said through broken teeth and a swollen face.

"Yes, but I turned them down."

"What do you mean you turned them down?"

"I hired an attorney, and he's going to get us more money."

"Ma... I'm happy with fifty-thousand," I said.

"I know it sounds like a lot of money, Michael, but it'll be better if we get more."

"Yeah... 'If' we get more."

"Look, Michael, if they've already offered us this much, then a lawyer can probably get more."

"Ma, this is what I want to do. Take the money and put it in an account until I'm eighteen. It will be a lot of money by then..."

"Michael, I know fifty-thousand sounds like a lot of money now, but you'll see. I know what I'm doing."

"Ma..., I don't care if you know what you're doing. I'm the one sitting here with his face smashed in. I want you to accept the fifty grand for me."

"It's not a good idea, Michael."

"Mother," I said sarcastically. "I stepped off the curb, if they get some kinda of witness that says that, I could get nothing. I don't care if you think it's not a good idea. I can buy a fucking house with fifty grand. I want my lawyer's phone number because I want the fifty grand."

"Well, 'I' am your guardian, and 'I' make the decisions in your life."

"Well, considering that you are living in a mental hospital for making a bad decision in your life, I don't think you're in a position to make a fucking decision about my life. I want my lawyers fucking number..."

"You little fucking bastard," my mother said under her breath.

I don't know what had gotten into me, but I was glad it did. Here was a chance for me to take all the emotional pain away and have something to look forward to in a few years, and instead my mother wants to make yet another bold decision in my life. I was fucking furious at her. I asked her one more time for the phone number of the lawyer she hired. When she said she wouldn't do it, I rolled over and pretended like she was dead.

My mother sat there for an hour and talked to the back of my head. Then she got up, told me everything was going to be all right, kissed the back of my head for some reason, and left.

After she left, a nurse came in to check on me. When she realized I was up and alert, she pulled back the curtains surrounding my bed and asked me if I would like to have dinner. I told her I was starving and that I would love to have dinner. When she left, I could see that I was in a large room with three other kids in hospital beds. After a few minutes, I started up a little conversation with the other kids.

"Wow, it's good to see you alive," one of the kids said.

"Yeah, we thought you were going to die so we asked the nurse to move you," another kid said.

"Gee, thanks," I answered.

"Sorry. We thought you would die and turn into a ghost or something."

"So what happened to you?"

"I got hit by a bus."

"Really? Wow, cool," the third kid said.

"Cool...? Yeah, I guess..."

A little while after that a nurse started to bring in some food. One kid had a turkey dinner, and the other two got cheeseburgers. I could hardly wait for my food because I was starving. Finally a nurse brought me my tray and sat it on the table. Then she pulled a big syringe with a rubber tube out of her pocket and uncovered my tray.

"What the hell is this?!"

"Well, because of the damage to your lips and gums, all your food has to be strained."

"Strained...? That's baby food."

"Well, I'm sorry, but this is what you're supposed to eat until your mouth heals."

Well, I guess it's only fitting that I miss out on two dreams today; one was fifty-thousand dollars, and the other was a cheeseburger.

I ended up staying in the hospital for two weeks, and then I went back home.

CHAPTER 3

BOY'S TOWN

I stayed at home for the next couple of weeks, and I didn't go to school. Even after my mother told me that I should be well enough to go back, I still didn't go. My grandfather even got tired of pouring water on my head each morning. Then my mother called me one day and told me that I was going to have to move and live somewhere else.

Halfway through my complaint she told me that I was going to be moving up the block to Marcus Capeeto's house. At first thought, I didn't like the idea but then after talking about a few other places I could be going, moving up the block had a nice sound to it. Marcus lived in a big twelve room house with his family, which consisted of Debbie and Joe, his parents, then in order of age came Denise, Freddy, Marcus, and then Jenny.

After I moved in, adjusting to sharing Marcus's small room, and sleeping on a cot, was a little rough but I soon managed. Marcus and I went to different schools. He was now in, what was called, a 600 school. It's a school you go to when no other school wants to take you. All the loony birds, from other schools go there. The place had cages on the windows, and a guard at the front door. After breakfast we'd head our separate ways unless we came up with a better idea like cutting out for the day. Eventually I grew to enjoy living at Marcus's house because it made me feel like I was part of a big family, which made me forget about mine. One of the things I liked about it was that everything was regimented: Get up at a certain time, eat at a certain time, and go to bed at a certain time, unlike at my house where I could just about make my own times for these things. Then I started to go to work with Marcus and Freddy on the weekends. They worked for their father who did all the maintenance on a bunch of big buildings in Manhattan; it was hard work at times but it was good pay.

Sometimes I would go over to my house, and it was very strange. My grandfather had moved out by now and was living with my Aunt Marie. It was a bit of a surprise because nobody bothered to tell me he was moving. My life was teaching me that things just happen for no reason, so I just had to except it, whether I wanted to or not. Without my grandfather around, my mother had asked one of the tenants that we called Uncle Phil to collect the rents. When I'd go there, it was like my home was functioning without the main ingredients. My mother's car was in the driveway, there was a big pool in the backyard, my stuff, my mother's stuff and my father's stuff was scattered throughout the house, but that was all that remained, aside from memories. It was eerie, like stepping into a weird time capsule.

One day I was down on 34th Avenue by Bench Park playing two-hand touch football with Marcus, Dave, Herman and little Johnny DeSilvio when a group of girls came over to the store near where we were. There were about seven of them and one guy nick named "Chick."I kinda knew one or two of the girls from the neighborhood. Being that Marcus and I went just about everywhere together these days I thought it was a little strange when he stopped playing football for a minute, ran over, and started talking to them. After he was done, he ran back over to the huddle.

"So what's this, Marcus? Are you holding out on the girls?"
"No, I met them over by the park one day, and I told them to stop by. But I didn't think they would. But there are a few cute ones. You want me to introduce you to them?"
"Yeah, that's cool."
"All right I will, but I'm after the one named Adrienne."

After Marcus introduced me to them, I invited them all over to my house to hang out after the football game. I made sure that they all knew that they could come and hang out anytime they wanted to because there wasn't any fear of my parent's coming home. At first, after explaining why my parents wouldn't be around, they didn't want to go. I then told them not to worry because if anything happened, Marcus and I would be outnumbered by them. After they agreed, I think Marcus had the same idea as I did at that point, which was to end the football game as soon as possible. When we got done with the game we all headed over to my house. They stayed until dinnertime, and then they told us that they would probably see us again.

"Wow, not a bad catch, Marcus. Do you remember all their names?"
"Well, I think so. There's Adrienne, Jane, Lisa, Edith, Mary, Teresa and Corky's sister, Alice. Did you decide which one you're going to go for?"
"Hmmm, I don't know. If you're already going for Adrienne, that leaves me with six to choose from."
"Yeah, but what about that guy named Chick?"
"Well, I don't know, Marcus. He seems like one of the girls if you ask me. So, you can have him."
"Well, no thanks. I'm sure they'll come back though," Marcus said as he tightened up and admired his biceps.

By now, after I went to a dentist appointed by the bus company, a temporary bridge was made for my teeth. Being that it made me talk with a lisp when I wore it, I didn't wear it much. The way I figured it, if it took me this long to learn how to talk without my front teeth, I didn't feel like learning how to pronounce words all over again, so I threw it in a drawer. Aside from my teeth I didn't have any other long-term effects from getting hit. Pretty lucky, I guess.

I went to visit my mother up at Creedmore. She looked fine for the most part. The ward that my mother was in was a co-ed section, so men and women wandered in and out of the day room. There was this one guy the guards had nicknamed Mousey; he reminded me of a scary-looking elf. Mousey was the type of patient who, no matter what you said to him, would stand there and repeat, "Yeah, Okay.... Okay"

This one time he came over to where my mother and I were sitting, and he started trying to have a bit of a conversation with us. I really wasn't in the mood to have a conversation with him that day, so I just pretended that he wasn't there. By now he was standing behind my mother and facing me, and he kept repeating, "What are you doing? What are you doing?"

About twenty questions into this routine he started shaking his arms with his hands in his pockets. Finally I asked my mother if Mousey needed his medication. When my mother asked me why I had said this, I explained what he was doing. My mother turned around to look at Mousey, and then she said, "Oh, Mousey get the hell out of here. Cut that shit out, and go inside and watch TV. Come on now, I mean it."

Mousey looked at my mother for a second, then hung his head low, and slowly walked out of the visiting room, even though his hands never missed a beat.

"What the hell was that all about?" I asked.
"Well, Mousey cuts the pockets out of his pants and walks around masturbating all the time."
"Get the hell out of here. He was masturbating that whole time?"
"Yes, Michael."
"Well, from now on, make sure he's never standing behind me when I come to visit."

Like I said before, visiting my mother was always an adventure.

One day while Marcus and I were hanging out over by Bench Park with Dolly Schlishman and Karen Pango, and a kid I knew from Catholic school named Kirk Castro walked over to us.

"What are you guys doing in my park?" he asked.
"Excuse me, you are joking, right?" I asked.
"Do I look like I'm laughing?"

After I realized that he wasn't joking, I said, "Kirk, I don't know how big you think you are, but if you make me get off this bike I'm going to kick your ass from one end of this park to the other. So now, you leave."

Kirk looked at me like he was shocked for a second, and then as if he wanted to kill me before he turned and walked away. Years later, in a weird way, he would get even with me.

Marcus and I were working on our bicycles in his two car garage one weekend when we heard some noise coming out of the steeple overhead. Marcus got a little scared and started to yell up there that he was going to go inside and get one of his father's shotguns and start shooting holes into the ceiling if somebody didn't come out of there. Within a couple of minutes, Freddy, his older brother, stuck his head out from the trap door that led up there and said, "Cool out, Marcus. We're up here drinking some beers."

"Really? Then let us come up."

"Well... all right, but wait a minute."

On that note Marcus ran up the ladder, and I followed right after him. When we got up there, I couldn't believe how big it was up there.

"Wow, this would make a cool clubhouse," I said.
"Yeah, but it doesn't have a floor. There's just a bunch of old boards we put up here."
"Well, I've got some big sheets of plywood down at my house. We could use them."

After Marcus and Freddy asked their parents if it would be okay, we started to turn the steeple into a clubhouse. It turned out to be pretty good timing, because it was starting to get cold out and now we would have a place to hang out.

By now Marcus and Adrienne were a steady item. I had started to date Edith, but being that her parents were very strict with her, I decided to start dating Lisa instead. I had known Lisa from Catholic school, and I thought she was cute then. Now that the steeple was done, Marcus and I decided to take the girls up there one day. Getting up into the steeple was not an easy task, though. You had to balance yourself on a ten-foot ladder and then hop off the top step onto your belly, which would now be the floor of the steeple, and then drag yourself in. It might sound like an easy task for a guy but for a bunch of girls, it was almost life threatening. It took us close to an hour to get all seven of them up there, and then after we got them all up there, they started worrying about how to get back down.

Marcus and I managed to calm them down in a little while after we started to joke about how we now had a captive audience. Then Jane reminded Marcus and me that there were seven of them and that they were probably able to beat us up. Lisa reminded the other girls that I had taken karate classes when I was younger, which made them all quite for a second or two, and then Lisa suggested that they would have to get me first because of that. After we hung out up there for a couple of hours, we started to help the girls back down and somehow in the process Edith fell off the ladder. Fortunately she didn't get hurt, but it was a long time before we were able to get them back up there again.

When Christmas came around, my mother was able to send me some presents to put under Marcus's family's tree. She also managed to get me some nice things for my birthday in January.

All in all we had a pretty mild winter, and one night Bobby Marnell, Eddie Russo, and I were hanging out over by Bowne Park. We had heard that it was going down into the teens that night, and we shared a bottle of brandy waiting for the edges of the pond to refreeze so we could climb onto the thick ice out in the middle.

We waited and checked the ice for a couple of hours, and finally it seemed like the pond was as frozen as we were. In order of weight I was the heaviest, then came Bobby, then Eddie. Eddie made it on first. Then Bobby found a spot, and then after a few close calls I finally got on. We stayed on the ice fooling around until we were really cold, which was about three hours, and then came the task of trying to find a way to get off the ice. Of course Eddie, who weighed about one hundred pounds, had no problem getting back off. But as for Bobby and me it was becoming a bit of a challenge. Every time we would get close to the edge of the ice it would start to crack under our weight, and we'd have to run back towards the center.

After we tried for hour to get off the ice, it was only about ten degrees. Finally in a bit of frustration I told Eddie that I was going to run as fast as I could and dive towards the edge. Being that I had a long distance to cover I knew that I wasn't going to be able to make the entire span, so I wanted him to grab whatever part of me that made it to the concrete and pull me out. I rehearsed what I was going to attempt with Eddy about two times, and then I backed up to get a good amount of space. I took a running start, and just as I was going to kick off for my leap, the ice broke underneath me, and I made a frantic dive towards the stone edge. I landed on the thin ice on my stomach with my hands holding onto the stone edge where Eddy was standing. As I was lying there, I looked up at Eddy and said, "Eddy... fucking grab me!" No sooner had I said that than "Splash!" I fell through the ice.

What really sucked about this was that the water that I had fallen into was only two feet deep, but because I had been lying flat on the ice, I was now wet from my toes to my armpits. Whereas, if I had just fell in and walked to the water's edge I only would have been wet up to about my knees. I jumped out of the water faster than I had fallen into it, while I felt like I was going to have a heart attack. Then I looked at Eddie who was still standing there with his mouth open and said, "Thanks for nothing." I really didn't know what to do for a second, but I decided to run home to Marcus's house. I was about twelve blocks away from his house now, and by the time I got halfway there, my clothes were already frozen solid.

When I got to Marcus's house Debbie was in the kitchen. She took one look at me and said, "Oh, my God! What happened to you?"

As I explained what had happened I tried to take off some of my clothes, but I couldn't because they were still frozen. Eventually after standing in front of the stove for a few minutes, I was able to get some of them off, which allowed me to start thawing out. A few days later I saw Bobby, and he told me that he had found a way off the ice a few minutes after I fell in, and he was able to walk off.

My cousin Dino was still running away from the home he was at from time to time and staying at my house, while I was living at Marcus's house. It was kinda nice to be able to walk down the block to my house and visit with him while he stayed there. Being that my grandfather wasn't living there any more, Dino had to either fend for himself or rely on me to get him some food. This meant that I would have to sneak food out of Marcus's house for him, or Dino would have to steal some food from the local supermarket.

When Dino first started running away from home, Aunt Linda or Uncle Richie would stake out the house for a little while and usually catch Dino within a couple of days. After he had gotten caught the last time, Dino stopped coming and going from the front of the house and now would cut through my neighbors' yards in order to come and go. Oddly enough, whenever Dino managed to stay away from the home for boys he would always call his mother to let her know that he was all right. This time he was able to stay at my house for over three weeks before he got recaptured.

I rode over to Ronnie and Russell's house on 169th Street. They hung out with a bunch of older kids over there. A few of them were a little nuttier than my cousins, and one or two were a lot nuttier, although they were all pretty nuts. I remember one thing they would do that I thought was insane. There was this elevator in this one building that everyone had learned how to stop between floors. The "game," if you will, was to catch some friends in the elevator between floors and then piss all over them. I was actually amazed the first time I saw this game. I couldn't believe that these guys would get a kick out of this until I walked over and saw the guys in the elevator scrambling around trying to cover their faces while three other guys were peeing on them.

"C'mon, Mike. Pee," Russell said.
"Well, no," I answered.
"C'mon," he said reassuring me, as the other guys scrambled like rats in a box.

I laughed to myself and then said to my cousin, "I don't know all of them. They might kick my ass when they get out."
"No, they won't. They'll just catch us in the elevator one day and piss on us."
"Well then... that's okay, I'll pass on this one, enjoy. Thanks for asking though," I answered.

One of the guys Russell hung out with was named Jimmy Duguid; you'd have to be crazy not to know that he was. I remember the day I saw him pull up to the corner, jump out of a smashed car, and run right past us.

"What the hell was that about?" I asked.
"It looks like Jimmy almost got caught in a stolen car by the cops again," he answered.

About an hour after that, Jimmy Duguid came over to where we were hanging out.

"Any cops show up?" he asked.
"No," my cousin answered.
"Did you steal that car?" I asked him.
"Yeah, it takes two seconds once you've got an ignition rigged."
"Wow, that must be hard to do," I said.
"Naaa, it's easy. Here, look, I'll show you how to do it. Besides you never know when you'll need to get a car for yourself one day," he answered."

I went to visit my mother up at the State Hospital. I told her about Dino getting caught at the house again, and she explained that she was sorry to hear about it.

"Well, you look a lot better, Mom."
"Yeah, but I feel like shit. I've got to get the fuck out of this place."
"Yeah, I know what you mean."
"Do you really—!"
"No, Ma ... I guess I don't."

Visits with my mother were always enjoyable.

School was over; summertime was here. Marcus and I rode our bikes over to Whitestone pool one day. A lot of kids went there in the summer. Marcus and I would spend most of the day watching the older girls in their bathing suits with stupid looks on our faces. As we were taking notes on them, one day I saw my old friend from Catholic school, Neil Mc Grorey. I heard that he had open-heart surgery not too long ago. After he ran over, I could see the scars he had on his chest.

"Wow, Neil. They really cut you open, huh?"
"Yeah, I know. It looked like I had a big zipper on me."
"Sorry I didn't come see you when you were in the hospital."
"Aww, don't worry about it," he answered.

Neil, Marcus and I stayed at the pool all day right up until suppertime, and then we all rode our bikes back home. We had a great day together.

Dino called me at Marcus's house one day; it had been a while since the last time he had gotten caught at my house.

"Hey, Dean. What's up?"
"Mike, my mother had me put in a worse place this time."
"Shit! You're kidding me, right?"
"No, I'm not."
"It's worse than the other one?"
"Yeah, it is. I've been here two weeks and I got into five fights already, and I haven't won them all."
"You're shitting me?"
"No, I'm not. But I'm all right"
"So what's gonna happen. Are they going to keep you there?"
"I don't know. They're talking about keeping me here for a while," he said.
"Shit, that sucks," I said before he had to hang up.

Then about a week later out of the blue I got another call from Dino.

"Mike, I know how to break out of this place, but I don't have any money to catch the train or anything. Besides, this guy I met, Billy, wants to come with me. Can you get a car?"
"Well, I don't know anybody with a car, Dino."
"Mike, see what you can do. I've got to get the fuck out of this place; it's bad here. I'll call you in two days at about nine o'clock, okay? I've got to go now, bye."

It bothered me to think of Dino in a place like that. I knew Dino could fight, but he wasn't really a big guy and I'm sure some of the bigger kids were messing with him.

One day, Marcus, and I were riding our bikes over to Bobby Marnell's house when all of a sudden Marcus takes off flying across the street. I didn't know what he was thinking, but it wasn't the first time I thought that about him. The only thing I see is a girl walking with her back towards us, wearing a halter top, and shorts. As the girl looks over her shoulder in Marcus's direction I realize that it's Adrienne. Marcus jumps off his bike, lets it crash, and starts screaming, "You fucking whore!"

The next thing I see is, Marcus, pull down her halter top, and then trying violently to rip her top off, while he's screaming. "Everybody look at the fucking whore!"and starts laughing like a madman.

I was in shock, and couldn't believe what I was seeing, but I knew she needed help. I dropped my bike, and ran to help her. By the time I got to her, Marcus, was literary twirling her around in circles with her halter top wrapped under her armpits. I slammed into him, grabbed him in a bear hug, and screamed at him to let her go.

Marcus lost his grip on her top and, Adrienne, tumbled to the ground like a ragdoll.

"Adrienne, go. Go, I got him."
"Yeah, go you bitch, get the fuck out of here."
"Marcus, I swear, shut the fuck up or I'm gonna slam you on your head."
"Go home bitch! You want to break up with me! Fuck you!"
"Marcus, I'm warning you."

He calmed down a bit, after I said that, and I held him against the fence while, Adrienne, got up, and hobbled down the block with her arms covering her breasts. When I saw her get to her house, I let him go.

"What the fuck is wrong with you? You'll be lucky if you don't get arrested."
"I don't give a fuck.," he said as he jumped on his bike, and rode away.

Man, what the fuck was that? I wonder if they should increase his medicine, and I wonder if I should tell his mother about this.

I was very surprised when Dino called me the next night instead of two days later, like he had said he would.

"Mike, I've got to get the fuck out of here!"
"Whata' ya' mean?" I asked.
"I got my ass beat today."
"Why? What happened?"
"This big black kid came over and took my milk at dinnertime."
"So how did you get your ass kicked?"
"Well, I couldn't just let him take it. If I did every other big kid would think that I was fair game so I ran up to him and punched him in his head," he explained.
"I guess by the sound of things it didn't work, huh?"
"Well, that's funny, I mean, it didn't seem to work when I was getting my ass kicked, but after the fight, some of the other big guys that I didn't know were coming over to me and calling me psycho pup and slapping me on my back and congratulating me for standing up for my shit. But now I've got my privileges taken away from me."
"So what are you going to do?" I asked.
"I'm outta here, I don't care where I go, I'm gone... me and Billy are busting out. Can you get a

car?"

I looked around Marcus's house to see if anyone could hear me and then I said, "Russell's friend Jimmy showed me how to steal a car. Maybe I could try to steal one to come and get you."

"Well, look, after dinner in the mess hall, one of my jobs is to take the garbage out. That's how I met my friend, Billy. After we carry the garbage outside were going to bolt. We'll be out there at six o'clock tomorrow night. If you can make it, cool. If not, don't worry about it. I'll be all right."

Dino gave me directions just in case I could make it, and then he said," Wish me luck. I'll call you if I make it."

After I got off the phone with Dino, I went over to my house to see if I could find any keys to my mother's car, but I couldn't. Then I went to see if I could do the trick with the ignition like Jimmy had shown me on my mother's car, but it didn't work. I called Marcus's mother from my house later that night, and after a little bit of pleading, I got her to let me sleep at my house that night. I thought about my situation and Dino's, and I wondered if I would just make a bad situation worse by stealing a car. I kinda knew it wasn't a great idea, but I wasn't going to leave Dino standing out on the street by himself either. After thinking about it one last time, I decided that I didn't care what happened to me, because I couldn't just sit around and not try to help Dino.

I figured that I would try to "borrow" the little old lady around the corner's car later that night. At the very least I thought she wouldn't come out and kick my ass. Once I got there I couldn't believe how easily Jimmy's little trick worked on her car, and I was very surprised when the car started on the first try. By the time I got to the corner I didn't know whether or not I should floor it and get the hell out of there or just calmly turn on my blinker and go for a little ride. There was half a tank of gas and nobody around, so I decided to go for a ride. I felt like a big shot, a 13-year-old big shot.

After I drove around for a little while, I decided that I had better put the car back, so it would be there for me tomorrow night. After that I went back to my house.

The next day, even though it was still light out, I decided to leave early in case I got lost, which I did. But I got there early enough to find my way around town in Long Island. Then at about a quarter to six, I went and parked over by the garbage cans next to the institution where Dino was. A little after six, I started to get a little worried, but then sure enough Dino came out with some other kid carrying garbage bags. I tooted the horn and he looked at me, smiled, and then said something to the kid behind him. Then they both dropped the garbage bags and ran towards me. I had rehearsed this thing in my head a few times and found myself startled when Dino jumped in the car and yelled, "Start the fucking thing already!" I started it and hauled ass out of there.

"So who's this guy?" I asked.
"Billy, the guy I told you about."
"Where do I gotta take him?"
"Well, actually he's got nowhere to go either, so I figured he could come stay with us for a while."
"Yeah, but first let's go to North Port, Long Island. I've got a friend over there named Mike Viale, he can get anything, and I want to get some weed," Billy said.

"Wait a minute. First of all, I don't know if this lady reported her car stolen. Second of all, if she did and I get busted, it'll be for having weed also," I yelled back.

"No, you won't," Billy answered, "If you're going to get busted for the car, you're going to get busted for the car. Second of all, I'll tell them the weed is mine. What's the worst they're going to do? Send me to a home? Besides," he added, "it's on the way anyhow."

"Yeah, what the hell? I've never smoked pot, and I feel like celebrating anyhow," Dino said.

"All right, fine. But we can't hang out all night. I've got to get this car back, and Dolly might call to check up on me," I said.

It took Billy a while to find Mike, but he finally did. When they came back to the car, there was a girl with Mike, real cute, and she seemed a little bit older than the rest of us. Mike was about my age but seemed older. Billy came over to the car and introduced everyone. Then he asked me if I would give Mike a ride with us into Queens because he had to pick up some stuff.

"He'll make it worth it for you," Billy said.

"Yeah," Mike said. "What do you want: money, pot, drugs?"

"He'd like a little bit of each," Billy answered for me.

I figured what the hell; I had to go back to the city anyhow. We all piled in the car and left. As I was driving back to the city, Mike started to fool around with the girl he was with, which was a little funny with three people in the back seat. It was Mike, then the girl, then Billy. After a few minutes the girl said to Billy, "Move your legs over, so I can suck his dick."

Billy looked over at Mike, and Mike said, "C'mon, move your fucking legs."

About a minute after that I heard Billy say, "Oh, man, this is torture. I haven't been this close to a woman in eight months.

Then I heard the girl say from behind my seat, "I'll bet you really want some of this then, huh?"

"Want some?" Billy said. "Shit, I'd cut off my right arm for some of that."

"What? You want some of my dick, too?" Mike asked.

"Naa, Naa, Naa, no thanks, I haven't been away that long. I was talking about getting a blowjob, not giving one. Thanks anyway," Billy answered.

It was dark out by the time we got to my house. Mike made a phone call and said he'd be back later and left with his girl. I called Debbie in case she had called me and told her that I was in for the night. By the time I got off the phone, Billy had rolled a joint, lit it, and then passed it to me.

I looked at Dino, and he said, "C'mon, Mike. It's a celebration for my breakout." Then Billy reached into his denim jacket and pulled out some cassettes.

"Where the hell did you get those from?" Dino asked.

"Well, I didn't care about any of my other shit, but I wasn't going to leave my Elton John tapes there for anyone else. Do you have a cassette player?"

Before long we were smoking more joints and listening to "Funeral for a Friend" by Elton John. It's a good thing I had taken back the car already because I was getting pretty smashed. The only problem was that I wasn't able to put it back in the same parking spot because someone had taken the spot, but at least it was pretty close.

After I don't know how long, Mike came back. He started pulling all kinds of drugs out of his pockets. Each time he did, Billy said, "Wow!"

"I tell you what," Mike said. "I'll give you thirty bucks, some pot, and a little coke if you can drive me back in the morning."
"He'll do it!" Dino answered.

I looked at Dino while he was shaking his head up and down and said, "Well, all right."

While Mike started to separate my portions, I asked Dino what I should do with the coke.

"Fuck it. We'll do it. We're celebrating remember?"
"Yeah, but I've never done it before."
"Don't worry. I'm here. I'm not going to let you get fucked up."

After about an hour we were all pretty buzzed when out of the blue Mike's girl said, "You know... I'd like to fuck all you guys. You're all cute..."

Dino, Billy and I stopped dead in our tracks, and then we all looked over at Mike. He looked back towards the three of us, shrugged his shoulders, and said, "Go for it." As my jaw dropped so did Dino's and Billy's zippers.

"But wait a minute. I go first," Mike said.

Then he bent her over the couch, lifted her skirt, and was in. While Mike was taking his turn, I whispered to Dino, "Dean, I never got laid before. What do I do?"
"Really...? Cool! You'll love it. Just watch what we do, and start taking notes real fast."

I sat back and found myself amazed that this was actually happening. Dino and Billy were waiting as patiently as possible with their soldiers standing at attention, while Mike and this girl were thoroughly enjoying themselves.

Mike finally got done, so Dino and Billy moved in. By now the girl was like a ringleader in a circus telling who to stand where and put what in where.

Shit, I thought. I'm still fooling around with girls' boobs, and this girl has got a party going on. There's a whole big world out there that you don't know a thing about, Mike.

Dino got done, and now it was my turn. I stood there for a moment unable to move. Mike looked at me, then at Dino, and shrugged his shoulders.

"He's never had sex before," Dino said.
"Ooooo! A virgin," the girl said.
"Don't talk with your mouth full," Billy joked.

Oh, great, I thought. Now everyone knows I never had sex before.

"C'mon," Dino said in a huff as he walked over and undid my belt. "Take your pants off."
"Okay, now take your dick and put it right there," he said.
"Where?"
"Right there."
"Where? I don't see anything."
"Come over here," Dino said as he grabbed me by my erect appendage and led me towards my fate.
"Okay, wait, wait, now push," he commanded as he gently tugged at my manhood.

"Whoaaaa," I said out loud as my virginity melted away. Then I stood there for a moment, unable to move for fear of exploding.

Dino jumped behind me grabbed my ass cheeks and thrust them back and forth.
"Back and forth, Mike. Back and forth, just like this," he said.

On the sixth thrust from Dino, I exploded. Wow, now I know why guys fight over girls, I thought.

Once we were all done, the girl got up and went into the bathroom.

"Okay, now you guys all owe me," Mike said.
"Oh, no, you never said we had to pay for that before we started," Dino answered.
"Well, Okay…, then this one's on the house."

The girl came out of the bathroom with her makeup on and dressed and said, "What do you have to eat? I'm starving."
"Look in the kitchen and see what you can find," Dino said.

She found eggs and potatoes and started cooking for us and talking like nothing had happened.

Even thought I felt great, I was still a little shocked by the whole thing.

"So wadaya got, this whole house to yourself?" Mike asked.
"Well, kinda," I answered.
"Yeah, Billy told me about your mom and pop. It's fucked up, but don't sweat it. Parents can be real assholes sometimes. When I was a kid my stepfather used to get drunk, come home, and beat the shit out of me. After a while, though, I'd just roll up into a ball and take my licks. But what really pissed me off was when he'd beat on my mother. I swore one day when I got bigger I'd kick his ass."
"So whatever happened? Did you kick his ass?" I asked.

"When I turned thirteen, I figured I was a man. A few days after that he started hitting my mother again so I stepped out in the hall and yelled at him, "Motherfucker, leave my mother alone!" He walked over to me and said, "Oh, so you think you're a fucking man, huh?"

"So I said yes, and he punched me square in my face. When I woke up I realized that I was staring at my bedroom ceiling. I didn't know how I had got there until I tried to stand up, and I realized that he had punched me so hard that he knocked me through my sheetrock wall. My feet were still in the hallway. Then I got up and went to wash the blood off my face in the bathroom. My stepfather walked past the bathroom and went into my room. He came back, threw two shopping bags at me, and said, "You're a man now. Here's your fucking clothes. Get out.""

"Fuck. What did you do then?" I asked.

"Well, I didn't want to get punched in the face again, so I left. I went and slept in the park that night over by my house. Then I learned how to survive on my own real fast."

"Did you ever go back home?"

"Yeah, I went home about two months later. But some nights my stepfather would come home drunk, open my bedroom door, and tell me to leave. It went on and off like that until I finally left.

After hearing Mike's story I thought to myself...You know, Mike, maybe your life didn't turn out bad at all. Maybe it could have been worse. I had it pretty good for a while. Maybe it was time for a little bad. But shit, I think I could have learned my lesson a little easier than the one I was handed.

The food was ready, and after we ate we decided to make the trip out to North Port now instead of the morning, so I went and borrowed the car again, and we all went for the ride back to Long Island.

Food was a little bit of a problem the first few days that they were living there, but it was soon solved. Dino and Billy would take turns stealing stuff from the supermarket in order to keep themselves fed. I was still living up at Marcus's house, so food wasn't a problem for me.

One morning I went over to my house and noticed that there were a lot of doughnuts and apple pies lying around, so I asked where they all came from.

"Oh, this supermarket left them stacked up in the back of the store for us outside, and we got tired of going back over there every couple of days so we took a bunch of them this time," Dino explained.

"Yeah, I wish you'd let us use that car. We could get enough pies to last us a week," Billy said.

"Really? You can get enough food for a week?" I asked.

"Yeah, and there will be pies there tonight," they added.

"Well, boys, let's go shopping tonight," I answered.

That night we took enough pies to last a while, and we ate two of them on the way home.

A few nights later, back at Marcus's house, I made the mistake of trying to calm Marcus down while we were in front of his pool table. Even though Marcus was my best friend, every now and then he would freak out and get violent, and this time turned out to be a bad one. We were playing with our slotted electric cars, on a track set-up in his basement. I noticed that my tire had come off on my car, so I grabbed it off the track to fix it. Out of nowhere, Marcus screamed, "What the hell are you doing, I was beating you!!"

He grabs a pool stick off the pool table, and swings it at my head. I ducked, and then charged him. I slammed into him, and I get him into a headlock. Then, with his back towards me, Marcus reached down, grabbed a pool ball, and whacked me in the forehead. Thank God, I saw it coming otherwise he would have got me right in the face. At first I couldn't believe he did it. I mean it's not like this was the first time Marcus had freaked out on me, but this time he really hurt me, and then I snapped. I turned him around and strangled him until his eyes rolled, and he went limp. Even after he slid to the floor coughing, I felt like whacking him with a pool ball. I left him lying there and then went upstairs to go look in the hallway mirror.

Joe, Marcus's father, was watching TV, in the living room and said, "What have the two of you been up to? I thought I heard some yelling downstairs."

I looked in the mirror and saw a lump, which seemed like Mount Everest on my forehead and said, "What have we been up to! I don't know what you've been up to, but I've been trying to prevent myself from getting killed. Look at this fucking lump!"
"Hey! Don't talk that way in my house!" Joe yelled.

Hmmm, Mike, this might be a way to cause a fight and get thrown out of here. I thought for a second, but then I reminded myself of how I had seen Joe hit Marcus once or twice and decided that pissing him off might not be a good idea.

"I'm sorry, Joe. I've just never had a lump this big on my head," I said.

As I leaned forward into the light to show Joe the lump, I could hear Marcus gasping for air and whining in the basement.

"Holy shit! He really did give you a whack," Joe exclaimed.

Then his father jumped off the couch, pulled off his belt, and ran towards the stairs. Marcus, who could have overheard the conversation, hissed weakly, "NO...NO, NO."

The next thing I heard was Marcus running around full of life, yelling for his life. I felt a little bad for Marcus after a minute or two, but hey, this lump is still there and he could have hit me in my face if I didn't see it coming.

The next time my mother called, I told her that I no longer cared to sleep there any more, but she told me that I had to stay there.

"Why? There's no school now. Just send me the money you've been sending Debbie, and I'll get my own food," I reasoned.
"No, you can't go shopping and cook for yourself."
"That's right. I forgot. I'm a kid. Right Ma... Fine, then I'll eat at Debbie's and stay home. Besides, there's not enough bedrooms in Marcus's house, and I'm getting tired of sleeping on a cot mattress on

the floor in Marcus's room. Sometimes I feel like his puppy. I didn't do anything wrong. I'm tired of being punished for it. I want to live in my own room for a while."

"I'm sorry. I didn't know you were sleeping on a cot. I thought you had your own bed."

"Well, there's four kids here, and they all had their own rooms before I came."

"All right, listen. Stay there for a few days, and I'll talk to Grandpa and see if he wants to leave Aunt Marie's and come home for a while. But I won't promise you anything."

Even though my mother said that she would see what she could do about my living arrangements, I decided to sleep at my house the next few days with Dino and Billy, the fugitives.

One night my cousin Russell showed up with his nutty, friend, Jimmy Duguid. They had a bunch of beers, and we sat around and got a little drunk. After a while Jimmy asked if anybody wanted to go out for a ride in his car.

"What, you've got a car?" Billy asked Jimmy.

"Yeah, but it's stolen," Jimmy said.

"You never told me that fucking car was stolen! George will kill me if he finds out I'm in a stolen car," Russell yelled.

"Yeah, but if I would have told you that it was stolen, you wouldn't have come for a ride either, right?" Jimmy added.

My cousin looked at Jimmy and didn't say a word. It came down to neither of us wanting to be called a wuss for not having gone out for a ride, so we all went.

I thought about how this had been the fourth or fifth time that Russell or his brother had come over and stayed out all night. Maybe it was just because they knew Dino was here, or maybe not. Well, anyway, they knew they could always stay here if they wanted. By the end of the night, Jimmy had bragged about how he sometimes sold the cars he stole and made some money. He also managed to teach everyone else how to steal a car, after we got done joyriding around that night.

A few days later my mother found out that I had been staying at home and complained to me about it. I figured I'd test how secure Creedmore was and told her that I didn't really care how she felt about it, because I was going to stay home, but I would still eat at Debbie's house. My mother started yelling at me as if I was a child, expecting my obedience, because she was still my mother. I told her that I was going to make the first decision in my life, and deal with my own consequents, if she didn't mind, and hung up.

Well, what's the worst that could happen if she doesn't break out, Mike? No more food at Debbie's? Fuck it, that I could live with, I thought.

After I spent about a month living at home and roaming the streets with Dino and Billy, Mike Viale stopped by. He was dressed in new clothes and looked pretty good, but unfortunately he didn't bring any girls with him.

"Hey, what's up, guys? Man, you're a sorry-looking bunch," Mike said.

"We've all seen better times," I answered.

"You got any money? Any food?"

"Well, we've got doughnuts, and apple pies, up the ass. We've been snatching them from the supermarket at night after they make their delivery, and I've made a little money selling them to other stores in the neighborhood," Billy said.

"Yeah, we've been eating doughnut soup, doughnut salad, toasted doughnuts, and topping it off with doughnuts for dessert. I'm so sick of doughnuts, and apple pies, I'd be glad if I never saw another apple pie as long as I live." Dino added.

"Well, I hate to say it but you ought to see my fridge," Mike explained. "Well, listen, I figured you guys would be in rough shape. That's why I stopped by, aside from taking care of some business. I got a hold of some credit cards; they're stolen. I've already gotten myself a wardrobe, and you can get food at some places. I'll give you the cards, and you decide. You've got to use them soon though," he added.

"I don't know, Dino. I think we can go to jail for this," I said.

"Yeah, I know, Mike, but Billy and I have been living off your hand-me-downs since we got here. Look at my sneakers. There falling off my feet. Besides that, we could get enough food for a month."

"Listen, one of these cards is a platinum card, so don't get stupid and try to buy a thousand dollar TV set." Mike added.

"Mike, we're just gonna get food and some clothes," Billy reasoned.

Mike told us how we should use the credit cards, and left in a little bit.

After talking about it for a little while, we ended up going down to Main Street for some clothes. We window-shopped for a while and talked about doing it, and then we finally did. Each one of us ended up getting ourselves a little wardrobe, and then we decided to call it a night because we didn't want to press our luck.

While we were leaving Main Street, I bumped into a friend's older brother. After we said hello to each other and kept walking, Billy said to me, "Mike, I know that guy from the neighborhood, he sells pot."

"Really?"

"Yeah, and I was just thinking, if I asked him what he wants from a store, maybe we could trade it to him for some pot that I could sell, so we could make some money," he added.

"Do you think we should take another chance with the credit cards?" I asked.

"Yeah, why not? I guess we've already crossed the line anyway," he answered.

Billy ran off and came back a few minutes later.

"Okay, he says he wants a big radio, and he'll trade for that."

We decided to go for it one more time, so Dino and Billy went inside the department store while I waited outside with the packages that we had already gotten. I put myself in a position so I could see the checkout counter from outside to watch them. Then after a few minutes I saw Dino go over to the register. He was about to sign the receipt when these two people came over said something to him, and the three of them walked away. After a couple of minutes I wondered if I should leave, because it didn't look good. The only problem, I thought, was whether or not I could carry all the bags by myself and not look too stupid.

My mind was made up for me when the two people and my cousin came outside, and I was told that I should come inside now. My cousin, who was standing there in handcuffs, looked at me and said, "Do the bird," which meant split in our lingo. Then I looked at the big guy standing there waiting for my reaction, and I felt that he could run pretty fast, too, so I decided to go with them.

The police came a little while after that to officially arrest us. They took us over to the 109th Precinct, and I went into a small holding cell behind the desk sergeant. They took Dino somewhere else. Oddly I didn't feel scared, considering this was my first arrest, I was more concerned about getting sent to one of the places that Dino had been running away from. After I sat there for a little while, a cop took me out and explained that someone was coming from the home Dino was at and they would take him back. I was going to Central Booking in Que Gardens. The cop took me over to the bathroom to take a leak and told me that I was lucky that it wasn't the weekend, otherwise, I'd be there with all the wackos. Well, here goes, Mike, I thought. When you get to Central Booking at least you'll get to see where your mother was when she got arrested.

After I got processed, the cop walked me over to an empty holding cell.

"Okay, turn around, drop your draws, and spread your cheeks."
"Excuse me???"
"Turn around, pull your pants down, and spread your cheeks."

As a million thoughts were racing through my head, I said, "Why would I want to do that?"
"It's not a matter of you wanting to do it. You have to do it, its procedure."
"Let me get this straight, you want me to pull my pants down, and turn around... for what reason?"
"I gotta see if you're hiding something."
"Like what, a school bus?"

On that note, I heard the prisoners in the cells next to me start to laugh.

"What are you, a wiseass!?"
"Officer, this is the first time I've been in jail, and someone's asking me to turn around, and pull my pants down. I don't get it, I'm a little confused."

By now, the guys in the holding cells are howling with laughter.
 "You stupid ass, I gotta see if your hiding any drugs or anything."

Seeing that he was getting a little angry, and frustrated, I yelled out to the other prisoners, "Did anyone else have to do this?"
"Yeah, stupid, we all have to do it," a prisoner said back to me.
"Fine, I don't like the idea of this, but I'll do it."

I hung a moon at the cop, while watching him over my shoulder, then he shined a flashlight at my butt, and then told me to zip up.

"You gotta do this to everybody you arrest?"

"Yeah."

"Jeeze, I actually feel bad for you now. You need a little time out or something?"

"Get the fuck over here, and get in this cell, you little wiseass."

Once I got in the cell with the other guys, having heard all different kinds of stories about jail, I decided to stay up all night. I got transferred over to Queens Criminal Court in the morning; it was an unpleasant ride. Since I got there late, I wasn't going to get the chance to be in the first batch for morning court, I was told. While I was there, in the holding cells, I met some interesting people but I didn't like the feeling of being a caged rat.

That afternoon I got a Legal Aid lawyer appointed to me, and he asked me for my home phone number, so I gave him Dolly's number and explained my situation to him a little bit. One of the things he told me was that I could have an option of going into a program and get this off my record, or I could take my chances and take it to trial, I opted for the program, and my lawyer got me released that afternoon. When I got outside, I took a deep breath and thought, Man, this fresh air never smelled so good.

I sat outside the courthouse for about ten minutes, thinking about my freedom, and then wondered how I was going to get home from there with no money. I guess I'd have to sneak on the train. Hope I don't end up back here like that black guy I was in with at the holding cell who was arrested for sneaking on the train. Fuck it, I'm too tired to walk six, seven miles back home, I thought.

When I got to the train station I saw a cop standing there and told him about my situation. "Well, why don't you walk?" he said. I explained my reasoning to him, and showed him my court papers, he thought about it for a minute or two then he let me go onto the train.

Surprisingly Billy was there when I got home; I did kinda wonder what happened to him. He explained that he had no time to do anything to help Dino because they grabbed him in two seconds, so Billy ran.

"What happened to you?" Billy asked. "You were outside. Didn't you see anything happen?"

I told him what happened, and Billy said, "Shit, I would have grabbed as much clothes as I could and just ran."

After a few days at home it was becoming harder and harder for Billy and me to keep ourselves fed. I guess one of the main reasons for that was because I didn't like to go "shopping." In the past he and Dino would both go "shopping." Between the two of them, there was always food on the table. Then one day out of the blue-my mother came home.

"What are you doing here?" I asked.

"I borrowed a key and snuck out. What happened to you and Dino? I didn't know he was living here with you," she said.

I couldn't believe it; I was actually in a bit of shock that my mother was actually standing here busting my balls again like she would in the old days, almost as if nothing had ever happened. I didn't know whether to answer her or just laugh out loud at the absurdity of it all. Then I thought to myself, Shit, she does look a little pissed off. Maybe she broke out of Creedmore. I think I'll just play along and answer her questions for now.

While my mother and I were talking about my living situation, Billy walked in.

"Who's this?" she asked.
"Well, this is a friend of Dino's. He was staying here with him."
"Oh no, he can't live here. This kid's got to go back to his family."
"He doesn't really have a family," I reasoned.
"No, I'm sorry I have enough trouble thinking about you. I can't go back there thinking about another kid living here," she answered.

By this time Billy, knowing of my family history, was agreeing to everything my mother said. After I talked with her for a little while, she decided to let him stay that night though.

I explained to my mother the program that was offered to me, and my mother agreed that it sounded like a good idea. My mother hung around the house for a while and then called up a cab to make sure she could get back in time, as she put it. When the cab got there, she reminded me that Billy and I could stay there that night, but Billy would definitely have to leave. She said she'd check and see if Grandpa wanted to come home again. Then she gave me some of the rent money she collected, and she left.

"Wow, what a trip, man," Billy said. "You must be bugging out. How long has it been since you've seen your mother at home?"
"A pretty long time," I answered. "Shit, this sucks. If my mother's really got a key, then you've got to leave," I added.
"Yeah, but believe me, if your mother wants me to leave, then I'm gone, man. I don't want her getting mad at me," Billy answered.

The next day Billy took the train out to Long Island to see some old friends. He ended up staying out there a few days before he came back.

"Well, what's up? Did you find a place to live?" I asked.
"Well, I had a great time, but I couldn't just ask anyone yet for a place to live," he answered.
"I'm gonna need a couple of days."
"Well, do what it takes, I guess," I answered.

A few days later, I spoke with my lawyer about my court case, and I joined the court-appointed program. The program I went into sent me over to Jamaica Hospital; basically I was a janitor. It might not have been so bad if the real janitor helped me out a little, but I guess for him it was a free ride. The only other bad part about it was that I worked on the floor that the nurses called the dying floor. I didn't have to do this full-time, but even the little time I had to do there became too much. I ended up calling the program and asking them if I could be moved, and after a week they put me as a stock boy down in the basement, lifting boxes. Heaven, I thought.

I was still living at home with Billy when one day Debbie, Marcus's mother, stopped by.

"You know, Michael, your mother thinks you're living at my house. And what is this boy Billy still doing here?" she said.

Being that I didn't have much of an answer for her, I didn't say anything.

"She's going to call my house tonight at 6:30, and she wants you to be there. Besides, you know that school is starting soon," she added.

When I spoke to my mother that night she read me the riot act, and she added that Billy had more than enough time to leave, and even threatened to call the cops on him. She also mentioned that there was a good chance that she would be coming home also.

My grandfather moved back home within a few days of that call, and Billy, moved out to Long Island. Gramps still had a problem waking me up in the morning. He'd give me one or two wake-up calls, and if I wasn't up by then, he'd dump the pot of water on my head. It still did the trick

A short time after that, school started. I would now be going to JHS 189, on Sanford Avenue. The only good thing about starting a new school was that my cousin Russell went to the same school again, so basically we didn't go. I ended up not going for the first month of school until my mother found out. I guess someone at school also found out, because now I had to report to the guidance counselor once a week to check in. I was still cutting classes, but sometimes I would sneak back in just to let the guidance counselor think I was in school that day. After seeing the guidance counselor a few times, he felt comfortable enough to ask me about my personal life.

"So, Mike, when do you think all your problems with school started?" he asked.

At first, being a bit of a private person, I didn't feel like answering him, but then I thought about it for a minute and figured I'd see what kind of a guidance counselor he was made of.

"Weeellll," I started, "I guess it all started when I came home from Catholic school one day and saw a bunch of cop cars on my lawn."

"Really? Go on," he said.
"Yeah, so I go inside my house and find out that my mother shot and killed my father that morning."
"Excuse me...!?"
"Do you want me to bring you a fucking newspaper article?"

Once he realized I was serious, I saw years of study drain out of his face while I waited for his educated answer.

"I, I... don't know what to say," he stammered.

"Well, I guess you know how I felt. So, you want to know when I lost interest... Gee, I don't know. Let me think about it, um... I don't like my teachers, the kids make fun of me, I don't know-you pick one, I'll go with it," I said sarcastically.

When he started to pry about my response, I realized that maybe I shouldn't have opened this can of worms with him. I assumed he knew about my past because a few teachers at my old school had the newspaper articles, and I thought it was something that would just follow me throughout my school life. Once he realized that I had clammed up, he said, "Okay, Mike, I guess you don't want to talk about it anymore today, so I'll stop. But listen, if you ever feel like leaving any of your classes to talk, you can come here, and I'll give you a pass, Okay?

Cool, I thought. Maybe I should have told him sooner.

The living arrangement at home lasted a month or two, until I made the mistake of telling the guidance counselor that my grandfather was taking care of me.

"You mean to tell me that a 78-year-old man is taking care of you?" he said.

Not long after that, my mother told me that I was going to have to move to Aunt Marie's.

Man, what a crock of shit, I thought. First of all, Aunt Marie lived outside of the school zone but she decided to let Russell and Ronnie go to the same school because of their friends, so it was twice the walk. Now this meant I'd have to wake up earlier and I'd have to share Russell's room and single bed with him. I mean, what the fuck? I was getting so sick of this shit. Not only was I bouncing around from place to place, but I had already learned this crap they were trying to teach me at school when I was in Catholic school. Why should I have to waste my time and learn it again? I shouldn't even bother going anyway. The next time I spoke to my mother I read her the riot act.

"Look, Michael, I know it's a pain in the ass, but you shouldn't have said anything about Grandpa taking care of you. Here's the deal though: Either you go live with Aunt Marie, or they're going to put you in a home until I get out."

"Gee," I said." My choices seem endless."

About a day or two later I packed up a little bit of stuff, kissed my grandfather goodbye, and rode over to my Aunt Marie's with George when he got off work. It was all such a pain in the ass, especially since my grandfather had just moved out of Aunt Marie's.

That night I had difficulty falling asleep. Not only was it a new environment with me sleeping in someone's bed with them but to top it off Russell would grind his teeth while he slept. By the time I fell asleep, Marie woke us up for school. We ate a little breakfast and walked through the Queens Botanical Gardens to get to school.

"Fuck school. Let's go back to sleep," Russell said.

"Where? In the street?"

"No, I know a place we can go."

We walked about a block and a half and then came upon some row houses.

"Who lives here?" I said as we walked up to the front door.

"Nobody. This one is abandoned."

We went inside and walked up to the second floor, and I was a bit surprised to see a bunch of guys sleeping on the floor in the living room.

"Who the hell are these guys?" I whispered.

"I don't know, but I might know someone. Don't worry. It's all right."

"Really?"

"Yeah... hey, there's Ronnie Kershner. I told you I'd know someone."

After that we found a spot to lie down on the floor, and we went back to sleep.

"Hey, Russell, Russell, it's 11:00. Are you going to school to get some lunch?" his friend Ronnie said.

"Naaaa, we've got some money. We'll get a slice of pizza or something," Russell answered.

We got up a few minutes after Ronnie left and, when we did, I was surprised to see that everyone else had left. I asked Russell if everyone who was sleeping there went to our school, and he told me that they didn't. Everyone from the neighborhood just met up there to hang out during school.

"Shit, man," I said. "This is a whole empty house. Why don't we see if we could buy it or something? Then we could charge everyone to sleep here."

"You're fucking nuts... C'mon, let's get something to eat. I'm starving."

After we ate, we wandered down to Main Street and stayed there until school hours were over, and then we headed towards his house. We took the short cut through the Botanical Gardens again and headed for the park on the hill that was down the block from his house. When we got up there, a bunch of kids our age were there. Russell introduced me to everyone; that guy Ronnie was there, too. One thing that I thought was pretty cool was that there seemed to be more girls than guys there.

Over time I got to know everyone at "Turkey Park," as we called it. That kid Ronnie and I even had a few of the same classes together. Three months into the school year, and we still hadn't seen each other yet... go figure. When we did finally meet up, I realized that we were both a little nutty at school. Sometimes Ronnie would come over to one of my classes and yell under the door, "Hey Mike! I'm cutting out now with some girls. They said they've got beer and some pot at home. Do you want to come?"

"Not now, Ronnie," I'd yell back. "I've got to wait for this class to end first. Wait for me by the handball courts, Okay?"

"Okay," he'd yell back.

"Are you done now?" the teacher would ask.

"Yes."

"Good. May I get on with class"?

"Okay."

"Thank you."

One night we were hanging out over at Turkey Park, and one of the girls came up with an idea for a game that I thought was pretty cool. Being that it was going to be me against eight girls, I liked the idea from the start. It turned out to be a kissing contest and guess who got to be the judge. They told me to lie down on the slide, and then they covered my eyes. One by one they took turns kissing me, and I had to pick 1st, 2nd and 3rd place winners.

Each time a new round would start, the kisses got better and better. One girl who had bad breath kept getting annoyed because I wouldn't pick her, and she started to open up my pants and said, "Let's see if he could tell who can suck his dick the best."

OOOOOOOO, please, please, please, I thought, as I waited for events to turn in my favor. But they took a vote and decided not to do it. Then I called them all a bunch of chickens with the hope of them taking me up on my dare, but they didn't.

Russell and I basically had the same routine day after day when it came to school, but after a little while the cops started to raid the house where we would sleep. It wasn't long after that they boarded it up. Now it was starting to get cold outside, so we'd go to school just to keep warm at times. One day we found out that some bigger kids had broken into the Park house at Turkey Park. When we went inside we realized that there was electricity in there, so it didn't take long before we found a mattress, a heater, and even a TV. Man, it was great. We could stumble out of bed, eat breakfast, and then walk down the block and go back to bed or watch TV now.

I went to visit my mother, it took a while for the visiting room to quite down until we could talk, not that there were too many visitors there. The patients were all acting a little crazy that day. The visiting room was an open room with a small archway that led into the quad she was in.

"So how's things?" she started.

"Who me?"

"Yeah, you."

"Life's fucking great, Ma. It's never been better. I love bouncing around."

"Look, Michael, I know it's rough, but it could be worse. You could be in a home or a place like this, Okay!" she answered.

I paused, looked around the room, and thought, What the fuck am I doing in this trip? I'm sitting here arguing with my mother about my living conditions that she has no real control over, and she's trying to make sense of it by showing me her living arrangement because she killed my father, while I'm sitting in a nuthouse with a bunch of crazy people asking me over and over, "Do you got a cigarette?" "Got a cigarette?"

Whew! Michael, cool out. Keep your head together, I thought.

"Guess you're right, Ma. It could be worse," I said dryly.

I stayed for about an hour and then decided that I didn't want to take the buses home too late so I left. Sitting on the bus on the way home, I reminded myself that it probably could be worse.

One day when I happened to be in school, the boys' dean, Mr. Hersch, called me to his office. Shit, I thought. I haven't even been here that much. What could I have done? When I got there, I asked him what I had done now.

"Mike," he started, "it's just been brought to my attention that even when you're in school you're not even in any classes. You've been thrown out of every class you have. For math class you go to the main office. For English class you come here. For Social Studies you go to the girls' dean. For Science class you go to the principal's office. I've even heard that sometimes you're seen in the lunch room for 5th, 6th and 7th periods. But that's not why I called you here. I looked at your school records, and I know you're a smart kid, so I'm going to give you the chance to prove it. I'm going to have you moved up a grade on a trial period for one month, but if you screw up once, you'll go right back, no ifs, ands, or buts. Now, you can try it, or you can go on the way you're going. The choice is yours."

I thought about it for another minute and said to myself, Yeah, that would be great. Even though it's late in the year, I could hack it.

"Sure, I'll give it a try."
"Remember, Michael, screw up once and you will go back into 7th!" Mr. Hersch reminded me.

For three and a half weeks I worked my ass off until one day I whacked some wiseass in the head with an onion in science class. Mr. Hersch didn't even have me come to his office. "Bam!" I was back in 7th before I knew it. Some of the other kids in my old class were like, Where were you?
"Well, I took a little vacation with my parents," I'd explain.

Honestly, I was very disappointed with myself. I was given a shot, and I blew it.

About a day or two later I was still in a pretty shitty mood because I had failed to stay out of trouble at school. You could say that it was just a simple matter of not being able to behave myself. But I had a "reputation" to live up to. I guess having a reputation comes with a price, and my prize, was getting returned to the 7th grade. Instead of going over to Marie's house after school, I went over to my neighborhood. I met up with some of my older friends over at Bench Park, and I got high. About an hour later, Jimmy Duguid showed up with a stolen car, and I decided to go for a ride with him. We cruised all over the place and, by the end of the night, he told me I could have the car if I wanted. Fuckin' a-right, I thought. At the very least, I wasn't going to have to take two buses back to Marie's house tonight.

I figured that I should call my Aunt Marie and make up some excuse, because I really didn't feel like going over there. After arguing on the phone for a while, I kinda got an okay to sleep at home that night. Then I headed back over to Bench Park. When I got there, I saw Jimmy Marnell, but figured I should ride around the area first to see if it was safe to park by him. Then I pulled up to Bench Park and said, "Hey, Jimmy, you want a ride anywhere?"

"Oh shit, where did you get a car from?"

"Jimmy Duguid gave it to me," I answered.

"Yeah, let's go for a cruise," he said.

We decided to drive over to the Whitestone Bridge. When I got there we parked, grabbed the beers Jimmy had gotten, and walked under the bridge. After sitting there talking for a while, Jimmy pulled out a pipe and said, "Hey, did you ever smoke opium hash?"

"What is it?" I asked.

After he explained what it was, I said, "Sure, what the fuck?" We sat under there for a few hours just getting buzzed and talking. Then at about 1 am. Jimmy said he had to get home because he had school in the morning.

I was pretty high by then, and I had to drive Jimmy home with one eye shut so the road didn't look cross-eyed, because I was so high. Jimmy even threatened to take the car away from me once or twice, but I told him that Jimmy D. said I couldn't let anyone else drive. I dropped him off by his house on 154th Street and, instead of going home, I headed up to Bowne Park to see if anyone was still hanging out. After I circled the park once, it seemed like everyone had gone home so I stopped the car, got out, and drank one of the beers that Jimmy had left.

This is it, huh, Mike. This is hanging out being cool. Actually it just about sucks, probably because I'm by myself, I reasoned. Yeah, I need a piece of ass tonight is what I need, but where the fuck am I gonna find one? I mean, shit, I'm only 14. I know, I'll go into Manhattan. I've seen whores down there. Fuckin' a-right, I'm outta here. Besides, I've got enough gas.

It took me longer to get to Manhattan than it did to find some ladies of the night once I got there. After riding around the area for a little while, a prostitute walked over to the car and knocked on the window while I was waiting at the light.

I let the window down, and she said, "Hey, honey, do you want some action?"

"Well ah, no," I beamed.

"Oh, cause the reason I ask you, honey, is cause you rode around the block four times, ya' know?"

"Well -------."

"Look, my pimp wants to kick my ass, and he's been driving by, and he's waiting for me to be alone. So could you just give me a little ride out of here?"

"What does your pimp call alone? Driving on a side street with one other person?"I questioned.

"Ya' know, alone," she said as she opened the door and hopped in. She closed the door and then said "Okay, go!"

"Where?" I asked

"Anywhere. Just get me outta here."

As we rode around she told me the ins and outs of the business and explained that she would go back to her pimp and tell him that I was a good trick and give him some of the money she was hiding from him.

"Well, why don't you just take that money and come stay with me? I got a nice place we could stay at."

"Yeah, right, you look like a kid. What'd ja' do, take your father's car and go out tonight?" she joked.

"No, it's stolen."

"Oh, get the fuck out of here. The one guy I pick tonight has a stolen car, and I'm going to get busted for that. Shit! I'd rather get slapped around by my pimp instead."

"Don't worry about it. I'm driving cool. You can see that," I said.

She looked back and forth for a second and then said, "All right, but don't show off and get stupid, O.K.?"

"Don't worry about it," I answered.

She had blond hair and brown eyes and looked pretty good. She told me she was 25, but she looked a bit older.

"Ya' know," I said, "you don't like your pimp beating you up, why don't you just leave?"

"Well, it ain't easy, okay? Besides, what the hell do you know about having it rough?"

"What the hell do I know? I'll tell you what the hell I know. How do you think it feels to come home from school to find out your mother shot and killed your father?"

"Get the hell outta here. Really?" she asked.

"I'll give you my name; you can go look it up in the library on their microfilm, okay," I snapped at her. "And if I can live through that, you can live through your shit, too, if you want."

"Who knows? Maybe you're right," she said, as she gazed out the window.

"You know I'm right. It's hard, but you don't need anybody."

After we drove around for a little bit more, she explained that it was probably all right for her to go back now, so I could drive her there.

"By the way, what's your name?"

"Well, my street name is Dixie."

"What's your real name?"

"Well, you're not supposed to tell."

"Oh, come on. Who the hell am I going to blab to?"

"Well, I'd rather not, okay?"

I asked her to go into a deli to get me some beers before I dropped her off. She told me that I could come back and see her if I was ever around again because she worked the area.

"Hey, next time I come around, do you think you'll let me have sex with you?"

"Hmmm, well, you are kinda cute."

She leaned back in the car, kissed me on the cheek, and said, "We'll see, baby. We'll see."

She came back with the beers, and then I drove her over to her area. She kissed me on the cheek again and left. I drove around the city for a little while, thinking about how odd, and nice it was to be able to talk to a complete stranger about life. It was getting real late, by now, so I decided to head back home.

By the time I got into my area, I had drunk most of the beers, and I decided that I wanted to drive by the luncheonette to pay my respects to my father. Being that I wasn't allowed to his funeral or anything, this is where I went, the last place he was alive. Each time I'd go there I'd usually sit on a car and talk with my father. But this night, probably due to the buzz I had on, I talked out loud. Good thing nobody walked by; it would have looked like I was crazy, talking to the store.

After I said my peace, I figured I'd drive by Bowne Park one more time and see if the older guys were bullshitting or not about hanging out all night at the park.

When I got there, it was empty, so I started for home until I decided to pull over for a minute to get a chance to view some of the food I had eaten today while I puked it up. After that sightseeing trip, I thought it might be better if I lay down in the car for a minute, so I did.

"Knock, knock."
"Oh...my fucking head," I thought.
"Knock, knock, knock."
"What the fuck is that?" I thought. I looked up and saw a cop standing outside the car knocking with his billy club.

Shit! I wonder if I should start the car and try to split. Wait a minute, Mike. Maybe they can shoot you for trying to get away.

"Come out of the car, and let me see your hands," the cop said.

They arrested me and took me over to the 109th Precinct, and then I went to Central Booking again.

Well, the place hadn't changed a bit. I hoped I could get some food. I was starving, I thought when I walked in.

After I got strip searched, photographed, and printed, they took me over to the four holding cells.

This is fucking great, Mike. Everybody else is either going to school or cutting school by now, and you're sitting here, maybe going to jail this time. I guess you don't fuck around when you fuck up.

When the police had asked for a phone number, I gave them my Aunt Marie's. I didn't want them to think I was on my own because they might put me in a home this time, I reasoned. Being that it wasn't the weekend, it seemed like I would be able to make afternoon court.

I rode over to Queens Courthouse on a chain gang, that's where they have everyone attached to one another with one long chain that has handcuffs attached to it. After we got to the holding cells, we each got Legal Aid lawyers assigned to us. Somehow my lawyer was able to get me released without any bail. This time I was smart enough to get some train fare off the lawyer after I got his business card.

When I got outside I thought, man this air never smelled so fresh. I said this again to myself as a little joke because jail has the smell of fear, dread, hopelessness, sweat, vomit, piss, shit, semen, and death all wrapped up in one, to name a few. When I got home, to my house, I called up Debbie, and asked her how I could call my mother because it was an emergency. Debbie said that either she'd call me back or have my mother call me at home. It turned out that my mother called me.

"Ma."
"Where the hell are you?"
"I'm home."
"How did you get there?"
"Well, I guess you heard. They let me out."
"What the hell am I going to do with you?" she asked.
"Look, Ma, I had a rough night."
"Did you get beat up or something?"
"No, but almost," I lied for sympathy through a slight hangover.
"Yeah, Marie told me you were arrested. She's really upset about it."
"Look, I know George slaps around Ronnie and Russell, but I'm not going there to get slapped up. I'm going to stay at home with Grandpa for a few days, all right?" I said.

My mother didn't answer me, and then she added. "What's going to happen with court now?"
"I don't know. They might send me to a home," I lied.
"What about a lawyer? They assigned you got a lawyer, right?"
"Yeah."
"Okay, give me his phone number."

Whoops, think fast, Mike, I thought. I pretended to fumble through some papers, and then I told her I lost it.

"Oh, Michael, now you've got to call the courthouse to try and get it. I can't call from here."

Whew... "Don't worry, I'll get it."
"How long until you go to court?" she asked.
"About three weeks."
"Okay, then get his phone number and address and mail it to me, but do it tomorrow."
"All right, I will."
"You know, I can't believe you did this. I've got to go. I'll talk to you soon."

My Aunt Marie thought I might be a bad influence on Ronnie and Russell. That was a laugh, so I moved back home with Gramps. I didn't really bother going to school much; all I had to do now was just hide somewhere in the house or in the garage again.

As it turned out with my new court case, somehow my lawyer got the case quashed, which amazed me.

Sometimes I'd go up to school just to hang out with some of the guys. One day while I was up there, I met up with Ronnie Kershner, and he had his sister's new chopper bicycle. Ronnie was real protective of his sister's new bike; he didn't even want me to ride it. Finally I convinced him by telling him that I could ride the bike through the walkway in the fifteen-foot fence and grab the pole that you walked under as you went through, and he could catch the bike when it went out from between my legs. I explained to him that I would do a similar feat when I was younger.

"No way. You're nuts. Really?"
"Yeah, I'll do it," I answered.

It happened to be the end of the school day so all the kids and people we knew were in their homerooms. Ronnie yelled up to get some kids in our homeroom to look out of the windows and watch me kill myself. One of the people who rushed to the window was this girl I was dating named Caroline. Now I had an audience. Ronnie ran down and stood in place as I rode down to the end of the schoolyard. Everything was set to go and "Bam," I was off. First gear, second gear, third gear.

By the time I got halfway across the schoolyard, I realized that I was going much faster than I did as a little kid, but I didn't have an audience back then either. As soon as I came up to the top pole, I grabbed it. Because I was traveling so fast, the force spun me upwards and then I crashed into the fence overhead, let go of the pole, and dove towards the ground.

After I hit the ground, everybody at the window and a bunch of kids outside were cheering and asking me to do it again. I look up at what sounded like a moose laughing and saw Ronnie holding his stomach and laughing his ass off as his sister's bike whizzed past him and crashed into the wall. I looked down at my wrist that was hurting and saw that I had dislocated it. Remembering what happened the last time I waited two hours for a doctor to set a bone I decided to try and pop it back in place myself while it was easier, before the swelling. I lay my right arm down on the ground and slammed down on my wrist. "Snap!" it popped back in place.

"Ronnie, shut up. I broke my fucking arm!"

Ronnie grabbed his stomach tighter, held one hand out in front of himself, and gasped, "No, no, don't fucking tell me that," as he fell to the ground from laughing so hard.

By now all the kids at the window were clapping and cheering, "One more time!" There would be no repeat performance this evening, I thought.

"Ronnie, it's not fucking funny. I broke my fucking arm!" I yelled.

"I know. I'm sorry. I can't help it. You had to see it. It was great," he answered.

"I can't even go to the hospital because I don't have a parent or guardian to sign for me, Fucko."

"I'm sorry. I'll stop laughing. What do you want to do? I can't get my mother to do it. She kill me for not being in school, and for stealing my sisters bike," he said as he wiped the tears from his eyes.

"I'll have to go to Marcus's mother, Debbie. Maybe she can go with me."

Debbie did manage to get my mother to call the hospital so the hospital could get permission to put my arm in a cast. The doctor thought it was a very odd dislocation until I told him that I re-set it myself. "Well, you do pretty good work, young man. Maybe I can get you some part-time work around here."

A few weeks after that while I was hanging out in the schoolyard again, a friend of mine named Ricky Stills came outside into the schoolyard with a group of kid's and one older person.

"Hey, Ricky. What's up? What are you doing out here?"

"Omen, our teacher, lets us come out for some fresh air and to have a cigarette."

"I haven't seen you around much. What class is this that you're in?"

"It's not regular school, Mike. It's called Project 25. It's a drug program," he said.

"Oh, really? Then I guess your teacher wouldn't mind if I lit up this joint I have."

"Get out of here. You won't light it," Ricky said.

"Why not? He can't do anything to me," I said as I lit it.

Then I took a nice big hit and blew it in the direction of the other kids.

"Hey...! What's up...?" A few kids yelled with smiles on their faces.

"Nothing, dudes. Just chilling out, smoking some weed."

"Hey!" Omen yelled. "What are you, a wiseass? I'm sitting here with a bunch of kids from a drug program and you're smoking pot in front of them."

"I know. I'm just showing them the errors of their ways," I explained.

"Aren't you supposed to be in school?"

"Yeah."

"What school do you go to?"

"This one."

"Oh, really. Well, do me a favor. Just go sit downwind and smoke that thing, okay...?"

"Yeah, fine."

I took one last big hit and blew it in everyone's face before I walked away.

I spoke with my mother today. She told me that there was a good chance that she was going to get out of Creedmore.

Shit, I thought, and I was having such a good time.

She started talking about coming home and how nice it would be. She also implied that things would be a little different when she got home. I started to wonder if I was happy or sad about her coming home, because I really wasn't in the mood for any family nicey nice psychological bullshit or having someone telling me what to do any more under the conditions that I had been living.

Sometimes I was amazed that she was able to keep our house from in there. I did tell her that it would be nice for her to get out because it seemed a little nutty there. She laughed and said, "Yes, Michael, just a little, though. Hey, are there any friends you want to say goodbye to?"

"No."

"What about Mousey? I know he likes you."

"No, that's okay, Ma. I'll write him." We joked.

"Well, I'm going to have a court date in a few weeks, so wish me luck, okay?" she said.

"What do you mean? You have to go back to court?"

"No, it's not that kind of court. It's like a court here at the hospital, with doctors and nurses."

"Really? That sounds interesting. Maybe I could bribe someone by offering to cut their grass for a few weeks."

"Yeah, that would be nice. Well, I've got to get off the phone now."

"Good luck, Ma. I'll talk to you soon."

About a week after this I got thrown out of J.H.S. 189 and placed in Project 25. The program Director explained to me that most of the time was spent in group counseling with time set aside for learning. There were a set number of counselors for each phase of the program. Phase One had only one counselor, the colored guy named Omen whom I had smoked a joint in front of.

"Now your ass is mine!" he told me the first time I met him in private.

I knew Ricky and a few other kids in Phase One, so it wasn't too hard to adjust. I guess I had been sent there because I hardly went to school and because of that joint in the schoolyard. But boy, did this place teach me about drugs. The age group went from about fourteen, to seventeen, so whatever I didn't know about drugs, the seventeen year-old sitting next to me did.

Being that our school day let out later than regular school, friends of mine would climb up on the cages that covered the windows on the second floor and yell into the window. "Can Mike come out to play?" It went over big with some of my classmates, but the counselors were un-amused, so much so that they'd threaten to keep me there much later in the day and have me help the janitor. Luckily I got my friends to stop.

I skipped out on the program a few days after starting it. Instead I hopped on the train and went to check out the world. I always liked to ride the train and watch all the people going to work. I still liked to study and observe them, I guess to try and somehow compare what I was doing and how I was living. I ended up at Grand Central Station. I calmly walked through the station while all these people were scurrying about to the point of almost knocking you down to get to work. They would be running around in their grown-up school uniforms, while giving me little sneers for not being dressed to code. I grabbed a coffee and a doughnut, and then I sat down and watched.

I thought some of them were so hypocritical at a glance to sneer at me while running around to kiss the ass of someone else who could, if he wished, just cut off their heads on a whim.

I certainly wasn't running around kissing anyone's ass these days. Maybe they just didn't like the freedom I had on my hands, I reasoned.

I had seen my father have to fire some people so I knew what that was about. Then I'd sit there and wonder if this was all it was about, and think that school was supposed to deliver me here. I was so far removed from school at this point, I didn't even know how smart or how dumb I was any more. I was too busy trying to figure out how I could make a buck and keep myself fed at ages thirteen, and fourteen, in between places to live. I couldn't give a flying fuck about A B C's and fractions any more.

Once or twice I did try to get a real job to make some money in the neighborhood, usually at construction. But then once I did, I'd bust my ass all week long, and get paid. Then I'd look at my two hundred dollars and say to myself, This guy thinks I'm a fucking elephant for two hundred a week. I've got to quit, or I'll be dead in a month. I would pick up the paper and call up some other jobs that looked easier, or looked like jobs I would like. I'd call for Bank Manager, Veterinarian, Gynecologist, Motorcycle Salesman, you know, fun stuff. The first thing I'd ask about is pay. After that I'd be all ears. This would be until they asked me about my experience, of which I had none. This would usually end the informal interview.

I'd usually wander around the city thinking along these lines and watch the changing of the seasons, as I liked to call them. Morning rush hour, lunchtime, homeward bound, and then nightfall. Then another series of seasons would begin. But this day I would go home with the homeward bound crew. I couldn't tell whether they looked worse in the morning or now, but one thing was for sure- not many of them looked happy.

When I went back to the program the next day I caught hell and, aside from having some of my privileges taken away, I was also told, in so many words, that there was going to be a higher price to pay. Within a month everybody in my class moved up a phase except me, for some reason. It sucked hanging out with Omen now, because nobody else was in the class. After I made a stink about it, they decided they would let us hang out with the other three phases that would stay together all the time. At least I had company now.

I got news that my mother was coming home, and then bam, she was home. In the beginning it was like she wasn't even my mother. It was like straight talk without pulling very many punches. There wasn't any bullshit kid stuff any more for the most part. I didn't realize it at the time but my mother was re-orienting herself with the real world while trying to get into mine. She didn't go out much at first, but then gradually she went out on the back porch. She eventually got the hook on that, and she was running all over the place in a little while. We didn't speak a lot but soon she started conjuring up rules and battle lines.

My mother also started to get a little nutty with some of the rules from the Project. The one we fought the most about was how I wasn't supposed to hang out with any of my old friends. To try and reason with me, she said that I could invite as many friends from the program that I wanted to my house, so I did. I invited about six people but only Ricky Stills, Scot "Pete" Pete, and Tommy Faye showed up. Tommy lived around the corner from me so I knew him from the neighborhood. He was the kid whom I had seen get his head bounced off the concrete by Danny Barbuto when I was in the first grade.

We hung out and had a half-ass time. My mother also got me a puppy around this time, a female German shepherd. I named her Bobo. Being that I had a little time on my hands because of the curfew rules from the program, I was able to teach Bobo a few tricks after about a week.

My mother took on another tenant; his name was Frank Leadera. He was a patient at the hospital where my mother had been. My mother had talked a lot about helping out people from the hospital, and she also told me she could get paid for doing it, not that I liked the sound of living with crazy people.

Frank seemed like a nice enough guy, he was very quiet, not like some of the other nuts I had seen at the hospital. After he was settled in for over a week, I still hadn't seen him come out of his room twice though.

After being in Phase One for seven months, I finally got promoted into Phase Two. Being that Phase One was a two month exercise, I believe some type of default upgraded me. Whatever the reason, it was nice to be able to feel like a part of the group and to finally be with friends and all the people whom I had already met while they passed through Phase One while I was there- especially since I started to feel like I was the poster boy for the first Phase.

After a while at the project I started to fit in with the whole group and get a little popular, maybe to popular. One day a guy I had met in class asked me if I could get him some pot. Because I wanted to fit in, I told him I could. He looked at me for a long minute and then said, "Okay, then get me an ounce."

"Yeah, sure, no problem," I answered.
"Tell me when you get it, and I'll have the money ready."
"Well, if we do it, we do it in the morning. I don't want that much weed sitting in my pocket all day."
"Yeah, yeah. Of course, we'll do it in the morning."

A few days after that it was time to meet. Joey was one of the other popular kids within the program, just like I was starting to be. We had planned to meet in the hallway before class and exchange items, but he never came. He stiffed me. It's funny because I almost thought he was just talking out of his ass anyhow, for some reason, so it came as no surprise. After he didn't show up, I walked into one of the few classrooms that were reserved for us within the school.

I was a little late, and we had a school class now, so I went there figuring that I wouldn't have to deal with the counselors about my lateness. After I was in class for a little while, the teacher sent one of the kids out of the class. A few minutes after this, one of the counselors named John came into the class, which was odd. After some students looked at him, he placed his finger to his lips, to quiet them, and walked towards the back of the class where I was sitting. He bent down next to me and said, "Why are you late?"

"Well, I know that I'm late, but couldn't this wait until class was over?"

"No, I think it's something we should discuss right now."

"Fine, we'll discuss it right now, okay? My alarm went off late, so I woke up late. So what do you want to do, shoot me?"

"What's that bulge in your pocket?" he asked me.

"What- this? It's nothing. It's a handkerchief."

"Let me see it."

"Why, you've never seen a handkerchief?"

"No, it's not that. I just want to see yours."

Something doesn't smell right about this, Mike, I thought.

"Step into the hall with me, Mike."

Basically there was no way out of the set-up, so John, the counselor, received an ounce, and I got shit from all the counselors and put back into Phase One.

"I got your sorry ass again? I guess you didn't learn your lesson the first time around," Omen said my first day back with him with his new class.

Then I got balled out from my mother when I got home. Just when things were cooling down between us, she started clamping down again. It really made me start considering options about myself, namely about being on my own.

A few days after that, I came home from the Project, and there was a strange car in the driveway. When I got inside, my mother introduced me to a married colored couple that she had met at Creedmore. I said hello, and my mother told me that she had cooked a good big meal, so we should get started. I figured she wanted to make a good impression on them for some reason, so I went along with it.

We sat down and ate and talked just about nothing throughout the meal. When I got done, I got up and started to walk out of the kitchen.

"Michael, listen," my mother said. "You're going to spend the weekend at my friend's house."

"Excuse me?" I asked.

"It's just for the weekend," she continued. "I've got some friends coming over, and they're going to sleep here. So it might be better if you weren't here."

"Uh Ma, I could just go to Marcus's house or Aunt Marie's or something, you know."

"Yeah, I know but then you might hang out with some of the people that the program said you couldn't hang out with."

I was very angry at the fact that my mother had put me in a situation where I wasn't able to speak my mind with strangers present, but I soon got over it. I decided that maybe if I did speak my mind her "friends" might decide that they wouldn't like me to spend the weekend there.

"Well, you know, Ma, first of all, I don't know these strangers, although they seem like nice people. And I don't think we have a lot in common, so if you want me to get lost for the weekend, why don't you throw me a couple of bucks and I'll keep myself busy."

"C'mon, Michael. Don't give me a hard time with this. It's just for the weekend."

Whoa, Mike, maybe your mother wants to have a guy come over, and she wants to be alone with him. I mean, it's not like she's done that in the past, but why would she be trying to get me out of the neighborhood? Maybe she's afraid I'll come home and surprise her? That might explain why she put you in this awkward situation, but it's fucking bullshit that I've got to go with these strangers, I thought.

"Fine Ma. I'll leave for the weekend, okay? I'm going to go pack something."

"Well, I've already packed something for you. We can leave now," she explained.

"Well, it's nice to know that we set aside some time to talk about it. Fine, let's go."

We didn't speak much for the first half hour into the ride, and that's when the whole situation started to smell funny, because any questions I started to ask were given stupid answers. Finally I couldn't take it any more, and I felt like I was being set up for something.

"So where the fuck are we going, Ma? Canada?"

"Hey, boy. Don't speak to your mother that way," the colored guy said.

"And who the fuck are you to tell me how I can speak to my mother?"

"I'm the guy who'll pull this car over and give you what you need- a good ass whippin', boy," he said.

"No, no, Harold. That's okay, just keep driving. Michael, just simmer down, okay? We're almost there."

"Big fucking deal, I don't even want to be "there" in the first place. That's supposed to make me feel better, that we're almost there?"

"Hey, boy, watch your mouth," I was told again.

The conversation went on like this for about another hour and half until we arrived at our destination. It was a huge field stone house, with a gravel driveway. One thing I found odd at first glance was that the lights were on in every room, and there were quite a few cars parked in the driveway. When we got inside, I looked into the living room on my left and saw a few kids of different ages and color sitting around watching TV. I knew then that I was set up.

I felt enraged, and betrayed. All this talk, and actions, over the last two years about me not being sent to a home, and here's my mother delivering me to the wolves.

"So you must be Michael. Your mother told me so much about you. I'm sure you're going to have a great time living here," some big fat fuck told me. I looked at my mother, and she looked away from me.

My mother stood there and chit-chatted for some time until I was told to go upstairs and meet some of the other boys. As I walked up the stairs, I noticed that the place hadn't been painted in a long time. I got up to the boys' bedroom and noticed that there were about eight different types of beds all over the room.

There were a few smaller kids lying around up there, and after a few seconds this little guy came over to me and said, "You must be a new kid, huh?"

"Yeah," I answered.

"Well, let me tell you the ropes then. Unless they've got another cot somewhere, you'll have to sleep in bed with someone. But don't sleep with Joey; he wets the bed. Your parents are still here, right?"

"My mother still is," I answered.

"Well, if you brought any good stuff with you, you better give it to her now; otherwise, you'll have to fight the bigger kids downstairs to keep it, like that gold chain."

"Come on, it's not that bad here, is it?"

"Well, you're kinda a big kid so you won't get it from everyone. But yeah, it's fucked up here," he said. "But there's one guy named Dan... he's the worst."

"Is he big?"

"Well, he's only a bit bigger than you."

The kid I was talking to was a bookworm type, and I really couldn't understand why he might be here.

"Well, what does he do to you?"

"Let's say I get a package from home with some treats in it. He'll take them from me, and if I don't give them to him, he'll give me a few whacks in the head until I do," he explained.

After a few minutes of talking with this kid, my mother's colored friend came upstairs and dropped off two suitcases.

"Your mother wants you to come to say goodbye," he said.

"Tell her she can go fuck herself," I answered.

Harold glared at me and then he left. I started to talk to this kid again, when he whispered, "Oh, shit! There's Dan!"

"Wow! New stuff for me," Dan said, as he bent down to open my suitcase.

"Get your fucking hands off my shit!" I barked at him.

Dan, who probably hadn't had anyone talk to him like that in a long time, said, "Oh, uh, I was just fooling around." Then he turned around and left.

"Wow!" the smaller kid said. "Can I be your friend? I'll let you have my bed!"

"Sure, no problem. You can be my friend."

"Wow! Hey, did everyone hear that? This guy's my friend."

By now three or four other little kids came around us and started chirping.

"I can't believe that you scared Dan," one small kid said.

"Yeah, you should beat him up. He's real mean to us," another one said.

After having established a small fan club, I felt like pulling Dan's shit out of the dresser and taking his spot. I felt kinda bad for the little kids; they didn't seem bad enough to belong in a place like this, I thought.

I was given a drawer or two from some of the kids, and then I started to unpack.

"You should still hide some of your good stuff," my first friend said. "Besides Dan there are a couple of older kids on the other side of the house. They're not supposed to come over here, but sometimes they do."

Eventually a cot was brought up for me. "Here, you can sleep here," I was told.

After I got settled in, I lay down on my cot and thought about my situation.

"Man, this is some shit. I don't know why my mother took me all the way out here to cut me loose. She should have done it back home where I had some friends. That's some shit how she set me up. So what now, Mike... what's your next move? Got any tricks up your sleeve this time?

I lay there for about an hour, in a bed that stunk, and then the colored guy who spent two and a half hours driving me there came upstairs and said, "Pack your stuff. Your mother changed her mind."

I could actually hardly believe it. I leapt up as slow as possible, for effect, and dragged my ass over to my dresser, packed, and then left. I didn't say a word to anyone all the way home.

A day or two later my mother told me that she felt really bad about taking me to that home, but she thought it would be a good thing for me.

"So what changed your mind?" I asked

"Well, the place looked like a dump. I thought it was nicer."

"Well, I guess I should thank God, that they hadn't painted in years, huh?" I answered.

The next weekend my mother let me stay out late. I ended up over by Bench Park on Saturday. Tina, my old babysitter, was having a bit of a reunion with her friends. They had all hung out at Bench Park before us, and now they hung out two blocks away at the Murray Hill Bar. The guys had their motorcycles out with them; there were some pretty cool Harleys. I was the third generation who would inherit the park from Jimmy Marnell and the age group he hung out with, if all went well. It was a little funny but you could see the magnetic chain reaction right down the line. The older guys knew some of the younger guys, like Jimmy and his age group, and Jimmy knew some of my friends, and I knew some younger kids and their friends from the neighborhood.

That night I met up with Marcus and another friend of ours, John Slocum. He was sometimes called Little John. His father was known as "Big John Slocum," who was a black belt in karate. Big John dated one of Jimmy "Peck" and Dolly Schlishman's older sisters. Peck and Dolly were in my age group.

I also knew Big John. Sometimes about six or seven of us would challenge him to a fight at the big sandbox up at Bowne Park. He'd always win and kinda whip our asses in the process. I used to think it was fun, until I realized that no one was running in to get him after I'd attack. He'd calmly whack me around and gently kick me out of the sandbox, if you will. Then he would chase around the chicken ass guys and gently kick their asses.

On this night Little John, Marcus and I teamed up and rode around half the night on our bicycles. At about 12:30 Marcus had to go in, so I asked John what he wanted to do.

"I don't care. I don't have to go home if I don't want to."
"That's cool. I was like that for a while. Hey, do you want to sleep over my house tonight?"
"Sure, why not?"

When we got to my house, my mother was still up, which wasn't uncommon.

"Mom, John is going to sleep over tonight, okay?"
"Well, wait a minute. Does his mother know?"
"Yeah, she knows," John said.

John and I watched TV until about 4 am, and then we snuck out and rode bicycles around the neighborhood. The next morning bright and early, my mother knocked on my door. After I let her in, she told me that she thought that there was something wrong with Frank, our new tenant. I asked her what the problem was, and she told me that Frank had locked himself in the living room last night, and now he wasn't answering the door when she knocked on it. I was very tired from being out late last night so I told her that he was probably just sleeping.

"Michael, I pounded on the door and he's not answering."
"So what do you want me to do?" I asked.
"Climb into the window and see if he's all right."

After a bunch of mumbling and grumbling, I went downstairs to do it. When I got down there, I knocked on the door a few times, but Frank didn't answer. So I went outside and opened up the window. When I looked inside, Frank was lying on a beanbag chair we had in the corner. He was lying on his back, with his hands at his side, like he was sleeping. I called him a few more times, but he still didn't answer, so I looked at my mother and asked her what she wanted me to do.

"I think you should climb in the window and see if he's all right. I know he's supposed to take some medication in the mornings, but I didn't hear him at all this morning."
"Yeah, but what if I go in there and wake him up and he freaks out on me?"
"Michael, just go in and see if he's all right."

After I climbed in the window, I noticed that Frank's eyes seemed open, which was odd. I walked over to him and called him again as I kicked his foot and got ready to run in case he bugged out on me. But he didn't move. Then I leaned over and slowly touched his hand, and he was ice cold.

"Ma! I think Frank's dead!"
"Michael, don't fucking tell me that!"
"I'm telling you, Ma. I think he's dead."

After going through the same routine of calling, kicking and touching again, I told my mother to call 911. A little while after that an ambulance pulled up and the paramedics verified my views. When they were done, they packed up and started to leave, without Frank.

"Aren't you forgetting something?" I asked.
"Oh, we don't take the bodies. After the police come, they'll send for the meat wagon."
"Well, how long will that be?"
"Who knows? Sometimes it can take all day."

I didn't know it at the time, but whenever there's a dead body at someone's house in the city they assign a cop to stay outside your house until it gets picked up by the morgue. When the cop arrived, he told us that some Detectives would come by in a little while to ask us some questions. Shortly after that, he went outside. I went back into the room Frank was in, and I was just staring at him. It was eerie, and odd, to see someone in their death pose. I was a little upset with the fact that there was a cop car sitting outside my house. That, along with the thought of an unmarked police car out there in little while, made me angry with the situation. Just when things were calming down for us in the neighborhood, this has got to happen.

As I was staring at Frank I thought to myself, "Of all places, why the fuck did you have to die here!?"

Right after I said that, for some unknown reason, the door behind me slammed shut. My first thought was to poop myself, my second thought was to make the sign of the cross, apologize, and get out of the room as quick as I could. Thankfully, I went with my second thought. Once I got out of the room, I knelt down, said a prayer for Frank, and then went outside for some air.

As it turned out, they came to take away Frank's body at dinnertime, just in time for my neighbors to get home from work and accumulate in front of my house. Half of them ran away when they saw the body bag being carried out of my house.

A few days after that, my mother told me that she had contacted John's mother and found out that his mother thought he was staying at his father's house the night he slept over. John's parents had been divorced for some time. John had told me that he would bounce back and forth between them.

"How did you find out?" I asked.
"I spoke to Debbie, and she found out. So if he ever decides to sleep here again, I will be calling his

mother."

School was ending soon for summer vacation; unfortunately the program didn't. It went on through the summer with shorter hours. I was not pleased to hear this at all. I realized by now that getting into trouble only prolonged my agony there, particularly in Phase One with Omen. The only way I was going to get myself out of here was to get my mother to think that it was senseless for me to go there also, I surmised. It took me an awfully long time, but finally I started to win my mother over to my point of view.

One of the ways I did this was by telling her that, after almost eight months in this place, I had only been in Phase Two once whereas people I had started the program with were already in Phases Three and Four. Even after some of them had gotten into trouble and one or two people had gotten arrested, they were never put back into Phase One. The deal, if you will, my mother made with me was that if I was "good" for a period of time and they didn't put me into Phase Two, she would agree with me on quitting the drug program.

Her period of time lasted almost three months, and by that time I was ready to quit the program on my own before my mother decided to take me out of it. Now that I was out of the program, school had started and I wasn't enrolled, nor did I care about being enrolled in school any more. Fortunately for me at the time it seemed like my mother didn't care whether or not I went to school any more either. Within a short amount of time, I started slowly to revert back to my old ways with my old friends, which meant staying out late and getting stoned.

Then one morning after having stayed out all night, my mother told me that she was selling the house.

"Why do you want to sell the house?" I asked.
"Well, you know that I've always liked living in the country, so I was thinking of getting out of the city and living there."
"So why don't you just go and rent a place upstate like you did when I was younger and live there sometimes?"
"Well, I just don't want to worry about this big house any more. Besides, there's nothing really here for me. I've got no good memories here."
"So if you sell the place, do you plan on giving me some money so I can get a place in the city?"
"Well, no. I was thinking that I would get a big house up there with maybe a barn, and we could both live there."
"Well, it sounds nice, Ma, but I don't want to go and live in the country."
"Well, it wasn't much of a choice, Michael. I'm selling the house, and we are moving upstate."

With that statement my mother and I got into another one of our arguments. By the end of it, I was given the ultimatum of either moving out right now and getting my own place or moving upstate that weekend to stay with some friends of hers until she came up in a month. I decided to move out. But after living out on the streets for almost two weeks, with no money and no place to go, I had to agree, reluctantly, to her plan.

CHAPTER 4

COUNTRY ROADS

My mother rented a van, and I packed some stuff. When we left, Marcus and my dog Bobo came for the ride. So did a few joints. What really sucked was that she didn't tell me where we were going. After we passed Albany, I started to wonder how far upstate I was going. We ended up driving about five and a half hours north of Queens, up to a town called Morehouseville in the Adirondack Mountains. Just to give you an idea of how small the town was, it was inside of another larger town, and there were only nineteen people of legal voting age.

When we got to my mother's "friend's" house, I was introduced to the Wenzels. There was Billy Sr., Billy Jr., and Marie, Billy Sr.'s wife. After a little bit of small talk I was told to take my things inside, but I was also told to leave my dog outside so it wouldn't bother their dog, which pissed me off. When that was done, Marcus and I took a walk down the one-lane road to a small bridge.

Once there, Marcus and I sat down and smoked a big fat joint. Afterwards we were fooling around, jumping from rock to rock around the stream, until my dog Bobo fell in the water. I just about jumped in after her to get her out of the freezing water. By the time we walked back to the house, Bobo's fur was starting to freeze. When we got into the house, I was again told that they were afraid my dog would fight with their older dog, and they suggested I take Bobo into the van and turn on the heat. Marcus and I got the keys from my mother and went into the van and wrapped Bobo up in some blankets. I was half serious when I told Marcus I should split, leave my mother up there, and drive back home. He agreed but warned me that my mother would probably kill us once she got back to New York.

It wasn't too much later that my mother came out and said it was getting late and she and Marcus would have to leave soon because it was a long drive back. I kissed Bobo on the lips, and gave Marcus a hug goodbye, and started to get out of the van.

"Aren't you going to give me a kiss goodbye?"

"Ma, you're dropping me off, in the middle of nowhere, to live with people I don't know. I'll get you next time, okay?

On that note, I got out of the van, closed the door, and watched them drive down the road.

I went in and told the Wenzels that I was going to take a little walk. They said that would be fine, but I would have to be in soon because it was almost nine o'clock, and it was a school night. I smiled and thought to myself that this is not going to fucking work! Then I walked back down the hill and sat under the bridge, cursed the situation I was in, and smoked another joint. I sat there until my ass froze from sitting on the rocks, and then I went "home."

I got in about nine-thirty and went upstairs to my room which was also occupied by Billy Jr. Thank God at least there were two beds, but only one television and that was downstairs in the living room. They must've thought I had a bad stomachache because I went to the bathroom about every forty-five minutes to smoke a cigarette out the window. The last time I came out of the bathroom, Billy had gone to bed and shut out the light. I made sure I hadn't forgotten to curse anything happening in my life up until now, and then lay in bed for a couple of hours until I fell asleep.

The next morning Billy's mother woke us up at about six-thirty so we could get ready and take the bus to school. I'd say, besides getting up that early, the second worst thing was their reluctance to give me a cup of coffee. After a lot of persistence on my part, they decided I could have a half cup each morning. I was still a few months shy of my fifteenth birthday, but had already been drinking coffee for years.

We went outside to catch the bus, and I swear it had to be at least ten below zero. We stood out there for about ten minutes until we heard the bus engine in the distance, but it still seemed like forever until it got there to pick us up. I got on the bus and looked for a seat. While I looked around, a girl named Norma grabbed my arm, pulled me onto her seat, and suggested that I could sit there, which seemed cool to me. Billy sat a few seats behind me and introduced the girl he was sitting with as his girlfriend, Melissa, and then he introduced me to her younger sisters and to some of his friends.

The ride to school took forty-five minutes because our bus route was "out in the sticks," I was told, and one of the farthest away in the district. My new school was in a town called Poland, just like the country. I hate to admit it but the ride was so long it felt like we had driven to that country. I had to laugh when we first drove up to the school, because it looked just like the school in the Archie series comic books. There were no people hanging out in front of the school, no graffiti, and no cages on the windows. I had been told to go to the main office when I got to school that morning.

After I found my way there, they asked what grade I was in. I wondered if I should tell them the grade I was supposed to be in but figured that maybe I shouldn't because I might not be able to keep up with the class work, so I lied and said I was in the ninth grade. Actually by this time I hardly remembered what grade I was supposed to be in, but I figured I could handle the ninth grade.

Then they made me a program card, and I was told how to get to my homeroom. There I met some of the kids in my class, and they seemed innocent enough. After a few days, I was given a locker and was able to find my way around. One of the things I noticed was that, unlike city schools where the teachers show up at the institution that is mostly run by the inmates, the country teachers showed up like it was a place of business and ran it that way. I also started to notice some of the girls noticing me after a while. It was pretty nice and getting better because the older girls seemed to be making themselves attainable.

Maybe it was the new kid on the block type of thing, but that was okay with me. In fact, it was great until eleventh and twelfth grade guys with names like "Bear" and "Tree Top" with massive builds from working on the farm started bumping into me and warning me to stay away from their girlfriends. This presented a problem since I was stuck in the same building with everyone all day, and I didn't know who their girlfriends were. I didn't really feel like asking them at the time that I was being bumped into in the hallway whom I should stay away from.

From my experience in the city schools, I was amazed at a couple of things. When one of the teachers shouted for the class to be quiet, they would actually shut up and start shuffling toward their seats. I hadn't seen anything like that since I was in the fifth grade in Catholic school. They also had a class called Study Hall. It was one period during the day when kids of all different grades would get together and do homework or study together. I'm not sure it would work in a city school because the older kids would probably have the younger ones doing their homework or worse.

Life in my new home was too boring, though. I would do whatever I had left of my homework and then go take a walk for excitement. There was about two or three feet of snow on the ground, so I wouldn't be able to walk out too far into in the woods, which I loved to do. I'd usually end up walking down the road a mile or two and then turn back. I still had some weed on me, so every now and then I'd smoke a joint. My only minor problem was running out of rolling papers, so I had to fashion a pipe out of a soda can. Just to give you an idea of my surroundings, there were about five houses in a quarter-mile area, and only two of those had full time residents. Otherwise it was all woods for miles. One day while I was out walking, I spotted some kids running around who looked to be about my age. I wondered who they were but didn't go introduce myself. I asked Billy Jr. that night if he knew who they were. He said they were kids we rode the school bus with. I asked him to introduce me to them the next day, and he said he would.

The next day he introduced me to the Lewis kids on the bus, whom I had seen while walking. There were two brothers: Ricky was two years older than I was, and Ronnie was younger but bigger either of us. They had two sisters: Dawn was about my age, and Sara who was only about two. Dawn was extremely developed for her age. After a few days I started going up to their house. It was an old three-story lodge with a bunch of rooms. I'd go up there and help them chop wood or help them with some of their other chores while I tried to get to know their sister a little bit better.

After being in school for a few months everything was going pretty well for me. I was getting 80's and 90's on my school tests, and I was actually getting to like this school thing once again. The only thing I didn't like was the vice principal. The reason I didn't like him was because he would walk the halls with a big paddle, and he would paddle people with it. He would walk around as if he was some type of tough guy. I'm sure from the look on my face he knew I thought he was an asshole and didn't like him. He used to be a drill sergeant in the Marines, and he treated us like new recruits. I would really like to see him try this shit in some city schools with some city kids. I'm sure he would have had his ass handed to him in about a day or two. I guess he thought he was still in the Marines and could rule with an iron fist from what I had heard and seen.

One day some old school records from J.H.S. 189 arrived at my new school. I was told to report to the vice principals office. I walked into his office and, with a smirk on his face, he said that he had reviewed my records and they showed I hadn't finished the eighth grade. Even though I was doing very well in the ninth grade, he decided I would have to be sent back to the eighth grade. He then handed me a pile of books for the eighth grade classes and said I should go to my ninth grade classes today and return those books at the end of each period.

"You know, I'm really supposed to be in the tenth grade. I didn't get left back because I couldn't do the work. I got left back a few times because I never went to school. I mean, look at my test scores now. I'm getting 80's and 90's on my tests, and I didn't even start here at the beginning of the year. Considering how well I'm doing in the ninth grade now, couldn't you just let me stay there now?"

"So basically you'd like me to reward you for lying to me."

"...Well, no."

"Oh, good, so you can see my point of view. Here are your new books and your new program card. Goodbye."

I picked up my new books and program card, thanked him sarcastically, and walked out of his office.

I elected to go to each of my classes and return the books right then and there. I walked into each class, interrupted the teachers, and explained I wouldn't be attending their classes any more. After that, I got my jacket, left school, and walked around town for a while. It felt a little odd when a few people on the street asked me why I wasn't in school, so I had to make up a bullshit story for them.

In the city you could hang out in the stores and play pinball and nobody bothered to ask you anything. But now it seemed like the whole town was watching me. I decided to stay out of the handful of stores and walked around until it was time to catch the bus home.

It was discouraging to have to go back to the eighth grade or school at all the next day. It was funny, but most of my teachers were the same ones I had for ninth grade classes. I'd say the worst part of being back in the eighth grade was doing schoolwork I had done at least twice before in other schools. I wasn't at all enthusiastic about it, and my scores dropped to 70s or less as opposed to my ninth grade scores. During all this, my mother wrote and said she was going to come up and visit me. My only response was to write back one word: Why?

After school I would usually do whatever homework I had and then walk over to Ronnie and Ricky's house. Sometimes we'd shoot at old cans with rifles in their backyard. For the most part there was nothing else to do so far out in the country.

After a few months my school records from Project 25 the drug program, were sent up. Their records stated that I hadn't finished the seventh grade. Yeah, you guessed it; I was sent back to the seventh grade. I wrote a sarcastic letter to my mother explaining what was going on and thanked her for sending me there. By the time she called me up to say she would try and do something, I didn't give a fuck about school any more. I reverted to my city kid habits, found the smartest kids in class, and told them they were responsible for doing my homework every day. There wasn't much they could say since I was turning fifteen and twice their size. I didn't study for tests and still got scores in the 80s and 90s, so it was a fucking joke.

The teachers eventually caught on to the fact that I had other kids doing my homework, and they told me not to do it any more. I didn't have to say it but my attitude was like, "Go fuck yourself." I kept it up, and eventually I was sent to the vice principal's office.

He told me to come in and sit down. I told him I'd rather stand. That statement pissed him off, as I intended, but what could he do about it? He told me if I didn't stop having the other kids do my homework, I would be suspended. I suggested that maybe he should just throw me out of school now. He put on a phony smile and said, "Oh, I wouldn't want to do that just yet. I'll save that until I catch you doing drugs at my school."

After he smiled, I asked him if he was done with me. He said that he was, so I left his office.

In the meantime one of the girls in my class had a crush on me and offered to do my homework and use different handwriting. How could I refuse? Every morning we would meet where the school buses dropped us off, and she would give me my homework. I'd make it a point to say hi to her in the hallway when she was with her girlfriends. She would brighten up, and she and her girlfriends would start chattering like a bunch of hens. This worked great for a while until the teachers caught on, because we always had the same wrong answers, and I was once again warned by the vice principle. I figured, Fuck it, and stopped any attempt at turning in any schoolwork. I'd sit in class and do my time until the bell rang. I would have cut class but there was nowhere to go. Besides dickhead was always roaming the halls, looking for anyone who might be cutting class.

My mother called to say she was going to look for a house to rent in the area and move up there. I told her sarcastically how nice that sounded. She said she had a little surprise for me; she was going to bring my friend, John Slocum, with her. I asked her how she managed to trick him. I'd bet she was lying when she said John was looking forward to it.

A funny thing about the weather this far north was not having a season you could call spring. The people around here even renamed it mud. Even though the snow would be melting, there were days it would freeze at night and then snow on top of it. But I can tell you that even this was better than ten or fifteen below zero every other day. By the time all the snow would melt and dry up, it would be summer. But unfortunately, for me, there was still snow out now.

My mother called with bad news one night. My dog Bobo had gotten hit by a bus and was in pretty bad shape. She said she would see what she could do for Bobo and call me back later. It made me feel like shit, and I wondered why Bobo was out running around buses anyway. Of all things, she gets hit by a bus like I did. Later that night my mother called back and said she'd taken Bobo to the New York Animal Medical Center in Manhattan. The doctors there said Bobo would need steel rods in her leg and a hip replacement. That was the good news. The bad news was the three thousand dollars they wanted to do the work. I knew my mother didn't have that kind of money to spend on my dog, and I certainly didn't either. My mother asked me what I wanted her to do. I had a few choice words for her but elected not to use them. I didn't hide the sarcasm when I said, "Mom, do what you have to do with my dog. Oh yeah, thanks," and hung up the phone.

After I hung up the phone with her I went for a walk in the woods to clear my head. I hated feeling helpless and knowing I couldn't do anything for Bobo. After I found a place to sit down I thought about how pissed I was at my mother for bringing me up here and for not watching my dog. Then I wondered if I'd ever see my dog again. I just couldn't believe that she would let my dog run around in the street like that, and now she calls me with this story about how it's going to take three thousand dollars to fix Bobo. I sat out there for a few hours, and then I wandered back to the Wenzels' house.

My mother called back before I went to bed. She told me not to worry because Bobo was being operated on right now. I asked her, in disbelief, how this was possible, and she told me that she talked to one of the doctors there and that she practically begged him to help her do something. After some persistence he told her he would work on Bobo as an outpatient in his office. She said that he would volunteer his services, but she would have to pay the seven hundred dollars for the new hip and the steel rods. Then she joked and asked me if I had any money to chip in, which I didn't think was too funny. As it turned out, Bobo made it through the surgery, which made me very happy.

Billy and I would throw the Frisbee or football around, but for the most part he would play with his guitar. He wanted to be a Rock 'n' Roll star. I usually went off on my own to Ronnie and Ricky's house. I'd have to say that I enjoyed hanging out at Ronnie and Ricky's house. Besides, their sister was cuter than Billy.

My mother wrote me a few weeks later and told me she had bought an older van and that she was going to come up and visit with Bobo and bring some of my things. She ended the letter by saying that she was going to try and leave in a week.

A few weeks later she called and said she was leaving that day with Bobo and that I would see her that night. I thought it sounded nice to be able to see my dog and get some of my things.

Later that night I got a call from John Slocum. He said, "Mike, you won't believe what happened tonight."

I asked him how he got this number and why he was calling me. He told me he was coming up with my mother to surprise me, but that was a little impossible now because my mother had flipped the van over. I asked if they were all right, and he told me they were fine.

"What about Bobo?"
"Don't worry; she's fine. But check it out, Donald came with us."

Donald was a young guy of about twenty years old but he was about twelve mentally, not his fault or anything. We knew him from the neighborhood.

John told me they flipped over about three times and that Donald had been lying down in the back with Bobo. He went on to say that, as the van was flipping, he saw Donald, who was pretty tall, in an X position with his hands at the opposite ends of the roof, his feet planted on the floor. As the van was flipping with Bobo bouncing around, Donald was yelling, "Whoa, Alma, stop the van, stop the van!" John said it was real funny because only moments before they were laughing about Donald snoring, and he must have been dead asleep just before the van started flipping. He told me it was a good thing they had crashed when they were just coming into town because the Fire Department was there in minutes.

Then he said that he and my mother had gone through the windshield and ended up outside the van, but Donald was still inside, moaning. By the time they got their wits together and ran to the back door and tried to open them to get him out, the Fire Department showed up. When one of the firemen broke open the back doors, Bobo tried to attack him. I guess because she saw him in his uniform while he was holding an axe.

John told me that they were at the hospital getting checked out and that they were going to get a hotel for the night right after they could prove to the doctors that Donald didn't have brain damage, that he had come there that way. Then we hung up. Well, I guess my mother was here.

I don't know how it worked out, but my mother ended up staying at Ronnie and Ricky's house once they made it up there the next day. I went and visited everyone. I hate to admit it but I was happiest to see my dog. She looked like a big daisy. She had on a huge collar that surrounded her head to prevent her from chewing at the stitches that ran down the length of her thigh. Aside from a slight limp, she was fine but not fully recovered.

My mother stayed in the area for a few days. I didn't realize it at the time, but she had looked around for a house to buy or rent. I had a great time up there with Slocum and Bobo. Donald hung out inside, instead of out in the cold, although I can remember the one time when Donald came out while we were having a snowball fight. He went back inside, looking like Frosty the Snowman insisting that he wasn't going to get into any more snowball fights with us after that.

Ricky was sixteen and had a learner's permit, so his mother used to lend him her car from time to time. Ricky used to get a kick out of cutting into the snow banks while he was driving along at a moderate speed. So while John was there, Ricky got his mother to lend him the car. We went out for a ride, and Ricky was demonstrating, for John, how he would rooster tail the snow while he was driving for John. I guess he made the stupid mistake by giving me the steering wheel from the passenger seat. Not that I couldn't drive from that side, but I guess because of what I did while he was driving.

We were going along, and I was cutting more and more of the snow bank while I was steering, and Ricky was starting to give the car more and more gas. When all of a sudden, I don't know why, I cut the wheel hard right into the snow bank. Poof! The lights went out, I had literally buried the car, it seemed.

Ricky started saying, "Oh, you fucker, you've gone and done it now. Oh, you fucker!" I've got to say that, because it was black inside the car, I got a little nervous that Ricky might pop me in the mouth, so I jumped into the back seat with the other guys. His brother, Ronnie, cooled him off and told him not to worry because we'd all dig the car out. We decided that we had to be in pretty deep because we couldn't open up any of the car doors.

We opened up one of the back windows and fortunately the wall of snow covering the window was only a few inches thick. We all climbed out the window. When we got out and looked at the car, there was only a piece of the trunk and back bumper sticking out from the snow. There were five of us with one shovel, and it still took us an hour to dig the car out. It didn't get funny until the car started, and then we all had a good laugh.

John, Donald, my mother, and Bobo left a few days after that.

I remained in the seventh grade for two months and with only a month of school left I was put back into the eighth grade. At the end of the school year I was informed that I'd be held back in the eighth grade because I didn't have enough time in it to be promoted into the ninth grade. But who cared any more? Summer vacation would be starting soon.

My mother called. She told me that John liked the idea of moving up there. I told her I always knew John was crazy. She added that she might have rented us a house up there. She assumed that I would be happy. I guess she really didn't know that I was still trying to figure out a way to get my hands on some money so I could get the hell out of there.

Meanwhile the weather started getting warmer, more mud during the day. That winter season we got about 365 inches of snow so you can imagine there was plenty of it to melt.

Mary, Billy's mother, at the place I was living, was babysitting two small boys named Chris and Chad from down the road, which in country talk, I learned, could mean a city block or two miles. They were the school bus driver's grandsons. His nickname was Sarge, from having been in W.W. II. Sarge was directly related to Chad and Chris's mother, Donna; her husband's name was Brian. I got to know the kids pretty well. They were like five and seven. Chad was smaller and younger, but he was a little tough guy. He liked to fight and get tossed around. Chris was the complete opposite.

Brian had lived in a house over by the post office on Route 8 in Hoffmeister when he was younger, and now it had been empty for a while. My mother had asked Mary about any houses for rent in the area, so Mary asked Brian about that one. Brian didn't own the house because, as he told us later, he had been adopted but he called the family and found out that they would be willing to rent out the house. It sat on forty acres, but it was a somewhat strange configuration for a house because it had been added onto a few different times. It started out as a one-room cabin, and two more houses were added to turn it into an eleven-room house.

My mother ended up renting the place, and within a couple of weeks she, John, Bobo, and I moved up there. I thought it was one of the coolest houses that I had ever lived in. To be honest, it was a lot better than sharing a bedroom with Billy. It was an eleven-room, house and I could choose any room I wanted. There were so many rooms in this house, we were able to pick a room we wanted for the summer, and one for wintertime. The reason we were able to do this was because the summer rooms didn't have any heating pipes, whereas the winter rooms did. There was one major problem with the place though; it hadn't been painted or redecorated in at least twenty years. My mother soon fixed that problem. She bought John and me a ladder, paintbrushes, and some paint, and put us to work.

In the meantime it was still chilly out at night, so we all slept pretty close to the wood stove in the living room. John took the room that was attached to the original cabin. My mother, took the couch with a hideaway bed and slept in the big room in the cabin that became the living room by day. That was also where the wood stove was situated. I took a room that was in the bigger addition, attached to the living room by a small hallway.

She made up for that by taking the upstairs master bedroom for all her personal belongings. I took a room at the top of the stairs. John took the bedroom next to me up there for his summer room. John was happy with his winter room, because he felt it was centrally located. It was close to the wood stove so it was always warm, close to the bathroom, and close to the kitchen. I liked my winter room because it was more private.

Brian, Chris and Chad's father, was very helpful while we got settled. My mother had become good friends with him and his wife, Donna. Donna was a nurse at night, and Brian worked days for the town. My mother offered to babysit Chris and Chad from time to time. John and I, being city kids, might have been a little rough on them from time to time, but personally I grew to love the little squirts, except when I would catch Chad whacking Bobo with a shovel or something.

During the days it was getting pretty warm out, and one day I made the bad assumption that the water might be warm enough to take a dip. We had been walking up French Road, and there was a deep stream over by the town barn. I suggested to John that we should take a swim. He said he was game, but he wouldn't go first because he thought it might be too cold. I figured that, if I was going to do it, the best idea was not to check the water temperature, so I stripped down to my underwear and jumped in. I don't think that in my life I have ever been submerged in anything colder than that fresh water stream. The one thought banging in my head was that somehow before I passed out I had to get John to jump in. Even though I wanted to pop out of that stream and run screaming, I calmly broke the surface with my head and said, "Ahhh, the water feels great!"

Now take into consideration that John and I had been checking the stream temperature for about two weeks, so when I came up out of the water John still had his pants and shoes on. While the first stages of hypothermia were setting in, I was saying to John, "Come on. Don't be a pussy. The water's fine." While he observed the situation, I waited patiently for him to get undressed while my legs and arms were going numb. He finally got undressed and leapt up high in the air to jump in, at which point I leapt out and yelled, "It's fucking freezing! You're going to die!"

John looked at me wide eyed as he tried to swim through the air for the shore. I ran for my clothes up on the road as John splashed into the water. By the time his head popped out of the water, I had my pants halfway on and scooped up the rest of my clothes and his, and started laughing as I ran down the road towards our house. In the meantime, John seemed to have somehow jumped out of the water faster than he had gone in. He was yelling, "You motherfucker, you could have given me a heart attack!" as he ran after me down the road. I threw pieces of his clothes in the air as we ran. We got a good laugh about it later on, and both agreed the water felt as if it was thirty degrees.

Eventually the weather got warmer, and one day we got invited by Ronnie and Ricky Lewis to go over to High Falls, the local swimming hole that was "down the road a bit."

So after driving about twenty miles we got to High Falls, and it was beautiful. When you first got there you'd have to cross a steel bridge that was about thirty feet long. It passed over the West Canada Creek. I thought it was a weird name for a creek that was as wide as seventy feet from shore to shore in some spots. At High Falls it got very narrow for the water to go over three waterfalls, which were to the left of the bridge as we drove over it.

After the waterfalls it got calm for about twenty-five feet with high double cliffs on the left and a smaller cliff of about six feet high on the right. Then that channel went from eight feet across to about fifteen feet across, where it got much shallower and created rapids. The width got larger as it reached the bridge and much deeper. It went from about a three and a half-foot depth in the rapids, to about twenty feet deep under the bridge, which made the water move more slowly again as it made a left turn on the other side of the bridge around a huge boulder.

We got out of the car and, from sitting on the bridge looking at the waterfalls, I could see a large flat boulder on the right where other people were sitting and sunning themselves. Ricky told me that, about eighty years ago when the government hired lumberjacks to clear the land for timber, the lumberjacks in their spare time took some dynamite to blow up the rocks and made the waterfalls and scenic area around the bridge.

The water surface was about thirty feet below the bridge. When we got there, Ron climbed over the side and asked, "Do you think I should jump?" I didn't get scared for him because I thought he climbed over the railing and stood there a little too calmly. John, on the other hand, told Ronnie he didn't think he should jump. Ronnie looked at him and said okay and then jumped. I have to admit, it looked pretty cool. By the time Ron had made it up the trail, I was already over the railing getting up my courage to jump.

Before I did, Ron and Ricky came over to me and told me the rules. Number one, go in feet first. Number two, keep your arms at your sides when you hit the water. Number three, don't jump out too far or the momentum will send you onto the boulder in front of you. Number four, don't jump to the left because there's a ledge about seven feet under the water that you'll hit. I sized up the situation and had the rules repeated one more time and jumped. I figured if Ronnie hadn't died when he did it, I could copy what he did and live, too. Man, what a rush. The wind whistling past your ears and the sights rushing past on the way down, and then splash! You'd hit the water and go down about ten feet.

The first time I did it, I opened my eyes and looked up from underwater, It looked like I was in some type of weird, large hole. Then I swam up and broke the surface. When I did everybody was clapping and cheering. John kept saying that he couldn't believe I'd just jumped like that. While I was still in the water, I noticed a big thick rope hanging from under the bridge, so I swam over. Then I swung out on it and dove into the water before going up and jumping off the bridge again. We were having a great time down there when Billy Wright, a kid we rode the school bus with, came over to the bridge. He sat there for a few minutes and hollered down to ask about the water temperature. We told him it was fine. Then he gave the thumbs up signal and proceeded to climb to the top of the bridge. I asked Ricky what he was doing, and he said some people are crazy enough to jump off the top of the bridge. I could hardly believe him at first; the top of the bridge was about fifty-five feet from the water.

Billy climbed up, took a deep breath, and jumped. I swam over and started to talk to him about how he did it. He was a few months older than I was, but we were about the same size, so I had to get some pointers from him.

He took me up to the top of the bridge and told me to watch everything he did. He said the most important thing was to only step off the bridge because you drifted twice as bad from this height toward the rocks. He looked at me and said, "Okay, watch." Then he stepped off the bridge and that boy was gone, like outta here. Man, what a rush, I thought. If jumping off the bottom was a trip, this must be the ultimate. He came back up and showed me one more time. I guess he thought I was going to jump, too, but my courage was still busy sizing up the situation.

I didn't jump, but I sat there contemplating it for a while. Ronnie Lewis was bigger than I was, and he had been swimming here for years and still hadn't jumped from the top. Ricky, who was older, wouldn't even consider jumping from the bottom. He thought we were all nuts. John still didn't have his courage up to jump from the bottom, and neither did Billy Wenzel, the kid I used to live with.

After a while I went over with the other guys who were now jumping into the waterfalls. There were three waterfalls separated by two cliffs. The waterfalls were about twenty feet high and the cliffs were about twenty-seven feet tall. The falls in the center was called the Big Bopper. It was twelve feet across, and about three-quarters of the water went through it. The other two took the remainder of the water, with one being larger than the other.

The game over there was to see who could dive the closest to where the waterfall hit the whitewater below. The water was pretty deep under the falls, about fifteen or twenty feet, so you didn't have to worry about rocks. Sometimes you would jump into the white water and the waterfall's undercurrent that broke the surface would just keep you in place.

Billy Wright told me about a rumor that some people had actually been able to climb in behind the waterfall, but it seemed a little too nutty for him to try. I thought about this and figured that, if I was able to do this, it might be a way for me to get even with him for calling me a chicken shit for not jumping off the top of the bridge, if I didn't kill myself in the process. One thing I could agree with him about was that it did seem like a nutty thing to try. We stayed there until the mosquitoes really started coming out at dusk, and then we left. I didn't realize it at the time, but all the activity knocked me out and I slept like a baby that night.

My mother brought home some kittens; two of them were brother and sister, the third was a stray, and the fourth one was a Manx. A Manx looks like a small bobcat. They're born without a tail and walk like a bobcat. Since he was the smallest, the other kittens would knock the shit out of him when they were playing. Poor thing, they played with him like he was a mouse, and when one got done with him, another one would jump him. After a while we would break up the little wrestling match whenever they would get a hold of him, but unfortunately we weren't there all the time and he still caught a beating or two. He was the same color as Morris the cat on the television commercial, so we named him Morris.

Ricky and Ronnie came over to pick us up a few days later. They were going over to High Falls, and it wasn't as if we had anything better to do. We went and had a great time over there, but as far as the bridge-jumping status nothing had changed among any of us. During the ride home I was pretty pissed at myself for not having jumped off the top of the bridge, not that the other guys would let me live it down after watching me climb up and down a few times during the course of the day. I told them they could all go fuck themselves, because I had jumped off the bottom of the bridge the first time I got there. John still hadn't jumped off the bridge, and after all the years Ronnie and Ricky had been going there, only Ron jumped off the bottom of the bridge, so there. When John and I got home, we had a nice meal and I went to sleep.

The days we didn't go to the falls started to get pretty boring. I mean, for one thing there were only three channels on the television, and just to give you an idea, you had to drive twenty miles north to Pesco Lake just to get a pack of gum. John and I had to keep coming up with new adventures and games to keep from going stir crazy.

One day we'd climb the mountain across from the house. The next day we'd cut the end of a tube sock off and slide one of the cats in until its head would pop out the other end. Then we would tie a knot at the end by its back feet so it looked like a sausage with a head on it. This was when the fun would begin. Now don't get me wrong; it's not like we would hurt them, I loved all my animals. My dog Bobo would occasionally chase the cats from time to time, and when she would catch them she'd nibble on them as if they had fleas. Once we got the cat into a sock, the cat would usually look up at you as if to ask, "Okay, what the fuck is going on?" with a half look of boredom.

Then John or I would walk over to the front door, open it, and yell, "Bobo! Get the cat!" The look of boredom on the cat's face would change to "Oh shit!" and almost instantly the cat would become the fastest inchworm you have ever seen. Sometimes they would do pretty well and get two or three feet before Bobo would catch them. Once she caught them, she would pick them up and prance around with her trophy until we could catch her and let the cat go if she didn't do the flea bit on them.

Another game we had was rock fights where we would both get a bucket of rocks, make up boundaries, and try to hit each other with the rocks. Luckily we were both pretty quick so neither of us ever got injured badly. Then one day John came up with a new game. He came over to me and said, "Okay, this is how we play. You get a bucket of rocks and sit on the front porch, and I have to ride past you as fast as I can on the bike, and you have to try and hit me." I looked at him for a second, like he was nuts, and said, "Cool, I'll play."

He came whipping by the first time, and I was only able to throw three or four rocks at him before he was out of bounds. Then he came past the second time and the same thing, three or four throws and nothing. I realized it was taking me too long to reach down into the bucket and reload so I put about four or five rocks on the railing as John made his turn to head back into enemy territory. I put another four or five in my left hand just as John rode into bounds.

"Whoosh!"
"Bam!"

The first shot hit the bike. My second, third, and fourth shots missed. Whoosh! The fifth shot was a direct hit in the rib cage. John's jaw dropped open as he grabbed his ribs and crashed head first into the drainage ditch.

I was jumping up and down yelling, "Yes! Yes! A direct hit!"

John was saying something garbled while I was ranting and raving about how our hero was an expert marksman. John was still saying something quite garbled as I walked over to the drainage ditch. I have to say John looked pretty pathetic lying in the inch-deep stream of ditch water with the bicycle twisted around his ass. But hey, he thought of the game, not me.

He repeated himself for the third time, but he must have finally lifted his chin out of the water, because this time it sounded more like, "You broke my fucking ribs."

I helped him out of the ditch and then helped him over to the porch to sit down. After a while he was able to breathe a little better, and he suggested that it was his turn at bat. I tried to get out of it by saying that I would have never decided to play if I knew that I would have to be a driver also. But he didn't buy any of it, especially with his ribs still throbbing. I figured, what the hell? He was hurt, so how well could he throw now?

All I had to do, we agreed, was make three passes. I made the first two without getting hit, but on the third attempt he nicked me in the back of the head. I didn't crash, but my fucking head was humming. I went over and sat down on the porch with him to lick my wounds, and we both unanimously agreed that we shouldn't play this game any more.

Ricky, Ronnie, and Billy Wenzel stopped by today. You guessed it, High Falls. No sooner did I get in the car when everyone started busting my balls. It was like, "Hey, Billy, you're in for a real treat today. You get to watch Mike do some bridge-sitting." John said.

Ronnie interrupted with, "Yeah, if you watch real close you'll get to watch Mike climb all the way up and all the way down."

I guess the ribbing was just what I needed, because when we got there no sooner did we park when I pulled off my t-shirt and climbed to the top of the bridge. Then I looked down and thought, "Fuck it. All I have to do is take one step, and it's a done deal," and jumped. Everybody ran towards the bridge, yelling, "He did it, he did it."

I'd say the weird thing I was thinking on the way down was that, even though I knew I was jumping from a higher distance, I kept waiting to hit the water. I started to think I'd never hit, when "Splash!" I hit.

When you're swimming in fresh water, the deeper you go down the colder the water gets. You can feel the temperature changing as you go down. I went from warm to freezing in what seemed like a split second. Then I sat down there for a few seconds to enjoy the cold water a little bit, but also to put in their heads that maybe I wasn't coming up. When I looked up, I realized I had let myself sink to about twenty feet and that I might be in a bit of trouble with the amount of oxygen I had left. Then I did something very stupid. I looked down to see how far from the bottom I was. It was dark and murky, and I thought I was seeing the bottom of the stream. I figured the best thing for me to do was swim down to the bottom so I could kick off with my legs and get a better start to the surface. Then I turned upside down and headed for the bottom... wrong answer.

After swimming another five or six feet deeper, I realized I was fucked, so I stopped, turned right side up, and started clawing for the surface. I looked up towards the sky, and it seemed miles away. I thought I might not make it.

My mother was a very good swimmer, and I remembered what she told me when she was teaching me to swim. She had explained that when you are swimming underwater and you want to go further, slowly start letting your air out because it will give you a few more feet. I had started to do that for a few seconds, and by the time I let out all my air I still hadn't broken the surface. I swore I would not stop moving my arms and legs, and I would die with them moving. I knew I had to be near the surface, but I thought my lungs were about to explode. Luckily I instinctively inhaled just as I broke the water's surface.

Everybody up on the bridge was clapping and yelling, "All right! He did it!" If they only knew, I thought. I floated on my back and took deep breaths of that beautiful air.

Ronnie jumped off the bottom of the bridge, and John said, "Fuck it. If he can jump off the top of the bridge, I have to jump off the bottom."

He climbed over the rail and yelled, "Don't forget the Alamo!" right before he jumped. Fucking nut, what did a place in Texas have to do with jumping off a bridge?

He landed while I was still floating on my back, amazed at myself for jumping off a fifty-five foot bridge. I lay there and evaluated the whole situation that had happened. The determination of finally climbing up the bridge, the courage to jump, the exhilaration of jumping into the air. The comfort of hitting the water safely, the travel, and brief meditation. The stop and realization, the thought and motivation, the try and desperation, fresh air and exasperation.

Then Ricky shouts, "Well, I can't let the city slicker beat me in my own backyard," and he jumped off the bridge with his goofy red hillbilly hat and all.

A lot of scores were settled with the bridge that day. I decided that if I was ever going to be crazy enough to jump off this thing again, I'd have to do it now. I got out of the water and walked back up the trail. When I got up there, I got a bit of a standing ovation from everyone. I started to climb up the bridge again, as someone called for a drum roll. When I got to the top of the bridge, I looked down and thought that I really must have been nuts. I felt the urge to sit down and stare at the height again but knew if I did that I probably wouldn't jump, so I looked up in the air and stepped off the bridge.

Whoosh! I could hear and feel the gust of air hit me from under the bridge as I jumped.

Splash! Ahhh, swim, swim, swim. I was good for the day. All the guys were cheering and jumping off the bridge themselves by now. I ended up having a great day at High Falls.

One day we went over to the Patero household; we went over to have dinner and meet some neighbors. It was the first time I had ever met Melissa's parents. Billy, the kid I used to live with, was still dating Melissa, the oldest. I knew her and her sisters from the bus ride to school, but John hadn't met any of them yet.

Melissa's parents' names were Donna and Dick Patero. I had heard that he wasn't in good shape, something to do with his liver. There was another guy there named Leo Foss. He was pretty cool, loud and outspoken. The Wenzels were there and my mother, John and myself. Everybody was talking and getting along pretty well, so I decided to go out back and have a smoke while they were talking. No sooner had I lit up than the two youngest girls came out. I wondered for a moment if I should let them know I smoked cigarettes, and then I decided the hell with it and took a drag. They squealed and looked at each other, then squealed again, and said, "Ooh, he smokes." I personally thought it was kind of cute. I had been smoking for at least two years by then, so it was no big thing to me.

While I was out there talking to them, their cat came running toward us chasing a chipmunk. The chipmunk looked around and then up at me. I swear his look said to me that I was a hell of a lot better choice than the cat. He ran smack into me, scrambled around and ran straight up the inside of my pant leg. The cat stopped and so did the chipmunk, about four inches under my groin.

The cat looked left and right and then up at me in bewilderment and then slowly walked away confused. In the meantime I was telling the girls to call the cat, but they couldn't stop laughing about it. By then the cat had disappeared. I figured the only safe way to get the chipmunk out was to pull down my pants. That solution had two minor drawbacks. I didn't like the idea of pulling my pants down in front of ten- and eleven-year-old girls from the school bus and letting them see me possibly get bit in the nuts. The second reason is that I wasn't comfortable with the possibility of someone walking out of the house and seeing me with my pants down, jumping around, and holding my nuts in front of two little girls. I asked the girls to go in the house because I had to open my pants up, and they said, "No way! We want to watch this."

"You're not going to watch me take my pants off," I said as I looked to see if anyone had heard me.

Patty asked what the big deal was, since they'd seen their daddy in his underwear. After a minute or two I figured I didn't have time to get into it as I had a more pressing matter at hand. I slowly opened my pants and started to pull them down. By the time my underwear was showing, the little girls were going, "Oohhh." When I looked up at them, they were doing the dramatic googly eyes routine. I stopped for a second, took a deep breath, and started pulling them down again. I pulled them down until I saw the head and shoulder of the chipmunk. He had his little paw on his nose with his eyes squeezed shut. He opened them slowly and looked around. Then he looked up at me, looked left, then right, and jumped out of my pants, and ran like hell. We all laughed, and then I got my pants pulled up. As we walked back inside the house, one of the girls said as a joke that she was going to tell that I pulled my pants down in front of them.

Leo was the first person I ran into when I got back in the house. He was a Don Rickles type who would jokingly compliment you as he was putting you down. I figured I would tell him what happened outside, in case I had to cover my ass.

Leo got to talking with my mother and offered to take John and me up to his camp for the weekend. He said he had taken Billy, Ronnie, and Ricky quite a few times over the years, which my mother had verified. At the time, though, she thanked him and said she would think about it.

Dinner was great; everybody who came had brought something, almost like Thanksgiving, although I could see that Dick didn't have the same type of food the rest us had, he was on a special diet, due to his condition. By the end of the night after a few conversations with Ronnie and Ricky's mother, my mother said that it would be nice to let us get away for the weekend once in a while, if Leo didn't mind. John and I had already spoken to Billy about what was what with Leo, and Billy said it was cool to go to Leo's house because he lived in a three-story cabin that led down a hill to Pesico Lake. Billy said that sometimes Leo would buy shotgun rounds and let him shoot at old cans in the backyard, so naturally we were very interested. It sounded a lot more interesting than having rock fights out of boredom.

After a course of time, we ended up going over to Leo's house. When you first drove up to Leo's place it looked like a three-room cabin, but it was actually built on the side of a hill so its size was misleading. When Leo opened the door, instead of entering the house you were in a small hallway with a staircase in front of you and a doorway on your right. The staircase led down one floor into the main living section. On the right was a doorway where there were extra bedrooms. We went in and got a look at the first set of rooms at ground level on our right. They were neat cedar-lined type rooms. Then we went down the stairs to the living room. There was a kitchen, living room, bedroom and a bathroom on that level. There was also a balcony that overlooked the lake where Leo's boathouse was. I found out later that under the balcony there was a screen-enclosed room with a three-sided cellar room made out of cinder blocks behind it. I thought the place was one of the best little cabins I had ever seen.

Leo had picked up a few boxes of shotgun shells before we got there. He had already asked my mother if it was okay, and we shot off the rifles that night. Leo also had some cool souvenirs from World War II. He had been in on the Normandy landings. John and I were both war buffs and went gaga over some of the stuff. He had an SS Officer's small sword, a luger pistol, a few bayonets, and a handful of German medals. We stayed at Leo's cabin that weekend and had a great time. It was a good change of pace.

Mary Wenzel had said that her niece was thinking of buying the old town store that had been vacant ever since I had been up there. It was right across from the original old one-room schoolhouse on Route 8, that was right out of a storybook time, and much too old and small to use any more. Besides, the outhouses for the school had fallen down about thirty years ago. They did eventually move up about a month later, and after a little time they bought and opened up the store.

I met Brian's brother, Jack. His sons' names were Billy and Timmy. They were both a couple of years older than we were. Billy had lived in the city of Utica, so he considered himself to be pretty sharp, which made John and me laugh; Timmy was more of a country type. They were pretty cool to hang out with.

My mother told me that she was going to go to New York and bring a load of things up from the city. Before she left, she arranged to have Brian come over at night at about ten o'clock and then in the morning to check on us. Unfortunately the morning for Brian was six or seven, but it was pretty cool of him. He made sure that we were okay and all.

The store was open now, and we had met Mary's niece's kids by now. Sometimes John and I used to call them up at night and ask if it was too late to come over. Too late to come over meant an hour and a half from now. That's the amount of time it would take for John and me to walk the three miles to get there.

Some nights it would be bright from all the stars; other nights it was only lit by the moon outside when we'd walk there. But some nights it was so dark that we would have to follow the white line on the road. I mean, you couldn't even see your hand in front of your face. To top it off the only place there were streetlights on that stretch of Route 8 was by a home or intersection. At times under one of these conditions you could hear noises in the woods, some close and some far. In the beginning I have to admit it we never paid attention to them, but after a while you'd hear these noises and start to take notice of them. A few times we heard what sounded like branches snapping but wrote it off as a deer getting spooked. By then we had seen what it looked like when a deer gets spooked in the daylight. They didn't care what was in front of them, and they'd just start leaping away, taking everything in their paths, mainly branches. You can hear the branches snapping and breaking as they run through them. But for good measure, we started carrying a couple of rocks with us.

When we'd get to the store, we'd buy some stuff, hang out a bit, and then head back. Whenever we would start out on our voyage back home, we would wish we were at the opposite end of French Road and Route 8. We lived at the intersection of French Road and Route 8, and oddly enough the store was at the same named intersection at the opposite end. Either way you looked at it, it was a six-mile walk round trip.

One day while my mother was still away, she called and asked John and me if we would mind babysitting Chris and Chad. We both knew how to take care of ourselves, and I was pretty sure Chris and Chad would have a good time for the most part, so we said we wouldn't mind. After cooking dinner one night, I remembered that the garbage had to go out in the morning, so I put the trash bag out the front door to remind myself.

After dinner the four of us relaxed in the living room. The kids watched television while John and I read war books. I don't know why but I've always been fascinated with real war stories ever since I could remember. I guess I liked reading about real-life stories of people overcoming hardships.

While we were sitting there, Chris, who was seven, got up and walked over to the front door. I was watching him because I thought it was a little odd for him to walk over to the door because I hadn't heard anything there. He pulled back the window's curtain and looked out. I observed him do what appeared to be a little dance, and then he put back the curtain. Then he calmly walked back to the pull-out bed, and lay down with his brother, then continued watching television. I asked Chris what that was all about. He looked at me and said innocently, "Oh, there's a bear on the porch."

I said, "What? Are you nuts? You must be seeing things."

He looked back at me and said, "No, I'm telling you there's a bear on the porch."

"You're dreaming, kid."

Then he said, "I'm serious. There's a bear on the porch. Go look for yourself."

I put down my book and started walking towards the door, as I told him that there better be a bear on that porch after I got up.

I got to the door, pulled back the curtain, dramatically thrust my face towards the window, and looked right into the face of a bear. There was only a piece of glass and about fourteen inches between us. He looked like he was sitting cross-legged, Indian style, with the garbage bag between his legs, digging through the scraps.

Then he looked up at my eyes and appeared to nod his head and shrug his shoulders as if to ask, "Can I help you?"

At this time I figured he didn't want to break through the window and smash my face, so I decided to somehow make John a part of the fun, because he was watching me and waiting for my reaction. I calmly put back the curtain, walked back to my chair, sat down, picked up my book, and started to read it again.

"So? What happened?"

I put my book down and said, "There's a fucking bear on the porch!"

John got up and walked to the door, speaking to me in the same tone of voice I'd just used on Chris. Then he looked out the window and said, "Holy shit! There's a fucking bear on the porch!"

I looked at him and said, "Yeah, I know."

John ran off to his room and jumped back out with a baseball bat. I looked at him and said, "John, if that bear comes in here, I hate to tell you this, but you'll be fighting him alone. I'm going to show him where the clean sheets are and the pantry. Then I'm going to take the kids and sleep on the roof."

He looked back at me with panic and asked, "What should we do?"
"You should put down the bat, sit down, pick up your book, and read, because fortunately he doesn't look like he's trying the door handle."

John agreed timidly and sat down with the bat across his legs, but he couldn't read his book. I'd have to admit that I was a little frightened also, but I figured there was no sense in making a bad situation worse with the kids who were now looking around wide-eyed at us.

After a little while I joked to Chris and told him to go see if the bear was still there, and he said, "No way! You go look."

Then I turned to John who was still sitting with the bat across his legs and said, "Well, you certainly look like a likely candidate."

He looked at me, smiled, and then got up and walked slowly towards the door. John looked out the window and then strained to the left, then towards the right. John looked back at me and asked, "Do you think I should go out there?"

I glanced around the room and said, "Well, I could probably grab the kids in time and then make it upstairs to the roof if anything bad happens to you."

Besides, I thought, who was I to stop his balls from learning a lesson?

He slowly opened the door, stepped out, and started walking out gingerly.

"I don't see anything, do you think he's still out here?"
"Well, go out a little further,"
"Why?" He said as he walked out a little more.
"Because, I heard that bears like their prey to get far away from their holes before they attack."
"Get the fuck outta here!" John said, as he ran back inside.

Fortunately nothing was out there. He came back in, and then we all had a good laugh about it.

The next day Ricky and Ronnie came over with their mother's car. The first thing I asked them was if they knew that there were bears around here. Ricky and Ronnie smiled at me, and then Ricky said, "Why? You didn't know there were bears around here, you dumb fucker?"

I said, using country slang I had learned, "Well, fuck you, numb nuts, you should've told me by now!"

We all started laughing after I explained what had happened last night.

My mother came back; she had brought up an eighteen-foot rental truck with her this time. John and I were at the Lewises' house the night my mother drove up, so she came over to pick us up.

We asked her why she had such a big truck, and she said that she had brought a lot of our stuff and things for our friends with her. She added that when she packed the truck, she had put our stuff in first, and now our things were in the front of the truck so we couldn't get to it until we unpacked the truck. She explained that we would have to help her make the rounds and drop that stuff off before we could get to ours.

The next day we went and made the rounds to a few people's houses. John and I rode in the back of the truck and joked that we were practicing to become Santa's elves.

After a couple of stops the truck was getting pretty empty, and I could start to see some of my stuff. She had brought up about half of my comic collection, which I'd hoped she hadn't because I realized that it would make it more difficult for me to take off one day if the opportunity presented itself. She had also brought up a few televisions, my stereo, a few air conditioners, and a stand up freezer unit.

My mother said the last stop was going to be Ricky and Ronnie's house. While we drove there, the freezer unit started sliding around in the truck because it hadn't been tied down. We had the back doors open, and after having a few close calls, we told my mother to slow down a bit. When we got to the Lewises' house we dropped off a bunch of things for them. When we got done, my mother asked Janet if the boys could come over to my house and help us get the freezer out, which they did.

On the way over to my house the four of us rode in the back of the truck. We took turns riding in the freezer, while the other three guys took turns sliding the freezer back and forth for effect. Rick was the only one who was a little leery about going into the freezer. He had a bad case of claustrophobia. But by the time the third guy was done, Ricky's manhood was being tested. After we finally got him in there, John came up with the idea of catching it after we would tip the freezer over.

We slid the freezer back and forth once or twice, and we could hear Ricky going, "Whooaa, whoa," just before we tipped it over.

He shot out of it like Superman, hit the ground, and rolled over to the doors. He leapt up, saw what we had done to him, and with a crazed look in his eyes said, "You crazy fuckers, don't you ever do that to me again!"

We were like, Sorry dude; we were just fucking with you. Ricky calmed down a bit, and then he said he thought the truck was flipping over.

After we dropped the freezer off we drove Ricky and Ronnie home. We stayed there for a bit and then decided to leave. John said it was getting a little cold out, so he was going to ride in the cab. I decided to ride in the back. My mother said that, if I was going to ride back there alone, I would have to keep the doors closed. Then my mother got in the truck and told John to lock the back doors on me. When he came back, I told him to leave them open because I was going to have a cool ride back home.

For some reason when I felt my mother put it into gear, I jumped out, locked the doors, and then I hopped up on the bumper. My mother had started to move by now, so I quickly scrambled up the hinges and onto the roof. As we started up the hill, I thought to myself that it felt a little spooky up there at night with the cool mountain air. By now I was sitting over the cab in front of the truck, pretending to be on a motorcycle. After we reached the top of the hill, I noticed that my mother started driving a little faster than usual, so I decided to hold on a little tighter. When she kept on going a little faster, especially around curves, I thought it might be a good idea to go and center myself in the middle of the roof. I figured that maybe they were trying to give me a bit of a ride. But after a few more turns, it was getting harder and harder to hold onto the roof.

By this time I had already spit into the palms of my hands to try and get some suction or traction to avoid my hands from sliding. I got the feeling that they were now trying to scare me a little bit, but I wasn't about to start banging on the roof or yell just yet. But I did hope she'd take it a little easy around Dead Man's Turn that was coming up.

But no dice, she was barreling right along towards it. I decided to start banging and yelling, and to my surprise they started yelling right back and joking with me that they had no brakes. Dead Man's Turn was one of those twenty-five mile per hour turns, and they started into it at about fifty-five miles per hour. I didn't think I was going to make it and remember asking God to let me die quickly if it was to be. It was a left-hand turn and halfway through it I was actually riding on one hand, one foot, and twenty-five percent of my right ass cheek. The worst thing about Dead Man's Turn was that a stream ran under it directly in the middle of the turn. The tube that was under the road was about fifteen feet high, and then there was about five feet of dirt on top of that so it would have been a big drop for me. That's not to mention that the truck roof sat about another twelve feet above the road, and we were driving about forty-five miles per hour now.

While we were going through the turn, I could hear John and my mother howling, "Whoopee."

I'm thinking to myself, "What do they think? I'm Superman or something?" I swore I was going to kill them if I lived through this, and "Whew," I made it through that turn.

But the ride wasn't over yet. It lasted another mile.

In between hanging on for dear life, I thought to myself, You know, this would be a fitting way to die after surviving getting hit by a bus. When we finally stopped down by Route 8 I leapt off the truck. It felt real good standing on the ground. Then I walked over to the driver's side and said to my mother, "Whata' ya' fucking nuts? You could have killed me! I was on top of the truck."
"Oh, my God," my mother said. "I thought you were inside."

My mother apologized and asked me to get in the cab of the truck. I shook my hand at her and said, "Na, thanks anyway, but I'll walk the rest of the way."

The Lewis boys drove over the next day. Ricky asked me if I had any apples left on our apple trees. I looked at him strangely and said, "Yeah, why? What the hell do you need with apples?"

He explained that they also had apples out in the car and that they were going to go over to the dump to feed the bears. John and I were like, Cool, we've got apples. Let's go.

The dump, it turns out, happened to be on French Road, which interested us even more especially since this happened to be the same road John and I would use to walk to Ricky and Ronnie's house at all hours of the night. I couldn't believe my eyes when we got there. I hadn't seen so many bears in one place in my life. I looked at John as if to say "Holy shit," and he looked back in acknowledgement.

When we stopped, Ronnie and Rick got out with their apples, walked over to the wire fence, and started tossing some apples towards the bears. Ricky looked back at me, smiled and said, "Oh yeah, big tough city kids afraid of a few bears."

Nothing for nothing, but there were about fifteen bears out there and only wire between us. But I still grabbed the apples and told Ricky he could go fuck himself as I got out of the car. John, hesitantly, followed shortly after me.

At first the bears were about twenty-five feet away from Ricky but, after we tossed them a few apples, a few came closer. It got to the point where they were on one side of the fence and we were hand-feeding them. It was amazing; never in my wildest dreams did I ever think I'd be looking at a wild bear eye to eye like that and hand-feeding him.

Fortunately, not that it would matter, black bears aren't that large, so I felt a little bit calmer around them, until we ran out of apples. Needless to say, we left a few minutes after that.

It was getting late in the summer now, and a lot of fruit trees in my backyard were heavy with fruit. There were also blueberries, raspberries, boysenberries, and strawberries growing wild. John would go out some mornings with Bobo, some drinking water, and a big basket. By the afternoon I would see him coming back from the woods with his lips and fingertips stained from the berries. The best thing about this was the huge basket of fruit he would bring back, a day's toil if you will. John had seen my mother make pies, and he would experiment making all different types of pies. Some were destined for history, and others were destined for the raccoons that night.

My mother would go out to some of the local auctions and get a lot of different types of food- everything from homemade cheese to slaughtered chickens, and her usual supply of knick-knacks.

One night she came back in a truck with three horses; one was a young colt. When she got out she told us that they were going to the slaughterhouse if nobody bought them. She also admitted that she made the mistake of looking into their eyes when no one was bidding on them. We put them in the small two-story barn across from the house and unloaded some hay from the truck that delivered them.

The next day we took them out to try and ride them. It turned out that the two larger ones we were able to ride. The colt was only a few inches taller than I was at the time, so he wasn't big enough yet, we figured. We didn't have saddles, so it was a bit difficult to stay on at first. After a few falls, I started to get the hang of it. John took a little longer to learn how to stay on the horse. I can still see him galloping off into the briar bush and coming out with burrs stuck in his hair and clothes as the horse would gallop off into the sunset without him.

We all went to High Falls again. I tried to teach John how to dive off the high cliffs on the left side of the falls. There were actually two sets of cliffs on that side. The higher one sat back in the bushes a bit. The thing I was really trying to teach him was how to angle one's dives as to prevent oneself from hitting the third cliff that sat about three feet under the water. Then you had to break surface instantly in order to avoid crashing into the other side of the rock cliff.

I must have sat there with John for twenty minutes and let him watch me do it a number of times, before he stepped up to bat. I talked him through the whole thing one more time about how he had to make a shallow type of dive as opposed to a high dive. He told me he had it down and proceeded to dive high into the air. I looked right at him and said, "You fucking asshole! You're a dead man."

John's eyes shot open the size of saucers as he tried to desperately flap his arms like they were bird's wings to avoid his fate. There was no time for me to reach him, so the only thing I could think of was to stick my head underwater and see if I could tell how much damage he was about to receive. After John hit, he came up to the surface in a dead man's float, and I thought he was dead. Then after a minute, he looked up at me with crazy eyes and said, "Mike, help!"

I knew he was hurt but couldn't help criticizing him. He looked at me and said, "I know, Mike. I'm an asshole. Help me."

I thought that he had hit his head but, as it turns out, his head cleared the cliff but his whole right side was scraped and bruised from his armpit down to his toes. I helped him onto the rocks where he sat for most of the day.

School was going to start soon. Great, I'd get to see all the little kids from the seventh grade.

One day Billy and Timmy Taylor came up to the Lewis house, Brian's kin, if you will. Their family had a camp about two hundred yards southeast of Ricky's house out in the woods. Billy had come from the "Big City," and he had brought some weed and beer with him. When he pulled out that first joint I had to hang onto it for a few minutes. I hadn't seen one in ages. John and I decided to call my mother from the Lewis house and tell her we were going to sleep at the camp. Then we hiked up into the woods to the cabin with them. We partied till about two in the morning until we fell out. It was a little uncomfortable sleeping up there on old cots with no pillows, but I didn't mind too much after partying all night.

School started and the only good thing about it was that Norma, the girl I shared a seat with on the bus, had grown up nicely during the summer. All the other kids seemed happy to be back at school; to me it was no big deal considering my academic career by now.

That weekend we went to High Falls. The water was getting colder, which meant that fall was right around the corner. I told John that this was probably the last chance he would have to jump off the top of the bridge, but he wouldn't budge. I did figure out how to climb under the waterfall that day. There happened to be a few rocks that jutted out on the smooth large rock inside the falls. Once in there you were so close to the water that the falls would rush down your back in some areas. It probably wouldn't be so bad if the water had been a foot or two thick, but it happened to be about ten feet thick. With one slip you'd be gone.

After about an hour, I had shown John how to get under the falls and went to get Ricky to show him. I went in first, and Ricky came in after me, so when it was time to go back out, Ricky was the first one exiting. It was very tedious stretching from rock to rock, and when it came time to grab the last rock, you had to shove yourself up and outwards with your arm strength in order to catch the last rock while the water level was about chest deep. Unfortunately, Ricky missed the last rock and fell under the water.

I leapt to the next rock that Rick had just pushed off from in order to get closer and try to help him. The odd thing about how Rick was positioned in the water was that the force of the water from the falls was keeping him pressed against the cliff wall, and his head was still under water. I kept calm and tried to figure out a way to get his head above water as he reached around in the air like an octopus. I assumed Rick still had some air left so I still had some time to think.

I wondered if, while he tried to find something to grab onto with his arms thrashing around like a crazed man, maybe he was standing on some type of ledge because he wasn't moving. I figured the only thing to try would be to pull him up by his arm towards the last handhold, and he could push off from there. If not that, at least I might be able to get his head above water, so I grabbed one of his arms and pulled while holding on to my handhold with one hand. No sooner had I done that, his head popped out of the water, and I must say he had on the craziest face I'd ever seen on a person. Then he scampered up my body like a squirrel going up a tree. His weight pulled my other hand off the handhold I had, and I fell into the water now.

Fortunately I was still calm when the waterfall pulled me under. Even though it seemed like minutes it probably took less than a second for me to make my decision. I had already swum to the bottom of this little channel under the falls, and I knew it was about fourteen feet deep. I also knew from trying to get under the falls that underneath the turbulent white water it was calm. The best thing to do, I figured, was to head in the direction away from the turbulence while I was underwater. Fortunately I wasn't bounced around long enough so that I didn't know my up from down, so I swam down away from the falls and I have to say that I was pretty glad when it worked. I had reached the calm water, now I could swim away from the falls for as long as I could while holding my breath, and then I'd come up floating like a dead man. I wanted to teach Ricky a lesson and scare one or two of my other friends who were watching just for good measure. As I was floating, John landed on top of me and pulled my head above water.

"What the fuck are you doing?" I gasped.
"Oh, shit, Mike. I thought you were dead," he answered.

After I climbed out of the water we all sat on the rocks and had a good laugh about the whole thing.

School was getting easier. By now I was a shepherd with a flock of trained sheep to do my homework. It's not like it was all take. With some of the girls, I would have to sit with a few of them at lunchtime or pretend that the girls doing my homework were my girlfriend from time to time. There were also one or two younger guys who would do my homework, and I would protect them from some of the bullies. After a little while, though, it needed restructuring. What I had unknowingly done was create little Frankenstein monsters with the guys, and they started taking me over to bigger and bigger guys to beat up, which got to be a hassle. It took a little time but I did straighten out the rules with them after a while.

I'd say the best thing about school was the bus ride to and from school. I did mention that I sat with Norma, didn't I? I thought we came as close to having sex without anyone watching at times, but this lasted until I got called down to the vice principal's office one day. When I got in his office, he said to me, "I'm going to ask you this once, and only once. Did you have sex with Norma on the school bus?"

I looked up at him and said. "No."

Then he said, "What if I told you that I had witnesses?"
"Well, I'd tell you they were full of shit."
"Oh, Yeah?!Well, I have a roomful of kids you ride the bus with as witnesses and you, young man, are suspended, wiseass."

I guess he thought that this statement might devastate me, but I was like, Cool, no school for two weeks.

By the time I got back to class, somehow the story had spread. By the end of the day, guys I had been in fights with were coming over to me and congratulating me, so yeah... I was walking around doing the stray cat strut. That was until I got on the school bus and saw a mound of schoolwork I was required to do in order to re-enter school after my suspension. When Norma got on the bus, I nodded at her sympathetically, and she nodded back. I also found out that I had a new seat on the bus. Norma also had a pile of work, but she only got suspended for three days.

When I got home, I gave my mother the note from school, and then I sat back and expected her to start bitching about it. She looked at me, shook her head back and forth, and said, "I can't believe you. You're something else, and you have sex with a girl on the school bus. What are you, a fucking animal?"

I figured I'd be a bit of a wiseass and said, "Well, it's not like I could bring her home and tell you I'm going upstairs to get laid."

My mother didn't say anything. She just shook her head again and looked at the pile of work I was carrying. She asked if that was the amount of work I had to do before I could go back to school, which happened to be about forty pages thick. I told her it was, but I wasn't going to do all this work just to go back to that dump.

"No, you'll be doing all that work;" my mother said.
"You know what? Just send me to a different school. I can't stand that place."
"I can't. There aren't any other schools up here."

As it turned out, my mother and John helped me out with some of the work, so I went back to

Poland Central High.

One night the TV weatherman it said there was going to be a blizzard. My mother suggested that we go out and pick up some things in the yard, and some neighbors called to say the same thing. John and I both talked her out of it by saying that we would do it in the morning. We all went to bed, and I couldn't believe my eyes in the morning. There were at least three and a half feet of snow, and it was still coming down. The snowflakes were about two inches in diameter, the biggest I had ever seen. By evening they had all the roads open. In the meantime, John and I had to cut a path across the road to the horses. When we got done, we got Bobo and had a pisser in the snow.

Leo dropped off his snowmobile at the Lewis house, so Ronnie called and told us to come over. My mother didn't want to take the car out, so John and I walked there. Even though it was a school night and we'd have to walk home, too, it was well worth the journey. The thing I liked best about learning to ride a snowmobile was that you could do all the things you'd love to do on a motorcycle without the risk of falling onto the ground. Besides, if you did, it was a shorter drop to soft snow. We had a pretty good time that night. After a couple of hours, though, we were pretty tired. Rick said that, if the three of us could fit on the snowmobile, he'd drive us home. John and I weren't in any shape to walk, so we made sure we all fit.

It was decided that we would have Thanksgiving dinner with Brian, Donna, Chris and Chad Taylor. When we got over there in the morning, Donna and my mother started cooking dinner.

By early afternoon John and I were helping my mother set the dinner table. The table sat in front of a big picture window with a view of the road. While we were setting the table, I saw Ricky Lewis drive by pulling a flat bottom rowboat attached to the back bumper with a chain, and Billy Wenzel and Ronnie were sitting in the boat. As John and I looked at each other and smiled, I heard my mother say, "Oh, no. Don't even think about it."
"Why not?" I asked. "It looks pretty cool."
"Because you could get killed," my mother said.

We managed to con our way out of the house with the promise of not doing it and ran down the road to meet up with the guys.

We waited in the woods with snowballs, and after a few minutes they came back down the road. When they got in our sight, we hit the car once or twice, but what we were really waiting for was Billy and Ronnie in the boat. We bombed the shit out of them with snowballs.

Ricky stopped at the bottom of the road, and they waved for us to come down. When we got to the car, Billy and John got in the car, and I jumped in the boat with Ronnie. We drove up to the Lewis house, and John and Ronnie switched places. Then we turned around and headed back towards Chris and Chad's house. Rick was pretty good at pulling the boat. He knew how to cut the wheel of the car and make the boat weave back and forth like a pendulum. That weaving also meant there were a few close calls with snow banks.

When we got near the Taylor house, Ricky started honking the horn while we shouted and waved.

I'll never forget the look on my mother's face as her jaw dropped when she watched us sliding by in the back of the boat. We stopped at the end of French Road and got the car and boat turned around. I told Ricky, unless my mother was out standing in the road, not to stop and just keep on going. I figured I could only get in trouble once, but I could ride in the boat a few times before that happened.

After an hour or so, the boat started coming apart at the seams because of scraping on the dry spots on the road. One sign of this was the sound when the ice ran out and the metal boat hit the bare asphalt. There were also a lot of sparks.

Eventually everyone had to go home to eat dinner, so John and I would be dropped off first. Ricky told us he'd give us a great ride on the last run, and he lived up to his word.

We were doing about seventy miles per hour on the straight sections of the road. Then we had to pass the one-lane bridge just below Billy's house where I used to live when I first moved to the area. It required a bit of maneuvering at slow speeds, let alone the speed we were traveling at now. Ricky had to slide us through the bridge using the momentum of the car because the bridge was on a curve. He got us through, but now because of the higher speed, the boat was sliding along the driver's side of the car because of the pendulum like effect. Just then a car came over the hill, and we were in the path of a head-on collision.

The car was about twenty-five feet in front of us. We were close enough to see a family of four with the shocked looks of people who couldn't believe they are going to be hit by a rowboat. Only God and Ricky knew what Ricky did to get us out of it, but the next thing I know is we were on the passenger side of the car riding the snow bank sideways until Ricky got us straightened out.

We arrived at the Taylors' in a bit of a daze and got out of the boat. I looked at Ricky and said, "Wow, what a great ride."
John added," Yeah, and great driving, too. Thanks."

When we walked in the house my mother started yelling at us, "Don't you know you could have killed yourselves?"

I looked at her and said, "I know Mom. Believe me I know."

School still sucked for me but John was actually, doing well. He was getting eighties and nineties on his tests. By then I had done this grades work so many times I got seventies and eighties without even trying. I was also fooling around with a new girl on the school bus whose name was Lori. She had some accident when she was younger that had damaged her vocal chords. She spoke in a whisper, and I would joke with her and pretend I couldn't hear her when she would ask me to put my hands under her shirt.

One day I had the horror of finding the colt dead when I opened the barn door. After I was sure he was dead, I pulled his body out of his mothers view. I sat outside with his body for a while and decided I wanted something to remember him by. He was such a spunky little horse. I decided to skin his neck and make a vest out of it. Once done, I had the horse mane going down the middle of the back of the vest. I had learned to skin animals from some of the old-timers in the area. Every now and then they would toss me a deer head to practice on.

After I told my mother about it, she had someone come over and pick up the body for a fee. We had the other two horses checked out by a vet, and he said the mare had worms pretty bad and gave them to the colt, and that's probably why he died. The other horse was fine, but after talking it over, we asked him if he knew of anybody who might want the both of them. It was too much of a hassle taking care of them. I had fallen more than once on the snow taking them water, even though Brian had plowed a path in the snow with his truck. Another problem was spilling water on the path, and after the course of time it turned into an ice skating rink. The vet said he might know of someone, and in a few days they were gone.

Christmas had come and gone; it was lean but nice. Billy and Timmy Taylor were up for the holidays. They'd pick us up on their snowmobiles, and we'd hit the trails. It was considered a pretty warm day out at fifteen degrees without the wind chill factor. On a day like that, you'd have to wear a ton of clothes. I'd start with a pair of long Johns, one pair of wool socks, and a pair of regular socks. I wore a sweater and two pairs of dungarees, my leather jacket, and an Army coat over the top of everything. Last but not least, a facemask, regular hat, two pairs of gloves, and snowmobile boots. The theory up there was if you got hot in the winter, which was rare, you could take something off but better to be prepared than not.

This was a good set-up for riding the trails, but when we would go to school in the mornings we couldn't wear that many clothes. We'd catch the school bus at about six-thirty in the morning, and in order for John and me to get an extra fifteen minutes in the morning, we'd let Sarge pass our house and pick up some other kids first. He'd honk the horn for us as he went by so we could have an extra few minutes to get ready. That was when we'd get dressed into our school clothes. That usually meant sneakers, pants, a shirt jacket, and maybe gloves. Sarge had to come back towards our house by the post office that was fifty yards from our house in order to make his left turn to head up French Road to pick up more kids. It sounds like no big deal, but try it at twenty below, and with wind chills it would feel even colder. Sometimes it was so cold we would scrunch ourselves between the storm door and the inside door of the post office just to keep warm. The kids on the school bus thought we were nuts when they'd see us standing out there, instead of getting picked up at our house.

So like I was saying, we were out on the snowmobiles and were hitting the bars along the way as it got colder out. Some places had old-timer's bartending and, because of all the clothes you had on, they'd assume that we were old enough to drink, or it was a matter of them being too lit themselves to care. We were also hitting on a few joints that day, so we were getting a little toasted.

On the way back we decided to take a different trail. It was about a half mile shorter as opposed to the other way that went past a few bars. It was still about a four-mile trip and, because of that, we wouldn't have the chance to stop and warm up anywhere. Timmy's headlight didn't work, and it was getting late, so we decided to go for it. About three-quarters of the way back, Timmy was honking his horn, signaling Billy to stop. Billy finally got the message and pulled over, and Timmy said, "Billy, give me your mask. My face is freezing."

As Billy leaned back towards us he yelled, "How can your face be cold? You're wearing a scarf."

"No, I'm not," Timmy yelled back.

Billy got off his snowmobile and started walking towards us. As he got closer, I saw his eyes shoot open in amazement as he looked at Timmy's face. Then he pulled off his helmet and face mask and thrust it towards Billy.

I could tell something was out of whack because of the way the whole thing went down, so I said, "Timmy, let me see your face."

My jaw dropped, too, when I saw his face. The condensation from his breath had frozen on his day-old beard growth, and he looked like he had a beard of snow. "Holy shit!" I exclaimed.

Timmy looked at me and asked, "What? What's wrong?"

"Look in your mirror, Timmy," I told him.

He looked at his face and then back at me and said," Holy shit! My face is frozen!"

We stayed there for a little while until his face thawed out, and by then we were all pretty cold. I couldn't tell if my fingers were numb from the cold or because the strap I had to hold onto was under Timmy's big butt so that he was sitting on them as we rode. Whatever the reason, I couldn't feel my fingers. By the time we got back to my house, it was getting dark so Timmy and Billy decided to make the four-mile run home instead of coming in to warm up. I told them to give us a call when they got home, so we could make sure they got there. By the next day I found out that the reason that my fingers were tingling was because my fingers were frostbitten.

Regardless of how I felt about having to live in the country, I learned some simple things about life and how other people lived. The first year we lived there we didn't even have a washer or dryer. My mother had found this thing called a washing stick that we would use to wash our clothes. It was shaped like a funnel with a broom handle coming out of the thin end. We would put our clothes in the bathtub to soak, and then we had to pump this up and down I don't know how many times, until the clothes looked clean. In the winter, we'd lay our clothes on large baking trays around the wood stove to dry. In the summertime, we hung them outside.

John and I actually enjoyed doing the laundry this way because we would get a great workout. That and the weight set we were working out on led us to believe we were getting huge. It was the first time I had ever stuck to a weight training routine. It gave me a little more confidence while in school. I was able to press one hundred and ninety pounds over my head two or three times. Not bad for a sixteen-year-old who stood five foot ten inches tall.

John and I were getting pretty bored during the day. I mean, how many times can you do this, that, or the other over and over again? We were even tired of inventing things to do with our free time. I guess my mother was aware of it, and that's probably why she started letting me and John take the car out a few times by ourselves. She knew I could drive, because she had taught me years ago on country roads. It was funny how she'd tell us what time to be home. She would say, "Michael, there's a half tank of gas in the car, so come back when there's a quarter of a tank."

Our car was a powder blue 1971 Mercury Marquis with a four-twenty-nine cubic inch motor. Man, did that baby have a passing gear. We'd usually go rip roaring around on country roads. But the best was when we would hit the Jones Road. The Jones Road was a two-lane dirt road that was hardly used any more. It started by the West Canada Creek Bridge and ended at High Falls. It was about a five-mile trip with no streetlights, houses, or phones. It was pretty reckless, but I'd have the car going sideways at about sixty miles per hour after coming out of a turn.

As time passed and being that it was getting warm out now, my mother would let us have the car during the day, and we'd pick up the Lewis brothers and head for High Falls. We always made sure to take the Jones Road there and back now that I was driving.

Sometimes John and I would wonder if we should plan an escape back to New York City with the car. We always concluded my mother would find out we were okay and staying back at the house, but then she'd probably freak out and want to kill us for leaving her stranded up there. We also didn't want to deal with the risk of having to siphon gas all the way back.

Even the distraction of getting the car from time to time couldn't erase the thought of wanting to go home to the city. John was doing pretty well in school, but I had lost any ambition for it long ago, and I was just going through the motions. John even admitted that, even though the schools were a better environment, he was still pretty homesick. So now I had John on my side to bolster my argument with my mother for wanting to go back to the city. Finally after a lot of complaining and arguing with my mother, she told us that we would go back to the city at the end of the school year. John and I could hardly wait for the school year to end, and fortunately we didn't have to. We managed to get into another argument with my mother before the end of the school year and, in frustration, she said that we would leave now.

CHAPTER 5

BACK INTO THE ABYSS

The plan was to pack the car with as much stuff as we could and drive back to New York City. My mother would come back in about a month with a truck and get the rest of our stuff, she said. That I didn't mind, but I was totally against the plan she had about leaving Bobo up there until she came back. I told her that the dog could sit on my lap, but she said it would be too crowded. When I asked her why it would be too crowded, she explained that Brenda, an older girl I had fooled around with and who had become friends with my mother, wanted to see New York City for the first time, and my mother had agreed to take her. She told me not to worry because Brian and Donna Taylor would look after Bobo until she came back up. I didn't like the idea and asked her one last time.

"Are you sure you're going to come back for my dog?"
"Yes," she answered.
"And you're sure you'll come back for all my stuff?" I asked.
"Yes, I'm sure," she answered again.

A day after that we had the car packed and set sail for home. We were counting the hours back home, and I do mean hours. There was so much stuff in the car we had to drive pretty slow. The car was also using a lot of gas, so my mother decided to stop and fill the tank one last time which should get us home, she reasoned. We stayed there a few minutes to stretch and use the bathroom, and when I came back out, we stood there for a few minutes and watched the sun go down until everyone was ready to go.

There wasn't much conversation going on for the next hour except for Brenda and her excitement of finally getting to see New York City. While Brenda was explaining how she might like to stay and get a job, the rear driver's side tire blew out just as we crossed a bridge. My mother was trying to keep the car straight by counter steering but soon we were in a tailspin. As the car was midway into the spin, I looked at her and she shrugged her shoulders and took her hands off the wheel, which wasn't of much use to us any more anyhow.

As the car spun around we slid to the left across four lanes of traffic, and the passenger side of the car slammed into a large curb just past the bridge. After we came to a stop, my mother broke the silence and asked if everyone was okay.

We all looked at each other and said yes. I got out to look at the damage, and the first thing I noticed was that we had two flat tires. I couldn't tell right there and then in the darkness, but the frame looked like it was probably damaged, too. After that, I got into the car and drove it over to the shoulder of the road. My mother thought she'd seen a sign for a rest area that should be up ahead a little way. She said we should drive the car there, and that way we'd at least get something to eat while we decided what to do.

It sounded fine, and a lot better than sitting around in some damn cornfield by the side of the road. At about this time a trucker stopped and asked us if we needed any help. My mother asked me if I wanted to ride with the trucker to the rest area with Brenda, while she drove the car to the rest stop, but I said, "Well, being that you wouldn't let me drive all the way down here, I guess I can get to now."

"Fine, she answered, "I'll ride with Brenda, and you and John can drive the car."

Shortly after that, they left and John and I headed out. As it turns out, the rest area was about two miles down the road and halfway there both rear flat tires had fallen off the rims. John and I were getting a big kick out of the rooster tail of sparks coming off the rims when I slammed on the gas pedal. I was driving with the lights off, which made the ten to fifteen feet of sparks look even more dramatic. After what seemed like hours of driving at ten m.p.h., we were finally able to see the lights from the gas station at the rest area. As I got closer, I could see from the light off the signs that the gas tank was almost empty. I thought about it and figured that there was no way I could have used three-quarters of a tank of gas to travel two miles. I stopped the car and asked John, who had been riding on the trunk, if he smelled any gas from where he was sitting, and he said yes. Then I got out and stood a few feet away from the car and lit my lighter. I looked down on the ground and saw wet spots. Then I looked under the car from a few feet away and saw gas dripping from the gas tank. I looked at John and said, "John, if you and I are ever in a situation where sparks and gas are involved at the same time, do me a favor and let me know you smell gas."

When I got over to my mother, she told me she had called her friends, Big Joe and Little Joe. They were going to come up and get us in the morning. We were only a little over an hour from the city, and it was only about eight-thirty at night. I wondered why we had to wait until morning but figured beggars couldn't be choosers.

The car was stuffed with mostly things my mother had gotten from her flea market trips, probably destined to be put behind the walls in the attic with the rest of her treasures. It was difficult trying to get any sleep sitting up in a car seat. I didn't want to lie down on the ground for fear of waking up with an ear full of bugs. I finally did get to lie down on the hood of the car after it cooled off and managed to get some rest.

In the morning, when Big Joe and Little Joe showed up, my mother had already spoken to a mechanic at the rest stop. He said he could fix the car up for about two hundred. I told her to forget it, and Big Joe did as well. In the daylight you could see that the frame had been hit by the curb, but my mother insisted that she really liked the car and the mechanic said he could fix it. Whatever, I thought.

It was one of those real hot, humid mornings, and while we were unpacking the car and loading it into their van, I thought I'd give my two front teeth, which I didn't have, to be swimming in High Falls right then.

As we re-packed, my mother joked about how she had gotten into an accident moving upstate, and now she had gotten into one moving back.

One of the terms for my release from upstate was that I had to promise my mother that I would go back to school. It really sucked when I heard that I would have to go back to J.H.S. 189. The school was a three-year school for seventh, eighth and ninth grades. I was in the school for about two and a half years along with Project 25, and had never gotten out of the seventh grade, it seemed. Here it was almost two years later, and I was going into the eighth grade again. I mean, even if by some fluke I got promoted and never got left back again, I'd be about twenty years old when I graduated.

My mother went to school with me with my school records that first day so there wouldn't be any more screw-ups, and spoke with the guidance counselor. He took one look at me and said while he was laughing, "There's no way I could admit him to this school. Look at the size of him. He'd run the whole school. He's bigger than most of my 9th graders, and you want me to put him into the eighth grade?"

As it turns out, I got sent to Flushing High School with a class full of kids who were left back a year or two at some time or another, and now we were all sharing the ninth grade together. The first thing I noticed was how disrespectful the kids were to the teachers. For instance, let's say the teacher was writing something on the blackboard, and he or she would turn around and say, "Class, please be quiet." Half the class would stop talking, and the other half would tell the teacher to go fuck herself. I'm not saying that this would happen in all the classes, but it would happen more often than not. The teacher would be teaching to about half of the class, all of whom would sit up front so they could hear while trying to pay attention, as the rest of the class would just do their own thing.

The second thing about going there were the drugs. With the snap of a finger, you could get just about any drugs you wanted. Then there was the problem of having the willpower of even making it into school. For instance, on any given day you'd walk up towards the front door of school, and the first thing you'd meet up with was a group of guys and girls walking away from school. They'd say something like, "Hey, Mike, my parents are at work, and we're going to go to my house, hang out, get high and hopefully invite some girls and have some sex. Do you want to come?" So socially speaking you're supposed to say, "No, I want to go learn how to add fractions for the fourth time."

Then once you got close to the front doors, there would be another group of people taking the last few hits of a joint or popping some type of a pill or another, while trying to sell their wares. The final obstacle was when you'd walk through the front door, and kids would stop and say, "Fuck this," then turn around, walk back outside, and leave. Then you would go into your class, try to hear your teacher, and get some homework as a prize. I put up with about two weeks of this bullshit before I said to myself, I can't deal with two weeks. How the fuck am I going to do about four more years? So I stopped going. I'd say about the only thing school had done for me the last two weeks was to put me in touch with my old buddies.

After a while my mother stopped asking if I was going to school. That's not to say that it came about easily. My mother suggested that if I wasn't going to go to school, then I should get a job. Then one day I met up with my buddy Aaron who had been working up on Northern Boulevard at the carwash for some time after school on the weekends. I told him I needed to work, so he got me a job with him. I would get a couple of bucks an hour, under minimum wage, of course, and we'd split the tip box among four to six guys. So now I was a professional car swabber, which meant it was my job to wipe the excess water off a car when it came out of the washer. Some days you made shit; other days like Saturday or Sunday, you could make 100 dollars, or more, which wasn't bad for a sixteen-year-old.

I worked there for about a month or two, and then I started getting bored with my job and the pay. I remember the day I made the mistake of asking Ira, the owner, if I could have a raise. He lectured to me about how I was fortunate to have found him and this job, and that he was allowing me to have the opportunity to put a couple of bucks in my pocket, because technically he didn't really need anyone out there swabbing the cars down and making his customers feel obligated to give me a tip, etc., etc. Bottom line – I guess there wasn't going to be a pot of gold at the end of this rainbow. I decided to apply for a few other jobs, but let's face it, at sixteen years old without much work experience, who's going to give you a second glance or give a fuck for that matter?

I had learned through my Aunt Marie that my cousin Russell had ended up with a pretty good job in Manhattan. He had started out in some bar as a busboy and had now worked his way up to part-time bartender. I asked her for his phone number, but she told me that she didn't have a steady number for him or my cousin Ronnie since they had left home at about sixteen years old. I figured, "Shit, if Russell could do it, why couldn't I?"

The only part of the puzzle I didn't know was that Russell had gotten himself a phony I.D., so he would appear older. I got the paper and looked for some jobs in Manhattan one day. I set up about ten interviews for the following day. I got up early the next morning and squeezed onto the bus with the masses. Even though traveling on the crowded bus was a little uncomfortable, I was pretty happy about it. I looked at it like it was the beginning of my "rite of passage," you know, like becoming a man. I thought about it being a small price to pay, traveling in order to get my hands on my first check. Ahhh, and what I would buy with my first check, I thought. I got off at Main Street and made my way to the turnstiles, or corrals, one might say, of the subway station to take the number 7 train to Manhattan. I got onto the train but didn't get a seat; I realized that I wasn't fast enough. It had been a long time since I last rode the trains. I used to ride with Marcus to go work with his father. You had to have a quick ass in order to get a seat on the train in New York.

All the job interviews I had set up were for busboys in either bars or restaurants. When I got to 42nd Street, I switched trains to go downtown into the Village. I had always liked it there, not too many skyscrapers amongst other things. When I got to the first place and went in for my interview I walked into the manager's office. He asked me if he could help me, so I said, "Yes, I'm here for the job, as a matter of fact."

He looked at me and said, "How old are you?"
I told him, "Sixteen and a half, sir."
"Sorry, you're too young," he answered.

Wow, I thought. That certainly knocked some wind out of me.

Before I left, I decided to go into the bathroom to check myself out.

Hmmm, hair is fine, clothes are clean, there's no snot hanging out of my nose. I wonder what the fuck is wrong with him – I thought. Ahhh, fuck it, I've got nine other job interviews to go to. The only bitch about it is that I had to do a lot of traveling along the city, but it'd be worth it, I figured.

People were still running around trying to get to their jobs on time when I got back on the train. I came to realize that I had kind of screwed up a little when I made my appointments. I made them after each phone call instead of trying to map them out first and then scheduling them, because my next interview was uptown and then I would have to travel all the way back down here. But what the hell? It'll be worth it.

At the second interview, the guy explained that he could probably use me for deliveries. I asked him what I would make, and he said, "Probably tips."
"What else would I get paid?" I asked.
"Nothing, just tips."

Shit, I thought, I can remember making deliveries at my father's pizzeria, and sometimes the people wouldn't tip at all. I don't have any time to travel all the way here to possibly make money for the day, so I told him I'd call him back.

The next job was for a bar-back in a bar, which was like a busboy in a restaurant. The guy spoke to me for a few minutes and said that I was too young to work in a bar. I said, "Yeah, but my cousin works in a bar and he's not much older than me."

He answered, "Well, that may be. But you're too young to work here! Goodbye!"

Ahh, fuck him, I thought. I wouldn't want to work in this dump anyway.

The next one was at a diner. I was starting to get a little discouraged, and I was a little surprised when I made it past the interview. I guess telling him about how I used to run my mother's and father's luncheonette kind of made him interested. Then I went out with him to go over my job duties. It was lunchtime about now, so it was a little busy.

"Okay, the first thing you'd have to do in the morning is make the coffee. Then get all the creamers out of the refrigerator and make sure they're all full. Then after the customers start coming in, you have to set up the tables. After they leave, you take the dirty dishes and start loading up the dishwasher. Then go back out, break down the tables you just set up, and clean dishes. After the dishwasher is full, you turn it on and if you see, like now, the dishes start piling up in the sink and you start running out of clean ones, start cleaning the ones in the sink. Then after breakfast, it starts slowing down. First thing you do is check the creamers. Oh I forgot, in the morning you have to have at least two pots of each coffee regular and de-caf on the side, so keep your eye on that. So lunchtime, first thing, you check with the cook and whatever he needs done – you do for him. Clean lettuce, make tuna fish, get butter, whatever he asks – you do. Oh yeah, that goes for the waitresses, too. Then you do just about the same thing for lunch as you did for breakfast. It's just about the same routine for dinner, but by that time my son usually comes in after school and helps out. But always make sure you have plenty of coffee. It's a bit of a long day, but you'll get used to it. I know I'm forgetting one or two things, but you'll get the hang of it. You'll work from Monday to Saturday, and I'll start you at, let's say…$200 per week. Do you want to start now?"

I guess when he saw my eyes open up to the size of owls; he probably mistook that expression for me being overjoyed. What he didn't know was that I was about to ask him if he was shitting me.

"Well, I have a few more interviews to go on today. Is it all right if I call you back at about dinner time?"
"Sure, sure," he said. "And remember that's $200 a week – cash."

After I left I thought to myself, Shit, I can make two hundred on a weekend working at the car wash, fuck. I hope Russell didn't start out like this. I could have gotten him a job at the car wash too.

The rest of the interviews were much of the same story. At about a quarter to eight at night, I walked around the city trying to find my ego, which I had lost on my last interview. After a while I started to get a little tired and decided to start heading home. I took a different route back home and ended up having to change trains at 79th Street in Queens, to catch the number 7 train. As I was changing trains I stopped into the bathroom to take a leak. It was about the most pleasurable thing I had felt the whole day.

While I was peeing, this guy walked in and stood by me at the urinal. I glanced over at him because it didn't seem like he had opened his pants before he stood there. He caught my eye and said, "Hey, kid, I'll give you ten bucks if you let me suck your dick."

I laughed to myself and said to him with a frown on my face: "If I let you suck my dick, you'll give me ten bucks!"
"Okay, okay, make it twenty because you're so handsome, but that's it, only twenty," he answered.

Shit, this is the best job offer I had all day, I thought. "That's all right. I'll pass, but thanks anyway," I said.
"You know, you're not on 7th Avenue, honey. You're in Queens, and twenty dollars is good money for Queens," he answered.

I told him, "Look, I didn't come in here to get my dick sucked. I appreciate your offer, but I came here to take a piss – that's all."

He started to talk again, saying, "Well, maybe we could go to my place and have a drink or something and …"

I interrupted him and said, "Bye. Thanks. See ya', toodaloo," as I zipped up and walked out the door.

As I was riding the escalator upstairs I thought, Shit, maybe I should go stand by the women's bathroom and see what happens. I did, but I didn't get any offers, so I left.

It was kind of late when I got back to Main Street, and I was pretty glad to see that Hurdy Gurdy, a restaurant, was still open. I walked in and picked up a menu, when this guy started calling me from down on the other end of the counter.

Well, low and behold, Ronnie Kershner, my buddy from high school. We hadn't seen each other in a few years, and we started bullshitting about some of the crazy things we had done in high school. Then I asked about some of the people we hung out with in Turkey Park. As Ronnie started answering me, he picked up a doughnut and stared at it. I said, "Ronnie, what the fuck are you doing?" He looked at me, smiled, and then proceeded to squish the entire doughnut into his mouth.

He had managed to take three to four chews before he spotted someone who came walking out of the back room. Then he frantically tried to destroy the evidence with one swallow, which I thought would be a tremendous feat if accomplished, which it wasn't. In a split second, his expression changed from smart-ass to distress as he managed to choke himself on the doughnut. Having almost choked to death myself once, I knew he still had a little time on his hands and figured that instead of getting all worked up, I'd let him see if he could figure something out for himself. Besides that, I wasn't in any big rush to stick my hands down his throat like my mother had done to me.

We had eye contact, but no such thing as the Heimlich Maneuver then. By now Ronnie was wide-eyed and pointing at his throat to try and tell me what I already knew, which was that he was choking. I was still hoping that he'd figure this thing out for himself. I mean, Shit, he still has about 40 seconds' worth of air left in him. Then finally after what seemed like hours, he dove head first into the slop sink, turned on the water, and started making weird gurgling noises as dishes and stuff started falling off the counter around him. At this point the guy who was walking out from the back said, "What the fuck is going on?"

I looked at him and said, matter of factly, "He's dying."

Ronnie stood up, looked at me with a crazed look, and said, "Gee, thanks for getting upset and trying to help me, Mike. But don't worry. I got it under control."

"Ronnie, look. You know I love you, but if it was your turn to die, who am I to interfere? Besides, you know in your heart I would've come to your funeral."

He looked at me and said, "You fucking nut, I could've died."

Ahh, it was good to be home.

I went over to Ricky Dale's house today; his mother told me that he had moved back out to North Port, Long Island, with his father. I asked her if she had his phone number, which she did, and then I went up the block to see if Donde was home. When I got there, his mother answered the door. She was happy to see me and told me that "Donde" wasn't home, but to check at Bowne Park because he'd probably be there. So, I walked a block and a half over to the park, and sure enough he was there. I hung out with him until he had to go home and then for the fuck of it I went down by 34th Ave. to Bench Park, one of my old hangouts, on the way home.

When I got there I saw some people were hanging out, so I stopped by to see if I knew anybody. Jimmy Marnell was there; so were Jimmy "Peck" Schlishmen, and Joe De'Silvio. They were all happy to see me and, yup, you guessed it, a bunch of joints were lit up. Marnell asked me what I was up to, so I told him I was working up at the car wash. Jimmy said, "Aw, fuck that. I'll front you some weed to sell. You could probably make more in two days than you could working all week at the car wash."

I stayed there till about 4 in the morning and when I got two blocks away from my house I wondered if I should go home, and go to bed, or if I should walk two blocks in the other direction to the car wash and find a place to sleep over there. I could probably fall asleep in the back by the door and get awakened in the morning when they opened up for work. Then I thought I must be stoned. Oh, yeah, I forgot, I am. I guess I'll go home and go to bed for a while. When I got home, I lay in bed for a while and thought about Jimmy's offer until I dozed off to sleep.

I got up late for work, threw my clothes on, and ran down the block to work. When I stepped outside, it was one of those hot, humid, sticky days already. When I got there, Ira came over to me, frowned, and said, "You're late!"

I'm thinking to myself, Thank God you told me, Ira... I might have been confused the whole fucking day. Oh, man, he's still standing there. I hope that he doesn't want me to come up with a mental blowjob for an excuse. Shit, he's still there. Oh well, here it goes.

"I'm sorry, Ira. My dog ran out and got hit by a car," I said.
"Well, all right. Just make sure it doesn't happen again!" he said and walked away.

Muskie, a guy who worked there, looked at me and said, "Shit, Mike, how many dogs do you have?" Then we all had a good laugh.

I felt like shit, no sleep, hung over, hot and sweaty. Every time someone wouldn't throw any chump change into the tip box, I'd think to myself that offer of Jimmy's was starting to sound better and better. By the end of the day, I made just about $100 I figured that after I'd throw my mother a few bucks, I'd have a pocket full of nothing. After work, I went home and fell asleep.

I woke up about ten that night, grabbed something to eat, and went over to Bench Park to see if Jimmy was around. When I got there, Jimmy was hanging out with Peck. I asked him to give me the breakdown on what I would make moving the shit, and he told me.
"When can I start?" I said.
"Right now if you want."
"All right, fine. I'll give it a shot."

On that note Jimmy reached into his pocket and pulled out an ounce of weed. But then he said, "Mike, remember. Don't go smoking this shit up when I front it to you. I don't want to have to knock you around."

As I walked away, I reminded myself that Jimmy was a little bit older and about twice my size, so I probably didn't want to get knocked around by him. I walked up to Bowne Park, and there was a bunch of people hanging out, so I asked if anyone wanted to cop any weed. Ricky Dale happened to be there, and he asked me if I had brought some down from the mountains. I laughed and said that I did, and then Ricky explained that he had just driven in from Long Island that night. After we got done talking, everybody bucked up, and I had my first sale underway. I figured, Shit, that was pretty easy. I might as well go ask some of the older guys on the other end of the park if they want any. I asked Donde to lend me his bike, and I rode over there.

The guys who hung out over by the park house were a little bit rowdy, but I had met some of them through other older friends. I rode up and said, "Hey, does anybody want to buy any weed?"

I looked around at the faces and realized that I didn't recognize anyone, but what the fuck? So one guy says, "Why? You can get weed, you little shit?"
"Yeah," I said feeling a little brave. "Why? You want some or not?"

They talked amongst themselves, and then one of them said, "Sure, we'll take an ounce. What's the price?"
"Seventy-five bucks," I said while trying to calculate my piece of change.
"Seventy-five bucks! It better be good shit, kid, and you don't get the money until I see the shit."
"It's fucking great, you'll love it, and then you'll probably be looking all over the place for me to get some more," I told him.
"Well, it better be, you little wiseass," I was told.

I explained to them that I had to take a little ride to go get the stuff, and then I pedaled my little ass over to Jimmy and told him I needed more weed.

"Here, Jimmy. Here's some money I already made. I've got to have the other one fronted to me again, and don't fuck me up. It better be good shit, or I might get my ass kicked."

Jimmy looked at me as I handed him the money and said, "How much of the first ounce do you have left?"

I opened up the bag that I had left, and then Jimmy said "Not bad. I guess you're a little business man now. But are you sure these guys are cool?"

I thought about it for a minute, because I wasn't about to tell him that where I was selling this was where I had met some guys through him. Then I figured I'd better not; otherwise, he might drive over there and do the deal himself. I told him that I knew they were cool, because they were smoking some hash when I got there.

"They got hash? Find out how much they want for it, all right?"

"Yeah, no problem. I will."

Then I rode over to Bowne Park by the bigger guys. When I got there, a few more of them had shown up to hang out. I rode over to the guy I had been talking to and said, "Hey, I got it. Where's the money?"

"Hold on," he told me. "Let me smell it first," which he did. Then he looked at me and said, "Hey, you're right. It is good. Now scram before I kick your ass!"

I hollered at him, "Hey, fuck you, man. I need to get the money or the weed back, or I'll get a beating."

"Oh yeah? Well you're going to get two ass kickings tonight if you don't scram, kid!"

Great, I thought. If I don't get this weed back, not only might Jimmy kick my ass, but I won't make any more money, and I don't want that to happen. Besides, if I show Jimmy that I already got a few lumps for standing up for myself, he might let me off the hook. I took a deep breath, wished that I had gotten a little more stoned before this, and said, "Fine, kick my ass, and show everybody what a big man you are!"

Then he walked over to me and threw me off the ten-speed bike onto the ground. I jumped up and yelled at him, "Give me the fucking weed, man!" hoping some of the other guys would hear me and maybe cut me some slack.

I think it might have worked, because one or two guys started saying: "Ohhhh, we got a little tough guy here."

Then I looked through the crowd of about fifteen guys and saw Moose, an older guy that Jimmy had introduced me to years earlier. Moose was a little slow in the brain but big on muscle. I yelled, "Hey, Moose! These guys are trying to steal my weed!"

Moose looked at me and said, "Hey, Mike! Who's trying to steal your weed?"

That was it. I was in. As ugly as he was, he looked like a fucking angel with wings to me at that moment. Moose was twice this bum's size, and I could see his eyes widen as Moose looked around for the culprit. Now I felt like a big shit, and I said, "Yeah. This guy right here, Moose, and he just threw me on my ass, too."

The other guys started backing away from this guy as Moose walked towards him. It was great to see him starting to shrink into a mouse. "No, Moose. I was going to pay him. I was just fucking with him until he wised off, that's all," he lied.

Moose walked over to him, smacked him off the top of his head, and said, "Well, don't fuck with him. He's a good kid. Hey!" Moose yelled out as he picked me up by my armpits and stood me on the park bench. "Does everybody see this kid? Well, nobody fucks with him unless they want to fuck me! All right? He's a good kid, and he's been through a lot of shit. Fuck, a bus even hit him, and he's still here. Look, show them your teeth, Mike."

Which I did, and a few of the other guys went, "Ohhhhh." Then a few of them said, "Okay, Moose, he's cool. Nobody'll fuck with him."

I felt so good that I wanted to hug Moose, but I knew he'd kick my ass if I did, so I didn't. The guy who whacked me walked over, paid me, and said, "Sorry, kid."

Oh, I swear I wanted to take a poke at him.

After that was over, Moose and I sat down on the bench and started bullshitting. Then he leaned over to me and pushed a small spoon under my nose. I asked him what it was, and he said, "Don't worry. If anything it'll put some hair on your chest. After I snorted it, he dug it back into his vial and said, "Here, you'll need at least two hits."

While we sat there, I remembered that Jimmy wanted to smoke some hash, so I asked Moose to get me a price on the hash from the guy who had been filling up bowls of it. Moose said he'd check it out. While Moose walked over to the guy, I sat there and felt like a big shit hanging out with the big guys now, smoking joints, and getting high. To think all it took was getting tossed onto the concrete once and having a little luck that Moose was there. It could have very easily gone the other way, though, and I could be waking up licking my wounds, headed for another little thumping.

Moose came back over and told me the guy had blonde hash, and he gave me the price. I said, "Moose, this guy isn't going to fuck me if I come back with the money, is he?"
"No don't worry, Mike. I'll throw him a beating if he does."
"All right, I'll be back in a little bit."

By this time I started to feel a little buzzed, so I asked Moose what he had given me. He looked at me, smiled, and said; "A little speed, Mike. It'll make the night go by faster."

I hopped onto the bike and rode over to the other side of the park. It was "Donde's" bike, and when I pulled up, he said, "Where'd ya' go?"
"Well, it's kind of a long story, but I went to go and sell some weed to the park boys," as they were called. "I got thrown off the bike, almost got my ass kicked, and almost got beat for the weed. But lucky for me, my friend Big Moose was there, so he settled everything for me. Then I hung out with the boys, smoked some hash, did some speed, and then rode over here."

Donde looked at me and said, "You didn't fuck up my bike, did you?"
"No, Donde, I got thrown on the concrete – not your bike. But I'm fine. Thanks for asking."

Somebody else in our crowd said, "You can get some hash or speed?"
"Well, I don't know about the speed, but I can definitely get some hash."
"Cool, get me some."
"Yeah, me, too," someone else said.

I told these guys I would, but I would have to get the money up front. They said fine and paid me. I went to get back on the bike, and Donde said, "Oh no, don't take my bike. You're going to fuck it up."

I reached into my pocket, pulled out a bunch of twenties, and said, "If I fuck up your bike, I'll pay for it, all right?"

Donde looked at me for a long second, and then said, "All right. I might not be here too much longer, so if I'm not, leave it behind my house next to the pool.

After that I started to ride the bike over to Bench Park and felt like I could ride forever. I guess the speed was kicking in.

When I got to Bench Park, I told Jimmy that they had some hash and the prices on it. As I started to count out his money, he said, "Fuck it. Take the money, and score me some hash." So I sped back over to Bowne Park, waved at my guys, and went over to the park boys.

I went over to Moose and told him how much hash I needed. He said, "Shit, you got that much money on you?"
"Yeah," I answered. "Look," I said as I pulled out a small wad of twenties.
"I guess you do. Hey, Headly, Headly, come'ere."

Headly wasn't his real name I found out, but everyone just called him that because he always had some type of drug on him. After he walked over, Moose told him how much hash I needed and warned him to do the right thing with me. I gave him the cash, and he handed me back twenty dollars and walked over to his car. Moose pushed the spoon back under my nose twice, and I thanked him. Headly came back and handed me a big chunk of hash in a sandwich bag. After he walked away, I said, "Moose, you gotta show me how to break this stuff up. It's going to three people."

Moose said he would, and then we walked over to an empty park bench.

"Now, who gave you how much for what?" he said as he ripped the sandwich bag in half and pulled out the tinfoil from my cigarettes. I told him the breakdown, and he explained in one breath, "Okay, this piece is for this guy," as he pulled off a little piece of the chunk. "This piece is for this guy, and this big piece is for the other guy. Now you made ten dollars off of this one, fifteen off this one, and twenty off this one. Not to mention the twenty Headly handed back to you. This piece," he said as he pulled off a small piece from the largest chunk, "is for you, and this piece," as he broke that in two, "is for my teaching lesson," and threw it in his pocket. Now come on, let's get you a beer, and go smoke some of Headly's hash. Oh yeah, and I'll tell him to hook you up any time you need something."

Then we went back over to the group and caught a buzz. Before I left, I got Headly's phone number. Then I rode back towards my guys on the other side of the park. I didn't realize it but I was pretty ripped by then. I also made some cash and some hash. I got over to my guys, and they immediately sparked up some hash and joints to celebrate the arrival of the hash. I stayed there a bit, smoked up, and then headed for Jimmy at Bench Park. As I rode over, I thought it must be amazing that I haven't crashed on the bike yet. When I got up there, Jimmy had just finished rolling a joint and, as I came to a stop, he tossed it to me and said, "Here, spark up."

I looked at him and said, "I don't know. I'm pretty ripped."

Jimmy said, "Don't worry. Here, sit down. Smoke some weed, and then I'll make a sandwich in a bowl with the hash and some weed. You do have the hash, right?"
"Yeah," I mumbled.
"Cool," Jimmy answered.

As I sat back on the bench, I realized that I had gotten more stoned tonight than ever before.

Needless to say I got to work late the next morning. Ira looked at me and said, "I know, I know, your dog got hit by a car again, right? Just get to work."

It turned out to be another hot sweaty day. Eventually I started working there less and less, and I got my own bicycle to make my rounds, which started to get a little bigger.

Over the course of time, I completely stopped working at the car wash. My thinking was, what the hell, I've been paying someone else for me to get high. Now I was getting high for free and putting a little cash in my pocket, just by doing a little running around. Eventually I saved up a couple of hundred and bought myself a little car to scoot around in. It was a 1970 Cutlass Supreme. That's not to say that it was legal. I had thrown a pair of plates on it and would only go out with it at certain hours.

By now I was hanging out at three different locations. One area was at Bowne Park. I had met most of these guys from the time I went to St. Andrew's Catholic School. I would hang with them and the guys from their neighborhood. Then I would hang out at Bench Park with the guys from my neighborhood. And finally, I would hang with the guys that I had gone to public school with over on 149th and Northern Boulevard, over at the Raven luncheonette and Volcano Pizzeria. With the three locations, I was keeping myself busy and high. But for the most part, I started hanging out more and more over at 149th, probably because there were more girls than guys hanging out there than at any of the other spots.

Another reason why I liked hanging out there was that most of the guys and some of the girls were into sports. For instance, we would play handball against the wall on the side of the luncheonette, but I don't mean for an hour. We'd start playing at about 10 – 11 at night, and sometimes we'd still be playing at 3 or 4 in the morning. But the best part about hanging out there was football; four of us were fanatics. It was Tony, Cody, Eddy Mc Allister and I. All we needed was an excuse to play day and night, rain or shine-we loved our football.

We played on concrete so we'd usually play two-hand touch, but occasionally we'd play tackle and not the type where you'd just run into the guy. We made it a rule that you'd have to put the guy down any way possible, except for punching him in the face. But it would come close to that sometimes. We wouldn't play this way very often because it would sometimes take a week or two to heal. Another guy I hung out with over there was Joey Gatto. It was funny, but my mother had hung out with his father at times when they were kids in Astoria.

I drove up to Bowne Park, to see if any of the boys were hanging out. Nobody was there when I first got there, but soon everybody showed up. Ricky Dale showed up with his brother Bobby again. They had both come in from Long Island where they lived with their father. Their older stepbrothers, Michael and Robert, were with them, too. Then Donde showed up with Gerald and Pete.

I had first met Pete in the drug program I was in, and he started hanging with me and my friends back then. We stole Gerald from another group of guys after he had gotten into a fight with a bunch of twelfth graders at their graduation party. He beat up four guys out of a group of ten he was fighting with before the cops came and broke it up. Not bad for an eighth grader.

"Pete, holy shit – I haven't seen you since the project. What are you doing here...? I heard you were in a home."
"Yeah, I was for a little while. Then when I came back, I met up with Donde."
"Yeah, he's been hanging out a long time now," Donde said. "Your cousin Dino even drives up from time to time," he added.
"Yeah," Ricky said, "I forgot to tell you Dino lives out by me now. He's been dating some girl named Robin."
"Dino ended up with me at Camp Mc Cormick when I was there, and after about eight months Dino broke out and got away," Pete said.
"Get the fuck outta here."
"Yeah, one day this new kid moves into our barracks, and I look and it's fucking Dino. I had a great time there after that," Pete added.
"Wow. Small world, huh?" I said.
"Yeah," he answered.

About an hour later, Frank Tamaro, Joe Coulon and Steve Catalano showed up with two other guys. These guys were more like Robert and Michael's age. After a while, some of us started smoking some more pot and drinking beers, amongst other things. Then I don't remember how it started, but someone started to hang moons at cars as they passed by.

The next thing you know it was four, seven, twelve of us out there walking around with our pants around our ankles, waving at cars as they drove by. After about fifteen to twenty minutes of this, it all started to dwindle down back to one guy, Steve's friend. So he stood there for what seemed like another five minutes. Then all of a sudden, a cop car rolls up to the intersection.

We all started yelling at him that there was a cop car behind him, but he didn't believe us. Now the cops were staring at us, wondering what we were yelling about, which would have given him plenty of time to pull his pants up. Instead he sat there with his back towards the cops, telling us to go fuck ourselves because he knew that there were no cops behind him.

At this point the cops had seen him, and they started to turn the corner towards him. He must've seen the headlights shining on the trees and then on us, because he turned around and said, "Oh, fuck!" Then he dropped his beer, bent over, and grabbed his pants from around his ankles, which happened to fully moon the cops, pulled them up, and started to run into the park.

We all started chanting, "Go, go, go," as he ran. I don't know why he ran into the park instead of across the street into the backyards, but I guess he had his own plan. The park offered no cover, and the cops had jumped the curb and were now chasing him through the park in their car. He made it all the way to the other side of the lake, which was about 150 yards away, when another cop car entered the park on the other side. He was fucked. To make it even more comical, he decided to jump into a bunch of newly planted bushes that were only about 12 to 15 inches high. We were laughing our asses off, looking at each other going, "Shhhhhh... he's hiding."

We walked over there as the cops were writing him some tickets, and they told us to scram or we'd make it worse for him, so we went back to our benches. He came back over about a half hour later.

As it turns out, Steve's friends were brothers, and when the one brother came back, his older brother was ranking on him, telling him what an asshole he was for getting caught. This went on for about another fifteen minutes until the other brother, who said nothing up to this point, said, "Oh yeah, well, when we left home today, I thought I'd do you a favor and grab your wallet for you. But I guess it turned out that I did a favor for myself by giving them your I.D."

The other brother didn't believe him so the summons was shown to him, and he said, "You motherfucker," which led to another chase around the lake. We were all screaming again, "Go, go, go." He caught him on the other side of the lake, and they started going at it until we all ran over and broke it up. Needless to say, it was a very comical night.

Jimmy Duguid stopped by today; he had a habit of doing that from time to time since I came home. His new thing was starting a wrestling match with you until he started to lose, then he would grab your nuts and squeeze them until you yelled "Uncle." Unfortunately, it was only a matter of time before this sick game got passed on to other people I knew at Bowne Park and Bench Park.

So this day Jimmy stopped by with a 1973 Plymouth Grand Fury. It was similar to the ones that the cops in my neighborhood would use as undercover cars. He pulled up with it, and the first thing I asked him was if it was stolen, and he swore it wasn't. He started bragging and going into much detail about how fast the car was. I told him the car was probably a pig and didn't move at all, so he offered to give me a test ride in it. I didn't have anything better to do, so I took him up on his offer.

We started out on 150th Street, and headed towards Whitestone until we got to Bayside Lane. He had already blown one stop sign and screeched the tires as he made his right hand turn, so I sat there yawning, with my hand up covering my mouth for dramatic effect. We caught a green light up on 154th Street, and we were passing Bowne Park doing about 80 m.p.h. I sat there and made sure he knew I was totally un-amused and bored. By now he was taking his short little breaths, which would signal that he was getting frustrated or crazy, depending on the circumstances. So he slams on the brakes and made a hard turn on the right into Bowne Park. Fortunately, it was a weekday at about 2 in the afternoon so the park wasn't that crowded. I sat there and asked him if he noticed the squirrels playing with each other as we flew past the trees. By now his face was turning red from frustration as he hauled ass the three blocks it took to get to Northern Boulevard, which is one of the busiest streets in Queens.

We stopped at the red light, and he looked at me and said, "So, you want to play rough, huh?"

I yawned again.

Jimmy looked left, then right, and reached under his seat, pulls out a flashing light, like the cops use, and put it on the roof of the car. He plugged it into the lighter and hit a switch he rigged to sound like a siren. Then he started inching out through the red light. When other cars saw him, they started to slow down, and Jimmy nailed it and made a left turn. Now he was weaving in and out of traffic as we started picking up speed. Meanwhile Jimmy's got this stupid, determined look on his face. By the time we were doing 70 m.p.h., down Northern Boulevard, I was starting to get a little nervous, although it was pretty cool watching people stop or swerve out of your way thinking you were a cop. But after the lights turned red for us and he was still doing seventy, I knew I had to say something. I could just sense him wanting me to say "Uncle," which made me hold out for a few near misses with other cars. Finally I said, "All right, Jimmy... Uncle," which I knew he was waiting for me to do, so he just had to slam on the gas and go faster. I had to bite my tongue and let him go faster because I now knew he was trying to make me scream like a bitch and beg him to stop. So I did the opposite. I looked out the window and calmly said, "Jimmy, if you don't slow down or stop, I'm going to punch you in the head."

He looked over at me as we were swerving through the cars and said, "If you do that, we'll probably crash."

As I continued to look out the window, I said, "The way I see it, we're probably going to crash anyhow so I might as well get a shot in on you before we do."
"I don't think you'll do it," he said, so I tried to but he dodged the shot.

Now we're swerving in and out of traffic, lights flashing, sirens blasting and me throwing punches at him as he's laughing and yelling, "A'ha, I got you!" I managed to get in one or two good body shots, which might have made him slow down and stop but I'm not sure.

Once we stopped, he looked at me all serious and said, "Man, you're a tough one. Everyone else would start screaming once I flicked on the siren."

After that we drove over to 169th and Crocheron Avenue, to see if Scott Pete or other guys were around. We drove around for a while and ran into Vinny Wenzel. He came over to the car and started talking to Jimmy, and then said hi to me after he saw me and asked about my cousins. Then he started telling Jimmy that Detective Lizio had come over to his apartment one day with another cop to question him about some things. Vinny said he had nothing to hide, so he let them into the apartment.

"So, Jimmy, he starts asking me about that store that got broken into up the block, and I tell him I don't know shit about it, and then out of the blue him and the other cop grab me and toss me onto the floor. So I'm not fighting back or nothing, and as I'm laying there, he lights up a cigarette and keeps asking me about the store up there. So I tell him I don't know shit about it, and this cocksucker burns me with a cigarette. I go to yell, and he puts his hand over my mouth, burns me, and asks me again. He does this four or five times, Jimmy, and I finally told him."

"Told him what?" Jimmy asked.

"I told him you did it... What the fuck was I supposed to do? He was burning the shit out of me, Jimmy," Vinny answered.

"You know you're fucked up, Vinny."

"I'm sorry, Jimmy, but what was I supposed to do?"

"Well, good thing you told me. At least now I can come up with an alibi. All right, I'll see you later."

Vinny said, "I'm sorry, Jimmy," as we drove off.

"Jimmy, do you believe that?" I asked.

"What? That Vinny told on me?"

"No, I mean the part about Lizio burning Vinny with a cigarette?"

"Yeah, he probably did it. He's a scumbag. There's even some talk that he's the bag man for the mob," Jimmy explained.

"What do you mean, like he's in the bag?"

"I don't know. I'm not 100 percent sure, but he's been with some real shady characters, ya' know, talking about the weather."

My mother started busting my horns about the hours I was keeping and not working... so she thought. She added that she thought it would be a good idea for me to get my G.E.D. She also said that she had spoken with Joey Gatto's father, and he said that it would be a good idea for his son to get his also. This way, my mother explained, she could drive the both of us over to Queens College together.

"Great, I'll think about it," I told her.

"Well, think about that or think about moving out," she said.

I decided that checking out the school thing might be a little easier than finding an apartment right now, so I elected to go.

My mother dropped Joey Gatto and me off at Queens College to take the tests for the G.E.D. There were two tests to take, one for reading and one for math. We sat down for the tests, and we were told that we were allowed a certain amount of time for each test. Then we were asked if there were any questions. After that we were told to begin. The reading test was first, and after I got done, I looked around and realized that I was the first one done in the whole class. It scared me a little bit, so I went back and checked some of my answers. After that, we did the math test. This time I hadn't finished the whole test before the time ran out. When the tests were over, we had a bit of a break time while we were being scored. I asked Joey how well he thought he did, and he wasn't sure about it.

After about a half hour, we went back in to get our grades. The teacher would call out your name and then give you your grade, and then she asked you what was the last grade you finished in high school. When she got around to me, she said, "Michael, 13.6 reading, 10.5 math level."

"Aw, shit," I said, thinking about how fast I had gotten done.

The teacher said to me, "Michael, do you have a problem with this?"
"Well, yeah, 13.6 reading. Doesn't that mean I failed the reading test? I mean it only goes up to twelve, right?"
"No, actually the reading test goes into two years of college, which would be a score of 14. By the way, what was the last grade that you completed?" she asked.
"Completed...? Well, that would be the 7th grade."

She looked at me and exclaimed, "No way. Impossible." Then she made a cross reference with some paperwork that my mother had obtained and made me take in. She looked at it, and then under her breath she said, "Holy shit, you're right."

By now I was starting to get a little embarrassed because some of the other kids were staring at me. But I really got embarrassed when she got up and said that she was going to get somebody to talk to me.

As soon as she left the room, I said, "Joey, fuck this. I'm leaving."

Joey looked at me and said, "What are ya' crazy? Stay here. Maybe they'll just give you the G.E.D. and be done with it."

When the teacher came back, she told me that someone would be down shortly. After a little while another teacher showed up, called my name, and asked me to follow him. I'm thinking, Oh yeah, baby, give me the G.E.D., and I'm outta here.

We walked into a little room, and then he sat down, introduced himself, and told me his title and position, which sounded pretty fancy. I asked him why he had brought me in here and if he was going to give me my G.E.D. He said, "I can't give you anything. That you'll have to do a little work for, but I am going to offer you a scholarship to attend this college."

Oh great, I thought. I didn't even want to come here for an hour, and now he's asking me if I want to spend a few years here.

"Look, I'm grateful for your offer, but I can't deal with school any more. I've had my fill of it."
"Michael," he said, "college is not like junior high school. It's much different here. Young people come here because they want to be here, not because they have to be, and I think if you give it a try you would see that. I think considering that you only completed the 7th grade, even if you tried a little bit you would do great."
"I can't. I don't have the time for homework or spelling words any more." I told him.
"Michael, do you realize that right now you are smarter than half the kids who completed the last four years of high school and have graduated?" he explained.
"I guess I do now. But really, all I came here to do is to get my G.E.D. so I can get my mother off

my back. That's all," I said.

Then he said, "I hate to tell you this, but I really think you are making a terrible mistake, and I wish you would reconsider."

"Look. Don't take this the wrong way, but it wouldn't be the first and probably won't be the last mistake I'll make. But no, I can't, but thank you for your time. Oh and please, don't say anything to my mother about this, O.K.?"

"Well, I think I'm professionally obligated to tell your mother."

"Listen, boss man, you tell my mother about this, and you and I are going to have a big problem."

"Excuse me!?"

"Listen, I don't mean to talk to you this way, you seem like a nice, caring man. But I'm done, I can't. I can't deal with this school bullshit anymore. I'm done."

"Okay, I won't. This conversation is between you and I, but if you would like to reconsider here's my card. You can call me any time. Good luck to you, young man," he said.

We shook hands, and I walked out of the room.

When I got back to the main room, the class was being let out. I met up with Joey and explained to him what had happened. He asked me if I was going to do it, and I told him no, that I couldn't deal with school any more. I ended up having to do a few study classes to ready myself for the main test and eventually took it and passed with a pretty decent score. At least I thought my mother would be off my back for a while. It kinda sucked that I felt this way about school now. There was a point in time when I really enjoyed school. But sadly, I wasn't in a position to override the personal decisions that individuals made for me over the years, of how smart, or how dumb I was while attending school.

"Pete" stopped by my house today; he asked me if he could borrow my car for a little while, so I told him it wouldn't be a problem as long as he had it back to me in about two hours. I didn't hear from him for five days, and when I did he called and said he thought he might have blown the oil pump on my car. I said, "I don't care what you did. Just get my car back to me."

That day when I came home, I saw a trail of oil leading down the block into my driveway. When I put the car on jack stands to check it out, I saw a piston rod hanging out of my oil pan. It wasn't the oil pump he had blown; it was the motor. I stopped by his house and asked him what he was going to do about it, and he offered to get me another motor. Well, so much for driving. I guess it's back to the bicycle for now.

One day a friend of mine, Joe "Dust," gave me a hit of mescaline which is similar to a light hit of acid. I liked it, and in no time at all I was getting more and more of it. We were also making some pretty constant runs to Harlem to score angel dust, P.C.P. That's how Joe had gotten his name, Joe "Dust." He would also score his heroin up there. He was crazy for the speedballs, which is when you mix heroin with cocaine. I'd snort it sometimes, but he loved to shoot up with it. I still liked taking mescaline a little better, and after a while I got up enough money to score a couple of hundred hits. Then it was off to the races. Joey "D" and I would make these weird combinations with heroin and mesc. One night we mixed mesc, and cocaine, but the wildest was when we would mix mesc with angel dust. When I say mixed, I don't mean in a test tube, I mean in our bodies. We'd get so twisted that I'd usually wake up stoned the next day. That's not to mention that by now I was doing three or four hits of mesc. I guess I was building up a tolerance to it.

My birthday had come and gone by now, seventeen... whoopee. Scott Pete had paid for another motor for my car. He got it from Aaron's friend up at the carwash. He was still working there, and everybody joked with him that he was probably sleeping with Ira and would be part owner soon. I made a few runs with Ricky Dale out to North Port in Long Island. Dino was still living out there, and so was Mike Viale. They were both doing fine. That's not to say that Ricky always got along with the both of them all the time.

Everyone that I was hanging out with liked mescaline and started asking me for more and more of it. My thoughts were like, Hey, if they're going to do it and buy it off someone it might as well be me selling it to them. Before no time I was copping a thousand hits at a time. I'd get them for $900 and sell them at three dollars a pop. Technically, it would seem like I was making a pretty good profit, but between bartering for other drugs, paying off my debts, and losing some in card games, which people loved to be in with me, I'd barely have enough to get the next thousand hits. I was also consuming quite a bit of it by now. I'd pop eight hits at a time, not to mention taking part in anything else that was going on.

When you keep yourself this high for a long amount of time, you don't even notice your realities walk right past you. Nor do you start to care, unfortunately. By now I kept myself so stoned most of the time I wouldn't see my realities frantically waving their arms in desperation right in front of my face. Realities such as, a good job, a house, a wife, kids, a future. The only things that matter when you're high, are right here, and right now. Everything else just fades from view.

Jimmy Duguid stopped by today. He had a different car. This one was a 1970 Dodge Demon. I asked what had happened to his Fury, and he told me that he had wiped it out while being chased by the cops one night. I asked why he was being chased, and he said that Guy Balsam had ratted him out and told the cops it was stolen.
"Oh, and this one isn't, right?"
"No, I swear I bought this one," he said.
"Yeah, your ass, Jimmy."
"Well, anyway I got even with Guy. I snuck up behind him and busted his ankle with a bat, so keep an eye out for the cops," he explained.
"So what...? You stopped here because you think I'm stupid enough to take another ride with you, Jimmy?"
"No, I stopped by because I've got a friend of mine looking for a room to rent if your mother's still renting."
"What is he, a fucking bum?" I asked.
"No, he works. He's got a business. He's a liquidator of stores that go out of business, and he needs space to store his stuff," he told me.
"What kind of stuff?" I asked.
"You know,.. all kinds of different stuff. It's hard to say. I mean, like, let's say a store goes out of business. Well, he sells whatever he can for the guy and keeps what's left over for himself. And then he usually sells that stuff, too. So I mean, don't worry he always has money, and even if he didn't pay you

rent for some reason – you could always keep his shit."

"Well, it doesn't sound half bad to me if he's got his own business. I'll have to pass it in front of my mother first." I said.

"No, I understand. You talk to your mother and then let me know and I'll…"

Before Jimmy had a chance to finish, a car swerved into my driveway and two guys jumped out. Jimmy's eyes popped open, and without saying a word, he jumped out of his car and took off like a bat out of hell down my driveway, into my backyard, and jumped the fence, with the two older guys chasing him and cursing at him to stop. After he got away, the two guys came over to me, and one of them said, "What were you talking about?"

"Who the fuck are you?"

"We're cops! That's who the fuck we are."

"Yeah, big shit, are you here to arrest me? If not, get the fuck out of my yard. You're on private property now," I explained.

"Oh, you're a wiseass, huh? What's your name?" The other cop asked.

"You're the cop; figure it out. That's your job, ain't it?"

"We'll see you around, wiseass," one of them said as they left.

Meanwhile, while I was aggravating them, I couldn't help worrying if Jimmy's "new" car was stolen. But the cops got into their car and left without even looking at it.

When I went inside, my mother asked me what the yelling was about outside, and I told her that some kids were playing tag through the yard.

"Listen, I spoke to Jimmy, and he said he has a friend that needs a place to rent to store some stuff."

"Yeah, but if he's one of Jimmy's friends, is he all right?"

I told her I didn't know for sure, but Jimmy had said the guy was in business, so he must be all right.

"Well, I'll check him out first and send him over for you to meet him," I told her.

After that my mother went inside, and I popped another hit of mesc and made myself a sandwich.

About an hour later Jimmy Duguid called on the phone. "Mike," he panted. "Did they take my car?"

"No, Jimmy, it's still here. When are you going to move it?"

"Listen, I got a better idea. I got a spare key under the seat. Get the car and meet me on the other side of Northern Boulevard. I'll be at the Long Island Railroad station. Then we'll go meet Jimmy Morgenstern. He needs a place soon, and he always has money on him."

"Yeah, I guess that sounds okay. Hey, wait a minute. This car's not stolen, is it?" I said.

"No, Mike, I swear it isn't. I'll show you the papers when you get here," he said.

"All right, but don't expect me to be there in two minutes, though, I'm going to drive around a bit and make sure I'm not being followed by your friends. When I get there, I'll toot the horn five times so you'll know it's me," I explained.

"All right, Mike. Thanks. I'll be waiting."

After about ten minutes I went and picked him up. He asked me what had happened with the cops, and I told him.

"So what's the story with this guy Morgenstern? How old is he? And if he's got a business, why is he looking to rent a room?" I asked.

Jimmy said, "Look, Mike, he's 36 and he still lives at home with mother. He's kind of slow like that but he's a cool guy, really. I wouldn't send a murderer to your house, but his mother wants him to move out."

We went to go meet Morgenstern over at his house up on Bell Boulevard. We talked, and, I figured he seemed harmless and actually a bit goofy, and I believed that I could throw him out on his ear in case there were any hassles with him over at the house. After talking for a little while, he explained to me that he didn't even need a place with a bed just yet. He just wanted a place where he could store some stuff. I said that he could rent the basement, but he would still have to talk it over with my mother. Morgenstern added that he could use a place pretty soon, so maybe he could meet my mother the next day. I told him that it might be all right, and I would give my mother his number. We finished talking, and then Jimmy and I left. When I got home that night, I told my mother about Morgenstern and that I felt that he would be all right as a tenant, and she could call him tomorrow some time to meet him. She said, "Well, as long as you think he's all right then."

When I woke up the next day, my mother told me that Jimmy Morgenstern had stopped by. She said that she had rented him half of the basement to store his things, and he told her that he wasn't quite sure if he was ready to rent a room just yet. She explained that he could pay her week to week on the rent, and she was quite happy when he gave her a whole month's worth of rent. He started moving in his things that day and then for the next few nights. The basement had its own entrance so it wasn't like he was bothering anyone.

Marcus, and I were driving around one night looking to score some weed. Every place we stopped was dry, like a desert. We kept driving father, and father, from our neighborhood when all of a sudden, he veers the car over the double yellow lines, and I see he trying to run over two cats. They had ran into the street, chasing each other. He missed one, but I heard the other one hit the floor board under the car as he starts laughing like a hyena.

"Ahahahahaha, I got one, he said as his head was turning straight into my fist.

I couldn't have timed it any better, my fist crashed straight into his face, and I hit him with such force that his head bounced off the driver's side passenger window. He just started to lose control of the car when, Bam! I punched him again, this time in the side of his head. And, again, his head bounced off the window. By now he had totally lost control of the car, and we were heading straight for construction barricades.

Oddly for me, this was all taking place in slow motion, and for a strange reason, I felt happy. It wasn't just for the poor cat he had hit. It was also for everybody that Marcus had attacked, violently, out of nowhere, for his own reasons over the years. Everybody in the neighborhood, in our age group, had a "Crazy Capeeto" story, or scar from him. I had several. It's not that I was scared of him, I felt bad for him. Every year his circle of friends got smaller, and smaller. For some dumb reason, I decided to stay friends with him. The look of surprise that was on his face when he saw my fist about to crash into his face felt so liberating, from holding myself back over the years, and seeing that same face, on his siblings, and friends, I almost wanted to punch him again. It was like, here's a taste of your own medicine, how do you like it?

We crashed into the barricades, just missed a parked car, and a tree, and ended up on someones front lawn. He screamed at me to get out of his car, and I told him he better shut the fuck up before I dragged him out of the car, beat his ass, and drove home alone. Even though I had always stuck up for him, this time he had crossed the line with me. Needless to say, it was quite a while before we spoke after this night.

One day Tony Morealass stopped by to ask if he could borrow a wheelbarrow from me because he had gotten a landscaping job around the corner. Tony was a friend of mine whom I had known from the 1st grade. I wasn't sure if this was another one of his bullshit stories or what. It wasn't the first time he had come over to my house to ask to borrow something. Two other times he had come over and pulled the same story. Like the first time he came over, he wanted to borrow a drill because he swore he had a job going on and that he'd give it back when he was done, which he never did. Then the second time it was an electric hedge trimmer, and I told him, "Tony, you didn't even bring my drill back, and now you want me to lend you something else?"

Then he'd start crying and telling me how he couldn't believe how I couldn't believe him and how he swore on his mother's grave that he would give it back to me and pay for the drill and all. I guess he must've mistook the look on my face as a look that believed him, because actually, I would get so sick of looking at him standing there crying over a hedge cutter that I'd say, "Here, Tony, take it and go. Goodbye." It's not like I really cared about the stuff. I probably had six drills and four hedge cutters anyway. Who knows? Maybe that's why he'd ask me. So this one day he wants a wheelbarrow and I tell him, "Tony, I don't care what you do. But I want my wheelbarrow back, and if you don't have it back to me tonight I swear I'm going to your parents' house, bang on their door, and ask them for it."
"No, Mike, I swear. I swear I'll have it back to you," he swore.

About an hour after this, I had to go make a run to the store, so I got in my Cutlass and headed towards Bench Park. Guess who I see running towards me with a color TV in a wheelbarrow... Fucking Tony. I stopped the car and raised my hands in the air as if to say, What the fuck are you doing?

Tony stopped, looked left, then right, and said, "Do you want to buy a TV? It works."
"No, Tony... I don't want to buy a fucking TV. Just give me back my wheelbarrow," I told him as he ran off down the block with it.

A few nights later, Eddie Mc Callister and I were playing the chicken shit game. That's a game where you press your forearms together, and drop a lit cigarette in between them until one guy chicken shits out. Unfortunately the night we happened to be doing this, the both of us were on about six or seven hits of mesc and tripping our balls off, with neither one of us moving. So while we're on our third cigarette, I tell Eddie about the wheelbarrow thing with Tony. He said, "Shit, you didn't know that about him? Him and that guy Cody are always breaking into people's houses. If he didn't know you, he'd probably try your house, too."

After Eddie told me that, I started wondering if Tony was coming over to borrow tools or to case the joint.

"Did you ever break into anyone's house?" I asked.
"No, man. It's not my scene," Eddie answered.
"Yeah, me either. Hey, Eddie, this cigarette went out. Do you want to call it a draw?"
"Does that mean you gave up, Mike?"
"Eh, fuck you! Light it back up, Eddie."
"All right, we'll call it a draw, Mike."

A couple of weeks later Jimmy Morgenstern asked my mother if she could rent another room to him. He told her he would do the same thing and give her a month's rent for it, so my mother decided to rent him another room.

My cousin Dino drove in for the weekend with Mike Viale to stop in and say hi. We went into Manhattan and had a pisser for two days nonstop. Then I went out to Northport with them for a few days. My cousin Dino picked up two girls out there. Dino, Mike, and I partied and had sex with them in a hotel all night, until we told them we had to leave and go back to the city in order to drop them off. Dino was always good for the girls. Even when we were kids, from time, to time, he'd bring home a party girl after he would run away from the boys homes he was at. Another thing that was nice was that he usually shared them with me or anyone else who was around. I swore if he could find gold as fast as he could find pussy, we'd all be rich. Shortly after that, we dropped the girls off, I drove back home.

When I got there, I decided to do a load of laundry, so I got some stuff together and went down to the basement to do a load. The basement was split into two sections. On one side we had a small apartment with a laundry room in it, and the other side was an open room with the boiler in it. That's where Jimmy was renting. The staircase and a small hallway down the middle separated the two areas. When I went down the stairs, half the stairs and most of the small hallway were cluttered with Jimmy's stuff. After I filled up the washing machine, I went upstairs and told my mother to tell Jimmy he had to move his stuff when she saw him, because I couldn't get down the stairs.

Pete stopped by my house. He asked me if he could stay over for a while because he had gotten into an argument with his stepparents, and he wanted to give it a few days to blow over. I told him that it wouldn't be a problem.

Dino stopped by again a few days after Pete did. He had a little cutie with him. Brown hair, nice build, and she had on a pair of short shorts. It's a good thing he shared her before Pete fell in love with her, because Pete wouldn't let her out of his sight after he was with her. I guess he was afraid she might jump our bones if he did. It was a little difficult having sex with her in the house without my mother knowing about it, but we managed to figure out something. After a few days, the three of them went out to Long Island.

A couple of days later, I was outside cutting the lawn, and Tommy Fay and Cody showed up. Tommy pulled out some gold chains and asked me if I wanted to buy them. I looked at the two of them and said that I wasn't interested in buying any. We hung out in the driveway for a little while, and Jimmy Morgenstern showed up. When he got out of the van, I told him that he had to get his stuff out of the hallway and off the stairs. He apologized and said that he had called and spoke to my mother about giving her the rent and she had mentioned it to him. Then he said, "Hey, Mike, what size waist are you?"

"Why?" I asked.

"Because I got in a whole load of jeans. Maybe you could use a pair."

"What kind are they?" I asked.

"What? Are you kidding? I only get the best. I got Lee's and Levi's," he said.

"What? You're going to give them to me?" I asked.

"Yeah, I got a bunch of them. And what about sneakers? Do you need a pair?"

"Well, I guess it wouldn't hurt if I got a new pair."

"What about your friend here? He certainly could use a pair."

We all looked down at Cody's raggedy ass sneakers and nodded in agreement.

Jimmy said, "What size do you take?"

Cody looked up and said, "Size 9."

Then Jimmy opened the back of his van and started rummaging around until he found a pair of size 9 Puma's. He handed them to Cody and said, "Try these on."

Cody opened the box and exclaimed, "Wow, cool!" Then he yanked off his old sneakers.

I thought it was a little odd, but quickly decided that I wouldn't turn him down on his offer. Then Jimmy handed me a pair of sneakers. Cody's eyes were the size of owls after he got on both of his sneakers. I started taking off one of my sneakers as Cody said, "Hey, Jimmy, do you want to buy some gold chains?"

I looked at Cody and raised my eyebrows as if to suggest that he might screw up everything by saying something like that out of left field, especially taking into consideration where he might have gotten them. Then Morgenstern looked at Cody and said, "Let me take a look at them."

He looked at them for a few minutes and said, "How much do you want?"

Well, I guess Jimmy probably doesn't go to church on Sundays for the least part.

Cody and Tommy turned to each other, spoke about it, and then Tommy said, "Seventy-five each."

Jimmy exclaimed, "Sold!" and took out some cash and paid them.

After talking for a little while, Jimmy asked us if we could help him take a few things downstairs. Besides, he reasoned, you'll have to help me get some boxes out of the van in order for me to give you some jeans. I knew there would be some catch for having gotten the sneakers. We helped Jimmy unload his van and put the boxes downstairs. When I first got down there, I didn't realize that he had brought in a lot more stuff, because now the place was loaded. We made some room and started putting the boxes down, and Jimmy said out loud to me, "Hey, Mike, these guys aren't going to rob me, are they?"

I looked at Tommy and Cody and said, "I don't know. Are you going to?"

Tommy looked at me and said, "Shit, Mike, you know me. I've lived right down the block from you my whole life."
Cody added, "I ain't gonna rob you. Mike knows where I live, too."

I looked back at Jimmy whose face changed to calm and said, "Well, I guess they're not going to rob you."

Jimmy handed out some jeans to us and then asked me if my mother had another room he could rent. I told him I wasn't sure but I would ask my mother about it. When we got upstairs, Jimmy gave his number to Tommy and Cody, and then he left.

"Shit, did you see all the stuff he had? Where did he get it all, Mike?" Cody asked.
"He's got some kind of liquidation business, and he gets it from there," I said.

Cody asked me what type of business that was, so I explained it to him.

"Shit, I'd like to get into that kind of business," Tommy answered.
"Yeah, so would I," Cody agreed.

We talked for a little while, and then I told them I'd see them later.

Gerard stopped by a few days later; we hung out and worked out a little bit. He told me that John Slocum was back in town, and he asked me if I had seen him. I hadn't but I asked Gerard how he knew John was back in town.

"Because he's living with his father, Big John, a few blocks away," he said.
"Where did you see him?"
"He's hanging out up at Bench Park."

After we finished working out, we stopped over by the park and ran into John. It was good to see him because we hadn't seen each other since we had come back from upstate. We started hanging out together a lot after that day.

When I got home for dinner, John Cody was sitting out in front of my house. I walked over to him and asked him what was up, and he told me that he was waiting for Jimmy Morgenstern to come over because he had some gold chains he wanted to sell to him, and Jimmy said to meet him here.

"Well, what the hell do you have to meet him here for? Why don't you meet him in front of your house and sell him some gold chains over there?"

"I'm sorry, Mike. I didn't know it bothered you. I won't do it anymore," he answered.

"It's not only a matter of it bothering me. I don't need my mother asking me why my friend is selling gold chains to her tenant," I said.

After I got inside I sat down for dinner. While I was eating, my mother told me that Jimmy had asked her if she had another room for rent and that she was thinking of renting him my father's old room.

"Why not? It's not like it's a shrine or something," I said sarcastically.

My mother didn't say anything, and I walked out of the kitchen with my food. I guess that was her way of trying to ask me whether or not I minded. She ended up renting him the room. A little while after that, I ran into Jimmy out in the hallway, and he asked me where Cody lived, which I thought was a little strange.

"Why do you want to know?" I asked.

Jimmy looked at me nervously and then said, "Well, because I didn't tell him to meet me here to buy gold chains off him."

"Yeah, well, it's not too cool, especially in front of my house."

"Don't worry, Mike. It won't happen again," Jimmy said.

About a month after that, I heard that Cody got arrested for breaking into someone's house. Not my thing, but I wasn't going to end the friendship just because he was an idiot. Then I saw him a few days after he came home from jail. He told me that they might put him away for a little while.

"How much did you make from that adventure?" I asked him.

"Shit, less than two hundred bucks," he answered.

"Oh yeah, Cody. I would have definitely jumped on that deal," I said sarcastically.

"Yeah, right. Tell me about it."

We talked for a little while longer about what he thought his options were, but even after talking about it for over an hour his options seemed very limited.

In my spare time these days, I played a lot of two-hand touch football over at 149th Street with kids who lived in the neighborhood over by the Raven Luncheonette, which was one of my stomping grounds. One day while I was over there, Joey Gatto asked me if I wanted to go play full contact football. He told me to bring my helmet and shoulder pads so I could try out for a small league he and Gene O'Donnell played in. I thought it sounded cool, and I eventually joined the team with them. It's funny but, being that I didn't always make it to practice, I wouldn't be allowed to play during the games, so it turned out that I got hurt more at practice than I did in the real games. I still had a great time, regardless of that. The defensive coordinator was a young guy I got along with real well. He'd let me play what was called "monster man" on defense. That meant that I could play any position at any time while I played. I did real well at that position, but like I said, being that I didn't always make practice, the other guys got to play more than I did.

Aside from that, I'd spend my days getting high, selling drugs to get high, working out, and being a seventeen-year-old bum.

One day while I was sleeping late after a night of partying, my door got kicked in and two guys rushed my bed. I don't know why, but ever since I was a kid, I started putting a baseball bat next to my bed, so I went for it. That little fumble for the bat was all it took, because after that I started trading and catching blows while I was sitting up on my bed. I always had a hard time getting up in the mornings, but this was definitely not one of those mornings, I thought, as I started catching more blows than I was giving. A few minutes after that, they yelled out that they were cops, and I told them they should have said that sooner. Well, that's cool, I thought, because this thing was starting to get out of hand. While they held me down, they told me that they had a search warrant for my house. One of the rooms they wanted to search was Jimmy's new room in the attic. A minute or two after that, some other cops came into my room. Then I heard a bunch of other cops run upstairs.

Man, what the fuck is this about?

A minute or two later, I heard them break down a door. Then a few of them came back down and said, "Yup, we got it. It's upstairs!"

As one of the cops read me my rights, I asked the other one why I was being arrested.

"Because you're in possession of stolen merchandise," he said.
"But someone else lives upstairs. Why should I get arrested?" I asked.
"Look, this is your house, right?!"
"Right," I answered.
"So you're getting arrested for possession of stolen property," he said.

Man, this is some shit. Aside from messing around with drugs, I've kept my nose clean this whole time, and now I'm going to get busted for something I didn't even do.

In the course of breaking down some doors, they reported back to one of the detectives watching me and told him that they had hit the jackpot. About an hour later I asked the cop why I hadn't been taken to the police station if I was arrested and they had found what they wanted. He explained to me that they might wait for my mother to get home. This way they could take us both in one trip.

Man, this is a turn of events, I thought. My mother is probably outside watching the house instead of me this time. Unfortunately just before they finally decided to take me to the police station, one of the detectives opened up my desk drawer and found an ounce of hashish. A little while after that, they took me to Central Booking, but not before all my neighbors watched me come out in cuffs and get into one of the many police cars.

While being driven over to Central Booking by a detective in an unmarked car, I hoped that my mother didn't come home. Otherwise, she would be charged with possession of stolen property too, once she arrived. Then they might send her to the nuthouse again, I thought.

After getting printed and having my bologna and cheese sandwich, I was told that two detectives would be personally delivering me to Queens Criminal Court. Unfortunately I had to wait for seven hours to pass before that happened

"Man, what the fuck did you do?" a prisoner asked me.
"Why do you ask?" I answered.
"Because detectives never come back to drive someone over to the courthouse. We all go on a chain gang and take a ride in the paddy wagon," he answered.
"Believe it or not, I didn't do anything," I answered.
"I hear you, brother. Neither did I," the guy said.
"Yeah, none of us did," someone else added, as they all laughed.

When it was my time to go I was put into a pair of handcuffs and frisked by the detectives. Then we started to walk outside.

"Fix your hair, kid. You're gonna be a star."
"What'a ya' mean?"
"There's a TV crew outside."
"No shit."
"No shit!" he answered. "Do you want to talk to them?" he asked.
"Yeah, I'll tell them I was framed. I'm sure they never heard that one before."

When we walked outside, bright lights lit up the night. A female reporter asked me something, but the detective said that I had nothing to say. Well, so much for stardom, I thought.

After being dropped off and processed at the courthouse, I didn't get to make night court, and finally the next day I got to meet my assigned lawyer. He told me that my mother had been arrested also.

When I got into the courtroom, the DA told the judge that he wanted my mother and me charged together. Then they talked about bail.

"Well, Your Honor, under the circumstances of what was recovered, I would ask for $100,000 bail," the DA said.
"Holy shit! What did they find?" I asked my lawyer.

My lawyer looked at me, smiled, and said, "A lot of stuff. I heard that it was a few truckloads to be exact."
"A few truckloads! From where?" I asked.
"All over the house is what they're saying," He answered before he went to talk to the judge.

"No, Your Honor. I don't agree. I feel that the defendant's past record doesn't reflect the magnitude of this arrest and, as you know, there is another party involved. So I would request that bail be set at $50,000, and Michael be R.O.R.'D."

The judge answered, "I feel that there is more to this case than meets the eye myself, so I'll grant this motion."

"What does that mean?" I asked the lawyer when he came back over to me.
"Shh, you're going to get out," he said.

After a few more minutes the court talk ended. My lawyer turned to me and said, "Okay, look, you're going to be released on R.O.R., with a $50,000 bond. That means if you leave and don't come back to court, you'll have a $50,000 bail once they catch you, and then they'll probably raise it more than that."
"Well, what about my mother?" I asked.
"I don't know. I'm not sure about what's going to happen to her," he answered. Then he looked at his watch and said, "Well, it's after 5. The clerk's office is closed; you'll have to call tomorrow to find out about your mother. I have to run now. I've got another case coming up. Here's my card; call me in a few days."

He gave me his card, and then he started to leave.

"Wait! I need to borrow some money for the train," I said.

He looked at me for a second, and then he handed me five bucks. "Call me, and remember we've got to be in court in two weeks," he explained.

As he walked back towards the holding cells, I thought, Thank God I'm outta there.

As I walked out of the courtroom, down the main hall towards the door, I looked at the cops, the relatives of other defendants, and defendants, who were there. I told myself that it looked like one big mess... and now I was a part of it again.

When I stepped outside, I stopped and took a deep breath of cool air. Man, I can't believe how nice this smells. But I need to stop experiencing this smell.

As I walked to the train station I thought about what could possibly be left in my house after a few truckloads were gone. I guess this was the second phase of my test, huh, God? First my father, then all my possessions. What's next, my house? My life?

When I got home Jim, the nice guy who still rented the "raven's room," let me in.

"Mike, how are you? Are you okay?" he said.

This was the second big bust for Jim; he had been there the first time back in 1975, poor bastard, I thought.

"I'm fine. Are you okay?" I joked.

"Mike, they were here for two days taking stuff out."

"From where?" I asked him.

"From everywhere. They broke the doors down even after your mother gave them the keys," he answered.

"You saw her get arrested?"

"Yes, she told me that if you were to get out, I should give you the rent money."

"Cool, do you have any now? I'm starving."

"Yes, here's fifty for now. I'll give you my key for the new lock I put in, too. Make a copy, and give it to me tomorrow."

When we were done talking, Jim went back to his room. I walked around the house to see what was gone. Each floor had been stripped bare, and anything of value was now gone. All of the things that my mother and father had bought over the years and more than half the stuff from behind the walls that my mother had packed away from when she went to flea markets years before my father died. They even took my father's old rifle collection and all the tools he had. After I got done walking around, I went into my room. All my expensive things were still there, and I wondered what was up with that. Between this and the stuff we left upstate, the house was pretty bare, I thought.

The next day I was finally able to track down my mother, and I found out that she was being held at Rikers Island Prison with $100,000 bail. After calling to find out the visiting hours, I was put on her list, which would enable me to go see her. So I made plans to see her the following day.

Once I got to Rikers Island, I had to wait for the prison bus to take me over the bridge to the right building. Then I had to go through a metal detector and empty my pockets. Of course I had forgotten about a big pocketknife that was inside of one of the pockets of the Army jacket I was wearing. Luckily I remembered it before anyone found it, so I volunteered it. The guard laughed at me as he confiscated it from me. Then I flunked the I.D. test and had to catch the next bus off the Island without seeing my mother.

A few days later I was able to get proper I.D., so I went back and got to see her.

"Michael, can you believe this shit?" my mother said over the telephone through the glass between us. "I told the cops that the rooms they were taking the stuff from were rented to Jimmy Morgenstern, and they didn't care. Then after they cuffed me, a cop walked over to me and said, "Alma... Alma... Alma... I finally got you for something!" When I looked at him I realized that I would see this guy once a month over by the luncheonette that we used to own, talking to your father. All that time I didn't know he was a cop. I thought he was in some kind of business with your father. It was right around the time that I cut back on my hours and didn't have to work there as much. But who the fuck is he to tell me something like that? But don't worry, it will all work out in a little while. And we'll get back all our stuff, and then we're going to sue their balls off."

Aside from that, we had a normal conversation, I guess. Then I left.

By now the word and the newspaper articles were out in the neighborhood about my arrest. People were either real friendly, or they'd totally avoid me for the most part. Some of my friends even told me not to come by their houses, because they were told by their parents that they couldn't hang out with me any more. On the outside I just blew it off as nothing, but on the inside it brought back similar old feelings of being some type of space alien. Over time it started to bother me again.

Great, I thought, here's some more newspaper articles for someone to throw in my face at some point in time. After a while of having to explain myself to certain people, I figured the hell with everyone, let them think what they wanted.

My friend Gerard and I still hung out together. He was one guy who was smart enough not to show his parents my newspaper articles. Both of us started lifting weights again in my basement like every day. It was something that would make me feel good about myself and, aside from that, I felt it was the one thing nobody could take away from me or tarnish in any way. I guess I was also building a protective shell around myself in some way and making the pain go away through pain. I wasn't really aware of it at the time, but I was starting to get immune to mental and physical pain, which is not always a good thing in this world. The drugs I was taking might have helped with this belief a little bit.

I found Jimmy Morgenstern's phone number about a week or so after getting out of jail, and I called his house a few times. Each time I did, his mother told me he wasn't home, until finally one day she told me he moved out. Then I got a hold of Jimmy Duguid. Being that the police didn't want to believe anything, I figured the best thing to do was to speak to Morgenstern myself. Talking to Jimmy Duguid was a start in that direction.

"So is there anything else you want to tell me about this guy, Jimmy?!"
"Mike, I swear I didn't know he would bring stolen stuff into your house. I just thought your mother could use the money, I swear."
"Well, where is the motherfucker? He never answered the phone, and then his mother told me he moved out."
"I don't know. I heard he's laying low, and that could mean anything. I even heard that he went to Florida." Jimmy said.
"Well, when you see him, you tell him he better write me, call me, or see me, before the shit hits the fan," I said.
"All right Mike, I'll put the word on the street. Hey, how did this whole thing happen anyway?"
"I'll tell you how it happened. You know that little shit ass John Cody I hung out with?"
"Yeah."
"Well, he started to hang out with Morgenstern, and then he got busted for robbing someone's house. So for some reason he decided to take down some serial numbers off of some of the shit Jimmy had, and he gave them to the cops so they could check and see if any of the stuff was stolen. Guess what? Two of the things were stolen, so they got a search warrant for my house. What I don't get is why he didn't tell them that it was Jimmy's shit. Or maybe my father's brothers have some pull in the 109th Precinct, and this was their way to get my mother. Who the fuck knows? But I'll tell you one thing for sure, they cleaned the house out. They took everything, and the way I see it, one way or

another Jimmy's fucking responsible for this. So tell him he better get in touch with me. I'll see you later."

"All right. See ya'," he answered.

Every time I walked into my house and saw that all the stuff that was gone, it really pissed me off. That's not to say that I wasn't angry about my mother being away, but I had already dealt with something of that magnitude. Besides, at least she wasn't facing murder charges this time, I reasoned.

My mother was finally able to get out on bail a few weeks later. Her bail got lowered to $20,000, so she put the house up as collateral. She also had gotten a new lawyer named James Fury. It's funny but I could remember like it was yesterday how she would fight with me to get up for school. These days she would fight with me to get up so we could go to court together. The last time I was arrested I didn't mind going to court because I was wrong and I had to go. Now not only wasn't I wrong, but I got to go with my mother to face charges of possessing over a halfmillion dollars' of stolen property, as they claimed. What a fucking joke, I thought. If I had half a million dollars' worth of stuff, would I have been walking around with a few bucks in my pocket all the time? I'm sure I would have squeezed in a Corvette or a motorcycle somewhere, if I was able to amass that much shit.

Whenever our lawyers would tell the DA about Jimmy Morgenstern, he didn't want to hear it, even though it turns out that he had a long criminal history.

After about a month or two, it just became routine to have to go court every two weeks, and each time it would get postponed for another two weeks.

One day out of the blue, my cousin Dino and Mike Viale showed up from out on Long Island.

"Mike, we heard what happened from Ricky Dale. You all right? What the fuck did they take? Ricky told me it was like ten truckloads or something," Dino asked.

After I explained the situation to them, Mike said, "Mike, that's fucked up. And this Jimmy don't show up or nothing to take his rap?"

"Not even a call. No, nothing," I answered.

"So who is this guy? Do you know anything about him?" Mike asked.

"I guess he's some big-time thief."

"Even though he's not being charged with anything, he didn't offer you anything for bail or a lawyer?" he asked.

"Nothing. Like I said, not even a phone call."

My mother came home a little while after my conversation with Mike and Dino; she was real happy to see Dino. She asked him how he was and how he was making out on his own. Dino told her he was fine and he was sharing a house with some other people out on the Island. Dino ended up staying at my house for a few days, and my mother said she didn't mind if Mike stayed, too, because he seemed like he was very polite. Dino and Mike had some money on them, so it wasn't like the old days. They went and made sure we all ate steaks every night.

I still hung out at 149th and Northern Boulevard around this time. In the past, a bunch of us would play two-hand touch football all night long, but for some reason I didn't play much football these days. Being that John Cody had gotten back to the neighborhood way before me, nobody had a clue that what had transpired with me was because of him. I really wasn't in the right frame of mind to ask him if he had done this to intentionally hurt me and my family, or if he had done it with the impression that the police were only going to go after Jimmy Morgenstern. How do you ask somebody a question like this without ripping off his head and getting charged with something else?

At the time there were a lot of neighborhood guys hanging out, so he acted as if he could avoid me and still hang out. Then one day when he got close enough to me, I told him what an asshole I thought he was. He came near me as he was saying, "I don't want no trouble with you, Mike." Then BAM, he jap punched me in the mouth.

I ran towards him and beat his ass to the corner until we fell to the ground, and then Tony Morealass ran over and broke it up when Cody started yelling for help. For that and other reasons, I still have my doubts about Tony not knowing about his best friend's intentions before the whole thing went down. After that night, the crowd I hung out with was divided in my favor, so Cody stopped hanging out.

A few of the guys were dating some of the girls who would hang out with us. I started getting friendly with this girl named Monica Abbananto. I had known her from high school, and being that she was very shy back then, Ronnie Kirshner and I would get a kick out of talking sexy to her, when we were in school. A bunch of us over there also started getting high with some real drugs. It started out slow, and then it just built up to a whole range of different things almost overnight. One night I got so buzzed up, I coaxed Monica into carving her initials onto my shoulder with a pocketknife. Her initials were "M.A." I guess it was either some ritualistic thing for me, or I must've been real high.

I was hanging out by 149th Street a few days later, and Tommy Faye stopped by. He looked good, he was dressed up in new clothes, and he had a nice tan and some gold on.

"Man, what happened to you? Did you win the lottery?" I asked Tommy.
"Nah, I went to Florida with Jimmy Morgenstern for a few weeks."
"Really? So what did you get, a little cozy hotel room by the beach?" I inquired.
"Fuck no, first we went to Disneyland and stayed there for a week. Then we went down to the Florida Keys, and then we stayed in some fancy hotel on the beach at Fort Lauderdale. I'll tell you, Mike, Jimmy must've spent ten or fifteen grand."
"So what did you have to do, sleep with him?"
"Yeah, fuck you. I don't know why he took me. Not that I give a fuck, though. I had a great time," he answered.
"Did he happen to mention anything about me getting busted?" I asked.
"No, why? You got busted for something?"
"Well, yeah, but it was no big deal."
"So why would Jimmy know something about it?" he said.
"Well, no. It's just that Jimmy might have heard something about it before he left because he lives at my house, that's all."

I talked to Tommy for a little while longer and made up a story about what I had been busted for. Then we both walked home towards our houses. When I got to Tommy's house, I asked Tommy if Jimmy had come home from Florida with him, and he told me that he did. Then I walked home.

When I got home, I was surprised to see that Dino and Mike were just finishing up painting the kitchen.

"What's up with this?" I asked.

"Well, your mother was saying how dark and dingy the kitchen was, so we decided to paint it for her. It's a surprise," Dino said.

"Yeah, so you can finish cooking the steaks out on the barbecue," Mike said.

"Not steak again?" I moaned.

"Man, fuck that. You remember when we were kids and we'd starve at night or split a can of soup? Well, those days are over, Mike. From now on, whenever we're together, we eat steak. I don't care if it's coming out of our fucking ears. We eat good from now on as long as I'm around," Dino said.

"Listen, I just saw Tommy Faye. He just got back from Florida. He told me he was down there with Morgenstern and that Jimmy had blown about ten to fifteen grand down there with him. That's some shit, huh?"

"That's Tommy from down the block, right? He used to hang out with us when your mother was away?" Dino asked.

"Yeah, that's him," I answered.

"He's home now?" Mike said.

"Yeah, I just walked home with him."

"Well, I think we should invite him over to our barbecue," Mike said.

Dino and Mike cleaned up, and then they walked over to Tommy's house. I finished cooking our steaks and threw on another one for Tommy. They came back about a half hour later with Tommy and two six packs of beer. My mother hadn't gotten home yet, so I put her food on the side. Then the four of us sat down to eat.

After a little bit of small, talk the conversation turned towards Morgenstern.

"So what's up with this Jimmy guy? I hear that he has some type of a salvage business," Mike asked Tommy.

"Well, uh, yeah, that's what he told me."

"Really? That sounds like a good type of business."

"So he's home at his mother's house now, right?" Dino asked.

"Yeah, that's where he's staying," Tommy answered.

"Oh, because his mother told me he moved out," I said.

While we were talking, my mother came home with some shopping bags.

"Oh, my God, what did you do to the kitchen? It looks great!"

"I thought you would like it, Aunt Alma. Me and Mike painted it for you," Dino said.

"Hey, I helped clean the brushes," I added.

"Yeah, you lazy fuck. Ooops, sorry, Alma, I didn't mean to curse," Michael said.

My mother gave Mike a little frown, and then she said, "Oh, thank you. It looks so nice in here now."

Then Dino got up and said, "Don't worry about the grocery bags. I'll put them away. Oh yeah, Mike put your food in the stove. Here, I'll get it."

My mother took her food, and she went inside to watch TV, while we resumed our conversation.

"So tell me something, Tommy. Does this guy Morgenstern know anybody?" Mike asked.

"What do you mean?" Tommy asked.

"You know, does he know any mob guys? Is he a big guy or a little pussy?"

"Well, he's bigger than any of us, and I know he has a gun or two. Why do you ask?"

"Hey, what the hell are you guys talking about?" my mother said as she walked back into the kitchen.

"No, nothing. Nothing, Aunt Alma."

"I heard you talking about guns and Jimmy Morgenstern. Listen, once this thing goes to court, that bastard Jimmy will get what he deserves. So don't go and try something stupid. There's enough trouble going on here. All right?!"

"Yeah, no, I hear you, Alma. I was just wondering what kind of a guy Jimmy was," Mike said.

"Well, that's all you guys better do is just wonder about it. He's going to get his, believe me," she explained.

As my mother walked out of the kitchen, Tommy asked me if Jimmy had skipped out on paying the rent, so I told him that he did. After dinner, Tommy left, and Dino, Mike and I went over to Bench Park to hang out.

The next night after dinner, Tommy Faye came over. Dino had answered the door, and he yelled for Mike to hurry up because they were ready to leave. By the time Mike ran down the stairs, I asked Dino where they were going.

"Well, nowhere, Michael. It's a surprise."

"Don't worry, Mike. You'll like it," Mike said.

"Yeah, we'll be back in a little while," Dino added as they left.

I didn't feel like going out that night, so I worked out a little bit, and then I went up to my room to watch some TV.

About two hours later I heard someone come in the side door. Being that none of the boarders used that door, I figured it was probably Mike and Dino, so I went down to see what this surprise thing was about. When I got down to the kitchen, Dino was there and he seemed a little out of breath.

"What's up? What's the matter?" I asked.

"Where's Mike? Did he show up yet?" Dino asked me.

"No? What's going on?"

"Look, Mike. Don't tell your mother, all right? Me and Mike had talked to that prick Jimmy. He was supposed to give us ten grand, so we could give it to your mother for court costs, because he didn't want to turn himself in. But Jimmy lied to us, and he went to pull out a gun. So Mike started to kick his ass. Mike chased him while Jimmy was screaming across the street, and then some guys ran out from this bar and grabbed Mike to stop the fight. So I grabbed one of the sawed-off shotguns that Mike brought...."

"Guns! What fucking guns?" I asked.

"Well, Mike thought that Jimmy sounded like he was bullshitting on the phone, so he brought some guns with us."

"Oh, fuck, Dino. What happened!? Is anyone dead?!"

"No, no, no. I took the gun and shot it into the air to scare the guys that were holding Mike, so that maybe they would let him go, but they didn't. After I did that, Jimmy started screaming like a woman and ran over to some guy's car who was at the red light, and just jumped in the guy's car, and then the guy took off."

"What about Tommy?" I asked.

"Tommy came back here with me; he's outside."

"What did he do?" I said.

"He drove the car to meet Jimmy."

"Dino, what the fuck...?"

"Yeah, yeah, I know... but we were trying to get some money for your mother from that motherfucker," he answered. "But don't worry, you and your mother won't get in any trouble."

Dino paced in the kitchen for a few minutes and then decided that it might be better if he left, so he did. I went back into my room after he left and lay down.

Man, I thought, this is fucked up. Mike's probably in jail, and Dino and Tommy might go there too now.

The following day my mother told me that she was going to take on another boarder. She said it would help with the lawyer's fees.

"What I want to do, though, is let you take your father's old room which is bigger and rent your room."

"What do you mean? I've got to move my stuff tonight?" I asked.

"No, the guy is going to come by tonight to see if he wants the room, and then he'll move in at the end of the week," she said.

"Yeah, okay, fine. I can move out by then."

The guy who came over to see the room seemed pretty cool. His name was Dave, and he worked in Manhattan as a chef. Dave decided that he would take the room after looking the place over, so that meant that I would have to start to pack and move upstairs.

After dinner the next day, I decided to start packing up some of my stuff and sorting through it. About an hour later my mother called me and said that Dino was on the phone. "Yeah, Dean, what's up? Where are you?" I asked.

"I'm still in Queens. I slept at Adelchie's house last night. His dog Petey is a nut and kept me up all night. Listen, I found out that Mike got arrested last night. I'm not worried, though. Mike wouldn't say anything; he'd keep his mouth shut. But I feel real bad about it."

"That is fucked up," I said.

"I know, I know," Dino answered. "Don't worry, though. Nothing is going to happen. I'm going to probably sleep here tonight again."

"All right, call me if you hear anything about Mike, okay?"

"All right, I will. I'll talk to you later."

"Bye."

"Bye."

After talking to my cousin, I went upstairs and packed some more of my stuff. About an hour after that, I heard a loud knock on the door. Ah, fuck it, I thought, someone else will get it. Then I heard it again, this time louder. I heard my grandfather yell that he was coming to get it, and then I heard a bunch of people raising their voices while running around. "What the fuck is going on?" I said out loud.

I walked out of my room and stood at the top of the stairs. When I looked downstairs, I saw a bunch of guys running around in the hallway. The light was only shining from the kitchen, so it was hard to see down there. Then I heard my mother say, in a raised voice, "What are you talking about? You must be nuts!" in a raised voice.

I walked down the stairs and saw my mother turn back around to face the guy who had just handcuffed her. It was Detective Lizio. "Looks like I got you again, bitch," then BAM, he punched my mother square in the face.

"You fucking cocksucker!" I growled as I started to run down the stairs to get at him. He looked over his shoulder and yelled to some other cops, "Get him." They all looked at me, and then they started to charge their way up the stairs towards me.

The next thing I knew I had the 1973 defensive line of the Oakland Raiders bum rushing me. I knew that this was one fight that I couldn't win, so I turned around and started heading for the three small windows at the top of the stairs, so I could jump out of them like I would do for fun when I was younger. As they were leapfrogging over each up the stairs to get me, I felt someone grab my leg. I yanked it free and ran up a few more stairs. Then someone grabbed my other leg tighter. This time I turned around to yank my leg free, and this huge lineman leaped over the top towards me and hit me in the throat. As my body slammed onto the landing, I attempted to squirm out from under him. Then a few more cops jumped on top of him to put more weight on me while he still had his forearm pressed into my neck. I felt my throat close underneath the weight of them, as a few other detectives who were standing around started kicking me for good measure.

After a moment or two, I realized that it was no accident that this cop's forearm was pinned into my throat, while the other detectives were on top of him. Once I realized this and just before I felt like I was going to pass out, I attempted to spit in his face without the use of my lungs. Most of it landed back in my face, but I think I got my point across, because one of the other cops slapped this one on his shoulder and said, "Okay, he's had enough." He gave me one last shove for good measure. Then when he got up, the other detectives sat me up and cuffed me.

I didn't realize it at the time but Jim, from the "raven's room," had come out during this and got so scared that he ran back into his room and dialed 911, because he didn't know that they were detectives. While I was sitting on the landing, I asked one detective if he could get my sneakers. He kicked me in the mouth and said, "Shut the fuck up!" A few minutes after that I heard a radio call on someone's walkie-talkie. Then I heard them start saying, "Who called for backup?"

In the next fifteen minutes I heard a bunch of sirens, and about ten more cops ran inside my house yelling. A few minutes after this, they decided to take me to the station house at the 109th Precinct. The detective who was now watching me was the same one from the last time I was arrested. He uncuffed me to let me put on my sneakers.

"Hey, do you think I'm going to Rikers Island this time?"
"Yeah, you probably will this time, Mike."
"Well, then, I better wear my shitty sneakers from what I've heard."

Then just before he led me downstairs he paused, looked at me, and then at my desk drawer.

"Awww, there's nothing in there."
"Yeah, but I'll just check it out for the hell of it," he answered as he opened up my desk drawer and pulled out an ounce of hashish.

Well, that's fitting, I thought, two busts in two months with two ounces of hash.

When I stepped out the front door, I was amazed. It looked like a bad Christmas light show from all the flickering police lights. I hadn't even known that there were this many cop cars in my neighborhood. A TV camera crew was there, and so was the whole neighborhood for blocks around. The two-lane street in front of my house was shut down, and it took ten minutes of jockeying cars before they could drive me away. I saw a bunch of my friend's faces in the crowd along with the scorning faces of some of their parents and my neighbors. Oh well, I thought, there goes the neighborhood again.

They kept me handcuffed in the holding cell for about two hours, and then Detective Lizio, the one who punched my mother, walked over to my cell and said, "Who's got the key?"

He opened up the cell and told me to follow him. Then he took me into a room that only had a table and said, while I was cuffed, "So you've got a problem with me punching your mother?"

I realized that I was in the "beating" room and that there were five more cops sitting at their desks right outside this room, so I decided to keep my mouth shut. But, what a scumbag, you want me to verbally defend my reaction to you for punching my mother in her face, while my hands are cuffed behind my back. Well, who knows, I guess that's how a pussy handles his shit. After standing there for a minute, or two, and not saying anything to him, he took me back into my cell and cuffed one of my hands to the bars. I wanted to stick my thumbs in his eyes, and blind him, but common sense prevailed.

My mother was arrested, and brought in a little while after that, and I asked one of the detectives what she was charged with. "The same thing you are: attempted kidnapping, attempted murder, and assault with a deadly weapon," I was told.
"What? Get the fuck out of here!"
"I'm serious, and if we find the sawed-off shotguns, then it's gonna be worse."
"What sawed-off shotguns? I don't know what you're talking about. I didn't do anything."
"We'll let the judge figure that out, okay"

Just before they took me to Central Booking, that same cop came over and said, "Well, they just found the shotguns. It looks like you're fucked!"

After I got to Central Booking, it was still pretty early so there was a little bit of room to lie down in the cell. But after a few hours, the cops didn't have a spare cell to strip search any new prisoners in, so they would tell the rest of us to face the wall while the new prisoners flashed the cops their anuses, which I always found oddly amusing.

At the Central Booking holding cells, the male and the female cells share the back wall, and there was a vent at the top of the back of the adjoining walls, so you could hear conversations on both sides. Whenever a female was brought in, all the guys would start whooping and hollering every time that a female guard would tell the female prisoner to get undressed for a strip search. After a while, I've got to admit, I'd started yelling along with them. Then a little while later, I saw them bring my mother in. Everybody started to get a little rowdy, until I said, "Hey! Shut the fuck up. That's my mother!" After a bunch of them started to believe me, they all raised their voices in conversation to block out the sounds coming from the other side as a kind gesture.

A few minutes later, my mother and I talked through the vent for a little bit until they came to take her to the hospital. Her nose was broken, and she needed a stitch or two on her lip, she told me.

About an hour after she left, my cousin Dino was brought in. They put him in my cell with me after he was strip searched.

"How the fuck did you end up in here?" I asked.
"Well, you won't believe this, Mike, but I went to stop by the house, and when I saw so many cop cars there I thought that the house had blown up or something. So I ran over to the house to see if everything was okay."
"Oh, no, don't tell me."
"Yup, I walked over to the house, and somebody asked me who I was. After I told them they said, Great, now we don't have to look for you. Then I got handcuffed."

An hour later, which must've been three in the morning by then, Tommy Faye was brought in. As he walked past us Dino yelled, "I knew it! You rat bastard! You ratted us out."

Tommy didn't say a word as he was led to a different cell, and Dino kept questioning Tommy even as he was being strip searched.

"No, I swear, Dino. I didn't say anything," Tommy answered.

Tommy might not have said anything, but the detectives he came in with decided not to put him in the cell with us anyhow.

A little while later, a police guard came over and told a bunch of us that we had to move to another cell. He called out names and then said, "Let's go!"
"Hey, what about my cousin, Officer?" I asked.
No, he don't go-different time schedules."

Dino and I looked at each other, and I said, "Well, take it easy, Dino."
"Yeah, you too, Mike."
"Bye."
"Bye."

They put me on a chain gang in another room, and we left a short time later. As we rode in the paddy wagon, one of the prisoners found out that we weren't going to make it to night court, so we were going to spend the night at a police precinct somewhere else for the night. When we got to our destination we were given our own small cell and told to give them our belts and our shoe laces before we went to bed, just in case anybody decided to hang himself. After we got settled in, a police officer came over to my cell and said, "Hey, kid, here's your article. Good luck, you're gonna need it."

Then the guard tossed me the paper, and the story went like this: "Female Fagin arrested after her gang of youths attempt a kidnapping." After some sketchy details, it gave a reference to the other charge that was pending.

Well, Mike, I guess you really hit the big time, huh? Nice work, kid, nice work indeed. I nodded to other end of the cell and gestured; Goodnight, Mom; goodnight, Dad; goodnight, John-boy. Then I rolled up my shirt for a pillow and went to sleep.

They got us up at about six the next morning and gave us something to eat that wasn't moving, and then we hit the road. I met up with my cousin Dino when I got to the Queens Criminal Courthouse. We were going to both go up before the judge together. I had already thought long and hard about whether or not I would get bail, and I didn't like the look of it considering I was already out on $50,000 bond. Just before they took my cousin and me out to court, we were thinking of ways we could get some money together, in case we got bail.

Well, we got bail all right; the bidding started at $1 million. The judge intervened and finally lowered it to $500,000 on each of us. I don't know how my cousin didn't hear it, but I said dryly, "Dino, we got bail."

He smiled until I told him how much. We were charged with conspiracy to commit murder, attempted kidnapping, assault, and possession of two sawed-off shotguns. As we were led back to the holding cells, I noticed that the courtroom audience was much quieter now.

Instead of going to Rikers Island that night, we were split up again and sent to different precincts to spend the night.

The next morning I was back at Queens Criminal Court, and I ran into Mike and Tommy in the holding cells. Being that Mike was already talking to Tommy, I considered it a neutral setting and didn't say anything about Dino's accusations. While the three of us were there, we talked with our assigned lawyers, and then we were told that my mother would be in court with us. My cousin Dino was brought into the cell a short time later. It took a little while to calm Dino down, but we decided to talk reasonably about things because, after all, Tommy was in there with us.

"Look, guys, I'm the only one they can charge with attempted murder 'cause I hit him," Mike said.
"But what about the gunshot that was fired? Doesn't that connect the shotgun to the crime?"
"Well, they didn't find a shotgun on me at the scene, so that's something that they have to prove. So if I cop out to the assault charges, what could they charge you guys with...? A sawed-off shotgun? How...?"
"Well, how did my mother get involved... or me for that matter?"
"I guess you got arrested because that's where they found the shotguns," Mike said.
"But how did they know that the shotguns might be there?"
"Well, that's what the fuck I've been saying, guys. There was only one person with me when I brought the shotguns back to the house, and that motherfucker is standing right in front of me. Tommy, are you sure you didn't open your fucking mouth?" Dino said.
"No! I didn't say anything! They found the shotguns after a few hours, didn't they? If I would have told them, don't you think that they would have found them sooner? Besides that, I'm in jail, too, so if I ratted everybody out to save my own ass, I shouldn't be here, right?!" Tommy answered.
"I'm telling you, Tommy, I better not find out you did," Dino stated.

A little while later Dino took me to the side and said, "I don't like it, Mike. Tommy is the weak link in all of this. I say we beat shit out of his ass now, and tell him he'll get worse if he yaps."
"Look, Dino, I have my doubts about Tommy also. But something don't add up here. If Tommy ratted on us, why the fuck would they put him in here with us in the lion's den? That don't make sense. I'm thinking maybe they ain't got shit on us, and they're waiting for one of us to break. That's why maybe it's better not to throw Tommy a beating and alienate him from our pack, because then he'll feel like he doesn't have anybody in here, and then he could become dangerous to us. Besides, remember what Grandpa always told us: Always be friendly with your enemy, this way you'll know what he's up to."

Dino nodded his head at me, but I knew him, and I knew that he was half a step away from throwing Tommy a beating. So I was going to have to keep the peace between them, at least until we found out more information.

Just before the four of us got into the courtroom, I thought it was funny that some of the court officers were putting on their gun holsters. Two other ones even had their billy clubs out. I said hello to my mother as I sat down next to her in court and gave her a small kiss on her cheek. Family reunions, don't you just love them?

We were told exactly what we were being charged with again. The lawyer's, Judge, and D.A. talked about this, that and the other, and then we were asked if any of us were going to post bail. After we replied that we weren't, we were told that we would be going to Rikers Island.

We all got split up again, and I got ready to go to the "Rock."

After they processed us and we got downstairs, they took me over to a different holding cell. I found out that Mike, Dino and Tommy were going to Rikers Island, but I wasn't. As it turned out, I ended up going to a small police department to spend the night again. By the next day I was back at the Queens Courthouse and in the same cell that the other guys were put in before they went to the "Rock."

After a few minutes, this one large black kid put his foot next to a smaller black kid's foot and said, "Hey, man, what size sneaker do you take?"
"Size ten. Why you ask?"
"Because them motherfuckin' sneakers is mine once we get on the bus!"

The bus ride really sucked because we went the same way that we would drive if I was going towards my house, and the entrance way to Rikers Island was in the same area as the Pizzeria we used to own.

As I stepped off the bus, I heard the large black guy talking about his new sneakers.

"Look at my sneakers. Ain't they beautiful? Look at your sneakers. They ugly. Your momma don't love you, boy," he sang to the smaller kid who had just lost his sneakers on the bus ride over, and had tears running down his face.

When we all got off the bus, we walked through a door into a large staging room with a bunch of cells in it. Then we walked into the first cell on the right and were taken off the chain gang. The cells on my side were all about 10 x 30 with a toilet. On the other side, there were smaller cells where it seemed like the guards kept the troublemakers. Once we were released from the shackles in that first cell, some prisoners were phased out to some of the other cells and then into the prison itself. I don't know why, but I was the only one left from my busload until the next batch of people arrived.

When the door opened with the new batch of prisoners, a blast of fresh air came in with them. I made sure I breathed in every last drop of it before it dissipated. I might not get another one for a long time, I thought. One of the things I noticed, which I thought was strange, was that even though it was a little chilly outside, the walls were sweating from condensation.

I stayed in that cell all day and into the night until I was the last person there. Then I dozed off at about 2 a.m. At 4 a.m. a guard came over and opened the cell.

"Oh, I didn't know anyone else was in here. Oh, well, listen. You guys better not fuck around, Okay?" the guard said.

Being in a half daze I said, "Whoa, whoa, whoa. What are you saying? Who are you putting in here with me?"

Then this voice answered, "Don't worry honey, it's only me, a faggot. I won't touch you," the faggot said.

"Fine, and I won't touch you either," I said.

"Oh really, Well, I'd be the best piece of ass you ever had," he said.

"That's okay, I'll take your word for it, honey," I answered.

As he walked past me, in the darkness, I noticed that he was carrying a pair of high heels and had a small feminine build, so I figured there wouldn't be a problem and I went back to bed.

About a half hour later, a black guard walked by and said, "Oh, no, this won't work. You can't stay in there."

I looked up to see what he was talking about, and I didn't see anything but the faggot sleeping on the other bench like I was. The guard came back over and opened up the cell, and then he escorted me past three half-empty cells, stopped, and put the key into the door of a packed cell. I looked into the dark cell and saw about twenty-five to thirty black guys sleeping on the floor and on the benches and not one white guy. I looked over at the guard as he swung open the door, and he said, "Welcome to Rikers Island. Step inside please."

"You gotta be shittin me, you're gonna put me in this cell?"

"I'm not shittin you, step inside."

As he slammed the cell door behind me he said, "Have a good night."

After he closed the door, I thought, Well... trial by fire. I stood there for a minute or two, and I wondered if I should just jump into the middle of these guys and start swinging while they were still asleep, or if I should wait until they all woke up in the morning to see if any shit would hit the fan. The experience made me realize that racism, was still alive and well, on both sides of the fence. There's no way he should have put me in that cell, and he knew better.

After standing there for a minute or two, I realized that I was being rude, if you will, by staring, so I figured I'd stop wondering and sit down on the floor. There was just enough room for me to stretch my legs out, so I did. About twenty minutes later, after I was sitting there contemplating my overall situation, the white guard who put the homo in my cell walked by, gave me a double look and said, "Who the hell put you in there by yourself?"

I pointed at the colored guard, and the white guard said, "Yeah, it figures. He's a fucking asshole. Did you put him in there?"

"Yeah," the colored guard said.

"Well, give me the fucking key."

"Well, there's a rule that no prisoners are supposed to be left with the homos overnight."

"Well, you could have put him in another cell. Besides, I'm the one that put the homo in his cell, and I outrank you, so I'll take the heat for it."

I have to say, the sound of the lock opening was one of the sweetest sounds I'd ever heard. I may be a little nuts, but I wasn't stupid. I viewed that room like an "odds" kinda room. My odds on getting into a fight with someone in that cell looked good, let alone getting my ass kicked by the whole room.

"SLAM!"

"CLICK!"

"Oh, hello, honey. You home?"

"Yes, dear. I'm sorry. It'll never happen again, I swear."

I have to say that the faggot's voice was the second sweetest sound I had ever heard, and seeing his heels even almost looked good in a weird kinda way.

I had already given this cell the bye-bye, as a blip of time, but it was nice to be back home. I lay down on the bench wide awake and very aware of my situation. It was all a bit of a humbling experience to a degree.

After sitting there for a few minutes, I thought about my odds inside the prison. I was in a large room that I considered to be the first outpost before going into the prison complex. The strange thing about being in this room for so long was that I almost had too much time to contemplate what I needed to prepare myself for, instead of just being thrown into my fate, whatever that may be. Being that I had passed most of my time watching a lot of different faces going inside, it also made me wonder about the odds of some of the new prisoners that I had seen during the day, because a few of them didn't look like they had a chance.

It was close to morning now, and I thought to myself that I'd better get some sleep because I didn't know what tomorrow held for me.

By the time I woke up, the cell had started gathering people for their morning run to court. I got up at about 9 o'clock after it started getting a little noisy. Then I could hardly believe it, but Dino came in. We were pretty glad to see each other, and I wondered if we might be placed together somewhere. About an hour later, Mike Viale came in. It was nice to be in a room where we held the favor over the rest of the cell, almost like family. Quite a different feeling than I had this morning when I was told to change cells, I thought. We talked about our case for a bit, and a few things didn't add up is what we concluded.

"Look, we got two ways to do this thing," Mike started. "I kicked someone's ass at a bar and got hit with assault charges a while back, so I'm probably going to get hit with some time again, because it'll be considered to be another violent crime. I could cop out to it, and they might let you guys go. But if I do, you motherfuckers better keep my commissary stocked. Or the other option is that I go with you guys, and we don't do anything until we see what they've really got against us."

"I guess you stay with us, and either we all do time or we don't. All right, Dino?" I said.

"All right, we'll stick together. If we all go down, we all go down," he answered.

"Now what about Tommy? You know him; I don't. Is he a punk?" Mike asked.

"You know him better than me, Mike," Dino said as he looked at me.

"I don't know. He's a bit of a talker, but I think he's stand up. But like I told Dino, Mike, I don't think it would be a good idea to alienate him from us right now," I said.

"Yeah, but there are still some missing threads that I don't like," Dino said.

"Well, let's wait and see what happens at court today. Maybe they'll reduce the charges somehow," Mike suggested.

Ironically we were told that we were on hold, and if called, a special van would take us to court. I guess the D.A. was also wondering how to move on this case. It turns out that we never went to court that day, so we stayed in that cell past lunch and dinner until about two in the morning.

A guard came in about this time and called out our three names with some other names. I was a little amazed finally to hear my name called after seeing all these other guys go before me all day long for two days now. Then they took us into a long hallway where there were three guards.

"Strip!" one of them said.

Fifteen guys looked back and forth at each other for a second or two, and then we started to strip.

"Put your clothes out in front of you!" we were told.

After the guards checked our clothes and the front of our bodies, the guard yelled, "Turn around, bend over, and spread your cheeks!"

Some of us laughed, and other people grumbled. Personally I again thought it was funny that we had to moon our captors.

Then they called out the first three names. These guys trotted out the hall into a doorway that they were pointed to.

"Well, we're all still together," I said.
"Yeah, but let's see what happens." Mike answered.

After a while they called out our three names, and we trotted into what were the showers.

"Hey, Dino. You know, I am a little horny," I said.
"Yeah, right. Fuck you."

When we got inside there was one guard standing there. "All right, stop the line!" he barked. "Garramone, Baiardi , Viale...you guys Italiano?" he asked in a different tone.

"Yeah, and we're all related."

"You're all here together?"

"Yeah."

"What's the charge?"

The three of us looked at each other, and Mike said, "Assault, attempted murder, conspiracy to kidnap, and possession of sawed-off shotguns."

The guard shook his head and said, "Fucking buncha nuts... All right, listen, this place is punk city, so if anybody tries to take your shit, you're better off punching him in the face and take your beating if you have to. Otherwise, everyone will try to take your shit, you understand...?Now, do you want to take showers?"

We all looked at each other and said no.

"All right, then move along!"

"Do you think they'll keep us together?" I asked.

"No, they'll split you up. Now move!"

The next room we walked into was a medical room, and I was surprised to see a female nurse in there. A guard who was standing there said, "Okay, one at a time."

Mike looked at me and said, "The nurse needs to jerk you off to get some semen, so she can check and see if you have any venereal diseases. We had to do it when we first came in."

"Really??" I asked.

"Yeah, cum fast so we can get outta here," Dino added.

I could hardly believe it but I figured what the fuck. The nurse took my blood pressure and then told me to turn around, pull down my pants, and wipe a Q-tip on the tip of my dick, which I thought was strange. After I got done, I turned around and handed the nurse the Q-tip. The nurse looked at me and said, "Pull your God-Damned pants up."

I stood there shocked for a moment, and then I yanked my pants up as fast as I could and ran out of her office while I heard Mike, and Dino, laughing their asses off. When I got out in the hall, I could see that everyone was getting separated into groups.

When Mike and Dino came out, I gave them the middle finger, and they both pointed at me and called me a sucker. We were all put into different lines, and then they started giving out pillows and blankets. One of the guards pointed to me and said, "Garramone, you're going back this way."

"Why?"

"Well, they don't know where to put you yet."

"Mike, Dino, take care. I'm going back."

We all nodded at each other, and then the guard yelled, "C'mon, move!"

Well, so much for staying together, I thought.

As I walked back towards outpost1, I thought it would have been nice if we could have stayed together, but fate seemed to play an odd role in this place. When I got back to the main cell, the faggot with the high heels was still there, but nobody else was.

"I knew you'd come back for me. You just couldn't live without me. C'mon, admit it," my new wife said.

"SLAM!"

"CLICK!"

After our hello's I went into the dark cell and sat back down on my bench.

"So where did you go? And why are you home so late?"
"Well, I went to go check out the showers and then the nurse's station."
"Oooh, sounds kinky."
"Not that kinda checking out, honey. Then they told me that they didn't have a place for me so they sent me back here."
"Oh... Hey, you're not like a maniac or something, are you?"
"No, I'm cool."
"You're not going to grab me and try to rape me, are you?"
"Well, not tonight, honey. I've got a headache."
"Oh, okay," he said in almost a sad tone.

After that I rolled up my shirt and made a pillow to lie down with. Well, another night in the fun house. I wonder if I'm going to get out. Maybe this is the closest I'm going to get to be out in years. What a fucking mess, I thought.

The next day the new guys started piling in about 7 a.m. I skipped the breakfast call again and slept till nine. I stayed all day in that cell, watching faces come and go. I wondered which ones were going home and which ones were coming back. Most of them were smiling and cutting jokes about getting "Cut'em loose Bruce" as a judge. About an hour after dinner, a bunch of guys started to come back from court, and Tommy Faye came into my cell from a new busload that had just arrived.

"Tommy, over here."

When I looked at him, his eyes looked glassed over.

"Mike, what are you doing here?"
"I've been here for days. Where were you?"

"I was at court."

" ... Tommy, let me ask you something. Where did you get arrested?"

"At my house."

"Why did they come to your house?"

"I guess because I'm the one who called Jimmy and told him to meet us at King Kullen supermarket that night."

"You know, it's really fucked up that my mother got arrested with this bullshit."

"Yeah, Man. This is fucked up. There are some big charges."

"Yeah, I know, but I was talking to Mike and Dino, and we're all going to hang tough and see what happens. We don't think they can make everything stick together. Do you know what I mean, Tommy?"

"Huh? Yeah, yeah, I hear you."

Tommy got shipped off a little while after that meeting, so I went to sleep after two guys got done fighting over a pair of sneakers.

"Hey, wake up!"

"Huh?"

"You're being shipped off."

It turns out that I ended up in that cell all day, and after dozing off it was about two in the morning by now.

"Where am I going now?"

"You got a nice room with a view," the guard said.

I walked down the hall, and I was given a sheet and a pillow case.

"Where do I get the pillow?"

"We ain't got none left!"

"Oh, well, thanks for the sheet."

"C'mon, move!"

We walked down a few halls until we were buzzed into a secured guard area. There were two long halls joining out from the center of the guard booth. They glanced at my paperwork and then buzzed open one of the doors.

"Walk down to cell #13, and then walk in!"

As I walked down the hall, I thought it was a little odd that one of the cells on my right was open with a prisoner sitting on his cot. I glanced at him while I walked by, and he looked back at me. When I got to my cell, I saw that my wrought iron bed didn't have a mattress on it. Instead of yelling down the hallway and waking everyone up, I started to walk back.

"What's the matter?"I heard over the loud speaker.

"I ain't got a mattress!" I yelled back.

"Aw, man, shut the fuck up!"

"Yeah, shut the fuck up!" I heard some of the grumpy inmates say.

Over the loud speaker the guard told me to come back to the guard post. After I got there, the guard opened up what he called the south side and told me to walk down the row and see which cell was vacant so they could buzz me in to get a mattress.

After I got one and went back to my cell, I put the sheet on the mattress and fell right to sleep, first time in a bed in days.

"Whirrrr, Crash!"

"What the fuck!"

I bolted up and saw that my cell door was open. It was still dark outside, and I watched as guys walked past my cell door.

"Hey, what the fuck's going on?"
"What do you mean...what the fuck's going on. It's breakfast time."
"Oh."

Man o' man, I'm starved. I could go for some eggs and sausage right now, or pancakes, I thought.

I got dressed and walked down the hall still half sleeping and dreaming of bagels. The line formed a horseshoe, and I watched as some guys grabbed a whole loaf of bread as they walked away from the line.

"Hey, how much bread can you take?" I asked someone next to me.
"All you want," I was told.
"Trust me, the bread is the only good thing here at breakfast," he told me as I made my way to the middle of the horseshoe.

Whatever was being served up as the main course started to make an odd sound whenever I heard it hit someone's plate. As I turned for my portion, the server wound up and "Splot!"

"Damn, what the fuck is this shit?!"
"Check dis' mutherfucka' out. He thinks he's in the motherfuckin' Holiday Inn. Das strawberry jam and rhubarb. Welcome to Rikers Island. Would you all like some clean towels and sheets for your room, sir?"

By now a few guys around me were laughing. It was the biggest pile of jam I'd ever seen in my life on a plate.

"They woke me up this early for this shit and no coffee? Yo, guard, you don't have to wake me up for this breakfast any more!" I informed him.

I grabbed my two by four box of cereal, my milk and orange and then threw the rest away. After that I went back to my cell, ate a little, and went back to sleep.

I slept until lunch, and then we were sent to eat in the day room. The day room had a TV in it and was attached to our main hallway, or quad as they were called. After lunch you had to go back to your cell until dinnertime. It had only been a day, but already I started to feel a little claustrophobic. This cell was much smaller than the one I had spent days in when I first got here. At least I had a window in my cell that I could see out of, which made me feel a little better. Those windows were tight as a drum, though. I checked them out like a squirrel looking for a nut.

We were let back out at dinnertime to eat in the dayroom again. Now this was getting impossible, I thought. I didn't mind not having any utensils for breakfast or lunch, but now we're having rice with shredded chicken. After I sat down, I looked around to see what all the other inmates were doing to eat. Most of them would break off the molded edge of the styrofoam plate and shovel food with it. While I was eating, a black guy got up and walked over to another black guy's tray, picked up his unopened milk, and walked away.

Remember, Mike, if anyone tries to take your shit, you've got to hit him, I thought to myself. I'd have to say the only thing I really worried about at that time was not knowing that much about my case and facing those charges. I didn't want to go and hit somebody and make things worse for myself. It was already a delicate situation, I thought.

We were allowed to stay out in the dayroom after dinner until eleven o'clock, and then we were sent back to our cells.

When I got to my cell that night, I lay down and contemplated whether or not I could stay in a cell this size for a number of years. While I was lying there, I noticed an inmate kept walking back and forth in front of my cell about every half hour or so. The fourth time he passed, he stopped and said, "Hey, you. I didn't get anything off the last guy that was in this cell."
"Yeah, so?" I answered.
"So I'm gonna make damn sure I get something off your ass!"
"Man, the only thing you're gonna do with my ass is kiss it, motherfucker!"

The guy answered, "No, I ain't gonna be kissing it. I'm gonna be kicking it."
"We'll see, motherfucker."
"Yeah, we'll see," he said as he walked away.

The next morning a guard woke me and told me to get ready for court.

"Court? What do you mean court?"
"You've got twenty minutes to get ready for court. When the door opens, come out and walk to the guard's station."

Shit, court, I thought, then I sat up and looked around my cell. Well, all I came in with was a sheet and a pillowcase, and I don't need them. Fuck, I should have eaten some breakfast this morning. Then

I got up and looked into my metal mirror.

Hmm, Michael, you look like shit. I guess I got everything then, I joked with myself.

Dino, Tommy, Mike V., and I met up to go to court at outpost 1 in the holding cell again that day.

"So, Tommy, how'd they pick you up again?" my cousin Dino asked.
"I told you, man. I was at home." Tommy answered.
"All right, listen. We've got bigger things to talk about," Mike V. said.

As they were talking about our case, I thought about what my mother might have on her mind at this time. She's going through the same shit I am right now. What a bad fucking dream with shit still looming, I thought.

"Baiardi, Viale, Garramone, Faye. Let's go!" a guard yelled out.

We stood up as three guards came in, did a monkey cuff on us, and then cuffed the four of us together. A monkey cuff is when they got the feet involved so it's difficult to walk. Instead of putting us on a bus, the four of us were led to a paddy wagon. After we got inside, Mike said, "Oh shit, I hope we're not going to a Federal prison on the sawed-off shotgun charges."
"What do you mean?" Tommy asked.
"I don't know. I think it might be a bigger charge," he answered.

When we got to Queens Criminal Court, we were hustled past a bunch of inmates in cells and taken directly upstairs. After we ate something, all of our court appointed lawyers came into the holding area. They were explaining to us that we were there because my mother had to go to court, and they weren't sure if we all had to go together or if they were going to try my mother separately.

"Michael," Dino said, "you don't think your mother would drop a dime on us, do you?"
"For what? She's got no reason to."
"Yeah, I guess you're right."

A short while after our lawyers had left, they came back and we were told that we would all be charged together, but because they didn't have enough court officers available, it was decided to leave us back here. Then a few hours later, we were told that my mother had gone to court by herself and that we'd have to stay in this cell until dinner time. Then we would be taken back with all the other prisoners.

In the holding cell, the one thing you could almost pick out by smell was inmates who had gotten back from court and the smiling and joking ones that were just brought in from the world. One good thing about the new ones was that they gave away cigarettes like nothing.

This time when we took the ride back on the bus, I observed the outside world again. It was strange to watch the people and kids my age going about their business through the bus windows. Man, you take all that for granted, I thought.

We were separated shortly after arriving to outpost 1 on Rikers Island and got sent to our cells. In a funny way, it was almost nice to be back in this cell. But before long I was pacing like a lion in my new cell, feeling a little claustrophobic. That was the real thing that started to get to me about this place. I managed to fall asleep in a little while, and then I heard, "Hey, motherfucker, I'm happy to see you back!" It was that fucking Spanish guy again.

"Man, fuck you," I said.
"No, fuck you."

This motherfucker, I thought.

"Man, fuck you. I'm going to bed. Come back tomorrow night, you fucking ghost, and I'll argue with you then."
"Yeah, come back tomorrow night. I don't feel like listening to you guys argue," another inmate yelled out.

A few others let out their two cents about it before my "friend" moseyed along.

The next day at dinnertime I noticed that the guy who walked suicide watch was out in the day room.

Great, I thought. He's hanging out with those two big Spanish guys, so now not only might I get hit with another charge for kicking his ass, then I'll have to fight one or both of these guys.

That night while I was sleeping, someone threw a cup of water on me. It must've been a ghost because by the time I ran to my door nobody was there, so I went back to bed.

The next afternoon the doors opened, and a bunch of inmates started yelling, "All right, commissary time."

"What the fuck is commissary time?" I asked a black guy across from me.
"It's commissary time, man. We go get us some Twinkies, some cigarettes, socks, anything you want," he answered.
"Shit, I'm gonna get me some shit then," I said.

When we got to the end of the hall, I thought it was pretty strange that everybody else wasn't coming with us, but I figured that maybe they didn't need anything.

It's funny, but we lined up in two rows and walked out into the hall almost like we were school children. I noticed that there were a lot of other inmates out in the hallway, too, probably also going to the commissary, I figured. Once we got there we waited our turn, and then our unit went up to the commissary window. The colored guy who had the cell across from me was doing a little bit of a dance by now, singing, "Gonna get me some Twinkies, yea, yea, gonna get me some cigs, yea, yea," while he was doing a little James Brown dance.

"What's your name?" I was asked by an inmate from behind the glass window.

After I told him, he said "Nope! I don't have you down on the list."

"What list?"
"Whata'ya' trying to play games?"
"No, what list?"
"The list that tells me what's in your kitty."
"Huh?"
"The money people send you."
"Fuck, I don't think anyone sent me money."
"Well, that's why you ain't on my list."
"Oh, shit. I didn't know you ain't got no money," the colored guy from my quad said.
"That's all right. I should have known that you needed money here for this."
"Well, I'll tell you what. You can have a Twinkie and some of my cigs."
"Well, I ain't sucking your dick, motherfucker," I joked.
"Don't worry, I don't want you to suck my dick. I want to fuck you in the ass," he joked.

While we walked back towards our quad, I ate my Twinkie, very slowly to savor it. Just as we got up to my entranceway, I noticed a few of the other quads standing in the hallway. Most of them were holding bags, so I figured that they had also gone to the commissary. All of a sudden I heard someone get slapped in the head.

"You better give me some of your shit, motherfucker!"

I turned in the direction of the slap and saw Tommy standing in another line with his head low while some black guy said, "I'm telling you. Better put me down for some cigarettes, motherfucker."
"Hey! Don't put your hands on him, motherfucker!" I yelled out.
"Who the fuck are you, motherfucker."
"I'll tell you who the fuck I am. I'm the motherfucker, who's gonna kick your ass if you touch him again."
"Well, he might have been your bitch then, but now he lives with me, so he's my bitch now, motherfucker!" he answered.

Having remembered some of the jail lingo, I said, "Yeah, motherfucker, what makes you think I won't have your ass had, for a carton of cigarettes!"
"Yo', my man, right here, right here, I'll take that bet," someone in his line said.
"You ain't got no cigarettes, man," my quad mate said in a low voice.
"Shut the fuck up!" I whispered back to him.
"Oh, yeah, yeah. Dat's right, motherfucker! He'll have your ass had! Don't fuck with his homeboy!" he yelled.
"All of you, shut the fuck up and move!" a guard yelled.

Shit, I guess Tommy didn't know the ropes of punching someone in the face first and asking questions later, I thought.

When we got back to our quad, a bunch of the other guys were mulling around, saying, "What ja' get? What ja' get?"

Some of the inmates started sharing their stuff with their friends as soon as we got back. Then one inmate I had started to get to know saw me empty handed and said, "What the hell did you get?"
"Two cigarettes and a Twinkie," I answered.

As my colored friend walked to his cell, he said out loud, "Remember, man, don't go back on your word. You gotta give me a piece of your ass now. You ate the Twinkie."
"Shit, what do you think I'm Snow White and I ate the poisoned apple, motherfucker?"
"That's right, motherfucker. You my Snow White now. Make sure you wear something silky and brush your teeth. I'll see you tonight. Don't be late now," he joked as he walked away.

At lunchtime I found myself a small pencil. As funny as it may seem, it kinda meant a lot to me because it was the only thing I owned in there. Out in the world I probably would have thrown it away because it was so small. Now all I needed was a piece of paper so I could write myself a letter, I thought. It was the same thing with the phone calls that we'd get to make once a night...Who the fuck was I going to call? I mean, first of all, my friends all lived at home with their parents, and I'm sure their parents didn't need to know where I was. Even if the phone was given to one of my friends, what was I supposed to say, "Hi, I'm in jail. I've got two bails set at $500,000 Uhm, send me money for Twinkies, I'll talk to you later." Besides, I'm sure everyone had a new newspaper article of mine now for their collection.

After dinner that night, I started to walk back to my cell with my pencil, when a guard called out to me and told me that I had court tomorrow. Besides doing push-ups for half the night, I was pretty bored, so I went to bed early.

"Hey, motherfucker! Get up!"
"Fuck you!" I answered, thinking I'm not in the mood for this guy's shit tonight. "No, you better get up, asshole!"
"Man, fuck you! Go hang yourself," I said.
"No, you better get up!"

Man, this shit has got to stop, I thought. I slowly opened my eyes to argue with this guy and saw the reflection of flickering flames on the ceramic block wall.

"Fuck!"

When I jumped up, I saw that he had tossed a flaming wad of toilet paper onto my bed. I knocked it off my bed and then drop-kicked the door where he was standing. I was so enraged, that I probably would have killed him if I got a hold of him. By the tone of my voice and the look on his face, I could tell that he knew that he had crossed the line with me, and he took off down the hall. A few minutes after that, a guard walked over to my cell.

"Hey! What the hell is going on here?"

"Hey, guard, listen. That guy that walks suicide watch is not my buddy. So any time he's by my cell, he's waking me up and fucking with me. He's not talking about the weather. So if you could do something about it, I'd appreciate it."

He looked at me slowly and said, "We'll see," and then he walked away. His answer almost sounded like an invitation to a club.

The next morning I figured that I'd better get some breakfast because it was going to be a long day. I decided to try the jam I was given, and it was the worst thing I had ever eaten. While I was force feeding myself, I noticed that a little mouse had gotten into my cell.

"Hey!" I called out to the black guy across from me. "There's a mouse in my room!"

"Is it a little brown one, or the black one?" he asked.

"It's a brown one."

"Oh, that's lil' shit. The black one's bigger, and we call him big shit. They make their rounds the day after we go to commissary to stock up on their shit."

"What are they in for, killing a cat?"

"No, I think they both in for armed robbery. Give lil' shit some Rice Crispies. He likes them."

After lil' shit and I had breakfast, I went back to sleep for about an hour until I was called to go to court.

When I got to outpost 1, Dino, Mike, and Tommy were already there. Because Tommy had someone on the outside, he had himself some cigarettes. But Mike had some shit; he looked like Santa Claus. First, he had on a blue goose down jacket and then underneath that he had on a denim jacket. He also had cookies, candy, eight packs of cigarettes, a gold chain, three watches, and a new pair of sneakers.

"Where the fuck did you go shopping?" I asked.

"Well, I'm good at playing cards," he answered.

"Good. You must be a great fucking card player, Mike. I'd just like to know what you used for your opening bet on your first hand," I suggested.

"Eh, he used his fucking ass, right, Mike," Dino said.

"Yeah. Fuck you," Mike joked back at Dino.

"So, Mike, why do you have all this shit with you? You plan on getting out or something?" I joked.

"Shit, fuck that. I'm not leaving my stuff in my cell. Mike... we're in jail, remember? Someone will rob my shit if I leave it in my cell," he reasoned.

Mike split up his stuff with the rest of us just before the bus came. As small as my portion would seem like out in the world, in jail it seemed like I was a millionaire.

After we got to court, our lawyers came out to talk with us. They said we might end up in court with my mother again. After sitting in the holding cell for half the day, two guards came over and

217

started to take Tommy out of the cell.

"Tommy, where are you going?" Mike said.
"I knew it. I knew he was a rat!" Dino yelled as he jumped up.
"We're all in this together, Tommy," I reminded him.

Tommy glanced back at me as he walked out of the holding cell, and the guard said, "Shut up. His lawyer wants to talk to him."

The three of us sat there for another three hours before we got called to court-without Tommy.

"I don't like this, man. I've still got bad vibes about Tommy, guys," Dino kept insisting.

Just before we were taken into court, three guards came into the small holding cell and put handcuffs on us. Then they told the guard at the door that they were ready. The guard then opened the door, looked out, and said, "Is everybody ready?" Then we were taken into the courtroom.

I was surprised to see my mother sitting there, but I was even more surprised to see that there were three guards standing behind our chairs and they had their guns on, unlike the last time when the guards behind us only had their billy clubs.

After ten minutes of court talk, the D.A. said, "Your Honor, the District Attorney calls as his first witness for the State... a Mr. Thomas Faye."

"That motherfucker," Mike said.
"I told you! I fucking knew it. We should've beat his ass when we had him," Dino said.
"Shut up," a guard behind us said.
"Yeah, what's worse than that is you gave him some of our cigarettes and candy, Mike," I said.
"Yeah, that motherfucker. I forgot that."

The guard behind me placed his hand on my neck and started to squeeze his nails into my throat.
"I told you guys to shut up!" he said.

As I pulled away from the guard, I said out loud, "Man, get the fuck off me!"

Tommy was walking up to the front of the courtroom, as the judge said, "Hey, keep it down over there!"

While Tommy was being sworn in, the guard behind me whispered in my ear, "You better keep your mouth shut before you and I take a little walk into the back, wiseass!"

Under the circumstances this was one of the last things I felt like listening to, so I turned my head towards him and said, "Oh yeah, tough guy? Well, if you're so tough, why don't you take me outside the building, take my cuffs off, and we'll play a little winner take all?"

Great, just what I need. A guard who's into necrophilia because that's what I'll be in a few minutes once Tommy opens his mouth- a fucking dead guy, I thought.

"Mike, shhhh, I want to hear," Mike V. said.

Tommy talked about Mike and Dino, and then he talked about his interpretation of what my mother said after she had heard us talking about Jimmy Morgenstern in the kitchen that day, but he said nothing about me.

"Any further questions, gentlemen?"
"No, Your Honor."

After a little court talk, the judge told the court officers to take us back to the holding cells.

Hooray for our side, I thought.

"Listen, Michael, Grandpa is going to send you a little money, okay? What the fuck is that carved in your arm?"
"Oh, I let this girl carve her initials in my arm."
"What the fuck was her name, MA?"
"No, she forgot to put the dots at the end of the letters."
"Oh, my God, it looks like you carved, MA, on your arm. I'll see you later."
"All right, Ma," I answered as she was led to the woman's prison entrance.

The three of us were then led back to where they kept the male prisoners by three armed guards. Dino kept saying, "I knew it was him. I knew it. I told you guys from the start."

After we were un-cuffed and put in our cell one by one, I said, "Hey, asshole, I'm un-cuffed now!"

My guard looked at me and said, "Fuck you!"
"Fuck you, too, asshole!" I answered.

When we got back to one of the main holding cells, our lawyers showed up a little while later. One by one, our lawyers called us over to the bars separating us, and told what kind of deals the D.A. was offering us. Dino went first, and when he came back he said he was offered 1-3 years. Mike came back and said the same thing. I followed my lawyer, and after we sat down, he said to me, "Well, you've got the same charges they do, but you've also got one other charge against you."
"Well, that's good," I said sarcastically.
"Yeah. They're offering you 6 years state time, but they'll probably try to give you 14 years Fed time for possession of sawed-off shotguns, like your mother," he said, as he laughed under his breath.
"What the fuck is so funny? Did somebody tell a joke!?!" I asked him.
"I'm sorry, but it is a little funny," he said.
"There you go again! So, he's offering me twenty years? I'm fucking seventeen-years-old, and he's offering me twenty years?"
"I'm sorry, Michael. But that's what he's offering you. Okay, look, they're not offering your

mother any deal like you guys, and it looks like someone is going to get the gun possession charge. They're going to try to show that your mother called together this meeting. Then they're saying that, because the guns were found in her house, that she was in possession of them. Because you lived there too, there's a little gray area about charging you both with the guns but their gonna try. They're also considering changing the charges, but I'm not sure. They might stick to the old ones.

After he explained that to me, he said, "Now, here's the worst part, guys... guys... they'll give you these deals if you all turn state's evidence against Alma, your mother," he said, as all the lawyers looked at me.

The slight enthusiasm we had left the room immediately, and I explained to my lawyer that I couldn't give state's evidence against my mother.

"Not me."
"Me either."

We all agreed.

"Well, then, I'll tell the DA that the three of you turned down their deal. You know, Mike, I think the reason they're being so hard on your mother is because this is the same DA she was up against in '75."
"No, don't tell him I turned the deal down, tell him I told him to go fuck himself."
"Well, I can't tell him that."
"Give me a piece of paper, and I'll write it down so you won't have to say it."
"Michael, c'mon, you don't want to piss him off."
"Why not? He already told me to go fuck myself by offering me that kinda deal. Rat my mother out, and, get twenty years!?! You know what, you're right, I'll change that now that I think about it. Tell him I said to suck my dick."

The three of us didn't say much on the bus ride back to Rikers. Too much to think about, I guess.

When we got into the first cell at outpost 1, along with the other guys who were in this cell, there were three colored gay guys in there with us. The funny thing about them was that you could see that they were three different kinds of fags. There was the street hustler, a transsexual I already had the pleasure of meeting, and the last one who was a queen. Their intelligence seemed to go in the same order. A few of us started to talk to them, and after a little while it seemed like everyone in the room was involved in the conversation.

It turns out, the hustler explained, that at a young age he was thrown on the street and started having sex with men to survive. The transsexual explained that as a child he was the youngest with three sisters.

"The reason I'm gay," he said, "is because my parents couldn't afford to buy my sisters dolls so they used me as one. They would dress me up with makeup and put women's clothes on me. After a while, I started to like it, I guess."

"Well, I've always been a woman, honey child," the queen said with a wave of her hand. "Ever since I was a baby," she added.

"If I'da had a few hundred more, I wouldn't even be here," the transsexual said. "I'm already half a woman."

"What do you mean?" the queen asked.

"Well, I've already got the breasts!"

"Oh, no, you didn't." the queen said.

With that, almost as if it was an invitation, the transsexual put down her heels, opened up her flannel shirt, and showed us a real cute pair of tits.

"Damn! I've been here six months, and I ain't seen titties in all that time," Seville, a skinny black dude from my quad, said as he stood up.

The transsexual, realizing her mistake, started closing up her shirt faster than she had opened it.

"Come on, honey. Let me just play with them."

"Hell, no!"

"What you mean no, woman?"

"Come on, Seville. Let her alone. We were just all talking," someone said.

Well, now I guess I know all I need to know about faggots, I thought.

About an hour after that, a big black dude came in. He had come in from upstate for a new charge they found on him, I learned. He wasn't in that cell for more than a minute before he said, "Oh sit'... a gold mine."

"Uh uh, honey. You're gonna have to kill my ass before you get any!"the queen said.

"Nobody would want your ass anyhow, bitch. You're too big and bony like a man. You're too ugly," he said to the hustler. "But you're just fine, honey child. We need to talk."

I don't know what the two of them talked about, but it wasn't long before the transsexual was sucking someone's dick in the open toilet stall for this big guy. At that time the three of us happened to be sitting close to the stall, with me being first. Well, it sure didn't look like it was any different from another type of blowjob, I thought while I watched.

"Yo! Mighty Whitey, you want some play? Whatcha got?" I was asked by the transsexual's new manager.

"No, that's all right. I'll pass," I answered.

"What about you?"

"No, thanks, I'll pass too," Mike answered.

"And you?"

"Uh..."

"Dino, you don't want any of that shit!" I said.

"I don't know, Mike. That blowjob is starting to look real good. Besides, I don't know how long I'm gonna be here, ya' know," he answered.

"Get the fuck out of here, you horny fuck. Go back to your cell and jerk off."

"I will... but I ain't got soft hands, you know, and that looks reeeal soft."

"C'mon, Dino. You don't need that shit."

"All right, but remember this, Mike. If I do big time you owe me a blowjob from some nice looking girl when I get out."

"All right, fine."

Just like usual, I was the last to go back to my quad late that night. Well, nice to be home, I thought. After thinking about how big that black dude was today, I decided to do a few extra push-ups that night.

The next day I slept through breakfast and went out with everyone for lunch. As I was walking towards the dayroom, I saw the guy from suicide watch standing with his big friends by one of their cells. He smiled at me as if I wouldn't do anything to him, but his expression changed when I changed direction and walked towards him. He started to undo his belt and then wrap it around his hand. I don't know why the guards let him use this belt with the big belt buckle on it, but I knew he used it as a weapon. I walked straight up to his face, looked into his eyes, and said, "The next time you fuck with me... I'll kill you, motherfucker."

I stood there a second, ready to take my licks from all three of them until we both realized that his friends weren't going to jump in. I stood there for an extra second or two, staring into his eyes. Then I turned and walked away.

"Hey, Mighty Whitey. Don't worry about him. He's just a big mouth. I saw your charges. You're all right, you hear?" his big friend said.

"Yeah, I hear."

"Listen, my name's Papo, and his name is Mopy. What's yours?"

"Mike."

"Well, look. You're cool with us, so don't worry about us jumping in on your fight if you need to take care of business."

"All right, that's cool," I said as I nodded my head at the suicide watch guy and walked towards the dayroom.

After lunch, I shot the shit with Papo and Mopy, much to the suicide watch's dismay. It turns out that Papo was in for killing a kid on his prom night. Shot him in the chest while robbing him. Unfortunately I wasn't really in a position to tell how stupid I thought he was for shooting some kid for a handful of coins. Mopy had an interesting story, though, I thought at the time. It turns out that two years ago Mopy got sentenced on some charges because his good friend turned state's evidence on him.

"When I was in the courtroom, just before he opened his mouth, I said, 'If you open your mouth, I'm gonna shoot you.' He did. So I did." Mopy explained.

"How the hell did you shoot him? You had a gun on you in the court room?" I asked.

"Right after I did my two years for that charge, I went back to my neighborhood, found out where he was, got a gun, and shot his fucking ass."

"Get the fuck outta here. You're shittin' me," I said.

"Yeah, man. We're from the same neighborhood so I heard the same thing," Papo added.

"So how'd you get caught?"

"Well, I didn't realize it, but there were two cops sitting in a cop car down the block."

"Yeah."

"Yeah, so they come running down the block, and we started to have a shoot-out."

"Really? So how'd they get you?" I quizzed him.

"Well, they shot my ass five times, so I gave up."

"Fuck, I guess I'd give up too, if they shot me five times."

"Show him. Show him, man," Papo said.

Mopy looked at me and pulled off his shirt to show me the strategically placed bullet wounds on his body. The last two shots, he explained, hit him in the gut so he had a colostomy bag attached to his side. We talked until it was time for lock down and then went back to our cells.

I took a shower that night after dinner. Luckily I had found a small piece of soap in the showers. It's kinda funny but this was the first shower I had taken since I had gone there. I figured that, after hearing about all the rumors about jailhouse showers, I should check out the quad I was in for a few days before I took a shower. One of the rumors I did find to be true was that, of all the things you didn't want to be in prison that was even worse than a rapist, was being a child rapist. A rapist only got spit upon and beat up by a few people, whereas a child rapist would get it from everybody.

After my shower I took the soap to my cell and washed my socks, underwear and shirt. Then I did my push-ups and sit-ups. It was a routine by now. I knew you had to be in shape in this place. After that I laid down on my cot, after I checked on my pencil.

So, this is it, huh, Mike? Seventeen years on this planet, and you finally arrived. What a fucking trip. What a fucking ride.

Being that my shirt was still wet from washing it in the showers, I went to sleep without using it as a pillow. I'm not sure, maybe because of the shower, but that was the best sleep I'd had since I got there.

The next day Seville came over to me and kept telling me that he wanted to be the new houseboy. The houseboy is usually a big guy who is a go-between from the guards and the inmates. He's there to keep order for the guards. Our guy happened to be this huge white guy; his arms were bigger than Seville's legs. All through lunch and then at dinner Seville told me how he was gonna be houseboy and what he was gonna do to that big white boy. Then about a half hour after dinner, Seville turned to me and said, "Okay, man, I'm going for it!"

I always considered myself to be a man of logic so I said to all one hundred and ten pounds of Seville: "Seville, that boy will beat your ass!"

"No way, man. Don't talk like that, man. You'll bug me out."

"Okay, you do what you want then. Go get him, tiger."

"Yeah, yeah, that's right - I'ma get him."

With that in mind Seville strutted his little ass across the dayroom floor, stopped in front of the big white dude, and slapped him cold in the face.

Holy shit! I thought. This little motherfucker has some King Kong balls on him.

The white guy stood there with this dumb surprised look on his face for about ten seconds. Just as Seville was asking him if he needed some more, the white guy slapped Seville in the face so hard that his little one hundred and ten-pound body flew over the table. Then he proceeded to slap his prey over the picnic tables like a bear chasing a rabbit.

After the tenth time he whacked Seville, we all started to convince him that Seville was "well done."

Situations like these test your friendships, but it pays to have rational thoughts about friendships in a place like this.

After the white guy was done speaking his mind to Seville, a closer friend of Seville's checked on him. "I'm okay. Just don't move me for a little while," Seville moaned.

Then he sat there for another ten minutes until he pulled himself up. As he left the room limping, he turned to me and said, "Now, I have everyone's respect!"
"Well, you certainly got my respect... for something, Seville." I answered.

The next morning, a bunch of guards woke us up and stood us outside in the halls, most of us still in our underwear. Then they took everything we owned and threw it in the hallway. It was an assortment of clothes, combs, toothpaste, fruit, milk, juice and letters from home. Then they stomped on everything until it was crushed.

"Holy shit! What the fuck did we do?" I asked the guy across from me.
"This is not funny!" a guard shouted.
"Do I look like I'm laughing?"
"What do you think this is? Some kind of fucking joke!" he yelled at me.
"Shhh, Mike, it's shake down. It's all right, Officer. He don't know. He's new," the inmate next to me said.

Oy vey, just what I need. Another lesson in here, I thought to myself. The coup-de-grace was having to get undressed and present your anus to the guard. Fitting, I thought, after they just got done stomping on all your stuff.

Shake down, I learned, is when the guards are looking for some sort of contraband. After I got back in my cell and saw my pencil, it made me glad that I didn't own anything.

Two guys got into a fight, and one guy got the shit stabbed out of him real fast that night. While the guards tried to take care of him, he looked into my eyes and died. After that, I found myself to be in a very serious mood that night locked in my cell, taunting myself with the insanity of my freedom and possible long incarceration. The depth and reality of my new society really hit home. With all the uncertainties I was juggling, there was one thing I knew, and that was that if I ever got out of this place, I'd never, ever, come back. But while I was here, I had to double up on my exercising, so I could put up a good fight if my day came.

We ended up having shake downs for almost a week, sometimes twice a day, but always at different times. I did eventually find out the reason. The guards had found half of a hacksaw blade on the south side, and they assumed that the other half was on our side.

Over the next couple of days, without going to court, my bail had gotten lowered to $1000 from $500,000. About a day after that my grandfather had it paid. I can't tell you how nice it sounded the day the guard came over to my cell and said, "C'mon, you're bailed out. Let's go."

I stopped by a few cells on my last long walk down the hall to say good-bye to a few people. They all wished me good luck, but none of them could really look me in the eye. I took the money that was left in my commissary account, and then I asked about the bus schedule. I was told that I'd take the bus out with the visitors, and then I'd get dropped off out front by the bridge. It was the same route I'd taken when I'd come up to visit my mother, only now I was somewhat of a "free man."

CHAPTER 6

ENTER THE THUNDER DOME

After getting processed I was let out into the visitors' area, on the free side. To see people talking, laughing, chewing gum, and reading a paper seemed amazing to me. I felt as if I was watching a play. It felt weird to go from inmate to visitor so quickly. I took the bus ride back into the world over the bridge with the civilians and, after I got dropped off, I sat at the bus stop in a bit of a daze. I marveled at the fact that twenty minutes ago I was a prisoner, and now I was out in the world with twenty bucks in my pocket. I took the first bus that came by. I felt that it was a good thing I got out early because at least I didn't have to ride the bus all the way home with the rush hour people while I looked like a bum.

The first thing I did when I got home was to thank my grandfather for bailing me out with a big hug. There were things that we could have discussed, but the bond we had surpassed anything we should talk about. Instead he just looked at me and told me to be careful because he liked me. The second thing I did was to take a nice, long, hot shower to try to wash the prison stench off me. After that I walked around my house and I realized that everything of value that was missed the first time around was gone this time, even all of my shit. I called up my friend Aaron, and he was happy to hear that I was home. "Don't go anywhere. I'll be right over," he said.

I don't know how he did it, but after he got there, Aaron talked me into going to the movies with him. I decided that going to the movies was the least of all the evils that he had in mind for my homecoming celebration. After we drove over there and parked, we started to walk towards the two big lines for the movie when all of a sudden I just froze.

"I can't go, Aaron."
"Why? What's the problem?"
"I don't know. I just don't want to be with that many people right now."
"What?! What the fuck do you mean??"
"It's like you're asking me to go see a movie, and I just got done living one."
"What are you worried about? You got big in jail."
"It's not that kinda worry, Aaron. It's something else."

When we got back to my house, Aaron went and got us a few beers for my celebration. I also happened to meet the new boarder, who had moved into my old room while I was on vacation, in jail. He seemed like a pretty cool guy; his name was Dave, and he had spent some time in Vietnam.

After a week or two, I was a little better adjusted to my surroundings, and I started hanging out with some friends. So one day I was up at Bowne Park hanging out with Peck, Jimmy Marnell, Joe De Silvio, and Freddy Capeeto. We're sitting around drinking some beers when Jimmy decided to light up a joint and then another one. "This is your coming home party, Mike. Enjoy," he said as he passed the first joint to me.

About a minute after that, Freddy and Joe got up and started to toss around a Frisbee. Soon Peck and Jimmy joined into their game. So now I was the only one sitting on the bench with all the beers, hitting on a joint, watching these guys playing catch in front of me.

"Slam! Slam! Slam!"

Hmm, that's funny. That sounded like three car doors closing, I thought. When I turned my head to look, I saw a police car with two cops and some kind of Police Captain walking towards me. Oh fuck, they're hitting me with some other charge, I thought, as I crushed up the lit joint between my fingers.

"Hey, don't you know Mayor Koch passed a law two days ago, stating that you couldn't have an open beer container out in public?"
"What? Get the hell out of here."
"Get the hell out of here nothing. It's a $500 to $1000 fine."
"No way!"
"Let's go. Let's see some ID."
"Shit, I don't have any ID on me, but you can ask those guys over there. They're my friends."
"Ha! You think I'll be asking those hooligans your proper name?"
"Let's go. Empty your pockets."
"Empty my pockets for what?"
"So we can take you down to the station house."
"For what?"
"Until someone can come down to the police station with some of your ID to claim you. Or if you keep it up, I'll charge you with vagrancy or something. Now empty your pockets," he said while the two other cops spilled out the beers.

Man, I thought, with two open cases, this is the last fucking thing I needed. As I went through the motions the guys never missed a beat playing Frisbee. Just before they put me into the police car, I shouted out, "It's all right, guys. Thanks for asking. I'll see you later."

When I got over to the 109th Precinct, I told the cop to go upstairs and verify my name with one of the detectives. Finally after I asked him several times, he did. Two minutes later, Detective Lizio came downstairs, looked at me, and said, "Who him? No, I've never seen him before."
"Yeah, thanks for nothing," I said.
"Any time," he answered.

After about thirty minutes I got to talk to "Uncle" Phil. by phone.

"Uncle Phil."
"Yeah?"
"Listen, you've got to do me a favor. You've got to go in my room, get my wallet, and take a cab over to the 109th Precinct so I can prove who I am. I'll give you money for the cab when you get here, okay?"
"Yeah, okay. I'll see you in a little bit," he said without asking any questions.

After Phil went there, I was given a summons to appear in court by one of the cops, and then we took another cab back to my house. Being that only a short time had passed, I figured I'd take a gamble on the guys still being up at the park, so I told the cab driver to take me there. Sure enough, they were still there with more beers, playing Frisbee.

"Gee, guys. Thanks for sticking up for me. Didn't you see them roll up on me?"
"Well, look, Mike, nothing for nothing, but every time you get arrested these days it's usually not for little shit, ya' know. So we decided that it might be better if we pretended that we didn't know you," Jimmy Marnell replied.

Well, I guess I'm no longer a Musketeer, 'All for one, and one for all'

A day before I had to go to court on the possession charges, I got a call from my lawyer on the other case.

"Mike, I've got good news. They might drop all charges against you."
"Great. What about my mother?"
"Well, I don't think they're going to do anything like this for her, Mike. I think they're going to hang her. Sorry."
"Well, thanks. Thanks for everything."
"Okay, I call you when I find out for sure."

The next day before court I spoke with my lawyer, and he told me that we were still waiting on the DA to either drop the charges or proceed with the case. When I walked into court, the judge said to me, "Well, it's nice to have you back. I heard you went on a little vacation."
"It's nice to be back, Your Honor," I answered.

Like usual, the case was postponed for another few weeks. Well, a postponement is better than a sentencing.

I ended up getting a construction job with Gerard working in Manhattan. After work he'd come over to my house, and we'd work out for hours. I'd usually take a little time and money out each week to send some things to my mother, Mike, and Dino at Rikers. One thing I really hated was when my mother would tell me to get her some bras and underwear. My mother took a size 44 DD bra, so I'd always get funny looks from the sales girls. I'd write some letters, but what do you say to someone who's in jail, so I'd usually send post cards.

I was in the basement working out alone one night when I heard a knock at the side door. When I went to check it out, it was Tina, my old babysitter. "Hi, how have you been, Michael? My God, you're getting big."

It was dark out, but I could see that Tina was still pretty hot. She also had two girlfriends with her who were both knock-outs, especially since they were all a few years older than I was.

"So what's up? How've you been?" I asked.
"Well, I was wondering if we could get high here."

Shit, my hormones thought, Tina with two other hot babes. Fucking a' right you can.

"Sure, why not?" I said.

We all went downstairs, and I figured I'd continue working out. As we spoke, Tina's girlfriends kept saying, "Ohhh...Look how strong he is. He's got a hot body"

When I saw them take out a spoon and a needle, I said, "Exactly what are you getting high with?"
"Well, we're going to shoot a little heroin."
"Do you want some?"
"Yeah, we can make him work it off," the another girl purred.
"Well, I go first," the other girl said.
"No, no, no, let's not even go there," Tina said.
"Oh, come on, Tina. Just because you would never have sex with me, don't stop me from getting some now," my hormones instigated.
"No way. I knew you since you were a baby. I don't even want to think of you having sex with my girlfriends."
"Okay, so go upstairs and watch some TV then."
"Yeah, Tina, we'll take good care of him. We won't break him."
"Look at him. He's gorgeous. Come on, Tina," the other girl said.
"....No, I can't. I mean, you guys can't..."

By now, as we were talking, they had prepared their stuff, and they were shooting up one by one. Then one of the girls said, "Here. Here's some for you," as she pressed the needle towards me.

"Well, wait. You don't shoot up, do you, Michael?" Tina asked.

So here I am with three hot chicks who just shot themselves up, and what am I supposed to say, No, I'm a pussy. I'll just snort some? "Yeah, I shoot up. But I can't do it by myself like you, Tina."

On that note, with my muscles and veins popping, the two girls jumped me like vampires, caressing my arms.

"Oooh, let's get him here."

"No, let's get him over here."

"No way are you sticking a needle in that vein. I'll fucking pop," I said.

After the three of us agreed on a vein, the girls shot me up while Tina frowned.

"Mmmm. Tina, he smells good, too."

"No, I already feel bad about this. Let's go," she answered.

We all stood up and headed for the stairs, and I said, "Hey, Tina, how long is this going...to...take...to... wow."

I managed to get up the stairs, kissed them all goodbye, and then sat down on the steps, stoned off my ass. I literary nodded out, and woke up three hours later.

The next day when I came home from work, there was a new black Mercedes sitting in my driveway running. I approached the car cautiously to try to get a look at the two guys inside.

Who the fuck could this be? Cops don't drive new Mercedes, I thought.

"Whoa, Mike, be cool. It's me, Vito... Vito from Corona, your father's friend. You used to come over to my house on the Fourth of July and blow off fireworks."

"Oh, shit! Yeah, how are you doing?"

"I'm doing great, Mike, great. How you doing?"

"I've been better."

"Yeah, I know, kid. I heard. Come on, get in the car. We'll go have a drink and shoot the shit."

He told me that he was sorry to have heard about my father and asked me what happened to me after the shooting. After I told him, he asked me why my uncles didn't come pick me up.

"I don't know. Maybe they were afraid that they'd piss me off, and I'd shoot them or something."

"I read about your last bust in the paper. It's too bad about your mother, though."

"Yeah, it's a real fucked - up deal."

"It's too bad we lost contact," he said. "I probably could have helped you unload some of that shit you had."

At this point, I figured that there was no point in bursting his bubble until I heard what he came to say, so I just sat back and listened.

"So, what are you doing for money these days?"

"I'm doing construction in Manhattan."

"Mmm, construction - hard work. Listen, Mike, how'd you like to do a little job for me? It'll get you back on your feet. You know what I mean?"

"What kind of job?"

"Well, you like to travel, right?"

"Yeah, so?"

"Well, you'd have to take a little trip to Vegas. Of course, everything would be paid for, and you'd stay there and watch this guy for me."

"That's it?"

"Well, no. Then I want you to whack this little Jew bastard for me. He owes me a lot. The job will pay you five grand plus expenses. But that's also because I like you."

Remember, Mike, if I'm going to end up doing time for anyone it's gonna be for me. For my reasons, number one. And number two, I'm not going back to jail, especially now, I thought.

"What's there to think about? You'll be put up in a nice hotel, we'll give you some broads to have fun with, you'll get a tan, do the job, and come home."

"Well, don't get me wrong, I appreciate the offer. I just got to think about it."

"All right, Mike, you think about it. Now if you want to get in touch with me, you call this Laundromat and ask them how much they would charge you to clean ten pounds of velvet. That will let me know you're in, and I'll stop by your house, okay?"

After I got dropped off, I sat on my back porch and said to myself, So what do ya' think, Mike? You want to be a hit man?

There was a very small battle in my head for a few minutes, but I already had a taste of what it felt like to be a victim of this type of circumstance first-hand... and it was a bitter taste. One that I wouldn't want to be the cause of for some other family.

I got word back to Vito that I would pass on his job a few days later.

Tina would still stop by just about every day. She would shoot herself up, and then she'd shoot me up and leave. Sadly, her girlfriends weren't with her. One day after about three weeks of this, I was coming down the stairs, and I got such a sharp pain in my stomach that I grabbed my stomach and fell down the whole flight of stairs. I sat there for a few minutes and realized that I was probably becoming addicted to heroin.

Man, if this type of pain comes after three weeks, I can just imagine what it will be like in another month. I decided, while sitting up at the bottom of the stairs, that I was done with this shit at any cost.

The first couple of days were a little rough, but it got easier after I told Tina she couldn't shoot up here any more.

I brought home two little black cats that seemed a few days apart in age. One of them I caught over by Bench Park; I named him Buckwheat. The other one I pulled out of a dumpster by Western Beef, a huge supermarket over on College Point Blvd. This one had extra toes on his feet; I named him Stymie.

My buddy John Slocum worked over there; so did my old school pal Ronnie Kershner. These guys would put in a full day at the market, and then they'd do all night security work outside. Sometimes I would hang out with them all night. They'd take turns sleeping, so each one of them would be refreshed by the morning. To keep warm, they'd keep a fire going using broken pallets in an old oil drum. But after a while, they'd get real cold so John would grab a plastic milk crate and yell out, "Ten million degrees," and then he'd toss it into the barrel. Man, those milk crates would burn. You'd feel like you were getting sunburned if you were too close to the fire. After that, you'd start out with a clean slate and could withstand another hour or two of the cold. Sometimes you had to do what it took to get your hours in somewhere. I'd always try to get something indoors for extra money when it started to get cold out.

We all went out one night for Aaron's birthday. He was trashed by the end of the night, and he fell asleep in the car. I told Johnny boy to ride to some prostitutes, because I had promised to get Aaron a blowjob for his birthday.

"Yeah, but Mike, he's out of it," Peck said.
"That even makes it better," I answered, "because I'll get him one, you'll witness it, and he'll have to be content with it because you'll have witnessed it."
"Aww, that's fucked up. The boy's gonna get some play, and he won't even know it," John said.

When we got there, fortunately Aaron was still out like a light.

"Okay, John, now drive around until you find a real ugly one," I said.
"Oooh, that's cold."
"How about this one?"
"Nah, we can find worse than that."

This sort of exchange went on until we all agreed on the ugliest and oldest one we could find.

"Hi, honey. Any of you guys looking for some action tonight?"
"Well, one of us anyhow, sweetheart," I said. "It's my friend in the back seat. He wants a blowjob. How much?" I asked.

She looked in the back seat and said, "Hey, what's wrong with him?"
"Aaa, he's just passed out from drinking."
"Wait a minute. You Italian?"
"Yeah..., why?"
"He ain't dead, is he?"
"Why? You got something against blowing dead guys?" I joked.
"No, but I'll have to charge you more money," she answered.

To prove to her that he wasn't dead, I pinched Aaron's nose closed until he gasped for air.

"Okay, honey, that'll be $20 then," she said.

John, Peck, Jimmy, and I climbed out of the car at her request. Then she climbed in and started talking all this honey shit while she was fishing to get his joint out of his pants. We were standing outside, drinking and joking about it, when all of a sudden Aaron starts howling, "Whoa, whoa, get the fuck out of here," and starts kicking at this poor old bitch. Then the prostitute starts kicking and slapping back at Aaron. The three of us were pissing in our pants until it seemed like it was starting to get a little too wild, so we jumped in the car and broke it up.

"What are you, fucking crazy? I could've had a fucking heart attack. I wake up, and this old ugly bitch has my dick in her hand. Yo', that's fucked up, Mike." Aaron gasped.

As I was laughing, I said, "I'm sorry, Aaron. I'll make it up to you. After all, it is your birthday. Find a cute one you like, and I'll pay for that one, too."
"Shit, after that cow I don't think my dick wants to ever come out of my pants."

We all got blowjobs that night, and then we left. Little did I know that in a short time, one of us would be dead.

I had a party at my house on Halloween night. I invited a bunch of my friends from all over the place. My friend Ricky Dale rode in from Long Island on his motorcycle and then passed out on the couch all night long. After about two hours of hanging out, someone told me about another party that was going on close by, so a few friends and I decided to go. As I was heading towards the door, a girl walked over to me and said, "Hi, I'm Patti. I live around the corner."

"Oh... hi. Listen, I was just heading out to another party with a few of the guys. There's beer and soda in the refrigerator, and there's still some food left."
"Wait a minute. This is your party, and you're leaving to go to another party?"
"Yeah, but don't worry. You'll have a good time here. There's food, beer, music and anything else you might need," I said to her as she stared at me with a strange look.

The other party turned out to be a little party, and I figured that maybe I should have stayed and talked to that girl, Patti. She was kinda cute.

After staying at this party for about a half hour, we decided to go over to Dunkin' Doughnuts. Once I got there, I couldn't believe my eyes when I saw Tommy Faye standing in line. Because of pending legal shit I had, I decided that I didn't really want to start too much shit. But I couldn't contain the need to humiliate him a bit, especially with the buzz I had on.

"Na, he don't want a doughnut. He wants a hunk of fucking cheese, because he's a fucking rat!" I said.

Tommy looked at me and turned white, like he should have, and then looked away without saying a word. Being that there were quite a few people in the store, I said, "Go ahead, Tommy. Why don't you tell everyone how you sold my mother out to get your pretty little ass out of jail? And while you're at it, tell us how you ended up being that black dude's bitch in jail."

With that, someone grabbed me from behind and threw me into the cigarette machine. When I jumped up, aside from Gerard, Donde, Tony and Hector Morealass, and Brian Brawly, there were only about four faces I didn't recognize.

Mmm, just what I wanted, an excuse to kick someone's ass, I thought.

"So who's the fucking tough guy?" I said as I glanced over the faces again, and then "BAM" the guy standing on the left of me grabbed me and threw me into the cigarette machine again. Motherfucker! Well, at least now I had a target, I thought, as I sprang to my feet.

Then I heard "Wham" just before I spun back around in time to see my target back pedaling past me. I jumped him like a horny dog in springtime. Tommy's other friend tried to jump in, but he was distracted when my friends kicked him in his fat ass.

Gerard, who was drunk and had just spent his last two dollars on a coffee and a doughnut, was trying very hard to tiptoe through the brawl to go have his coffee, when someone smacked it out of his hand.

"Motherfucker!" Gerard said as he tried to kick the guy who slapped down his elixir. "Crash!" went the plate glass window he hit instead.

By now you could hear police sirens heading our way, so everyone started to scatter. As I ran outside, I saw that Tommy's two friends had caught Donde over by a parked car and were throwing about 100 punches a minute at him. Fortunately from what I could see, nothing was landing. I beaded in on the guy who was bending down with his ass facing me and, wham, I kicked him so hard that his head slammed into the fender of the car they had Donde pinned against. The other guy turned around after the noise and said, "There he is, get him," and started to chase me.

"Owww. My ass. I can't run. You get him."

Just before I took off, I looked at Donde. He smiled at me for helping him while he was making his getaway before the cops got there.

By the time I got to the end of the block, I heard a car peeling out, so I put it in high gear. I made a right at my first corner, and then a left at the next, and ran behind a parked car in someone's driveway. A car screeched around the corner and for some reason pulled right into the driveway I was in. I turned and ran towards the small driveway fence these people had and read the small "Beware of Dog" sign just as I hopped over it.

Hmm, I thought as I landed on the other side, the lesser of two evils, I hope.

I hit the ground and almost ran into their German shepherd, who had the same surprised look on his face as I did. We both did a small little sidestep, passed each other, sized each other up and, bam, I was gone over their backyard fence. As I hopped over the fence I hoped that someone had followed me; the dog wouldn't let the next guy go, I thought. A few days later word on the street was that I had beat up Tommy's uncles.

During that next week I heard my buddy Ricky Dale got into a motorcycle accident. I was told he had been sliced open by a guardrail as he slid on top of it, like a hot knife through butter. He died twice in the ambulance and once on the operating table, but they managed to stuff everything back into him, aside from two feet of his intestines and his spleen. He also managed to puncture one lung and collapse the other one, while breaking all the ribs on his right side. The doctors gave him a forty percent chance of pulling through it.

Christmastime was here. I had started working with a construction company, and I was booked until the 24th but then I'd have two days off. The last night on the job, a few of the different trades were having a little party over at the elevator shanty on the 23rd floor. I had seen shanties before, but nobody ever had one like the elevator operators. These guys would have two- or three- room shanties with a TV, microwave oven, lounge chairs, couches, and beds, and sometimes they even had bathrooms complete with showers. "It's in case you don't want to go home to the wife, lad. You could tell her you slept at the job," I was told.

After I had a few "tastes" I walked over to a window without glass, sat in the window sill, and watched the sun go down behind the World Trade Center. It was a memorial picture in my mind.

Well, Christmastime in New York, you can smell it in the air, I thought. I hope my mother, Mike and Dino got the things I sent them in time. I guess that about does it for my shopping list, except for the bottle of wine I've got to get for my grandfather. Boy, remember Christmas in the old days, Mike? Now that I think about it, I guess I had it pretty good by being an only child and all. Well, at least I had some good ones to last me through all the shitty ones now.

"Well, party's over, lad. Now go home and see if you can get the missus to give your candy cane a lick or two," I was told.

New Year's Eve sneaked up on me pretty quickly, so quick that I didn't have time to make plans. But after a while, I did manage to run into a few of the boys.

"Hey, Mike, what are your plans tonight?" Peck asked me.
"I don't know. I don't really have any. Why?"
"Well, Joe De Silvio and Joany are going with me and Chrissy to Manhattan to watch the ball drop. Do you want to go?"
"Nah, I hear it's nothing more than a big mess. Besides, I heard only the tourists go there to get mugged."
"Yeah, well, none of us ever did it before, so we're going to go."
"All right, see you next year."
"Yep, don't forget to write."

Instead of making any plans I stayed in the neighborhood and worked on forgetting my way home.

The next morning Bobby Marnell came over to my house and let himself in.

"Hey, Mike, did you hear?"
"Hear what?"

"Peck got stabbed last night. It looks pretty bad."

"What? What do you mean?! Where?"

"Before they got to see the ball come down, some guy in a blue pickup truck cut him off so Peck raced after the guy and caught him by a red light."

"Yeah!?"

"Well, then Peck walked over to the guy's truck and told him what an asshole he was, and then they got into a little bit of a fistfight, and somehow Peck got stabbed. Joe said that he thought the fight ended pretty fast after he saw Peck get punched in the stomach, and when Peck walked back to the car and sat down, Peck said, "I'm stabbed... he fucking stabbed me.""

"What about the guy?" I asked.

"He took off."

"Well, how is Peck now?"

"I don't know. I heard it went through his liver, and they can't stop the bleeding. Look, I got the phone number to the hospital. I'll call now. Where's the phone?"

While Bobby got the phone and dialed it, I thought to myself, Peck's a strong young guy. He should pull through, but that thought was interrupted by Bobby moaning, "No... don't tell me that... not Peck. Really? Aw, fuck. All right, I'll get off the phone. Mike...Peck's dead."

After Peck's funeral a bunch of us chipped in and got another headstone installed in Bench Park for Peck. It was put right under Joe Magun's, another young neighborhood guy who was killed.

My birthday came next, 18... I guess I'm a man now.

John, my friend who lived with me in the country, came over a few days after that and told me that he had a nice birthday present for me.

"Yeah? What is it?"

"Well, it's a double date."

"Double date, your ass. I'm not going out with some ugly broad so that you can get laid."

"No, Mike I swear. Her friend is just as good looking as my date. She's your type too, with long black hair."

"You serious, or are you shittin' me?"

"No, I swear."

"All right I'll go, but if she's ugly, I'm gone."

"Okay, no problem. C'mon, get dressed."

It turns out that John wasn't shittin' me. The girl was as good looking as he had said, and she had long black hair down to her ass. Her name was Asia. The one John was with was named Wendy; she had long blond hair, and they both had a few tattoos. We went out and had a pretty good time. After talking for a while, we found out they were both from Milwaukee. I also found out that Asia had a 1-year-old daughter.

Eventually John and Wendy stopped seeing each other, but Asia and I got to be an item over the next few months. I really liked Asia, she was only a few months older than I was, and we got along great. But I wasn't ready for the whole baby thing. It was pretty hard for me to do but, after being with her for a couple of months, I decided that I was going to break up with her. I went over to her house one day and brought about two hundred dollars' worth of food and diapers with me. "I know this is going to seem weird, Asia," I said, "but I can't do the baby thing. But listen, if there's anything I can do for you, just call, all right? I'd still like to be your friend."

Then I kissed her and left.

I took another one of my therapeutic trips into Manhattan. I would take them from time to time to get my head straight about shit in what I felt was a neutral setting. Another thing I liked about being in the city was that just in case I happened to talk to myself out loud, nobody would mind or pay attention.

What triggered this one, in an odd way I guess, was breaking up with Asia and the thought of Peck's funeral. Eighteen years old and laid up in a coffin. Peck had a few sisters, and it wrenched at your gut to see them so sad. Stabbed- just like that dude in jail.

It just goes to show, Mike, I thought, You've got to be on guard in the world. That's what I've got to do... train to be on guard 'cause I'm not going out like my father, Peck, or that dude in jail. No sirree', my motherfuckin' ass is slipping on a bar of fuckin' soap, that's the way I'll be going out, something real stupid, I thought as I rode the train into the city. I'm also getting tired of some of the people in my neighborhood, too, the way they look at me as if I'm a fucking leper. The way they stop and freeze when I walk by or cross the street when they see me coming, they look at me like I'm a homicidal maniac. I still try to say hi to some of them, but I know they're just being extra polite for a reason.

After I got to the city I walked around, hit a few bars, and then headed for Central Park. Walking into Central Park is always refreshing for me after getting my fill of the city's mayhem.

So, bottom line, Mike, I thought as I sat on a park bench, no matter how nice you are to people they still choose to treat you like you're a time bomb. So you know what? Fuck 'em. Act like one. I mean, what are you really scared of in this life anyway, emotional pain? Physical pain? Been there - done that. I just gotta be cool and on guard at all times.

By now I had walked until it was way past midnight, and just to prove this new theory to myself, of being cool and on guard and acting like a time bomb, I decided to walk into any dark area of the park where one wasn't supposed to walk. It was some kind of ritual thing for me. After a while, I did run into two tough-looking guys, so I purposely walked towards them. After we nodded our heads at each other, I walked by and realized that it's true. It's better to confront your fears head on instead of thinking about how bad they might be. If nothing else, at least you could sense what was coming and be prepared, as opposed to being surprised when you would be more vulnerable. You just had to know how and when to use the volume control with your inner voice and emotions, I reasoned. I wasn't really happy with my life, and I kinda knew I was heading down the wrong road. But what was I gonna do? Ask a stranger for guidance? After filling my head with a bunch of reasons and healthy answers, I left Central Park at about 3 am and went home.

In theory it was a good set of beliefs, but they started to mutate over time as I started doing more and more types of drugs, and I started acting more and more like a time bomb. Being that I was already proving a little point about myself to others about being as hard as steel, drugs were another tool in that direction. If someone I was with had three shots of whiskey, I'd have six. If someone did four lines of coke, I'd do ten. If three guys shared a dime of angel dust, I'd smoke one by myself. These things alone started to make my peers think I was nuts. That's not to mention that I was working out every day on drugs and getting huge. I lied to myself that somehow, with the help of drugs, I'd overcome the feeling that bothered me. I guess that's why they call some drugs hallucinogenic; it makes things seem like they aren't.

The more something inside me screamed out that something was wrong, the more I tried to drown it with alcohol or numb it with drugs. I'd get up and, bam, I'd get high before my inner voice could speak up or knew we were awake. I knew I was traveling down the wrong road, but how do you jump off a train that seems to be traveling 100 mph? Especially when peers around you who are involved with drugs look at you like something's wrong with you for standing close to the doorway, ready to jump.

Woe to the inner emotional workings of an individual who knows this and can't jump, because the next volley is even more destructive. Now there's inner shame involved. Wait a minute, you think, I'm strong, I'm good looking, I'm street smart, I can take care of myself. How can this little voice bring me to my emotional knees? Then months later comes the second alarm. That's when your resistance to your drugs or alcohol builds up, and your inner voice tries another route of escape.

'Don't you feel bad that the only way you can function is if you place your soul in a bottle of formaldehyde?' 'What? Who said that? You motherfucker, don't tell me how to live my life!' you scream internally as you look for some type of inner phone you can rip off the wall. 'Okay, okay, you want to talk? Here, see if you can talk now!' you say as you double up on everything you were taking in the first place.

There are two ironies at work here the whole time, and the first one is that the stronger the people are emotionally, the more drugs they have to take in an attempt to silence their strength or to blind the view of the road they're on. The second is that, in the long haul, it's easier to jump off the train as soon as you can, because you'll find out once you do jump that the train wasn't really moving; it was all in your head. Some people jump off with no time to lose. Still others elect to ride to the end of the line with whatever circumstances come with it.

People will paint their own canvas from the ideas they have about themselves and their surroundings. If you want to be a lawyer, you'll act like one, and then you'll talk like one. Then you'll dress like one, buy a lawyer's car, and live in a lawyer's house. You'll even listen to lawyer's songs. Then you'll enhance your canvas' colors when you decide whether or not you'll be a good lawyer or a bad- ass lawyer. From my position in life at this point in time, I decided to use black, purple and red for my canvas. My theme song was "Fade to Black" by the Rolling Stones. "All aboard!"

My lawyer on the shotgun case called me today.

"Mike, good news. They dropped all charges against you."
"Well, that's a relief."
"Yeah, I'll bet it is."
"What about my mother?"
"Well, her case is going to trial along with the others."
"Great," I answered.
"Yeah, that must be a tough spot to be in. Well, you're a smart young man. Use your head in this world. All right? Take care."
"Yeah, thanks. Take care."

Well, I certainly didn't look it, but I felt 300 pounds lighter.

Over the course of the next year, on this case everybody got sentenced. Dino and Mike got hit with one to three year sentences, my mother got hit with five and a half to fifteen years for being the mastermind, they said. I spent my time working part-time, partying all the time, and working out every day.

My buddy Ricky had finally got out of the hospital. When he had first gone into the hospital, his hair was pretty long, but now he looked like Jesus Christ. His stomach and chest looked like he had a big zipper sewn onto him, and he walked a lot more slowly. He even lost some weight, as if he could afford to. But Ricky was still Ricky, and in no time he was back to getting high again. There were some nights where he would get so high up at Bowne Park that we would literary have to carry him home and drop him off at his mother's doorstep.

I really couldn't believe it, but it just so happened to be April Fool's Day when I got before the judge on my first case. I sat down and figured I'd be in for the same bullshit of the case getting postponed for a few more weeks, and I can honestly say that I was very surprised when halfway through it, the judge said to the DA., "I'm sorry, but you've had almost two years to get ready. Case dismissed!"

Then slam went the gavel.

"No way?!" I said to my lawyer.
"That's it, Mike. You are free to go," he answered.
"Yo, wait a minute. He can't say April Fool's Day, can he?"

My lawyer laughed, and said, "I should tell that to the Judge. Your Honor..."

I grabbed his arm and said, "Don't tell him I said that. I don't want to piss him off."
"Don't worry the case is over. Your Honor, my client expressed his concern in whether or not you were going to tell him April Fool's?"

The judge laughed, and said, "I should do it just to watch the expressions on everyone's face."

The DA looked over to me with gritted teeth and said, "I wish he would change his mind."

That was it, almost two years of this shit, and it was over. It's kinda funny, but this was the first day my mother chose not to come to court from jail, where she was doing time for a case that happened because of this case. When I got outside, I still couldn't believe this case was over. As I stood there in a bit of shock, I tried not to make eye contact with anyone on the steps of the courthouse for fear of someone shouting out April Fool's and dragging me back to court. After that, I decided that I needed to celebrate, so I went and got lost in Manhattan for two days.

About a month after my court day, I ran into Fran, my neighbor from across the street.

"Michael! Why haven't you stopped by to visit me?" she scolded.
"Well, I'm sorry, Fran. I figured you thought I was some kind of nut, like everyone else does."
"I've known you for your whole life- since you were a child, Michael. did I ever tell you that?"
"Well, no."
"Then you get your butt over here one day this week. Do you hear me?"
"Yes, Fran. I hear you."

Fran had been like a second mother to me when I was growing up. Sometimes her daughter, Ronnie, would babysit me when I was younger, and I did miss them a bit. As odd as it may sound, it actually felt nice to be scolded by Fran today.

Later that night, I happened to be over by the Raven Luncheonette with Jimmy Duguid. We were sitting there getting high, when all of a sudden a car skidded to a stop in front of us. Four guys jumped out and started to chase Jimmy around back, so I ran after them. By the time I got back there, they had caught Jimmy and were trying to wrestle him to the ground. I started grabbing them and yanking them off him. At about halfway through them, Jimmy looks up at me and says, "It's okay, Mike. They're cops. They got me."
"Yeah," one of the guys I had thrown said. "We're fucking cops, and you're under arrest now."
"For what?"
"For trying to help him get away," he said.
"Bullshit, I didn't know you guys were cops. You didn't say anything. All I see is four guys jump out of a car and start chasing a friend of mine and then start beating on him. I didn't know what the fuck was going on."
"Well, you know my face now, motherfucker, so watch it," the detective said.

By now they had finished handcuffing Jimmy, and they started walking towards their car.

"Hey, wait a minute. What's your name?" a different cop said.
"Uhm... Michael."
"Yeah? Michael what?"
"Michael Garramone."
"Thee Michael Garramone?"
"Yeah, "THEE" Michael Garramone," I repeated.

"Oh shit," he said. "We should arrest this motherfucker, too."

"Na, na, na, I'm clean, man. I've been clean ever since my last arrest a long time ago."

The cops talked to each other for a minute, and then one of them said, "Aw, fuck it. We got what we were after. Let's go."

Whew, that was fucking close, I thought, as they left.

A day or two later, I went over to Fran's house across the street. When I got there, Barbara answered the door. After talking for a second or two, I realized that I hadn't been standing this close to her in years. She looked so sweet and innocent, and it was like a breath of fresh air talking with her. We chatted for a few minutes until she asked me what I was doing there. I explained that I had ran into her mother, and she threatened to beat me with the wooden spoon if I didn't come and visit. Barbara laughed and said. "The wooden spoon, like when we were kids."

She invited me inside, and I could tell from the light that she certainly filled out her clothes in a very nice way these days.

"Well, mom's on the porch watching TV. Don't be a stranger, Michael," she said as she walked back upstairs.

When I walked onto the porch, Fran said, "My goodness, look at you. You've really grown."

"Well, I work out a lot these days," I said.

Fran and I talked until about two in the morning about a lot of things, and then I hugged her and went to leave.

"Wait a minute, I want your phone number. I want you to promise that you're not going to wait for years to let me know how you're doing," she said.

After I did both these things, she added that I should take Barbara out once in a while. "You know, she's like a sister to you, not to mention that Ronnie misses you, too."

When I left, I actually felt a lot better for some reason. I guess it felt nice to talk to someone who cared about me.

When I got to my front door, Ricky was sitting there, petting Stymie my cat.

"Where the fuck were you all night?" he asked.

"I was across the street."

"I've been looking for you all night, man. I went to Harlem and got the monster 'D', man."

Monster D was slang for P.C.P.

"Well then, spark it up, my man," I said.

Since Ricky's last major motorcycle accident, he was still riding, and he had gotten into two minor ones. He still had a cast on his arm from the latest one. After we smoked a dime or two, Ricky said that he had the munchies and wanted to go get a coffee and a donut.

"C'mon, I ride ya'."
"Fuck that, I'm crazy - not an idiot, Ricky. We'll walk."

Ricky had on a Walkman radio; it was the type you put in your ears like ear plugs. We each put one in our ear and walked four blocks like a pair of Siamese twins joined at the head to go and get our coffee and doughnuts. When you're high on "Angel Dust," a lot of things become socially acceptable. We got there, and I grabbed a soda. Ricky inhaled his doughnut and coffee before we even got out of the store and complained about still being hungry, as we walked around the side of the building.

As I kept walking, I noticed that the dumpster was loaded with day old doughnuts. "Hey, Ricky. Here's a whole pile of doughnuts for you," I joked as I grabbed one and lobbed it over my head at him.
"Whoa, doughnuts!" he said as he looked into the dumpster.
"Don't even think about it, Ricky," I yelled back to him as I kept walking.

After I didn't hear him answer me, I looked back to see Ricky flicking "bad" donuts into the air, while he took a bite of the good doughnut innards before the others hit the ground. I started laughing so hard that I was begging Ricky to stop. Ricky, who was as stoned as I was, looked at me, shrugged his shoulders, and kept eating. By now I was hysterical and trying to crawl out of view of him. After he had his fill and I regained my composure, I went back into Dunkin' Donuts to get a soda for the one I dropped out back from laughing so hard.

While we were back in there, we ran into an old friend of ours, Joe O'Neil.

"Did you hear that Pete got busted?"
"No, for what?"
"Well, I heard that he went into the diamond district in Manhattan and tried to hit some jewelry stores in a building."
"Really? So what happened?"
"Well, that's the funny part. I heard that he planned on hitting this place because it was in a small building next to a big parking garage. You know, the ones that have a few parking levels to it. Anyway he planned to hit the place with this other guy he was with and then run upstairs cross over the roof, onto the parking garage, and then hide in the trunk of a stolen car he parked there."
"That sounds pretty stupid. So he got nailed leaving the parking garage?"
"No, here's the funny part. After him and this other guy got into the trunk, this girl he started dating was supposed to go in and claim the car with the ticket she had, and then drive the car out with them inside."
"And?"
"And she chickened out and left them there. About two days later, one of the people who worked there heard people yelling from inside the trunk, so he called the cops and they got nailed."

"What a fucking genius," I said.

We had a good laugh envisioning Pete living in a trunk for two days with a roommate.

The next morning I heard the lawn mower going and realized that Dave, the guy who was living in my old room, was probably doing it. I threw on a pair of shorts and went down to help him. When I got down there, I said that I'd help him, and Dave said, "You can help me by getting me a cold beer from the fridge, and by going out back and flipping the hamburgers I'm cooking."

After having some beers and burgers with Dave, I decided to go to Ricky's and see how he was doing after eating all those doughnuts. When I got there, his mother told me he was still sleeping, and she wanted me to do her a big favor.

"What's that, Helen?"
"I want you to take that motorcycle and put it at your house. He came home last night, and I think he was drunk. He's going to kill himself on that thing," she said.
"Yeah, but Ricky's my friend. I can't, like, lie to him about it."
"That's right. He's your friend, and he's going to kill himself on it, so I'm going to tell him that I don't want him to ride it until he gets it re-registered and insured, which also means he'll have to spend money to have all the lights and everything fixed on it. By that time, maybe he'll think it's not worth fixing, okay?" she said.
"Okay, Helen."

She gave me the key and a helmet and told me to drive straight home with it, so I rode around town for a while. Then I went home and parked it in my driveway.

A few nights later, I saw someone sitting in the driveway on the motorcycle when I came home. It turned out that it was Jimmy Marnell, and he was high as a kite on P.C.P.

"What are you doing, Jimmy?"
"Shh, man. I'm in Las Vegas."
"No, you're not. You're in Flushing, New York."
"I know, man, but I'm dreaming like I'm there."
"Oh, okay. I'll wait here until you get back then."
"Aw, fuck it, man. You blew it. You wanna get high? I got some dust."
"Yeah, what the fuck?"

After about a dime or so, I didn't know if I was hallucinating or if I did see someone through the basement window turn on the light and start making out with this big fat chick. When "whoever" got her shirt and bra off, I said, "Hey, Jimmy, do you want to watch a porno movie?"
"No. Why the fuck would I want to watch a porno flick with you?" he answered.
"Because it's live action. I'm watching it right now."
"Bullshit, where?"
"Look into the basement window."

Jimmy, who was a lot more stoned than I was, said, "Oh, shit, rewind it, man."

"Who do you think it is?" I asked.

"I don't know. It's your house. Who does it look like?"

"Well, nothing for nothing, Jimmy, but I don't know what anyone's naked ass looks like around here."

A few minutes later, we both realized that it was my friend, Aaron. After we watched him for a little while, Jimmy and I were moving our shoulders in unison, saying things like, Yeah, yeah, Aaron, right there, right there. Okay, a little faster, there boy, right there. Now get her leg up. When he got done, I said to Jimmy, "Watch me go down and scare the shit out of them."

Then I opened the side door quietly, ran halfway downstairs, and yelled, "Aaron, the cops are here. It's another raid! RUN!"

Man, let me tell you, that fat chick threw Aaron off her like a chicken bone, threw her clothes on, and ran out the side door without him. After that, I told Aaron it was a joke, and maybe he should go catch the girl he was with.

"Nah, that's all right. I didn't want to pay for a cab for her, anyway. It's cool."

When we got out to the driveway, Jimmy laughing so hard, he was crying.

"Man, I've never seen anyone move so fast in my life as that fat chick just did. She almost ran me over on the way down the driveway," Jimmy said.

After we all stopped laughing, Jimmy told me he needed a place to live.

"Well, you can live here, Jimmy, but you've got to pay rent."

"Yeah, no problem, Mike. I'm working steady at the transmission shop."

"Well, I'll ask my mother then, and see what she says."

By now my age group was slowly inheriting the Murry Hill Bar from the guys who used to hang out at Bench Park. One night Gerard and I were up there having a few drinks, and Freddy Capeeto showed up with Donde and Joe De Silvio. Freddy had his father's van, so we all piled in to go for a ride. After about an hour or so, we ended up over by a 7-11 store near Francis Lewis Boulevard and Northern, so we stopped in to get some beers.

When we went back outside, Donde was having a conversation - slash - argument with a bunch of white guys who were hanging out. Having known Donde for a few years, I could tell he was trying to feel them out to see if he could act like a tough guy. Besides that, "Donde" could get weird on you any second, so you never knew what would happen with him.

Instead of getting involved I leaned on a parked car and waited for what I thought would be any second for Donde to pop this guy and get this fight started. I didn't know what the hell they were arguing about, but still I waited, and waited, and waited. About fifteen minutes into this bullshit, I said,

"What are we doing talking? Arguing? Jerking off? Or leaving?"

Everybody grumbled for a minute or two, and then Donde started arguing with this black guy who was there with the other guys. After about two or three more minutes of our fearless leader arguing with this new guy, I said out loud, "Man, fuck this. I'm gonna go sit in the van."

By now it was starting to get ridiculous. But hey, I didn't start the fight so I didn't feel the need to finish it. Then the black dude starts mouthing off big-time, "Man, you all a bunch of pussies. I'll kick all your asses, even Mr. Cool with the hat on."

I used to wear my grandfather's black Fedora with a black jacket liner and leather fingerless gloves, very similar to the getup "Rocky" wore in one of his movies. It was like nature's warning device, like how a cat or a cobra puffs up to let you know that you're in for some shit if you fuck with me, I'm ready.

We were outnumbered, but that doesn't mean shit to someone on five hits of mescaline who already has a give-a-fuck attitude. Besides that, my outlook these days was that nobody could hit me as hard as a city bus. Anyhow, that was it. My cork had popped. Now I had a personal invitation to get involved in this bullshit fight, so in a typical New York style, with a Robert De Niro accent, I go, "You talking to me?"

"Yeah, I'm talking to you, motherfucker!"

With that comment, I flew out of the van. By the time I reached him he was back pedaling with his fists raised in the air. I threw two scissor kicks at his face, and he turned around and ran towards the store, jumped inside, and stuck a broom through the handle of the glass door to help keep it locked. The whole time he was running, he was yelling "That motherfucker know karate. I don't fuck with no karate motherfuckers!"

Then from the peanut gallery, I heard Donde say, "He don't know karate."

Instead of kicking Donde for getting me into his bullshit, like I felt like doing, I turned and systematically kicked each enemy to see if they wanted a piece of me. Starting with the closest person, as each one denied me a confrontation, I kicked the next one.

After kicking six different people I turned to kick the next guy and hesitated when I saw it was Donde. It took a lot of strength not to kick my friend in the face for being a wiseass and starting this fight. Before we knew it, two police cars screeched into the parking lot. The cops separated us into groups and asked each group their story. Each group told the cops that nothing had happened until the black guy said, "No way, man. That dude with the black hat assaulted each one of us. You need to arrest him."

"What?" the cop said. "You want to tell me that this one guy assaulted all seven of you guys?"
"Well, not me. I ran, man."
"Na, he didn't do nothin', Officer," one of the black guy's friends said.

245

"Yeah, he didn't do anything, Officer. We just all had a little argument, that's all," another friend of his agreed.

"All right, all right, where do you guys live?"

"We come from Bell Boulevard, sir."

"And you guys?"

"We come from Northern Boulevard and Murry Hill Lane," Freddy answered.

"All right, get the hell out of here and go back to your neighborhoods. If I see that van up around here tonight, you're all going to the station."

As we were driving back to our neighborhood, Freddy, looked in his rearview mirror and said, "Oh, shit."

We looked out the back window, and saw the colored guy barreling down on us like he was going to smash into the rear end of the van. Frankie swerved out of the way, at the last minute, and then we noticed that another car was right behind him. Oddly, they passed us, and drove in the same direction as the colored guy.

"Get those motherfuckers!"

"Yeah, but I can't fuck up my fathers' van," Frankie said."

"Don't worry, whatever happens to it, we'll get it fixed," I said.

We took off like a bat out of hell after them on that note. Being that there was a delay in catching them, they must have thought they were in the clear because we caught them in a cul-de-sac, as they were trying to turn around. Two guys ran over to the colored dude, and he locked his door. So, somehow, his driver's window got smashed, and the wolves pulled him out of the car, and proceeded to beat his ass. The rest of us descended upon his two friends, and as the fists started to fly, they yelled out that they weren't chasing us, they were trying to catch their friend before he did something stupid. We stopped, with raised fists, looked at each other, then told them to get in their car, and wait for the colored dude to get his ass kicked. After he got a nice little ass kicking we piled in Frankie's van, and left.

For the next couple of weeks I kept running into my neighbor Fran from across the street after she would park her car in her driveway. Now she was threatening to get the wooden spoon if I didn't stop by and visit her again. I kept telling her that I would stop by until one day I ran into her, and she said, "Well!"

And I said, "Well??"

Then she said, "Well!!"

Then I said, "Well... I was planning on stopping by tonight."

"At eight!"

"Yes, Fran, at eight o'clock."

"I'll see you then," she said.

I went over to Fran's house that night at 8:00 p.m. When I got there Barbara answered the door.

"Hi, Michael."
"Hi, Barbara."
"How've you been?"
"Fine. Yourself?"
"I'm okay. I guess you're here to see mom, huh?"
"Well, yes... I am."
"She's inside," she said as she opened the screen door.

As I started to walk past her, I thought, Mmmm, man, she smells good.

"Hey, Barb."
"Yes?"
"Do you want to go to the movies one day this week?"
"This is the second time we're in the same room together in years, and you ask me if I want to go to the movies?"
"Well...yeah."
"Well, I don't know. Word on the street is that you're a crazy man."
"Yeah, but you know I'd never hurt you."
"That's not the answer I was looking for, Michael."
"You know what I mean, Barb."
"Well, I'll tell you what. Connie's kids are coming in for the weekend, and if you want, you can come with me and the kids to go see the movie E.T. I promised I'd take them, unless you're afraid to be seen with a few kids."
"All right, that sounds fine to me. What time do you want to go?"
"We'll go on Saturday at 1:00. Do not be late, or I'll send the kids to get you."

When I got done talking to Barbara, I went inside and talked with Fran for a few hours.

"You know, Michael, one of the reasons I asked you to come over is because Barb has been telling me about some of the stories she's been hearing about you, and I wanted to see if you were all right. Understand this, Michael. I have three grown kids who already left the nest, and they each grew up differently. So if there's anything you ever need to talk to someone about, you know I'm here. All right?"
"All right, Fran. Thanks."
"All right. Now let me beat your butt in chess before you leave."

I was working in construction with Gerard now, so he used to stop by my house in the mornings to get me. We both used to walk to Main Street from my house and catch the Number 7 train into Manhattan for work. I was always a tough cookie to wake up in the morning, so it was a good thing that he'd stop by for me.

This one morning I was still in bed when I heard this really loud, weird bird singing. So I started trying to whistle the same tune back towards this bird. Mind you, I was still in bed and hung-over.

This goes on for about a minute or so when all of a sudden I hear, "What are you, a fucking wiseass?" It was Gerard.

I went to the window and said, "What the fuck kinda whistle is that?"

He answered, "So sue me. I don't know how to whistle."
"I guess that's why I had never heard that kind of bird before," I said.

Then I threw my house keys down to him and climbed back into bed. When he came upstairs, I really felt tired.
"I don't want to go to work. I feel sick, Mom," I joked.

Gerard pulled the blankets off me and told me to get the fuck up, so I did grudgingly. Then I got dressed, and we left. I was still half-asleep when we turned the first corner of my block, and as I looked down on the ground, I saw a roll of cash and started to swoop down to pick it up just as Gerard's eyes spotted it. After I grabbed it, I started to count it- $180. Then I looked at Gerard and said, "Fuck work. I'm going back to bed," while Gerard was cursing into the wind about the money I had just found instead of him.

He did talk me into going to work, though. I guess that's why I gave him less of a cut.

When we got to work, we were working with Mikey De'Nardo that day. Mikey asked us if we knew of any places for rent, so I told him that he could rent a room from me. He moved in by the end of the week. It worked out pretty well because now I would get a wake-up call by Mikey knocking on my door before Gerard would show up, and then we'd all leave for work.

I went to the movies with Barb and her sister's young kids on Saturday. After we got there and I got done getting popcorn and candy for the kids, I turned to Barbara and said, "Well, Barb, I guess we're playing the deluxe version of 'House' now, huh?"

She looked at me, smiled, and said, "I guess."

At the theater we sat with the three kids between us. It was very refreshing to hear Connie's kids oohing and ahhing throughout the movie. It made me think of a time when I was amazed at the world. But the ooh's and ahh's ended when it appeared that E.T. had died.

"Michael, E.T.'s dead," one of Barbara's nephews said through tearful eyes.

Oh, shit. Oh, fuck, what are you going to say now? Think, Mike, think.

It's funny, but the only thing I could think of was how upset I was as a child when I was at the movies with my mother and Bambi's mother died.

"Well, E.T.'s in heaven now, and he's with a bunch of other E.T.s now and..."

I could see that I was having as much luck with him as my mother had with me years before. Then three-quarters of the way through my explanation, E.T. came back to life in the movie.

"You lied to me! He's not dead," Amit said.

Oh, fuck. Well, there goes the neighborhood, I thought.

"Well, Amit, I knew he was going to come back to life. I was just kidding with you," I said as Barbara looked at me and smiled.

When we got back to Barbara's house I looked at her, nodded at the little boy, and said, "I think someone's packing a piece," as we walked through the front door.

"Huh...? Oh, I smell it now," she said.

Being that Barbara seemed to have her hands full taking off jackets and because I had never done it before, I said that I would change his diaper.

When I opened that kid's diaper, it looked like someone had smeared chocolate pudding from his belly button back to his ass cheeks.

"Oy vey! Vata' mess you made," I said with a distorted look on my face.

The poor kid looked up at the strange look on my face and started crying.

"You're crying? You gotta' see what I'm looking at," I told him, which made him cry louder.

I guess he did know what I was looking at.

"Barb! Barbara, come here. I can't do this. I'm a chicken. I can't do it."
"Michael! Don't make him cry like that!"
"I'm sorry, but I was just as surprised as he was, though. It's not my fault. I've never done this before. I didn't know what I was getting involved in."

As Barbara quieted him down and started to clean him, she said to him, "Oh yeah, big tough guy. He can get hit by a bus and get into fights, but he can't change a little poop in a diaper. Just wait till I tell his friends what a big chicken he is."
"Well, when you tell them make sure you show them a picture of that mess."
"Oh, stop it. It's just a little poop."
"No, no, no. When my cat goes to the bathroom in his kitty litter box, that's a little poop. What he did... is a masterpiece."

When Barbara got finished, she got up and went to throw away the artwork. Her little nephew sat up and looked at me with this pouting little face as if I didn't want to be his friend any more. So I said to him, "Look, I'm sorry, but you scared me. I didn't know you had that in you. C'mon, let's play with the coloring books, okay?"

It's nice how forgiving kids are, because we were coloring up a storm in no time.

When I got home that night, Jimmy Marnell was there. He handed me a wad of cash and said, "Can I have the front room in the attic?"
"Yeah, what the fuck," I said.

Later that night a bunch of us went into Manhattan to mess with some whores. We went downtown, but I wasn't interested in getting anything. I just went for the ride. After we found them we got out of the car and were bullshitting with some of the working girls. Needless to say, I was on a few hits of mescaline. So we were out there when all of a sudden this whore came over to me, saying out loud, "Oh, baby, I want you."

Like I said, I wasn't interested in any action, but I figured I'd play along. She came over to me and started rubbing her crotch on my leg. Then she says, "I'm horny; rub my ass," so I obliged her.

She in turn started rubbing my ass with both hands while she was dry humping me. Then she goes into this "Oh I thought you wanted some play but I can see in your eyes you don't want none of this." Then she started walking away.

The whole thing lasted like forty seconds. Then I remembered my cousin Ronnie telling me about this time a whore had rubbed his ass and took his wallet. When I checked my back pocket, my wallet was gone. This bitch must have been a ghost, because she disappeared into thin air. I noticed this black dude who had been standing around us, and I knew he was the girl's lookout so I said, "Where'd she go, motherfucker?"

He looked like a homeless dude, so I knew he wasn't her pimp, just a lookout. He wasn't about to be a wiseass with seven stoned out white dudes standing around him, so he gave me a bullshit line that all he was going to do was to ask me for a dollar so he could get something to eat. I guess that's why he was standing around for twenty minutes.

The bitch got me for $250. Well, shit happens. I'll tell you it wasn't the cash that bothered me so much- it was all my IDs and my phone book.

We hung around until everybody got their shit taken care of, and what really pissed me off was that I had even loaned some guys some money, before I got robbed, to get their blowjobs.

As we headed back towards Queens, I was complaining the whole ride back. When we got over to Queensboro Plaza, everybody was pretty sick of listening to me whine, so they chipped in and told me to get out of the car and don't come back until I got a blowjob. I figured what the fuck and found myself a cute little honey. It was pretty early in the morning now and getting light out, so to make sure that nobody got a free show I went behind a building, through a fence and into an empty lot with this prostitute. Then she started to give me a blowjob. No sooner than she started, and just when it started to get good, I heard someone lightly toot a horn. I look over in the direction of the sound, and there were two cops sitting in a cop car. One of them was shaking his finger at me as if he was scolding me, and the other one was shaking his head back and forth. I knew I was fucked, so I put my finger up to my lips while I'm still getting head as if to say, Shhh, be quiet. They both shook their heads no, and flicked me the thumb as if to say beat it. I looked down at the honey and said, "This is the best head I had in a long time, sweetheart, but these two cops over there want us to leave."

She stopped, looked around, and said, "Where? What cops?"

When I pointed, she looked, and then booked (ran). When I walked back to the car, everybody was joking with me about why I should be feeling better and asked why I wasn't smiling now, so I told them. They laughed about it all the way back to Queens.

We were, for the most part, calling Murry Hill bar our second home. At first we had to crack some heads to establish our realm, but once we did, we just about owned the bar.

We would smoke pot, deal drugs, and steal beer from the storage room. I don't mean a beer of two. We kept it down to a case on Friday night and one for Saturday; we didn't need to get greedy. This one night, these two dudes came in but they looked a little too preppy for the way they were talking. They fucked up, though, when one of them wised off to one of our girls.

Before I continue, I think I should give you a little more insight as to how things were inside our bar. A lot of the people who hung out, for the most part, had fucked- up home lives, if any, and were basically pissed off at the world anyway, and just looking for an excuse to go off on someone. From a stranger's point of view, you would have been better off having a beer in a tank full of piranhas.

For instance, let's say I got into a fight with someone. It wasn't uncommon for one, two, or three of my buddies to steal my fight from me, beat the shit out of the guy, and throw him out of the bar. It was nuts. Anyhow, so this guy wises off to one of the girls. I happen to be sitting pretty close, so I said, "You must be some type of tough guy, huh?" I guess he thought he really was because I was 19 and he was like 25 or 30, so he started mouthing off to me. I told him I thought he should shut his mouth before he got popped in it, and he said, "By who?"

I told him that it was probably going to be someone very close to him, and when he opened his yap again, I gave it to him, and the shot landed him on his silly ass.

That was it. My fight was over because the piranhas grabbed him. These two guys got their asses beat the whole length of the bar and then thrown out of the place. It was nice to have that kind of unity. We were in our own Vietnam. We also had a spice of 5, 7, 9, 10 years of our own friendships sprinkled in, which is sometimes stronger than support from your own family, as the case might be.

The bar cooled down after a little while. It was like the bar, as a unit, had to get some shit off on something. Then, blam, the front door swung open, and cops started swarming in. The guys who got their asses kicked were there, too. But it was very strange for, like, five or six cops to come for one call. They told all the guys to get against the wall, and for the girls to stay seated at the bar. But in the course of the conversations, cops kept showing up until there were, like, twelve cops plus these two guys who, as it turned out, were off duty cops. They were sore, in more ways than one, for getting their butts kicked. It looked a little bad for a few minutes, but it all finally came down to the cops asking the bartender what had happened. The bartender told the cops that these guys were being wiseasses with some of the girls and ended up catching a beating for it. The jury retired, and the cops bought the story my buddy the bartender had told them. After the cops left the bar, everything went back to normal.

Barbara called me at home one day.

"Hi, Michael. What's up?"
"Uhm, nothing. Just hanging out."
"Well, would you like to go out again, maybe without the kids? Or do I have to wait a few more years?"

There was a reason I hadn't spoken to her since our date. I decided that I didn't want to see Barbara, and it had everything and nothing to do with her. She was a nice girl, and I knew her since I was a kid. I was thinking that maybe she might really get hurt if she was around me or my element. Besides, I had given up on my future and my past, so what could a girl like her want with me? I mean, I could be dead tomorrow, and nobody would really give a fuck, especially the way I was going. But after talking with her and thinking about it for a few minutes, I decided that I did really want to see her again. So I said, "Well, no, Barb, you don't have to wait that long. We can go out again."
"I have an idea," she said. "Why don't we go to that same Italian restaurant that your father took us to when we were kids?"
"Well, yeah, okay. Let's do it next week."
"Next week?"
"Yeah, I'm pretty busy with work now, but next week looks pretty good."
"Okay. Call me. You have my number, right?"
"Yeah."
"I'll talk to you later."
"Okay, bye."

A few nights later Donde, Marcus, and I were driving around in Marcus's car drinking a few beers, and Donde kept asking Marcus if he could drive his car for a little while, but Marcus, and I kept arguing against it. The reason we were against this idea was because Donde really didn't have any respect for anyone else's property. It was pretty common knowledge that if you let Donde drive your car, he'd think he was Mario Andretti, and he'd race around the neighborhood like a nut. Finally after about a half hour of swearing that he'd be cool, Marcus and I agreed to let him drive with a bit of a threat behind it. Marcus let him take over at 150th & College Point Boulevard.

After driving around for about ten minutes and acting very cool about his driving, we got to an intersection with a red light. While we were sitting there, a van pulled up behind us and came right up on our bumper.

"Look at this guy. He wants to play," Donde said.
"Donde, don't fuck up my car," Marcus warned.

After we drove about half of a block, I realized that there was a black Trans Am tailing the van that was still on our bumper. Donde was driving slow on purpose so that these guys would pass us, but they didn't. They just stayed on our bumper. When we came to the stop sign at the next intersection and stopped, the guy in the passenger seat of the van jumped out with a baseball bat. "GO! GO! GO!" Marcus and I yelled in unison, especially since he was coming to our side of the car.

Donde slammed on the gas, and we peeled out of there. After a few blocks Marcus and I looked back and noticed that the black Trans Am had pulled out from behind the van and was tailing us at a safe distance. Being that Donde had already hit a few parked cars in his attempt to flee, Marcus and I came to the same conclusion.

"Donde, bang a U-turn and slam that fucking Trans Am!" I said.
"Yeah, do it!" Marcus agreed.
"Nooo!" he shrieked. "I'm going up the block and pulling into your driveway!"

Great, I thought, just what we need right now- a bitch at the wheel.
"What are ya', fucking stupid? Then they'll know where I live. Keep driving," I shouted.

Donde made the green light at my corner but missed the light at Northern Boulevard. By now the Trans Am was on our ass with the van right behind him. Then Donde stopped for the red light at Northern Boulevard.

"What the fuck are you doing? GO!" I yelled.
"FUCKING GO!" Marcus shouted.

In the second that Donde hesitated, the van swerved around the Trans Am and barely boxed us in. The passenger door popped open, and out came the dude with the bat again. All I can say for this guy with the bat is that he was lucky that Marcus or I wasn't driving as he ran in front of our car over to the passenger's side.

"Run his fucking ass over!" I yelled.
"Hit'em. Hit'em," Marcus agreed.
"Nooo! Ask him why he's chasing us!" Donde shrieked.

Marcus and I both looked at Donde who had the look of a deer caught with lights shining in his eyes as the front windshield went "Crash!"

Donde didn't budge. "Smash!" went the passenger window. It's funny, but in the slow motion moment when the shattered glass was ricocheting off the interior of the car and our heads, I thought at least he doesn't have a gun or we'd be dead by now.

"Fucking shit, DondeDonde!" Marcus said as he cut the wheel and slammed his foot onto the gas pedal on top of Adelchie's foot.

It wasn't a moment too soon because that next swing was going to hit some flesh, namely mine. Marcus's Impala smashed into the van, bent its door forward, and pushed it into another car that was waiting at the light.

"Whack!"
"Fuck! He got my taillight too," Marcus yelled.

The three of us got lucky because number 1, there were no cars coming as we screeched onto Northern Boulevard, and number 2, somehow Donde snapped out of his dream and grabbed the wheel again, although he still must've been dreaming when he figured that he could turn down a one-lane street doing 60 mph at the next corner. As he turned he sideswiped six cars on the left side of the street and then did the same thing to three more on the right side before he gained control. After he blew the next stop sign at 40 without looking, it was obvious that he was driving like a spooked deer now. Then he blew the red light at 60 M.P.H. and for a fleeting moment, I wondered if it might have been a better idea to get out and fight the guy with the bat.

By the time Donde made a quick right and then a left into Marcus's driveway, it seemed that we had lost the Trans Am and the van that was tailing us. In the process of Donde losing our tail he ended up smashing into Marcus's brick column fence and his sister's Camaro before he threw it in park, leapt out of the car, and ran away.

Marcus and I looked at each other and his newly mangled car with steam coming out of the hood. Marcus calmly looked at me and said, "Whata' ya' wanna do now?"
"I'll tell you what I wanna do. I want to go find that Trans Am and smash the shit out of it. They ain't got guns; otherwise, we'd be dead now."
"I know my car's all fucked up now anyway. We should. The only problem is that Donde must've put a hole in my radiator, and I wouldn't want to get stranded with those guys."
"Yeah, fuck it. We missed our chance now. Listen, Marcus, if you need any help with your car, let me know. Okay?"
"Aaaa, fuck it. I can tell you without even looking that it's all fucked up. Maybe you can just help me pull the motor."

Marcus and I parked the car down the block from his house and then agreed to call it a night but not before we joked about the trail of shit that ran down the block and led up to Adelchie's house.

For the next couple of days I asked around about the black Trans Am and the van that had a bent door, but it's like they were ghosts. Nobody knew nothing. Who knows? Maybe it had something to do with the cops we beat up.

One night I borrowed a car from one of the boarders at my house and picked up Ricky. As we started to drive over to Ridgewood to cop some angel dust, we ran into Patti, the girl who lived around the corner from me and who had come to my Halloween party. She was with her friend Karen and her faggy- looking dog Pom Pom.

"Hey, what are you girls up to?" I asked.

"Oh, nothing. We're just talking," Patti said.

"Well, why walk when you can ride?"

"Well, okay. C'mon, Karen, let's go."

Karen was a little more hesitant at first but finally agreed to come for a ride.

I was already a little buzzed up on some mescaline and found Karen's little verbal sparring matches with me quite amusing as we rode towards Ridgewood.

"Where are you taking us?" she demanded.

"We're going to take a little ride over to Ridgewood."

"Oh, no, we're not! You take us back right now!"

"Cool your jets. We'll be back in forty minutes. Besides, I asked you if you wanted to go for a little ride, and you said yes."

"You can't force us to go with you somewhere that we don't want to go. That's kidnapping."

"Kidnapping...? That's a serious charge, huh?"

"Yes, it is."

"Jeez, I guess you leave us no choice then. We'll have to murder you now," I joked.

Patti, who was a lot more easygoing than Karen, said, "Shhh, Karen, don't give him any ideas."

Once we got into Ridgewood I got a little lost so I kept trying to backtrack to find my way to the starting point, but I was having a bit of a hard time considering that all the mescaline had finally kicked in. But Karen still wouldn't let up. "You went through a red light!" she said.

"Don't worry. I'll stop twice at the next one."

"You're going the wrong way down a one- way street!"

"Don't worry. I'm only going one way on it."

"You don't even have a rearview mirror!"

"I do to," I said as I reached into the glove box and pulled it out. Then I flipped it back to her and said, "Here, if it makes you feel any better, you look out the back window with it and tell me if any cars are back there. Better yet, why don't you just fix your makeup with it?"

When I looked back, I noticed that Patti was trying to hold back her laughter.

We finally got over to the park, and then we went to cop some drugs, not that Patti or Karen knew what we were up to initially. When I pulled up, a bunch of zombies ran over to the car to sell their stuff.

"Oh, my God! Look at them! They look like a bunch of monsters, and I can't believe you brought us here to do a drug deal," Karen said out loud.

"Yeah, I am not too happy about being here either, Patti said.

I had to laugh because, come to think of it, the dealers did remind me of some monster movies I had seen, while they were reaching into the car for some money.

"You know, Patti, if you want, as a special favor, I'll drop off your friend Karen and that funny-looking dog with my friends over here."

"Oh, no, Pom Pom doesn't go anywhere without me."

"All right, you can keep the funny dog. But your friend goes."

"Nooo! Karen can't survive out there alone."

"I know. That's my point."

"No, Karen stays with me and Pom Pom."

"All right. All right, I was just trying to be nice."

After Ricky and I got what we came for, I started the car and drove away. About a block away from there an unmarked police car hit its lights, and I was told over their loudspeaker to pull over. Ricky had already started to smoke some dust with his head out the window, so I told him to put it out and hide it.

"Wait, wait, keep driving and let me get one more hit."

"What do you mean wait?"

"Well, fuck it. If I'm going to jail, I'm going stoned."

"That's right, and I'm telling the cops that you kidnapped us."

Karen pissed me off with that line, so for spite I threw the twenty hits of mescaline I had on me into her lap. As I pulled over to the curb, Karen and Patti were playing "hot potato" with the hits while the dog was barking.

"You better lose those things, Karen," I warned.

The detectives pulled us over and, when they came to the car, one said to Ricky, "Is there anything in the car we should know about?"

Then Ricky looks at him point blank and says, "Yeah, there's a bowl of dust under the seat that I was smoking."

Well, that was awfully brave of him, I thought. I just hope it will end there.

"Let me see it," the cop said as he smelled it and then put it in his pocket.

After that, they made us get out of the car, and then they took a look throughout the car. They even went through the trunk and through a bag of dirty laundry that was there. After about an hour I got a minor ticket for a taillight, and we were told to beat it.

After all their searching they never found the hits or the three bags of dust Ricky stashed... whew.

When we got back to Flushing, I dropped Karen off first.

"You're going to go by yourself with these nuts?" Karen asked Patti.

"Oh, don't worry, Karen. They're not that bad. Besides, if I don't show up at home tomorrow,

Michael lives around the corner from me so send the police over there."

During the ride back towards our neighborhood, I asked Patti if she really had to go home, and she told me that her father was probably going to yell at her for coming home this late as it was.

"Oh," she said, "don't drop me off in front of my house, though. Then he'll really have a shit fit."

After I dropped her off, I turned to Ricky and said, "Pretty cute, huh?"
"Yeah. Not too bad, Ralphie boy."

Gerard came to get me for work the next morning. Being that I was out with Ricky all night, I only got about three hours' sleep and was pretty much out of it. I must've left a door open because instead of calling me from outside he walked into my room and yelled, "Rise and shine, motherfucker." He then turned on the lights and pulled off my blankets.

Man, he was pretty lively for 6 a.m., I thought. Then he stuck some blow in my face and said, "Here, this'll wake you up," which it did.

We ended up doing some blow, and being that Gerard had one of the company vans that day we did some more coke while we rode to the first job site. At about noontime I went into a deli and got us both large bottles of apple juice. You don't really get hungry when you're wired up, so we hadn't eaten anything all morning. I had no idea that this combination of cocaine and apple juice works as the nastiest laxative I never wanted to try. I mean, when my cousins and I were kids, my cousin Ronnie found what he believed to be a large chocolate bar. We ate it not knowing it was Ex-lax and we were just about physically fighting for bathrooms. But trust me, that was a mere bag of shells compared to what was about to come.

By the time we got to the Brooklyn job site, we both had to go like bandits. I elected to grab a compound bucket and go to the bathroom in the basement at the job site. Gerard told me smugly that he was going down the block to the Chinese restaurant to use their facility. I wished him luck and ran to the basement of this total rehab we were doing. I swear it felt like I hardly got my pants opened before I exploded and figured that Gerard must have a stronger system than I did because of the fact that he elected to walk down to the restaurant instead of driving. When I got done, I went across the street to the deli and got some real food in me. I was up on the roof eating when I heard Gerard howl my name like an alley cat. Each time he called, it sounded more pathetic than the last. I mean, even when I answered him, he just kept howling my name. I couldn't see him as I was coming down the stairs, and I started to think he had gotten hurt or something. I asked him if he was okay, and he howled back that he wasn't. I asked him what was wrong, as he walked onto the job site, and he looked me in the face, frowned and said, "I shit myself."

"No way."
"Way."

We both repeated this, and then he told me that the Chinese restaurant was closed on Mondays.

He explained that he had almost made it back here and that he had on his jailhouse butt, which was a joke about how you should walk around in jail with your ass cheeks clenched together. I still couldn't believe that this well- built, strong young eighteen-year-old shit himself until he went into the basement, relieved himself, and then threw his underwear into the next room to prove it to me. He then asked me to run up the block and get him some pants or shorts to wear because we still had to run into Manhattan.

I went up the block to this very small clothing store and found the shorts area. They happened to have men's and women's shorts next to each other. I picked up a pair of men's denim shorts, but then I spotted the prettiest pair of pink shorts with butterflies on one pocket next to me in the women's pile, and I just had to get them for him. When I got back, Gerard was squatting in front of a fire hydrant letting the water run down the front and out the pants legs of his pants. I don't want to tell you what color the water was.

I have to say, though, Gerard certainly didn't appreciate me walking all the way down the block and going to the store for him after seeing his new, pretty, pink shorts. He put them on while grumbling, and we left for Manhattan a short time later.

We had two bosses, Frank and Squiggy, as we called him amongst ourselves. Frank was real cool. He was more of a friend than a boss. But Squiggy more than made up for being a typical asshole boss. When Frank saw Gerards, shorts, he laughed his ass off. Squiggy on the other hand was like, "What the hell is this getup?" As if Gerard would wear this getup on his own.

That day it turns out Gerard and I had to go and do some work in the building where the office was, before we left for another job site. It entailed going into office space where people worked at desks. I mean, you just had to picture Gerard standing there with a work shirt on, construction boots, and a tool belt with hot pink butterfly shorts. It was priceless. The rest of the day Gerard kept telling me that one day he was going to get even with me.

Gerard and Donde came over to my house that weekend. We had a good laugh talking about Gerard's new shorts. After that they asked me if I wanted to go with them to some clubs out on Long Island. I told them that I wouldn't mind going with them, but first I had to cook dinner for my grandfather. So I told them to come back in a little while. Sometimes worrying about preparing my grandfather's meals before I could make plans for myself bothered me, but hey, he did it for me when I was a kid. Now he was my responsibility.

They came back in an hour in Donde's father's Mercedes, and we went out to the Island.

Since we really didn't know the clubs out there, we were doing a hit and miss on them until I came up with a little game plan to avoid paying any door fees. Donde would stop out front, and Gerard and I would get out and walk over to the front door. Gerard would start up a conversation with the doorman, and I'd walk past him into the club without saying a word. Being that Gerard and I weighed about 160 and we were doing 4 sets of tens, benching about 250 pounds, we usually didn't get much lip. If we did, Gerard would say as I kept walking, "Oh listen, he's a little crazy. But don't worry, I'll go get him. Besides, he's on his medication tonight. So what time are you open till?"

Once inside the club, I'd walk around and check out the girl situation. Then I'd check out the men to women ratio. When I got done, I'd either walk right past Gerard and get back in the car, which was a cue to leave, or I'd wave to Donde to go park the car. Then we'd hang out for a little while, talk to some of the girls, and decide if we were going to get any action. Part of the fun was watching Donde use his famous one liner. It went like this: "Hey, if I spend some money on you tonight, do you think I'll get laid?" The real funny part was not that he had the balls to say this. It was the reaction on some of the girls' faces and the fact that he'd get laid the most out of all of us.

After hitting a few more places, we were all pretty toasted, so we decided to call it a night and headed over to Slouch's apartment. He was an old friend from the neighborhood, and since he was on vacation, Donde was watching his apartment. On the way over there, Donde remembered that Gerard and I would have to sleep on the pullout couch together, which started a bit of an argument. After a little while though, we all cooled out, and I reclined in the passenger seat and relaxed. After about fifteen minutes Donde said, "Look at this fucking asshole."

"Huh? What?"
"This guy over here," he said as he pointed out my window.

I glanced out my window and saw this guy who was a little bit older than we were, driving in a beat-up older car. I thought nothing of it, so I rested my head back on the seat and closed my eyes again. Then the wind hit me in the face as Donde yelled out my opened window, "So what's your problem, asshole!"

"Aw man. What the fuck? I was sleeping," Gerard said.
"Ahh, don't worry about it. Adelchie's going to get into a fight with someone. Go back to bed."

As we kept driving, they kept arguing and arguing. Finally Gerard sat up in the back seat and yelled out, "Hey, I got a good idea. Why don't you guys pull over and beat the shit out of each other?"

"I'da stopped over a half mile ago and whipped your buddy's ass, but he's a big pussy, it seems. A big pussy in a car that his daddy bought for him," the other guy said.

"You want to fight, asshole?" Donde reconfirmed for some reason.
"Let's go, motherfucker. You and me one on one," the other guy said.

I've got to admit that I think the guy had a set of balls to be yelling into a car with three dudes in it, but it was no skin off my back because it wasn't my fight.

The guy pulled over, and Donde stopped about ten feet in front of him and finally got out of the car. Gerard and I turned around so we could watch through the back window as Donde approached his foe. Then they both stood there and started arguing again.
"Come on, man. Hit this motherfucker," Gerard said.
"Hey, Gerard, you wanna get out and kick both their asses for waking us up?" I joked.
"Tell me about it. We should."

After a few minutes Donde turned around and started walking back towards the car as the guy got back into his car.

"Boy, you really taught him a lesson," I said when he got back into the car.
"Yeah, the promo was bigger than the fight," Gerard chipped in.
"Aw, go fuck yourselves," Donde answered.

As Gerard and I slid back into our positions, Donde started the car and drove.

After about two minutes Donde said, "Look, here's this motherfucker again."

I lifted my chin again and noticed that his car was riding alongside of ours.

"Look, don't start no bullshit again, all right? You had your chance and blew it, so just keep driving. I don't feel like hearing you guys in stereo again."
"Yeah, enough's enough," Gerard chipped in again.

The cold wind in my face felt like a premonition of a headache to come. No sooner than my window opened, they started at it again like two schoolgirls.

"Aww, man, what the fuck? Not again with you two," Gerard said while he was lying down.

As pissed as I was getting, I was resolved not to get involved in this fight.

After about another ten minutes of this shit, the guy said, "You know what? You're all a bunch of pussies. I'll kick all your asses."
Jeez, this guy's got balls. Maybe he's a little bigger than I thought, I figured as I raised my head up to get a second look at him.

"Yeah, you, the guy with the string tied around his head, I'll kick your ass."

I had worn a thin black piece of silk on my head that night as a bandanna, so that's what he was referring to.

"Who me??"
"Yeah, you asshole!"
"Oh, shit, that's funny," Gerard said.
"Oh, yeah? What are you laughing at, you fucking poodle!"
"Oh, shit, that's funny. He called you a poodle," Donde said.
"What? You called me a fucking poodle? Pull over. I'll kick your fucking ass!"
"No, Gerard. I got this motherfucker. Pull over, Donde," I said while Donde was already, oddly, pulling the car over.

When we stopped I jumped out and started walking back towards the guy's car. After he stopped, he got out and while standing behind his door he started to size me up. Then he bent down and grabbed something from under his seat. At that point my street senses kicked in. For me that meant slow down and look at my situation as an outside observer. Then, to list my options real fast. Because he had such a set of balls with three guys in a car, I assumed the worst, that he had a gun. I wanted to be able to do more than just sit there as, how should we say, a duck, so I kept walking towards him, I glanced from side to side, looking for an escape route, and went over my options. We were stopped in an industrial area that had commercial buildings built side to side of each other with no alley ways. To make matters worse there weren't even any cars to duck behind if he started shooting. It didn't take long to realize that there were no options, "quack-quack." Meanwhile in the background, I heard Gerard yelling, "What the fuck are you doing?!"

I slowly looked over my shoulder while keeping pace and noticed that Donde had let his foot off the brake, and was slowly creeping away with the car while looking in the rearview mirror. I guess he saw this guy reach under his seat for something also. Well, if nothing else, one thing was certain, and that was if anything was going to go down, I was going into it alone now.

By the time I turned back around, the guy was standing straight up but holding whatever he had gotten behind his car door. I took a deep breath and said, "That's right, motherfucker. You'd better take something out from under your seat, because I'm not going to sit around and bullshit with your ass for an hour." Then I stopped walking and said to him, "Now if you want to fuck around with me, let's get it on!"

He paused, looked at me, and said, "You know... your buddy's driving away and leaving you here."
"Well, obviously, he's a pussy. So he can go fuck himself."
"Look... I ain't got no beef with you. It's your asshole buddy I wanted a piece of."
"Yeah... well, I think I want a piece of his ass too now."
"Tell your buddy I'll still fight him one on one as long as you guys don't jump in."
"Oh, I'll tell him. And believe me, we won't jump in."

I turned around, and as I walked back to the car, I laughed to myself and thought, Look at this shit. One minute I'm going to rip this guy's head off, and the next minute I'm negotiating a fight deal for him.

When I got back to the car, Donde sneered, "So what happened, Mike ? You didn't want to fight him?"
"Well, actually he said he really didn't have a beef with me, so he didn't want to fight me. But he still wants to fight you as long as Gerard and I don't jump in."

Gerard laughed and said, "Oh, shit. Well, I guess you still got a fight on your hands, Donde."
"I ain't going out there to fight him. He's got a gun or something," he said.
"You're sure you don't want to fight him, right?" I said.
"Yeah, fuck that," he answered.

I stuck my head out the window and yelled, "Naa, dude, he decided that he doesn't want to fight you. Take it easy. Good night." Then I flicked my finger forward and said, "Fuckin' drive."

261

After the guy zoomed past us, I said, "So what's this bullshit? You start a fight and then leave me there?"

"Well, I thought he had a gun," he said mater of factly.

"Oh, I see. So you figured that there was no sense in you getting shot right over this."

Nothing was said after that, so we drove along for another fifteen minutes until Gerard said, "Donde, where the fuck are you going? We've been driving for an hour."

"Well... I'm a little lost."

"Then pull over to that doughnut shop. I want to get coffee, and you can ask for directions, too."

We all got out and got some food while Donde got directions, and then we sat outside and started to eat when, so help me, the guy Donde was fighting with drove by, tooted his horn, and waved at us.

"That's it. I'm gonna kick his ass. C'mon, let's get him," Donde said.

Gerard and I looked at each other and shook our heads. Gerard said, "No, this is what you're going to do. You're going to sit down, shut up, and eat your fucking doughnut, or Mike and I are going to get up, kick your ass, take the car, and leave you here."

"Well, fuck you. I'll just leave you guys here!"

"No, I don't think that's going to happen either," I answered.

I don't know. Sometimes Donde was straight up and would handle his own shit; other times he got weird on ya'.

The following day, after we got back, I decided to give Barbara a call and ask her out to dinner like we had planned. She told me that she still wanted to go to the Italian restaurant that my father took us to as kids, so that's where we went. Once we got there, Barbara started reminiscing about when we were kids. She just didn't get it, though. For her it was only 8-9 years ago; for me it was like decades. I could tell from the conversation that she wanted to get involved with me, and who knows? Maybe if it was some other girl I wouldn't even be thinking like this. But this was that funny little blond girl who used to call me from across the street for an hour when we were children. How could I invite her to hell? She should be dating some rich kid who went to college or something like that, I thought. I sat there and listened to her describe old fairy tales about my life until I interrupted her and said, "Barbara, I'm no good for you."

"Oh, stop it. I know you're a good person. I remember when you used to ride around the neighborhood on your bicycle, saving poor animals."

"Yeah, I still do that now. But I'm still no good for you," I told her, even as a part of me wanted to hold her and kiss her.

"How about the time you boosted Marcus up to Inga's window and let him stand on your shoulders so he could kiss her, and you fell down, and etc...etc..."Well, Mike... I thought, just shut up and enjoy the night.

Gerard and I dropped some acid the next night. We worked out as usual until the acid really kicked in, and then we went out. We decided to head up towards the Raven Luncheonette to see if anyone, namely girls, were hanging out. While we were there, Manny, an old friend of mine, showed up.

"Hey, Mike, you got any mesc?" he asked.

Being that I was still dealing on the side, I had some on me, so I sold him some. After we hung out for about a half hour, Manny said, "Hey, you guys want to come with me down to Nobody's?"

Nobody's was a club down the block from the luncheonette, and there usually were some nice-looking girls hanging out there.

"I don't know. You wanna go, Gerard?"
"Ohhh, maybe it's not a good idea, Mike. The street lights are starting to melt for me," he answered.

While we were standing there, I noticed that there were two guys standing in front of the club which was about forty yards away, and it looked like they were staring at us. I glanced at them for a second and then slowly looked away. Maybe you're just high, I thought.

After another minute or two, I looked back and saw that one of the guys was standing with his hands on his hips, and he nodded his head in an upwards position towards me. So I yelled down the block, "Can I help you with something?"

The guy with his hands on his hips yelled back something that I couldn't understand, so I yelled back, "Look, I can't understand you, but if you want to get your ass kicked, come down here. Otherwise, take a fucking hike. Gerard, can you back me up?"
"Yeah... I'll keep one eye closed and just push one towards me," he answered.

They yelled back something I couldn't understand again, so I waved from down the block for them to come over and yelled back, "Com'ere – com'ere," as a spider would say to a fly.

They both said something to one another, and then they started walking towards us.

"Oh, I got a bite, Gerard."
"Yeah, I see. Reel them in nice and slow," he answered.

Then a very funny thing happened, almost like an optical illusion. As they got closer they got smaller, and we got much bigger. You could tell it was happening to them also, because their pace started to slow down a bit.

"Which one you want, Gerard?"
"Well, I'm a little stoned, so give me the smaller one tonight."
"All right. Hey, Manny, I'll try to save you some leftovers all right?"
"Shit, I can tell right now there ain't gonna be no leftovers," he answered.

Then the bigger one of the two walks up to me and starts saying in a Spanish accent, "Hey, what's up, my friend?"

While I was sniffing out this response, he started to put his arm around my neck like he wanted to be friends. For a second I let him put his arm there but then he made the mistake of trying to grab me in a headlock. I slipped my head out from under his arm and started throwing a flurry of punches at him. Gerard, who had already broken his leash, was throwing a barrage of punches from his side at my guy, while the guy tried to cover up in between us.

While this was happening, I saw the guy's friend from the corner of my eye as he scrambled around to try to find a stick or something. Just as he picked up a 12-ounce beer bottle, Manny, who was carrying a portable umbrella, smacked him full face with it. With Manny's next shot, smacked the beer bottle out of his hand, and it shattered onto the ground. By now I was taking body shots and thought, Man, this guy hits pretty hard. His friend started to scramble again for something, but this time with a flick of a switch Manny's umbrella elongated, with the strap still tied around it, now it looked like a sword. With one arm raised in the air, Manny started poking and slapping this guy in the head and body, and he yelled out each time he made a jab at him. By now I had already started throwing stronger punches, and oddly enough the punches I was receiving seemed to be heavier also.

The guy standing in between us had his arms covering his head and was slightly bending down when a strange thing happened. Being that I could see Gerard's face now, I noticed that every time I threw a body shot, Gerard would grit his teeth and crinkle his eyebrows at me, and then I guess he noticed the same reaction from me.

Come to think of it, Mike, this guy's got both hands covering his head. Gerard and I must be punching the shit out of each other. We must've both thought the same thing because as our punches slowed down to a trickle, so did the shots we were receiving. Gerard and I smiled at each other as soon as we stopped, and Gerard said, "Man... this is good acid, huh?"

The guy we had been throwing bombs at took off like a Chihuahua that had been nipped in the ass, while Manny continued to flog his guy with his umbrella.

"Okay, Zorro... that's enough. You can let him go," I said.

After Gerard and I stopped laughing, and the other guy took off, I said, "Manny, what the fuck was up with that? You looked like a swordsman."

"Oh, I used to practice fencing for a little while when I was in the Navy."

Once the dust had settled I realized that I had somehow lost my father's watch that I had been wearing, and I asked Gerard and "Zorro" to help me look for it. After about ten minutes I did find one, but it wasn't mine. It was a nice trophy, though. A few minutes later I did find mine about ten feet away.

About twenty minutes after bullshitting about our fight, Zorro said, "Hey, ya' know, I was at this party earlier but I left because nobody had shown up yet. It's over by Parsons Boulevard and Sanford Ave. You want to go check it out? There should be some girls there by now."

"Yeah, why not? Come on, Gerard. Let's go."

After we got to the building, we went up to the fifth floor where it was. It was pretty happening now because there were 25 to 30 people there. After we got some cups and filled them up at the beer keg, we headed towards a room that smelled like pot was coming from it. As we made our way over, I saw Harold hanging out in the middle of all these people I didn't know, sparking up a bunch of joints. Harold was this much older black dude who was pretty cool. He would hang out with us by the luncheonette and sell everybody weed.

"Yo', Harold. What's up?"
"Wus up, my man?" he said.
"What are you doing here?"
"I come to the rescue," he joked.

One thing about Harold, though, he never sold bags, only joints. I bought about ten of them from him. Then Gerard and I moseyed on over to the window to spark up a few of the joints I had just bought. While we were standing there, Gerard said, "Yo', Mike, watch this," as he dumped his beer out the window. I looked out the window just as it rained down on two guys downstairs. The two guys looked up and started yelling, "You maricon hijo de la gran puta, motherfuckers."
"Yeah? Fuck you! You spic motherfuckers!" Gerard yelled back out the window.

Aside from the music, all the conversation in the room stopped.

"Hey, you fucking gringos. In case you haven't noticed, we're all spics at this party!"

Gerard, who was peeking on acid by now, hadn't heard this, and was still yelling out the fifth floor window down to the street at these guys. I was hitting him in the ribs trying to make him shut up, but he just kept on yapping. Finally, as the hits to his ribs were getting stronger, he looked at me, then at the room, and realized that he had fucked up. Gerard grimaced at me, and then we looked at the room full of people, then out the window, then at each other.

"Gerard," I whispered, "we're either leaving this party through the window or we've got to fight our way to the door. Now, I don't know about you, but I never learned how to fly, so get ready."

"Yo, Mike, I'm fucked up. Don't leave me here."
"All right, listen. When I turn around and start walking out of the room, put your hand in my back pocket and follow me. But listen... if I stop... start swinging, okay?"

I turned back to the guy who had just updated us and said, "Obviously we've overstayed our welcome. And I'd like to apologize for my friend here, he's tripping on acid. So if you gentlemen don't mind, we'll be calling it a night now," and started walking towards the door, not knowing what to expect, with Gerard's fingers placed firmly in my back pocket.

Luckily we got out of that room with only a few bad press reviews. As we walked out, I looked at Harold who had his hand up to his forehead as if he just got a bad headache. I winked my eye at him, and he looked up at the ceiling and rolled his eyes at me. I had one quest in life now, and that was to feel the coolness of the front door handle in my hand, I thought, as we slithered towards it. Once we got outside, I looked at Gerard and joked, "You fucking asshole."

"Yeah. That was a bad one, huh?"

"Bad...! I'm surprised we don't look like Swiss cheese from knife holes."

As we headed home we joked about really calling this night a night, while we purposely looked both ways for traffic at each intersection on the way home.

A few days later I was hanging out with Ricky, and he asked me if I wanted to buy his motorcycle that was still at my house. Even though it was a little beat up, it still had plenty of balls for a 750. We agreed on a price of $600 and then we shook on the deal.

"But you've got to give the money to my mother, because she cosigned the loan for me," he said.

That night I went and paid his mother, and she told me that she would send for the title because Ricky had lost the last one. A few days after that, I told my mother over the phone about my purchase, and she had a fit.

"Who the fuck are you to spend $600 on a motorcycle when I'm the one that pays all the bills in that house? You should give me that money for bills!?!"

"All right, Ma. I'll get the money back."

"Where do you get the balls?" she started.

"I heard you the first time, okay? I'll get the money back and give it to Uncle Phil."

"And if you don't like it, you can get the fuck out," she continued.

"All right, Ma, I'm gonna go now. Nice talking to you, bye."

"Yeah, bye."

I went over to Ricky's house the next day and asked his mother to let me have the money back because I had to pay some bills.

"Oh, no. You wanted the motorcycle so you bought it. A deal's a deal, and that's that," she stated.

"Oh, I agree with you, Helen. A deal's a deal, but my mother's busting my horns about paying some bills at the house. So do me a favor, will you? I'll give you my mother's address in jail and you write her and tell her your point of view for me, okay? Or better yet, just mail her the money, okay?" I said then I left.

That night Ricky called me and told me he had a check for me.

"What the fuck am I supposed to do, Ricky?"

"I know. You don't have to explain it to me, Mike," he said.

About a week after this Mike Viale called me from the prison.

"Hey, Mike, how you doing?" I said.

"Actually, I'm doing great. I'm getting out in two weeks."

"Fuckin' cool. Do you want me to come and pick you up?"

"Na, that's all right. They give you bus fare to get home once you get out. Besides, I'm all the way up in Attica State Prison."

"Well, you know you've got a bed over here."

"Yeah, I know. Thanks."

"You don't have to thank me for that, bro. Just tell me the time and day you're leaving, and me and Gerard will come get you at the bus station, all right?"

"All right, that's cool."

"See you soon."

"All right."

Dino called me about a week later from jail and told me that he might be getting out also.

"Yeah, I go before the parole board in two days," he said.

"Well, just so you know, Mike called me, and he's definitely getting released. So I think you should have a good chance, too."

"Really? Where's he going when he gets out?"

"Well, I told him to come here. Why, is there a problem between you two?"

"No... it's nothing. Nothing at all."

"Really? You don't sound so convincing."

"No, it's nothing. Well, that's news I can use, though, when I go up before the board about Mike getting out."

"It should be, because Mike had the assault charge and you didn't."

"Yeah, I know, but with my luck one of the guys on the parole board's wife is sleeping with someone who looks like me."

"Yeah, right, or got a speeding ticket on the way to work that day."

"Well, wish me luck."

"Good luck."

"All right, I'll talk to you later. Hey, what about your mother?"

"Na, she got nailed again."

"Man, that's fucked up."

"Yeah, I know."

"All right see ya'."

"See ya'."

Barbara called me; we had set up a date to go out last night, and I stood her up. I was hoping that she'd get pissed off enough to tell me to go fuck myself, which she did all right. She caught me while I was hanging out in my driveway with Gerard that day. She had my friend Nicky Cardone and this girl Danielle from down the block with her when she showed up. As she stormed over towards me, Gerard said, "Uh oh, you're gonna get it now."

"So who the hell do you think you are to stand me up on a date, huh?"

"Well, I'm sorry."

"Oh, you're sorry. Do you know what a God-damn telephone is? Huh?"

Boy, she was pissed. I had never seen Barbara this pissed off before, and I've gotta say she looked kinda cute. But what really started to piss me off was the way Danielle was staring in my face like she thought she was going to pop me. Danielle was a big tomboy, and nobody had ever seen her with a boyfriend.

"So who's this? Your bodyguard?" I said as I pointed at Danielle.

"And what if I am?!" Danielle answered.

"Danielle, look. Let me tell you something. I don't give a fuck if you're a girl. I'll knock you the fuck out if you want to be a wiseass."

"Well, go ahead. Do it!"

"Nicky, come here a minute."

Nicky and I walked over towards my front porch, and I said to him, "Nicky, what's up with this bullshit? Since when is it Danielle's concern about what happens in Barbara's social life?"

"Well, before I tell you, you got to promise you won't hit me," he said.

"Tell me what?"

"First, promise you're not gonna slug me."

"Nicky, I'm not gonna hit you. You're a friend of mine."

"Promise?"

"I promise."

"Okay, well, look, you know Danielle is hot for Barb, right?"

"No, is she really?"

"Yeah, she is."

"So?"

"So she's had the hots for Barbara for a long time."

"Yeah?"

"So when Barbara called my house, and told me she wanted to come over here, Danielle happened to be at my house."

"So?"

"So when Barbara came over to my house, Danielle tried to talk her out of coming here. That's all."

"Oh, so Danielle came over here with you to kick my ass and show Barbara that she's a better man for her, huh?"

"Well, I don't know about that, but maybe."

"Okay, look, Nicky. When we go back out there, you'd better pull Danielle on the side and tell her to watch her mouth with me, because I will knock her on her ass, okay?"

"Yeah, all right. I'll tell her," he said.

After we went out front and Nicky pulled Danielle to the side, I walked over to Barb who was talking to Gerard and said, "Listen, I'm sorry about last night. Let me make it up to you tonight. All right?"

"Well, I already made plans for tonight."

"Okay. Well, if you're not doing anything tomorrow night, maybe we could go out then, Huh?"
"Well, call me tomorrow, and we'll see."

As they left, I blew a kiss at Danielle and said, "Bye, bye, honey."

She flipped me the middle finger and then left.

"I don't know, Mike, I think the big one has the hots for you, to be honest" Gerard said.
"Yeah, fuck you, too," I joked.

Gerard and I went to pick up Mike from the bus station, but he never showed up.

"Shit, maybe he didn't get out after all," I said.
"Yeah, but why the fuck would he tell us to meet him here?"
"I don't know." I said.

We hung around for another two hours just in case he missed a bus or two, but he never showed up. Gerard and I decided to drive back to Queens and see if there were any messages from Mike. When we got there, Mike was sitting on the steps drinking a beer.

"Mike! How the fuck did you get here?"
"Man, when I got off that bus and saw the daylight of Manhattan, I just walked out of the parking garage into the city like a moth to a flame. I never even made it inside the bus station, sorry."
"No big deal. C'mon, give me a hug."

It was nice to see him out, but I still felt a little guilty about the whole thing. We went out that night and partied our asses off to the point where we had to carry Mike back two blocks to the house and put him to bed.

The next day at work, Gerard and I were dragging ass because we both had hangovers. We happened to be on the same job with Mikey and Aldo, who was Squiggy's cousin. About an hour later I heard someone yell out, "Wooow." Being that I didn't hear anyone yell out for bandages, I figured everything was okay. Then about five minutes later I felt some type of shock on my arm, and I let out a yelp. When I turned around, Aldo was standing there holding two long wires that were stuck into a wall socket. My eyes were now open wide, and I was very awake.

"What'a ya', fucking nuts?" I said as Gerard ran in laughing.
"He fucking got me, too," Gerard said.
"You fuckinga upa now?" Aldo said with an Italian accent.
"Yeah, I'm fucking upa now," I answered.
"It'sa good for a hanga over," he said.

Shit, come to think of it, I don't feel a hangover any more, I thought.

"Yeah, Aldo it worked good. But do me a favor. From now on just get me coffee, all right?"

At lunchtime Mickey told Gerard and me that he was really thinking of buying a motorcycle for the summer.

"So what are you going to buy, Mikey, an 1100?" Gerard said to Mikey who was about 5'6" and weighed about 130 pounds.

"No, I was actually thinking about getting something smaller to scoot around on."

"Hey, Rob over at the pizzeria is selling his little 450. That would probably be good for you," I mentioned.

"Yeah, but I don't want to buy a piece of shit."

"No, the thing's like brand new. He babied it."

After work we went to check out the motorcycle, and Mikey bought it right on the spot. Rob let him use the plate to get it home so we ended up joyriding it all night. I got the plate to Rob the next day. The one thing I couldn't understand, though, was why Mikey still chose to ride back to work with us in the work van instead of taking his motorcycle.

"Fuck that," he would say. "I'm not going to get run over during rush hour."

That Saturday Mike V. cooked a big barbecue for everyone; he even set the table. Then he put all the food out and slapped Gerard's hand when Gerard grabbed a hamburger. "Don't touch anything. Grandpa!" he yelled. "Come on, it's time to eat."

My grandfather sat at the head of the table. Mike said, "Here, Grandpa, I got you some good wine," and poured him a glass.

After he poured it, Mike looked at me and winked his eye. I closed my eyes and nodded my head back at him. Dave from upstairs was there also. It was Friday so he already had on a little buzz. He was out there with his famous shorts again, you know, the ones where his nuts would hang out when he sat down.

After a while, we all had a little buzz so Gerard and I came up with an idea. We went inside and got some straws and then we went outside and started shooting spitballs at Dave's nuts while he was sitting on the steps of the back porch, drinking beers and telling stories. Dave must've really been juiced up because, by the time we were done, there were spitballs on his knees, his shins, his feet, the wall, and his nuts, but he didn't feel a thing. We had a good time, but most importantly my grandfather had a good time also. Even though I was taking care of him, I still thought I didn't spend enough quality time with him. I guess I wasn't able to separate the two actions Sometimes when I was home I'd put Benny Hill on the TV for him and sit and watch it with him. It was funny, but the first time I put it on he said, "Looka' dis! You see whata disa women do? I'ma no believe. Ina' my country, they puta them in jail ifa dey where clothes likea dat"

He was referring to the scantily clad women. I asked him if he wanted me to change it and he would say 'No, it'sa okay, I'ma watch it.' Once he knew what time it was on, I would come home, and he would be watching it himself.

My Aunt Marie would take the bus and come and see him from time to time. Sometimes she'd spend the night. It was good because my grandfather would be in a good mood for days. My Aunt Linda on the other hand came and got him once in two years.

Dino got paroled. He told me not to bother with picking him up because he would just jump on the train and come over. The day he came home we hugged each other. He looked me in the eye and said, "You owe me a fucking blowjob."

Gerard looked at me and said, "Hey, if you guys want to be alone, no problem I understand."
"No, I lost a bet with him when we were in jail."
"Too much information. I don't want to know any more."
"Fuck you, Rod," I joked.
"Is Mike still here?" Dino asked.
"Yeah, he sleeps on the front porch."
"Where am I going to sleep?"
"Well, everything's filled up now, but you can either stay in the front porch with Mike or take the room in the basement."
"I'll take the room in the basement," he said.

The first two weeks Dino was home, he really tried to get a good job. He'd get up early with the paper and go out all day. Every day he came back with nothing. I knew his ego was taking a bit of a pounding, so I'd make sure that I'd have dinner waiting for him when he got home.

"Dean, maybe you're going for jobs that ain't right for you. I mean, let's face it. You're 19 with no experience. Maybe you've got to start little for a while and then go for something better."
"I don't know. Maybe you're right. But I'm trying, Mike. I'm really fucking trying."
"I know, Dean. I tried myself at one time, but then I said fuck it. I work construction now. Yeah, I break my ass sometimes but you know what? Sometimes I make more than the suits I ride the train with, ya' know, so fuck it. Let em' smile in my face, because they can kiss my ass and they know it."

All in all though, everything was pretty cool on the home front. Between me, Mike, and Dino there was always food on the table, and my grandfather would sometimes cook us a nice Italian meal, or between all the guys who lived at the house we'd have a big barbecue. Besides that, Dino and Mike would pick up the slack with my grandfather so that was real cool. Dave took over full responsibility of cutting the grass and taking out the garbage, and we all took turns cleaning the bathroom or patching things up around the house. Dino also seemed to get along better with Mike, for whatever that was about. We were like a family now at home, but the nights were still pretty wild.

By now we had a clique of about twenty people from the neighborhood who would hang out in the Murry Hill Bar at different times; it became a second home in a sense. If someone came to my house to look for me and I wasn't there, the second place they'd look was the Murry Hill. Now that Mike and Dino were out, we were more of a fist than just a finger in the sense that if someone fucked with me, they'd have to be prepared to be fucked with by Mike and Dino and vice versa with the three of us.

To look at it from a distance, first you had me. I was working out every day, and when I wasn't working out I was half out of my head from some type of drug. Then you had Mike, who had a punch on him that would split skin and knock out teeth with one blow. Then there was Dino. He was smaller than Mike and I, but man, what a bite, he had. I mean, understand this; Dino for more than half his life now had either been in some type of home or institution where he was the little guy. After years of taking his licks, he learned how to give them back to someone even quicker.

"Ya' see, Mike, I'm a little guy," he'd say. "So I've got a little window of opportunity where that fight's got to be going my way in the first thirty seconds or I'm a dead man."

For instance, this one night Mike and I were playing pool in the Murry Hill, and this guy about my size walked in with these metal studded biker bracelets on. He came in, looked around, and then walked over to the pool table and placed his quarters down behind some others. So I was playing Mike in a game, and I was actually winning. You don't usually beat a guy who's been playing pool in the joint for two years that easily. But strangely enough, I did beat Mike this game. After we were through, Dino walked over, picked up his quarters, and started putting them in the slot.

"Hey! It's my game. I'm up next."

"Na, man, my quarter's been sitting here for a while. Besides you just walked in five minutes ago," Dino said.

"I know I did, but that's my game!"

"Look, just wait your turn like everybody else, okay?" Dino said as he racked up the balls.

"Yeah, it's his game," Mike said after I broke up the balls.

"Oh, is it?"

"Yeah, it is," I said as I took my next shot.

"Oh, then I guess... I'm sorry. Here, shake my hand," he said sarcastically.

"What? Look, I don't have to shake your hand. You come in, bust my balls for no reason, and then tell me to shake your hand? Thanks, but no thanks," Dino said as I bent down for my next shot.

"So what? Are you a pussy now because you can't shake my hand like a man?" he said as he walked over to Dino and I took another shot.

"WHACK! WHACK! WHACK! WHACK!" I heard as my ball dropped in the pocket.

I looked at Dino who had just whacked this guy in the head several times with a pool ball from off the table. Then he flipped him to the floor and slammed his face on the floor a few times. Then he flipped him over and punched him in the face a couple of times. When he got up and reached for a pool stick, I yelled out, "Dino! Dino! He's done!"

Dino hesitated for a moment, and then he proceeded to drag the guy out the length of the bar and roll him out the front door. It was similar to an ant dragging a chicken.

"Okay, whose shot is it?" Dino said when he came back in as Gerard walked outside to check on the guy.

"Well, it's still mine," I said.

"Oh, come on, I've been gone a half hour and you're still shooting."

"Hey, I'm sorry. I stopped to watch the half-time show."

"Oooo," Gerard said as he walked back in shaking his head. "That guy's toast. It might be a good idea to call him an ambulance."

"Really?" I said.

"Yeah... really," Gerard answered.

"Come on, come on, take your shot," Dino said.

I handed the stick to Dino and told him to shoot as I walked outside to check on the guy with Gerard.

When we got out there, Gerard said, "I dragged him over here to the light pole and propped him up."

This guy was fucked up. I never knew that someone could get lumps on top of lumps until today.

"Oooo, look at this one over here," Gerard said.

"That's nothing. Look at this one."

"Phuck you!" the piece of meat said through swollen lips.

"Aww, shut up or I won't call an ambulance for you," Gerard warned.

"You tell that motherphucker that I'm coming back here to kick his ass."

"No, I don't think that's what you want me to tell him right now, especially in your condition. Besides, he's my cousin, so you better shut up before I kick you in the face."

When I went back inside, Dino kicked my ass in pool. I guess he was on a roll.

A short time later an ambulance pulled up. After they put the guy in the ambulance, one of the drivers came inside.

"Does anyone know what happened to this guy?"

"Yeah," Mike said, "He got into a fight and lost."

"That's it?"

"Yep."

"You guys do some nice work over here, 'cause I'll tell ya', this guy's a masterpiece."

"Maybe we ought to start signing them," I joked.

Gerard and I had to drive to the Brooklyn job the next morning before we went to Manhattan, so I was able to get in a little snooze before we got there. Then out of nowhere I heard Gerard say "Holy shit, I don't believe it."

I opened my eyes, still half-groggy, and said, "What? What's the matter?"

"Look at those fucking nuts!"

By now I realized that we were down the block from the job site, but I still didn't know what he was talking about.

"What? What are you talking about?"

"Look at the job site. More specifically, look towards the roof," he said as he pointed.

"Holy shit!"

Frank, our boss, had wanted us to come to this job to put up scaffolding so we could set up these two neighborhood guys Frank had hired. Slip and Tony were about our age but they were a couple of dee's, dem, and doe's type of guys. Slip was about 6'4" and weighed about 280, whereas Tony was about 5'8" and weighed in at about 145. Frank had sent them to this job to put up vinyl siding on the four-story building. Being that the scaffolding hadn't arrived yet, they decided to start without it.

The ingenious idea they came up with involved a rope and an old tire. Slip had tied the rope to the chimney, wrapped it around his waist, and lowered Tony down in an old tire. To make matters worse he was swinging Tony back and forth, so he could nail the long strips along the side of the building. When we got out of the truck, Gerard yelled up, "What the fuck are you doing?"

Tony and Slip looked at each other and then back at us, as if we were the idiots. Slip said, "Like Frank told us to do, some siding."

"That's not what I mean. What are you doing with this rope and tire? You're gonna kill Tony."

"No, I ain't. It's a good strong rope. I brought it from my house," Slip said.

"Yeah, I checked it out before I climbed over. It's good," Tony chipped in.

Somehow Gerard convinced them that it wasn't a good idea. Then we set up the scaffold after it came, and went to a Manhattan job site.

After work that night, I went out again with Barb. We were seeing a lot more of each other these days, but I still wouldn't take her out to my bar. The last thing I wanted to picture myself doing was explaining myself to Fran on how her daughter got slugged during a barroom brawl. Even though I felt close to Barbara, I still wouldn't allow myself to get closer to her. It had been a long time since I had allowed myself to be this emotionally close with someone I cared about. Also because I hadn't spoke to or with anyone about myself for such a long time on this level, I found it difficult to relate to it. After a while though, I just allowed myself to enjoy my time with her. I'd probably be lying if I didn't think that I wouldn't enjoy having sex with her also, but there was no need to rush anything.

John Slocum stopped by my house one day. He hadn't seen Dino yet, so they were happy to see each other.

"So where you staying now, John?" Dino asked him.

"Well, I was living out by my mother for a little while; now I'm back in Queens living with my father."

"Big John?"

"Yeah."

"Shit, I haven't seen him since he used to kick our asses at Bowne Park in the sand pit when we were kids, and he would teach us karate moves. How's he doing?"

"He's fine. Man, that was a long time ago," John said.

"Shit, motherfucker, I still got a twitch from them beatings," I joked.

"Yeah, I know what you mean. He's fine though. He works on Wall Street now," John answered.

"Hey, what are you doing tonight?" Dino asked.

"Nothing really."

"Come out to the Murry Hill, man. I haven't seen you in years. We'll celebrate."

"Yeah, John, come out with us," I added.

"Yeah, of course, man," John answered. "But if it gets cold tonight, you've got to lend me a jacket, Mike," he explained.

After we ate something that night, we headed out for the "Hill." Being that it started to get cold out, I decided to lend John a jacket. I opened my closet, and John said, "Let me borrow your suede Daniel Boone jacket."

"If I loan you this, John, you better not fuck it up. I'm serious. If you get into a fight or something, you'd better take it off."

"Come on, Mike. I'm not gonna get into a fight tonight."

That night we were having a good time celebrating with John, and while we're hanging out, about five strange guys came into the bar. Nobody paid them much mind for a while, until I saw Mike getting into a little hassle with one of them. I walked over to see what was up, and I heard the two of them having a calm, quiet argument along the lines of somebody about to get their ass kicked. Mike looked at the guy and said calmly, "I think maybe it's a good time for you and your friends to leave."

The guy got half a wiseass sentence out and "Crack!" Mike hit this guy so hard and fast that I flinched. I heard something hit the floor, so I looked down and saw this guy's tooth lying there. He put his hand to his mouth and started walking towards the door while a melee broke out with his friends. It's funny, but most of the girls there knew the routine, and they would bunch up in the corner somewhere and give us plenty of room. Part of the fight ended up by the front of the bar, and I saw one of their guys go down. As he went down next to John, who was minding his own business, he grabbed a hold of my suede jacket and ripped the pocket. John stood there with his mouth open, looking at my pocket for a second until I yelled, "John, look at my fucking jacket! I told you not to fuck it up, didn't I!!!"

"Oooo, you motherfucker." Whack! Whack! Whack! John started punching the guy. "John! John! Take my fucking jacket off!" I yelled out half-joking with him.

"I, (whack) can't, (whack) do that, (punch, punch) right now, Mike!" he answered as he got involved in the fight.

By now it was obvious that these guys were trying to fight their way towards the door, but just like a cat with a mouse, we kept them around a lot more than they cared for. The fight did finally get up towards the door, and one by one we tossed them out until they were all outside. After a minute or two, the guy Mike had hit started pounding on the door with a crowbar.

"Come on out, you motherfuckers!" he kept yelling.

"John, when I tell you to, open the door, okay?" Mike V. said.

When the guy came back and started banging again, Mike yelled, "Now."

John swung the door wide open. Mike hit the guy who was standing in the doorway with a crowbar smack dab in the forehead with a beer bottle.

Being that the door was on a spring-loaded hinge, we were able to watch the guy as he rolled his eyes up in the air and tried desperately to maintain his balance as the door slowly closed.

After they bounced something off one of the windows, we decided to come up with a plan to end this bullshit. There was only one way to settle this, and that was to open the door, bum rush them, and beat their asses again.

"What if they got a gun?" John said.
"They ain't got a gun. If they did, they would've come in and used it by now," Mike theorized.
"On the count of three, open the door," Mike V. added. "One... two... three!"

We were poised like a bunch of thoroughbreds waiting for the gate and then, bam, we were off. The first guy to get hit was the guy who got clocked with the bottle. I've got to say, though, that the look of surprise on their faces was priceless.

We beat most of their asses back into their car, and then we beat the shit out of their car. After a minute or two, I figured out why nobody was sitting in the driver's seat yet. I heard somebody giving out loud moans. I turned around and saw Donde jumping up and down like a kangaroo on the chest of the guy we had already knocked down. He must've had the keys to the car. Each time Donde was ready to land on him again, the poor bastard would tighten up and get ready for the next landing. After two of them that I saw I said, "All right, Donde, you're gonna kill him."
"I know... that's what I want to do," he said bravely.

The third time he leaped in the air, I pushed him off target. I knew the guy was hurt because of the way he was trying to scramble back to his car.

By now guys were jumping up and down on the hood and roof of the car as the guy was trying to start it.

"Man, that car better start!" I warned.
"Yeah, you better get out and push the motherfucker," Dino said.
"All right, all right, man. We'll push it; just stop kicking our asses," one of them yelled.
We agreed, so they got out and started pushing it as we smashed beer bottles against the car.

After they got halfway down the block, we all piled back into the bar.

"A shot of whiskey for everyone who was in the fight," Mike V. said.
"All right!" Donde yelled.

"Shit! I didn't see you fighting. You were just beating the shit out of someone we had beat the shit out of. But don't worry, you can get a beer out of it for effort," Mike V. explained.

At about three in the morning, when there were only the steadies left in the bar, Dino and Mike got into a little argument. It seemed though that Dino was doing all the arguing. I walked over and said, "Come on, guys. Let's go outside."

Once we were out there, I asked Mike what the problem was.

"Check this out, Mike," Mike V. said. "You know what he's arguing with me about? He's pissed at me because when we were in the joint I had heard that Dino was having a little problem with a situation, so I had some guys take care of it for him without asking him. And now he thinks I'm telling everyone out here that I was handling Dino's shit for him in there."

"Are you?"

"No."

"So, Dino, what's the problem?"

"What? Just because he says so, you believe him?"

"Why should he lie? Everyone knows you can handle your shit, so what's the problem if Mike helped you with some shit in the joint? I'm sure he would have appreciated it if the situation was the other way around between the two of you at the time. It's called looking out for each other," I reasoned.

"Yeah, but this was different. After that, everyone in my quad was saying shit like I was Mike's boy!"

"So what? Who the fuck are they anyway?" I answered.

"Dino, I can see the hate in your eyes for me right now," Mike V. said.

"That's right, and if I had a knife in my hand right now, I'd fucking stab you in the heart!" Dino said.

"Over this?" Mike asked.

"Yeah, over this!" he answered.

Mike looked at Dino and said, "Wait a minute." Then he turned around and walked back into the bar.

I turned to Dino and said, "Come on, Dino. What the fuck?!"

"You don't know, Mike. You weren't there."

"So do you think you'll ever see those guys in jail again?"

"No!"

"So what's the problem?"

While Dino was thinking up an answer, Mike walked back outside, handed Dino a knife, and said, "Here, stab me!"

Dino took the knife out of Mike's hand, smiled, and then stabbed him on the left side of his ribcage. Then Dino walked back in the bar.

Mike and I looked at each other, and then he frowned and said, "The little fuck stabbed me."

I turned my head to look at the knife sticking out of Michael's side and said, "Shit, Mike. You all right?"

He looked at it and said, "Yeah, it didn't go too deep."
"What do you want to do?" I asked.
"Well... I guess pull it out."
"All right, look, I'll pull it out, but if it starts bleeding real bad, I'm gonna put it back in to stop the bleeding. All right?"
"Yeah."
"Then we'll hop in a car, and I'll bring you to the hospital."
"All right," Mike answered.

I pulled the knife out, and it started to bleed a little bit more. But at least it wasn't gushing and, after watching it for a couple of minutes, Mike decided not to go to the hospital.

When I went inside and got a bag of ice for Mike, I saw Dino sitting at the bar staring straight ahead.

"Dean, that was fucked up," I said.

He just looked straight and didn't say a word.

I went back outside and helped Mike clean up a bit. Then we went to my house because Mike wanted to rest. I decided to stay at the house so I could check on him from time to time throughout the night. He ended up being all right, and the next day he was just a little sore as he put it. Dino made up with Mike a few days later, but it wasn't all kissy huggy from there on in.

A few days after that, I was out with Barbara again. She was telling me cute innocent stories about her brother's daughter and what she did last weekend. I thought, Man, for two people who grew up the same, we're a world apart now. I was amazed at her seriousness and concern about her situations because they didn't fit into my realm of thinking at all any more. But as odd as they sounded, they still felt very refreshing to hear about with such sincerity on her part. We ended up fooling around a little bit at my house, but I only walked away with a limp, and blue balls that night.

Mikey stopped by the "Hill" tonight. He was pretty happy, so he bought us all a round at the bar.

"So what's up, Mikey," I said.
"Nothing, I just got back from a little trip I took with the motorcycle this weekend, and I feel good."
"Cool, you should take a trip like this every weekend if you're gonna come back this happy and buy us all a round of drinks," said Dave, who also happened to be hanging out.

Being that we didn't have anything else to celebrate, we decided to toast Mikey's happiness.

After we helped close the bar that night, Dave said that he was too drunk to walk home so Mikey said he'd ride him there.

"Hold on, Mikey, you don't ride too good on your own. As a matter of fact, being that nobody had heard from you, we were all wondering if we were going to have to chip in for your headstone. Look, being that Dave's twice your size and you're both a little drunk, maybe you shouldn't ride him." I said.

Mikey insisted, and Dave was too drunk to care so off they went.

Gerard and I figured they were only traveling about two blocks so we let them go.

As any knowledgeable motorcyclist could tell you, leaning with the rider when and as he drives is what a passenger is supposed to do. What was happening here was that Dave was swinging his arms over his head singing some stupid song, which was causing Mikey to weave back and forth as they rode up the street. I turned towards Gerard just as he was turning to me, and we both said, "I'll bet you ten bucks..."Then we laughed and joked about not wanting to take each other's bets before finishing our sentence. After that, we both turned to look up the street to watch their progress.

"Man," I said, "it looks like they might make it."
"Yeah, but look how close Mikey is coming to the parked cars on either side of the street."
Right after they got out of sight, we heard their crash, and Dave started to howl like an alley cat at the appropriate time. Gerard and I ran up the block and saw Dave flat on his back, yelling, "Ooooo, my leg! My leg!" Mikey, who was all right, was walking around in circles mumbling to himself.

When I got over to Dave and touched his right leg, he howled again. Well, at least I found out where he was injured, I thought. As I proceeded to inspect his leg, Dave proceeded to yell out loudly each time I rolled his pants up to the next level. I knew Dave's leg wasn't broken, because the first thing I had done was to lift it slightly in the air to check that before I started. I thought that maybe he twisted his knee badly because I still hadn't seen any blood so far.

After I got his pants rolled up to his knee, I said, "Dave, there's nothing here!?!"

He squinted up at me and moaned, "The other leg!"

Because Dave might have been really hurt, I decided not to slap him as I started on his other leg. In the meantime, Mikey was walking back and forth saying, "I can't believe I did this to my friend. How could I do this? Dave, I'm sorry."
"All right, Mikey. Cool out," Gerard said to him.

I went through the whole procedure with Dave on his other leg while he was howling. Then I checked them both out again and said, "Dave, I think you're all right!"
"I am...? Really...?" he answered.
"Yeah, now get up before I hurt you," I joked.

He stood up and said, Ow. Well, it's not that bad."

Mikey who was still mumbling said, "Dave, I'm sorry. Here, I'll ride you the rest of the way home."

"Okay," Dave answered.

"Wait a minute... This ain't a good idea, either," I said. Mikey insisted, and Dave was too drunk to care, so off they went on the motorcycle again.

They started weaving down the block, and then "Bam" they crashed again. This time Dave was standing and Mikey was howling. I looked at Gerard and said, "This one's yours."

A few nights later I was up at the Hill trying to avoid this girl named Maryann. We were in a bad stage of a courting arrangement. I had flirted with her one night but decided against it because I figured it might be a one-nighter. Being that she was friends with Jackie Lenhart and some of the other girls who hung out, I didn't want to create any type of rift. But now there was a worse one with Maryann, because when she asked me point blank if I was interested, I said no. So now it was like a woman scorned type of thing.

A little while later Donde showed up with this guy Freddy. I had hung out with Freddy a few times, and he seemed cool. After they were there for a little bit, I said, "Come on, let's get outta here, and go somewhere else."

"What's the matter? Maryann after you again?"

"Yeah, I think for sure she's gonna kick my ass today," I joked.

We left and headed down Northern Boulevard towards Bell Boulevard to check out a club called Camouflage.

We didn't get more than six blocks into our voyage when Donde started yet another argument through my window with some clown. During their argument I looked over to see that the guy was eating a full slice of pizza, so I decided to kick back with the seat and wait for that slice to fly into our car.

After about five minutes of his bullshit, Donde started calling this guy's mother names and told him that he had her last night. I was thinking, Shit, this guy's got the patience of a saint because I'da flung that slice a long time ago.

As I peered forward to see if he was still eating the slice, "Splat!" it hit me full in the face. Donde was hysterical with laughter as the hot sauce stung my face. My first reaction was to punch his head through the driver's window, but fortunately my logic kicked in. We were in the outside lane doing about 45 mph, and there was heavy traffic coming in the opposite direction. I'm sure we would have gotten into an accident. But I was so mad, I had to tell myself twice not to do it.

"Cut this motherfucker off, and stop him!" I said as I wiped the sauce off my face. As usual Donde was more than happy to oblige.

When our cars stopped, I ran for the guy's door yelling, "I'm gonna kill you, motherfucker!"

"NO! NO! NO! I didn't mean to hit you, man. I meant to hit your asshole friend, but I didn't want to throw it, because I was afraid I'd hit you!"

I was so pissed I swear I could have flipped his car over by myself.

"Please, man. I don't want to fight you. You'll kill me!"

As car horns were beeping to get by, I thought that I must have looked like a madman standing here in traffic with pizza sauce on my face. When I looked back down at the guy, he was smiling.

"What the fuck are you smiling about!?!"
"I'm sorry, man. It's a little funny, though."
"It ain't fucking funny!"
"You're right, man. I'm sorry, you're right. It ain't funny," he said as he corrected himself.

I turned around and got back into the car and said, "Take me home!"
"Pull him out of the fucking car, man," Donde said.
"Man, fuck you. Take me home!"
"Why are you pissed at me? I didn't throw pizza at you. Come on, we'll all go out."
"I'll tell you why I'm pissed. It's because you start these fucking bullshit fights through my window to get me involved in them. Then once I'm involved, you remember how to pull a car over instead of you pulling over and fighting your own bullshit fights. I'm telling you, Donde, turn this fucking car around, and take me home now!"

Nothing was said on the ride back to my house, but that was fine because I was done with him to a large degree.

I ran into Mikey over at the house one day, and he told me that he was going to have two weeks off from work. He wanted to take a road trip into the country or something.

"So why are you telling me?" I asked.
"Well, I wanted to know if you wanted to come with me." he said.

Yeah, I could use a little vacation, I thought. Besides, Mikey probably doesn't want to drive the whole way, so I said yes.

After some talk and with a little fanfare, we left on the motorcycle for Florida, of all places, from the Murry Hill a few nights later. Halfway through Jersey it started pouring rain, but I kept riding. It was coming down so fast that I got soaked immediately. After a few more minutes, I asked Mikey if he wanted to pull over or keep riding, and he yelled back, "Go for it; I'm fine."

We drove for another hour but I had to stop soon, because the wind against my wet clothes was making me freeze. So I decided to pull into the next rest stop on the turnpike and get some coffee. As I walked into the front door of the place, I noticed that my boots were sloshing from being soaked.

"Hey, Mikey, look at my boots," I said. "There's bubbles coming out of them!"

"Really? Mine are pretty dry," he said as I looked over towards him.

"Hey! Your whole body's pretty dry. What's up with that?"

"Check this out. While we were riding, I noticed that if I stayed in this little air pocket behind you, I wouldn't get soaked. But if I sat back comfortably, I'd get soaked by the rain, so I sat in the pocket."

"Tell me the fuck about it. For a while there I started to think you might be a faggot or something, because it felt like you were sitting in my pocket. Look at you. You're fucking dry."

"I know," he said as he laughed.

"Yeah, fuck you. You're buying anyhow."

After drying out in the air-conditioned place for a while, and almost freezing to death, we had some coffee, and decided to get going because it was a long way to Florida. Fortunately, it had stopped raining by then.

We rode for about another hour and a half, and then I decided to stop under an overpass to smoke a joint. Then we headed out again. The real pain in the ass about this trip was that, since the motorcycle was only a 450cc, it was only doing 67 miles an hour because of all of the weight we were carrying. I watched the speedometer as we slowly got up to speed, 45...55...60, and "POP" went the tire. I looked down and noticed that we had a flat on the rear tire, so I slowed the bike down and pulled onto the shoulder of the road.

Mikey started cursing about the bike breaking down, while I started cursing about not having a tire patch kit. We stopped, assessed the situation, and decided after several moments to get off at the next exit, which was closer than the one we left, and see if there was any type of as station around. The bitch about it was that the next exit was a mile away. I would have ridden the bike, but I didn't want to destroy the tire rim. So instead, what I did was start the bike up, put it in gear and trot alongside of the bike.

I set upon the task and had gotten about a quarter mile when I decided to glance back and see where Mikey was. When I looked back, I saw that he was about a quarter of a mile behind me, still yelling at the moon. I didn't know what he was bitching at though, I was the one who was still wet and now jogging with his motorcycle. I kept going and then, after a little while, I looked back and Mikey wasn't even in sight any more. By the time I got to the next exit, a car pulled up and let Mikey out; the little bastard had hitched.

When we got to the toll booth, I stopped the bike and rested for a minute. No sooner than I had stopped, it seemed like the toll collector called me on the loud speaker and asked me to come over to him. I walked over to him, and he asked me what I was doing there. I explained my story to him, and then he told me that I couldn't just sit there, on 'his' highway, and I would have to move. Just great, I thought. I asked him where he expected me to go at 4 in the morning to get a flat fixed. He told me there was a place in town, to stay on the road till I saw a flashing red light. Then to make a left, keep going down the road a piece and blah, blah, blah. Then after all that, he told me that they opened at 8 in the morning. I went back over by the bike and spoke to Mikey. I told him that I could call Dave at the house to see if Dino was sleeping there that night before he left for work, so that Dino could make arrangements to pick us up if all else failed. Because it was 4:00 a.m. and I knew that Dave had to get up early for work, I chose to let him sleep until 6 in the morning before I called.

As we were talking this over, for a few minutes, a state trooper pulled up. He asked me what the problem was, so I told him. Then the state trooper told me that I couldn't just sit there and that I should move down the road a couple of hundred yards. It seemed kind of a difficult thing to do, taking into consideration that the exit ramp after the toll booth was only 120 feet in length before you'd have to make either a left or a right.

"Look, what's the difference if I'm sitting on that side or this side of the toll booth?"

He said, "Look, son, I don't care what the difference is. You can't sit on my stretch of highway, so move it."

I figured that this guy must have had too many jelly doughnuts in his time and that maybe I'd better not press my luck with him. I grabbed the bike, started it, and then started walking past the toll booth.

"Ticket please."

I don't know why, but it seemed strange him asking me to pay and all with me walking the bike through the toll booth, especially since once I got the tire fixed, I'd have to go through this same toll booth to either continue my voyage or go home. I paid the ten bucks, walked about fifteen feet, and stopped by the phone booth. After talking about our options, Mikey lay down in the grass and went to sleep. I sat on the bike, put my ankles on the handlebars, and rested until 6 am, then I called Dave.

He sounded like a sleepy teddy bear when I woke him, and in all the time I knew him I never heard him talk that way, so it sounded funny. I asked him about three times to see if Dino was there and to wake him up so I could talk to him. Dave went on his voyage, and I waited.

As I was waiting and putting more change in the phone, I noticed that a bunch of rabbits were all over the grass by the phones, eating as they watched me. After a minute or two, maybe because I was stoned, I imagined that they had been listening to my conversation and were waiting for its conclusion as they stared at me.

My cousin got on the phone, and he sounded a little worse than Dave, so I knew he must have gone out that night. I asked him if he could wake up Frank Capeeto in a little while and see if he could get his father's van to pick us up instead of us looking for this bike shop on foot. He started telling me all this yahoo about, "Don't worry. The troops are on the way." I told him to call Frankie and call me back. He called back and told me in a sleepy voice that he had gotten no answer at Frankie's and that, after he got a little more sleep, he would call Frankie back and set something up, not to worry.

When I hung up the phone, I looked at the rabbits and they all seemed in agreement: They were thinking, Sure, sure, your cousin is coming with a van to pick you up. It's not like he's going back to sleep and forgetting all about you. After looking at the rabbits, for some reason, I knew I was on my own. I walked over to the motorcycle, sat down, and started to take the tire off with the little tool kit that came with the bike.

It was daylight out so, when I got done, I woke Mikey and told him I was leaving. Then I started walking down the road carrying the tire. Half-awake, Mikey said, "Yeah, I'll wait for you."

It was only 120 feet to the intersection but since I had decided to carry the tire and rim instead of rolling and chasing it down the road, the heat was really starting to get to me. No sooner than I had crossed the three-way intersection, a station wagon pulled over and opened the window. The cool air from the air-conditioned car hit my face, as they asked me if I needed a ride anywhere. It was like a dream come true, and I jumped at the opportunity.

After we drove for a little while, I started talking to the occupants. They were a cute little country family of modest living. The mother of the brood was the most talkative, so talkative that I told her, in a nice way, she missed her street.

As we were driving along, I thought for a moment about how I must've looked when she picked me up. I had on black combat boots, black jeans, a black cut-off T-shirt, a black feather earring hanging out of my ear, and a six-inch knife in a sheath strapped to my belt. I must've looked like a fucking Rambo or something when they picked me up. Thinking about this for a moment, I asked her if she had any fear about picking me up.

"The way we feel about, let's say being killed, is that if the Lord tells us it's our time to go, it's our time to go, and that's not going to stop me from helping someone in need," she answered.

The conversation went on like this for a little while until we got to the place and I got the tire fixed. After that she dropped me back off at the toll booth, and we said our goodbyes. Then I started to put the tire on while Mikey slept. After I got finished, I woke up Mikey and drove over to the toll booth to the same guy from last night. I got my ticket for the thruway and then asked the guy how far he thought "down the road a piece" meant. He asked me why I asked, and I told him the place was over four miles there and back. Then I told him, "You see me walking off carrying a motorcycle tire. Maybe you could've said something."

He answered smugly, "You got a ride. What are you crying about?"

"Yeah, fuck you, too, asshole," I waited for his reply, and after there wasn't one I left.

Mikey started whining when I took the turn to go back to New York, but by then I was in no shape to drive to Florida from Jersey. When I got back home, I went and slept for a little bit.

When I woke up, it was about 5:00 in the evening. I showered and then went to do a load of laundry up on Northern Boulevard. After I put a load of wash in, I went and stood in front of the laundromat. Gerard got off the bus at the stop across the street. I knew it was him immediately, but he stopped walking and was squinting his eyes towards me from across the six-lane street, so I played it off as though I was looking at him to start a fight. As Gerard was trying to look over my glare to see if it was me, I gave him the middle finger. He gave it back and then smiled. Then he crossed the street and asked me what I was doing there because I was supposed to be halfway to Florida by now.

"What are you talking about? We didn't go anywhere. We went to a topless club, picked up two dancers, screwed them half the morning, and then I came home, got some sleep, and then I did laundry."

Gerard said, "Really? That's cool."

Then I told him the truth, and he told me I was full of shit, that I probably did go out and get laid. I had to actually prove this story to him with Mikey's version.

Instead of giving up on taking a trip to Florida, we decided to head north and see the house I used to live in. I heard it was abandoned and wanted to go there and see if any of my things were still there that were left behind. If the house was in really bad shape, instead of sleeping there we could always stay with some people I knew up there, I told Mikey.

We hung out and bullshitted for a while with Gerard that evening, and we decided to leave that night. Then we repacked the bike and left at about 7 p.m. By car it's normally a four and a half hour trip, but on this little motorcycle it took us seven and a half hours.

When we got to the house, it was dark outside so you can imagine how dark it was inside. I told Mikey to come in with me while I tried to get the electric on, but he was having no part of it, especially after I told him that he had to climb in the broken window with me around back.

The house had huge windows with big panes of glass; each piece measured about 2' by 3' and there were four to a window. Mikey was more afraid of a bear in the house than a person. He had heard about my bear story up here.

The only things I had on me were a knife and a cigarette lighter. Just as I started climbing in the window and getting second thoughts about doing it, Mikey asked me for the bike keys as I went in. After I told him to go fuck himself, I told Mikey that when I had left four years ago I had taken out the fuse for the electric, but that meant that I had to go down to the basement. Mikey agreed that it would be great if I could turn on the electricity, as he stood outside.

The only problem about the basement routine, I thought, was that when I was living there four years ago, I didn't even like going in the basement with the lights on. I swear it felt like someone had died down there. It was more of a cold cellar made of piled rocks and dirt floor than a basement by today's standards. I asked Mikey one more time if he would come with me, but he still swore he'd rather sleep in the garage or in the grass for that matter than go inside the dark house and into the basement with me. I took a deep breath, called him a pussy, and walked towards the basement door.

It was weird in there because the whole house was like a time capsule from when I had left. Even though I only had the light of my lighter, everything looked just like I had left it. I walked over to the basement door, checked my surroundings, and then turned off the lighter to allow it to cool for my trip into the basement. At that moment it was so dark and spooky I figured that it would be a great time to get mauled by a bear or jumped or shot for that matter. I clicked the lighter on and started my voyage into the unknown.

I have to tell you, though, as that cool damp air from the basement hit me, I think one of my nine lives jumped out of me and went to wait with Mikey. When I got over to the fuse box, the new fuses I had put there years ago were still there. I put one in and "bam" Thomas Edison's invention sparked to life right in front of me. When I heard the refrigerator go on, I knew we were home free now.

When I got upstairs, I turned on some of the lights and a radio. Mikey came over and tried the door, and then he knocked. There were no cars on the road at that hour, so I knew it was him, but I still said, "Who is it?"

He said, "It's me, Michael."
"What do you want?"
"I want to come in."
"Why?"
"Because I'm cold and I want to sleep in a bed."
"Go climb in the window on the other side of the house."

I knew he wouldn't because there weren't any lights on that side yet. Mikey then pleaded, "Come on, Mike. I was scared, man. That's why I didn't want to come in with you."

I made sure I let him beg for a while before I finally let him in. We started a fire in the wood stove and found some canned food so we heated it up and ate it. I slept in my room that night, and it was strange because we had made the decision to move back to the city so fast that hardly anything was packed. My mother had promised me that we would come back for most of this stuff that was lying around, but we didn't. What really bothered me was that she had left Bobo with some people, and she never came back to get her. I had left clothes in the drawers, old school books, models of cars I had made, and pictures. It was like for a few moments I could be 15 again with not only the thoughts but all the props in place.

While I was sleeping that night, I don't know what it was, but it felt like someone grabbed my ankles and pulled my legs towards the end of the bed. Two thoughts came to mind: one was physical muscle cramps from the long ride, the other was that the thing in the basement had finally got me. I figured, though, at this point it could do whatever it had to and lay there for a second or two, waiting for the worse, and then I jumped up. Now I figured that there was no way I could go back to sleep without settling this fear once and for all, so I smoked a little hash and went down into the cellar. When I got down there I turned on the light, looked around, talked openly to any type of ghost that might be there, then I turned off the light, and told him that, if someone was there, it should now do anything it had to. I stood there in the dark until the feeling went away, and then I went upstairs to sleep.

We went over to High Falls the next day, and there were No Trespassing signs posted all over the place. I found out from someone who was there that the kids' summer camp that I had gone to in the area had bought the waterfalls and the surrounding cliffs we used to dive off.

After climbing up the bridge and looking down at the small area between the rocks that we used to jump into, I thought to myself that I must have been fucking nuts at 15 and 16 to jump off. It scared me now.

We swam and hung around until a sheriff came and told us we'd have to leave the watering hole. I stopped by my grandmother's house on the way back from High Falls to see if Franny or Billy still lived there. When we got there, I could see that my grandmother was still as nutty as ever. I never could understand how my grandfather hooked up with her, but good thing he did. Nana told me that Franny had moved out and that Billy would be back tomorrow, so I told her I would stop by then.

That night we spoke to Gerard about him coming up. It would be hard with three on a bike, but I was sure that we'd figure something out.

I was egging him on about how great the wind felt in your hair on the ride up and how nice it felt to be cruising down these country roads. I was actually trying to get him to jump on the Amtrak and come up because I dreaded the 350-mile ride back on this little bike. It was O.K. to ride around the neighborhood, but on the highway it felt like you were riding a moped. I guess I must've said something right, because Gerard did come up after work on Friday.

When I went to get him from town, I managed to lose the helmet with a small camera and an ounce of weed. Bummer. I didn't realize it until I got to the train station. I figured that Gerard would wait, so I drove back to see if I could find the helmet and stuff, and then I drove back to where I had heard some people beeping a horn at me earlier, which was about six miles from the train station. But no such luck. When I got back to the train station, Gerard threw his hands up in the air and said, "Fuck, I thought I got off at the wrong train station. Where the fuck were you?"

After I explained to him what had happened, I asked Gerard how much money he had on him. He told me, and then I told him that we had to buy a helmet. The cheapest one we found was like 70 bucks, and then we drove the 40 miles back to the house where Mikey was waiting. Gerard told me that he had brought up some angel dust with him, but we decided to wait for a special occasion before we smoked the P.C.P.

When we got to the house, Mikey was there with a pile of my comic books. Mikey looked up at me, put the comic book down, and said, "This is the most relaxing vacation I ever had!"

It was quite comical because there he was, sitting in some house with no food, no TV, one change of clothes, and a pile of comic books. We decided to go out and get something to eat, so we went about four miles "down the road" to a bar and restaurant. We had to do it in a set of two rides. We tried three on the bike, but it seemed like it could be deadly on this little bike. While I was there, I called my Uncle Billy and told him to come up and meet us. He showed up with a few country friends of his a little while later.

After we had dinner and a few beers, we went outside. We decided, after speaking with these guys for a little while, that we should spark up a joint up with some angel dust in it. None of them had ever smoked "dust" before, so we made sure it wasn't straight dust. But these country dudes thought they were little bad asses now. It was cute.

After we got a little buzz, the country dudes suggested that we go to another bar where there were some girls hanging out, so we got ready to leave. Gerard went with the guys in the van because he said his ass was still sore from riding on the back of the motorcycle. Mikey and I drove behind them on the bike when we left. I don't know if the guy drove the way he was driving all the time, or because he was high, but it was bad. He was weaving all over the road. Mikey and I were laughing our asses off, figuring that Gerard was freaking out, which he confirmed when they stopped. The rest of the weekend was pretty quiet, but the three of us really had a good time.

Gerard almost decided to ride the bike back but declined at the last minute. He gave us all his money, except for like five bucks, and then took the comfortable train ride home with a hundred-pound duffel bag I loaded up for him with some of my things from the house. Mikey and I got home late that night without incident.

A few days later, after we got back, I walked into the Murry Hill, and Asia, the girl I used to date, was working as the bartender.

"Hey! Asia... what are you doing here?"
"Michael... how are you? What are you doing here?"
"I hang out in this bar!"
"Oh, shit. That's funny; I didn't know that."

We got to talking, and I found out that she was still single.

"Have I got a guy for you. Good looking, Italian, and his name is Michael."
"Really? How long have you known him?"
"I've known him a long time. Speaking of time, you remember that shit I was arrested for?"
"Yes?"
"Well, he just got done doing time for it."
"Oh..."
"But trust me, he's a nice guy."
"Yeah, and probably as horny as a jack rabbit."
"Well, that may not be all that bad for you, you know," I joked.
"Well, bring him in tonight, and let me see if he's a lunatic."
"Sure, no problem. Hey! Wait a minute. He might have been here already."
"That would be funny if I had already met him, huh?"
"Yeah, it would be," I answered.

I took Mike over that night and, after talking with each other for a few days, they went on a date. When I saw Mike the next day, I asked him how everything went. He told me that it went great, and he thanked me for setting him up with her.

"Hey, Mike, I've got a friend of mine who just got out of the joint, and I was wondering if he could stay over for a little while."

"Well, is he a psychopath?"
"No, he's cool."
"What's a little while?"
"Well, he's got an old lady out here. He just wants to cut loose for a few days before he goes home," he explained.
"Well, I guess for a few days it won't be bad."

When I met Timmy, he seemed all right, a little quiet. But I guess he was just getting readjusted to the world. By the time two weeks had passed, though, Timmy came out of his cocoon. At first, his staying there wasn't really much of an issue, but when he started trying to find his rank in the pack is when a few problems started.

I pulled Mike aside one day and said, "Mike, you know that you'll always have carte blanche with me, but Timmy's starting to step over the lines of being a guest and acting like one. If he doesn't get it into line, he's gotta go."
"Oh, I'm sorry, Mike. I didn't know you felt that way. I'll keep him away from the house more often and see what his plans are, okay?"
"Yeah, no problem," I answered.

Barbara and I went on another date. She gave me another dose of sanity, and it was refreshing. At the end of the date we stopped at my house and fooled around. She had to be home early, though, so I walked her across the street, limp and all.

Mikey came down into the basement one night while Gerard and I were working out and said, "Hey, I'm going to walk over to Jack in the box to get some fresh air and tacos. Do you guys want any?"
"Yeah, sure, here's a bunch of money," Gerard said. "Get some tacos for me and Mike."

After Mikey hadn't returned for about two hours, we both started to wonder what had happened to him. Needless to say, we were both also a little pissed because we were hungry. If he wanted to go hang out, he shouldn't have told us he'd come back, we agreed. When he finally did come back, we were really pissed because he didn't have any food on him.

"Mikey, where's our food?" we asked.

Mikey stood there with a distorted look on his face and finally said, "I think Andy and his friends just killed some guys!"

Andy Biaz happened to be a nutty school friend of mine.

Mikey explained to us that he was at Jack in the Box, and a few dudes started to hassle him while he was ordering, asking him for some money. Then when he went to pay, one of the four guys tried to grab his money. Mikey, who wasn't much of a fighter, then said that he paid for the food and left.

"But these fucking guys followed me and start trying to grab my food and shit. They were nuts. Then by the time I crossed the street in front of Firestone, Andy happens to pull up in a car with a few guys and said, 'Mike, are these guys bothering you?' And I said, 'Yeah, man. They're trying to take my food and my money.' Then Andy and his friends jump out of the car with baseball bats and start hitting these guys."

I was a little shocked because I never had a grown man cry on me before, and I didn't really know what to do or say about it, but I knew I had to try something. I put my arms around him, patted him on the back, and said, "There, there, Mikey. It's all right. It's all right."

After Mikey settled down, Gerard said, "So what happened to our food?"

"You know, you're a sick fuck. I'm telling you that I think somebody died right in front of me, and all you can say is where's my food!?!"

"Look, Mikey, I'm sorry you had to witness something like that, but I didn't know the guy who might be dead, and I'm still hungry," Gerard answered.

"Here, take the motorcycle and get your food, all right?" Mikey answered as he threw Gerard his keys and some money.

"Mikey, you really think Andy, and his friends killed these guys?"

"Mike, it would be a miracle if this guy lived. Each time they hit this guy in the head, it sounded like a bowling ball bouncing off of the concrete."

"So what happened after that?"

"Andy and his two friends got back into their car, and then Andy told me to get in, but I didn't want to get in because then I'd be an accomplice."

"So what did you do?"

"Well, I started walking away, and Andy followed me and yelled for me to get in again. So I thought that he might hop out and whack me with the bat, so I got in."

"Then what?"

"Then they ate the food I was carrying. After that, we rode around for a while, and Andy started to tell me that if anything happened with the police, I'd have to be his alibi and that he did it to protect me and we were outnumbered. I told him I'd do it, because I was afraid that he might kill me, too, if I said no, but fuck that!"

"Mikey, you gotta go to court for him. He did save your ass after all."

"Mike, look, if I knew he was going to kill someone I'da let those guys rob me and take a beating. I didn't ask Andy to kill someone for me."

Andy did get arrested, and Mikey turned down the request from Andy to come to court for him. He also refused my advice after I told him that, even though it was bad that Andy, and his friends had killed someone, he should still go to bat for him. I told him that the least he could do was go to court and tell his version of what happened, but Mikey wanted no part of it.

On the homefront, I started to get the idea that Barbara enjoyed giving me a limp every time we would see each other, which was quite often now. As a matter of fact we had spent a lot of time wrestling, but nobody got pinned yet. To be honest I was getting tired of the "virgin" routine, and I felt I needed to be with a woman soon.

After one night of a "session" with Barbara, I took her over to the Hill. It was early, so I figured that there shouldn't be any problems. When I got there, Asia was bartending and Mike was playing pool. Asia asked me if I had heard the good news yet, and I told her I hadn't and asked her what it was. She told me that she and Mike had gotten married that morning. I was a little shocked at first. I mean, I knew that they would be good for each other, but I didn't think that they would go and get married in just a few weeks of knowing each other. Then Mike walked over, smiled, and showed me his wedding ring. I hugged him and then kissed Asia, and we had a few drinks to celebrate.

"I hope you don't mind, Mike, but I'm moving in with Asia," he joked.

I laughed and then said, "Hey, wait a minute. What about Timmy?"
"Don't worry. He's going to move in with me and Asia for a bit."

When Mike and I went to play a few games of pool, I walked past Barbara and she had the female look of, "Your friend can get married, but you can't, right!"

After Mike and I played pool, Dino came in arm in arm with ugh... Maryann.

At that point in time, I don't know which one of us disliked each other more.

"Hey, Dino, did you hear that Mike and Asia got married?"
"Yeah, Maryann and I are next."

He then smiled at her and kissed her. Well, life is funny, I guess.

We had a few toasts and then Dino and Mike went in the back to play pool. The bar wasn't that crowded yet, but as the night progressed more and more people showed up. By the time Mike and I were playing a game of pool, my friend Gene O'Donald's brother "O.D.", as he was called, came in with his best friend. O.D. had a few at the bar and then he and his friend made their way over to the pool table.

After we spent about an hour of drinking and playing pool together, comments started to go back and forth between O.D., his friend, Mike, and Dino. I had my back turned towards O.D. and his friend, and I was just about to take my shot when Mike picked up a pool ball and said, "Shut the fuck up!" he threw it at whoever was standing behind me, towards the front of the bar. Then I heard the ball go "thud" against soft flesh.

Then without warning, Dino picked up a ball and threw it. "Thud," I heard it go again. Now the two of them were clearing the table. I basically stayed in the same position I was in to take my shot, because they were sailing the pool balls over my head through the doorway now and chasing O.D. and his friend out of the bar with flying pool balls. I have to tell you, though, from my vantage point, the whole thing was hilarious. I was looking up at Dino and Mike, and they both looked like they were at tryouts for the N.Y. Met's baseball team.

Dino was now squinting with one eye closed for better aim before he threw his ball. The other funny thing about it was that I could hear the pool balls sailing clear across the bar and hitting the front wall, and then I would hear the ones that were hitting their mark. It went something like this, Whoosh, crack (wall), Whoosh thud, owww! (self-explanatory).

When they started this fight, there had been quite a few people in the bar, but by the time I turned around after it was over, I couldn't see anyone. Then someone asked if it was over yet. After I said yes, I walked over in the direction of the bar, and I saw Asia, Barbara, and Maryann huddled in the right hand corner. Then people started to come out from behind the jukebox, the pinball machine, and the end of the bar. Just about this time "Weedhopper," PeeWee's older brother, came into the bar and said, "All right, what the fuck is going on in here?"

Mike, who still had a pool ball on him, said, "Shut the fuck up," and then threw his pool ball. It caught Weedhopper in mid-step and bounced off his forehead before it hit the ceiling. Before his foot touched the ground, Weedhopper spun around and, without another word, wobbled out of the bar.

"That was a beautiful shot, Mike," Dino said.
"Why, thank you, Dean," Mike answered.

I had to agree on this because Weedhopper was a bit of an asshole. Asia started yelling at Mike, saying that he swore he would stop fighting and stay out of trouble. He looked at her and said, "Look, I'm sorry, but they started it. So chill out."

Everyone who stayed in the bar peeked back out from their hiding places again and asked if it was really over this time. Dino and Mike both looked at each other, agreed, and told everyone that it was. After a few more minutes, the front door slowly opened, and some of the people who had managed to run out of the bar meekly asked if it was all right to come in now. I didn't know it, but about ten people managed to run out. It looked kinda funny when they all filed back in and sat at their drinks and money that they had left behind and started carrying on as if nothing had happened. I never heard what happened to O.D. and his friend, but I did hear that Weedhopper got eight stitches on his forehead.

The day of Halloween I had come home, and for some reason I was in a bit of a hurry. After running up the stairs, I noticed that no one was in the shower, so I decided to jump in it now before anyone got home. I ran up the next flight of stairs, kicked off my sneakers, and pulled off my shirt. I turned to my left to get my shower things and, as I turned, "Whap," something hit me right under my right shoulder blade. For a brief second, I thought that maybe I had gotten shot, because I didn't know of anything that could move as fast as whatever had hit me. But because I didn't see an exit wound on my chest I figured that maybe it wasn't a bullet.

Maybe it's a ghost, Mike, I thought. It is Halloween, and you are in your father's room.

"D...Dad?!?" I questioned out loud.

I sat there for a second or two not knowing what to expect, and then I slowly turned around to see nothing, absolutely nothing.

Wait a minute, Mike. I know something hit me in the back.

As I was facing the opposite direction now and thinking about my situation, I heard a noise over my left-hand shoulder. At first I wondered if I should either throw a punch or run, but I figured to myself if anything could move this fast, Mike, it could whip your ass before you knew it. I slowly turned around and didn't see or hear anything.

Whoa, Mike, I thought. Maybe you're having an acid flashback. I heard they happen.

Then I heard the noise again right in front of me and still didn't see anything. Oh, that's it, you must be tripping, Mike, 'cause there's nothing there.

The room was lit from the setting sun, so I couldn't see all the way down to the floor from where I thought I heard the noise. I bent over and started to feel the rug to test my sanity. Then I felt something small and furry, so I grabbed it, and it was a fucking sparrow.

Holy shit! How could a bird fly through a window that had a two-by three-foot opening in it at that speed and have the exact timing to have a collision with me?

The bird was still alive but dazed, obviously. I stood there amazed for a minute or two before I placed it on the table next to the window. I left him there and, when I got back from my shower, he was gone.

Man, that was spooky, I thought as I got dressed.

After that, I called Barb and asked her what time we were going to meet. She told me that she would be done at about 10:30 because she had to get her nephews, that were visiting, ready for a party. So I told her that she could meet me at the "Hill" when she was done. My thinking was that I'd leave with her once she got there, So she wouldn't be there for any crazy shit late at night. After I went downstairs, I ran into Mikey and asked him if he was going to take his motorcycle out tonight. He told me that he wasn't crazy enough to take it out on a night like this, so I asked him if I could take it, and he said all right. Then I went for a ride to get some weed.

I rode around for a while, and then I headed over to the Hill about 9:30. Everybody was stopping by to show off their costumes, and a few people asked me to come with them to some parties they were going to, but I decided to wait for Barbara instead. Chris Petrello, Peck's old girlfriend, stopped by. She was dressed up as a black cat. Man, did she look hot, I thought. I turned down her offer to go to a party and watched her wag her tail out the door as she left.

Mikey stopped by a little later and asked me my plans. After I told him that I didn't really have any, except to wait for Barbara, he said that he wanted to stick close to the house so he could stay away from the nuts that would be out tonight. After ten-thirty came and went, I started to get a little pissed off. Asia was working that night, so Mike was there with her.

"Ahh, don't let it get to you, Mike. Barbara probably got suckered into watching the kids all night," Viale said.

"Yeah, Mike. But at least she could have called here and let me know so I could go do something."
"Yeah, that's true. Maybe she didn't want you to go out and do something, though. You know how girls get sometimes."
"Yeah, who knows?"

Hey, wait a minute, that's funny. Maybe she's standing me up on a date. All right, this is what I'll do. I'll hang out here tonight, and if she doesn't show or call, that's it. "Finito," as Grandpa would say.

By about one in the morning, people started showing up after parties. "Fran the man" was there with her boyfriend, and so were Jimmy Marnell and his girlfriend, Vicky. Fran wasn't all that big for a girl, but we called her that because she had kicked some guy's ass years ago and the name just stuck. Then Lo and behold, Barbara strolled in. I looked left, right, then said, "What happened? You forgot your purse here or something?"

"I'm sorry, Michael. I'll make it up to you."

Yeah, probably with another case of blue balls, I thought.

"Fine, then let's get out of here. I've been here all night."
"Well, let me say hi to everyone and wish them a Happy Halloween first."
"Yeah, hurry up, though all right?"

After a little while she was ready so I started to say good night to a few people as we left. I thought about staying put for the night, but being that I had been there all night I decided to split. I only had one helmet, so I gave it to Barbara as we walked to the door. Then I stopped to say good night to Vicky.

"See, I told you Barbara would show up. She likes you, I can tell. But where are you guys going to go now? It's late. Why don't you just hang out here?" Vicky said.

I stopped to think about what Vicky said, but then I looked at the clock, and it said, 1:23, the same date as my birthday. I thought it was odd, and a sign, that I should leave.

I gave Vicky a peck on the cheek and explained to her that I needed to get some fresh air and that maybe I might be back in a little bit. Then I walked out with Barbara.

"We'll stop at my house, and I'll get another helmet. Then we'll go to this party I was invited to, all right?"
"Don't be mad at me, Michael. I told you I was sorry," Barbara said as I sat on the bike and started it.

The bike was a little cold, so I decided to ride to the corner and back to warm up the motor.

As I was heading back to the corner, I looked at Barbara and wondered for a second if I should just drive right past her and go meet Chris, but that thought changed when a car screeched around the corner heading right for me.

I looked at the couple in the car, and they were both facing each other, arguing. This guy had made the corner pretty fast, and he wasn't looking. He was hugging my right side of the one-lane street. I tried to pass him on my left. Just as I was doing this, he compensated for his wide turn without even seeing me. The last thing I thought about just before he hit me was if I was going to end up out in Northern Boulevard to get run over by some other cars.

I had been going about 45, and he was doing at least that when we hit head on. The last feeling I had was my body crashing into his car. I don't remember landing on the pavement after I bounced off his car, which could have been a good thing. I lay there for I don't know how long, but the first thought I had was that another car was going to come and finish me off. I was face down, so I decided to push myself up to my knees to try and crawl out of the street. I was able to raise myself twelve inches, spit out a tooth and some blood, and then I went back down with the same speed at which I had just pushed myself up.

"Okay, Mike. Let's try this again, and then we'll have a nice stiff drink at the bar," I said out loud to myself.

I pushed myself up again, and it felt as if someone put a foot on my back and gently pushed me back down. This time on the way back down, I opened my eyes and saw a big pool of blood, and I thought, Fuck, not again.

"Can somebody move my body, please?" I yelled out just before I blacked out. The next time I opened my eyes, I saw Mike Viale wiping my face with a bloody bar rag.

"Mike, don't die on me, motherfucker. Don't die!"

It was a really sad sight, and I had to look away...! Oh, fuck, Mike. I just looked away from Mike and my body!

I turned my head back, and I realized that I was standing about fifteen feet away from us. Then I looked and saw Barbara. She was still standing in the same position, holding the helmet with her mouth wide open, but I didn't see the car or the guy who had hit me.

People started to come out of the bar by now, and Mike started to yell for some more rags. Then Fran the man came out of the bar with her older boyfriend, George, and screamed, "No! No! George! You've got to do something! What am I gonna tell his mother!"

George grabbed her in his arms as Fran sobbed into his chest. I looked back at Mike and my body.

It all seemed to be happening in slow motion. After a moment or two of watching everything, I thought to myself, Fuck it... What the fuck do I have to live for? My life has been fucked up so far. What should I do? Go back and see how much more fucked up it's gonna get? Besides that, now my body's all fucked up."

Everybody was outside now, and I saw the guy who hit me pull up. He got out of his car, walked to the back of the crowd, looked towards my body for a second, and then at all my friends. He turned around, got back in his car, and drove away.

Yeah, you better leave, I thought; otherwise, you'll be lying next to me.

So this is it, huh, Mike? Just another city kid who died in the gutter. I thought about this for a second, and the sound of it really stung me somehow.

Yep, this is just the way you were supposed to end up, everyone will say. You know what, Mike? Doesn't it fuckin' sicken you how much bullshit you had to live with? Doesn't the thought just sicken you that, after all this, you're going to die in the street like a stray fucking dog? I never even lived my life, I'll never see Europe, I'll never get married, and I'll never have kids. Wait a minute. My life may be fucked up here, but I don't know where I'm going now. And what happens if I take too long to make up my mind and my body dies...? What if some type of door closes while I'm thinking? Maybe I'll become a fucking ghost, Mike, and stay here forever. Fuck it... I know I'm all busted up, but I don't want it to end now, especially like this! Besides, Mike, who the fuck will bury you??

The next thing I remember was being tossed into the back seat of a car, which woke me up. I tried to get up, and I heard Mike say, "Sit still, Mike. We're in the police car. We're going to the hospital, okay? Don't worry, I'm coming with you."

Then I heard one of the cops say, "Damn straight you're going with him!"

When I got to the hospital, Mike and one of the cops slid me out of the back seat, put my arms over their shoulders, grabbed me by my waist, and then carried me in like a scarecrow.

"Motorcycle accident. Where do we put him?"
"Hold on..., hold on. I'll see if we can bring him right in."

After we stood there for a second or two, the female voice said, "Okay, bring him right in."

As we started to move, I heard a voice say, "Yeah, and don't get lost when you get in there!"

Then I heard Mike say, "I don't know what the fuck your problem is, asshole, but you ought to get it checked out!"

After half a step, I felt Mike, who was on my right, get pulled backwards.

"What are you, a fucking wiseass?"

Now that no one was carrying my right side, I started to fall towards the ground and "Crack," I heard somebody get nailed.

As I started to hear a scuffle break out, the cop who was holding up my left side dropped me onto the ground. I don't know why, but it felt good to be on the floor. I guess because it was nice and cool, and I felt like I wanted to go to sleep anyhow. But after I got stepped on and kicked once or twice, I yelled out, "Excuse me, but can somebody get me the fuck out of here? I'm already fucked up."

I must've passed out after this, because the next thing I remember was waking up while I was lying down on a table with strange people pulling my clothes off.

"Wait a minute! Wait a minute! Where the fuck am I?"
"You've been involved in a motorcycle accident, and you're in the hospital now," I was told.
"Yeah, yeah, I know that, but what hospital?"
"You're at Flushing Hospital."
"Nope, get me outta here!"
"Excuse me?"
"I was here once before, and I don't like it here."
"Would you like us to call you a limo?"
"Nope, just throw me in a cab, and take me to Booth Memorial. I've got money on me."
"You know, my friend, you're in very bad shape, and by law we have to work on you here and now. So I'll tell you what, when we're done with you, you can call a cab, champ. Besides that, let me ask you something. Would you walk into a tattoo parlor, kick the artist, and then tell him to give you a tattoo?"
"Oops!" I said out loud because his comment shut me right the fuck up. Besides that, I was getting a little bored so I decided to pass out from the pain.

The next time I woke up, it felt like I had a hot knife being twisted in my chest.

"Doc! Doc! I think I'm having a heart attack!"
"Where is the pain?" he asked.
"All over my left side and by my heart! Oh, fuck! Oh, fuck! I think I'm having a heart attack."
"Okay, look. You're not having a heart attack."
"How the fuck do you know!?!"
"Because we have you hooked up to a monitor."
"Oh. Then what the fuck is this pain I'm feeling?"
"I'm not sure. That's why we're sending you to get X-rayed."

After he said that, I decided to pass out again.

"Mike! Mike! I'm here for you!" I heard Dino say.

It was nice to hear Dino's familiar voice. He stayed with me as they rolled me over on the stretcher to get X-rayed, and he told me that he'd be right outside the door.

"Don't fucking die on me, Mike!" he warned.

"All right, Dino, I won't. But if I do, tell my mother I said bye."

As I got wheeled into the room, the guy pushing me said out loud, "Hold on, Doc. I've got one more for you."

I looked over to see the colored X-ray technician taking off his white hospital jacket. Then he stopped and said, "Awww, shit, man, I was just leaving. Can't you get somebody else to do it?"

"No, I can't. You're here, so just do it, okay?"

"Gee, I'm sorry, man, but do you think you could take five minutes out of your fucking life and click a few X-rays for me? I'm fucking dying over here, ya' know!"

"Great, my last patient and he's got to be a wiseass," he said.

As I was being pulled onto the X-ray table, I could tell with my eyes closed whose hands were whose, because somebody didn't seem to care about being gentle. After the other person left, things started to go smoothly until he told me to lift my left arm over my head. The left side of my body was the side that had taken the impact, and everything hurt on that side. I let out a slow, low growl as I attempted to perform this trick for him and winced in pain as I tried.

"Come on, this is the last one. Just raise your arm over your head, will you?" he said.

"What do you think? I'm a fucking pussy? I'm trying, man!"

I heard him walk over towards me, and I assumed that he was going to try to help. Then he grabbed my wrist and snapped my arm straight out over my head. The pain was so intense I would have passed out if it hadn't been for my anger.

"You fucking cock-sucking motherfucker. I'll fucking kill you!" I said as I grabbed for him with my right hand.

He yanked my hand off and said, "You're not gonna be killing anyone, motherfucker. You're all fucked up now, so shut the fuck up!"

"Stand me up, motherfucker! Stand me up against a wall, and I'll kill you, motherfucker, even with one hand!"

"Shit, you better shut up before I take a pillow and smother your ass, motherfucker!"

I can't believe this, I thought. I'm in a hospital, and I'm getting into a street fight with this motherfucker, and I'm injured and can't move?!

"DINO! DINO!" I screamed.

"Shut up, man!"

"No, you better kill me now, motherfucker! DINO!" I yelled again.

I screamed Dino's name until I heard him banging on the door. In between screaming for him to break the door down, I heard him arguing with someone outside to open the door. When they finally did open it, Dino ran in and said, "Mike! I'm here! What's the matter!?!"

"Dino, smash this motherfucker's head open!" I said with my left arm still stretched over my head.

With each word or sentence out of my mouth, the pain was excruciating but I had lost it, and out of my mind with anger, I didn't give a fuck.

"He's crazy, man. I just touched him, and he started screaming that he was gonna kill me!"
"Well, did you hurt him?" Dino asked.
"No, man, I took it easy with him!"
"Yeah, you better change your tune, motherfucker," I said.
"Mike, cool out a minute."
"Cool out? Dino, this motherfucker tells me he's gonna put a pillow over my head and suffocate me!"
"Did you fucking tell him that!?"
"No, man. I'm telling you, man, he just went nuts on me for no reason!"
"All right, fine. I'll take care of it. Dino, take this motherfucker's name, the date and what shift it is because I will come back and take care of your ass, motherfucker!"
"Mike, come on."
"Dino, I'm telling you, take this motherfuckers name!"
"All right, Mike, I'll do it. Just calm down now, okay?"
"Look, I've got one more X-ray to do then he's done, okay?" the guy said to Dino.
"All right, Mike. Let him take the last X-ray, then you're done here all right?"
"Fine, but you stay in the room!"
"No, you can't stay in here with him," the hospital guard said.
"Fine, you take your fucking X-ray, then you come back in and put me on the stretcher, Dino, because if this motherfucker comes near me, I'll rip his fucking eyes out."

When the last X-ray was taken, Dino came in and helped me onto the stretcher. As the X-ray tech walked past us, I said, "See you when I get better, cocksucker!"

After he left, I decided to pass out from the pain again. Six hours after that, they took me back for more X-rays, but by then my "friend" had already left. One hour after that, a doctor came over and said, "Okay, Michael, I've got good news for you."
"What? I'm gonna die?" I gasped. "You're finally going to put me out of my misery?"
"Well, kinda. You see, because you have such muscle mass in your chest, we couldn't tell from the first X-rays, but now we see that along with breaking all the ribs on your left side you've got a collapsed lung, too. And that's what's been causing you all the pain."
"Collapsed lung? So what does that mean? I'm only gonna have one lung?"
"No, no, no, we'll take care of that," he said as he and his assistant started to gather surgical tools and put on gloves.

"Well, what does that mean? You're going to put an air pump down my throat?"
"No, what the procedure calls for is for us to make an incision between your fifth and sixth ribs and then we'll insert a tube that will be hooked up to something like a pump," he explained.
"Incision...? Cutting...? Well, you're going to knock me out, right?"
"Well, actually we can't because you have head injuries. So what we'll do is give you a local

anesthetic."

"A local? That's what they use to pull your teeth or to stitch you up, right?"

"Yes, it is."

"And you're going to cut me open on that?"

"Yes."

"Fuck! Well... let's do it before I change my mind," I said.

The doctor sliced between my ribs four times and then jabbed the scalpel into the fresh wound as he cut about two inches long. Well, that wasn't that bad, I thought.

"Whoa!" I hollered, "What the fuck is that?" I said as a sharp pain pierced my body.

If you can, for a moment, try to imagine sticking something with the diameter of a dime through a paper cut between two ribs. Yeah, ouch!

When he made a second attempt, I grabbed his hands and said, "No, that's it. Fuck it. I'll live with it."

"You can't live with it. Now come on, I'm almost done," he lied.

"All right, look then. If you're going to do it, then shove that thing in and don't stop until you're done, okay?"

I've got to tell you, I'd been through a lot of pain this night, but this was the worst. This hurt more than the accident itself.

"Grrrrr, man. Fuck! Are you almost done?"

"Almost."

I looked down while he was working, and I saw blood all over the table.

Shit, man, they didn't even clean up after the last person that was here, I thought, until I looked at his gloved hands and saw them covered with blood. After he got done busting my cherry, he put a stitch or two in and told me he was done.

"Gee, I don't know if I should kiss you or kill you, Doc, but thanks."

Then I decided to pass out from the pain. Unbeknownst to me, I spent the night in intensive care, and then the next day they put me in a regular room.

CHAPTER 7

HOUSTON, WE HAVE A PROBLEM

Ouch! What the fuck was that? I opened an eye and saw a nurse walking away.Bitch, I thought.

It's dark... I'm in a room... there's window's... I'm still alive... Okay... I... sleep.

Ouch! I opened an eye and saw a nurse walking away again. Bitch, I thought, dark... window... sleep.

Ouch! Bitch...dark...sleep...

Ow...! Bitch.....sleep...

"Ow! Hey! What are you sick, or something? You come in here every five minutes to just stab me or what?!"

"Oh, my God. You scared me!"

"Yeah, well, you've been scaring me, too, lady."

"I haven't been coming here every five minutes. You've been unconscious for five days, and I've come in each morning."

"Well, then I've got a good way to wake someone up- stab them in the ass every morning for five days. I'm telling ya' it works."

"I haven't been stabbing you in the ass. I've been giving you your injections."

"Injections? Shit, they hurt like hell."

"Well, now that you're up, I'll alternate them on either side of your butt, O.K.?"

"Hey, how bad am I?"

"Well, I'm not going to lie to you. You hurt yourself pretty bad, and we were wondering if you were going to pull through."

"Hey, I'm not tied down to the bed, am I?"

"No...? Why do you ask?"

"Because I can't move."

"No, you're just sore. Well, I've got to go on calls now. It's good to see you up. Bye."

I fell back asleep shortly after she left.

The next morning I woke up on my own. It was still dark out, and for a moment I wondered why I was awake. After another minute or two though, I dozed off.

"Ow! Fuck!"

"Oh, you're up?"

"Yeah, I'm up. I was waiting for you, I think."

"Why...? You wanted to hit me?"

"No, I just wanted to get ready."

"Oh."

"Hey, you know, nothing for nothing. You're probably a nice lady and all, but you're starting to become a pain in my ass, so I think I'd like to end this relationship."

We both had a good laugh, and then I asked her what time it was.

"I've come in here every morning at 5:30, and it's 5:30 now."

"Shit, I think I'm going to wake up at 5:30 every morning for the rest of my life and look for you now. This is 'thee' worst alarm clock I've ever had."

"Well, don't worry, because you might not need the shots any more. But you've got to stop pulling that intravenous tube out of your arm or else."

"Yeah, well, I just hate these things."

"We all do, but they're there for a reason."

She said she had to go, so I went back to sleep.

I woke up at 5:30 the next morning, but the nurse didn't show up. This time I stayed up because I didn't want to get surprised again. Well, now that I'm up, I might as well do a body check, I thought. I can see my feet, so my legs are still there. Now... can I move them? Right leg... good. Left... not so good. Oh shit! I thought as I grabbed my dick. Whew! But what the fuck is this tube? Oh well, at least it's still there. Okay, my left arm is shot, and so is my neck. I can't move either one of them. Now... my face.

I raised my right hand and started to feel every inch on my face. Hmmm... swollen lips okay, fuck... my eye... what is this? It must be a bandage... that's why I probably can't open it. Hmmm, these must be stitches. No, it's dried blood. Here, these must be stitches, yeah. Okay, let me see the forehead; this side's good... Wow, this side's fucked. Now my head... what the fuck? This feels like concrete. Shit, it's all over my head.

After I checked on the tube in the side of my chest, I noticed that the sun was coming up. Well, Mike, it's a new day and you're still here. So let's think, Mike. What was the last thing you were doing?! Hanging out with the boys and getting high, right? Well, that's it, I'm done with that, I've had my fun. Now, God, we're even, okay? I'm sorry for cursing at you the night after my father died. I know you don't owe me anything, but if you could cut me a little slack on this one, I'd really appreciate it.

A nurse came in a little while after that, and while she was checking on me, she asked me what happened to the intravenous needle. She got a little annoyed after I told her I pulled it out. We ended up having a battle about this for a few days, but she finally won after I woke up one day and saw that she had stuck it in my hand and then wrapped it up with three rolls of tape like a catcher's mitt.

A doctor came into my room a short time later that day. The first thing I did was to ask him about the tube in my dick. He told me it was a catheter and that everybody who was unconscious got one. Then I asked him if I had both my eyes. He told me that I did, but that one was swollen shut.

"How long do I need the tube in my chest?"
"Well, at least a week."
"Now, what's up with my neck?"

"As far as I can tell, you probably stretched, strained or pulled every muscle and tendon in it. But if you weren't so physically fit, you probably would have broken it."

He went on to list the other damage I received, which amounted to thirty stitches over my left eye, seven in my cheek, and about another six in my lip. I fractured my left cheekbone and broke my nose, which, I learned, they wouldn't set for another five days.

"You broke all the ribs on your left side and collapsed your lung, and you also have road rash on part of your face, your arm, and both your knees."

The questions he couldn't answer were why my teeth were numb, why I had the constant taste of blood in my mouth, and why there was a bone sticking up into the skin in my shoulder. But he did tell me that once I got a little better he would send me to get it X-rayed again. Then he told me that he had to go see other patients.

Well, I guess all you have to do now is heal, Mike, I thought.

The next day I was lying in my room, and in walked Mike Viale and Asia.

"Mike! You motherfucker! I thought you were gonna die on me!" he said.
"Yeah, me too, Mike. Me too. Mike, come here. What happened to you?" I asked him.

He walked closer to me, smiled, and then lifted his sunglasses off to show me two black eyes, a broken nose, two missing teeth, and about fifteen stitches over his eye.

"What the fuck happened to you?! You look like you were on the bike with me!"

Asia looked at him and said, "Go ahead, tell him. Tell him what happened."

Mike looked at me with the look on his face of having rehearsed this too many times with Asia and said, "Well, do you remember the night of the accident when I was carrying you into the hospital with one of the cops?"
"Yeah, why the fuck did you drop me on the floor?"
"I didn't drop you. I got pulled away from you by my hair by one of the cops."
"What…? Why…?"
"I swear I didn't know what it was about, Mike, but this one cop was being a real asshole that night. First he started when I had you out in the street. Then after we put you in the cop car, he was fucking with me all the way here. When we got to carry you inside, like a real wiseass he tells me not to get lost inside."

"Yeah, I heard something like that."
"So I looked back at him and said, 'You know you've been talking to me like an asshole all night while my friend's dying, and I think you should cool out.' Then he grabbed me by my hair, so I turned around and dropped the motherfucker."
"No, Mike, you didn't."
"Yep. Dropped him right on his ass."
"And gave him about fourteen stitches," Asia added.
"Then what happened?"
"Well, then the other cop, a security guard, and an ambulance driver jumped me."
"So that's how you got fucked up?"
"No."
"What do you mean no?"
"Well, after they arrested me, another police car came and picked me up. Then they took me to Kissena Park, you know over by that bicycle track, and beat the shit out of me for about fifteen minutes until another cop car came over, and then they beat the shit out of me."
"Get the fuck out of here."
"Man, a different car pulled up every so often, and then those cops got out and beat my ass and

left."

Then Asia said, "I called the 109th until 5:30 in the morning before they finally told me he was at Booth Memorial being treated for injuries he sustained while being arrested."

"Yeah, you know what was fucked up, though?"

"What?"

"After the cop I hit got stitched up, he came over and beat my ass, too."

"Michael, I just bailed him out an hour ago, and you know where the first place he went was?" Asia said.

"No, where?"

"Here," Asia said. "He said he wasn't going anywhere until he saw you."

"Aww, come here and give me a kiss, Mike."

"Hey, cut that out. I'm starting to get jealous," Asia said.

"Michael."

"Yeah?"

"Do me a favor, okay?"

"What's that?"

"No more motorcycle accidents, okay? I don't want to go through that again."

"No problem. Neither do I," I said.

"Yeah, no more motorcycles, Michael. I can't take them either," Asia answered.

"So, Mike, what are your charges?"

"Huh, Get this: assault on a police officer and possession of a stolen vehicle."

"What...! What do you mean...?"

"Mikey had reported the bike stolen to the cops at the scene. That's how this whole thing got started," he said calmly.

"You're shitting me!"

"No, he's not, Michael. I saw his charges," Asia said.

"That little motherfucker," I said.

"It's almost too late now, but tell him to drop the charges if you see him. I don't want to see him, because I'm afraid I'll kill him," Viale said.

"I'll get word through Gerard. I can't believe that shit," I added.

Mike and Asia hung out for a little while longer, and then they left. I couldn't help but feel bad that once again something in my life had such a huge impact on Mike's life.

The doctor came in the next day and asked me how I felt. "Like shit," I answered.

We went through my usual complaints about my shoulder and my jaw, and then he left. Man, I thought, this fucking sucks. I'm 19, and I feel like I'm ninety; I can't even move. I wonder how much better I'm going to get. I hope it's a lot more than this 'cause this sucks. You know what I think? The more I lay here, the harder it's going to be to heal and get up later, and I've been in bed since I got here.

After thinking about this, I decided to try and sit up. It was especially difficult to do because I had to pull my head up by my hair; it was the only way I could move it. After about three attempts, I was finally able to perform this trick. But my head started throbbing like hell, so I decided not to even try to stand up. After that, I figured that I had done my exercise for the day, so I lay down and took a nap.

I got another visitor the next day, Gerard. The first thing he did was to walk over to my monitor and pick it up.

"Hey, what's this?"

"Put it down, man. It's attached to me!"

"Oh, shit, sorry. Where...?"

"Right here," I said as I lifted the sheet to show Gerard the tube in my chest.

He scrunched up his face and said, "Oh, shit. That looks like it hurts!"

"It did. Trust me, it did. Where's Dino at?" I asked.

"Well, he's been running around lately with that wiseass Timmy. I don't know, but I think Timmy's been up to no good."

"Well, do me a favor. If you pass the house tonight, tell Dino to stop by."

"All right."

"Hey, Gerard. Check out this bone that pops out of my shoulder when I try to move it."

"Wow, does that hurt?"

"Yeah, it hurts like hell, but the doctor tells me it's nothing."

"Listen, Mike. I've got a little surprise for you."

"Yeah, what's that?"

"Well, she wouldn't take no for an answer. Barbara wants to see you."

"Yeah?"

"Yeah, she's in the hallway right now."

Great, I thought. I didn't really want her to see me in this shape. That's why I didn't want any visitors, but what was I supposed to say now?

"Well, tell her to come in."

When Barbara walked in, I could see her try and suppress her shock.

"Oh, you don't look that bad," she said.

Even though she was telling me how good I looked, I could see the tears forming in her eyes.

"Well, at least you're out of the woods now," Barbara said as she bent over to kiss me.

"Yeah, now all I have to do is climb over the mountain," I answered her.

"You know, the night you had your accident, somebody found your watch, and the alarm was beeping on it every hour after I got home all night long. It beeped like that for days, and even though it scared the shit out of me, I hoped it wouldn't stop."

"So how did it look?"

"What?"

"The accident."

"I didn't see anything. I heard a crash, looked around, and then heard your body hit the ground.

That's when I looked. I hate to admit it, but I just froze. I stood there holding the helmet in shock. Even after Michael came out of the bar and went over to you, I couldn't move. I stood there until they took you away in the police car, and then somebody drove me home."

"Well, remind me never to take you on any bank heists," I joked.

"I'm sorry."

"Ahh, don't worry about it. There was probably nothing you could do anyhow," I answered.

Gerard and Barb were shocked to hear about what had happened to Viale. Then they were even more surprised to hear that Mikey was the cause of it. I explained to Gerard that he needed to have a word with Mikey about the charges against Mike as soon as possible, and he said he would. Both of them hung out for a couple of hours, and then they left.

The next day, my friend Aaron came to see me, but he wasn't able to keep a straight face like some others.

"Oh, Mike! Fuck!"

"You're making me feel real good over here, Aaron, and in about two seconds your visit is going to be over!"

"I'm sorry, Mike. I didn't know you got this fucked up, though."

"One..."

"Okay, okay, I'm sorry. Hey listen. When I came to visit you, the lady at the desk sent me over to a social worker. They wanted to know how they were going to get paid, so I told them about your situation with your parents. The lady didn't believe me, so I told her that I'd bring her some newspaper articles tomorrow."

"Great."

"Well, it might turn out for the better 'cause there might be a way that she can have your bills paid while you're here."

"Well, that would be nice."

"Yeah, I'll work on it tomorrow. Hey, what's this?"

"Leave it the fuck alone. It's attached to me."

Aaron hung out with me for about two hours before he left, and my doctor stopped by a short time after that.

"So how are we feeling today?" he asked.

"Like shit. When are you going to set my nose... after it heals?"

"Well, we can't take you downstairs until your lung heals."

"What about my shoulder?"

"Well, it's kinda the same answer."

"What's this concrete shit in my hair?"

"What- this?"

"Yeah."

"It's nothing. It's dried blood."

"Well, maybe I could get some water here, so I could wash it out."

"I'll remind one of the nurses about it after I leave."

The doctor left a little while after he checked on the tube and listened to my lung.

That night Dino came to see me. He walked in with Maryann, Timmy, and Timmy's old lady.

"Oh, Mike. You look fucked up," Dino said.
"Yeah... fuck you, too. Thanks for visiting."
"I'm sorry, cuz. You didn't look this bad the night of the accident. I'm surprised."

While we were talking, I noticed that Maryann had a smirk on her face.
"Get that fucking bitch out of my room!" I yelled.
"Mike, come on."
"Dino, she's sitting there smirking in my face. Now get her out of my room, or all of you fucking leave."

Everybody left but Dino.

"Mike, what's up with you, man? That's my girlfriend."
"Yeah, well, let me tell you something now, Dino, that I never told you before. I didn't like her two months before you got out, I didn't like her when you started dating her, and I didn't like her after you moved her into the house without telling me. I especially didn't like her whenever we sat down for dinner and she'd sit there smiling in my face as if to say go fuck yourself. But being that you're my cousin and I love you, I didn't say anything to you, okay? But she's not going to sit here, and give me that same face. So from now on, just keep her away from me, okay?"

"Fine, whatever. I didn't know you felt that way," he said. "Listen," he added, "We're going to Atlantic City for the weekend. We're going to blow some money and have some fun."
"Really? Why don't you buy a car or some clothes like you said you needed?"
"I will, I will. Once we get back, all right? We'll be back on Sunday, okay? Come here, let me give you a hug. I'm glad you're still alive, Michael. Oh, yeah, before I forget, Grandpa went to live with Aunt Marie."
"Oww, watch my tube."
"What tube?"
"Never mind."

We hugged and kissed each other on the cheek, and then he left.

Late that night the nurses brought another patient into my room. It was an old guy; he looked like he was in bad shape from what I could see. After the lights were shut off and the curtains were drawn, he started moaning, weeping and yelling. I figured that he was in a lot of pain or something, so I didn't say anything about it and tried to get some sleep. The next morning I asked the nurse quietly what his problem was, and she told me that he was just old.

"Well, he sounds like he's in pain. Is there anything you can give him?"
"No, because he didn't have an operation or anything. He's just afraid."

My doctor walked in a few minutes later.

"So how are we feeling today?"
"Like shit."
"Oh, come on. You must be feeling a little better."
"No, really, I feel like shit again," I answered.

As he checked on my lung and then my tube, I asked him if he was going to let me get my nose reset, and he said no.

"Well, what about my shoulder?"
"Can't do anything yet about that," he answered.
"What about my top palate? It's really killing me."
"It's probably just aches and pains from your cheekbone," he said nonchalantly.
"Well, thanks for stopping by, Doc," I said as he left.

Gerard came up with Jimmy Marnell and Jimmy's girlfriend, Vicky, the next day. Gerard and Jimmy came into my room first, and then Jimmy explained that Vicky wanted to see me.

"I don't know, Jimmy, I don't think it's time yet."
"Oh, come on. I'm sure she's seen worse, all right?"
"Yeah, I guess."

Vicky walked in with a smile on her face, and then she turned and looked at me. When she saw me, her jaw dropped open, and tears started streaming down her face. She stood there for a few seconds and then ran out.

"Told ya'. It's not time for female visitors at all. That's one of the reasons why I didn't want any visitors. It makes me feel like I'm a sideshow act. Gerard, you tell them downstairs that I don't want any more visitors than the people who have already come to see me, okay?"
"All right, Mike. I'll tell them," he said.

After we talked for a little while, Vicky came back in, but she tried not to look at me.

"It's all right, Vicky. You can look at me."
"It just hurts to see you in so much pain, Michael," she said without looking up.
"It's all right. It doesn't hurt that much anymore. It's all numb now," I lied. "But I will tell you one thing, Vicky. The next time you tell me to stay and hang out, I'm not gonna move a muscle until you say it's okay"
"Oh, Michael. I did tell you that, didn't I?" she said.
"Yeah, but I didn't listen, I wish I had."
"Hey, Gerard. Did you see Mikey at work?"
"Nope, he must have been on another job site."
"Jimmy, if you see Mikey tonight at the house, you tell him to drop the charges on the motorcycle

then, all right?"

"Yeah, no problem. I'll tell him. Gerard told me all about it," Jimmy answered.

It was nice to see that Vicky was still with Jimmy. She was the total opposite of him and, as hard as it was for her to do so, she kept him in line. My friends left before dinnertime. It's a good thing they did; otherwise, they'd have to watch me eat this shit they call food. I didn't have a TV or a phone yet, but it didn't matter because I had a lot to think about.

My shoulder wasn't getting any better, and I knew something had to be broken in there. I still couldn't lift my arm, and I had been here over a week. But, come to think of it, I still couldn't move my neck or get out of bed. The more I thought about not being able to get out of bed, it pissed me off, so I figured I'd try again. It took three attempts just to sit up, but I was determined to stand up. Finally I was able to stand and take two steps, one forward and one back to the bed. I felt like an infant trying to walk. After that, I took a nap.

Gerard came back to visit me the next day with Barb.

"Mike, listen, I've got some bad news for you," he said.
"Well, I'm in a good place to hear it, I guess."
"It's Dino."
"Is he dead...?"
"No, he got busted with Timmy out in Atlantic City."
"For what?"
"Armed robbery."
"What...? Armed robbery...? In Atlantic City? How did you find out?"
"Your friend Maryann came over to the Murry Hill tonight and told me. But from what she said, it seems like Dino really didn't do anything kinda."
"What do you mean?"
"Well, according to her, they were in Atlantic City having some fun, and Dino and Timmy went to a liquor store. While they were there, Timmy pulled out a gun and decides to rob the place. She said Dino had told her when they came back that he was picking some wine for her, when Timmy pulls out a gun and yells out, "This is a stick-up. Nobody move!!" Dino said he couldn't believe what Timmy was doing. Then some guy came running out from the back of the store with a shotgun, so Dino hit the guy so he wouldn't shoot Timmy. Then Timmy took the money, and they left."

I couldn't believe what Gerard was telling me, and I asked him how they got arrested.

"Well, here comes the real stupid part. They leave there and go back to the hotel. After about an hour, they decide that maybe they should leave Atlantic City and come back to Queens, so they packed up and left."
"Yeah?"
"So they're driving for about twenty minutes or so, and Timmy says that they've got to go back to the hotel because Timmy left his gun under the mattress."
"No! Don't tell me," I said.
"Yeah, so they all complain about it, and Timmy starts yelling, 'My fucking fingerprints are all

313

over the gun,' so they go back to the hotel. When they get there, Timmy finds one of the maids and tells her to let him back into the room. The maid tells him to wait a minute 'cause she has to get the keys, and while they're waiting for her to come back, the cops walk over and tell everybody that they're under arrest."

"Huh?"

"The maid had already found the gun under the bed and gave it to the guy in the front office, who happened to be talking to the two cops that came over to retrieve it, when Timmy pulled up and asked to be let back into the room."

"Man, I knew that Timmy was an asshole. You know when I knew for sure? The day that Mike told me that Timmy's old lady said that she needed the car, and Timmy got into an argument with her because he wanted to go out. So he walked outside, opened his trunk, grabbed a baseball bat, and smashed every window in the car. Then he walked back inside the apartment, flipped her the keys, and said, 'Here, go use it now!'"

"Yeah, I always thought he was a bit of a wiseass, too, especially when he was staying at your house for a while," Gerard said.

"Man, that's fucked up. Fucking Dino just got out, and now he's back in on a big charge."

"Yeah, I know."

The three of us talked until visiting hours were over, and then they left.

I felt real bad about Dino getting busted. I knew he shouldn't have gone to New Jersey for some reason.

That night the old man next to me started howling and moaning again. He had been doing it for about five days in a row by now. I hate to say it, but I really wasn't in any mood to hear him tonight so after about an hour I said, "Come on, man. Shut the fuck up!"

"But I'm dying!"

"Tell me about it. If I could get out of this bed, you'd be dead already."

"No, I'm really dying!"

"Well, look. We've all got to die some time. You've got to decide if you want to live or you want to die. If it's your time to die, you can't worry about anything in your life, because it's all meaningless now. Believe me, there's nothing to it. I've already died twice, and it's nothing but one last exhale and you're gone," I explained.

"Really?"

"Yeah, really."

"But I'm all alone."

"No, you're not. I'm here, remember? Look, if you want I'll say a prayer for you," I said into the darkness at him.

"Really...? Would you...?"

"Yeah."

"Okay."

At first I would have said anything to shut him up so I could get some sleep, but then I figured, what the hell, I'll say a prayer for him.

God, look, I know I haven't prayed to you in a while, but shut this guy up... I'm sorry... I mean that in a nice way. Either let him get better and live, or just take him. Don't let him suffer, okay? In the name of the Father, the Son, and the Holy Ghost. Amen.

"There, okay? I did it."
"That fast?"
"Look, buddy, I haven't prayed in years, okay? And you happen to be the first person I prayed for and I don't even know you, so give me a break, okay?"
"Did you really pray for me?"
"Yeah, I did."
"Okay. Thank you."
"Good night."
"Goodbye."

He was quiet for the rest of the night after that, aside from crying for a little bit, but at least I was able to get to sleep.

The next morning I decided to sleep past breakfast, but I woke up after I heard a couple of people talking and moving things around. "Hey, what's going on over there?" I said as I started to pull my curtain back.

A nurse walked over, grabbed my curtain, and said, "The patient next to you passed away last night, so the orderlies are here to take him away."
"He died last night, and you're taking him away now?" I repeated.
"Yes."

Fuck, I thought. I haven't prayed in years. Maybe I should have prayed for a million bucks last night instead.

Aaron and Gerard came up to see me that day. Aaron told me that he straightened out my bills with the social worker downstairs so that they would all be paid now. After they hung out for a while, I told Gerard just before they left that I needed an Ace bandage, a piece of wood and maybe some tape and a cane.
"What? Are you planning to make a break?" Gerard asked.
"No, I just need the stuff. Don't forget."
"All right," he answered.

That night Gerard came back with Barb. He didn't forget my stuff, but first he told me that he had seen Mikey and that Mikey told him he was afraid to drop the charges now because he might get into trouble.

"Why's that?" I asked.
"Well, because he said that he thought that you were gonna die that night, so he told them it was stolen so he could get paid by his insurance to repair the bike."

"What? So you're telling me that he doesn't want to drop the charges?"

"Yeah, that's what he said."

"Okay, tell him if he doesn't drop the charges, then I want him to move out."

"Yeah, I'll tell him. So how you feeling?"

"I'm still hurting. As a matter of fact, I want you to help me out of bed so I can take a few steps. The last time I tried, I was afraid that I was going to fall down and really hurt myself."

Gerard helped me out of bed, and I walked as far as I could because I was still tethered to my "radiator." After that I lay back down.

"Okay, now let me have my stuff."

"What are you doing with that stuff?" Barb asked.

"I need it."

"Why?" she asked.

"Because this bone that pops out of place in my shoulder stays put when I press it down. It just pops out when I move it, and there's no pressure on it, so I was thinking that if I put a piece of wood on it and then tie it down with the Ace bandage, maybe it will stay in place."

"Oh, Michael," Barbara said. "Isn't that something the doctor is supposed to do?"

"Well, I've been telling him for days about it, and he still hasn't done anything for me. Although maybe once the doctor finds out that my bills are getting paid, now he might change his mind and help me out with this shoulder. But I can't wait that long. This bone is already trying to heal."

After a little while of working on it, Gerard and I rigged up something that didn't cut off the circulation in my arm but still seemed to work as long as I didn't move it.

"Hey, Barb, do you have a mirror?"

"What for?"

"I want to take a look at myself."

"Uhm, no, I don't."

"Don't worry, Barb. I know my face is fucked up because I can feel it. But I'm not going to jump out the window once I see it. I mean, fuck, I can't even stand up. I just want to see how it all looks on my face," I said.

"No, I don't have one, Michael."

They left, and a short time after I took a nap. Too much exercise for today, I guess.

The next morning when my doctor came in, he said, "What is that?" pointing to my shoulder. "Well, if you're not going to do anything, I am."

"It's not a matter of not doing anything. It's like I told you, we can't transport you to the X-ray room with the tube in you," he said.

"You know, Doc. My bills are being paid now."

"What does that have to do with anything?"

"Well, after talking to one of the nurses, she told me that she couldn't understand why the portable X-ray machine couldn't be brought into my room."

"Well...um...like I said, ah, we don't want to do anything until you can move around."

"Believe me, Doc. For this I'll force myself to move around."

"Well, then, we'll see if we can schedule something this afternoon."

"Thanks, Doc," I said dryly.

I didn't say anything about my nose or the numbness in my jaw that day. I figured I was going to get one thing taken care of, so I didn't want to press my luck right now.

About an hour later, someone did come to my room with the machine. All it took was about twenty minutes to take X-rays, and then they left. Two hours later my doctor came back into the room and said, "O.K. I found your problem. You have a broken bone in your shoulder. So what we have to do now is go in there, re-break the bone, set it, and then put in a few screws," he said matter of factly.

"You know what Doc? You're a fucking asshole. Now get the fuck out of my room." I guess nobody had ever spoken to him in this manner because he stood there with this stupid look on his face and said, "What...?"

"For over a week now, I've been telling you that there is a bone popping out of my shoulder, and you keep telling me not to worry about it. Now you come in here with your clipboard and tell me what I've been telling you? And you know why you didn't want to do anything for me? Because I didn't have any money to pay the bill in your eyes. So, as a Doctor, you're more than happy to let me go through life with these injuries. You know what? Get the fuck outta here!"

"What about your shoulder?"

"What, now that my bills are getting paid, you've got time for it. Fuck it, I'll live with it. I've already had practice!"

The next morning I had a new doctor because the other one refused to see me anymore. Thank God. The new one I got was nice because he actually came over to me and physically checked out my wounds and injuries instead of admiring them from a distance, holding a clipboard.

"Well, according to your charts, you look like you've made some progress there, Michael."

"What about this tube, Doc? When will it come out?" I said as a nurse came in.

"Well, Michael, your lung sounds good and, as a matter of fact, we can take it out right now," he said after listening to my chest again.

Man, that was music to my ears.

"Excuse me, nurse. Nurse, come over here and help me extract this tube," he said.

"Oh, no. I have to make the beds down the hall. Besides, I'm not that kind of a nurse," she said as she walked out of the room.

The doctor and I turned and looked at each other with the same stupid look on our faces, but not for the same reasons. Then he said, "Hold on a minute. I'll go out into the hall and get another nurse."

"Doc, let's do it now."

"Hold on a minute. Let me get a nurse."

"Doc, if you leave, I'm pulling this fucking thing out by myself. I'm sorry, I'm just sick of this thing, and I want it out. Why do we need a nurse?"

"Well, she has to push down on your chest so that no air goes back in as I slide the tube out," he said.

I don't know why it seemed odd when he told me this, but it did. Then I said, "Look, Doc, I've got two good hands. I'll do it, okay?"

"Well, I really shouldn't do something like this with a patient."

"I'm going to pull it out," I teased as I closed my eyes and grabbed for the tube.

"Okay, okay, let's do it right then. As I slide the tube out, you press down on your chest with your hands. All right?"

"No problem. I've got it."

Unbeknownst to the doctor, I would have told him anything he wanted to hear in order to get that tube out of me.

As he slowly slid the tube out, I swore for a second that I would ejaculate from pure pleasure, but I didn't. But then he kept pulling and pulling on it.

"Holy shit! How long is that thing?" I questioned him.

I don't know why but I thought the tube was only inside me about three inches. But this thing was about twelve inches long.

"Whata ya' gonna have, a bouquet of flowers at the end of it?"

"Come on, don't make me laugh," he said as he pulled the end of it out of me.

"Man, Doc, I swear that was better than sex."

"I'll bet it was," he said.

"So what about the hole in my side?"

"Well, you need to relax for a day or two and just let it close itself."

"No stitches?"

"No stitches," he confirmed, which didn't sound so reassuring, I thought.

"Hey, Doc, what about my nose?"

"Oh, yeah, I'll schedule it for you in a few days, he answered, and then he left.

It felt so good not being attached to the wall that I just had to get up and try to walk four steps away from my bed instead of my usual three.

After I accomplished that, I figured that I'd walk over to my nightstand and see if there were any old magazines in it. When I opened up the top drawer, I found a mirror sitting there.

Well, Mike, do you want to look at your masterpiece? You're going to have to see it sooner or later.

I hobbled back over to my bed and sat down. After taking a deep breath, I raised the mirror to my face. My God! I thought, now I know why Vicky ran out crying. I almost feel like crying myself. I looked like something that Salvador Dali had painted and threw away. My face was all contorted from the swelling and then mixed in with the dried blood, road rash, and bruises on my face, were little patches of stitches.

My nose was disjointed and, because I still wasn't able to wash my hair, the dried crunchy blood made it stand up in all different directions. But the one thing that really startled me were my eyes. Even though my left eye was still partly swollen shut and purple, I couldn't see any white in my eyes. They were both blood red aside from the hazel coloring. It looked like I had on a mask, but what made it even worse was that I knew I couldn't just take this mask off.

After that, I buzzed the nurse's desk a few times, and when a nurse came in, I sarcastically asked her for a mop bucket so I could wash my face and hair. She brought me back a basin with warm water and a wash cloth a few minutes later. Each time I washed out the cloth the water got darker and darker from my dried blood. After I finished my face, I washed my hair the best I could with one arm. By the time I was done, the basin water was reddish brown. Then I rang for the nurse again, so she could take away the water. When she came back, she told me that she would schedule to have someone come in and wash me up a little better tomorrow. I didn't say a word, because I thought it should have been done already.

That night Ricky Dale came up to visit me.

"Damn, Mike. That looks like it fucking hurts," he said.
"Yeah, it did, Ricky, and it still does."
"Well, I guess you and me and Joe O'Neil are in the same club now."
"O' Neil? What happened to him?"
"Shit, you didn't hear?"
"Hear what?"
"He got into a bike accident, too. As a matter of fact, he's here also."
"Joe's here?"
"Yeah, man, and get this. He's been here two months already."
"Really?"
"Yeah, I'm gonna visit him, too, tonight."
"Well, what happened to him?"
"Check this out. He was riding down his block, and he was cruising along at about 45-50 when all of a sudden this lady starts to pull out of a parking space. So Joe starts hitting his horn, but the lady just kept going. So Joe sideswipes her car and then crashed into a bunch of parked cars on the other side of the street."
"Well, it sounds bad but two months? He's been here for that?"
"Yeah, but get this. When he hit the lady the impact cut his leg off, he broke his back, and just before he went down, a bumper caught him in the jaw and ripped half his jaw off. Then when he was on the ground, the gas in the bike caught on fire and gave him third degree burns on his back."
"No shit!"
"No shit, man. So even though you're bad, Mike, it could be a hell of a lot worse."
"So how bad is he now?"
"I don't know. I just heard myself about it last week. So now that I'm here, I'm going to go visit

him for the first time."

Ricky hung out with me for a bit, and then he went to see Joe.

A little while later he came back to my room, and I said to him, "So what's up? How is he?"

"Well, I'll tell ya'. He don't look bad at all really. I mean, he don't look good, but I expected him to look a hell of a lot worse."

"What about his back? Is he paralyzed?"

"No, he's not."

"And his jaw?"

"It doesn't look that bad either. They took a rib out and rebuilt his jaw. The one thing that does look strange, though, is you remember that Joe was about 6'2"? Well, now he lost like thirty or forty pounds, with this long hair, and he's sitting in a full body cast up to his neck, with one arm sticking straight out in the air."

"Man, he must've gone through hell, huh?"

"Yeah, man, it looks that way. I'll tell you, Mike, and this should cheer you up. My accident was pretty bad, but Joe's looks worse to me, and out of all three I think I'd take yours, even though you took it full in the face. But I wouldn't worry, you were ugly even before your accident," Ricky joked.

"Yeah, fuck you, too."

"Well, listen, Mike, I've got to go before it gets dark out."

"Why?"

"Well, I took my motorcycle up here and the headlights ain't working, so I gotta split."

"Well, be careful, Ricky. Remember, the bed next to me is empty."

"Hey, that reminds me. How come they put you on this floor with all these old people who are dying?"

"I don't know, Ricky. Maybe they expected me to die, too. Who knows?"

"All right, I'll come up and see the two of you again soon," he said before he left.

The next day, after some nurse helped me wash up, my new doctor came in and checked out the hole in my side.

"Hey, you heal up pretty good. Listen, I'm going to have you scheduled to go down at four thirty to have your nose reset, okay?"

"Yeah, sure, that's cool. Hey, Doc, how are they gonna reset it? Does the other doctor have to give me a sock in the nose first?"

"Well, I'm pretty sure they have something a little more sophisticated than that these days, Mike. But it might be a good idea to tell the guy a few jokes or something when you go in there. I mean, after all he is going to reset your nose," he joked.

Some time after lunch, Mike Viale came up to visit me.

"Hey, champ, how you doing?"

"Not bad, not bad. I finally got rid of this tube in my side, so that's a plus."

"Yeah, let me take a look."

I lifted up my sheet and showed him my side.

"Hey, not bad. Now we've got matching scars. Remember the one Dino gave me?...Oops, sorry, Mike. I didn't mean to bring up Dino... Fucked up about him, huh?"

"Yeah, fucked up," I agreed.

"Well, you never know what could happen, Mike. Maybe he won't get that much time," he said.

"I hope not. So how you making out, Mike?"

"Well, I'm still facing both charges."

"Yeah, I know. Did you hear about Mikey?"

"Yeah, I heard. That little fucking prick."

"Tell me about it. I told Gerard to tell him to move the fuck out."

"Tell him he can move in with me."

"No, Mike, the last thing you need is another charge." We laughed. "I can't wait until I get out of here."

"When do you think that'll be?"

"I don't really know. It depends on how fast I can heal, I guess."

"Well, think of this, too, Michael. The longer you stay here, the more time you'll have to heal. You won't have to worry about feeding yourself or making any type of money right away, either."

"I know, Mike, but I really hate being in this place. I'd rather starve than be here."

"Well, I kinda know what you mean by that. I hate hospitals, too," he said. "But still you might want to give it some thought," he added.

"So how's Asia and the baby Natisha?"

"They're fine."

"That's cool."

"Hey, listen, I got a job."

"Really? Doing what?"

"Well, it's part-time right now, but you know the gas station right down the block from McDonald's and Jack in the Box?"

"Yeah, over by Firestone tires."

"I'm working there, night shifts."

"Well, hey, it's close to your house anyway."

"Yeah."

Mike and I bullshitted until they came up to get me to set my nose.

"So where you going now?"

"Well, there is this one wiseass downstairs who said he was going to break my nose, so I'm gonna go down and beat his ass," I said casually.

"What? What are you talking about?"

"Well, they're gonna set my nose today."

"Now? After all this time?"

"Tell me about it. Well, wish me luck."

"Break a leg. Hey, don't feel too bad. They never even set mine after they took me to the hospital," he added.

Mike and I kissed each other on the cheek, said goodbye, and I was off to have my nose broken.

"Hey, nice haircut, Doc."
"Huh?"
"Your haircut. It looks good on you."
"What do you mean?"
"Well, somebody suggested that I be nice to you. After all, you're gonna kinda leave a tattoo on me, right?"
"Oh, I get you."

The doctor shot me up with a "local," and then he stared at my nose for a minute while raising one eyebrow. He looked to the left, then to the right, and then straight in the middle. I almost wanted to laugh, because nobody had ever looked at my nose this way before they wanted to break it.

"Why are you smiling?" he asked.
"Oh, nothing, nothing," I said.
"Okay, ready?"
"Yep."

He placed his hands on my nose, and "crack" he broke it.

"Man! That sounded ill!"
"Huh?"
"Nasty. It sounded nasty," I said.
"Oh yeah, it does," he said as he put a stitch or two into my nose before he packed it with gauze.

"Whoa, hey, where are you shoving these things?"
"They've got to go up far to stop the bleeding."

He ended up pushing them so far up my nose, I could no longer breathe through it, but that was fine. At least my nose got set. After that 15-minute ordeal they took me back to my room.

The next morning when I got up, I felt like I had some energy, so I decided that I wanted to get out of my room. I buzzed the nurse and asked for a wheelchair, but after fifteen minutes I said fuck it, and decided to get up and force myself to walk with my cane. One, two, three, four, here I am at the bottom of my bed, Mike. You're going to make that big turn now, five...six...seven. I stopped at the end of the bed and thought, Well, this is it, Mike, no more bed to hold onto. If you fall, you're going down. If you do fall, at least try to fall on your right side, eight, nine, ten. The strangest thing about walking now was that not only was I walking slowly, but my brain had to slow down to adjust and keep up to my feet. I could never remember having to walk this slowly, although I must've as a baby at some time, but maybe not even then... eleven, twelve.

When I got to the doorway, I rested and wondered if I should go on. Then I noticed that the whole hallway was filled with old people in wheelchairs or walking with canes.

Shit, I thought. If they can get around, I ought to be able to get my 19-year-old ass around. Besides, maybe I can find a wheelchair.

I kept walking and got about fifteen feet down the hall when I noticed a cute little older woman, waving her hand for me to come near her. I smiled to myself and thought, I wonder what type of words of encouragement she wants to give me, as I started walking towards her.

After I got close to her, she looked at my face and then into my eyes and said, "You look like hell... something the cat dragged in."

I stood there shocked for a second and then said, "Yes, thank you. I almost died but I'm feeling much better now. Oh, and P.S. this is the first day I was able to crawl out of my bed, just in time to meet you. Thank you so much. Have a nice day."

Then I turned around and hobbled to my room.
That afternoon Gerard came up to see me.

"I've got to get the fuck out of this place," I said.
"Well, what does your doctor say?"
"Who cares what he says? I'll just sign myself out and go."
"Don't you think you should stay a little longer, though?"
"Probably, but I can't stand being in a hospital."
"Yeah, I hear you."
"Listen, Gerard, you've got to do me a favor. I need some clothes. The only ones I have are the ones I got into the accident with, and they're all ripped up and bloody. Get me some socks and underwear, too, okay?"
"Yeah, no problem. Hey, how's your shoulder?"
"Ah, it's fucked up, but I don't feel like letting them operate on it. They'll probably only give me a local in this place before they cut me open."
"So what's going to happen with it?"
"I don't know. Maybe it'll heal if I don't use it much."

Gerard stayed for another hour and then told me he'd probably see me tonight, because Barbara wanted to come up.

A short time after he left, Ricky came up.

"Come on, Mike. Let's go visit Joe," he said when he walked in.
"Well, I don't know, Ricky. I don't feel like walking around with just a smock on. All I have is my torn-up clothes from the night of the accident. Besides, I don't want everyone looking at me like I'm a freak."
"Fuck it. Put your clothes on. We're only going downstairs. Besides, you look fine."

After Ricky helped me to get dressed, we headed downstairs. By the time I was up to speed with my two-foot shuffle, we finally got to the elevator.

"Don't worry about it, Mike. I thought I'd never be able to walk this fast again after my accident, but I did. You will too after a while," Ricky said as the elevator doors opened.

"Oh, my God! The emergency room is downstairs. Don't move. I'll get you a wheelchair!" A nurse said from inside the elevator.

"No, no, no, I'm all right," I said to the puzzled nurse.

"All right...! Look at yourself!"

"No, you don't understand. I didn't have any other clothes to wear, so I had to put these back on. Look, its dried blood on the clothes. See?" I said as I pointed down towards the bloodstains on my white pants.

"My God, you scared the hell out of me. I thought you were lost," she said as we exchanged places on the elevator.

After the doors closed, I turned to Ricky and said, "I look fine, huh, Ricky?"

"Well, come on, Mike. You've got bloodstained pants and a torn-up shirt on, but your face looks fine, believe me."

"Yeah, okay, Ricky. I'll believe you," I said dryly.

I finally made it to Joe's room, and after we walked in, Joe said, "Damn, bro, you got nailed, too, huh?"

"Yeah, Joe, you could say that. But I see that you do pretty good work yourself."

"Tell me about it. I stopped counting my bills after they went over $60,000, ya' know."

"Shit, you've got me beat by a landslide. I got the $39.95 special."

"My bills were up there, too, I think I made them spend ten grand on morphine alone," Ricky added.

Joe looked over at Ricky and purred, "Mmmm, it's a wonderful thing, huh, Ricky? I'm on some right now."

"You said it, brother," Ricky answered.

"Fuck, about the only thing they've been giving me is aspirin and a local every time they have to cut me or re-break something."

"Do you have any type of insurance?" Joe asked.

"No," I answered.

"Awwwah, that's too bad because there's a whole world of drugs you're missing out on, brother."

"Amen," Ricky added.

"So how are your bills getting paid?" Joe asked.

"Well, to be honest, up until a few days ago they weren't getting paid, but Aaron worked out something with the social worker here, so now they're getting paid."

"Well, that's why you ain't getting no drugs, Mike. They ain't gonna give them if they ain't getting paid, my man. Besides, where the hell is your room anyhow? Ricky told me it was upstairs."

"Yeah, I'm upstairs with all the old people."

"Oh... you mean the dying floor."

"Excuse me?"

"No...Well... what I meant was that's what the nurses down here call it."

"Oh, that's nice to know."

"Ah, they probably didn't have any beds anywhere else when you came in, Mike," Ricky theorized.

"So, Joe, what happened to your jaw?"

"Come here, check it out. They took a fuckin' rib out of me and rebuilt one for me," he explained.

Joe had time to heal up, but I could see that he had been whacked, too, like me. But I've got to say they did some work on him, fixed him up well in spite of himself. We hung out and bullshitted until Joe received a visitor and it got awkward, so Ricky and I left.

By the time Ricky and I got to the elevator my legs were shot, and Ricky had to get a wheelchair for me because my legs were cramping up. As soon as I sat in it, Ricky started popping wheelies down the hall with me in it.

"Ricky! Cool out!"

"Don't worry. I've got you."

"Ricky, I swear, if you drop me, I'll kill you after I heal."

"I'm not gonna drop you, Mike."

"You better not."

When I finally lay down in the bed, I felt certain muscles twitching, muscles that I hadn't used yet to that degree.

Man, I've got a ways to go to get past this shit, I thought. This ain't all coming back in a week, Mike.

Ricky left a short time after that, and I really wondered where my life was leading or heading. I knew, amongst a lot of things, that things had to change in my life, big time.

I'm sure you didn't like the past, Mike. Did you? I questioned myself. So I've got to definitely change the road ahead. This is a wake up call, I reasoned. You've got to come up with a game plan to get straight with yourself and your life. Now, what's best for you? To hang out in this place and get fed and heal? Or go home and mend there? I've got some money in the bank, so I could survive for a while, that I know. But I don't know if I could take this place much longer. I think it's killing me in another sense. Well, I don't have to make a decision tonight, so tonight you can rest, I told myself.

Gerard came up that night without Barbara. After I got dressed, I took another short walk with Gerard. We went down to the visitors' room so Gerard could have a cigarette and, after smelling the smoke, I wondered how I had ever smoked at all. We bullshitted for a while, and I talked to Gerard about my idea of going home again.

"Well, I think you should stay here a few more days. But if you're going to go home, I'll drop some food off for you from time to time."

"You almost make it sound like I'm a leper."

"You know what I mean."

"Yeah, I know… thanks."

"So what's going on with the neighborhood?"

"Nothing. It's quiet for the most part."

"You still working out?"

"Well, I cut down a little bit. There's no one to work out with, ya' know."

"Shit, I can't even lift my ass out of bed. I probably couldn't even bench the bar with no weights on it. I know my shoulder wouldn't be able to take the weight. It still pops out of place from time to time from doing nothing. Imagine if I tried to put two hundred pounds on it."

"Well, you've still got to heal, ya' know. It's gonna take a little time. I know you don't want to hear it, Mike, but you could have been worse. You could have had nothing to work with."

"Yeah, I know. But now my teeth are getting fucked up."

"What do you mean?" Gerard asked.

"It feels like my top row of teeth on the left side are shifting so they sit inside my bottom teeth. I'm wondering if my jaw was broke or something."

"Well, all I know is that there's a reason they wired my jaw shut those two times I broke it. Maybe it's got something to do with your broken cheekbone. Besides that, what makes you think you could break your top jaw?"

"When I was a kid and got hit by the bus, along with knocking out some teeth, I lost some jaw bone fragments on top as well, and they told me that time that I had broken it, so I know it's a little weakened up there."

"Well, why don't you tell your doctor?"

"I've been telling both my doctors, but now at this point I'm afraid that they'll give me a local, then hit me in the face with a hammer, and wire me up. I don't think I'm into it right now. I'm starting to heal up, you know. I don't want to start all over again."

Within a couple of days, I decided that I was ready to leave, aside from everyone's advice. So one day I signed myself out and left. It was already mid-November, and it was a little chilly out, so I took my beat-up sweater out of my shopping bag and threw it on as I walked home. It was odd walking through some of the streets I had grown up on because I felt like a ghost, like I hadn't seen these streets in years. I headed towards Northern Boulevard and passed my old school J.H.S. 189 on the way. I even passed the doorway where we were allowed to smoke during times of the day when I was in Project 25, the drug program. I wondered what some of those guys were dealing with in their lives, if they had one.

After I hit Roosevelt Avenue, I made a right and headed towards the Long Island Railroad station. As I inched my way past the station, I watched a group of 12-year-olds play two-hand touch football in the street like I used to do.

Man, look at them, I thought. I'd give anything to be able to do that right now.

I made a left onto 150th Place and decided to walk one block out of my way and stop by the Murry Hill bar where I started this odyssey. I walked up the same block where I had made my return trip the night I got hit.

It's getting to be a shorter and shorter distance to the place where you died, Mike, the piece of ground where you died on this Earth, I thought, as I passed each parked car.

There was a car parked in the same spot where I remembered myself standing after I got hit, so I leaned against the car to envision it from that prospective again. Man, a split second and my life was changed again, Mike, I thought.

After I had stood there for a while, Brian Brawly came out of the Murry Hill and stood out there as if he was waiting for someone, so I called him. It was funny, because he couldn't recognize me from that distance, so I pretended like I was some old guy yelling at him as I was walking towards him, with my cane, telling him that he was a hoodlum for hanging out on the street like that. Brian would occasionally look at me with a confused dirty look on his face from second to second. When I got close enough, I said, "Brian! It's me, Mike!"

"Oh shit, Mike, I heard you died or something. How the fuck are you?"
"I feel like I'm dead. Thanks for asking."
"You had me a little fooled when you were walking towards me real slow with that cane."
"Well, that part's not a joke. I can only walk that fast. As a matter of fact, I think I'm going to be real sorry a little later that I did decide to walk all the way home."

After we stood there talking for a few minutes, Gerard walked out of the bar.

"Holy shit! Am I seeing a fucking ghost!"
"Yeah, fucking Boo!"
"Mike, what the fuck are you doing here?"
"I told you I was gonna leave."
"Yeah, but I didn't think you would, and this is the first place you come?"
"Tell me about it."
"How did you get here?"
"I walked."
"You walked all the way here!"
"Yeah."
"Shit, the last time I left you were huffing and puffing in the hallway."
"Yeah, I know. Besides that, I left an hour and a half ago."
"Get the fuck out of here," Brian said, "That's only a fifteen, twenty minute walk tops, and it took you an hour and a half?"
"Yep, and I don't think I should have stopped either. I think my legs are cramping up. I better keep going."
"I'd give you a ride but I don't have my car tonight," Gerard said.
"That's all right. I can walk."

I waited for the light to change and for the cars to stop down the block at the red light, and then I started to walk. By the time I just got to the other side of the six-lane street, cars were already whizzing by.

327

"I knew you could make it, Mike. I was cheering you on," Gerard yelled.

"I know. I heard you, you fuck!" I yelled back to him.

CHAPTER 8

HUMPTY DUMPTY

By the time I reached my house, the sun had just about set and the wind was blowing around the leaves from the naked trees. It almost looked spooky. I stood across the street for a few minutes, just looking at my house before going in.

Well, Mike, I joked, you're going back in for another round. I wonder what's next?

After sitting there for a few minutes, I decided that maybe I should go in before my legs tightened up and I couldn't move. When I got inside, I climbed the stairs to my room, lay down, and fell asleep.

I woke up the next day at about 11 o'clock in the morning. My body was aching, and when I stood up I was getting bad charley horses in my legs. After I made it down the stairs, I went to check the rest of the house. When I got into the kitchen, I made myself a cup of tea and then sat down and drank it. After that, I decided to check out the basement apartment where Dino had been staying to see what shape it was in.

When I got to the bottom of the basement stairs, I heard somebody putting a key into the side door.

Who the fuck could this be? I thought.

After the door opened, I saw that it was Maryann. She walked down the stairs right past me, looked over the apartment, then turned to me, and said, "Where is all of Dino's shit!"

I really didn't know what prevented me from cracking my cane over her head, but I didn't do it. I mean, she walked into my house, where she was never welcomed by me anyway, didn't say jack shit to me, and then turned and spoke to me with this fucking attitude.

"I don't know. I don't care, and you had better take everything you need to take and then get the fuck out of my face before I kill you, bitch! P.S., leave the fucking key!" I said.

She did what she had to do and then slammed the side door as she left.

A few days later, before Dino and I spoke, I got a fuck-you letter from him. What could I expect? Dino always did think with his dick when it came to girls.

Later that day I went back up to my room with a Bible I had found. I don't really know why I grabbed it, but I took it upstairs with me anyway. I had a bench with weights set up in my bedroom, and there was about 220 pounds on it. It almost made me cry to think that it would be a long time before I could lift it again, but I had stopped crying years ago. I walked over to it, tried to budge it, and nothing. It got me a little pissed off, so I figured I'd see just how much weight I could lift to find out where I had to start from. By the time I got down to just the bar with no weights on it, I was pretty discouraged. It only weighed 20 pounds, and I could lift it only twice. Then I sat up and got into one of those deep thought moods.

You've got one hell of a road ahead of you, Mike. Now I know when you told yourself to come back, you didn't really know what you were in store for, but it's too late for that now. You can't just lie down and die on this one. You've got a little fight ahead of you, but I know you can do it. This time, though, you're gonna do it right. No more fucking around, no more bullshit. Now you've got to work on your body again, and you need to make a lot of money, because I'm never going to find myself back in some hospital being treated like shit for one thing, and for another I just ain't living like this any more. I want to get my shit straight. I want to turn my shit around so that people can say, Look at that; He came back from hell and still straightened his shit out. What a fucking guy. Yep, that's what I want now, I thought.

I sat there and looked around my room, and I felt as if I was trespassing into someone else's life. I felt like I was in the room of some kid who had passed away.

The Bible happened to be sitting close to the bench, so I picked it up and held it for a minute or two, not knowing what to do with it. It had been a long time since I had held a Bible, let alone opened one. For a minute I didn't know whether to read it or if I should open it at all. I decided that I would hold onto it for a minute or two, clear my head, and then open it to any page and read. Just like when you play high or low with a deck of cards. When I opened the book and read it, it said, "If you are an evil doer and you have a following of evil doers, the Lord will not kill you. Instead he will strike you down and injure you so that your followers can gaze upon you to see the Lord's power."

I sat there as chills ran up my spine. I slowly raised my head and, when I looked out my window, the tree in my back yard had at least twenty of the largest ravens I had ever see at one time in my life.

By that night everybody in the house knew I was home. It was thrown together on short notice, but they gave me a little coming home party with the promise of a better one on the weekend. I was also told that Stymie and Buckwheat, my black cats, were fine and probably just running around somewhere. After a while, the party started to turn into a partying party, so I thought it best if I called it a night.

The next day Barbara came over.

"Michael, why did you leave the hospital? The doctor said it wasn't time yet when I spoke with him," she scolded.

"Yeah, I know but I had to get the hell out of there. The place was killing me."

"But what are you going to do now?"

"Don't worry. I'll manage."

"I know that, but at least you could have given yourself more time to heal."

"Well, the way I see it, I can heal just as fast at home, if not faster. I'll be fine, Barb."

After that we lay in bed together and watched TV the rest of the night. It was nice having her there. I mean, she smelled nice, she looked nice, and we had pleasant conversation. It was a big switch from lying in my hospital bed all night alone.

Over the course of the next few weeks, I grew much closer to Barbara in more ways than one. I guess rolling around in the grass kissing each other as kids finally paid off. My life was drastically changed now and would be for some time, so I really wouldn't have minded if Barb stopped coming over in the beginning, but she didn't, which really made me think about settling down with her. I mean, after all, I knew I always loved her.

Jimmy Marnell had the room next to me, but I would try to avoid hanging out with him because he was still getting dusted, on PCP, and I didn't want to take the chance of being tempted. Then there was another friend of mine who lived on the first floor who was dealing cocaine. He'd always have at least an ounce of the shit lying around on the table, not to mention that he and anyone who was there were usually high as a kite. Any time I did hang out, let's say to watch the N.Y. Jets lose a game of football, it would only be a matter of time before the joints and drugs would start flying back and forth. After somebody would pass me a joint, as difficult as it was, I'd say, No, thanks. Then everybody would look at each other and then at the joint and say, "Is there something wrong with the weed? Is everything all right?"

After a few times, I started to enjoy watching everybody else's reaction when I'd say no, because they'd look around at each other as if maybe they were doing something wrong. It turned into a little trick I'd use to make myself stronger, because I would feel stronger for not giving in. Feeling stronger at any level is what I needed at this point in time, so it worked out pretty well.

Mike V. had made it a point to come over my house every couple of days after I got home. He would stop by and bullshit for a while and then drop off a few bucks for my pocket. I felt guilty taking money from him, because he was married and had a child to think of now. Every time he would hand me money I'd take what I needed and try to hand the rest back to him, but he would push it back towards me. Then one day he said, "Mike, take it while I have it. We'll worry about it later. Besides, I took on another job now."

"Really? Doing what?"

"Well, I'm working as a janitor at McDonalds down the block from my other job," he said as he frowned.

"Well, it's just a job, Mike."

"I know, Mike, but it's pretty hard kissing ass for a few bucks, especially when I used to make the same money in a few days running around in the streets as a kid."

"I know, Mike, but you can't look at it that way. Do you think I liked any shitty job I've ever had? Well, I didn't. But you've got to put your time in while you keep your eyes and ears open for something better."

"I know. Besides, I promised Asia I'd straighten up for her and the baby and cut down on the drinking," he said. "Then I got a funny feeling that the reason they're not moving along with my cop case is 'cause they're waiting for me to fuck up so they can really nail me."

"I know what you mean, Mike. I ain't taking any chances on anything, either. I'm sure that a few people are pissed off that I skated on my cases."

"Why do you say that?"

"Oh, I didn't tell you. Get this. These two detectives come over to my house last week. So I let them in, and I'm standing there with my cane, all busted up, and they tell me that some lady got her purse snatched over by Weeping Willow Park."

"What? The park down the block from the 109th Precinct?" Mike asked.

"Yeah. So they say to me that the lady pulled out my picture from their mug shots. Okay, wait a minute, I said to them. I'm sure the two of you are aware of my arrests, and you think that I'm stupid enough to take some lady's shit ass purse right down the block from the 109th? My point, Mike, they were like two dogs in heat who wanted to dry hump my ass all the way to the 109th."

"So what happened with them?"

"Well, first I told them to take a look at my face and explained about my accident, and they suggested that I must've caught a beating since then. Well, what about my cane? How could I run with this lady's purse if, I can't even walk? So the cop says, Like I said, maybe you caught a beating since then. All right fine, I'll tell you what. I'll give you permission to go up to my room and open up the drawer in my nightstand next to my bed. In the top drawer you'll find a piece of paper from the hospital from when I signed myself out a week after this bullshit. And I think it even says something about being in a motorcycle accident. After one cop came back down with the paper, they stepped to the side and started to talk. Then they say to me, All right look, then, you shouldn't have a problem with standing in a lineup.

By now I started to get a little pissed off. So I said, Look, do you guys have a warrant, or are you asking me to come to a lineup? 'No, we don't have a warrant,' one of them answered. All right then check this out, take down the information on that paper and call my doctor, and if you still don't believe me, then come back with a warrant and arrest me, okay?"

"So what did they do?"

"They left, but I can tell you they really wanted to pin my ass to their chest and fuck that- I'm gonna rob an old lady's purse."

"Yeah, I hear ya', Mike. Hey, it's getting late. I've got to get to work."

"All right Mike. Thanks for stopping by and for the money."

"Mike."

"Yeah?"

"Don't thank me for the money any more, all right?"

"All right, Mike."

We gave each other a hug, and then he split.

Ricky stopped by one day after work.

"Hey, Mike, if you need work, Gus is looking for guys, and you don't have to move around that much at all because you'll work on a machine all day long," he told me.

"Where is it?"

"Over by the Flushing Bridge, before Shea Stadium. Do you know where the #7 train comes out? Well, it's right by that crane."

"Oh yeah, I always wondered what they did down there."

"Well, Gus, the guy who lives across the street from me, owns a shop over there."

"Is that the guy who does something with metal?"

"Yeah, he uses pewter, and he makes statues and frames out of it."

"How do you get there?"

"Well, I take the bus."

"Hmm, the bus. I still look a little fucked up with this cane and all, so I wouldn't want people staring at me all the time."

"Yeah, but once you get there, all you have to do is either stand there and polish something or sand it."

"Well, that don't sound so bad. Maybe I could even start walking there. I do need the exercise anyway."

"Yeah, walk along the bus route and, if you get tired, you could always hop on the bus."

"Well, let me think about it tonight."

"Yeah, sure."

"Hey, how's Joe?"

"Well, he's better but he's not that mobile yet. Believe me, I know. Been there, done that."

"Yeah, I know. I saw you, Ricky. How you making out with your gut?"

"Ah, the doctor told me to take it easy on beer, but a man's got to have a beer or two. How you doing?"

"Well, I've still got the aches and pains, and the hole in my side is definitely closed up now, so I've got a better breath. But my lung is still a little sore."

"Ah, it takes a while."

"I guess," I said.

Within a couple of days, I did start the job that Ricky offered. It was a bit of an adventure for me in the beginning, walking along the bus route to try and get my stamina back, but after a while I was able to walk all the way to work with my cane. I couldn't believe that after all this time I was still in this much pain, but I still managed to start felling better in another sense, with my mind.

Gus, our boss, was an interesting character. His wife's front office was connected to his office through a hallway. Then the hallway looped around and went through his workshop and connected back with the warehouse where we were. Every time Gus would come into the warehouse through his wife's office, he was calm and pleasant, but more than half the time when he came out from his workshop/office he'd be cursing and busting our balls, or else he'd throw Ricky out of the casting pit and start casting himself.

"Ricky," I said one day, "what the fuck is wrong with him?"

"Well, every time one of the molds he makes in his shop blows out, he gets pissed off because then he has to make a new one. Besides, you know he's a black belt champion, so nobody here is inclined to say anything to him about his outbursts."

Barbara and I made plans to go out and catch a movie, so I got home, took a shower, and waited to go out for a bite of dinner with her before the movie. I waited and waited until I called her house and spoke with her mother. Her mother told me that Barbara had gone out about an hour ago.

Well, so much for waiting. Maybe you ought to watch your step for the next few hours. Remember what happened the last time you waited for her, I thought.

After I had dinner that night, I went back up to my room, lay down, and watched TV. A few hours later Gerard stopped by.

"Mike, did you leave Barbara up at the Vinewood Bar?"

"The Vinewood? Why would she be up there? None of us really hang out there."

"Well, I just want to let you know that she's hanging out, getting a little friendly, especially with Tony Tesco."

"Really? Thanks for letting me know."

"No problem. Well, I'm going to stop in and see Jimmy and see what he's got in his bag of tricks."

Under other circumstances it might not have bothered me, and I probably would have kissed her off, but unfortunately for me, I had allowed myself to fall in love with her in the time I had been home. I decided to walk over to the bar, not to shock her, but just to let her know that I knew what was going on, so she could spare me any bullshit or promises.

As I walked into the bar, I looked around for a second and then headed towards the back. While I was making my way towards the back of the bar, Tesco stood up in front of me, facing me. I thought that maybe it was a coincidence until I saw the look in his eye. We stood there in silence for a second or two until he decided to step out of my way. Then I walked to the back of the bar and saw Barbara having a drink with some guy. She didn't notice me until I was standing right in front of her.

"Hi, how you doing?" I said.

She looked at me with her mouth open as if she wanted to say something, and I asked her if everything was okay.

The guy she was sitting with started to babble something about whether or not Barbara knew me, as she started to babble something on her own. I didn't pay any mind to the guy yapping, because I had already decided not to crack him one with my cane. What was going on between Barbara and I had nothing to do with him. Barbara asked me to come to the back of the bar where it was a little quieter, so we could talk.

In the middle of our emotional male-female conversation, a person I knew came over to me and said, "Hey, Mike, I just came in the bar, and I saw your buddy Mike walking past with Asia."

'Yeah, and?"

"And there was this guy walking behind him, cursing at him and calling him a pussy."

"No way!"

"Yeah, that's what I thought. That's why I'm telling you."

I thought the story so unbelievable that I walked to the front of the bar to see for myself.

"Where? Where is he?"

"Over there on the corner of Citgo gas station," he said as he pointed.

I looked across the street in that direction and sized up the guy following Mike.

"Ah, Mike can beat that guy's ass."

"Yeah, I know. So why hasn't he done it already?" my friend said.

Without thinking about it, I said, "I don't know. Maybe Mike doesn't want to be bothered," I said as I turned around, walked into the bar, and thought up another point to argue with Barbara.

After arguing with Barbara for a little while longer, I decided that I had enough bullshit for tonight so I stuffed $40 in her hand and told her to enjoy herself. Had yet another drink, and then I left.

The next day Mike stopped by at about ten o'clock in the morning while I was out on the back porch.

"Hey, Mike, what are you doing here? Aren't you supposed to be at work?"

"I quit," he said as he pulled a beer out of the bag he had.

"Mike, what are you doing drinking at this time of the day?"

"Why not? I should enjoy what's left of my life."

"What'a you mean? What the fuck are you talking about?"

Mike looked away from me and didn't say a word.

"Mike...! What's up? What's wrong?"

He looked back at me slowly and said, "Mike, I killed somebody last night."

"What...? Get the fuck out of here... I saw you walk past the Vinewood last night."

"You saw me there last night??"

"Yeah."

"Mike, that's the guy I killed."

"No way, Mike... Get the fuck out of here. Please, don't tell me that. I was going to cross the street, but I thought you could handle it. Mike, please don't tell me that!"

"I'm serious... Once we crossed the street and got to Firestone Tires, I snapped. I told Asia to keep walking."

"No, Mike..."

"Then I beat his fucking ass."

"Maybe he's not dead!"

"Mike, he's dead... Believe me."

It felt as though a ton of bricks landed on me and knocked my wind out after he said that.

"Oh, Mike, I feel so fucking guilty now. I should have gone out there."

"I wish you did, but it's all right. It was my fault... I should've listened to Asia."

"Are you sure he'd dead, Mike?"

"Mike, if anyone could live through that beating, I should carry a gun for protection. Besides... it's in today's paper."

Then he sat down, pulled out the paper, and told me the whole story. He had gone over to the Murry Hill to hang out with Asia while she was working and to walk her home when she got off work because their car was broken down. He was in there for a while, when this bar regular went over to him and asked Mike to buy him a joint and threw a dollar on top of Mike's money. It was the same guy Mike was always buying a beer or two for, from time to time. Then at the end of Asia's shift, they both got ready to leave.

When they got outside, the guy ran after them and told Mike to give him back his dollar. Then Mike told me he said to him, "After all the beers I've bought you, you're gonna come out here and bust my balls like I'm a thief? You know what? Go fuck yourself and your dollar." Then he told me that, after he started arguing with the guy, Asia grabbed his hand and told him she just wanted to go home, so he started walking.

"As Asia and I started walking, this guy starts following us while he's calling me out, so I go to pull away from Asia and she says, 'Mike, you promised. No more fighting. Besides, you've got that open case.' So I turn around and started walking again."

"And he kept it up after that?" I asked.

"Yeah. I guess he thought he was a bad ass because he had been in the Golden Gloves years ago."

"I know. I remember him shooting his mouth off about it from time to time."

"As I started walking again I turned back towards him and said, 'I'll catch up with you another time, my friend.'"

"So what happened?"

"He starts calling me a fucking punk and a pussy."

"I can't believe you didn't hit the guy right then and there."

"I know, tell me about it. While he's saying this shit, I'm telling Asia, 'C'mon, Asia let me kick this guy's ass, and then we'll go home, all right?' And she's like, 'No, Michael you promised me,' as we're walking. Mike, this guy follows me like that for three and a half blocks, and Asia is hanging on to my hand so I don't turn around and whack this guy. Ya' know, then I'm passing the Vinewood bar, and a few guys are hanging out. Then I walk past my gas station job and, Mike, I swear, it was like a movie because I crossed the street over by Firestone Tires and I come up to my other shitty job cleaning up at McDonalds. And while I'm thinking of all this shit this guy's yapping, and he says that he's gonna get a hold of Asia at work when I'm not around, and that was it- I popped. So I stopped, looked at Asia, pulled her hand off mine, and told her to go home. After she started to question me again, I looked at her and said, Asia, go home! And this cocksucker's saying, 'That's right honey, go home while I kick your husband's ass!' "

"So, Mike... ya' kill him?"

"Mike... I hear what you're saying, but you weren't there. And believe me, someone was going to die that night, and it wasn't going to be me."

By the time Mike finished talking, I could see by looking closer at his face that he was in some type of fight.

"You want to split? Take my ID and go?"

"Ahh, fuck it. I've got Asia and the baby here. I can't leave them. Besides, who knows? Maybe the cop case will get dropped, and I can have the charges reduced on this fucking asshole. Maybe to manslaughter and only do three years or something."

Mike stayed over for a few hours, and we talked. I couldn't get over the news. First Dino, now Mike. That was the last time I saw Mike in the world for a long time. He got picked up a few days later. Losing the two of them really put a dent in my emotions within that short time, because I felt like they were both a part of my family, and now they were both gone again.

A day or two later, Asia called me and told me that Mike had suggested to her that she tell me to go and pick up some of the hours he was working over at Citgo gas station. After contemplating it for a day, I decided to do it. I ended up getting a shift that started on Friday at 6 p.m. to midnight. Then I had Saturday off until 7 p.m. I'd work from then until the following morning at 6 a.m. which was two shifts and then go home, get some sleep, and then go back for the 4 p.m. to midnight shift. Needless to say, I'd usually end up being late the next morning at 7 a.m. for Gus. Then I'd find him in a bad mood that morning, and I'd have to hear him bitch. To make matters worse, my two black cats, Stymie and Buckwheat, were starting to follow me when I'd leave for work in the mornings.

At first it wasn't too bad, even though I was still walking on my cane, and I'd usually lose them around the corner from my house, but then they started getting smarter and running a little faster. Even though they were cats and they knew their way around, I still didn't like the idea of them following me farther and farther from home. I would run down the block and hide behind cars, trees, anything I could to lose them, and they would still find me at times. The real funny part about this was that, after a while, I'd stop and run around until I'd catch them and then carry them home and lock them in the house. A few times I would catch some of my wide-eyed neighbors, whom couldn't see the cats, watching me as it was happening. But before I could explain myself, they would just shake their heads at me and run off. I decided to stop trying. I mean, what the fuck, they all thought I was a nut anyhow. Then I'd end up late, and I'd try to explain this to Gus. He would just throw his hands up in the air and walk away.

Barbara stopped by one day, and knocked on my bedroom door. She said she wanted to check on me and see if I was all right. I was in a toss-up of whether or not I wanted to see her, but I gave in and saw her.

"So what's up?"

"Nothing... I just wanted to see how you were doing," she said.

"Why? So you could throw darts at me?"

"No, Michael. I just wanted to see if you were all right."

"Well, things are still fucked up, Barb. But you're welcome to come and see me as long as you like, to update your reports."

The conversation went on for about another ten minutes like this before she left.

Yeah, things were fucked up, especially my teeth, I thought. My top jaw had definitely shifted, and I didn't know how I could get them back in place without someone breaking something in my mouth. I had to get some money together to go to a dentist and see what he thought about it. Whatever it was, I bet it was going to cost a fortune. I wondered what was up with my bus case. Maybe I could get some money from there for this. I'd have to give my lawyer a call soon.

One of the first things I had to get used to at my new job at the gas station was Dukie, the watch dog. Dukie was an older German Shepherd that was basically trained to bite anyone who came into the office. So of course, every time someone would change shifts, you'd have to let Dukie get acquainted with you again. He was also a little blind, which made matters worse. This is probably why I got nipped once or twice by him while I was working in the beginning.

My mother had met a girl named Ann in prison, and since Ann was getting released, my mother let her and her boyfriend, Jim, rent the basement apartment. Ann was a little country girl who was also a little nutty. She did two years in prison because her boss wouldn't give her the two week's pay she had coming to her, so she went up to her job with a shotgun to get it, and ended up getting jail time instead. Her boyfriend, Jim, was all right, just a little nerdy, and he happened to be about 15 years older than she was. They had a Doberman named Tagon, too.

After a few weeks while I was working late one night, Ann was nice enough to carry a tray of meatloaf she had cooked for me all the way from my house to my job, which was about five blocks away. I never usually got the chance to get dinner for myself on Fridays, because of the travel time between jobs, so I thought it was pretty nice of her to go out of her way for me, I thought, as I swallowed it down.

When I got done eating it, I wondered if she had used the chopped meat I was going to throw out or if she used her own. I figured that she could probably tell that the one that I had was bad, so I didn't worry about it.

I kept working for the next two weeks in spite of feeling like shit, and I never even thought about the chopped meat being the problem. Besides, I needed the money, so I kept working. I've probably got a bug from being a little run-down from working so many hours, I thought. That's all.

Barbara called me on Saturday and asked me how I was. I told her I really felt like shit, and I asked her if she could do me a big favor.

"Well, what do you want?"

"Could you drop off two packs of cigarettes, I'm running low?"

"Michael, you started to smoke again? What about your lung?" she asked.

"Yeah, don't worry, though. My lung is fine, I guess."

She told me that she would drop them off, so I didn't have to walk to the store and go get them.

A few hours later, I decided I'd get them on my way to work. I was still walking with a cane and, now being sick and all, I was walking very slowly again. I was also pretty pissed at Barbara. The least she could have done was to call within four hours and tell me to go and get them myself.

After I got out to the front of my house, I could see why she hadn't gone yet. She was hanging out on her steps with Tony Tesco from the Vinewood bar. Barbara looked over at me, so I flipped her the middle finger and limped away.

After working my double shift that night, I slept like a baby when I got home. When I woke up in the morning, I shut off my alarm clock and stood up. No sooner after I stood up, I fell flat on my face from the pain in my stomach. As I gazed at the intricate stitching that was used on the rug in my room, I figured that maybe it was time to see a doctor. After calling to have somebody cover my shift at the gas station, I got to the hospital at 4 p.m. While I was there, other patients in the emergency room had me diagnosed with everything from appendicitis to cancer, which really improved my spirits.

Because my reasons for being at the hospital weren't "life threatening," as I was told, I finally got to see a doctor at about 4 in the morning.

About an hour after sticking his finger up my ass, the doctor walked in and said, "Well, I got it."

"What is it?" I asked as cheerfully as I could.

"Food poisoning."

"Food poisoning- that's it? And I feel this bad?"

"Well, let me put it to you this way. You probably wouldn't have felt this bad tomorrow."

"Really? Why is that, because it would have gotten better on its own?"

"No. Because by tomorrow, you probably would have been dead."

"Get out of here. From food poisoning?"

"I have never seen a case of it so bad in someone. Is this the first time you've ever heard of a doctor or something?"

"What do you mean?"

"Well, I'm sure you must've been sick, weren't you?"

"Yeah, sick as a dog."

"Well, didn't that tell you something?"

"I just figured it would pass."

"Well, it almost did, my friend. It almost did," he answered.

By 6:30 in the morning I had taken a cab home and lay down with a stomach full of medicine. I called in sick the next day and just sat around and watched TV for the most part of the day. I thought about that last incident with Barbara, and it really pissed me off. I decided that I was done with her 100 percent. I mean, after all the time we knew each other, the least she could have done was called or dropped the cigarettes off on my front porch. Shit, I could have even let someone else go for me if I knew she wasn't coming.

I turned the TV off and took a nap. Then about 6 p.m., somebody knocked on my door.

"Who is it?"

"It's me, Barbara."

"Barbara, what the hell do you want?"

"Well… can I come in?"

"Yeah, I guess." I said, even though I had just told myself I was done with her.

When she walked in, she placed two packs of cigarettes on my nightstand. I looked at them and then said to her, "What are you, fucking retarded? I asked for them yesterday."

"I know. I couldn't come over then," she said.

"You know, Barb, if you want to hang out with your new boyfriend, that's fine. But you could have called and told me you couldn't make it. Besides, with all the places there are in Flushing, can't you take this asshole down the block or something or go for a ride, instead of hanging on your front steps? I mean, is it some way for you to show me that you have a new boyfriend?"

"No, Michael, it's not that, believe me. I suggested that we go for a ride a few times, but he insisted on staying there."

"Well, besides that, what the hell do you want from me?"

"I just want to see if you're okay."

"All right, I'll tell you what, Barb. Why don't we make your life simple, okay? Just call me from now on, and I'll let you know that I'm fine. How's that for a deal?"

I don't know why it seemed like she had tears in her eyes, but she agreed and left. I clicked on the radio after that, and that new Rocky song was on, "Eye of the Tiger." The words really hit home. It was just the way I felt, I thought. "Just a man and his will to survive."

Well, Mike, you've gotten rid of drugs in your life, and hanging with the wrong crowd. Now your slate is clean, my man. I'm a little beat up, but I'm still here, and I'm still alive. It's time to get it right this time.

I talked with Asia, and she gave me Mike's address. I could write him now, because I was on his list. I gave Asia my phone number and told her to have Mike call me one night this week. When he did call, he told me he was sorry for not calling sooner, but he felt like there wasn't much we could say to each other, so he would just call Asia. He explained to me that the DA tried to put the two cases together, but the judge wouldn't allow it. But even so, now the judge knew about the cop case.

"Mike, if you want me to go to court on either case, it's not a problem. As a matter of fact, I think it might be a good idea."

"I know, Mike, but the fact remains the same. I hit a cop, and I killed someone. So it don't look good either way."

"I think you're wrong there, Mike, because there's more to the story than just black and white. But I'll go any way you want on this."

We talked about things for about another ten more minutes, and then he said he had to go.

I got up late for work again Monday morning. After locking my cats inside, I ran down to the bus stop.

When I got to work, I walked inside, and Gus happened to be standing there. He looked at me, rolled his eyes in his head, raised his arms, and slapped his hands on his thighs. So, in frustration, I did the same right back to him. He looked at me perplexed for a second or two, then shook his head, and walked into the office. Ricky was casting pewter in the pewter pit, as we liked to call it, and he was laughing uncontrollably.

"What the fuck are you laughing at?"
"You."
"Me? For what?"
"The way you just gave Gus back his shit, that's what."
"Oh, well, I'm not in the mood today. That's all."

After lunch, I tried to call back my lawyer who had the bus case again. This was like the fourth time in a week, and I finally got him. I was calling him for a few reasons; the first was for the status of my case with him, and the second reason was because I wanted to see if he knew anything about victim's compensation. I had heard that you could get some type of money from the city to help with medical bills. As I explained these thoughts to him, he would utter, "I see. I see." Then he said, "Well... I think you should find a lawyer who can handle the motorcycle case for you."

Just by the way he was speaking to me, I knew he was basically telling me to go fuck myself- in a nice way- but I decided to toy with him and asked if he could recommend anyone to me. He replied that he didn't know of anyone.

"Okay, fine. Let's move on then. What is the status of my bus case that you have handled for me for several years?"
"Basically... there isn't a status," he answered.
"So what has been your basic plan of attack over the last few years?!"
"Look, am I being fired?"
"Yeah, why not? If you can't even answer simple questions for me, I guess so."
"Fine, I'll send your portfolio and my bill to any address that you wish. Give the details to my receptionist."
"Your bill- for what?"
"All the work I've done for you."
"Work!?! You haven't done shit in over four years, and you want to get paid for that?"
"Well, if you say so, but I still get paid for my time. Welcome to the real world, kid. Good luck."

Then I heard a click.

I swear I was so pissed off I would have killed this motherfucker if he was in front of me.

The rest of the day dragged on until lunchtime. Luckily for me, Ricky had brought a few sandwiches with him, so we went and sat over by the crane by the dock. As we were eating, I complained about my lawyer to Ricky. Ricky looked to the left, then to the right, then at me, and started singing. "Sitting on the dock of the bay...Watching the tide roll away...Sitting here resting my bones..."

I smiled at him and joined him in singing.

I received a letter from my mother, telling me that she was going to be moved to a women's prison in Manhattan. It was on 27th over by the F.D.R. Drive. She sent me another letter once she got there, so I went to visit her.

I had to take one bus and two trains to get there, and then I had to walk about fifteen blocks. Unlike Rikers Island, what you had to do there was to stand outside, in the elements, and wait your turn to go in. When my turn came up, I went in and told them who I was visiting, and then I started to empty my pockets. Halfway through the procedure, the guard said, "Sorry. You ain't on the list!"

"What do you mean I'm not on the list? I've been on her list for years."
"Well, you ain't on our list!"
"C'mon, man. Cut me some slack. I'm coming to see my mother."
"Like I said, sorry. You ain't on the list!"
"Well, then get me any type of form that I need to be on your fucking list!"
"Hey, don't take your shit out on me!"
"Believe me, my friend, if I took my shit out on you, I'd be back in the joint. Now, either get me the form, or get someone over here who knows what I'm talking about."

After about fifteen minutes somebody with a few more pins on his shirt came over. They gave me a form and then told me to mail it in.

"Well what about the stuff I bought her? Can I leave it for her?"
"No, you have to take it back.'

Man, I was pissed off, not only couldn't I visit her but now I had to carry two bags of food, and a bag of new clothes back to Queens. About halfway back to the subway station, I ran into a homeless lady, so I gave her all the food. But I took the underwear and bras. The homeless lady looked at me strangely while she thanked me and walked away.

Oh well, at least my load was lighter, I thought.

A few nights later while I was working at the gas station, Tesco pulled into the gas station with Barbara in his car. He hung a U-turn and then parked by the Vinewood. I guess he wanted to show me his prize. A little while after that, I watched as this young hoodlum type walked straight for the front door while I was sitting inside.

Boy, he's gonna be in for a surprise if he walks in and I don't say anything about the dog, I thought.

He walked to the front door, smirked at me, and then walked inside. Because I wasn't sure what his reason for walking inside was, I didn't say anything as Old Dukie scrambled to attention and peeled out in one place until he started to get traction on the linoleum floor. The guy glanced at Dukie and then looked at me. I figured he had three choices at that point: 1) To get bit by Dukie, 2) To run back outside, or 3) To tell me why he was there real fast.

"Okay, Dukie. Okay, Dukie. It's me, Henry... It's all right!"

Dukie ran over to him, caught a scent, and then he was cool.

"Man, weren't you going to say anything to Dukie?"
"Why? You look like a smart man," I said still not knowing why he was there.
"My name is Henry, Henry Vega. I know all the guys who work here, and I used to hang out with your buddy Mike," he said as he petted Dukie.
"You used to hang out with Mike, huh?"
"Yeah."
"What's his wife's name?"
"Asia,' he answered.

Even though he had the right answer, I still wasn't sure about his reason for being there, so after talking for a little while about people we knew in the neighborhood, I asked him if he wanted to get us some food over at Jack in the Box. He said he didn't mind, so I pulled out a fifty and handed it to him. We looked at each other for a second, and then he smiled, took the fifty, and walked out. Well, I thought, this is one way to see where he's coming from. Besides, I'll only lose 50 bucks.

After I sat there for about twenty minutes, I figured he showed me his colors. But then he came walking back.

"Sorry, there was a line. I'll bet you thought I split, didn't you?"

I hunched my shoulders and said, "Yeah, I tested you with 50 bucks."
"I didn't come here to take your shit, Mike. I know you were good friends with Mike Viale, and me and Mike were friends. Ask him next time you talk to him."

I nodded my head, and we both sat down to eat. Man, I was hungry. These double shifts were bad, but not being able to get something to eat at times was the worst, especially when I didn't have the chance to stop and bring anything before I got here.

While we were eating, a car pulled in for gas. Henry looked over at the car and said, "I got this one, Mike," as he hopped up and walked out the door.

Henry was about 17 years old. He had on the same face as I did, which was one that didn't smile often. I could tell that he was similar to me at that age and wondered if he had any family. After he got done pumping the gas, he came back in, handed me the money, and started to finish his food. It was 3 a.m. now, and I watched as some people were leaving the Vinewood bar. Barbara and Tony came out, and they walked over to his car. Tony had a smile on his face as if he knew he was gonna get some action. I smiled and hoped that Barbara would keep him blue-balled for at least half the time she kept me that way.

Henry hung out with me the whole night and even helped me check out at seven that morning. I said goodnight to Dukie, then to him, and started to leave.

"Hey, I live by your house. I'll walk with you, all right?"

"Yeah, all right," I answered.

When I got home I went to sleep for a few hours. When I got up, I flipped on the TV to see the New York Jets winning at half-time 17 to 0. But by the time I got ready for work around 4, they were losing 28 to 17 as usual. Fucking Jets.

My mother got in touch with me a few days later. She told me that I was already on the list and that they were probably just busting her balls because of all the people she helped out while she worked in the law library. Now that everything was squared away with that, I told her that I would come up and see her on Saturday afternoon when I had some time off. She gave me another list of things she needed, and then we hung up. It felt a little funny going to see my mother, because even though we were still in touch often, I hadn't seen her in at least a year after she got shipped upstate.

When I got up to the prison on Saturday, the same guard was there. I looked at him and said, "Gotta be on the list, huh?"

He looked at me and then looked away without saying a word.

As I walked into the visiting room, a couple of the female inmates who were there said hello to me. I didn't think it strange until one or two of them said, "Hello Michael." I found an empty seat and sat down at one of the tables. After a little while, my mother walked into the visiting room. It was nice to see her, but it really sucked to have to see her in prison. After we hugged and kissed each other on the cheek, we sat down to talk. One of the first things I asked her was how a few of the women there knew my name.

"Are you kidding? Why do you think the visiting room is so full? They practically killed themselves to be here today, because they all wanted to see how handsome you were in person."

"Get outta here."

"I'm serious. I think every woman in here has a photocopy of your picture in their room, and I don't even want to tell you where some of them might be kept," my mother explained.

I ended up staying there for about two hours that day, and then I started my journey home.

The subway station was on the perimeter of a park, so I sat down on a park bench and thought about my life for a while. I thought about Mike, Dino, my mother, my father, and myself. Man, what a fucking ride, I thought. Physically I was doing much better now. I wasn't walking with a cane any more, but my teeth had definitely shifted from my jaw not being wired shut after my accident. Aside from that, I was just trying to get my head and my shit together.

They say you learn from experience, Mike. Well...I guess you're a fucking genius by now, a regular Albert Einstein. That's all in the past now. I've got to work on my future now.

I sat there and wondered how it must feel to have a "normal" life. You know, mothers and fathers may fight occasionally, maybe get a divorce, with no death, no arrests, jail, accidents or financial ruin. I mean, what the fuck do I need all this experience for? What- am I gonna write a book or something? Just all bullshit, Mike. A big waste of my fucking time, 'cause after all that, here I am, still at square one in life.

After I sat there for a while longer I realized that there were things inside the Army jacket I was wearing, so I started to go through the pockets. I found some old phone numbers, a bandanna, and change, and then I found a little bag of weed. Imagine that, I thought, It's a good thing that they have a coat room in the hallway before you go into the visiting room, unlike Rikers Island. What if you took your jacket inside with you when you went to visit at that prison, and a guard would have told me to empty my pockets, and like an idiot I would have handed him a bag of weed without knowing it. That would have been great.

I hadn't smoked weed in a long time. I could probably use a hit or two right now, I thought, as some young guy was walking towards me.

He looked kinda cool, so I asked him if he had any rolling papers on him.

"Well, I don't have any on me, but I got some at home." he said.
"Oh, really. And where's home?" I asked.
"It's right down the block from here."

After thinking about it for a minute or two I said, "Yeah. Why not? Let's go."

As we walked towards his building, I noticed a couple of prostitutes lingering around it. Then just before we got to the door of his building, he stopped, turned to me, and said, "If I bring you upstairs you're not going to rob me or anything, are you?"

Man, I thought, this would be too easy.

"Naa, I'm sure you ain't got nothing I want anyhow," I answered.

Just before we walked in, I noticed one of the prostitutes gently smiling at me while she was nodding her head for some strange reason.

After we got into his apartment, he took my jacket and then handed me some rolling papers. I went and sat on a barstool in his apartment and started to roll a joint. The young guy came back over after I finished rolling and handed me a beer, so I handed him the joint to light. A few minutes later he asked me if I would like a back rub because he was a masseuse. I figured, what the fuck, I could use a little back rub. Besides if he tried something stupid, I'd break his ass. He rubbed my neck and shoulders for a little while, and then he walked around in front of me and told me to lean my head back and relax. He rubbed my neck for a minute or two, and the next thing I knew he was kneeling between my legs asking me if he could suck my dick.

"You... want to suck my dick?"
"Please... can I? I'll pay you." he asked.
"You want to suck my dick, and pay me? Go ahead. Knock yourself out."

Well, Einstein, I thought. You want to chalk this up as another experience or what...?

On that note he opened my pants and buried his face in my groin. Being that I was straight, it was a very odd situation. I sat there in disbelief while this guy was attempting to suck my dick while wrestling with the thought that I was letting him. Then he opened his pants and jerked himself off while he kept his head buried between my legs.

After he was done, he jumped up, closed his pants, and told me I had to leave before his boyfriend came home.

"Here," he said as he pulled some money out of his pocket, "Here's thirty dollars but you've got to go now."

I closed my pants, took my jacket from him, and headed towards the door. Just as I got to the door he said, "Oh listen, I get off work the same time every day, and if you fuck me, I'll pay you more."

I looked at him and said, "That's all right. There's not going to be a repeat performance after today."

After I got outside, I looked at the crumpled money in my hand and then at the same prostitute who was still out there. She looked at me, and said, "That's right, honey. You got to make the money. Now you hold your head up high."

Great, I thought. Now I'm a fag and a fucking whore.

That following weekend when I was working my second job on Friday night, it was pouring out. But fortunately the gas station wasn't really busy. I was pretty grateful for that, because there wasn't any shelter from the rain by the gas pumps, and I was beat from my first job that day. When a customer did pull in, I reasoned with myself that I should have had at least 10 people by now, so I lifted my collar and prepared to get wet. When I ran outside over to the driver's window, the guy opened it a few inches and said, "Excuse me, but could you tell me how to get to the Whitestone bridge?"

My first thought about this guy wasn't too nice, but I figured I'd be nice and give him directions real fast as the rain beat down upon me.

"Okay, when you leave the gas station you make a right, then you take Northern Boulevard down to 150th Street, then make another right, and take that to 20th Avenue. At 20th Avenue you make a left, and go down about three blocks, and you'll see the sign for the bridge."

"Well," he said. "that's not the directions I have. The ones I have said to go to...etc...etc."

"Sir," I interrupted, "I just gave you the exact directions, and I'm getting fucking soaked. If you don't want to listen to my directions, fine. But I'm not going to stand here and debate with you about directions, so, good night. Thanks for stopping by," I said as I turned and walked into the gas station.

By the time I got back inside, I was pretty much soaked. I took off my leather jacket and started to dry myself just in time for the next customer. A lady pulled in, looked over at me, and then beeped her horn. It was still pouring out, and I dreaded the thought of getting soaked again, but I couldn't tell her to leave.

"Yes, ma'am. What'll it be?"
"Fill it up, check my tranny fluid, and the oil," she said with a smile.

Great, I thought, this bitch wants to keep me out here for an hour.

I set the pump on automatic and then went to check her fluids. After I checked the tranny fluid, I told her to shut off the motor so I could check her oil.

"Well, I never heard that you shut off the motor to check the oil," she said.

"Well, that's nice, ma'am. But I think I've pulled a few more motors out of cars than you have," I said as the rain continued to fall.

"Well, I think you're wrong, so just check the oil with the car running."

I went through the motions and told her that she didn't need any oil, because according to the dipstick, she had a mark of three-quarters on it. With the motor running and all the oil sloshing around, she had enough oil for wherever she was going. I told her she was fine, and then she asked to see the dipstick. After I showed it to her, she looked at it and told me that she wanted me to put some oil in her car. On that note I grabbed a screwdriver and a funnel because we didn't have the proper attachment for the cans of oil.

While the rain is beating down on me, it's times like this, that make you think, and wonder about your direction in life.

After I thought, and wondered, I stabbed the can, and made a hole on one side with the screwdriver. I attempted to make another one on the other side and oil shot out of the first hole, and hit me in my eye, on the side of my neck, and on my jacket. As I looked up I noticed that the lady was smiling about it, and for a second I felt like throwing the can at her head. I put the oil in her car, even though she didn't needed it, topped off her tank, and then told her what she owed me.

"Well, I shouldn't have to pay for a full can of oil, because you spilled some of it."

"Fine, lady. I'll tell you what, Merry Christmas, okay? Just give me the money for the gas, and I'll pay for the oil," I said, as the rain was beating down.

She paid me for the gas, and I turned and walked back towards the office. When I got there, I pushed the door open with enough force so that the door stayed open. Then I took off my jacket, grabbed the paper towels, and sat down behind the desk, wiping oil and water off my face. After I sat down, I noticed that she was still sitting there. She started her car, pulled up to the door, got out with an umbrella, and started walking towards the door.

"You know, I really don't like your attitude, young man!" she said as she walked towards me.
"Lady, don't come in here."
"How dare you tell me what to do!" she said as she headed into the doorway.
"Lady, don't come in here!!" I said as I slowly rose to my feet.
"Grrowl!" Dukie snarled as he scrambled towards her.

For a split second I felt like letting Dukie have his way with her, and I really should have, but I knew that he would really fuck her up. As I leaped over the desk to catch Dukie, I slammed my knee on the open drawer, fell over the desk, regained my balance, and lunged towards Dukie. I barreled into him with such force that I almost knocked him to the floor. Then I grabbed him by the scruff of his neck as he turned to bite me and I yelled out, "Dukie, stop! Dukie, stop!"

As this was taking place, the lady decided to grab the metal oil display rack that was next to her and shield herself with it, which caused fifty cans of oil to scramble away from the mayhem in all different directions.

By now Dukie's jaws were wrapped around my forearm but, because I had eased my grip on him, he didn't clamp down on me. Then I rose to my feet and grabbed hold of Dukie's collar, as I slowly got up. Dukie kept growling at the lady as she started to make another complaint, until I interrupted her and said, "Lady, get in your car and leave, or I swear to God I'll let this fucking dog go, and you can deal with him!"

She stood there for a moment with her mouth open and then put down the oil display, picked up her umbrella, ran off to her car, and left. I apologized to Dukie, petted him for a few minutes, and then limped outside to deal with the oil cans that were spread all over the parking lot.

By the time I got off at 12:30 that night, I was shot. I limped home, climbed the stairs, and headed for my room.

When I got up to the third floor, I noticed that Jimmy Marnell's door was open. Jimmy had been dealing PCP, angel dust, for some time now, but he was also smoking a lot of the shit, too, which happened to be the reason that Vicky had broken up with him a while ago. Aside from that, he had owed a few weeks of rent and my mother was starting to get on my case about it. The last thing I wanted to do at this hour was to try to talk to him about it while he was all stoned out, but I figured I'd better do it.

The lights were off in his room, but the radio was playing real low.

"Jimmy? Jimmy, are you there?" I said as I peered into his room.

As I took a step into his room, I could see his silhouette from the street light as he sat next to the window. He was sitting there not saying a word, with a gun pressed to his forehead.

Oh, this is great. Just what I fucking need tonight.
"Jimmy, what the fuck are you doing? Put the gun down."
"No, Mike, I'm done. I hate my fucking life."
"Yeah, so? Everybody hates their life at some point or another, but they don't blow their heads off about it."
"Mike, just leave, man, and let me do this."
"Don't tell me that, Jimmy. Because, believe me, after today the one thing I do want to do is leave and go to bed."
"So don't worry about this. Go to bed."
"Yeah, well, you know what I meant, and I ain't leaving. So what are you gonna do? Blow your head off, and traumatize the shit out of me."

I knew Jimmy was probably high on PCP. I just didn't know how high, and now that I could see tears dripping from his eyes, I knew that he was hurting. But I did know better than to try and rush him to grab the gun, so I stood there and kept talking with him to try to find out the reason why he wanted to end his life. Three hours later, at four in the morning, he finally told me his reason.

"My life fell apart when my parents divorced," Jimmy said.
"What...?!? What the fuck did you just say? You motherfucker! Give me that gun, 'cause I'm gonna shoot you now!" I told him.
"Oops. I said that to the wrong person, didn't I?" he said.
"You got the balls to tell me it's about your parents? I thought you killed someone or something, and after all the shit I've been through, this... this is your fucking reason?!"
"Well, what can I say, Mike? You're stronger than me."
"No, you know what the difference is between you and me? You're stoned out on angel dust and I'm not; that's the difference between you and me, Jimmy, okay? Now this is what you're gonna do. You're gonna give me the gun and the shit you've been smoking, and then you're gonna stay straight all day tomorrow, okay? And when I come home Sunday morning from work, if you still want to kill yourself, I'll fucking shoot you. Now where's your shit?" I said as I walked towards him.

After a little pause, Jimmy pointed towards his nightstand, and he said it was in the top drawer. I walked over to the nightstand and pulled out the whole drawer, turned towards him, held the drawer in front of him, and said, "Now, gimme the gun."

Jimmy glanced up at me, took the gun away from his head, uncocked it, and placed it in the drawer. I took a step towards him, kissed him on top of his head, and said, "Now go to bed, Jimmy."

It's funny, a few years ago I looked up to Jimmy like he was my big brother. And now, I'm his.

Within that next week, I unloaded Jimmy's shit for him, and put it towards his rent, and gave him back his drawer and his gun- without the bullets. After I asked him if he was all right, we never spoke about it again. About a week or so after that, I finally quit my weekend job because I felt like I had enough of a jump on my savings by now.

CHAPTER 9

THE PHOENIX HAS RISEN

Over the next year or so I started to do pretty good. By now I had two bank accounts and some decent clothes. I was back up to my old weight from working out, and my head was screwed on a little tighter. Unfortunately I couldn't say the same for Mike and Dino. They had both been hit with 5 1/2 to 15 jail terms. I still wrote to them and sent them cards, and I was still visiting my mother from time to time, along with shopping for her and dropping the stuff off.

By now I had quit working at Elias Art Metal and was working at a new place called Salsa Distributors. My buddy Aaron had stopped by my house one day and told me that this frozen food company he was working for was looking for a warehouse man. I took the job and, as it turns out, they were looking for an everything man, not just a warehouse man. I started working there at the end of the summer.

There was some team working in the office, Danny, who was German, and Ellen, his wife, who was Jewish. Anything missed by Danny's rules was usually picked up on by Ellen. When I first started there, I was taking three different busses which would take me about one and a half hours to get there. If I happened to have a car at the time, it would've taken me a half hour tops. After a while of working there, my duties grew. Now I'd also fill in for any salesman or helper who didn't show up that day for work. The company was based in Queens, but the routes were in Brooklyn, Bronx, Coney Island and Harlem. You know, nice quiet suburban areas... not.

There were two brothers who worked for the company, named Mike and Nabby. They were two black guys from Coney Island. Nabby was about 35 years old at the time, but he looked about 50. His brother, Mike, was my age. Anybody with any street smarts could see that Nabby had been through a few battles. I guess that's why we liked each other, because we shared something in common. Danny once told me about the time that Nabby showed up for work with a bunch of newspapers stuffed in his shirt with blood on them. As it turned out, he had been mugged on the train and stabbed, and he had put the newspapers in his shirt to stop the bleeding. Danny asked him why he didn't go right to the hospital after he got stabbed, and Nabby told him innocently enough that he had come to work because he needed the money. It never sat well with me when, a few months later, Danny fired him for coming to work with a little buzz on. I mean, everybody knew that Nabby liked to take a sip in the morning. Shit, I even stopped by a liquor store for him once or twice when I'd go on routes with him. He needed a sip like I needed a cup of coffee in the morning to wake up; otherwise, he would be grumpy all day. It's not like he would get stumbling drunk.

It's not like Nabby had to handle a corporate merger or anything. He was just a helper on the truck. His job responsibilities entailed loading up store freezers after the salesman made a sale. This was a job that Nabby had been doing for about three years and could do with his eyes shut. The day he got fired, I gave him a popsicle for the road. Then we shook hands, and he left.

One day my friend Jeff informed me that his brother, Sammy, had shot and killed himself in his car. It saddened me to hear this because I liked him. It's was a little strange because Jimmy, and Sammy, were best friends at one time. He told me that Sammy's car was for sale real cheap, so I bought it. It was a nice car, but it did have a funny smell to it from the dried blood I found under the seats. I bought the car on a Friday, and I was told I could use the plates to drive the car home and then get them back to Jeff on Monday.

I took the car home, and I decided to clean it up a little bit more. Aaron stopped by while I was working on it. We got to talking, and he asked me if he could rent the car for the weekend for about one hundred dollars. I figured, why not? It would help pay for the car. Then I told him he had to have the car and the plates back to me by Sunday night, so I could give them to Jeff. He agreed and then helped me clean it. When we got done, he gave me the money and left with the car.

I went to visit my mother at the prison on Saturday. Besides that, I just hung around the house, worked out, and listened to "Old Blue Eyes" Frank Sinatra. By eight o'clock on Sunday, I was a little pissed at Aaron. At eleven, I was angry, and by one in the morning I was ready to chew nails. I went to bed at about one thirty and got up at six, figuring I'd have to take the bus. Then took a shower, and went out to walk to the bus stop.

When I got outside, the car was in the driveway, so I figured that maybe I should go inside and check some of the rooms and see if Aaron was there. Sure enough, he was sleeping in the basement. I woke him up by cursing in his face, and he opened his eyes and moaned. I asked him if he was coming to work, and he moaned, "Yes." Then I told him that I shouldn't do it, but I would make him a cup of coffee, so he could get his ass moving. Then I went upstairs.

When I got back downstairs, he was still taking a shower. I told him to hurry the fuck up, because he was now making me late for work, but he still took twenty minutes. By the time he came out, I was pissed off again, and he said, "Mike, don't worry. We'll take the car and still make it to work on time." After thinking about it for a second or two, we got in the car and left. I hopped on the Van Wyck Expressway driving like a nut, I guess because I was pissed and didn't want to be late. When I got to work, the only parking spot I could find was one that sat halfway into a bus stop. I figured I would go inside, show my face, and then go out and move the car in a few minutes. I turned the car off, and Aaron said, "You can't leave the car here. You'll get a ticket."

I said jokingly, knowing I wasn't going to leave the car there, "Why should I care? They're not my plates."

"What plates? There are no plates on the car."

I laughed and said, "That's very funny, Aaron, but you are shitting me, right?"
He looked at me and said, "No, I took them off last night when I brought the car back. They're sitting in your basement."

I'll tell you, if I didn't love him, I would have killed him. The last thing I wanted to do was get hassled by some cop, especially in the morning. I threw him the keys to the car and told him to take my car home now, because I was not going to worry about it at the end of the day. Then he had the balls to tell me that he was going to be late for work so I said, "Aaron, you see me weaving in and out of traffic and speeding, and you don't say shit. You just sit there sipping your coffee, and now when I turn the car off, you tell me there's no plates on the car. Whata' ya', fucking stoned, Aaron?"

Aaron looked at me and said, "How am I going to get back to work?"
"Do you have any money?"
"No."

I flipped him a twenty and told him to take a cab; then I went inside. He came back about an hour later, handed me back my twenty, and told me he went back to my house, put the plates back on the car, and drove back. What a way to start the morning.

Danny and Ellen had two sons, and one of them was born with a facial handicap, as she would nicely put it. What it meant was that his jaw, and palate, were slightly deformed. One day Ellen started explaining to me about the number of surgeries that he had. She said that she was taking him to N.Y.U. in Manhattan, because she felt that it was the best place to handle the situation. When I heard Ellen explaining to me how much work had been done on her son and how much more needed to be done, it made me feel a whole lot more comfortable about my situation, so I decided to talk to Ellen about it. After I showed her my problem with my teeth, she said that she was sure that they could do something for me over there and that she would talk to the doctor and see if she could make an appointment for me to see what it would take to fix my teeth.

I got an appointment shortly after that, and I went. I met a social worker there whose name was Mrs. Huggins. It was a little odd for me at first, because Mrs. Huggins really seemed concerned. I tried to get Medicaid to help pay for it, but, at five hundred per week, they said I was making too much money. So they turned me down. After that didn't work out, N.Y.U. agreed to do the work, and wait until I could start making payments. I was amazed, and could hardly believe my ears when they said this.

As it turned out, I had two options. The first one was a procedure where they would put me under anesthesia and take a piece of bone out of my hip. Then they would re-break my top jaw and insert some of my bone and move my jaw out, set it, and then wire it shut. The other option was to try braces and a type of retainer that I would tighten every night. But I had to wear the thing 24 hours a day. I thought the braces would be a little more comfortable to live with, so I opted for that.

While Ellen was helping me get along in life, Danny kept asking me weird questions about if I had

353

been to jail, how long, how was it, and could I do it again? I answered him honestly, and I told him if I was ever to contemplate going to jail, it would have to be for a suitcase with about a million in cash before I would even think about going there again.

This conversation went on for about two months, give or take, and he always talked to me about it when we were alone. Finally one day I got a little pissed off about it, and I asked him what he was getting at. Danny looked at me and then asked me if I had ever killed anyone before. I told him that I hadn't, but that killing someone is not a problem. As a matter of fact, having died once or twice myself, killing someone is quite easy. Dealing with all of the consequences that follow is where the problems lie, in my opinion. I can't say that he understood what I meant, but we did stop talking about it for a while.

I kept up with my visits to N.Y.U. for the next few months, and it was great because my braces seemed to be working and in only a short time.

I went to visit my mother one day up at the prison. We talked for a while about various things, and then she started to explain to me that she thought that she would have a good chance of getting out the next time she went before the parole board. I asked her why she felt this way, and she explained to me that the first reason was because she had done the minimum time required on her sentence, which was already five years. The second reason why she thought she would be getting out was because she now ran the law library. She felt that the prison didn't really want someone with her intelligence handling inmates' grievances or getting their sentences reduced anymore, so they might be pleased to get rid of her, she felt.

"Yeah, Ma, but what if they're really pissed off about it?"

My mother gave me an interesting look and said, "Hmm, I never thought of it that way."
"Well, how soon is it before you go before the parole board?"
"About another five or six months."
"Well, maybe you should start throwing some sheep to the lions, just to soften them up," I joked.
"Yeah, right, tell me about it."

Unfortunately for my mother, as it turned out, she didn't make parole.

The next day at work I was talking with Ellen, and I happened to mention that I had an open case with the N.Y. Transit Authority.

"Well, why don't you have a lawyer working on it?" Ellen asked.
"I don't know. Maybe I just kinda lost faith in them. Besides, I don't really know any good ones."
"Well, I know this lawyer, and he's very good. Maybe you should give him a call."

I took Ellen's advice and called him one day. After I got done speaking on the phone with him for a little while, he seemed smart, so I made an appointment to see him.

After stopping by his office in Manhattan, I was impressed with him, and I decided to give him my case. After that I walked around the city for a couple of hours, and then I went home.

My grandfather, who was living back home now, was getting sicker more often these days, and I had to take him to the hospital once or twice. By now I was doing more cooking and all the shopping for us. There were times, though, when I didn't feel like coming straight home from work and cooking for the both of us, but I knew that I had to do it for him, just like he had done for me when I was a child.

As far as the house was concerned, Jimmy Marnell, Dave, "Uncle" Phil and Jim in the "raven room" were still living in the house. Jimmy was still getting high, Dave was still drinking but he was harmless, and the guy who used to deal coke in my house had moved out. Friends of mine would stop by occasionally, and we'd whip up a barbecue together. But for the most part, I just stayed home, worked out, and read books. I didn't go out much because most of the people I knew were still up to old tricks, and I couldn't be bothered with that stuff any more. These days I was more interested in keeping my shit together.

One day at work, Danny and Ellen told me that they were taking a three-day vacation this weekend coming up and that an older friend would be opening up the store. They told me that they would give me one of their cars for the weekend as long as I made sure that I was at the warehouse at 6:30 a.m. to open up on Monday, so I told them no problem.

I can't tell you why I picked that Sunday, maybe because I had my hands on a decent car, but I decided to go see my father's brother, Uncle Mike. My plan was to try to find my grandfather's house first, because I kinda remembered how to get there. Then I might be able to remember the shortcut that my father and I would always take over to my Uncle Mike's house, I reasoned.

By now I didn't really expect for my grandfather to still be alive, but it still seemed like the best option for me to try.

I didn't have any type of directions to go on, and the last time I was there I was 12 years old. A lot of shit had happened since then. But for the most part, I memorized how to get there, and I knew they lived on Beaver Damn Road, next to an apple orchard.

I left late in the afternoon and headed out to Jersey. I didn't know what to expect once I got out there, but I figured that I could either have the door slammed in my face, maybe get shot, or invited in. I decided that none of that really mattered to me, because I just wanted to know where my father was buried so I could pay my respects.

The drive was pretty somber, especially when I started seeing some old sights that I hadn't seen since I had driven this way with my father. I remembered a game we used to play called "Mustang." The first person to spot a Ford Mustang on the highway while we were driving would get a point. I'm not sure, but sometimes I think he used to let me win.

I finally reached Upper Saddle River in New Jersey. The only problem now was that they had built so many new stores on the main strip, it all looked quite different. It took a bit longer, but I found the street to get to my grandfather's house. Once I got on the street, I remembered it was supposed to lead me to a few other streets and landmarks I had memorized, but it didn't. The problem now was that they had either knocked down and rebuilt these huge houses or subdivided the big lots and stuck big houses between other big houses. I had heard that ex-President Nixon had a house in this area, and I didn't believe it until I saw the size of some of these houses.

After driving around for a little while, I thought that maybe they had knocked down my grandfather's house and that I was now looking in vain. But then as I was just about to give up hope, I found it. When I looked in the driveway I saw family-type cars in the driveway, and I knew that my grandfather wouldn't be driving these types of cars. Back in 1975, the whole family out here drove brand new Caddies, and after having seen some of their garbage trucks working in Manhattan, I assumed that they were still in pretty good shape financially.

After trying to find the shortcut to my uncle's for almost an hour, I decided to backtrack and start from the beginning. I got out to the main road and traveled up and down looking for the streets we used to turn down, to no avail. I kept ending up at this one intersection that was slightly familiar, and I would drive in either direction until I would get lost and then turn back.

Being that it was starting to get late and that I had tried to find the street a few more times, I figured I'd make one more attempt before I headed home. When I was about a block off the main intersection, I saw this house that they had turned into a real estate agent's office. Being that there was a car parked in front, I thought that maybe they might have some type of map of the area, so I pulled into the parking lot and turned the car off.

It was an odd-looking place in the sense that it also still looked like a home, and being that it was late, I thought maybe they were closed. I got out, and I started to head around the front of the car when this big puff of smoke came out from under the hood of the car. I figured that the car must've overheated, until I realized it didn't smell like steam-it smelled like rubber burning. I popped the hood open and jumped back in case flames were to jump out from under the hood, but fortunately there were none.

The smoke cleared, and I tried to look for the problem. When I couldn't find one, I got back into the car and turned the key. Nothing... not even a growl. I hadn't noticed it at first, but there was a little garage next door, real country like. These two guys were closing it up, and it was actually a mechanics garage. These guys had seen the smoke and started to walk over. While they were looking under the hood, a lady came out of the real estate office, talking on a portable telephone. She had rollers in her hair, so I could tell that she wasn't open for business. I guess she came out to see what was going on in her parking lot. By now both guys were checking out my car, and one guy looked up at me and said, "Yo,' dude. you're screwed. Your electrical harness caught on fire."

The lady must've heard this, because she offered me her phone to call someone. I told her that I didn't have anyone that I could call. She suggested that I call a cab, and I told her that I lived in New York City. Then the guy who had been looking under the hood said, "Even if I ordered the part tomorrow morning, it probably wouldn't get here for about two days," and suggested I squirrel up in a hotel. I told him that I would, but that I had to open up the store for my boss in the morning.

Then the lady said, "If you don't mind my asking, what are you doing here, being that you don't know anybody here?"

I explained to her that I had some family out here that I hadn't seen in quite a number of years and I had driven out here to see if I could find them. I briefly explained that I hadn't been invited and that it was a bit of a surprise. I told her that the reason I had stopped here was to see if she had some type of map I could look at, because I knew they lived across the street from an apple orchard on Beaver Dam Road. She told me that it wasn't an apple orchard any more; now it was a country club. Then she said, "Wait a minute, if you know their name and the street they live on, why don't you just look in the phone book?"

"Oh yeah, I didn't even think of that." Even though I had, I didn't call because I was afraid that someone might just hang up on me. Oh well, back to square one.

She asked me their names, and I told her Mike and Joanne Garramone. She looked at me a little funny and then walked back in the house. I went back to talking to the two mechanics. I felt as if they were my only chance of getting back home. Thank God, I thought, they were nice.

The lady walked back out of the house with the phone to her ear a minute later and said, "Michael?" I turned to her and said, "Yes?"even though I hadn't told her my name yet.

"I have your Aunt Joanne on the phone."

I took the phone from her, and my Aunt, whom I hadn't spoke to in years said' "Michael? Is that you?"

"Yes."

"O' my God, I can't believe it. Don't move. I'm sending your cousin's to come get you."

A number of feelings went through my mind, relieved, happy, weird, and slightly confused. Nobody had cared about me for so many years that it was odd hearing it in somebody's voice.

The mechanics gave me their card and told me to call them in the morning if I wanted them to order the part, and I thanked them. I asked the lady how she had gotten a hold of my aunt's number so fast, and she said, "Michael, your Aunt Joanne and I have been friends for years. We go to church together."

The lady waited and chatted with me and then went in to check on her kids. My cousins drove up in a new Jeep a few minutes later. Michael, whom I had liked instantly when we met as kids, was driving, and Robert, who was always aloof, was in the passenger's seat. It was great to see them. We awkwardly said our hellos, shook hands, and I climbed into the Jeep, and left.

We drove down some familiar territory that I had traveled during my very recent journeys and then turned left on a street I had missed. After a short ride, the street began to take shape, and then it became familiar once again. The apple orchard had indeed become a country club, and there were a few new houses built there. I blurred my eyes, and I could visualize myself driving down this familiar street years before. When we pulled down the driveway, even though it was starting to get dark out, I could still make out the Corvette, Mercedes, and Jaguar in the driveway. We went in through the back door by the pool. It took about twenty steps to get up to this door that let you into the back of the kitchen. I walked in, and it seemed like everybody was sitting there. My Uncle Mike was sitting there, my Aunt Joanne, and some of the other kids were also there. I didn't know what to expect, and then Elizabeth spoke and broke the silence. She smiled when she was done. Whew, there's one ally, I thought. Then we talked about going crab fishing when we were younger. A few stories came tumbling out after that.

We all started to get along after that, but I could tell that Mike was pissed, enraged, hurt and confused all wrapped up in one. I knew these feelings well, because by this time I had rolled up all of these emotions into one entity and would defuse them myself when necessary. The conversation eventually made its way downstairs, and as I walked down there, I noticed that the whole wall was covered with pictures.

After talking for a while longer, I noticed that the wall was full of pictures of my father growing up. I had been through some pain in the last several years, but this was a different kind of hurt. I was accustomed to looking at one beat-up old picture I had of him, but I wasn't prepared to see a whole collage from birth to death. Tears rolled down my cheeks, but I wasn't crying, the tears just found their way outside.

Mike started to talk now, but it wasn't that old family story kind of talk. He told me that on the morning that John had died he had twenty thousand dollars on him for a down payment on a sanitation route in Manhattan that Mike, Ralph, and John were buying. He added that he and Ralph had almost lost the route, and that routes didn't come easy in Manhattan. After I explained to him what my mother had told me years earlier about how someone must've taken it out of the store after her accident with John, Mike looked at me very unsure. Then Mike asked me if I knew what had happened to the money.

"Mike, I was a kid. What the hell did I know about twenty grand in a suitcase?"
My Aunt Joanne changed the subject by asking me about my missing teeth.
"How did you know I was missing some teeth?"
"I could tell," she answered.

If there was one thing I remembered about my Aunt Joanne, it was that she could just look at you and know what was going on without saying a word.

I explained to her about my bus accident and about my motorcycle crash.
"My God ! It sounds like you went through hell."
"Yeah, I was there a few times. But I'm better now."

We talked for about two hours longer until I realized that I still had to get home that night somehow. Robert made a couple of phone calls to some towing companies, and after hearing a few of the prices I told him to call a few limo companies just to get some kind of ideas on their prices. Oddly enough, it would have been cheaper for me to take a limo home.

After thinking about it for a few minutes, I realized that if I didn't take the car back with me

358

tonight, I probably would never get it home. I called back a towing company and gave them a time to meet me over by the car. After I hung up, I asked Mike if I could visit John's grave, and Mike didn't seem too happy about it. Then Joanne suggested that she would get the key to the mausoleum from Ralph and set something up with me so I could pay my respects. She also told me that John was buried with his parents, which I thought was nice. Mike told me that he had heard about me being in the newspapers two more times, and we talked about this subject for a little while until the towing company called and said that they were over by the car. It was time to go.

I shook Mike's hand and said goodbye, and then Joanne gave me a hug and told me to keep in touch. I took one last glance at John's pictures and then left with Mike Jr. and Robert. When we got to the car, we all got out, hugged in the darkness, and then I left.

After a little small talk with the tow truck driver, I settled in for the ride. It felt a little weird being driven home from my Uncle Mike's house, because it felt similar to when my father would drive me home after spending the weekend out at Jersey when I was a kid. Well, it might not have been one hundred percent, but at least I made some peace with some of the pain I had as a child.

By the time I got home, I had about an hour to get to work and, being that my car was at the warehouse, that meant that I would have to jump on three busses in a matter of minutes. For some reason I didn't have it in me, though. I felt burnt, excited, happy and sad, and the last thing I felt like doing was dragging my ass onto three busses to go to some bullshit job, especially after getting a second glimpse of the direction that my life should have taken. After thinking about it for a few minutes, I finally decided that I couldn't let that part of my past interfere with my obligation to the present. But I did feel like I needed some type of sleep, even if it was only twenty minutes. So I went inside, set my alarm clock for twenty minutes, and lay down.

About an hour later I heard my alarm clock screaming. Shit, I was late. I jumped up and ran down to the bus stop. Of course, whenever you're running late and at the mercy of others, life always seems to move in slow motion, and today was no exception. By the time I got to work, needless to say, Danny's friend was pissed. Even though he was pissed, I knew that the morning hadn't been so bad on him because David, the old warehouseman, had hung around to give him a hand. But I played my apologetic routine for him, just for good measure.

When Danny and Ellen showed up the next day, I had already made arrangements for their car to be towed over to the shop. Danny was a little pissed off at me for leaving his friend in a spot that morning, but he cooled out after I showed him all of my receipts to back up my story.

It's funny, but I wasn't really doing a whole hell of a lot around the warehouse these days. I guess it was because I kept on top of everything. As a matter of fact, it seemed like I was spending more and more time taking Ellen around on her personal errands. I mean, it wasn't like I was complaining but it was like 8, 9, 10 hours per week with her.

My teeth were finally straight, which was a major relief. I could hardly thank the people at N.Y.U. enough or Ellen herself for what they had done for me. I was especially grateful because I couldn't remember the last time anyone, let alone strangers, had done something for me.

I ended up working at Salsa Distributors for a total of two years, and I had managed to save about three grand. It was the first time, as a young adult, that I was doing well, and I was at peace with myself and the world.

One day my mother called me and told me that she wanted to put my phone in her name. When I asked her why she wanted to do this, she told me that she was getting out of prison and that she needed to start building up some type of credit. I didn't really mind putting my phone in her name on one hand, but ever since I had given her the number, she had been running up my phone bill to two hundred and fifty dollars a month. I wouldn't have minded if it was like this once in a while, but this had been going on for about nine months. God forbid if I would complain about it, because she would tell me matter of factly, "You're working steady; you can handle it." She also told me that she wanted me to tell Dave and Jimmy that they had to move out. When I asked her why she wanted them to move out, she told me it was because she didn't want any of my old crowd around.

"Look Ma, I don't know where you're getting your information from, but it's a little fucked up. Jimmy, all right. But there's nothing wrong with Dave. As a matter of fact, Dave doesn't even have to be asked. He enjoys cutting the grass and cleaning up the yard. He might drink a beer or two, but that's all. He's fine."

"I don't care. I want them both out," she said.

"Well, I'll tell Jimmy, but you can tell Dave yourself."

We spoke for a few minutes more after that, and then we hung up.

Man, I thought, this kinda sucks. I wonder if I'm next. I really don't want to be around here if she starts running that "rules" bullshit again. I better start saving money just in case the shit hits the fan again.

Ricky Dale stopped by my house today with Bobby, Jimmy Marnell's younger brother. Ricky told me that he was going to go and get his passport, because he was going to go and visit his father in South America.

"South America? What's he doing there?"

"He lives there."

"Since when?"

"Oh! Shit. I didn't tell you the story?"

"What story?"

"Well, about two years ago before my motorcycle accident, I was living out in Northport with him, and one day he comes home and says, 'That's it. I'm done, Ricky. I'm outta here. I'm done with the rat race. I'm leaving.' So he tells me that he's gonna take off and go and live in South America. You know my old man, Mike. Sometimes he talks crazy, and I thought he was shitting me this time. For a few weeks he was talking about it, and he kept asking me if I wanted to go with him. Then he buys a school bus, packs it, and a few days later, he comes home and says, 'That's it. I'm leaving, Ricky. Are you coming?' After I told him that I wasn't, he told me that the rent was paid for two months and left. About a month later I got a postcard from South America from my pops. He told me that he had bought a piece of property and built a small hut on it."

"Get the fuck outta here!"

"I'm telling you, I was shocked myself. Anyhow I'm going down to visit him in a month. You'll see. I'll send you a postcard from there."

After Ricky got done telling us about his planned trip, Bobby went upstairs to see his brother. He came down a little while later and said that his brother didn't look good and that there was no talking sense to him.

"I know, Bobby, and now my mother wants him to move out."

"Well, who knows? Maybe that will wake him up." Bobby said.

At work Danny started asking me about killing people again and jail.

"Danny, this is like the third or fourth time you've asked me about this. Who is it that someone like you- who has a nice house, a nice business, nice kids, and a nice wife- wants to kill, and for what reason?"

Danny looked around the empty office, then stared at me for a second, and said, "I want to kill this guy I bought the business from."

"Why the fuck would you want to kill him?"

"Why? 'Cause every month I've got to pay him about four grand, and it kills me. That fuck doesn't need the money," he said.

"Yeah, but Danny, this is not the time to be griping about the agreement you made about the size of your payments to him. Besides that, how do you think by killing him it's going to release you from your obligation of paying his family?"

"I don't think he has any family."

"Come on, a guy like that who doesn't need your money ain't got nobody around him?"

"Who cares? I just hate the motherfucker. Maybe you could just run him over with a car one day when he comes to get his payment."

"Well, don't take it personally, Danny, but I'm not a soldier for hire in anyone else's personal war. I've got my own personal reasons for that. Now let me ask you this. Let's say you kill this guy, and you don't have to make any more payments and you're going along for... 1, 3, 9 months and, Bam! You get nailed for it. What then, Danny? Could you look back and say it was worth it? You'll lose everything you have, everything you worked your ass off for, gone. Living in an eight by twelve foot cell, hoping some dude doesn't want to stab you over an orange."

"Yeah, well, I guess you're right."

Even though Danny agreed with me, his answer almost sounded more like a blow off towards me to change the subject. I really thought the whole conversation was strange coming from a mature, intelligent, successful businessman like Danny.

On the weekends my friend Aaron would work as a DJ at parties, and since he still lived at home, I would let him store all his records at my house.

One day he stopped by with Patti, the girl who lived around the corner from me. I still thought she was pretty cute, so I asked Aaron if she was dating anybody. After he told me that she wasn't, I asked her when she was going to ask me out on a date.

"What? I'm supposed to ask you out on a date?"
"Well, yeah, this is the eighties, you know."
"Well, you know where I live. You can come over and ask me," she said.
"Well, what about your father? I heard he was a nut."
"Well, I don't know who told you that, but you look like a tough guy. I'm sure you could handle it."
"All right. Give me your phone number."

After she did, I helped Aaron with a few more of his crates, and then they left.

I got a call from my mother. She had gotten paroled and wanted to know if I could come to Bedford Women's Facility where they had transferred her some time ago to pick her up. I told her I would, and she gave me the time and date.

On one hand I was very happy that my mother was getting out after five and a half years, but on the other hand I didn't know how happy I'd be once she got home. When the day came, I rented a car and drove up to Bedford, N.Y.

After I got there, the people at the prison made me wait another two hours before they let her out. First, I got her boxes, and then they let her out. I guess they were really going to miss her. It was good to see her, but I could tell in the light of day that jail had aged her. We hugged, said our hellos, and then left. I asked my mother if she wanted to get a good meal somewhere in town and, after being a little hesitant at first, she decided that she would. We went and had a nice lunch and talked about old times; after that we headed home.

On the way home, I got a little lost just about the same time that my mother and I were starting to have an argument. By the time I hit Times Square in Manhattan, my mother told me to pull the car over because she wanted to get out.

"Come on, Ma. Let me at least take you home, and then you can take the car, and go take off for a while in it."
"No, pull the car over now, and let me out," she said.

I pulled the car over; I handed her some money, and she got out. I stayed parked there for a little while until I saw her get lost in the crowd, and then I went home.

It was still daylight out by the time she got home, and after looking around the house, she walked over to me and said, "What the fuck did you do to the house!"
"What do you mean, what did I do to the house? I didn't do anything."
"What do you mean you didn't do anything? It looks like a shit hole here."
"Well, you know, Ma, five years of wear and tear on a house full of tenants is going to take its toll

on the place after a while."

"I can't believe you. I can't fucking believe you," she said as she walked away.

About a week after my mother was home, she asked me if I could borrow two thousand dollars from Danny and Ellen at work. When I asked her what it was for, she explained that she wanted to do a refinance on the house, and she needed the money for an application fee, and some of the money was going to be used to do some minor repairs. I was a little reluctant to ask them, but after my mother worked me over about how I had helped put the house in the shape it was in, I did. Danny said that he would do it for me regardless of what I wanted it for, but I would be responsible for it. I still had some of my own money, but I decided keep it on the side just in case things blew up with my mother, this way I wouldn't be left without a pot to piss in.

An old friend of my mother's named Danny stopped by the house one day. I hadn't seen him since he and his sisters used to babysit my cousins and me years ago. Whenever we would act up, Danny would dress up like the "Bad Lady" and scare the shit out of us. From that point on all my mother or aunts would have to do was mention the Bad Lady's name to turn us into little angels. After talking with Danny, he told me that his sister Geraldine was selling a pretty good car cheap because the transmission had blown in it. A few days later, I went and took a look at the Thunderbird and decided to buy it. Once I got it to my house, I askedFreddy Capeeto, to help me to fix it. A couple of days after that, we had it up and running for the most part, but it still needed some fine tuning.

During that week, my cousin Ronnie stopped by the house to say hello to my mother, and he brought Crazy Joey with him. Crazy Joe had lived across the street from my father's luncheonette, and he and my cousin Ronnie met there and had become good friends. Right then the two of them both had an apartment together in Manhattan. The both of them stayed over my house for a few days, and we all had a good time. Then one day Crazy Joe said that he wanted to go back to Manhattan. That meant that I would have to drive him to Main Street so he could catch the # 7 train. I figured that while I was heading over there, I'd stop to get some gas for the T-bird, so I took the plates off my car, that wasn't working, and threw them on the T-bird.

When I got there, I pulled up to one set of pumps and waited for the young colored kid inside to turn on the pumps. After waving to the kid, I politely waited a minute or two for him to turn on the pump.

Then I checked the pump and saw that he still hadn't turned them on. After waiting another couple of minutes, I was starting to get a little pissed off with him, so I walked over to the office, stuck my head in the door, and said, "Do you sell gas here?!"

Even though the kid was on the phone, he still took an extra minute to look up at me and say, "Yeah."

"Well, can I buy some?"

"Yeah, but umm, you've got to drive over to the other pumps. That one ain't working."

"And you let me stand out there for five minutes because you couldn't tell me that? Here, give me ten dollars on that other pump," I said as I handed him the money.

When I got back in the car, Crazy Joe asked me what the problem was.

"I don't know. Either this kid has a bad attitude, or he's afraid to speak to strangers."

Then I drove over to the other pumps, and the kid made me stand there and wait for another couple of minutes before he turned the pump on. When I got done, I sat in the car and, just as I went to start the car, four cop cars pulled up from the 109th precinct that was two blocks away and boxed me in. They jumped out with their guns drawn and yelled for everyone else around to leave. As this happened, I saw Crazy Joe reach for the door handle. While expecting a barrage of bullets to rain down upon me, I yelled, "Joey, don't do it, or we're dead!"

Joey stopped himself and froze, as the cops were screaming at us to put our hands on the dashboard.

"Now, Joey," I said calmly while my hands were on the dashboard, "is there anything you want to tell me? Anything at all?" I said to him calmly as we slowly made eye contact.

There was a reason we called Joe "Crazy Joe," and when he slowly looked away for a second I figured he was going to enlighten me as to why we had six guns pointed at us, staring death in the face. Then he looked back at me with a surprised look on his face and said, "Oh shit, Mike. You know what? For once in my life, I'm clean."

"Okay, cool, can you put your hands on the dashboard now, please?"

I can't tell you how good it made me feel to see him go from being a scared cat into a relaxed puppy.

"All right, Joey. Let's go through the motions here, and see what this is about now."

The cops made us get out of the car and, with our arms raised, then they frisked us.

"What's the problem, Officer?"
"Don't act stupid with me. You know what the problem is."
"If you say so, Officer."
"All right, now come over here and stand in front of the gas pumps!"

I didn't know what was going on, but I did see that this colored kid was now smiling from ear to ear.

"All right, you. Come out of the office. Is this them?" the cop said as the kid walked out of the office.
"Whoa, whoa, whoa, what the hell is going on here?" I asked.
"There was an armed robbery here a couple of days ago. Now shut the fuck up!" the cop said.
"Officer, I've lived here my whole life. Do you think I'm stupid enough to rob a gas station two blocks away from the 109th Precinct? And I'm dumb enough to come back to the same place in broad

daylight a few days later??"

"I told you to shut up!"

When I looked back at the colored kid, he had on a half-smile, a look of hate, and smugness, in his eye, but it had nothing to do with him getting robbed. After standing there for a few seconds, one of the cops keyed into his smirk and said, "Take a good look at these guys, kid. This is no joke."

We stood there patiently as this young colored kid was deciding our fate. While this is going on, a small group of colored kids his age showed up out of nowhere, and they started whooping it up. One of them starts saying, "Oh yeah, oh yeah, you got'em, you got' em. Dat's them.'"

The oddest thing I noticed about these kids was that they each had twenty dollar shopping bags of candy on them and it was nowhere near Halloween.

"Officer, these kids come out of nowhere, and they know we did this? And look at them. They each have a huge bag of candy. This is a fucking set-up, this kid robbed himself," I said to the cop standing next to me.

Crazy Joe had a stone cold stare on this kid the whole time, and I soon followed it. After another minute or two of this kid playing it off, he looked at one of the cops and said, "Naa, dat ain't dem." I wasn't sure about Joey, but I took a sigh of relief for me and this fucking kid's hide. Then the one cop asked me for my license, insurance and registration. Being that I didn't have all paperwork done on the car yet, I got nailed with a bunch of tickets, but it was definitely the lesser of three evils.

After the cop got done with running out of ink and left, I got back into the car. Joey looked at me and said, "Yeah, that kid got fucking robbed."

"Tell me the fuck about it. Instead of making a drop in the box, he made a drop in his pocket."

Joey didn't say anything as I started up the car, but then he turned to me and said "Mike, do me a favor? You got like a baseball bat or something?"

"Joey... what are you talking about?"

"I'm gonna bust this kid's ass for being a wiseass."

"Come on, Joey. Forget about it. It's over."

"Forget about it! Mike, do you know with my past record if this fucking, smiling punk would have picked us out, I'd be doing at least ten years."

"Look, Joey. Believe me, I know how you feel, but busting this kid's ass is not the answer. Let's just forget about it and call this one a close shave, all right?"

Crazy Joe looked at me for a long second and then said, "Yeah, all right, Mike... We'll call it a close one."

Within a couple of weeks, the refinance went through on my mother's house. Then my mother asked me if I would quit my job and work on the house full-time. Aside from her complaining that I was partly responsible for the wear and tear that the house had taken over the years, she told me that she would pay me for my time in one lump sum once the house was done, and she would get another refinance on it. The main reason I didn't like the sound of this was because, if for some reason we were to get into an argument and I had to move out, I'd be screwed without a job. Finally, after she busted my balls about it for about a week, every day, so I agreed to do it.

After I explained my intentions to Danny and Ellen and told them that I was going to leave in two weeks, I was asked about the two thousand dollars they had lent me. I assured them that they would have their money by the end of the week. I didn't want to tell them that I had already asked my mother about their money, and she told me that they could wait a little while longer for their money. I figured that, if worse came to worse, I could always go to the neighborhood loan shark and get their money for them. I figured I'd rather do that then use the emergency money I had stashed. Within two weeks I was working on my mother's house.

One day out of the blue, Patti, the cute girl from around the corner, called my house. I found out about it later on that night, after my mother told me that she had spoken with Patti on the phone for two hours.

"What did the two of you need to talk about for two hours?"
"You," she answered.
"Me? And exactly what did the two of you have to say?"
"Well, nothing really. But she sounds like a nice girl. I think you should go out on a date with her."
"Oh, really? Well, look, Ma, I appreciate your concern, but I don't need anybody to set up any dates for me, okay?"
"Okay, but she does sound like a nice girl, that's all."

A little while later I called Patti on the phone number that she had left me and asked her what she and my mother had talked about, but she didn't have too many answers for me, either. We ended up talking for about a half hour and, because she seemed to be expecting it, I asked her on a date and set it up for that weekend.

During the course of that week, I had been working long hours, and I actually looked forward to going out with Patti that weekend. The night of our date I got dressed up, picked up some flowers, and then rode over to her house. When I got there, Patti opened up the door in her sweatpants and then put a strange look on her face.

"What the hell do you want?" she said.
"Excuse me?"
"What... are you doing here!"
"I'm here for our date."
"Our date... was for yesterday!"
"Get the hell out of here."
"No, you get the hell out of here."
"Wait a minute. We had a date set up for Friday night, right?"
"Right, and today is Saturday."
"No way."

Patti looked at me a little funny and then said, "Are you serious?"

"Patti, I'm sorry, I must have got caught up with work and lost a day. You don't think I'd be dumb enough to stand a girl up on a date and then show up at her house the next day with flowers, do you?"

Patti looked at me funny again and then said, "You are serious. Well, nobody has ever stood me up on a date before."

"Look, I'm sorry, okay? I'll make it up to you tonight all right?"

"Well, you had better make it up to me," she said as she held open the door. "You can watch TV in the living room while I get ready."

Patti's mother came home a few minutes after that, so I stood up and introduced myself and told her that I was taking her daughter out on a date.

"You're not the Michael who was supposed to be here last night, were you?"

"Well, actually I am."

"Really? And Patti decided to go out with you again?"

"Well, why do you ask like that?"

"Because she was really mad at you last night, and said she would never speak to you again. That's why"

"Well, I explained to Patti that I've really been putting in such long hours rebuilding my mother's house that I must've lost a day."

Patti's mother and I talked for a little while, and then Patti came down the stairs and, boy, did she look good. We went out and had a very good time up on Bell Boulevard in Bayside. I took her home at about 2:00 in the morning, and I gave her a peck on the lips and then said good night. As I rode back home and thought about the nice evening we had just had, I wondered if I should get involved with Patti on a deeper level.

After working on my mother's house for a little while, the house was really starting to come along. But that's not to say that my mother and I were getting along that well. I stuck with the one-track mind of just getting the house done so I could get paid and then leave with some nice pocket change. Then one day out of the blue, my lawyer on the bus case called me and asked me if I would settle my case for $22,500.

"Twenty-two thousand five hundred?! Hell, yeah, I'll settle for that. Where do I sign?"

The lawyer explained that he could probably have a check for me in a few weeks and told me that he would call me when it was ready.

About a week and a half after that, I got a phone call from Ellen. She asked me if I could be expected to drop off their money. I apologized for it being late and told her that I would bring it to her.

"Oh, by the way, your lawyer called on your bus case. He said he wants you to call his office. I guess he thinks you still work here"

Right after I got off the phone with Ellen, I called my lawyer, and he told me he had a check for me.

"Well, when can I come and get it?" I said, wanting to go there right at that moment to get it.
"Well, how about a week from tomorrow?"

I thought his answer was a little strange at first, but I'd waited this long; another week wouldn't kill me, I guess.
"All right, that's fine," I said.

By now the house was really coming along. My mother had someone put in new windows, all 33 of them, and the house also had gray vinyl siding put on with white trim. She also had someone install a new boiler and a new rug on the three flights of stairs in the hallway. In the meantime, I did all the painting, paneling, tiling, and sheet rock. I also re-stained all of the paneling in the hallway and bedrooms that my father and I had put up years before.

My mother was also up to her old tricks again with garage sales and flea markets. It seemed like, every time I cleaned up one area, she'd fill it back up with this junk. But even though I thought she was spending money foolishly, the only thing I really cared about was that she finally gave me a check for Danny and Ellen.

I went over to Salsa Distributors that Friday afternoon, and for some reason something in the air felt strange. Ellen was sitting at her desk as was Danny, but Danny seemed very uneasy.

"Hey, guys, what's up? I'm sorry about the delay."
"Yeah, well at least I don't have to send someone over to your house to break your legs," Danny said.

Being that it was a little out of character for Danny to act this way with me and I didn't have a job to lose any more, I said "Well, you'd better send someone you don't like and someone who knows how to duck."

Danny looked at me for a strange second, and then Ellen said, "So tell me, Mike, what happened with your lawyer?"

"Well, he got me a settlement of $22,500."
"Really? That's great!" Ellen said.
"Yeah, and you know what, Ellen? I can't even express to you in words how grateful I am for you helping me with this lawyer and for getting my teeth fixed at N.Y.U. Danny, would you mind if I gave Ellen a hug and a kiss?"
"No, no, be my guest."

After a few minutes the workers started to come back in with a few of the trucks, and it being Friday, they came upstairs to the office for their pay. I said my hellos to them, and then Danny asked me to come with him while Ellen paid them. We walked downstairs and into the warehouse by the freezers.

"So what's up, Danny?"

Danny looked at me and then away for a second and said, "I want you to do me a favor," as he looked back at me.

Just by the way he seemed to be asking, I was pretty sure it wasn't about walking his dog or coming into work for a day.

"Well, what kinda favor, Danny?"

"Well, what I want you to do," he said as he looked away from me again, "is to break in here one night, and I want you to bust up the office. I also want you to take some bleach and wipe down the doors and railings, and I'll give you back this two grand you just gave me," he explained.

"You want me to break in here, trash the place, then wipe down the whole place with a bleach rag."

"Yeah," he said.

"Look, Danny... I don't know what you got yourself involved in, and I don't care to know, but like I told you once before, I don't sell those services. If I didn't know you so well, I'd swear it smelled like something that I don't want to be a part of. So good luck and if you don't mind I'm going to say goodbye to Ellen."

We stared at each other for a second, and then Danny nodded his head and looked away. I went upstairs, kissed Ellen on the cheek goodbye, and left.

The following week I went to my lawyer's office to pick up my check. After a little small talk he handed me some papers to sign and then gave me a $15,000 check.

"What's this? Where's the rest?"

"What do you mean? That's it."

"You told me I was going to get a $22,500 dollar check."

"Well, you did, but then we had to subtract all of the fees from it."

"Fees!? You mean to tell me you got $7500 in fees from me?"

"No... I only got about $1600. Your other lawyers who were on this case had to get paid, too."

"You mean I had more than one lawyer in this office working on it?"

"No, the other lawyers, the ones you had hired over the years."

"What!? There was only one lawyer, the first one, who ever did shit for me. Besides that, none of them did anything. They got paid, too?"

"Well, yes."

"What about the last lawyer I had? Did he get anything?"

"Well, he got the most money because he had the case the longest."

"How much did he get?"

"A little more than $5000."

"What! A little more than $5000 and he basically told me to go fuck myself. No, no way. Did you cut him a check yet?"

"Well, of course I did. I had to."

"Then I want to sue him."

"Mike, I'm telling you like a friend: Forget it. You're not going to find a lawyer that's going to sue another lawyer for you, and even if you did you'd be suing a lawyer. It would take years just to get to court, and cost you money. Next time you've got a lawyer you're not happy with, fire him as soon as possible because you'll be charged a fee even if he doesn't do a thing for you."

I'll tell you it really made me want to beat $5000 worth of shit out of that other lawyer, but society has its rules about things, I guess.

When I got back home that day my mother had just come home from some flea market and "Uncle" Phil was helping her to unload her car. For whatever reason, I didn't really feel like telling my mother my good news at this time. As a matter of fact, it took me a week to tell her the news, but it only took a few days for her to ask me to let her borrow it.

She explained to me that she was starting to run a little short on money. A lot of work was done on the house, but there was still a bit left to do. So because I wanted to see this thing through, I lent it to her. The deal we made was that she was going to pay me back my 15 thousand and another twenty thousand for doing all the work on the house. I really didn't agree on the price, but I just wanted to get the house done for her, get my money back, and move on with my life.

About one week after this, Ellen called me, and she sounded kind of frantic. She asked me if I could come over to the warehouse. Feeling a little leery about the place after Danny and I had our last conversation, I asked her what it was about even though I was afraid I knew what it was about.

"Michael... it's Danny. He was arrested for murder."

"Oh, Ellen. You're shitting me."

"Michael, would I shit you about something like this?"

"I'm sorry, Ellen. I didn't mean it that way. I'll be right there."

As I drove over there, I couldn't believe Danny really killed someone, and I really hoped that it wasn't the guy he had talked to me about. How stupid would you have to be to kill this guy, especially with the position that Danny was in with him, I thought.

When I got there, Ellen was very upset, and she ran over, hugged me, and said, "Oh, my God, Michael. What am I going to do? What am I going to do?"

After I calmed her down, we started to talk, and I found out that Danny did kill the prior owner that he was paying. To make matters worse, he killed him the night before I came to drop off their check and the guy's body was there in the freezer. It made me wonder even more if Danny was trying to set me up for it somehow.

"Michael, I need someone to run this place. I can't handle all these guys without Danny, and I don't want to be here by myself on payroll day. Listen, I'll give you whatever you want. What do you want? How about $800 cash per week, and I'll give you my new car to drive here?"

I knew the best thing for Ellen's survival emotionally and financially was to keep the business going and, because she had helped me, I needed to do something to help her. Ironically it felt slightly like déjà vu', because I had found myself in a similar situation some years back with my family. I pondered for a few minutes the idea of how I would manage to work here and finish working on the house at the same time. Then I came up with the idea to open her place at 7 a.m., work until 3, then go home and work on the house until nighttime. Ellen said that she would be fine with that, because she could get the guys to take in their own loads into the freezers and park their trucks at the end of the day. But she added that I would have to stay late on Fridays for payroll, so I agreed to do that for her.

On the drive back to Flushing, I wondered about Danny, my new workload, and whether or not I should explain anything to my mother about it. One of the main reasons I figured that it wasn't worth mentioning to my mother was because I basically got up late anyway, bought supplies, and then worked late into the night, so it shouldn't really matter. I did this for about a week and a half, and I was dog-tired, but I reasoned with myself that it would be well worth it when I was done because I was working both ends of my situation to benefit myself. By the time I'd get done with the house and get my money, I'd have a great job that I could do standing on my head, not to mention that Ellen was hinting at giving me a lot more money if I could run the whole thing by myself.

Then one day my mother asked me whose car I was driving, so I told her it was Ellen's.

"Ellen who?"
"Ellen, the lady I used to work for," I answered.
"What are you doing driving her car?"
"Well, she had a little problem over at the business, and I decided to help her out," I said, not really wanting to mention anything about the murder.
"Help her out?! And what about me? What about finishing the house? Weren't you supposed to help me?"
"I am helping you."
"When? When you're not working over there?"
"Look, Ma, I still put in just about the same hours that I did before."
"Do you understand that, if I don't have this house done, I'll have a big problem here, and then you'll have a big problem?"
"Yeah, I do. And do you get that if it wasn't for Ellen, I wouldn't have had the fifteen thousand to give you? I feel obligated to help her."
"I don't care how you feel, we need to get this house done!"

We argued about how I decided to manage my time for an hour, until there was no resolution on her part at all. She didn't want to hear it, and acted as if I was cheating on her, as crazy as that sounds. We both walked away extremely pissed at each other.

After I spent another two days splitting my hours, my mother basically flat out told me that, if I didn't quit working for Ellen, I shouldn't expect to get any money once she had the house finished by herself, now that it was almost done.

Man, I was pissed, and wanted to read her the riot act, but I figured I had to think rationally. Then decide what would be best for me. I couldn't just pin Ellen's ears to the wall and ask her what I could expect to make with her in the future, and I couldn't just walk away from my mother's house after working on it for six months and investing my money. As much as it killed me, I decided to give into my mother's wishes for my sake and the sake of the twenty thousand I had tied up over there.

I wrote Ellen a long letter and put it in the glove box of her car. Because I couldn't face her, I handed my mother Ellen's keys and said, "Here, you take her back her car."

My mother wasted no time and jumped at my request. To make matters worse, she asked Patti, whom I had dated a few more times by now, to follow her over there and then drive her back.

I really felt like a schmuck that day, but what could I do? She had me by the proverbial balls.

For the next couple of weeks after that, my life consisted of getting up, getting supplies, and then working on the house until 1 or 2:00 in the morning.

Patti and I had made a date for this weekend, and it was decided that I would come and get her over at her father's house. Being that her father was there that night, it happened to be the first night I had really spent any time with him. A few of the other guys in the neighborhood had explained to me that her father was a little nutty, but I liked to judge nuttiness firsthand on people before I make a decision. One of the things that were explained to me was that Rudy, her father, was always yelling whenever he was home. But after sitting in the living room for a little while, I could see that he did a lot of yelling on the telephone more than at anyone in the house.

Patti's mother, Alice, was Scottish and English, and her father Rudy was Italian, so it wasn't possible to understand what he was saying because he would yell in Italian. He and I didn't really speak much the whole time I was there, but I could still tell that he was a little nutty. After being there for about forty-five minutes, I asked Patti if she was ready to go out. After she told me that she was, I walked over to her father and in a gentlemanly fashion I said, "Mr. Rudy, what time would you like me to bring your daughter home?"

He glanced at the clock, then looked at me and said, "Nine o'clock."

I looked at the clock, turned back to him, and said, "Fine. Good night." Then I walked back into the kitchen and told Patti "Good night. I'll see you later."
"What are you talking about? Where are you going?"
"Well, it's a quarter to nine now, and your father said he wants me to bring you home at nine. So, I'm leaving."
"Oh, don't listen to him. We'll leave in a few minutes."

After a few minutes we did leave and, as we were walking out the door, Patti's father yelled out, "Patti, come home in one hour, and be careful. Do you hear me?"
"Yes, I hear you. I'll be careful."

As we closed the door, I said, "So what do you want to do for an hour?"

"Oh, don't worry. He just says that."

It was a bit of an odd situation for me to be in, because at this age I never really dated anyone whose parents I had to speak to in this sense, let alone to a parent with off the wall answers.

Patti suggested that, since I had worked all week, she would drive so we took her Mercedes 450 SL and went and picked up her friend Karen, who was with her boyfriend Ronnie. Then we went out to a bar in Great Neck. We stayed out pretty late and finally at about 2 a.m. we started to head back down Northern Boulevard. On the way back towards Queens, we decided to stop at a donut shop to get some coffee. After we got there and got our coffees, we sat at the counter, and each couple got involved in their own conversation.

"Listen, Patti. I like you a lot, but I don't really want to get involved in a serious relationship to the point of always having to know where the other person is and all."

"Good," she answered. "Neither do I, so let's make a toast to it," she said as she held up her coffee cup. We toasted, and then each took a sip of coffee.

After we got back in the car Patti decided to jump on the highway to save some time.

"Well, why don't you just stay on the side streets?" Ronnie said.

"No, don't worry. I'm fine. I know my way from here," Patti said.

As we got onto the highway, I looked back and noticed that for the first time tonight Ronnie was putting on his seatbelt.

"Oh, come on. It can't be that bad," I said.

"Says you," Ronnie answered.

Patti was driving fine for a while, and then she started to pick up some speed. Since I'd had the experience of driving recklessly before, it took me a while to say anything but by the time Patti was doing about 85 mph, I felt obligated to speak.

"Patti."

"Yes?"

"You're supposed to stay within the striped lines."

"Oh, I know."

"Well, you're also supposed to try to stay in one lane at a time."

"I know, but you see, I drive better when I drive faster and I'm just taking shortcuts."

"Excuse me?"

"Well, for instance, I'm here, right? And I want to get over there," she said as she pointed through a curve we were coming up to. "So why should I go through all these curves to get there?"

"Good luck," Ronnie said from the back seat.

"Because you're crossing four lanes to get there??" I said.

"Yeah, but it doesn't matter now because nobody else is on the highway."

"Yeah, but if while taking one of your shortcuts you happen to come across someone doing 55 or

60, you might crash into the back of them while you're coming around a turn."

"No, I won't. I've still got three other lanes to use to avoid them."

"Okay, Patti, whatever," I said as I grabbed my seatbelt and put it on for the first time in years.

She ended up getting everybody home in one piece, and then I told Patti to drop me off at home and I would get my car tomorrow. When I got out of her car, I couldn't remember the last time I felt this happy for my feet to touch the ground.

Over the next few weeks I continued to work on the house, and it was really shaping up. My mother had someone come to re-do all the concrete sidewalks, and we also had another small driveway with a two-car parking pad installed. Then one day I got up and walked into the kitchen to make myself a cup of coffee. My mother was sitting at the kitchen table with one hand on her forehead with her eyes closed.

"What's the matter?" I asked.

"You're not going to believe this."

"What?"

"Do you know the loan I took out on the house?"

"Yeah, it was for $65,000, right?"

"Yes, but being that I didn't have a job or any type of credit history, I had to go to a certain type of mortgage company."

"Yeah, so?"

"So the company I went to gave me the loan and told me it was with compounded interest."

"Yeah, so what does that mean?"

"That meant that if I didn't pay them their payment for the month, then the entire mortgage would double."

"What do you mean? The payment would double?"

"No, the entire $65,000 would double, and so would their payments."

"So what are you talking about? What happened?"

My mother closed her eyes, shook her head back and forth, and then said, "Do you know how I've always sent out any important things certified return receipt?"

"Yeah?"

"Well, this one time in my life, the most important time in my life, I didn't."

"And?"

"And the mortgage company sent me a letter, telling me that they didn't receive any payments for two months."

As I quickly tabulated two months of compounded interest, I said, "No fucking way."

"Now they tell me that I owe them $195,000."

"What? Get the fuck outta here."

"I'm serious."

"Fuck that. Start calling some lawyers."

"I hired a lawyer four days ago, and basically he told me I'm screwed."

"No, fuck this. Give me the guy's phone number."

"It's not going to do anything, Michael. I've been trying to talk to him ever since I got the letter, and he doesn't return my calls. They put me on the phone with someone else."

"Then give me his name and address. I'll go there myself."

"I...don't think it's a good idea for you to go to his office, Michael."

"Why? Do you think I'm scared of him?"

"No, I don't. I just don't think it's a good idea for you to go down to his office."

"Well, thank you for your opinion. Now give me his name and address, please."

"Look, Michael, maybe this is God's way of settling up with me for John or something."

"Look, Ma, if that's what you want to believe, okay, that's fine. But my time and money are also involved in this, and God's already gotten even with me enough, so give me this guy's name and address."

"No, I'm not going to do it. I'm afraid you'll go down there and kill him."

"Well, I can't guarantee that isn't a possibility, but it's better than sitting on my ass and not doing anything."

No matter how many times I argued with her about it that day, she wouldn't give me the guy's name or address. Unfortunately for me I didn't know that all I had to do was to go down to the city's assessor's office and look up the mortgage address for myself. I can tell you one thing, if I had gotten his name and address and he didn't come to terms with me on this, that his ancestors might have seen the money, but he never would have lived to see a dime. I would have strangled him until his eyes popped out of his fucking head.

Needless to say, my relationship with my mother deteriorated to another degree after that, especially since she was still busting my horns to finish so she could refinance the house, pay this asshole off, and hope that she came out with a little money. The only good thing she had going for her was that the real estate market was on fire in Queens. Korean families were coming into Flushing and literally buying up properties with bags full of cash. Even so, by the way I could calculate it, I couldn't see how there would be any room for extra money for me, after this now huge note was paid off.

Within a couple of weeks, the house was finished, and a few weeks after that my mother refinanced the house. She paid off the loan she had from the piece of shit mortgage company, gave me the Cadillac she had bought, and ended up with about 25 grand in her pocket. What a bust, I thought. I worked in this house for months so my mother could tell me she bought me a car. I was very annoyed with the whole situation and didn't miss any opportunity to argue with my mother about anything.

I guess my feelings at that time leaked into other things, because Patti and I didn't really see a lot of each other. Finally one day my mother and I got into another argument about her handling of the house and my money. When I was done saying my peace, she asked me to move out.

Basically I was broke at the time, but I wasn't about to take back my words, so I moved out that night. I didn't really take the time to look for a good place to live. Instead I called up a couple of friends and asked them if I could move in. Unfortunately one of the people I asked was Donde, and because I wanted to get out of my house in a hurry, I accepted his invitation without really thinking about it.

Adelchie's father had thrown him out about a year earlier. Fortunately for him, his father threw him into an empty apartment in one of his buildings. I knew "Delk's" apartment was only a one-bedroom, but I figured I'd get accustomed to sleeping on his couch after a few restless nights.

I moved in on a Thursday night, and after I had some of my stuff there, I found out that Donde didn't want me to sleep on his new couch. Instead I saw that he had put down a little sheet for me on the floor in the living room next to his front door, as if I was a puppy. Then he explained to me that I would have to be in by ten o'clock, because sometimes he liked to go to bed early.

"Well, why don't you just give me a key, Donde? Then I won't bother you when I come in."
"Well, try not to take it personal, but I really don't want to do that."
"Oh, that's okay. I won't take it personally, and I'll be home by 10:00 tomorrow night in case you want to go to bed early."

Even though I felt like reciting quite a few thoughts to him I decided, under the circumstances, to leave well enough alone. Because he didn't want me to use one of his pillows on the floor, I grabbed a pair of my jeans, rolled them up for a pillow, and went to sleep.

The next day I went out and looked for work. Then at the end of the day I stopped by Patti's mother's house. Because her parents had separated, her mother lived in a new house several blocks away from her father's house. Patti had moved in with her mother a short time after that. Her mother and younger sister weren't home yet, and after I "accidentally" pushed Pom Pom, her dog, off the couch we started to fool around a little bit, much to Pom Pom's dismay. Just about when the temperature was rising, her sister, Sharron, walked in with her boyfriend, Terry. Fortunately there was a small partition wall between the front door and the living room.

After a few minutes of all of us talking, Patti went upstairs, and Sharron went to take a shower. Terry and I lived pretty close to each other, but we didn't really know each other. After we made a little small talk about which people we both knew in the neighborhood, Terry said, "I don't know if you know this, Mike, but one of my older brothers used to work by your father's luncheonette. He'd go in there and have breakfast every morning."

Not knowing where he was going with this, I said, "Yeah, so?"
"Well, I thought you might like to know that my brother was sitting there having coffee the morning your pop was shot."
"Really? That's interesting. I'd like to talk to him one day."

We talked for a little longer until the girls came back, and by then I kinda figured that Terry was all right.

That night I went "home" at ten, so "father" wouldn't get upset. After I got in, I sat on Adelchie's precious couch and turned on the TV. A minute or two later, Donde walked in and said, "Listen, Mike, my girlfriend's coming over this weekend, and I'd like to spend some time with her."
"Yeah?"
"So I was wondering if you could sleep somewhere else this weekend."

"Well, let me ask you this, so I don't interrupt your privacy. The basement in this building has two entrances, right? Why don't you give me the key to the back door of the basement, and I'll move some tires and paint cans and sleep there?"

"Well, I don't think my father would like that idea."

"Well, how about this, Donde? I'll take my chances with your father catching me sleeping in your basement. I mean, after all, I've known him for about ten years or so, because to be quite honest and don't take this personally, your hospitality is killing me."

"No... I don't think that's a good idea."

"Okay... I'll make arrangements for the weekend."

"Okay, thanks. Oh yeah, and can you turn the TV down a little bit?"

"Yeah, Donde. No problem."

Well, what could I say. The motherfucker waited his whole life to get me in this position, so now he was pulling out all the stops. But this would be the last night for his performance, even if I had to sleep in my car tomorrow. Tonight, though, I decided I needed a good night's sleep just in case I had to do that, so I turned off the television and went to bed.

The next day I went to a few job interviews. One of the biggest problems I had was that I no longer had references for about the last two years of work because Ellen, I found out, had sold the business for about three-quarters of a million dollars and made a two-hundred and fifty thousand dollar profit.

I hooked up with Patti later in the day and explained to her my situation with Donde.

"Do you want to stay at my father's house? You know, he won't mind. He always has strangers sleeping over there. It's one of the reasons my mother moved out."

"What? I'm a stranger, too?" I joked with her.

"No, you know what I meant."

"Well, actually, your father's a little too nutty for me. Besides, with all that yelling he does on the phone, I don't think I'll get any sleep."

"Well then, I'll ask my mother if you can stay in the spare bed in the basement."

"Well, I don't know."

"Don't worry. She'll say yes."

Even though I had another friend or two who lived on their own, I knew I wouldn't feel comfortable living with them, so when Patti's mother agreed to let me stay there until I got on my feet, I took that opportunity.

At about the same time that I was trying to find a place to sleep, I had gotten very interested in the infomercials they had on at night about buying property with no money down. I was so interested that I actually went to one of the seminars.

After sitting through one of their seminars, I was informed that if I wanted to know more I could spend $350 for the books they were selling. I didn't have that kind of money to spend on books right then, so I called my mother and asked her to lend me the money for them. She thought I was a little nuts for doing it, but she agreed, so I drove over there, got a check, and then drove back and bought the books.

At night after I got done with the bullshit job I had gotten, I read all the books to see what I could find out from them. It's funny, but I already had a lot of fragmented thoughts about first and second mortgages, but I still basically needed one or two full sentences to thread my thoughts together. Even though it was an expensive piece of thread, it gave me most of the information. Now I was on a bit of a quest and started to call and ask some real estate agents some questions for the rest of the information. If any of them had the time they would answer some questions, but most of them didn't have the time. The ones who did basically told me that if I wanted to find deals like that, I should go to Montana or North Dakota because I wasn't going to find them in New York. I'd always thank them for their time and write down whatever they told me.

Unfortunately it was starting to become clear that, even though I knew the plan, the actual mechanics of the deals were a little more complex in order for them to get accepted by any banks, so I was still missing one crucial piece of the pie.

I stopped by my mother's house to get some more clothes. When I got there, "Uncle" Phil was in the kitchen.

"Mike, listen. Your grandfather is at the hospital. The paramedics think he had a heart attack."
"Which hospital is he at!?"
"Booth Memorial. I found him lying in the hallway, so I called 911. I'll wait here until your mother comes home. You go see how he is."

I ran out of the house and raced over there in my car. I had been through this routine a lot with him over the last few years, and I hoped it was just another false alarm like all the other times. Over the years my grandfather had been an anchor for me when I needed someone, and it pained me to think that his time might be up.

When I got to the hospital, I found out that he was already in the emergency room. In case this time happened to be the big one, I decided that there was no way I was going to not see or speak to him one last time. So without asking, I walked into the emergency room and peeked behind curtains until I found him.

"Grandpa! It's me, Michael!"

At first he looked at me as if he was dizzy, but then after a second or two he slightly nodded his head and slowly blinked his eyes. I tried to talk with him, but it was very difficult for him to answer, because I realized that he was having trouble breathing. While we were trying to communicate, two doctors and three nurses stood in the middle of the emergency room talking about a new restaurant that had opened up. They just happened to be raving about the excellent service that some of them had received in between my grandfather's gasps for air, as he tried to tell me he couldn't breathe.

I walked over to the group in the middle of the mayhem that surrounded us and said sarcastically, "Excuse me... but do any of you work here?"

"Well... yes," a doctor replied.

"Well, excuse me for interrupting your conversation, but my grandfather is lying in that room and he can't breathe so before somebody standing here finds themselves in a similar situation, can somebody take a look at him, or at least get him an oxygen mask?"

One of the male doctors who was a few years older than I was, laughed, smugly, and was about to try to intimidate me with all his weeks of aerobic classes until I stepped in front of him, looked in his face, and said, "Don't even go there, because you'll be lying on one of these hospital beds in the blink of a eye. Just do your job, and help my grandfather."

Within a minute or two the other doctor came over and started to check on my grandfather, while two security guards came over to escort me out. I looked at the security guards, told them not to take it personally, but I wouldn't be leaving this room until an oxygen tank was given to my grandfather. After it came, my grandfather was able to form little sentences with the oxygen, so before I left I took his hand in mine, and said, "Gramps, Do you think you're going to be all right?"

"Yes, yes, I'ma okay now."

"Okay then, I'm going into the emergency waiting room. I'll be right outside, okay?"

"Okay," he answered.

I kissed him on his forehead, then looked at him, and said, "You know I like'a you, Grandpa, right?"

"I know... I'ma like'a you, too."

After I was led out of the emergency room, I went outside to have a cigarette. While I was out there, I started to think about my life with my grandfather. I thought about his construction stories, his stories about Italy and when he first came to America. It's funny, but if he didn't do any of the things he did once he came here, I wouldn't be here. I also realized that he was the one person in my life who had spent the most time with me, more than my mother and my father, ever since I was a baby. I also thought about all the things that I still wanted to do with him before he left. Yeah, but don't think about that, Mike. He looks all right, he was talking to you, and he'll be fine. He's strong as a bull.

A short time after that my mother showed up. She hadn't experienced taking my grandfather back and forth to the hospital, because she had been in prison, and my grandfather hadn't been this ill before she went away, so she seemed a little more frantic about the situation.

"How is he?" she said with a worried look.

"He seems all right. He was talking to me. You can go see that nurse over there about his status."

My mother went in and spoke with the nurse, and then she was allowed to go and sit with my grandfather. After she came out, we stayed there for a while to see if he got any better. By the time we left that night, he was considered stable.

The next morning I called the hospital to see how my grandfather was doing, and I was told he was in a coma. I figured that my mother had already heard the news, so I drove over to the house. When I got there, my mother said she was glad I was there, because she didn't want to go to the hospital alone.

We drove to the hospital, and then we went up to my grandfather's room. Even though he was on a ventilator, I walked over to him and noticed that my grandfather's eyes were half-open, and what really made me realize that he was dead was that his eyes were one-dimensional. In other words, the color of his eyes didn't have any depth to them, almost as if someone had put a colored piece of paper behind a curved piece of glass. My mother started talking to him and running her fingers through his hair. She would ask me every couple of minutes my opinion of my grandfather's condition, but I didn't have the heart to tell her that I felt that her father was dead, so I just kept agreeing with her that he was all right.

After an hour of this, I couldn't really take it any more, so I said, "Ma... he's gone."
"No, Michael, don't say that. He's just in a coma," she said with tears in her eyes.
"Ma, he's gone."
"What makes you say that, Michael? You're not a doctor."

I didn't really want to tell her why I thought this, but aside from that reason, I just knew my grandfather wasn't there.

"It's his eyes, Ma. They don't have any depth."

Even after I told her that, she still didn't want to believe it. So I stayed with her for another hour, while she weighed the pros and cons as to whether or not he was still alive.

We left a little while after that, and a few hours later my grandfather's regular doctor called and told my mother he was brain dead. It was August 2, 1986.

The next day I went over to Gleason's funeral parlor and started to price everything for his funeral. Being that my grandfather had been in a union, there was money furnished by them for his funeral. My mother was a bit of a wreck, so I basically handled the whole thing. I didn't really mind, and even though it might sound odd, I felt good about giving him a nice funeral. After it was all arranged, I purchased a bottle of wine and asked the funeral director to put it next to his leg.

We had the funeral the next day and, as it turned out, we almost had too many limos and not enough people. Both of my aunts were there, but I didn't talk to my Aunt Linda. My mother decided, for whatever her reasons were, not to go to the funeral parlor. Instead she showed up at the church with one of her girlfriends. After the church service, we all followed my grandfather's coffin out of the church towards the hearse, and my mother started to get hysterical. I was glad that she was with one of her girlfriends, because I wasn't too sure if I could really handle consoling her. As cold as it may sound, after John's death and my two near misses, I just looked at death a lot differently at this point in time.

After the church services, we drove out to Long Island to my grandfather's mausoleum, but my mother was too upset and didn't come with us. Once we were out there, a priest said a few words and we all got to say our last goodbyes. When it was my turn, I kissed the top of his coffin and bid him farewell.

A few weeks after my grandfather's funeral, I happened to stop by Bench Park and hung out with some friends for a little while.

About a half hour later, Kirk Castro showed up. I hadn't seen him in the neighborhood in about a year or so, and he looked good. We got to talking, and I asked him what he was doing these days.

"Well, I'm working with my older brother, Ray. We put together mortgages for people."
"Get the fuck out of here. Do you know anything about second mortgages?" I asked.
"Shit, that's about all we do. It's called creative financing."

Just what I was looking for, the piece to the puzzle, I thought.

Kirk and I talked for a little while, and then he asked me if I wanted to see the big house he and his brother were buying over by Bowne Park.

"Yeah, okay. But first I have to stop at Patti's house."
"Patti... who? Patti from around the corner?"
"Yeah."
"No way. Are you dating her?"
"Yeah."
"Man, I had a crush on her for years when I was a kid. Do you mind if I come with you? I'd like to say hi."
"Yeah, sure, follow me over to her house. She lives by Bowne Park anyhow, so it's on the way."

After we drove over, Kirk went inside and said hello and started some small talk with Patti about when they were kids. We stayed there for about half an hour, and then we decided to leave. The house Kirk and his brother were buying was over by St. Mel's Catholic School. It was a big two-story brick, two-car garage house on a nice sized lot.

"Wow, it's a nice house. How much are you paying for it?"
"Well, my brother's buying it for about three hundred thousand, and the people are giving him a second mortgage on it. Being that the second mortgage overlaps the bank's mortgage, my brother's walking away with about 15 grand after the closing costs are paid."
"Really, no shit?"
"No, man, this is what I was talking to you about."
"So let me ask you this. If I found a house where the owner was willing to give me a second mortgage, could you and your brother get me the financing?"
"Yeah, as long as you structure it right and the numbers are good, it should be no problem. But understand this, for getting you the financing, my brother will probably charge you a little bit more than a regular broker, but he'll probably cut you some slack because you're a friend of mine."

Boy, this was just what my ears wanted to hear. Now all I had to do was find the right property.

After I left Kirk, I drove back over to Patti's house.

"Michael, I don't know what it is about him, but I don't trust him. I mean it's nice to hear he's buying a big house and all, but I'm telling you-don't do business with him."

It really came as a bit of a surprise to me that she would say this to me, especially after the conversation I had just had with Kirk.

"What do you have, little birds flying around or something?"
"What do you mean?" she asked.

After I explained to her the conversation I just had with Kirk, I said, "Come on, Patti. If he screws me, I'll kick the shit out of him."
"Yeah, but you'll still be screwed."

Even though the timing of her conversation with me was odd, and it put a little kink in my tail because she had been right about people before, I decided that I'd still go through with some of my plans with Kirk. If nothing else, I reasoned, at least I could find out more information that I needed on this type of financing.

On another note, with the living situation at Patti's house I was starting wear out my welcome, and I figured that, once I had one more paycheck under my belt, I'd go and find a place to live. That theory changed a few nights later after I came in at about 2 in the morning after hanging out with Ricky Dale that night in a bar. When I walked into the basement, I saw all my stuff packed and piled at the bottom of the stairs. There were a lot of things I liked about Patti, but her insecurity about me wasn't one of them.I was a little buzzed and tired, so instead of leaving I just plopped into bed and went to sleep.

"Click" went the basement light a little while later.

"Stomp-Stomp-Stomp-Stomp."

Oh shit, here she comes down the stairs. Maybe if I pretend I'm sleeping, she'll go away, I thought.

"Slap!"

"Get up! Get out! Just get out!"

I couldn't believe it. On top of a little hangover I had, she just slapped me in the back of my head. I sat up and started to laugh.

"What are you laughing about?"
"I can't believe you just slapped me in my head."
"Oh really. Do you want me to do it again?!?"

I was tired, a little hung over, and starting to get a little headache, so I decided that I'd try to make up with her instead of grabbing my shit and going to sleep in my car. It worked, but I realized that I had to get out of there soon.

The next day, against my better judgment, I went to go and stay with a friend who used to live at my house.

One of the main reasons I didn't really want to go and live there was because he was still dealing coke like he used to do when he lived at my house. The main problem I had with this was that he always kept strange hours and had losers over at all times. Being that I had known him for a couple of years and because I wanted to move out of Patti's mother's house, I figured I'd move there and save a little more money.

While I was staying there and working, I'd take any free time I had and I'd look for a house to buy. I figured the best thing for me to look for was something that I could rent out, and since I could do construction, I'd also look for something that needed repairs. Finding a house where I could live comfortably would come later, after I had one or two of these types of houses under my belt, I reasoned, because once I had money coming in from them, that rent would pay for my house. Eventually I hooked up with an Oriental female real estate agent.

I figured she would have some good insight into what was going on with the market, taking into consideration the explosion of Oriental people who were buying up Flushing. Being that I dressed sharp and drove a decent Caddy, she wasn't sure whether or not I had money, which was just fine, because she worked with me while she was trying to figure me out. We spent a couple of weeks working together, but I still couldn't find an ideal property that I wanted. I was looking for something that was a handyman special with a lot of rooms, in a decent neighborhood.

I stopped by my mother's house to get a few more of my things, and my mother told me that she took the money she got from the refi and bought a building in upstate New York, close to where we used to live. Still having a bitter taste in my mouth from our business arrangement, I said, "Oh, that's nice," and went about my business.

"Well, it's a four-story building, and on the first floor there's a bar."
"So I guess you're going to be a bartender, huh?"
"No, one of the reasons I bought it was because I figured that you could run it."
"That's an awfully nice gesture, but I'm not about to pack up and run some bar for you that's 350 miles away from here. But thanks anyway. Oh, and don't even think of asking me to go and work on it, because I won't."
"Look, just so you know, another reason I bought it was because I'm having a hard time paying the mortgage here, and I don't like what's going on in the neighborhood, the way it's changing."
"Good luck with it. I'm gonna try a few things around here."
"Well, listen, I'm not going to be around much, and the guy who was renting the basement apartment moved out. So if you want, you can stay there."

My mother's offer caught me by surprise, and I wondered why she was saying it, but regardless of that, it sounded a lot better than trying to sleep on my friend's couch. Sometimes I'd wake up while he was conducting business with some cokehead at 2, 3, or 4, in the morning, and it was quite bothersome considering that I had to be up by 6. Besides that I was getting tired of hearing him talk about how he made my week salary in half hour of business.

Within the next couple of weeks my Caddy started to give me problems. I took it to a few neighborhood mechanics, and they all told me it was probably the computer going haywire. I had more or less decided to move back home, so I figured I'd spend the money and take it over to the Caddy dealership. I took off from work one day, got up real early, and drove over there before they opened. By the time I got there at a quarter to eight, there were already two cars ahead of me. By eight o'clock, there were about 10 cars after me on line waiting for service.

They finally opened the garage door at about a quarter after eight, and somebody who was standing outside with a clipboard started to get information from people before they drove in. Finally my turn came up, and the guy with the clipboard started to wave me off, so I rolled down the window and said, "What's the matter? Don't tell me you're full already?"

"No, we ain't full. We just don't work on this model any more. They're too much of a problem, and they always come back after we fix them."

"Wait a minute. Are you telling me you don't work on these cars any more?"

"Yeah... that's what I'm telling you."

I stepped out of my car and said to him as I pointed at my front grill. "What does that say on my grill?"

"Cadillac," he answered.

"And what does that say on the big huge sign on top of your building?"

"Cadillac."

"Now tell me again what you said about my car?"

"We no longer do work on this model."

By now, one or two people started to beep their horns, and I said, "Well, then let me speak to a manager."

"I am the manager," he answered.

"You mean to tell me that after I save up enough money to bring it to you guys, because we both know I'm going to get charged an arm and a leg, I sit here for half an hour, take off work, and you're telling me that you don't want to work on your own car?"

"Look, kid, do yourself a favor, pull out the manifold and the fuel injection system. Put in a regular manifold and carburetor, and that will get rid of the computer on this car. Then you won't have any more problems with it, all right? Now do me a favor, and pull the car out of the driveway, so I can get the rest of these cars in. If you want, I'll talk to you a little more about it, okay?"

Instead of waiting, I shook my head, got back in my car, and drove off. Since I didn't really have the time to do this work to my car, I babied it for the rest of the week. In the meantime, I got most of my stuff back over to my mother's house. It was a good thing that I did because, by the end of that week, I was pretty sure the motor was blown.

At around the same time that this was happening, with my car, I had found a house with the real estate agent that would suit my needs. It was a narrow, three story attached house on Prince Street. It didn't have a lot of frontage, but it was deep. What I liked about the house was that it was mixed in with a bunch of business and factories, and it had a lot of rooms, so that meant that I wouldn't have to worry about the neighbors complaining about too many people coming and going while I ran it as a rooming house. It also needed some repairs, which could make the owner more interested in bargaining with me. After a few phone calls between me and the agent, I finally got the owner down to his lowest price. Now it came down to figuring out the right numbers, and dropping the bombshell on the real estate agent.

The reason I call it a bombshell is because, when I first met her, I vaguely spoke to her about second mortgages. She explained to me that they only have these types of deals in Alaska. The broker and I spoke on the phone a few times after that, and after a little bit of frustration on her part, she said to me, "Look, you do have money for a down payment, right?"

"Yes."

"Well, it's very simple then. How much of a down payment do you want to give him?"

"Look, I could give the guy a sixty-thousand dollar down payment if I wanted to, I lied. But that place needs a lot of work, and I'm not certain what type of money the bank will give me for that property in that condition."

"Well, look, why don't I come over to your place, and we'll sit down, get the seller on the phone, and see if we can work this out, okay?"

This was about the fifth time she offered to come over to my place, and I knew she just wanted to take a look at my surroundings to try to get a better feel of me. I had been doing business with this agent for a little while now, and this wasn't the first time that she had tried to invite herself over to my place. Basically because I didn't want her to see my bed in Patti's basement or to have a coke deal interrupt our discussion at my last home, I kept putting her off. But now that I was staying at my mother's house and it looked great, I felt a lot more comfortable about sitting with her at "home."

She came over about a half hour later and was quite impressed by my mother's house, not that I told her that it was my mother's house. After about ten or fifteen minutes of her trying to negotiate a down payment price with me, I said to her, "Do you think the owner would hold a second mortgage?"

"You know, I told you a long time ago that those deals don't happen here, and now you want me to insult the seller's intelligence and ask him to do something that I know he won't."

"Well, I don't agree with you. I think he wants out of that place, and he has a very low first mortgage. So any money he gets from my lender would be more than enough to relocate him somewhere else."

"When you say it like that, Michael, you make it seem like you don't want to give him any down payment at all."

"Well, actually I don't and I want you to ask him if he'll hold a $55,000 mortgage."

"That's well over the down payment amount. He'll never go for that."

"Well, can you ask him?"

"What for? He'll just say no anyhow," she answered in frustration.

"Okay, so it can't hurt anything if you ask, right?"

"No, I'm not going to ask him."

"Well, understand this, the only reason I haven't driven over there and asked him myself was because I didn't want to make you look bad or to make it seem like I was going behind your back to make a deal."

She glared at me for a second and then said, "Fine then. I'll call him, but if he says no, you need to tell me how much of a down payment you're ready to put down."

"Fine," I bluffed.

She picked up the phone, dialed, and then put her hand on her hip while waiting for someone to pick up.

"Hi, this is the real estate agent... Hi, how are you? Fine, thank you... Listen, I'm with the buyer right now, and he wanted me to ask you if you would hold a $55,000 second mortgage for him on your property instead of a down payment."

After a brief pause she said, "Really...?? You would...? Well, yes, you would be getting about $135,000 from a first mortgage. Well, okay, I'll tell him."

She hung up the phone with a shocked look on her face and then said, "Uhm, he said yes. He would go for it, so do you want me to tell the owner yes?"

"Well, I want to think about it for a day or two," I said.

I tried to hide a look of relief and smugness at the same time, but before I had the time to do so, the broker said to me, "Listen, if you don't want the deal, I'll take it."

"Whoa, whoa, whoa. Aren't you the one who was just fighting me because you didn't want to make a phone call, and now all of a sudden you're like a shark that smells blood."

"Yeah, but instead of jumping on it, you tell me you still want to think about it. I can't believe you. You get what you want and you're still going to think about it."

"I'll tell you what, I'll call you at home tomorrow about dinnertime, and I'll let you know if I'm gonna do the deal, all right? If I decide not to do it, instead of selling you my deal, I'll give it to you, okay?"

She stood there with a shocked look on her face for a second, and then she said, "Fine, call me tomorrow."

After she left, I beeped Kirk and went over the numbers with him.

"So, Kirk, if all the numbers come in, I could walk away with $25,000, right?"

"Yeah, that's if all the numbers come in."

"All right, fuck it. I'll go for it."

The next day I called the real estate agent and told her that I would do the deal. Two days after that, I had the contract made up, and then it was signed. My first deal was underway.

Over the next few days, I got all of my personal paperwork together and submitted my application to the bank. Then I sat back and waited to see what would happen.

In the meantime, my Caddy was dead, and now I had to take public transportation to work, which was a bit of a hassle. That weekend I went over to Marcus's house to see if his brother Freddy was home, and luckily he was. Being that Freddy knew a lot more about cars than I did, I wanted him to give me the final verdict on it. When he got to my house, he started the car up, frowned, and turned it back off.

"Yep, it's shot."
"Fuck!"
"How much money did you put into this car?"
"About $1,500."
"That sucks. Well, at least the body and interior are in mint shape."
"Yeah, well, I guess I can sit in it, turn on the radio, and pretend that I'm driving it."
"Well, you know what I meant."

As we were sitting in the driveway talking about the car, Ray, a mechanic who used to live in my mother's house, pulled up.

"Hey, Mike. How's it going?"
"Well, great, until my engine blew."
"Yeah, I saw the car sitting here, and I was going to ask you what you were going to do with it."
"I don't know. I'll probably come out every weekend, wax the thing, and pretend I'm driving in it, right, Freddy?"
"Aaa, fuck you," Freddy joked.
"Well, why don't you trade it to someone for a car that's running?"
"Where the fuck am I going to find someone who wants to trade me for it?"
"I'll trade you my car."
I looked down the end of the driveway, and Ray had a 1980 yellow and tan Buick Regal sitting there, and it looked pretty good. I looked at Freddy, then at Ray, and said, "Give me the keys. Let me take it for a ride."

After driving it for a few blocks, I came back, let Freddy check it out, and said, "You've got a deal. When do you want to do it?"

Within the next few days, I signed the title, we swapped cars, and I was driving again.

It was a pretty good thing that I had gotten a car, because Patti had started going back to Queens College to finish up her degree, and sometimes I would drive her there and pick her up. Her father was having some financial problems, so Patti told him to sell the Mercedes he had bought her to help out.

I made a phone call to the bank and the real estate deal I put together was starting to look like it was going to go through. About a week or so later, the drug dealer I used to live with stopped by my house. He told me that he wanted to go camp out and do some hunting up in the country this weekend, and he wanted to know if he could borrow my car. Being that I had just gotten a car back myself, I was a bit hesitant, but when he told me that he'd give me $250 for the weekend, I was like, "NO PROBLEM."

He stopped by Friday at about 5 p.m. and picked it up. Then he swore to me that he'd have it back no later than Sunday night. I warned him if I didn't have it back Sunday that he'd have to pay me an additional $75 on Monday. We agreed on it, and he left.

By Sunday night when he didn't return, I was pissed. But by Monday night I was furious, so I called my friend's sister. "Where's your brother?" I asked her when she picked up the phone.

"Michael... I guess you didn't hear."
"Hear what?"
"He got busted in a cop sting, trying to sell two kilos of coke."
"Oh, man. Are you serious?"
"Yeah, why?"
"Because your brother borrowed my car, and he was supposed to have it back to me by Sunday."
"Shit, well, the only thing I can do for you is give you the detective's phone number, and you can talk to him about it, I guess."
"Yeah, I guess. What the hell? I don't have any other options."

The next day I called the detective and told him who I was and asked about my car.

"Oh, well, you made my life easier. We were going to find you and bring you in for questioning," he said.
"Well, sorry to burst your bubble, but I guess I did your job for you then, huh?"
"Yeah, I guess."
"Well, look... I had nothing to do with this, so can I come get my car?"
"Oh yeah, sure, sure. Here, let me give you the address."

After he gave it to me, I asked him if the Long Island Railroad had any stops out there, and he told me it did. Man, that seemed a little too easy, I thought.

I got out there late the next afternoon, and I was taken into an interrogation room to wait for the detective. After about twenty minutes, he finally showed up.

"So, Mike... you ever been arrested for anything?"

I could tell by his tone of voice that we weren't going to be talking about my car for a while, and because I didn't have anything to lose, I figured I'd tell him what he wanted to know.

"Well, actually I did have a little problem with being arrested. They were both in 1981, I believe. The first one was for possession of stolen property, an estimated three quarters of a million dollars worth. You can find that newspaper article in the Queens section of the daily news two days after my bust. The second one was a few months later. It was for attempted kidnapping, attempted murder, and possession of two sawed-off shotguns. You can find that article in all three major newspapers."
"Well," he said with a smile, "I guess you keep yourself pretty busy."
"Yeah, but again, sorry to burst your bubble, but both cases were dismissed against me. So what

about my car now?"

"We'll get to that in a minute. So, you are friends with this individual, right?"

"Yep, I've known him a long time."

"And you were actually roommates with him?"

"Yeah, a little while ago I was."

"Well, we found mail and some of your personal items over at his house when we searched there. That's why I ask."

"Yeah, so?"

"So you want to tell me the whole time you were living there you didn't see anything going on, right?"

"Let me ask you this, detective. How many guns did you take out of his apartment?"

"Three rifles and two hand guns."

"So your question to me is why didn't I go and pull your name out of a phone book and call you about him, right?"

"Well..."

"Well, check this out. You can call all the detectives in my neighborhood and talk to them about me. I've been straight as an arrow for years. As far as drugs, I've been clean since '82 and you can even ask my friend this. Now if you want more proof than that, you can give me your coffee cup and I'll piss in it for you and you can have it tested."

"Don't be a fucking wiseass," he said.

"Sorry. Don't take it personally, but check this out. I may not be a rocket scientist, but I'm not stupid enough to travel all the way out here to pick up a 500-dollar car, if I was involved in this shit. If you really want to get technical, the dates on my mail at his apartment were from at least last month, so I was gone before any of this happened. So, look, what about my car?"

"So how did he get your car now?"

"He came to my house and rented it for the weekend for $250, because he told me that he was going to go camping."

"And you just gave it to him."

"Yeah, I could use the money."

He looked at me for a long second and then said, "You know, we have a new law out here that any vehicles we get in any drug busts, we get to keep."

"Fine. If you want to keep my car, keep it, it's a piece of shit anyhow. Now unless you want to arrest me, too, I've got a train to catch."

He looked at me again and then said, "Go ahead. Get your car, and get the hell out of here."

Ironically I had to pay 250 dollars to get my car out of storage, but I was more than happy to. Believe me, if I had gotten arrested for this bullshit, I'da' killed him.

As it turned out my whole week wasn't lucky, because the bank I went to get financing from came up short on the appraisal. There was no way I was going to go into this project without any cash to work with, so I went and put an application in with another bank. A few weeks later, the new bank came back short also, so I asked the real estate agent to talk to the owner and see if he would either come down a little in price or hold more paper on the property. When she said he wouldn't, I told the real estate agent that I still had another bank I was working with. At about this same time, I heard that my coke dealer friend was back on the street. The word was that he rolled over on his supplier and got himself off.

One day he happened to stop by my house and apologized for fucking me up with my car.

"I heard you had to pay storage fees on your car."
"Yeah, the whole weekend was a bust for me, too."
"Well, here's two hundred. That ought to cover it."
"Yeah, I guess. Oh, P.S., don't ever ask me to borrow my car, because I think you know the answer."
"Yeah, I won't."

We bullshitted about the old days for a little while, and then he left.

I hooked up with two more real estate agents, and I was also looking for houses on my own now. I guess I had the bug for it. While I was talking with Kirk about my new house search one day, he started to tell me about this one house he had all lined up for someone to walk into. He asked me if I might be interested in it. I told him that I might be, and I met him over at the house that day to take a look at it.

The house happened to be right down the block from where they used to hold the St. Luke's bazaar every year. When I pulled up in front of the house, I almost shit when I saw what house it was. Kirk was already standing there, and when I got out of the car said, "Holy shit! I can't believe it."
"What? What's going on?"
"When I was a kid at St. Luke's bazaar with a bunch of friends, for some reason I just felt like taking a walk..."
"Yeah, so?"
"So I walked down the block and got to this house on the corner, and I just stopped here and sat against a car. I couldn't stop staring at this house. I thought I was going nuts 'cause I couldn't or wouldn't move. I just kept staring at it for some reason."
"Oh, great. That must be a good sign then."
"Yeah, but what if it was a bad one?"
"Naaa, it was probably a good one. Come on, let's go inside."

I went inside and looked at the house, and it was kind of small but it was a legal two- family house. After I checked everything out, we said our goodbye's to the owners and went to have a cup of coffee.

"So what do you think?" Kirk asked.
"Well, I don't know. It's kind of small for a two-family and for what I have in mind."
"Yeah, Mike but it's set up so that there's 50 grand on the table. The appraisal's already in."
"Well, if that's true, Kirk, that's fine, but at $280,000 it's going to take about three grand a month to make up for that 50 grand. Like I said, the place is small. If I was to rent the downstairs with the garage I'd get about $850 per month. Then if I rented the upstairs I'd get about $600-650. That's $1500 per month at best. Right off the bat, the second mortgage would be 700 alone, so that leaves 800 to

cover the 2500 going to the bank. That would leave about 1700 per month that I'd have to automatically make on that money 30 days after I got it. Now, that's if I don't get a fucked-up tenant that I have to evict. Besides that, if this is such a great fucking deal, how come you're not doing it and you're giving it to me?"

"Well, because my credit is fucked up. Otherwise, I'da' done it already."

"I don't know. I need to have another type of income coming in before I jump into this one, even with the $50,000 on the table."

"Well, look, things aren't going well with me and my brother, and I'm going to go full time with Bernie's mortgage company. So what if we went partners on this one?"

"I don't know, Kirk. To be honest, having you come in as a partner for less of a cut of the 50 grand really doesn't make it sound all that much better. Don't take it personal. I just have to think about it. It's big numbers to be juggling."

"Well, let me know. I'll hold onto it for as long as I can."

"Now let me ask you this. Why do you think the numbers didn't come in on this first application I put in for the house on Price Street?"

"Well, I don't know. It could be a lot of things. Your credit isn't that strong, for one. Maybe you should apply for a credit card or two. I don't know if it'll help with this new application you put in, but it can't hurt."

"Yeah, I guess. I'll give it a shot."

"Now let me ask you something. What is it that you think is so great about that shitty little building on Prince Street?"

"Well, first of all, if the numbers come in, there will be some cash on the table. Second of all, it's in a real working section. I mean, right down the block is a huge Yellow Cab company, and I could probably fill the place up just with cab drivers alone. The place has also got a lot of rooms. I mean, shit. Aside from the kitchen there's like five small rooms downstairs, and it's a three-story building. I could rent each room for 75 to 80 dollars per week, and I figure I could make about 15 rooms there. Aside from that, now that this Korean real estate agent thinks I really know what the fuck I'm doing, she's telling me that in her community she knows of some people who rent out beds for 20 per night. At first I was like, Big deal, but then she tells me that they put bunk beds in the rooms and get like 80 per night for a room."

Kirk's eyes lit up after I said this. Unfortunately it didn't seem like they were lighting up in my direction.

"Really? Hook me up with this chick."

"Excuse me?"

"Well, I didn't mean it like that."

"Yeah, I know. But put your dick back in your pants anyway."

"Well, I guess that deal sounds a lot better now."

"Yeah. Well, if it does come off and I fill it up one way or another, then I've got no qualms about doing this one in Whitestone."

"Yeah, I getcha."

Over the course of the next week, I sent out several credit card applications. I also took a look at another handyman special with a new real estate agent. It was over in College Point about a block off 20th Avenue. Handyman special was a friendly term for this property. The owner was a jack of all trades, master of none. He demonstrated this by basically starting every project he could in the house and not finishing one. To put it nicely, the house was a wreck. I had taken Kirk along with me to this one, and as we walked through each room, Kirk rolled his eyes in disbelief at the condition. After we got done looking at it, we said our goodbyes to the owner, and we went outside.

Kirk still had on a face like he ate sour lemons, so the real estate agent turned to me and said, "You told me to bring you to a handyman special."

"No, that's fine. I know what I asked for," I answered.

"I'd like to know how you worded this one on your selling list," Kirk said to the real estate agent.

I talked with the real estate agent for a little while longer, and he left.

"Mike, come on. What are you, nuts? This house is a wreck."

"Well, understand this, Kirk. Not only do you and I know that, but even though the owner talked about all the ideas that he started, he knows it's a wreck, too. So I don't have to sell him on that point. But there's something more important about this place than that."

"Would could that be?"

"The house is a three-story, "legal" two-family, and he's using it as a one and his selling price is listed as a one-family. All I have to do is throw a kitchen upstairs and, bam, I make another 50 grand as a two-family."

"Oh, I getcha."

About two weeks later I got turned down for all the credit card applications I sent out. I also didn't get a high enough appraisal from the next bank I was dealing with, so it didn't look that good for my deal on Prince Street. Even though I got a little more money on the table from this bank, the only way I would be able to make the deal work was if I would be able to get the seller to hold a larger second mortgage with me. I called my real estate agent and told her to ask the owner if he would take a slightly higher note with me. Fortunately the real estate agent didn't have any qualms about asking this question anymore, so she got back to me pretty fast, and unfortunately the owner said no.

"You know, Mike, I think if you didn't take this long to ask him, he might have gone for it," she suggested.

"I feel the same way, too, but what could I do? It was out of my hands. Well, maybe it's not a total loss to everyone. You can take the deal, if you want. I'm done with it."

She thanked me for the offer, and we said we would keep in touch. It kinda hurt losing my first deal, but it also put a little fuel in my tank to get another one.

A few days later I picked up Patti from school and took her home. When we got to her house, her sister, Sharron, was running around the house all excited.

"What's up, Sharron? Why are you so happy?" Patti asked.

"Look, Patti, I got a credit card."

"Really, that's great. What's the limit?" Patti asked.

"Two- thousand dollars."

"What? Get the hell out of here. You're only 19. What did you tell them, you were a rocket scientist?"

"No, they mailed me an application telling me that I was pre-approved."

Really not believing that it was that easy for her, I quizzed her on the whole process that had taken place in order for her to be mailed a pre-approved credit card with a two-thousand dollar limit. After she explained to me that the only thing she had done recently was to sign up for college, I asked her if she would mind if I called the credit card company and talked to them, especially since I had just got turned down for one from the same company. Sharron told me that she didn't mind, not that I was going to give them her name, so I called.

"Hello, how are you? I have a question that I hope you can answer. I was recently turned down for one of your credit cards. Now, I have a job, I've paid many monthly bills and handled lots of money and obligations. So how is it that my girlfriend's sister, who just turned 19 and has never paid a gas, electric or phone bill and who doesn't have a job and lives at home, gets approved for a credit card with a two thousand dollar limit and the only thing she thinks she did to give anyone information about herself was to have signed up for college?" I asked.

"Well, that's it. She signed up for college classes. That's how we got her name."

"Yeah...and?"

"Well, you see it worked like this. Though your sister doesn't have any credit, our company feels that she will be a good risk because she has enrolled in college and will become a good customer for us after she's done with college," I was told.

"Oh, I see. But I've got to fill out an entire application, give you my work number, and urine sample, so I can get turned down?"

"Well, maybe your credit is no good."

"My credit is just as 'no good' as hers."

"Well, I'm sorry, sir. Maybe you can resubmit your application again."

"No, I think I should sign up for a music class at college in order to be pre-approved by your company. Well, thanks for giving me that enlightening information. Bye."

Sharron turned to me, put her nose up in the air, and taunted, "Well, Michael, you know how they like to give credit to mature and sophisticated individuals."

"Yeah, get outta here, you little wiseass," I joked back with her.

Now that my first deal was a dead issue, the deal in College Point was looking a lot better. This time, though, I didn't have the time for the real estate agent to decide whether or not they felt comfortable asking the owner to hold a second mortgage, so I drove over and asked him myself. He was a little leery about it at first, but after talking to his wife about it, he agreed. The only stipulation I had with him was about being a little flexible with the exact amount of the second mortgage, in case the appraisal didn't come in high enough. After pointing out a few features that weren't finished in his house and telling him that they were the reasons I had my doubts with the bank, he and his wife agreed to be flexible with me.

After I got done with him, I drove home and decided that in order to save time I would put in three separate contracts with three separate banks. That's not to say that banks like to hear this, but after talking it over with Kirk, he agreed that it would be a good idea to save time.

Patti called me today and told me not to worry about picking her up from college. She explained that someone would give her a ride. This went on for about two weeks until one day I asked her from whom she was getting a ride.

"Well... my teacher's giving me a ride home."
"Excuse me? What are you working on-your grades?"
"Oh Michael, It's nothing."
"Well, that's not what I wanted to hear."

Patti looked at me for a second or two and then said, "What?"
"Well, let me ask you this, Patti. It takes me about an hour to leave here, pick you up, and take you home. But now that someone's giving you a ride home, the same trip is taking you two or three hours, and you're gonna stand there and say, "What?"
"Okay, so I went out and had coffee with him once or twice."
"Oh, I see. And you were gonna tell me about it when? After he tried to make a move on you?"
"No, it's not like that. It's nothing."
"All right, fine. As long as it's nothing, then let him pick you up in the mornings, too."

After I hung up, I thought that maybe this wasn't what I really wanted to say, but I didn't seem mentally to have the time to deal with this bullshit. That's not to say I didn't care about her, but maybe I could have handled it differently.

I met up with Kirk, and he was just dying to show me the new office he had gotten at Bernie's building. We drove over there, and then Kirk introduced me to a lawyer who rented an office from Bernie; his name was Michael Ageges. Then he showed me his office.

"Well, it's not huge, and it doesn't have a great view, but at least it's mine." Kirk beamed as he leaned back in his office chair.

"Not bad, Kirk. It's pretty nice. So you'll be doing mortgages here with Bernie then, huh?"
"Yep, I just started full-time a few weeks ago, and I already got three deals going on."
"That sounds pretty good. Good luck with them."
"Thanks. Hey, you know, Mike, that deal with Richard in Whitestone is still available."
"Really? You haven't found anybody for it yet?"
"No, not really but it is still available, and I had another private appraisal done on it, and it still comes in right at the numbers."
"Well, I'll keep it in mind, but right now I'm waiting for an answer with College Point. Which reminds me, why don't you give them a call, and see how the appraisals went?"

Kirk called up each one of the banks and was told that one bank came in low, and the appraisal people in the other two banks weren't available.

"Make sure you call them for me tomorrow," I reminded him.
"Yeah, I will."

We hung out for a little longer, and then he drove me home.

Within a few days, I got my answers from the appraisal people. Another one of the banks came in low, and then the other one put an interesting deal together for me. In the first place, all the numbers came in on their appraisal, but then the deal they were willing to do for me consisted of the Bank holding $25,000 at the closing table in an escrow account. Once I got done fixing a few things on the house, then they would release the money after they sent back their appraiser to see if the list of things they would supply was complete. That night I went over to Kirk's brother's house to pick Kirk up, so we could go over the numbers and the list of requirements that was faxed to him.

When I got there, I noticed that the lawn was overgrown, and I made a comment about it after Kirk got in my car.

"Well, fuck it," he said. "I'm not gonna do it. Besides that, like I told you, I'm having bigger problems than that with my brother."

I decided that I didn't want to get into it with him and just left that conversation alone as we rode over to a diner. We got there, ordered some coffees, and went to work. By about our fourth cup of coffee we figured out that I would have about $25,000 to work with after closing costs were paid. Even though it seemed like a lot of money, it was cutting it close in my mind to do all the repairs, hire some people, buy supplies, and cover about 2,200 per month while I didn't work or have an income from tenants.

"Listen, Mike. I know you've turned down this deal once or twice already, but how about this? I'm working over here in the mortgage office, and I'm making pretty good money now. What if we went in as partners on the Whitestone house and the College Point house? Because this way you'd get $25,000 from Whitestone to help out with College Point and you wouldn't have to be responsible for the total nut in Whitestone. And if there's any problems with tenants in College Point, I can help out with that nut also."
"So what are you saying? You and I will split the Whitestone nut and if I need help in College Point you'll pitch in on that nut for a fifty-fifty split all around?"
"Well, yeah, I mean, look at it this way, Mike. If anyone can really get screwed, it's gonna be me, because everything will be in your name."
"Yeah, but on top of what looks to be a 2500-dollar nut in College Point, I'm gonna be responsible for about another 1350 in Whitestone in order to get $25,000."
"Yeah, that's if I don't rent out the upstairs in Whitestone. If I do rent it, let's say for $600 as a studio or 700 with the extra room. It'll bring down the nut in Whitestone even more. In the long run it helps us both out, Mike, because I need to get out of my brother's house, and you need more of a cushion to help you rebuild College Point in order to get them to release the 25 grand they're holding

over there."

"Well, that's another thing. If I take the time to break my ass over there to finish the house, then I'm supposed to split that money they release with you?"

"Well, maybe not 50-50, but remember, if I didn't help you to cover the nut in Whitestone, you wouldn't get that money from there to help out in College Point."

"Well, I don't know. It's not something I'm going to make a decision on right here and now. I'll have to think about it for a day or two."

"Okay. Yeah, I can understand that."

After I drove Kirk home, I went past the College Point house to talk to Mineo, the owner. I went to assure him that everything was all right and the bank looked like they were going to go through with it. At this point, I didn't want to explain to him about the minor setback, because it would mean that he would get a little less money on the closing table. I just wanted to go over and feel him out a bit. I now had a new option to go with which required involving Kirk, but I just wasn't 100 percent sure I wanted to go that route at this time. I spoke with Mineo for a little while, and then he looked at his wife, then at me, and said, "Well, Mike, there is one little thing my wife and I wanted to talk to you about."

Oh shit, I thought. Here it comes. After all this bullshit and running around, now he's gonna drop a bombshell on me.

"Well, what's that?" I said sheepishly.

"We don't want Cesar, our German shepherd, so you gotta take him too with the house."

Man, was I was relieved, amused, and quick with my answer. "Why not? He seems like a good dog."

I spoke to Mineo about the repairs and renovations I planned to do for a little while longer, and then I left after petting my dog.

About a week later my friend Aaron stopped by. After bullshitting for a little while, he said, "Hey, Mike. What's up with you and Patti?"

"Well, we haven't seen each other in over a week, but we still talk on the phone. Why?"

"So you guys broke up?"

"Not technically. We just got into an argument about something. Why do you ask?"

"Well, because I stopped by Jeff's apartment at about one in the morning, and Patti was hanging out with him."

"Really, Jeff?"

"Yeah, I just thought I ought to let you know."

"Thanks. I appreciate it."

"No problem. I've got to go. Call me tomorrow. Maybe we'll go out and have a drink."

"Yeah, maybe that's a good idea. I haven't gone out in a while."

After he left, I almost felt like calling Patti on this, but I figured I didn't want to act like a bitch, so I decided not to.

The next day Patti called me. "Hi, how you doing?"

"I'm doing fine... How about you?"

"I'm fine."

"Good. Good, how's Jeff doing?"

"I guess Aaron talked to you."

"I guess he did. So how is Jeff doing?"

"You know, Michael, don't let Aaron blow this out of proportion."

"You're hanging out at Jeff's apartment at 1 in the morning, and Aaron is blowing something out of proportion?"

"Well, I can tell what you're thinking."

"Oh, can you?"

"You know, Michael, I've known Jeff for a long time also. It's not like I just met him."

"So what does that have to do with you hanging out with him at 1 in the morning, Patti?"

"Nothing, but don't blow it out of proportion. We're just friends."

"Well, I'll tell you what. When you can come up with a better reason for being over there at 1 in the morning, especially since he happens to live about five miles away from you, give me a call, all right?"

"CLICK."

That night, after giving it a little bit of thought, I decided to take Aaron up on his offer. We started out hitting some bars in the neighborhood, and then we went to Bell Boulevard to check out some bars up there. We were having a good time and a few drinks until about 2 a.m., and then Aaron mentioned that he had to be at work by 7 a.m., so we left. After I dropped him off at his house, I was still in a partying mood so I wondered which bar I should go to. After stopping at one or two of the neighborhood bars and finding nobody around, I decided to stop by a topless bar over on College Point Boulevard and Roosevelt Avenue.

When I got inside, I could tell by the number of people that it was a pretty slow night, but being that I was already there, I decided to have a beer or two anyway. There was only one cute girl dancing there that night, and after her dance number was up, I decided that I'd wait and watch her dance one more time, then I'd leave.

After she came back on stage, she stood in front of me and danced there for practically her whole number. By now I was done with my beer, and I figured I'd throw her a five spot for entertaining me. I stood up, held out her tip, and waited a second for her to walk over.

"Here you go. Goodnight."

"Where are you going?"

I looked at her a little puzzled and said, "I'm going home... going to bed."

"No, you're not. You're gonna drive me home."

"Oh... all right... I guess I'm driving you home."

"I'm supposed to do one more dance, but fuck this, it's dead. I wanna leave. Wait by the door for me. I'll be there in one sec, all right?"

"Yeah, alright."

As I stood by the door, I wondered if something was up. Maybe some guy was bothering her, I thought, as I scanned the bar. As long as it's not the bouncer, I can kick anyone's ass in here, I reasoned. Hmm... wait a minute. Maybe she's got an ex-boyfriend coming to pick her up. As I was thinking about this, she came out of the back half dressed and said, "C'mon, I'm outta this dump."

I gave one glance around the bar to see if anybody was getting up, and then we left.

"So where am I taking you?" I said as we walked to the car.

"Brooklyn."

"Brooklyn! Fuck, I'm not gonna get back until 5 in the morning."

"Well, who knows? Maybe if you play your cards right, I'll let you sleep over."

"Or tell me to take a hike after I get there."

She stopped, looked at me, then unzipped her jacket, flashed me her tits and said, "You want to give it a shot or not? I can still call a cab."

"Well... you made your point... I'll give it a shot."

Just before I got to the highway, I stopped at an all night deli to get a soda.

"Do you want anything?"

"No, I'm fine," she answered.

As I got out of the car she said, "I've got plenty of condoms, you know."

"I'm... going in for a soda!?"

"Yeah, right."

"Yeah, right, your ass. You can frisk me when I come out all right?"

"Good, I will."

After I got back into the car, she patted me down quickly and then grabbed my groin for a second.

"All right, you're clean. Start the car. Let's go."

Being that Brooklyn is one of the boroughs that doesn't go by the street grid rules, I got a little lost. But after an hour I finally found my way over to her house. I pulled up in front of her house, gave her a peck on the cheek, and said good night.

"Whada ya' mean good night? Ain'tcha coming in?"

"Well, look. It's getting late and I've still got to drive back. So if I come in and chit chat for a while, I'll get home even later and probably hit some rush hour traffic to boot."

"Whada ya' talking about? Turn the car off and come inside. I'll letcha sleep over... But don't get fucking nutty on me once I let you in. You seem like a nice guy," she said with her now obvious Brooklyn accent.

I turned the car off and followed her into the three-story building. Lori had a small studio apartment on the first floor.

"What do you do, sleep on the couch?"
"Naa, it opens up into a bed."

I sat down, and Lori got me a beer. After a little small talk, she asked me to help her count the money she had made tonight. Then she pulled out two wads of bills from her purse. Being a little surprised at this I said, "What makes you think I'm not going to rob you?"
"I don't know. You seem cool enough not to."

While we were counting her money, she said, "Let me ask you something. Are you one of those guys?"
"Excuse me...? One of what guys...?"
"You know... one of those guys."
"No... I don't know... one of what guys?"
"You know, those guys that hang around topless joints and wait for the dancers to get off...?"
"What do you mean, like a pervert?"
"No, one of those guys that goes home with the dancers, has sex with them, gets paid, and leaves."

Whoa, dude, I thought. What a fucking career. "Well... yeah, I am. How much do they make?"
"No you're not, you're lying now."
"Well, look, don't worry about it. I like you, so I won't charge you for the first time."
"Yeah, right. You ain't a prostitute."
"Listen, I'll tell you what. You can be my pimp and line me up with work, and I'll cut you in for a piece of the action, all right?"
"Well, not while I'm fucking you."
"Yeah, but we ain't fucking."
"We will be in about ten minutes."
"Oh... okay."

Her take for the night was about $500, which I thought was great. Then she looked at me, then back at the cash and said, "Man... what a shitty night," as she stuffed it in her purse.
"You make more than this in a night?"
"Yeah."
"Shit, put a fucking G-string on me, and I'll dance for $500 a night all week long."
"Really? Do you want to borrow some of my costumes?"
"Shit, forget about the costumes. Just get me some work," I joked.

After a few more minutes of talking, Lori got up and turned down the light. Lori stood about 5'9". She had sandy brown hair about shoulder length that didn't know if it was in or out of a perm, a tight little butt, and large grapefruit-sized breasts.

"Do you want me to do a little strip tease for you?"

Man, what am I in, fucking heaven? I thought. "Yeah... that would be nice."

Lori turned on some music and slowly started to peel off her clothes. Needless to say, Lori had an incredible body. After she was totally naked, she started rubbing her pubic area while she did a few different poses for me. By now I was practicing on bursting my zipper. Then she walked over, opened my pants, and placed her head between my thighs. Unsure as to whether or not we would ever have sex again, I made sure that we had sex for three hours that night.

After we were done and slightly napping, I massaged her tight body. You know, Mike, I thought to myself, she has a really tight body, not an ounce of fat from what I can see. Maybe it's from all the dancing she does. Watch, with my luck she's is only 16 or something.

"Lori?"
"Hmm?"
"How old are you?"
"Huh...? I'm 26."
"Oh, okay, just checking."

I got up late that afternoon, had sex with Lori, and then made us some coffee. After we drank it in bed, I got up and slowly started to get dressed, assuming we wouldn't see each other again.

"Okay, listen. This is my schedule for the rest of the week," she said.

Then she started blurting out names of clubs and times that she would be home in the mornings, as a smile found its way to my face.

".... And this is my phone number. Either call me or be here tonight when I get home, all right?" she said.
"Yeah... I will."
"All right, come here and give me a kiss."

After I gave her a kiss, I left and drove back home. One of the things I felt about her was that she was a little tough guy, a little tough chick from Brooklyn. When I got home, I took a shower, got dressed, and then, I checked my answering machine- Patti had called me last night.

Over the course of the next week, I postponed the College Point deal and an answer for Kirk. I met with Lori several times at her house in Brooklyn after she got off, and I finally returned Patti's phone calls.

Patti tried to explain to me about her being at Jeff's house, and I wasn't sure if I should really buy it, especially since I was sleeping with Lori now. Then in the middle of everything I had going on, my mother had come back from upstate, and we got into another big fight about how I wasn't pitching in with any money. She asked me to leave again, so I moved out again by that night. The way I felt about it was that I had paid my rent over there for a long time to come.

I stayed with a friend of mine, and we hardly saw each other because I was spending time with Lori and her odd hours. So it was working out pretty good with my new roommate. Then one day Patti showed up telling me that she wanted to talk to me in person, so we went out and got some coffee. She started to feed me a story about how she ended up at Jeff's house and that nothing happened there between them.

"I can't believe that you could think that way," she said.

"Why shouldn't I think that way? First there was that teacher thing, and now this? I don't know, Patti. Your story isn't going down easy."

We talked for about another hour, and then I drove her back to her car, and she left. I wasn't sure how I would feel better about this situation by either talking to her, or by not talking to her at all.

I took a ride over to the Whitestone Bridge after I dropped her off, just to be in a neutral situation in order to think about a few things. I still had time with the College Point house, and I had Kirk pestering me about the Whitestone house from time to time. Under the circumstances of the College Point deal, the Whitestone deal started to look like a good option also. The only reason I didn't want to jump right into that one was because I didn't like the idea of being responsible for almost 6 grand per month before tenants, with my name on all the paper.

I've got to do something, though. I've got to take one of them, take Kirk as a partner, or find something else. I don't want to stay where I'm at for too much longer being indecisive, either. Okay, let me get back to that in a minute, I thought. Now what am I gonna do about this girl situation? I know Lori is a bit of a party girl, and I don't want to get too wrapped up with her for that reason. But, man, the sex is great with her. As for Patti, she's not a street girl but I have lost a bit of trust with her. Maybe I should drop both of them for now and just concentrate on becoming successful. That sounded like the best thing to do, but I was sure another part of my body would object to that idea. What is the most important thing to you, Mike? Being successful or being "happy," because I don't think I'm going to have the time, energy or money to do them both right now.

For the next day or two, I didn't contact Patti or Lori. I spent my time at the lumber and hardware stores trying to add up prices on the material I would need to complete the College Point deal. After doing this calculation and adding in my time factor and factors from people I would hire, it was close, almost too close on its own. When I got home, Lori called me.

"Where the hell have you been?"
"Well, I've been busy."
"Oh. Well, you better not have found another girlfriend, or I'll come over there and kick your ass."
"Don't worry, baby. You know I don't want you to do that."
"Are you being a wise guy or something...?"
"No, dear."
"Well, listen. I bought a new costume for work so I want you to come over and see me in it. Then you can take it off me and fuck my brains out."
"I think... I could handle that."

"Okay, honey, I get off at 2 a.m. so I'll be home by 3."

"Alright, I'll see you tonight."

"Okay, see ya."

I got over there that night at 3, and Lori showed me her new costume, which was a belly dancer. After she did a strip tease for me, she asked me to tie her up, blindfold her, and have sex with her. I have to admit that I didn't mind helping her with her request.

Having sex with Lori in general was great. I'd say the problem I had with it was that she was a screamer, whether she was tied up or not. I mean I've been with girls who were moaners, pleaders, directors, but I've never been with a girl who was this loud and vocal. She would yell out, "Fuck me" so loud that she'd almost embarrass me. We had sex off and on until about 5 a.m., and then we started to doze off. At about 5:30, there was a knock at her back door.

"Who the fuck is that?" I asked.

"Don't worry. It's probably Tony."

"Tony who!?!"

"Tony, the guy from across the street. I grew up with him; he's a crackhead. Whenever he runs out of money, he comes over here and borrows some money from me."

"So why don't you tell him to go fuck himself!?"

"Because he's a friend of mine, and he always helped me out when I needed it."

Lori got up, threw on a towel, and turned on the light. Being that the back door was at the side of the pullout bed, I pulled a sheet over my ass. Lori opened the door, and I looked at Tony with a frown on my face.

"Hey, man, I'm sorry to bother you," he said to me. Then he looked at Lori and said, "Lori, can I get a few bucks?"

"Yeah, Tony. You can have a few bucks, but stay out of trouble, all right?"

"Yeah, Lori, thanks. I will."

Then Lori closed the door and climbed back into bed with me.

"Are you afraid to say no to this guy? 'Cause if you are, I'll go out and beat his ass right now."

"No, it's not like that. Like I said, I grew up with him, and I feel sorry for him. Besides, I've got it now, and I he helped me when I didn't have money."

I didn't really like the idea of this situation, but good pussy overrides your judgment sometimes, as all guys know unfortunately. Besides that, I knew how it was when I was down on my luck and Mike Viale would come over and throw me a few bucks. But it was different. I wasn't out smoking crack. We woke up about noon, had sex for the third time, and then we went to get something to eat. We ended up at a fast food restaurant, and Lori complained that she lived in these places.

"Well, maybe one day I'll cook you something."

"Really? You would? Oh, you're Italian. You can probably cook good. Wow, would you really cook me a home-cooked meal?"

"Oh, come on. You're acting like you've never had one before."

"Well, when I was a kid my mother would sometimes cook for us. But that was years ago."

I looked at Lori for a second, and then I said, "Lori... where are your parents?"

"Well, I haven't seen my mother in two years, but I know through my aunt that she still lives in Brooklyn. I don't know where my father is."

"Why haven't you seen her in two years?"

Lori looked at me for a second and said, "Because her shitty boyfriend tried to have sex with me once or twice, and the last time I told her about it she slapped me in the face and called me a liar. So I left home."

"How old were you at that time?"

"Well... I was young."

"Really? That's some shit."

"Yeah, but fuck that. I think you're just trying to get out of cooking me dinner."

"No, I'm not."

"Okay, then come over Sunday and cook me some spaghetti and meatballs. I've got off Sunday during the day, Sunday night, and I don't have to be at work until 9 o'clock Monday night. Make sure you bring some wine and good Italian bread, okay? Please."

"Okay, okay, and what else should I get?"

"Besides condoms, nothing. Oh, don't worry. If you cook me dinner, I'll screw your brains out, so you better get some rest before then."

After we finished eating, I gave her a kiss goodbye and dropped her off at home.

When I got home, I got a message that a real estate agent had left me. I called him, and he explained that he had found "just what I was looking for," a handyman special. Being that I was keeping myself in limbo with the other deals I was kicking around, I figured I'd take the time to check it out, so we set an appointment for the following day at noon.

Patti called me a short time later. She told me that the car her father had bought her had broken down, and she wanted to know if I could drive her to school in the afternoons and pick her up until her car was fixed.

"Well, yeah... I guess."

"Oh, come on. Don't sound so happy about it. I'll make it up to you. Besides, you're not working now."

"Yeah... all right. What time do I have to be there?"

"Be here at 10."

"Listen, if I get there at ten, be ready, because I've got an appointment at 12."

"All right, I will."

"I'm serious. I don't want to come over and have to wake you up or wait for you to put on your makeup."

"All right, I'll be ready."

When I got there the next morning Patti was dressed and ready to go. Man, she looked good, long blond hair, nails done up, heels, the whole ten yards, I thought. She walked over to the car, got in, and gave me a peck on the cheek. Patti and I talked for a while on pleasant terms, but it didn't take too long before we started to argue about the whole situation between us. If I was to judge myself within the situation, I could say that it wasn't right to be involved with another person while having conversations in regards to resolving a situation with Patti, to a degree. On the other hand, how long did she have a similar situation going on with me?

When I really thought about it, there was a major difference between the two relationships. With Patti I had already been in a bit of a relationship; with Lori even though she was fun to hang around with and a great sex toy, I wasn't being honest with her about my feelings, and I started to feel a little guilty about that. I thought about that reason a lot deeper, and I knew I felt very uncomfortable about a bunch of guys throwing a bunch of money at her while she stripped for them. But then she handed me a piece of paper with all the addresses and phone numbers of the places she's working, and she came home and slept with me. So what I mean is that even though we were in a relationship, I wouldn't allow myself to truly believe it, maybe to spare my feelings if she just left one night, never to be seen again.

When I dropped Patti off at Queens College, she gave me another peck on the cheek and told me not to be late as she got out of the car. I almost felt like reminding her that her teacher would probably be more than happy to give her a ride home, but I bit my tongue instead.

After I dropped her off, I rode over to the handyman special to meet with the real estate agent. When I got there, I drove around the neighborhood for a little bit just to get a feel for the area. Then I drove over to the house. I was happy to see that the real estate agent had also gotten there a little early so we could get this underway. We said our hellos and then went inside and met with the owners. After our how do you do's, I started my physical investigation towards what I was looking for.

The house was a one-family, and it did need some work. The only thing that I didn't like about the place was that instead of having a bunch of small rooms it had a fewer bigger rooms, which meant fewer tenants for me. But even taking that into account, I still felt that I could make money on it as long as the numbers were in my favor.

By the time the real estate agent and I walked back out front, I had already determined what those numbers should be, so I turned to him and said, "All right, look. They're asking for 180,000. Now I think that's a little too high for the shape of the house, but instead of arguing with them about ten grand, I'll eat that as long as they do something for me."
"What's that?"
"I'll pay 180,000, but they've got to hold a 60,000 dollar second mortgage on the house for me."

The real estate agent stood there for a second or two, and then he said, "I can't go in there and ask them that."
"Why not?"
"Well, because... it's just not right. I've never heard of these deals before."

What I thought was a little humorous about this situation was that the real estate agent was about

45 years old, and he really hadn't heard of those types of deals, just like some of the real estate agents I dealt with before him.

"Well, look, it is possible as long as they agree to it. So just go inside and ask them. Otherwise, I can't do the deal because I feel that I'll be laying out too much of my own money. Besides that, remind them that I'm not arguing price with them."

"Well, I..."

"Oh, come on, what have you got to lose? About 7 grand for your pocket if you don't ask? Look, if they agree to it, I can get the financing, okay?"

The real estate agent put his hand to his chin, looked off into the distance, and said, "Okay." Then he walked back into the house.

After a couple of minutes he walked back out, shaking his head. He came over and said to me, "Well, they almost went for it but felt that they would need a little more money because of their high first mortgage. Now since you told me what numbers you could work with, I didn't make any type of counter offer."

"Okay, that's fine, because I wouldn't be able to work out this deal if they can't work with those numbers. Thanks for your time, and if you come up with any other properties like this, please give me a call."

"Well, okay... I will. Hey, are you sure you'd be able to get financing?"

"Yeah, I'm sure."

"Okay, I'll talk to you soon."

It's funny, but I noticed that the first couple of times that I spoke with real estate agents about these types of deals, it took me at least a week to feel comfortable enough to ask for a second mortgage. That's not to say that they were all accepted, or that all the real estate agents called me back to do business. But by now, I just didn't have time to mess around with these particulars. It was either yes or no, right there at the property.

When I got home I decided to call up the owner of the College Point deal, smooth him over, and stall for a little bit longer. I knew I had a limited amount of time left contract- wise, but I also knew that nobody had made an offer on his house prior to me for nine months. When I spoke to him he seemed a little nervous, but I calmed him down and then started to talk to him about his "knowledge" of some of the major repairs on the house. This had started just to soften him up for the time I needed to ask him to hold more money, unless of course I went with the Whitestone deal instead or at all.

He went on and on about all the things he had started and how nice they would look when they were done, but each time I asked him how much he thought, let's say a new toilet bowl was, he'd say, "Oh, you can probably get one of them second hand somewhere for real cheap."

I wasn't picking his brain for answers. I just wanted to make sure his mental calculator was working.

The following day I picked Patti up and dropped her at school. I hadn't seen Lori though, because we had a pretty big weekend planned, and I wanted to be rested up for it. After I picked up Patti later in the day she asked me if I wanted to go out and have a drink or two "as friends." I figured I had nothing to lose, so I said yes. A few drinks turned into dinner, and then Patti asked me if I could do her another small favor.

"Well, that depends. What is it?"
"You know my father has a new girlfriend, right?"
"Yeah?"
"Well, she hasn't been in the country that long, and my father's bugging me to take the both of them out to the movies."
"Yeah...?"
"I've been putting them off for a long time, and I was wondering if you could come with me so I don't have to go alone?"
"Oh, man, that's asking a lot, Patti. Couldn't we leave your father at home?" I said half jokingly.
"Oh, good, so you'll go."
"Whoa, wait a minute."
"No, you can't change your mind now. You said you'd go."
"Yeah, whatever, but you will owe me for this one."
"Okay, so I'll tell him this weekend then."
"No, actually I'm gonna be busy this weekend. Wednesday night would be better."

Patti looked at me for a second and then said, "Okay, fine."

After we got done having dinner, I drove Patti home. When we got there, she leaned over and gave me a kiss on my cheek, and then she left.

When I got to my friend's house that night, Lori had called and left a message that she wanted to see me tonight and that she would be home by two in the morning. Even though I was a little tired and we already had plans for the weekend, I figured I'd take a little nap and go over anyhow. I got there about ten after two, and Lori didn't show up until 2:30. She got out of the cab and ran over to my car.

"Ooooh, I'm so glad you came. I haven't seen you in days. Where the hell were ya'?" she said as she gave me a big kiss.
"Well, I've been pretty busy."
"Yeah, you better not be married with 5 kids 'cause I'll kick your ass."
"Yeah, but will you still fuck me?"
"Probably," she answered.
"Well, let's go inside so I can fuck you now."

When we got inside Lori shoved me backwards onto the couch, pulled my pants down, and placed her head between my thighs.

"Well, so much for resting for the weekend," I said.
"Don't worry. I'll take it easy on you tonight," she answered.

We had sex until about 6 a.m., and then we fell asleep. When we woke up at noontime, we had sex again. Then we took a shower together and went out to have some lunch. After lunch I drove her home and gave her a kiss.

"Don't forget now. Spaghetti and meatballs, candles, bread, and some good wine."
"All right. Come here." I said.
"What?"
"Here's that other kiss you wanted."

After we kissed, she walked away, looked back, smiled, and wiggled her ass for me as she kept walking.

Being that I was coexisting with Lori's work schedule, I figured the best thing to do was to go shopping now back in my neighborhood instead of scrambling around later, so I did. After getting all the food, I bought her a bunch of flowers and put them in my fridge for later. By the time I was done, Kirk had paged me, so I called him back. He asked me if I had made any plans with anything and then begged me to take him on as a partner.

"I don't know, Kirk. Sometimes I wonder about the whole thing of being partners."
"Mike, let me ask you this. If we went in as partners and I fucked you, what would you do to me?"
"I'd probably kill you"
"Exactly, and do you think I want to die? I've got a wife and a kid, and now I'm taking care of my sister-in-law's son, Nelson. I might even adopt him. So why would I fuck you?"
"I don't know. I'm not saying you would. It's just that I don't like putting myself in a situation where I could get fucked, that's all."
"All right, then. How about this? We'll go in as partners on both of them, and if you feel that you don't want the Whitestone house at some point down the road, keep the 25 grand you'll make over there, and I'll have my wife, Linda, buy the house from you."
"Well, words are fine and dandy, Kirk, but what if you back out and I'm stuck with everything in my name?"
"All right, then. How about this? I'll have the attorney draw up a contract that has Linda purchasing the house from you, and we won't date it."
"Yeah, and that can be torn up."
"No, it can't. Sal's a lawyer. He's not going to risk his job over a piece of paper. If you want, we'll even make up a private agreement that says the same thing."
"Well, I don't know. It sounds a little better. Let me think about it a day or two."
"You know, Mike, you've been saying that for a while now..."
"Yeah, so?"
"Well, I'm just telling you if someone else..."
"Yeah, yeah, if someone else comes along, you'll sell it to them. Don't forget you've been telling me this for a while now, too."
"All right, I'm gonna go," he said.
"All right, I'll talk to you later."

Sometimes when something seems too good to be true, it is. Something about the Whitestone deal with Kirk as a partner just seemed that way.

That night I got over to Lori's house at about 2:20; she wasn't home yet so I waited outside with the groceries and the flowers. By the time it was 3:30 I was pretty pissed because she still wasn't home like she told me she would be. I remembered the name of the club she was working at and even though I had never let myself, or had the need to call her at work before this night, I did. I drove over to a pay phone and got the number from information.

"Hello."
"Hey, how you doing? This is Mike. I'm calling for Lori."
"Who are you?"
I was smart enough to know not to say something to jeopardize Lori's job, but being that I was a little pissed off now I said, "I'm Lori's boyfriend!?"
"Aww, shit... I didn't know Lori had a boyfriend. Has anybody called you?"
"No... that's why I'm calling to see where she is!"
"Fuck..."
"Whatdaya mean fuck?"
"Look, Mike. I hate to be the one to tell you this, but...Lori's dead."
"What...!?!? What are you talking about??"
"Lori was waiting for a cab tonight and, after about a half hour the bouncer's younger brother offered her a ride home."
"Yeah?"
"Well, he must've been driving fast because the car flipped over. They got thrown out through the Ttops and died."
"No! No fucking way!"
"Look, Mike... I don't know you from a hole in the wall, and I'm not fucking with you. Here, hold on. Talk to the bouncer."

There was a short pause, and then I heard someone else's voice on the phone say, "What ...? Who...? Shit... Yeah, hey, Mike. Listen, it's true, man... Sorry. They're dead. They're both fucking dead, man. Look, the cops don't have a way of notifying any of Lori's next of kin, so I guess you can talk to them," he said as his voice started cracking.

I felt numb as he read off the phone number and name of the police officer in charge. When he got done the first guy got back on the phone and told me he was sorry because Lori was a good kid, and that she didn't fuck around with anything or anybody. She was all business, he said. Then he hung up. I wandered back over to my car and sat on the hood.

Naaa, this is a joke. It's a joke, right, God? A bad fucking joke, right?

The thought of Lori being dead stung. It stung real bad and real deep. I didn't know if I felt like laughing, crying or yelling out loud. It was a wave of anger, disbelief, shock and numbness. I mean, what the fuck? My number came up on the wheel again so soon. Aren't people supposed to have one or two upheavals in their lives and then move on? What the fuck was that all about? Here, Mike, here's a treat. Now it's gone. No matter how I felt or what I thought, I was pretty sure of something: Lori was gone. It really made me wonder if I was glad to have spent time with her or not. I drove around aimlessly for about an hour until I realized that I had to get rid of the flowers and groceries because I couldn't look at them any longer. I drove back to my friend's house and lay in bed thinking about Lori until it started to get light out, and then I fell asleep.

The next day I walked around in a daze from lack of sleep and disbelief. Halfway through the day, I felt pretty bothered about it and decided to pick up a couple of Valiums to calm myself down a little bit. A short while after that, I went back to my friend's house and tried to take a little nap.

By the time evening came around, I felt cooped up and tense. I decided to go out and try to be with some people instead of sitting by myself, so I hit one or two bars in the neighborhood. Nobody I knew was around, and I found myself sharing my drinks and my story with strangers. It wasn't great comfort, but at this point I'd take what I could get. After an hour or two of this, I drove over to the strip club where I had met Lori. It felt surreal just being there, and I found myself saying to myself, Okay, Mike, this is the first time you've ever come to this place, and there was no Lori. You never met her. As I sat there, tears started to roll down my cheeks. I didn't care if someone saw me. I really didn't give a shit if anybody did, but there'd be hell to pay to the guy who might say something wise about it. It's not like I was sobbing out loud, just warm tears rolled down my cheeks. It had been many years since that had happened.

No, Mike... she did exist, and she was a part of your life. Maybe a bit bigger than you knew. Oh shit, what about her body? Who's gonna claim it? Her family probably doesn't even know she's dead. Fuck... I've got to do something. Okay, her address book that she kept in her nightstand, she had her aunt's phone number in there. I had to get it and call her aunt and let her know what happened. Man, I was a little fucked up now but I had to do it. I couldn't let Lori lie in the morgue like that or, worse, get buried in a pauper's grave.

I made my way over to Lori's house in Brooklyn. When I got there, I decided that maybe I could get her back door open. I didn't think that there was any sense in telling any of the people in her building what had happened to her, because Lori did mention to me that she wasn't really friends with anyone who lived there. I felt that if I didn't tell anyone about what happened, Lori's stuff wouldn't be threatened, and her aunt could handle it. When I went around to the back door, I was amazed to find that it was open and that there was a small light on.

What the fuck is this? Maybe Lori's alive, but why would they tell me she was dead unless... what? Maybe she didn't know how to break up with me? Maybe the guy at the club was dating her? What the fuck? I really didn't know what to think now, but I did decide to find her address book.

After that and thinking about this situation for a minute or two, I picked up the telephone, and called the club that Lori had worked at. There was loud club music playing in the background when someone picked up.

"Yeah, hello."
"Yeah, is Lori there?"
"Lori... Lori who?"

"Lori, the girl who died over there the other night."

"Who the fuck is this?"

"This is Mike, her boyfriend."

"...Mike... listen, dude. I'm the one who spoke to you last night. Mike, Lori's dead, man. And don't take this the wrong way man, but I think you need to talk to someone about this, like maybe a priest or someone, ya' know?"

For some reason his words seemed to be true so I got my head together and said, "Listen, I know this sounds weird, but I went over to Lori's house to get her phone book to notify her family, and it's strange because her back door was open and there was a light on."

"Well, yeah, that does sound a little strange. But listen, the guy who died... his brother was crying in my arms last night, and I'm not a sick fuck, Mike. Mike... Lori's dead, okay? Listen, it's a fucked- up thing, but I gotta go now. Take care."

After I heard this I lay down on Lori's sofa bed with my head swimming. I grabbed one of her pillows and placed it under my head and it smelled just like her favorite perfume, a tear rolled down my cheek, and I fell asleep.

"Mike? Mike, are you up?"

What the fuck? Who the fuck is that? I thought as I opened my eyes. I looked over to my right and saw Lori's friend Tony sitting on the arm of the couch.

"What are you doing here?" I asked.

"What am I doing here...? I live here. Don't you know that Lori's dead?"

"Yeah, I know. How do you know?"

"This girl that worked with Lori last night lives in the area, and she told me."

"Oh, so I guess you broke in?" I said.

"No, I didn't break in. Lori had given me a key a long time ago to keep an eye on the place when she worked late. Well what are you doing here?"

"I came here to get Lori's address book so I could call her aunt and let her know what happened."

"Oh," he answered.

We looked at each other for a long second, and then he said without batting an eyelash, "Hey, Mike... can you give me some money?"

I almost felt like getting up and punching him in the mouth because I knew he had already gone through Lori's things. But instead I said, "Yeah, consider this as your last payment from Lori. It's nice to know you feel bad about it. Here," I said as I shoved twenty dollars towards him. He took the twenty, said thanks, and left. I almost decided to get up and leave, but by now the start of a hangover and the end of the Valiums made me decide to lie back down.

When I woke up the next morning, I was stripped to the bone- my money, my gold chain, my gold bracelet, and my diamond ring were all gone. That little cocksucker must've rolled me when I was asleep, I figured. I stood up, held my head, and went to the bathroom for some aspirins. Then I lit a cigarette and made some coffee. After I had two sips in me, I started to thumb through Lori's phone book. I found her aunt's number, took a deep breath, and called her.

I started our conversation by apologizing for being the one to have to break the news, and then I explained to her aunt all I knew.

Her aunt started screaming, "No. No, not Lori..." It felt bad to hear her Aunt crying but I felt like at least I accomplished something for Lori.

After I hung up the phone, I grabbed a picture of Lori and a little hat she used to like to wear. Then I took one more look at her little apartment, secured the back door, and left through the front door.

I walked over to my car, put Lori's hat in there, and then walked across the street to Tony's house. I knocked a few times on the door and, finally, an older woman stuck her head out the window and asked me what I wanted.

"Is Tony here?"
"Who are you? Police?"
"No, I'm a good friend of his... is he home?"
"No, he's not home."
"Well, when he comes home tell him Lori's boyfriend, Mike, stopped by to call for him, okay."
"Okay."

I got in my car and decided to drive around and look for the little fuck. I also stopped in every pawn shop I saw along my little cruise, but I didn't turn up anything. After about a half hour, I decided to go back to my neighborhood to get cleaned up.

I had given Lori's aunt a number where she could reach me, but I was still a little surprised when she phoned me about dinnertime. She was a little bit more composed by now when we spoke, and she explained to me that being that their family was Jewish they were going to have the funeral the next day. She thanked me a few more times, and we talked about Lori for a little while. Then she told me what time the family was going to be there and said that she would be glad to meet me. I didn't tell her, but I had already decided that, for whatever my reasons were, I didn't want to be there for the family end of it.

Lori's funeral was held in the middle of Greenwich Village in Manhattan. I always enjoyed going there, but I didn't know how true that would be any more after this. When I walked into the funeral parlor, nobody was there. I really hoped that it wouldn't be her in the coffin, but there she was, my little tough chick from Brooklyn, all dressed up in a pretty pink and white lace dress. It was heartbreaking.

I petted her eyebrows, and touched her lips, then knelt down and cried. After I was done, I lifted my head, and talked with Lori for a little while.
"Hey baby. It's me, I'm here... You look pretty, baby. But you know that... you always looked pretty to me. I wish you would have called me, I would've come got you. You'll always be in my

heart..., till the day I die, my tough little Brooklyn girl. Bye, bye, baby.

When I got up, I kissed her on the forehead, and startled myself, because I forgot how cold she would feel on my lips. After I felt a slight twist in my heart, I signed the reception book, and left.

I walked around the Village for a while aimlessly, just block to block, and then stopped and had coffee. After sitting there and thinking for a little while, I was glad to know that the driver had died with Lori also. I mean fuck, it was only fair, right?

When I was done with my coffee, I buttoned my jacket and then headed home. A little while after I got home, Patti called me.

"Yeah... Hey, Patti. What's up?"
"Okay, listen. We're all going to be ready in about an hour, and Zena wants to see "Married to the Mob" with Michelle Pfeiffer."
"Oh shit, I don't know, Patti... I don't think I can go today."
"Don't even try this. Zena's dressed, I'm dressed, and my father's taking a shower right now. So just come over in an hour. You promised me you'd take us."
"Yeah... all right. I'll see you in an hour."

Man, just what I wanted, to spend the rest of this day with her nutty father, I thought.

I drove over to Patti's father's house, went in, and said hello. Then we left for the movies. When we got there I went to get popcorn and soda for everybody while they went to find seats. When I got to our seats, the movie had just started, and Michelle Pfeiffer's character looked, talked and acted just like Lori. It was torture, heart wrenching.

I could hardly look at the screen and, when I wasn't looking, I heard Lori's voice through the character.

Patti asked me several times during the movie why I was holding my hand to my forehead, and I explained that I had a headache. What the fuck could I say? I sat and agonized through the whole movie, and I was so happy finally to see it end. After the movie, we went out and had dinner, but I didn't say much of anything. Then I drove everybody home, and they all thanked me for taking them out. I told them it wasn't a problem, and then I left and drove to a bar for a stiff drink.

The following day Kirk called me and asked me if I had made any decisions on anything we had talked about.
"You still want to do this, Kirk?"
"Are you kidding? Definitely!"
"Fine, do it, set it up."
"Fiftyfifty?"
"Yeah, fiftyfifty. But if you don't pitch in on the College Point house, that's going to drop to Zero."

The next day I went over to Kirk's brother's house and filled out all the paperwork that would be needed to do the Whitestone deal. Then I went over to the College Point house and had a bit of a heart to heart talk with Mineo to stall for time. I did this knowing that I had the other bank deal sitting in the wings with a different complex loan, but I figured I'd tell him about the complexities of that loan after I had some positive feedback from the Whitestone deal and really knew what kind of money I would be able to get from there.

That night I drove over to Brooklyn to try and find the little piece of shit who robbed me. I stayed around his house for about three hours, and then I decided to leave at about 2 a.m. Even if I didn't get my shit back, this little fuck was going to get a beating, I thought. By the next day Kirk called me and told me that he put the Whitestone house in with a few banks and that now, like all real estate deals, it was a waiting game. That night I went back to Brooklyn.

I got there at about ten o'clock, and the little fuck was hanging out by his house next to some closed stores with a friend of his. I parked my car around the corner, got out, and walked around the corner.

His friend happened to be standing a few feet away from him now and asked me what I needed, as I got closer. They were obviously dealing drugs, so I played it off and said that I was here to see Tony, because I didn't know this guy. He nodded his head and then turned the volume back up on the ghetto blaster he was holding. I walked over to Tony and, without him looking at me, he said, "Yeah, what'a ya need?"
"I need my fucking jewelry that you stole off me the other night, motherfucker!"

He stepped back with a shocked look on his face, composed himself, and then said, "I don't know what you're talking about, and I think you better leave before you get hurt!"

As he said this, I noticed my gold chain around his neck. I simultaneously punched him in his head and kneed him in the balls. He crashed backwards into the security gates of the store, and I rushed in for the kill. Just as I got another punch off on him, something crashed into the side of my head. I turned to my left and saw his friend holding a broken radio. Originally I had planned on taking Tony out quickly, so that I would be in a better position to deal with his friend if need be, but plans are made to be broken. In the time it took me to decide which person I should go for, his friend ran over and picked up a trash can to throw at me.

Being that Tony was lying on the floor holding his nuts, I guess my choice was made for me. As I ran towards his friend, I had to duck and let the garbage can sail over my head. He took off running, and by the time I chased him around the car and back onto the sidewalk, it appeared that Tony had his wits back and was about to stand up, so I kicked him real hard in the ribs. I turned back towards his friend in time to see him pick up the broken radio and throw it at me. I ducked and started to chase him again. As we circled the car again, an older green Riviera pulled up to the curb with three guys in it, nice and slow. The guy on the passenger side looked over towards Tony and his friend and said, "Hey. Is there a problem here?"

Not realizing who they were really asking, I walked over to the car, rested my hand on the roof, and said calmly, "Na, there's no problem here. I'm just kicking Tony's ass for robbing all my gold the other night."

As the three guys in the car slowly glanced at each other, slightly dumbfounded, I looked down into the passenger's lap and noticed that he had a jacket covering his hand, and it looked like he was holding a gun. They must be the look outs for Tony. Then the one in the passenger seat looked up at me, and said calmly, "Oh... all right. But make it quick, we don't need no cops around here." Then they drove off. Well, that's Brooklyn for ya.'

At this point, a little bit of common sense got in to me. As they drove away, I decided that maybe it wouldn't be in my best interest to be wrestling with five guys at one time if they changed their minds. I looked over at Tony and his friend as unfinished business as they took off running, and then I walked back around the corner to my car.

When I got in the car, I glanced at the baseball bat in the front seat and then resisted the urge to go back out and hit a few ground balls. Instead I decided to drive over to the police station and press charges against him. The way I saw it, I had given him the chance to give me back my shit, plus I kicked his ass. Now I'd just fuck him up again with the cops.

From driving around the neighborhood a few times looking for pawn shops, I knew the police station was only a couple of blocks away, so I drove straight there after getting rid of the bat. When I walked into the precinct, the cop at the desk said, "Holy shit! What happened? Do you want me to call an ambulance?"

I looked down at myself to try and see what he was talking about, and then I saw blood on the left side of my shirt from the shoulder down to my waist. The first thought that came to mind was how my friend "Peck," who had died, thought that the guy who stabbed him had only punched him. But I only remembered getting hit once in the head. I looked back at the desk sergeant and said, "I don't know... I only remember getting hit in the head."

By now the cop came out from around the desk and told me to lift my shirt. After I did this he glanced up and down at me and then looked towards my head.

"Oh, okay, here it is. It's a cut in your ear. You'll probably need some stitches but you'll be all right. So what happened?"

After I finished explaining my story to him, he told me that this Tony was the hard-on of the neighborhood and that he would get one of the detectives who had been working on a case against him. Then he pointed me towards the bathroom so I could wash up. By the time the detective came down I was cleaned up and had seen the cut in my ear and realized that it wasn't too bad, by my standards. I told my story to the detective, and he went on to tell me that this Tony had robbed a couple of old ladies in the neighborhood.

"Well, that's good. Now with this new charge, he can get some time out of it."
"Yeah, I wish... The problem is that the little old ladies were a little too scared to press charges

against him, so he walked," he said.

"Oh, really? Well, I'll tell you what, Officer. I'd really like to save you some paperwork tonight. So if we could go over there now and pick him up, I'd be more than happy if you could drop us off in a dark alley somewhere, and I'll beat him like a dog."

"Well, even though I love the sound of the idea, I can't do that because of my job."

I knew the detective was only slightly joking with me, so I tried a different approach with him.

"Well, actually what I meant to say was maybe you could drop us off somewhere, so I could talk to him about the errors of his ways and to show him what path his life is heading down."

The detective glanced left, then right, and then said to me, "Believe me, son, this is one punk that I'd love to bend the rules on. But I can't."

After talking for another minute or two, it was decided to take a ride past Tony's house to see if he was still there. When we got there, oddly enough, he and his friend were still hanging out. The detective turned to me and asked me if I saw him anywhere and I told him that he was standing right in front of us. They stopped the car, called for a squad car, and then arrested him. When we finally got back to the precinct, the detective gave me the case number and told me to call him in about two days to find out what he would be charged with.

Then he reminded me to have my ear looked at, apparently it was still bleeding. Being that it was getting late, I figured that instead of sitting in a hospital all night in Brooklyn, I'd go back to Queens and get it checked out. Fortunately it was a weeknight so the hospital wasn't that crowded when I got there. As usual, because it wasn't what they considered to be life threatening, I had to sit around until 3 am. When I finally got into the emergency room there, I noticed this girl who lived in the building next to me was there so I said hi to her.

"Do you know her?" a nurse asked.
"Yeah, she lives in the building next to me. Why?"
"Well, she just wandered in here, and she doesn't know her name or address."
"Well, I don't know her last name but she does live next to me, so if you want, I'll talk to the super at her building to tell her parents after I get stitched and leave."
"Well, okay, that would be good because we're not sure what to do with her. We don't want to just release her. Now let me take a look at your problem."

After I showed the nurse my ear and explained how I got it, she asked me if I had talked to any police officers. I explained that it happened in Brooklyn and showed her the report. Within the next two hours I got to see a doctor. He ended up having to give me seven stitches on the rim of my ear. When he was done, I went back over to the nurse I had dealt with, and she explained that my neighbor's boyfriend had found her and that she was okay now.

After I left, I got a cup of coffee and went home. Two days later I called the detective to see what was happening with the charges against Tony.

"Yeah, hey, how you doing?" he said.

"So what's up with the case?"

"Well, I found out that Tony copped out to a deal, and he got time served without probation."

"What the fuck? What the fuck did I waste my time going to you for? I should have just gone back with a baseball bat and broke his fucking legs."

There was silence on the phone for a second, and then the detective said, "Listen, I know it's frustrating. But believe me, I'm just as frustrated about it as you are. Now after thinking about it myself, the one good thing about it is that he's got another strike against him, so maybe that'll teach him a lesson."

"Yeah, well, maybe if you would have taken us for a ride and dumped us off, I could have taught him a better lesson."

"All right, so look," he interrupted, "what you need to do now is to bring up a receipt for your gold chain and then the DA will release it to you."

"Oh, come on, man. I bought that chain years ago. I don't know where the receipt is, and what about my ring and bracelet?"

"Well, I'm sorry, but that's what you'll need to get your necklace back. We didn't recover the other things, so you might want to check out a few pawn shops in the area."

After I got the name and address of the DA from the detective, we said goodbye and I hung up.

The most annoying part about this whole thing was spending the next two days, while that asshole was free, looking for someone to make me a receipt. After spending $20 for it, I got one from some kid at a jewelry store. Even though I didn't get everything back, it was nice to get my chain back. Patti called me a few days later and invited me out to dinner. Neither one of us had plans for that night, so I decided to go out with her.

"What the hell happened to your ear?" she asked me that night.

"Well, worse than that, it cost me that ring you bought me, too."

"What? What happened? Don't tell me you get robbed?"

"Yeah, I did actually."

Patti started to ask me the details of what had happened and, for obvious reasons, I really couldn't tell her the whole story, so I made one up for her. Within the next few weeks, Patti and I started to date each other again. By that time all the figures from the Whitestone deal were in, and I scored on it with all the numbers coming in. I called up Mineo and set up a time to see him. Then I went and reworked the College Point deal out with him. All systems were go after that, so I set up the closing for both of them days apart. The College Point deal called for me to get the closing costs paid, $25,000 in the bank's escrow account until completion, and I got $25,000.00 on the table to throw back into the house. The deal Kirk and I had on that one was that he wouldn't get anything as a partner until I got the money released and then, based on his input over there, it would be determined what he would get. I would be responsible for the first and second mortgages on that one by myself, until the money was released, and it was determined how much of a partner Kirk would be over there. It came out to about $2300 per month for College Point.

On the Whitestone deal, Kirk got $25,000, I got $25,000, and he would not only be responsible for the first and second mortgages but, in a short amount of time, his wife Linda would buy the house from me. Kirk moved into the Whitestone house after Richard and his family moved out, and I stayed put at my friend's place and waited for Mineo to move out.

By the time Kirk got settled into his new house, I had put together a team to help me rebuild College Point. I decided not to stay there while I was working on it because of all of the dust and debris. But my new dog, didn't seem to mind. I stopped by my mother's house, and she asked me if I had any money to put towards the property taxes for upstate.

"You see, Ma? That's one of the reasons I told you that I didn't want to get involved in that place."
"Well, I have nobody else to ask. Besides, you make it seem like it's a curse for me to ask you for money for something that's for your future."

Mother always did have a way of explaining herself, I thought, as if I would have chosen that investment for myself.

"Well, what's going on with this house?"
"Well, I'm a few payments behind."
"On a 300,000 dollar mortgage!?"
"Well, that's one of the reasons I'm trying to get that place running up there."
"I'll give you the 2 grand for the taxes up there, Ma, but don't ask me to come up there. I'm too busy anyway."
"Are you going to take Stymie and Buckwheat, with you?"
"No, I don't think I should because I'm not settled yet. Besides, they've lived here their whole lives. Why should I take them away now?"

Before I left, my mother asked me to go to the store for her for some groceries and a few cases of cat food for "Uncle Phil," so he could feed my cats and hers while she was upstate. So I did.

Even though I had my own personal feeling about losing fifteen grand with her on her house, it bothered me to see my mother having to try to hustle up an idea at her age to try to save her house. Sometimes the thought of it made me want to find the guy who screwed her on the first mortgage and really put him to sleep. I even went as far as thinking that I should stop what I was doing to help her, but I felt that if I could achieve my goals, there would still be time to do something with her house. But at this point I couldn't deviate from my plans.

The electrical wiring in the College Point house was a bit of a mess but, for the most part, it was functioning, so I didn't worry about it. My main goal was to shape up that house back into a two-family. I decided to turn the first floor into one pretty big apartment with a backyard and then to turn the top two floors into another apartment. Basically this was being done to get the house refinanced as a two-family. My real goal there income-wise was to still rent it out room by room as a boarding house once I was done.

The first thing I had to do there was to get a bathroom installed downstairs, so I decided to create one behind the kitchen. All I would have to do is take away a portion of the back bedroom. Then I would have to install a kitchen on the second floor. One of the biggest problems I faced in either of these proposed new rooms was that I didn't have any plumbing in place. I would also have to redo the large bathroom on the second floor because Mineo had also started a large project there and never finished it.

The bathroom up there was half demolished, half finished, and a whole wreck. One thing that I thought was real interesting was that the bathroom there had a 12- inch high raised floor. Originally when I questioned Mineo about it, he explained that he wanted to have a sunken tub effect in the room even though the floor only came up twelve inches on the tub. I found out the real reason once I started to demo the floor. It turns out that whoever started this project had decided that, instead of removing the broken plaster and tile from the bathroom, they would just raise the floor and leave debris under the new floor.

As far as the third floor, it originally had one big room with only two windows and two makeshift smaller rooms. I had decided a while back to turn the big room into two smaller rooms, for more income, and to repair the work that was done on the two smaller rooms. As far as the outside went, to put it nicely, it looked like shit. On the front of the house there was some siding that was at least two different types of house shingles. It was the same on the back except for the extension that was built on the first floor that was just covered in tarpaper. On the other side where my house sat four feet from my neighbors, nothing had ever been done there except for the first coat of paint that had been put on the house when it was originally built sixty years ago. Even though it looked like a mess I knew this Colombian guy named Chelo who could do siding, and he had already given me an estimate to do it all, with supplies, for 4 thousand dollars, which was cheap.

Another problem I had out front was that Mineo had put a soffit on the front of the house to try to create some type of effect. It hung down from the roof about 6 feet, ran the length of the house, and was about three feet deep. Out of everything he had done, this was the only thing that looked halfway decent, but being that he had never closed up the ends of it, every pigeon in College Point had a nest there. By now the thing had about two feet of pigeon shit in it and, aside from that, the wood was rotted. I figured the last thing I wanted to see happen was for the two feet of pigeon shit to fall on the appraiser's head when l was done, so it had to come down when the time came.

Long after putting word out in the neighborhood about needing some people to work, I was introduced to a guy named Kevin Shea. I got along real well with him, and I asked him how a Cuban guy ended up with a name like Kevin Shea. He smiled and showed me his profile and said, "I don't know. Maybe the milkman in my neighborhood was very handsome."

Kevin was a wood flooring man by trade, but he was also a good handyman. Ricky and Gerard were working full time with the union as carpenters, but within time they started to come over at night and help me throw up some sheet rock. I also got a commitment from two other friends of mine, Mike Baxter and John Carpenter, to sand the wood floors on the first floor and re-finish them for a set price when that time came. For the most part though, Kevin would be the only one who worked long hours with me into the night. Now that I had a few different guys working in there using power tools at the same time, the electric problem was starting to be a bit of a hassle. But I didn't have the solution to this problem in the budget yet, so it had to wait. For two months that's all I did. I didn't go out, I didn't enjoy myself, I didn't buy a car or clothes, and I didn't even get my teeth replaced. That just wasn't in the budget right now. I figured once I got refinanced, I could take care of those things later, along with helping my mother.

A typical day for me started at about 8 a.m. I'd go to Kevin's apartment and have some real Cuban coffee while he took a shower. Then I'd ride him over to College Point. Then I'd get any supplies that he, Gerard, Ricky or I needed for that day. I'd go back to the house, give Kevin his supplies, set myself up, and go to work. When I was younger I used to play full contact football. My position on defense was called "monster man," and it called for me to play any position that I felt that play would call for. That was the same position I held now working on this house. One minute I was a carpenter, a plumber, a painter, a plasterer, minor electrician or a roofer. Whatever it took, I filled the gap. Kevin and I would usually have to stop at about 4pm, and then I'd get dinner, eat, and then set up for Gerard and Ricky, if they showed up at night.

The first week they started to work for me, everything was fine. But by now instead of stopping by about 6 or 7 p.m., they'd wander in any time they felt like it. A few of the arguments we would have is when they decided to bring a half case of beer with them almost every night with their tools. As a friend, I could understand their point a little bit about wanting to have a beer or two after their long day in Manhattan. But as an employer or a person who needed to get this job done as soon as possible, it got to be a little annoying at times. My main problem with this was that, if they didn't come in with any beer, they would actually get some work done. But if they did show up with beers, it only took an hour or two for them to get a buzz and start throwing hammers at each other. Whenever they got buzzed, not only did their work output decrease, it got to a point where my argument with them was whether or not I should pay them for the amount of work they did or if I should continue to pay them by the hour.

Finally, friends or not, the rule was no work for them if they bought beer. After they would leave for the night and I had driven Kevin home, I would keep working and set up the next day for them and Kevin until one, two or three in the morning.

By now at least two months had passed, and it started getting cold out. Along with that knowledge, I also became aware of how poorly Mineo's plumbing job heated the house. As an example, he had removed all the cast iron radiators and replaced them with half inch baseboard radiators, this alone produces less heat. Then, he hadn't replaced any radiators in the three floors of the hallway, which meant that the hallway was freezing all the time. Instead of worrying about it right now, I decided to take the weekend off. I went out and had dinner with Patti, and then we caught a movie. It kinda felt nice to relax a little bit, but no matter how I tired I was, I couldn't stop thinking about what I still needed to get done at the house. The next day I stopped by Kirk's house, and some strange guy answered the door.

"Who are you?" I asked.
"I'm John. Who are you?"
"I'm Mike. Where's Kirk?"
"Uncle Kirk's inside."

"Kirk's your uncle?"

"Yeah, why?"

"Because you don't look that much younger than him."

"Well, actually I'm not."

"So you must be his brother Ray's son."

"Yeah, but I don't really get along well with my father. Hold on, I'll tell Kirk you're here."

I waited outside for a minute, and then Kirk came to the door with John, and said "John, this is Mike, my partner. If he ever comes to the door, just let him in, okay?"

After we bullshitted for a few minutes, Kirk showed me a bunch of new suits he had bought for work. It was funny, but I almost thought he expected me to be impressed, which I wasn't. Personally I didn't care how he spent his money. Just as long as he was taking care of the nut on this place, I could care less if he bought blue tutus for work. After we settled into the living room, I reminded him that his percentage of his partnership in the College Point house was getting smaller and smaller.

"I don't understand. What do you mean?"

"Well, here. Let me put it to you this way. I've been breaking my ass over there nonstop for weeks and, in all that time, you've come over to help two times tops for a few hours."

"Yeah, Mike, but I've been busy."

"Well, hey, I understand that you've been busy, but don't forget we agreed that your percentage depended on how you helped me out over there. I told you that if I was to do the whole thing by myself, you would not have a very large interest in the place."

"Yeah, but Mike, I've got a big note to carry over here. That's why I've got to put in long hours. I mean, shit, I hardly get to see my own son."

"Well, I understand that, too, Kirk. But remember when I asked you if you wanted to take your 25 grand from this house and help me blow out the College Point house, you said no. You didn't want to do that, and that's how we came up with the percentage deal, and that's what we're sticking to. Now if you're spending all your time working with mortgages and making money there, than hire someone to fill your shoes in College Point if you still want in."

By the end of the conversation, Kirk swore that he would spend more time over there, pitch in with money, or hire someone to fill his shoes. He didn't really convince me about it then, so I wasn't so surprised when he didn't fulfill his words to me.

It started getting colder out, and the little electric problem in College Point was getting to be a pain in the ass at times. That's why I was more than happy to hear from Kirk that this Greek kid, Billy, from the neighborhood, could come over and work for me for an hourly wage, being that he was an electrician. I of course would be paying the hourly wage, not Kirk. By now I had run all the plumbing lines that I needed by myself, so I could start on the tile work in the bathrooms.

I let Caesar, my dog, run around the house as a watch dog. The problem was that every morning when I got there to start work, I'd find all the places through the night where he'd go to the bathroom in the house. Being that he would take a shit in a different spot every day, Kevin would joke with me and tell me that once Caesar found a spot that he really liked, he'd always go in that spot.

Unfortunately he was still looking for that spot. No matter how patiently I waited for this to happen, the dog never really found a spot he liked. Even though it was a pain in the ass, I didn't mind too much now because the house was a bit of a wreck anyway with all the construction going on. But I knew it would be a problem once I started to put the finishing touches on things.

Kirk paged me one day and asked me if I could come over. After waiting for Ricky to show up, which he never did, I went over to Kirk's house.

"Yeah, what's up?" I asked.

"Well, I need to ask you for a favor, Mike."

"Yeah... how big?"

"Well, Christmas is coming up, and I don't have any money for presents for my kids."

"Whata ya' mean you don't have any money? I thought you were making money doing mortgages."

"I am, but you know how big the nut is here, and I'm just waiting on a few deals I got going on to close. It's just that with Christmas and all, a lot of people wait for the holidays to pass before they move into a new house."

"Kirk, let me ask you something. Everything is cool there with the mortgages, right?"

"Yeah, no, no, no. Everything's cool here. I'm just a little short for Christmas, that's all."

"Well, how much do you need?"

"Well, how about a thousand?"

"A thousand? What kind of presents do you need to buy?"

"Well, I've got Linda, my son, and Nelson, Linda's sister's kid."

"Kirk, let me explain something to you. This year I've got to buy presents for my mother, Patti, Patti's mother and father and her sister, Sharron, and nothing for myself. Now if I spend three hundred on all of them, that's a lot. You know why?"

"No..., why?"

"Because even though I'd like to spend three hundred on each of them, I can't, because it's not in my budget. Now you sit there and tell me that you need a thousand for you and your family. First of all, your son isn't even a year old, so he'd be happy with a light bulb. As far as your wife, she should understand because she's your wife. The way I see it the only person you should be worried with is Nelson because he's a nine- year- old boy. Aside from him, I don't see why you need so much money for Christmas."

"Because, Look, Mike, it's our first family Christmas in our new home. Besides, I'll pay you back as soon as I close on one of these deals I've got."

"All right, fine. But pay me back when?"

"Probably the first week of January."

"Fine, I'll give you a check."

Being that Christmas was a few weeks away, I decided to start putting longer hours into the College Point house. It got to the point where I didn't even know what day it was at times, and for a few days in a row I even slept there. Being that Kevin still needed a ride to work, I would just let him take my car home. What I really liked about giving Kevin the car at night was that I could call him by the end of the night and tell him what was needed for the next day, and he would bring the supplies the next morning, instead of me running around. It was one less thing I had to concern myself with.

One day Billy, the electrician, told me that for a couple of days he would have to shut down all the power while he was there in order to tie electrical lines in the main fuse box. Even though I really didn't like the sound of it, I decided to tell Ricky and Gerard not to show up to work. Not that they were keeping a definite type of schedule with me. Anyhow, I could use a break myself. Kevin was even starting to comment on how Caesar, the dog, and I were starting to look like brothers with dirt and plaster on us. I decided and confirmed with Billy that he could have two days by himself, uninterrupted for the most part, to take care of what he needed to while I took a break.

Kevin and I still worked for a few hours during each of those days, but once it would start to get dark we'd have to quit because lights were going on and off while Billy worked. Instead of waiting until Billy was finished working on these days I decided to just let him have a key to the front door, so he could lock up when he was done. Winter was coming, and it was even predicted that it might go down into the teens. Taking that information into consideration, I made sure to tell Billy to make sure he didn't forget to turn the fuse box back on so the boiler could kick on at night. Then I left.

The next day when I woke up, it was freezing outside. During the night it had gone down to 22 degrees; I guess winter was here. I called up Kevin and told him that I would come and get him in about an hour. Kevin didn't like the sound of that because, as he put it, sometimes an hour was much longer than an hour with me. Kevin was the type who liked to be set up and working by 7 a.m. Even though it was good to be that way, I could think of a lot of other things to do at that hour, like sleeping, for instance. Whenever I would pick up Kevin late he'd get in the car with this schoolteacher look on his face and scold me like one.

We went and picked up a few supplies, and then we drove over to the house. When we got there Kevin opened the door with his key, and I started to unload some supplies from the car. Kevin stood at the doorway for a second and then walked into the house. When he walked back out, he looked at me and said, "It's fucking cold in here."
"I know."
"No…, it's fucking cold "in here." Mike, there's no heat on in the house."
"What are you talking about? I left the thermostat on at 70."
"Yeah, but I'm telling you, there's no heat on in here."

For a minute or two, I thought that he was just busting my horns for picking him up late, but he didn't start to laugh. I stopped what I was doing and walked up the stairs into the house. When I walked through the hallway into the living room and still saw my breath, I knew Kevin wasn't joking.

"Fuck! There's no fucking heat! Kevin, run upstairs and turn the water on in the bathroom!" I said.

As Kevin ran up the stairs, I ran into the kitchen and turned on the pipes that still weren't connected to a sink yet. There was a slight hesitation for a second, and then water came out.

Thank God, they weren't frozen, I thought.

A second later Kevin yelled down that he had water up there, too.

"All right, Kev. Try the toilet, and leave the sink and faucets dripping," I yelled up to him.

I can't tell you how relieved I was that the water was still flowing through the water pipes. It meant that they hadn't frozen, so chances were that the heating pipes didn't crack either.

When we got done checking the water pipes, I went to go downstairs to see what had happened with the boiler. When I went to click on the basement light, I knew immediately what the problem was; there was no electricity on. If there wasn't any electric, that meant that the thermostat wouldn't click on for the boiler. I took out my lighter and checked the fuse box, and sure enough, Billy hadn't flipped on the main electrical switch to it. I crossed my fingers and flipped it on. No sooner had I done that then the boiler clicked on. Whew, I thought. Kev and I started working again, and I figured it would only be a matter of time before the house got warm.

After an hour, I started to wonder why it was still cold inside. I went downstairs and checked the boiler again, and it was off. I screwed around with it for a while, and then I went upstairs and played with the thermostat. When I turned the thermostat up higher, I heard the boiler click back on and figured that everything was okay. By the time a half hour passed and the house was still cold, I figured that something was wrong. I went back down into the basement and checked the water regulator; the system seemed full. Then I went upstairs and tried to bleed one of the baseboard heaters. When no water came out, I knew that I had some type of water problem. But just to be sure that it wasn't the bleeder valve, I unscrewed the threaded nut and then got a long thin screwdriver to poke into the valve head. With my first try, the screwdriver didn't go in. Then I shoved it in a little harder and heard a small crunch. When I pulled the screwdriver back out, there were ice particles on the end of it. Now I knew why the house wasn't getting warm. The heating system was frozen.

I didn't really expect the whole heating system to be frozen because the hot and cold water pipes were still running with water but, after thinking about it, the baseboard heater pipes that ran to the boiler were only 1/2 inch copper tubes. The water system, which was one inch lead pipes, would have needed to get colder to freeze up because of that. An older heating system would have two or three inch pipes feeding it, which meant that would need to get colder, or been effected by longer time in the cold. After I realized this I started to get a little worried that maybe the heating pipes had frozen and cracked. The next order of the day was to put the boiler up to 100 degrees and watch it closely, as I strategically placed electric heaters around the house, starting at the low points first, around the baseboard heaters. Then all I could do was wait and hope that the weather outside got warmer.

As the day wore on, I became aware of leaks in the heating system and prayed that each new leak would be the last. As the pipes were defrosting, Kevin and I kept on working in the cold. That night Gerard showed up with Ricky to do some work. Then Billy showed up a little while after that, while leaks were making themselves noticeable to me. I looked at Kevin and told him to tell Billy to leave now. Kevin talked to Billy for a second, and Billy turned around and walked out of the house. It's not that I considered him fired at this point; it's just that I knew how angry I was, and if Billy had said the wrong thing, I knew I would have stuck his head through a wall. I guess Gerard and Ricky knew that I was freaked out about the heating system, too, because they kept their complaints about it being cold down to a minimum. That night when we were done working, I turned the boiler down to 40, kept the water pipes dripping so they wouldn't freeze, and made up a list of how much copper tubing and baseboard heaters I needed to fix what was already leaking.

I got over to Kevin's apartment real early the next morning, because I knew I had a big day ahead of me. As a matter of fact, I got to Kevin's apartment so early that he had gone back to bed. After I woke him up again, he explained that he thought that I was going to show up at my usual hour, so he went back to sleep.

"Well, you might as well park the car and come up. Because it's going to take me a few minutes to get ready," he explained through the intercom.

When I got back up there, Kev was walking around in his underwear while he was making us some Cuban coffee. I thought it was funny, because usually I was the one walking around half asleep, and I had never seen Kev in his underwear. He took out some sugar and two coffee cups and placed them on the table. After that Kevin went to hop in the shower. As I sat in Kevin's kitchen, I noticed some candles he had burning in there with a type of shrine on some shelves also. There were pictures of saints and some rocks and beads and things spread on each shelf with the burning candles. I knew Kevin believed in Santeria as a religion but I never really asked him about it. On the bottom shelf, which seemed to be away from everything, was a birthday cake. I didn't remember hearing Kevin talking about it being his birthday or anybody he knew, but I assumed it was his to eat. By now the coffee was ready and I poured myself a cup and decided to look for a knife and a plate to get a piece of cake.

I was real hungry, and I wondered if I should just take a piece of cake without asking. After thinking about it for a minute I figured that maybe I should ask him just in case, "Hey, Kev, I'm taking a piece of cake, all right?"

The next thing I heard was Kevin slipping and sliding in the tub and then down his hallway as he yelled out, "NO, NO, NO!" The next thing I saw was Kevin standing naked in his doorway, dripping wet, yelling, "DON'T EAT THE CAKE!"

I stood there a little shocked with my plate and utensils, and I said, "Kev... it's just a fucking cake, man. Calm down."

As Kevin stood there soaking wet with his hand now, thankfully, covering his genitals, he said, "Mike, if you would have eaten that cake, there would have been big trouble."
"Why? Your girlfriend would have been pissed off?"
"No, man..., not that kind of trouble."
"Well, what kind of trouble?"

Kevin looked at me in silence for a second, and then he whispered, "Well, that cake was put out there for bad spirits..., it's like a gift for them. When they go in it, then you get rid of the cake."
"What do you think might have happened if I would've eaten the cake?" I whispered.
"Well, I don't know for sure... but you might have been standing here waiting for me with a knife, instead of coffee."

"Hmmm. Well, when are you supposed to get rid of the cake? I mean, when do you know they're in there?"

Kevin looked around the room, then at the cake, and he said, "Shhhh... let's not talk in front of the cake," in a very low voice.
"Oh yeah... okay. Well, I'm gonna go sit in your living room, okay?"
"Yeah, okay."

We spoke in hushed tones.

As Kevin turned around and walked back towards his shower, I walked into his living room and sat down. Okay, Mike, I thought, don't ever touch anything else in Kev's apartment unless he says it's all right.

Before going to work, Kev and I stopped by the supply house. I picked up the supplies I needed and two electric heaters. When we got over to the house, there was a pink notice and some type of summons taped to the door. Being that I never really had enough garbage to rent a big container, I unfortunately grew accustomed to placing that week's rubbish in front of the house until the bulk pick- up came once a week from the garbage company to pick it up. Somebody obviously didn't like my idea and must've complained about it. Their complaint would cost me 150 dollars and an additional 25 dollars a day for as long as it was there. So after Kevin and I got the supplies inside and set up the electric heaters, we went to work on moving the pile of garbage into the backyard.

The next few days were spent defrosting the pipes, putting up sheet rock, plastering and painting but, because it was so cold in the house, the plaster and the paint weren't drying.

"Hey, I've got an idea," Gerard said on one of the nights he and Ricky showed up. "Donde has got this big kerosene heater that looks like a jet engine. I'm sure if we could get it over here, it would make this place real toasty."
"Well, how much do you think I'd have to pay him to borrow it?" I said sarcastically.
"Ah, who knows? Maybe a couple of hundred dollars," Gerard joked.
"Well, I'm freezing my ass off upstairs. Let's see if we can get it now," Ricky said.
"Should I?" Gerard asked.
"Yeah, fuck it. Give it a shot," I answered.
After Gerard left, Kevin went back to work plastering in the kitchen, and I went back to work on the heating system. Anywhere I saw a crack in the copper tubing, or water from it, it led me to a leak as the system defrosted. Then I would cut out the copper tubing and either replace it or patch it with a coupling if I could.

Two things were extremely frustrating about this process. The first one was that as I heated up the pipe to solder it, ice that was somewhere down the line would start to melt. I'd have water back in the pipe which would make it difficult to solder it, because you can't heat the pipe up enough to solder when there's water in it. The second problem was that after I heated the pipe and successfully soldered it, I would become aware of a new leak 2 or 3 feet down the line after some more ice melted. But no matter how frustrating it was I knew that I couldn't afford to have a plumber come in and fix it, so it had to be done.

Gerard came back about an hour later with the heater and Donde.

"So I hear your heating system is fucked up," Donde said, with a slight smirk.

"Yeah... you could say that."

"Well, these guys came over to my house crying about how cold it was over here, so I figured I'd help out with the heater."

"Yeah, thanks. It looks a lot better than these electric heaters," I said as they brought it in.

"Oh, yeah, this will heat up this place in no time."

"Well, that's cool because I need to find all those leaks once and for all, instead of finding one here and there every half hour."

"Yeah..., so Billy fucked up your system?"

"Yeah, well, I was using him because I was trying to save some money."

"Well, I guess that didn't work out too good."

"Na..., it doesn't look like it did."

After Donde finished talking, he showed us how to work the heater. Then he took a walk around the house, and then he left. Meanwhile Kevin and I turned around to warm up our butts with the heater. I don't know why, but I was kinda surprised that Donde let me use his heater. I guess the sun, and moon, were aligned. Whatever his reasons were, I was more than happy he had them.

A few days before Christmas, Kirk beeped me and asked me where I was.

"What do you mean where am I? I'm in my mausoleum working."

"All right, are you gonna be there for a little while?"

"Yeah, why?"

"I'll tell you when I see you. I'll be there in five minutes."

Oh, great, what now? I thought.

When Kirk got there he looked a little disheveled, so I asked him what was up.

"Mike, I can't believe it. I came home today and Linda was sitting in the dark."

"What do you mean she was sitting in the dark?"

"They turned off my electric because I didn't pay my bill."

"Well, that's a good reason, Kirk. So why are you telling me?"

"Because I need to borrow 300 dollars for them to turn it back on."

"Wait a minute, two weeks ago you borrowed a thousand dollars off me, right?"

"Yeah."

"Well, when you borrowed this money, didn't you know you needed to pay your electric?"

"Well, yeah, but I didn't think they would turn it off at Christmastime."

"So what happened to the money I gave you?"

"Well, I spent it on Christmas presents."

I looked at him and said sarcastically, "Well, at least everybody's got presents, right, Kirk?"

"Come on, Mike. I told you I'd pay you back as soon as one of my deals comes through."

"Yeah... as long as I don't go broke in the process."

With all the shit I had going on, I almost felt like telling him to go fuck himself for being stupid enough not to give the electric company something to keep his lights on. But on one hand I couldn't see letting Linda and his kids sit in the dark and freeze. On the other hand, without the thermostat working, that system would also freeze up in this cold. I looked at Kirk, frowned, and then took my emergency check out of my wallet and wrote it out for three hundred.

"Thanks, Mike. Really, thanks," he said as he hugged me.

"Kirk, you're paying the mortgages over there, right?"

"Yeah, everything is fine with that."

"Fine, here." I said, as I handed him the check.

Fortunately Adelchie's heater had warmed the house up enough so that the heating system just about completely defrosted, and I could really start working on it. Unfortunately the next day he came over and told me that he wanted to work on his motorcycle in his garage, so he wanted it back. Well, I shouldn't complain. He did let me have it for almost three days.

It snowed on December 23. I told everyone that they could take a few days off and that hopefully, when they came back, I would have the heat on. Everyone agreed that it would be nice to have heat again, and Kevin even wished for some elves to stop by during Christmas Eve to fix the heat. I was a little tired, but I decided to run down to the liquor store and get a bottle of something to have a little Christmas toast with everybody, and then call it a night.

Being that it was still pretty early, I decided to give Patti a call and see what she was up to. She invited me over to her mother's house, but I warned her that I looked like shit. She reminded me that she didn't care about that. After I dropped Kevin off, I drove over to Patti's house. Patti gave me a little kiss when I walked in and offered to make me some hot chocolate.

"Yeah, that would be nice, I guess."

As I took my jacket off, Patti heated up some hot water.

"Here, come inside, and sit down," she said.

I went and sat in the living room, and Patti turned on the T. V.

"Let me take your boots off."

"No, that's okay. You don't have to do that."

"Just be quiet and relax."

Patti unlaced my boots and then pulled them off.

"Michael, why are your socks wet?"

"Well..., because I've got holes in my boots."

"Why do you have holes in your boots?"

427

"Well, it's just that I haven't had the time to go buy some. Besides that, I'm in the house most of the time, so it doesn't really matter."

"What happens if you step on a nail over there?"

"Is this a trick question?"

"No."

"Well..., then I get a hole in my foot I guess."

Patti looked at me, frowned, and then said, "What size boot do you take?"

"No, that's okay, Patti. You don't have to buy me boots."

"Well then, you need to get out and buy yourself some boots."

"All right, I will."

"When?"

"Soon."

"Okay then, I'll make you a deal. If you don't have new boots before Christmas, then I'm going to use my taste and pick you out a pair."

"What does that mean? I'll get a pair with butterflies on them?"

"You'll see."

Patti got up and made me some hot chocolate, and then we watched a movie together. It was rather relaxing, and it felt nice doing something other than construction day in and day out for a change.

After the movie, Patti asked me if I wanted to sleep in the basement instead of driving home, but I decided that it would be better for me to go home so I could shave and take a shower. The next morning, Christmas Eve, I went over just to check on things, I guess out of habit.

After I checked everything that I didn't need to check, I got a chair and sat in front of the picture window in the living room. I sat there and thought about my situation and proposed position in life.

I know you're killing yourself now, Mike. But first of all, it's better to kill yourself for yourself than somebody else. Second of all, it will all be worth it once you're done, was the conclusion I came to.

Christmas came and went. The weather warmed up enough for the pipes to totally thaw out, so I could work on them. While I was out in the neighborhood getting supplies, I ran into a real estate agent named Richard at College Point Realty. I had almost done business with him on another house in the area. I talked with him for a little while and explained to him that I would need tenants soon. He told me to give him a call when I needed him and then he left.

The pile of garbage out back was getting bigger, and by now I had to keep the dog in the basement. It started to get pretty bad down there after a day or two. Some mornings I barely felt enough energy to lift a cup of coffee to my lips, let alone start shoveling up dog crap. So it got out of hand pretty quickly.

It got to the point with the heating system that I had to give it one final push for more reasons than one, most of all so I could go back to work on something else, because I had already wasted at least two weeks on it. That day I went out and bought all the plumbing pieces I needed and set to work. I worked nonstop on it for hours. Kevin even started calling me Clint Eastwood whenever I whipped out the portable blowtorch to work on a pipe somewhere while whistling his tune from one of his spaghetti Westerns.

I started it at 10:00 in the morning and, by 4:00 a.m., I had fixed all the leaks and even piped out the heating system for the new bathroom. All I had left to do now was to tie these bathroom pipes to the old pipes in the basement. As I gathered up my tools, I decided that before I'd start it and finish the system, I'd have a ceremonial cigarette to start off the festivities that were about to happen. I could hardly believe it. After what seemed like countless hours of trying, I would finally finish it just in time for the warm spell that was due to come in the next few days.

My last weld was up in the basement ceiling, and as I stretched my arms up to the pipes, they ached from all the cutting and soldering I had done in tight spaces. Well, at least this is the last one, I thought. As I was heating the last tee, I mocked it and begged it to leak as I laid on extra solder. Suddenly in the mist of exhaustion, I got this incredible sensation on my left forearm. It was a little chilly by now, so I had put on a thin jacket liner. I tilted my head around my arm while I was soldering and looked at my forearm. I realized that it had to be coming from under my jacket. By now, it felt like a bee was stinging me, so I put down the torch and grabbed at my sleeve. I pulled my sleeve up and away from my arm and saw a big hunk of hot solder, stuck, smoldering on my arm.

As I yanked it off my arm, I swore I heard the copper tee mocking me. Well, I guess I should get a scar for finally winning this battle, I thought, as I walked over to turn on the boiler.

I stayed there until 5:00 a.m. so the boiler could build up pressure, and fortunately I could only find one tiny leak on a coupling. I figured that this one could wait until morning. Then I went downstairs, drained the system, took the dog for a walk, and went home to bed.

One of the last thoughts I had when I went to bed was that at the very least with the heating system working, nobody would complain about going to the bathroom in compound buckets in a little while, because now I could go back to installing the bathroom plumbing and putting in the fixtures. Around the time that the bathrooms were done, Kirk's older brother Ray died. I was a little surprised when Kirk asked me to come to the funeral, but I decided to go with him. On the day of the funeral, Ray's son John was there.

About a week after that, Kirk told me that he needed 2000 dollars to finish paying for his brother's funeral. Having very limited funds by this point, I said to him, "Kirk, why me? Why do you come to me with this?"
"Mike, please, you don't understand. I've got to pay this. What if they un-bury my brother?"
"They're not going to do that."
"Well, even if they don't, then they might put a lien on Linda's or my credit reports, and then I won't be able to buy the Whitestone house."
"You know, Kirk, this whole thing really hasn't been much of a partnership."
"I know, Mike."
"I know you know, and now at this point you need 2 grand, and you've got to ask me?"

"Mike, please!"

"You know, Kirk, I'm so thin right now that I've got to take a gamble with this guy at the bank passing me without everything completely done. Then I've got to take most of that money, finish the house, and refinance it, so I can go buy some new fucking suits like you do!"

"Mike, please. I've got to do this."

"If I do this thing, Kirk, this is not like the electric bill shit at Christmas. I need this money back fast."

"I know. I'll give it back to you fast. Who knows? Maybe after I go to closing in Whitestone, I can pay you from that."

"Why? You're planning on closing in two weeks?"

"Well, no. But I'm working on it, like I told you, I getting some appraisals done on it."

"Then don't plan on that, 'cause if I do this, that's when I want you to pay me back, in two weeks."

"All right, not a problem, Mike. I've got three deals I'm waiting to close on right now."

"Yeah, well. I still haven't said yes to it."

CHAPTER 10

THE PHOENIX HAS LANDED, AND WILL BE SERVED WITH A NICE CRANBERRY SALAD

After about another month of being chained to my masterpiece, I was surpassing all of the bank's requirements that they had set for me in College Point, and I was also running low on patience for Kirk's stories on paying me back the 2 grand I had loaned him. The time came when I started to get worried about running low on cash, so I picked up some part-time work with the Teamsters. The good thing about this type of work was that you could call for work whenever you needed it. But it wasn't as easy as it sounds, because if you can imagine there were at least 300 other guys trying to call the same two numbers for work at the same time. It was a little more difficult for me because my phone didn't have a redial button on it, so I had to keep trying manually. But at $18- $26 dollars per hour, depending on new or old merchandise, it was worth the hassle. The work primarily consisted of either moving stuff into a building or moving stuff out. But I'm not talking about one or two offices. I remember one job I got on where we were moving Olgelbe Advertising into their new location. Their new offices consisted of 15 floors in a brand new skyscraper.

When you work on some of these jobs, it doesn't take long before the foremen know which guys are workers and which guys are not. So when one of the foremen feels like you're a worker, it's almost a compliment if they come over and ask you if you want to work the next shift. In general, it's almost disrespectful if you say no to the foreman who asks you. For me, it was, like, okay, if I take the work, that means after I take the train home from Manhattan, I'll get home at about one in the morning. Then if I can get a few hours' sleep, I can go pick up Kevin at about 7 in the morning, and he can put up the bathroom doors and paint after I get done sanding some walls I plastered. All of this planning I did was for nothing, because as it would usually turn out, I would get asked back for almost every shift, while this job was going on around the clock.

On the last weekend I worked, I went to work at 7 Friday morning, and I left the job at 6Sunday night. I made $1700 dollars that week, but Uncle Sam took his $500 out of my check first, which left me $1200. It was a little rough to swallow, but not bad for only working a weekend. But even with picking up part-time work like this from time to time, it still wasn't enough. It was do or die, and I had to have the house inspected. I figured that if I set the appointment up now, it would still be about two weeks before the bank would send someone, so that should give me some time to tie up loose ends. Unfortunately, for me, I was told that they could send someone over in 5 days.

After sitting down and making a list of all the things I still had to do, it looked like I wouldn't have a moment to waste or just about catch any sleep. I called up Kevin and told him my plan of attack. "Don't worry, Mike," he said. "You can count me in, whatever it takes." I also called up Ricky and asked him straight up whether or not I could count on him. He said he'd finish up his work, and Gerald said he'd be there, too. Then I called up Kirk, my "partner."

"Kirk."

"Yeah?"

"I need you to come over to the house and help me finish it. The inspector's coming over."

"Well, gee, Mike. I'm a little busy these days."

"Kirk... I ain't asking, okay? I've been wiping your ass for months, and you still haven't paid me that two grand. Now, what days are you coming here to work?"

"Well... how about tomorrow at about 7 p.m. after I eat dinner?"

"Fine... I'll see you at 7."

I worked and slept at the house with Kev, like a dog, day and night for four days in a row, and Kirk still hadn't showed up. After working through the night on the last night with Kevin, I told him I was going to Kirk's house and get him.

"Mike... Don't go over there and kill him."

"I'm not going to kill him, Kevin. I need him to work."

It was about 7a.m. now, and as I drove over to Kirk's house, I figured that the inspector was coming at 4 p.m. so at least I'd get some work out of this little shit. When I walked into the house, Linda, Kirk's wife, was awake with the kids.

"Linda – where's Kirk?"

"Well, you know, Mike, Kirk was up real late last night working on some deals of his, so he decided to sleep late today," she said in a hushed tone.

"Linda..., I've been working four days straight and sleeping at College Point with Kev and a dog. Now, either you go in the bedroom and kiss his little cheek and wake him up, or I'm going to go in there to throw him out of bed. The choice is yours."

"Okay... I'll go see if he wants to get up now."

"No, you go in there and tell him to get the fuck up, and get his ass over to that house, or else he's going to be one sorry motherfucker, if he doesn't."

I stood in the living room until Linda came out and said he was coming.

"Fine... make sure it's now. Today, Linda," I said, just before I left.

When I got back to College Point, I picked up some breakfast for Kevin and me, and then we went back to the house.

"So, did you kill him?" Kevin joked.

"No, but almost."

After I explained to Kevin what had happened, he looked at me, tilted his head, batted his eyelashes, and said, "Hey, Mike... would you be my partner?"

"Fuck you, wiseass," I joked with him.

Kirk showed up about an hour later, and without saying hi or anything, I just told him what I needed him to do. We worked right up until the time the inspector came, and then I stopped to walk with him through the house.

As we did this, he kept writing in a little pad he had with him. When we got outside, he pointed to the side of the house and said, "It says here that you were supposed to put some type of sheeting on the side of the house over here."

"Well, look, according to the first appraiser I had here, he said all I had to do was throw up two pieces of plywood to cover up the damage over there. Instead of that, I decided to get the whole house vinyl sided. I've even got some estimates from some people. Now I know that was one of the requirements to have the money released, but come on, look at all the work I've done inside, a brand new kitchen, two brand new bathrooms, new floors, new walls, new ceilings. I mean, that goes over and beyond what I was asked to do from the bank. You don't think I going to do all that new work and then jeopardize this whole thing for two pieces of plywood, do you?" I said.

He looked at me for a second longer, as if he was expecting more of a mental blowjob, and then said, "Well, I guess you did do a nice job inside."

We talked for a few more minutes after that, and then he left. When I went back inside, Kirk was standing in the hallway

"So how did it go?" he asked.

"What do you care? In all this time I've been working here, you find time to come over three times. And now you're interested in the outcome. Look, I appreciate it, but don't worry about it now, okay...? As a matter of fact, you can leave now and go and get some sleep," I said as I walked away.

After Kirk left, I took Kevin out to get a nice meal, and then after dropping him off, I went home and passed out.

I took the next two days off to rest and planned my next moves. Even though it seemed that I would be getting the $25,000, I still had a bunch of work to do, and I needed to get some tenants in there. But before I split up the rooms into a boarding house, it would probably be a better idea if I refinanced this place as a two-family house. The only bitch about that was that I'd have to install the kitchen upstairs. But for the little money I'd lay out there in the long run with the refinance, I'd make out okay, I reasoned.

Within a few days, I received word that the bank was satisfied with my work and would release the money. The only problem with that was that it would take two weeks before I'd get a check. Being that I had some cash on me, I told my friend Chelo to come over and start to vinyl side the house. It was still cold enough outside to see your breath, but Chelo was from Colombia, and he liked the cold.

Besides that, when it came to money, Chelo was a go- getter. In the meantime, Kevin and I started on the plumbing for the new kitchen. One day while I was running around getting supplies, I ran into Richard from College Point Reality again.

"Hey, Rich. How you doing?"

"Not bad. How about yourself?"

"Good, good, I'm finishing up the house I was telling you about."

"Oh, how's it coming along?"

"Not bad. I think I see a little light at the end of the tunnel. Hey, Rich, I'm thinking of refinancing the property. Do you know of anyone I can use?"

"Well, if you're serious about it, I've got an ace over at a bank, but this guy's serious business, no bullshit."

"Believe me, I'm serious. I've got my ass invested over there, no bullshit."

"Well, what I mean by that is that this guy does like 20 to 25 closings a day. He did the closing on the old RKO Movie Theater on Northern and Main Street for about a Mil."

"Well, I guess that is pretty serious."

"When you're done and you're ready, give me a call, and I'll set up an appointment for you, all right?"

"Yeah, sounds good, Rich. I'll talk to you later."

Even though I didn't buy a house off Richard when I was looking, I liked him. I even stopped by his office and shot the shit with him and Margaret, the lady who worked for him, from time to time.

Shortly before I received the $25,000 from the bank, the house was just about completed, and I decided that it was time to give Richard a call. Another reason why I needed to do a refinance was because out of the $25,000, 10,000 had to go to the real estate agent for their commission that they didn't take in order for the deal to go through. That would leave me with about $15,000. I needed to get this all done in time because I had to figure out a way I could save my mother's house that she was now losing.

After I talked to Richard, he set up an appointment with his guy at the bank for me. I went to the meeting and explained that I felt that the house would appraise out at $300,000 after all the work I had done. At 80 percent loan to value that would mean that I'd get $240,000 on the table. Now even though with my second mortgage I owed $240,000 on the place, I knew after speaking with Mineo that he'd be more than happy to split the $70,000 dollar profit on the refinance now and then go back on with a smaller second mortgage, instead of waiting twenty years to get his $70,000.

I spoke with Mineo a day later, and he verified my point of view about getting 35,000 now.

The meeting Richard set up for me went smoothly, and the appraisal was done about a week later. The house did bring in $300,000 on an appraisal. A few days after that, Richard's guy at the bank called me and said that we'd close in a week and that he'd call me with a date. Ironically I got a call the next day and was told that the check for $25,000 was mailed out to me from the bank but from a different department.

Man, I thought, finally this is going to pay off for me. Once it does, the first thing I'll do is get my teeth fixed. Then, fuck everything, I'm going to pay off Kevin and a few people, and then I'm going for at least two weeks in the sun for a vacation. I could use it.

A few days later, I got paged three times from Richards's guy at the bank with 911 behind the numbers. When I called him, he said, "Let me ask you something. Do you think I'm some kind of fucking idiot!?!"

Having always spoken in business terms to him I was a little shocked, and I stammered, "Excuse me??"

"Do you own a fucking house in Whitestone???"

"Well... yeah. That's my partner's house. What's the problem?"

"Did you remember signing all the paperwork at the closing on that house?!!"

"Yes... but what's the problem??"

"What's the problem? Well, I had your credit report pulled and you haven't made a mortgage payment on that house since the day you bought it!!"

"No fucking way."

"What are you trying to do? Get me fired?"

"No, I swear to you, I thought he was..."

"Whatever – just lose my number, kid."

"Click!"

I must've stood there for two minutes with the phone to my ear unable to move. I couldn't believe that this fucking prick, who I had done all these things for, sat there, looked in my face, and told me time and time again that everything was okay. He knew I was putting every dime I had and my time into this other house for months. After the first month that he didn't make a payment, he knew that College Point was a dead deal for me, and he still had the balls to ask me for money.

My first reaction was to drive to his house and just beat him until he died, and I must say that I really liked the thought of that. But unfortunately my conscience popped in and came up with some other thoughts.

First, I'll ask Richard if he can pull up my credit report and see if it's true. If it isn't, I'll fax it over to Richard's guy. But if it is true, then I'll go and kill Kirk. No..., okay, Mike, you know that won't get you anywhere but sitting in jail, and you don't have time for that right now. You've got 25 grand coming to you in the mail. Okay, now he hasn't made a payment on that place in about 8 months, so that comes out to be about $10 grand. So, if I pay off that ten grand out of the twenty-five grand, pay off the 10 grand to the real estate agent, I'll have 5 grand left from that to live off of until I can refinance College Point. That'll free me up to get about 35 grand out of College Point on a refinance. I can still make this happen. I'll be ten grand shorter, but it can still happen. But that Whitestone house comes out of my name, and I put a lien on it for all the money he owes me, plus I break his legs. Yeah, that sounds good. Well, okay, Mike – we won't break his legs now.

After I got done thinking about all this, I hung the pay phone back up and called Richard. By the time I got there, he had already pulled my credit report and was shaking his head back and forth.

"Shit, Mike. Did you talk to your partner yet?"

"NO, not yet. I'm still afraid that I'm going to kill him."

"Well, that wouldn't be a smart thing to do."

"Yeah, I know. Well, I might still have a way out of this. Listen, if you can tell your guy at the bank that I'm real sorry about this and if there is anything I can do to make it up to him, I will."

"All right, I'll tell him, but he's definitely not going to do anything with you unless you clear up this mess first."

"Well, I might still have a way out of this mess. All right, I'm gonna go."

"Mike"

"Yeah?"

"Keep a cool head. You're a smart young man. Don't blow it over a shithead"

"Yeah, I hear you, Rich. Thanks."

I left Richard's, and I decided that the best thing for me to do right now was not to go see Kirk because I wasn't too sure if I would be able to control myself. Besides, from the looks of things, he wasn't going anywhere. Instead I went over to the supermarket, bought two big bags of peanuts, than I went to Bowne Park, and fed the squirrels some peanuts. That and waiting on tomorrow's mail seemed like a smarter thing to do. Although it was a very difficult thing to do with my mind racing, the squirrels seemed happy about my decision.

Needless to say, I had a very restless night's sleep that night, but finding out that I had a $25,000 check sitting at my lawyer's office made me a little happier, after speaking to Sal. That day I went over to Kirk's house at about 3:00pm. After he opened the door, I walked into the hallway and said, "Kirk, is there anything you want to tell me?"

He looked at me oddly and said, "No, nothing. Why?"

I took a deep breath, and I said, "I'm going to ask you one more time. Is there anything you'd like to tell me about this house, motherfucker?!"

"Mike... I swear... I was trying to do everything I could to make these payments."

"Oh, really? You didn't make one payment on this house since Day One and you got $25,000 on the closing table, for nothing. So what the fuck were you 'trying' to do!?"

"Mike, look, I didn't tell you this but one of the reasons I needed to get in on this deal was because I owed some people $20,000, and they were going to kill me if I didn't get it to them."

"That... was not my fucking problem... And what the fuck do you think 'I'm' going to do now?"

"Mike – look – please – I've been trying to get something going on over at Bernie's Mortgage Business for a while now, and I've got some big deals just waiting to happen."

"You've had these deals going on for months. They ain't happening. Try something new, fucko. Now while I'm sinking every dime I have into that other house, and you see me breaking my ass for months, not once do you think, Well let me tell him to stop knocking himself out because the party's over."

"Mike, I swear. I've been working on these mortgage deals, and I've had about eight of them out there. I didn't say anything because, if they come through for me, I'll be able to pay this place off and still have money left over."

"And what? While you're waiting on these things, I should just put a hold on my fucking life? I'm the only motherfucker who bailed your ass out! And you fuck me?"

"Mike, I swear, man. I'll even give you a piece of these deals!"

"What- these deals that you can't even make a dime off of!"

"Mike, they're going to pull through. Even if half of them pull through, I can still pay this house off. Look, Mike, if you want I'll even give you a part of these deals."

"The deals that never come through."

"Mike, a couple of the smaller ones came through. It just happens that I needed that money to live on at the time. Look. If you want, we'll go down to Bernie's office, and I'll tell him in front of you that you have a piece of everything I close on."

"I don't know, Kirk. I really feel like going with my other option, and that is to just strangle the fucking shit out of you."

"Mike, look, do you want to go over to Bernie's office right now, and I'll tell him that you've got a piece of these deals when they come in?"

Because everything I was working on had crashed and burned for the time being, I decided that I had some time to kill anyway. So I figured I'd call him on it, and I said I'd go. Besides, I wanted to see if these deals were bullshit also.

Bernie's office was in a large two-story building he owned, and he rented out two stores and a few offices out of it. Bernie himself was a heavyset guy who knew both sides of the street, and played them both. After I found parking, I walked over to meet Kirk who was standing at the front talking to somebody in a suit whom I had met before.

"Mike, this is Michael Ageges. He's Bernie's lawyer. He does all of the closings out of the office here."

After I shook Michael's hand, I said goodbye to him and walked inside.

"Yeah, Bernie rents Mike an office in the basement, so he's always got him on call," Kirk said.

Even though I really wasn't in a chatting mood with Kirk, I answered, "That's a nice place to have a lawyer for a switch."

Once inside Kirk felt the need to introduce me to all the people who rented office space or worked for Bernie for some reason. I really didn't care if Satan worked for Bernie. I was interested in taking care of business. Then we waited a few minutes for Bernie to finish with some of his customers before he was able to see us.

After a few minutes of fluff talk, I said, "Well, all right, Kirk. Let's talk shop now."

As Bernie looked towards me, Kirk said, "Bernie, how many deals am I waiting on?" Bernie looked back toward Kirk with a slightly confused look on his face and said, "You have quite a few of them."

"Well, look, Bernie. Anything that I close on, Mike gets a piece of, okay?"

"Fine. That's no skin off of my bones. Whatever you guys want to agree to."

"Well, let me ask you something, Bernie. How much does Kirk's deals amount to – roughly?"

"Roughly, if they all come through, about ten grand. That's if they all come through without him bringing in any other deals."

"Okay, so should I sign something here that says that I get a percentage of Kirk's deals?"

"Listen," Bernie said slightly flustered. "whatever deal you guys have between you is fine, but I'm not going to sign my name to anything that might legally bind me to some type of verbal agreement that the two of you have between you. Understand this, Mike, Kirk works for me; you don't. That's not to say that I don't have some understanding as to your agreement with Kirk, but if you guys break your agreement, I don't want to be held responsible for it."

"So I guess we're back at square one, Kirk."

"Mike, look. You know I've got these deals going on now. I'm not bullshitting you about them. Ask Bernie; I've been working on two of them for months."

"So what am I supposed to do, hold my breath until they happen?"

"Look, gentlemen, I really don't want to know any of the details of your agreement, so if you'll excuse me I've got some work to do," Bernie explained.

Kirk and I both recognized that as a cue, so on that note we got up. I shook Bernie's hand, and then we walked outside.

"Mike, I know I fucked up but I've been working my ass off on these deals. Remember how you said that I never came over to the house to help you?"

"Yeah."

"Well, I thought you were going to take me into the basement over there and make me part of the foundation."

"I can't believe you fucked me up like this. And what about Richard? Have you been paying the $600 a month second mortgage to him?"

"Yes, I've been paying Richard. I just haven't been able to cover the $1800 per month with the bank."

"You know, as fucked up as it sounds, I'd be better off if you paid the bank this whole time instead of him."

"Look, Mike. Maybe what I'll do is rent out part of the house to make some more money and ..."

"And maybe you should get a real fucking job!"

"Mike, I know you don't want to hear this, but you know I'm taking care of my wife's nephew, Nelson, and we put him in private school so that's extra money. Linda's not working because she's home taking care of the baby, and my nephew John just started working this new job. So how much am I supposed to charge him to live with me?"

"You're right, Kirk... I don't want to hear it. I don't want to hear how your personal life has affected my business plans and has taken a toll on me physically, financially, and now fucking emotionally. Not to mention that you also made me look like an asshole to a very good business connection at a bank, so fucking save it, all right? What about your father? Can you borrow the money off of him?"

"I can't just call him out of the blue and ask him for ten grand."

"Why not? It's practically what you did to me, and we're not even related."

At about this point, I decided that before I got myself aggravated and threw Kirk through Bernie's storefront window I would leave. Before I did, I told Kirk to go home, sit down, and come up with a few ideas, because I didn't feel like figuring out this whole thing by myself.

Instead of running over to my lawyer Sal's office, I decided to stop by a neighborhood bar in that area and think things through before my next move.

As I sipped a rum and coke, I wondered if I should believe what Kirk was telling me and see what he came up with, if I should just throw him out of the Whitestone house and rent it, or if I should beat the piss out of him and see if that would somehow or another motivate him some way. Aside from him, I had Chelo working on the siding, which was going to cost me a few thousand. Even though I had all of the major work completed, I still had some minor work to do on the bedrooms themselves, if I was going to put the rooming house theory into effect. Then there was the issue of what I should do with the $25,000 sitting at Sal's office. Out of that, ten grand was gone, so really all I had to work with was $15,000. It made me quietly laugh out loud and think that I should take the money and go to Atlantic City with Patti and have a real night on the town. Sal, my lawyer, had to notify the listing agents that he had received the check, so there was no finagling around with that ten grand.

By the time the second drink settled in, I decided to call Patti and see if she'd like to do something a little human, like going to a movie or dinner. I had been running so ragged the last few months that I could probably count on one hand how many times I had gone out with her, let alone spend some time with her.

Patti and I had very different upbringings, to say the least. She had an overbearing father who, in his own way, would try to do everything he felt needed to be done for his daughters, whether they asked or not. On the other hand, when I was being raised by my mother, she would allow me to challenge myself and suggest things that I might find interesting. Then while I raised myself for a while, I didn't have to answer to anybody or listen to anybody or even care what they said or meant. But there had been times before I got involved in the houses when I would be up at Bowne Park with Patti, and Rudy, her father, would pull up to the very large park in his Mercedes and yell into the park at 30-yard intervals, "Patty! Are you in there??"

The first time this happened, I looked at Patti, who had her face in her hands, and said. "Who is this crazy guy screaming into the park?"

Patti looked at me, and said, "It's my father."
"You're father? Why is he saying, Patty?"
"I guess it's his broken English, he doesn't say Patti, he say's Patty."

At first when we started dating, things like this got me very annoyed, and Patti and I would get into a few arguments about it until one day, out of the blue, Patti said to me, "If you had a daughter and her rough-looking boyfriend came over to the house to take her out, how would you treat him?"

Without hardly thinking, I said, "Well, I'd invite him inside and ask him if he wanted a beer."
"And then what?" Patti asked.
"Well," I said still not knowing that I was walking into a trap, "if he said yes, I'd throw him out of

the house."

"And you blame my father for the way he tries to look after me? You'd probably be just as bad yourself."

"Well... I...?! Who knows...? I probably would be, come to think of it?"

From that point on I looked at what I felt were interferences into my life by Rudy a lot differently. Being that my life had been very unpredictable for some time after I was alone, I always tried to plot my next course and my next step. Patti, on the other hand, was much more receptive and open-minded to things, similar to a leaf blowing in the wind, which I liked, and I was also afraid for her at times.

For instance, one time she had come over to my mother's house to get me while I was living there and I was just about to jump in the shower. I told her she could wait for me in my room until I was done and then went about getting my towel and toothbrush when my phone rang.

"Patti, get that."

"But it's your phone," she said.

"So what? Just get it. You know most of my friends."

"Hello? Who? No, there is no Tom here. This is Michael's phone," Patti said as I walked out to take a shower.

About twenty minutes later I walked back into my room, and Patti was on the phone. After hearing a little bit of the context of her conversation, I said, "Who are you talking with?"

Patti shrugged her shoulders and mouthed the words, I don't know.

"What do you mean you don't know? Is that the wrong number guy that called just before I went to take a shower?"

Patti put her hand over the receiver and said, "Yes, it is."

"Well – what the hell are you still doing talking to him?"

"Well, I can't hang up on him. He sounds lonely."

"Oh," I said as I walked closer to her. "You can't hang up on him because he sounds lonely?"

"Yes."

"Oh, okay," I said as I pushed down the receiver and hung up the phone, "Here, let me help you."

Patti, in her own way, got mad at me, which made me laugh. I reminded her that she was mad at me for hanging up on someone she didn't know, which somehow made her calm down. This is what I mean when I say I liked and feared her open-mindedness. Even the slightest thing around Patti at times turned into an adventure.

Fortunately Patti was home, so I made plans with her that night. Even though we had a great time, it was unfortunate that I couldn't really bounce off Patti major things going on in my life. She either couldn't really understand, or her opinion was to make the first move that would come to her without thinking of all the consequences. I guess opposites really do attract each other.

We decided to go out for some dinner and then go to a club in the neighborhood. Unfortunately it seemed that the harder I tried to relax, the more agitated I became for not being able to relax and enjoy myself. From time to time, while sitting in the restaurant, I'd find myself figuring out how much each table was bringing in, while Patti would ask if I was listening to her. After dinner we went out to a club, and even while we were there with the music blasting, I'd catch myself tallying up each bar. It made me recognize how badly I wanted to be in business, which would then turn around and make me want to go strangle Kirk again for fucking up on me. I know I couldn't have been much of a treat for Patti to be with that night, but she would still try to start casual conversations with me in between my plotting and planning. Even though by the end of the night it didn't seem like I was 100 percent relaxed, I figured that going out had allowed me enough time to think things out with a slightly clearer head.

Chelo was working on the vinyl siding in College Point, and he paged me the next day.

"Hey, Chelo, what's up?"
"Listen, Mike. I need some money for de supplies."
"How much?"
"Do you have about $800?"
"Yeah."
"Okay, then meet me at de house, okay?"
"All right, I'll be there in a half hour."

After I made some other phone calls I went over to the bank to get some money. Being that I had been a little stressed out the last few days, I hadn't really kept track of how many checks I had written out, but I only had about $2,000 left. I knew I was going to have to make some moves with either some tenants or the $25,000, but I just wasn't 100 percent sure which route I should take. The mortgage payments were going to be due in College Point also, so I also realized the fuse was lit on that end. I got the money, and then I went over to meet Chelo.

The siding was coming along nicely, and I had decided that, since I was there, I might as well go to work. Working always seemed to clear my head to the extent of being able to come up with some answers while being productive, instead of sitting in some bar whining to someone about my problems. One of the things that troubled me about the College Point house was that I didn't want to have a bunch of tenants running around before I was able to get an appraiser in there, because everything was new and squeaky clean so it looked great. But on a larger note, I needed the income. I reasoned that I could go to work with the Teamsters until everything worked itself out, but I knew that working itself out meant that I had to make a larger decision on a different level, which was what I should do about the Whitestone house.

It all felt like everything was too closely hinged on each other. There were still even larger pictures out on the horizons that I was doing all this work for things that were not coming together, such as saving my mother's house before it got too late and allowing myself, Michael, sane space to have a life in this battlefield. I'd always rule out that last one by telling myself that this was what I wanted, to be involved in something and to do what it took to accomplish it.

I kept working that day. By the time I broke for dinner that night at about 9:00, this is what I had come up with: Go to Sal's office, pay off the real estate brokers, take the $15,000, and blow it in

Atlantic City or double it there in one day. Get the check, pay off Whitestone, throw Kirk out, refinance College Point, then rent both houses, and get into some kind of business with the refinance money. Pay off Whitestone, have Kirk buy the house from me, be done with it, and look at the ten grand as another loss with him as long as I could refinance College Point. Pay off Whitestone, wait and see what happens with his deals, and refinance College Point, or throw him out, break his hands, then go to the bank with the keys for Whitestone, tell them the situation I was in, offer to give them back the house, and see what happens with them.

In a sense the house in Whitestone had come back to haunt me. I never really had a good feeling about it, and now it was preventing me from everything, it seemed. It was like a huge constipation in my forward progress.

My mother paged me that night at about ten.

"Yeah Ma. What's up?"

"What's up? I'm losing the fucking house over here, Michael. That's what's up."

"Yeah, I know Ma."

"What do you mean, 'Yeah I know Ma?' You know I'm losing the house, and that's all you can say, 'Yeah I know Ma!' You know, Michael, if you would have stopped what you were doing, got a job, and given me some serious help over here, with the rent money I've got coming in, I probably could have done something here."

I felt like telling her that if she hadn't been so stupid with making the payments in the first place, she wouldn't have been in this situation. But instead I said, "Well, you know Ma, if you would have given me this prick's name and address I might have been able to have done something then."

"Like what, Michael? Gone over there and shot him?"

"No, not if I didn't have to. I'd have made an appointment to see him on something made up, and then after I was in his office, I would have seriously suggested that he consider taking some type of payoff on his loan. There's no way I would have paid him $195,000 on his $65,000 loan after 5 months."

"It was compounded interest!" my mother yelled.

"I don't care if it was Martian money. Believe me, that motherfucker would not have seen a dime of that money if he didn't take a payoff. His descendants might have seen the money, but he wouldn't have enjoyed one dime of it."

"Well, that's still doesn't change the situation now. You could have pitched in."

"And done what? Move back home and help you pay off $3,000 per month for 15 years unless you decided to throw me out again somewhere down the line..."

"Click!" went the phone as my mother hung up on me.

It was just as well. I knew the conversation wasn't really going to go anywhere. She just wanted to blow off some stream.

After I got off the phone with her, I took a minute and calculated that, by now, the back payments on that house must be up to at least $25,000. I had hoped that my shit was doing much better by this time. I started to wonder if I'd be able to catch up with those payments by the time my shit broke, and I would actually be making some kind of money somewhere in some type of business. It didn't make sense to me to refinance College Point and throw money into the Flushing house, just to end up back at square one with $3,000 dollar a month payments.

Even though I was caught up in the middle of all this, I knew that I had to keep an eye out for some type of business I'd like to get involved in to make some money. If I held on to my two houses and saved my mother's house, I'd have to come up with $8,000 per month just in mortgage money. If I were to split up Whitestone and rent it, I could get about $1200 for the apartment with the attached garage. Then I could probably get about $450 for the small apartment upstairs that would be about $1,650 to cover $2,600. College Point is at $1700 with nothing rented there yet. If I left it as a 2-family I could probably get about $1500 per month over there. My mother's got about 2 grand coming in over there, so I'm short all around.

Now, if I rented rooms in College Point, then I might make out a little better. I could also take one of the rooms over there and not have to worry about getting a place to live. Maybe I shouldn't even pay Whitestone off. Maybe I should just give it back to the bank and worry about College Point and my mother's house. I never really wanted to get involved in that house in the first place. Man, it's strange. I'll never forget that day I stopped in front of that house when I was a kid walking home from the fair. I swear if I had known the trouble this house would have caused me in my future, I'da burned the motherfucker down. On that note, I decided that an hour's worth of thinking about it was enough for now, because I needed to get some sleep.

The next morning Kevin beeped me on my pager.

"Hey, Kevin. What's up?"
"Nothing. I finished that flooring job I was doing."
"Really? Do you want to come by and work?"
"Yeah, sure, but don't make it here by one in the afternoon."
"No, I won't. I'll be there in an hour."
"All right, I'll see you in an hour."

I took a shower and then picked up a coffee and went and got Kevin. Kevin had become a very good friend by now and, as a friend, I really felt like talking to someone about my situations. But as a businessman, I didn't think it was the right thing to do, so I didn't bring it up. After I got some supplies, we drove over to the house. When we got there, Chelo was working on the siding. I had given him a key to the front door already, so I wouldn't have to be there to open doors for him every morning that he worked.

As soon as we got there I let Caesar, "my dog," out of the basement. Ever since he took a crap on each landing one night, I decided to keep him in the basement. Now the problem was that he was still going to the bathroom down there, and I just didn't have it in me to spend an hour cleaning up dog crap. When I let Caesar out of the back door, I realized that it was about time that I did something with the mound of garbage that had accumulated in the backyard, especially now that the weather was breaking. My theory for letting the garbage pile up was that I didn't want to have to pay for a small dumpster each time I had a little bit of garbage. Instead, I thought it would be smarter to get one big dumpster when I got finished. Even if I were to rent Gerald's truck, it would take all day with at least two guys if the guys at the dump would let me take all this garbage there without getting suspicious. But I knew I had to do something soon. I had just recently got done repairing a few walls in the attic and re-created four rooms up there, so I sent Kevin up there that day to work. All he had to do was some light sanding, and then he could start painting.

About half way into the workday, Kirk beeped me a few times with 911's. Great, I thought, it better be good news. I stopped what I was doing and called him.

"Yeah Kirk. What's up?"
"Mike, listen, I closed one of my deals, and I've got about two grand for you. What should I do with it?"

I almost had to pinch myself, because he was becoming the last person I expected that from.

"You've got two grand, and you're actually calling me about it, right? This isn't some kind of fucking joke, is it?"
"No Mike, no bullshit. I'm serious. What do you want me to do with the money?"
"Okay, Kirk, fine. You've got two grand on you."
"Yeah."
"Okay, go pay my first mortgage on the College Point house, and then give me a check for Mineo on the second mortgage."
"Okay, fine."
"I guess I'll talk to you later then."
"Yeah, stop by tonight, and I'll give you Mineo's check."
"All right."
"All right, I'll see you later," Kirk said.

On one hand I really couldn't believe that Kirk had any money, but on the other hand I really hoped he knew better than to fuck with me with some bullshit story at the last minute about how the check he was given bounced on him or something. That night after I was done and had dropped off Kevin, I stopped by the Whitestone house. Kirk came to the door in his pajamas.

"Mike, look. Here," he said as he showed me two checks. "One is made out to Mineo, and the other one is made out to the bank. I told you I was waiting on these deals. Now all I need is for a couple more of them to come through, and everything will be cleared up again."
"Yeah, well, it's the down time that's killing me right now. I could have closed on College Point by now and been moving on to bigger and better things."
"I know. I'm sorry, Mike."
"Okay, well, fine. Give me Mineo's check, and here's the account number for College Point. You go to the bank and pay it. Kirk, I'm telling you these checks better not bounce."
"They won't, Mike. I swear it."

There were two reasons why I wanted Kirk to pay that month's mortgage. The first reason was because I wanted to see if he was being a man of his word. The second reason why I wanted him to make my payments with his checks was because I was going to get photocopies of his checks from Mineo and the bank, just in case the shit hit the fan somewhere down the road. I wanted to show his involvement in this, especially since it was the first checks that I had remembered him writing during our "partnership." Besides that, if his checks did bounce, I had some room to get myself out of the embarrassment time-wise.

I called up Mino and told him that, if he wanted, he could come over to the house the next day and pick up a check. When I did see him the following day, I warned him that it was a check from my "partner," so if there were any problems with it, he should just give me a call and I would cover it.

"Don't worry, Mike. I understand about your partner," he said. "I never liked him from the day I met him. He was just a bullshitter in a nice suit."
"Yeah. Believe me, I know."
"So what's up with the money that the bank was holding?"
"Well, I should be getting it any day now."
"Oh, that's good. At least the real estate agents will get their money. So how's the house coming along?"
"Well, pretty good. Come on in, and check it out."

I enjoyed bringing Mino into his old house from time to time, because he'd walk through each room and stand there and say, "Wow, you're really doing a good job here."

It made me feel good to hear it from somebody who really knew how much work was done. By the end of that day, Kevin had got done painting the new bedrooms in the attic, and then he started installing the doors. After a little while, I decided to call it a night, and I asked Kevin if he wanted to get a bite to eat somewhere.

"Yeah, sure. What do you feel like having?"
"I don't know. How about some Cuban food?"
"Sounds good to me. I know a good place over on Main Street."

We found parking close to the place, and the first thing I noticed when I walked in was that everybody who was working there was Japanese.

"Hey, Kevin, what's up with this? I thought we were going to eat Cuban food."
"We are," he answered.
"So why is everybody here Japanese?"
"Watch," he said as he started speaking Spanish to the waiter.
"Holy shit, they speak Spanish," I said.
"Yeah, but they are all from Cuba. You know what's really funny though?"
"No, what?"
"You can't tell, but they speak Spanish with a Japanese accent."
"You know now that you've taken me to see Cuban Japs. Let me ask you something. How does a Cuban guy like you get a name like Kevin Shea again? And don't tell me that story about the milkman.

What did you do, drop the O in front of Shea before you came to this country?"

Because Kevin and I were friends, he knew I didn't mean this to sound like I was a prick. So in an Irish accent, Kevin said to me, "Aye, maybe one of the little people was takin' a drink too much of the shamrock juice, and when they awoke they found themselves in Cuba. And while they were there, they found themselves a little senorita, mercy me, and the next thing you know we've got a whole pot of good ol' Irish Cuban babies, sez I." After we ate some very good Cuban Japanese food, I drove Kevin home. Then I went home.

The next day while I was running around in College Point, I ran into Richard from College Point Realty. After we said our hello's I explained to Richard that the house was just about done and that I was probably going to need some tenants for the rooms soon.

"So whatever happened with that money you were trying to get from the bank?"
"Oh, I got that. It's sitting at my lawyer's office"
"Well, what do you plan to do with that money?"
"I'm not sure. Why? You got any ideas?"
"Well, if something should pop up, I'll keep you in mind."
"Something like what?"
"You remember the guy at the bank I was telling you about?"
"Yeah, the guy I screwed up with?"
"Yeah, well, he's been throwing me some foreclosure deals here in College Point. Not a lot, but a couple, and maybe you might be interested in one."
"Well, yeah, that doesn't sound bad, Rich. Thanks for mentioning it."
"No problem. You've got the same number, right?"
"Yep."
"All right, I've got an idea of what you're looking for, so if I see something, I'll call you."

We said goodbye, and then I walked over to the hardware store. Man, there's a thought. It might not be a bad idea to hop into something else, but I'd probably have to ask Patti if I could put it in her name because my credit was screwed. Well, let's see what happens with it. Then again I could do it with Kevin also.

A few days later, to my surprise, I found out both of the checks I got from Kirk cleared. It almost made me wonder if maybe he was telling the truth about these deals he had. Over the next couple of days, Kirk called me from time to time and updated me on the progress of his deals. It almost seemed like he had done a complete turn-around. He even stopped by the house and offered to work. It made me re-evaluate my position with him to a degree. If he could take care of that headache with the Whitestone house, I could concentrate on bigger and better things, I thought. It seemed like ever since that house was thrown back into my equation, my whole mental thesis was knocked off its axis. I really just wanted the headache with that place to go away, even at the sake of trusting Kirk again. I decided to sit down with him to discuss the Whitestone house.

"Look, I want this Whitestone house out of my name. Unfortunately, in order for you to buy it with your wife, the payments need to be brought up- to- date. Now I don't suppose that you've got ten grand laying around, do you...? I didn't think so. So what you need to do is to get a bunch of applications from a few different banks and submit them."

"You know, Mike, things have changed a bit with the banks. That's one of the reasons I'm having so much difficulty getting my deals through."

"Yeah, I know. But you know what? Pull some fucking strings. I got involved in this fucking house because of you. You got money out of here that you didn't do the right thing with. You lived here for X amount of time and invited all your friends over to see your new house and how well you're doing at my expense. So now it's time to live up to your fairytale. Believe me, I'm more than tired of pulling your weight."

"I guess if you're talking about paying off the Whitestone house, you must've gotten the $25,000 released from the bank."

"Good guess," I said dryly.

"So what do you plan on doing?"

"Well, based on today's conversation with you, it should tell me which direction to go with you and this house."

As if it might have been a surprise, I did notice his ears perk up a little bit. I didn't really have to tip my hand to him, but I really wasn't in any mood to play games. All Kirk needed to do right now was say the wrong thing or act the wrong way, and I'm sure he knew his run with me would be over. After a moment of silence, I said, "So how do you want to play this?"

"Well, here's the problem, Mike. As you know I went to four different banks on the Whitestone house until I found a bank that would appraise the property high enough so that all the numbers would come in the first time. Now, this market we're in right now has basically peaked, so getting another good appraisal is going to be a little difficult. Then there's Richard's second mortgage."

"Well, as long as Sal's used for the closing, I'm sure there would be no problem with Richard's note floating for about an hour. I mean, after all, they are friends."

"Well, yeah, that would cover it, but that's if the appraisal comes in high enough. Then there's the case of going no verification or full "doc" with another bank. Usually no verification means that they'll loan you less money for the property."

"Yeah, I know. So what are you saying? Go full doc?"

"Well, yeah, because then I'll get at least 80 percent Loan to Value"

"So how are you going to accomplish that?"

"Well, I've got the paperwork end of it covered. I've got a problem when it comes to the bank statements."

"Yeah, so how do you plan on getting around that?"

"Well, what if you put the $25,000 into the account you had opened for me, and..."

"Yeah, right, Kirk."

"No, I'm serious. It would show up on my bank statement, and I could use that to go full doc with the bank."

"Nice try, but it isn't happening."

"All right, if you don't want to do the 25, then at least put the ten grand before you pay off the bank their back payments."

"Look, this is what I'll do. I'll put the ten grand into the joint account of ours, so that you can get bank statements. But the second I find out that the money's not there, Whitestone had better be paid off or else you better be living in Japan. But before I do this, we go to Sal's office and make sure that he'll cover you at your closing on this house, because they will be happening simultaneously."

"What do you mean?"

"By the time it comes time to pay this place off, you should already have several applications in for that house."

"So then that will be it, the end of our partnership."

"Kirk, the only partnership you and I had was in my head. And that ten grand is not a gift; you will owe me that money also."

"No, I know."

"Now, for the record, I'm amazed that I didn't handle this situation with you differently. Do not fuck up again."

"No, Mike, I'm telling you..."

"Kirk, I don't want to hear it."

Even though my brain thought that this sounded like a logical way to get this house out of my name, my gut really didn't agree with everything. But I ended up going with it anyway.

Being that it was going to take time before other things got rolling, I decided to start renting rooms in College Point. The first tenant I had was named Chris; Richard from College Point Realty got him for me. I got 160 bucks, a week's rent, and a week's security. My first tenant was born.

By the end of the month, the house was basically finished except for a few odds and ends. Now that it was warmer out, I hired a company to haul all the trash out of the backyard. They came with their own container and two colored guys for the labor. I had to throw the two guys an extra couple of bucks to clean up the basement's mess from the dog, but it was well worth it. I took them down there to show them what had to be done, and the smaller guy said, "Oh, man, look at the size of that shit. That fucking dog must be huge."

The other guy acknowledged this with a grump, especially since his buddy was the one who made the deal with me. He obviously wasn't too thrilled that he came to work that day. After that, I showed them where the hose was and what had to be done. As I started back up the stairs, I heard the smaller guy say, "Oh, shit. Here's another one, and another," as if he was on an Easter egg hunt.

"Man, shut the fuck up, and give me a box," the bigger guy yelled.

Chelo was done with the siding, but I wasn't done paying him off, which didn't make him too happy. Fortunately I had more tenants there, so I paid him from that when it came in, not that turning into a landlord was an easy task. I had about four tenants in total now, and aside from one of them, the headaches and the stories started. On paper your rent roll looks wonderful, but in reality until the money is in your account, every tenant is a bad tenant.

The time had come for me to really make a decision about Caesar, "my dog." He was a nice-looking big dog, but keeping him tied in the back or locked in the basement really wasn't good. The one person I figured would be the best one to go to with this problem was Rudy, Patti's father. Even though we might not have gotten along all the time, there was one thing I really liked about him, and that was his love for animals.

Rudy would come home from one of his voyages from the Bronx or Brooklyn at times with dogs or cats that he saved from the streets, as he put it. He would always make himself and everyone around him nuts until he found the right home for the animal. It was a trait that Patti also had, especially when it came to her beloved Pom Pom. After talking to him about it, we decided to take it out to his Persian friend Solly's house in Great Neck, Long Island, which was about a half hour away. I told Rudy that I wanted to go with him out there and check the place out with Caesar before I'd just give him away because, like I said, I did like the dog. I just didn't have time for him. We went out there, and as it turned out, Solly had a huge fenced- in yard which I thought would really be great for Caesar. After Rudy warned Solly, in his own way, that he had to take care of his new "son," I decided to let the dog stay there.

One day Richard from College Point Realty paged me. When I called him back, he told me about this deal that his guy at the bank turned him on to and that if I wanted to find out any more information I should stop by his office. I decided to check it out that day, so I explained that I'd stop by in about an hour. We sat down and looked at the numbers together, and they looked good. The house in question had gone into foreclosure, and the owners decided that they would be more than happy for someone at the bank to sell the place for them, which is where and how Rich got involved through his friend. The people had bought the place for $165,000 and, after owning it a few years, their mortgage was lower. But they could no longer make the payments. Rich explained to me that I could get the place for about $115,000, and he felt that if I fixed the place up, I could get about $200,000 for it in today's market, which I was also sure it could fetch, considering its location.

After talking about it for a little while, we decided to take a ride over and check it out. It was a nice two-story house with a one-car garage. Richard explained to me that it only needed minor cosmetics inside, which he was sure I could handle. When we got back to his office, I told him I was very interested in it and that I'd get back to him on it as soon as possible. As I took a ride back over to view the property, I figured that the way I could do it was to put it into Patti's name, in order to get a mortgage on it. Then I could do the cosmetic work on it while Richard listed it at his office. Shit, I'd be happy to get $160,000 for it, and I'm sure Patti wouldn't mind signing some papers to make a couple of grand in a couple of months.

Once I got back to the house, I called Patti and asked her if she was interested in getting involved in it, and she said she was. Being that I didn't have all the cash on me for the $15,000 that Richard explained would be needed, I figured that I would get the ten grand that was sitting in the joint account with Kirk and use that money. At this point, unless Kirk had a closing date, he'd have to wait until I did this deal, and then he could clean up the mess over there. Another month or two wasn't going to make a big difference anyway, I figured. Then I called Kirk and told him about my plans.

"So you want to take me in as a partner?" he asked.
"No, Kirk. Actually, I've still got a bitter taste about our last partnership, so I'm doing this one alone."
"Well, I don't think I can postpone the closing on this one for that long."
"What closing?"
"The closing I'm going to do on the Whitestone house."

"Wait a minute. Two seconds ago you asked me if I wanted a partner. Now you're doing a closing?"

"Well, that was a bad joke."

"A bad joke? You've got time to joke with me, motherfucker?"

"No, Mike. I'm sorry. I didn't mean it."

"Now what's this story on this fucking closing?"

"Well, I've been talking to the lawyers for the bank on the foreclosure on this place, and it looks like they will write off the payments and interest as long as I can get them back their original amount that they loaned."

"So that means that the ten grand is not needed to pay them off."

"Well, it's not needed for them, but now it's needed for the new bank because I'm going to show a larger down payment."

"How?"

"Sal's going to cover me at the closing. He just doesn't have it all."

"So when you say that you can't postpone the closing, what point is the whole thing at?"

"Well, they're going to send me a commitment on it."

"So if you're waiting for a commitment letter, you don't even have a closing date to postpone yet."

"Well, no. I don't have an actual date yet but, Mike, the market is getting soft on appraisals. I think if I don't do this thing now, I'm not going to be able to."

"So maybe I should just tack on the profit that I'm going to lose from the other deal onto you because of this shit, right!?"'

"Mike, look, man, I don't know anything about this other deal. All I knew was that I was trying my ass off to do the Whitestone deal."

"Fine, you do the fucking Whitestone deal, but I want to see the commitment as soon as it comes in, and if all the numbers aren't there after we sit down and look it over, I'm taking the ten grand for this other deal. Now, when are you getting the commitment?"

"It should be any day."

"Call me when you get it."

After I hung up with Kirk, I called Richard and asked him if he could give me a few days to put the deal together, and he said he would. He also told me he had another tenant for me in his office. I told him I'd meet the guy over at the house after I picked up some more paint for the two last bedrooms. When I got back to the house, the guy was there waiting for me. I walked in with the paint cans, put them down, and then showed him the available rooms in the attic.

"Well, what's up with these two rooms?"

"I gotta paint them."

"I tell you what," he said. "I'll paint both rooms for you if I can have this one and you use my labor towards my 1 week's rent and 1 week security."

I looked at the paint roller and paint brushes, then at him, and said, "Fine, but don't fuck up the new rugs."

"What about furniture?" he asked."

"I'll get you some from storage in my other house."

It's funny, but when I was a kid, my mother used to fight with me to help her get furniture out of people's trash to fill up the house for tenants when we first got the Flushing house. Now that's where I'd get all of my stuff for the tenants.

I called Kirk's house a few days later, and I didn't get an answer. I decided to drive over there about dinnertime to see what was going on with the Whitestone mess. The first thing I noticed when I got there was that none of the outside lights were on. The second thing I noticed was that there were no shades on the windows.

This motherfucker better be washing his windows, I thought.

I had a spare key to the front door, so I opened it. I went down the hall, walked into the living room, and saw that the house was empty. Then I turned on a few lights and walked through each room on the first floor. He had taken everything, even the dust balls. When I got upstairs, John's stuff was still in his room, which I thought was pretty strange. The more I walked through the house the angrier I got. The hardest part of my anger at that moment was not knowing who to be angrier with, Kirk or myself. In the middle of my anger, oddly enough, the one thing that kept popping into my head was the time Dino, Mike Viale, Tommy Faye and I were in the holding cells at Queens Criminal Court, and Dino kept saying over and over, 'I'm telling you we should kick the shit out of Tommy now. He's the weak link.'

Kirk was my weak link, and, I guess I should have just kicked the shit out of him.

The next thing I did was to drive over to the bank to go and see what I knew I was going to find about the ten grand that wasn't going to be there, which it wasn't. Then I went to a pay phone, called all my close friends, and put the word on the street that I wanted Kirk's head on a stick, and for anybody to call me if they saw him.

I woke up with something similar to a headache the next day, but not quite as painful. Even though I had some major changes in store, my brain was still focused on trying to pull off some kind of refinance even if it meant giving back the Whitestone house to the bank or putting my College Point house into someone else's name and doing it that way. I was still determined to get my money out of that place at any cost. Desperate men will do desperate things.

I went about my usual business of picking up Kevin, getting supplies, and getting to work. During the course of that day, I also made a few phone calls to try and locate any lenders who might be able to help me with my situation. I made a few calls that led me to some other phone numbers that I called. Either nobody would handle this loan, or someone was out of the office. After about an hour of phone calls with no luck, I decided to get back to work. At some point towards the end of that day, Patti called me and asked me if I wanted to go out with her to Manhattan. I decided that I could use a little break or time out for myself, so I accepted the offer. Her girlfriend from work, Megan, lived in Manhattan, so we stopped there first. Instead of there being a big rush to go out, Patti and Megan settled in to some wine and conversation. Before long though, I felt a little shut in sitting in an apartment in the city, so I told Megan and Patti, that I was going to take a walk. Megan, who was a really nice person and best friend to Patti jumped up and said, "Oh, I'm sorry. If you guys want to go out right now, I'll get ready."

"No, that's all right, Megan. Really, it's okay. You guys relax. I could use a good walk in the city."

Patti looked at Megan calmly and said, "It's okay. He likes taking walks. He even does it when he's over my house."

"Really?" Megan asked.

"Really, Megan," I said as I grabbed my coat.

When I walked outside, the air was cool and crisp with all the sounds and unimportant action going on. I don't know why, but I just loved it. Megan lived by the entrance of the Midtown Tunnel, so when I got to the end of her block, I made a right and headed downtown. I really needed to take a "think about everything and nothing at all" type of walk. The trick was to walk far and long enough to let my brain fizzle until I couldn't think of anything at all. Another thing I liked about walking in the city was that you could talk out loud to yourself, and nobody would look at you like you were crazy. It was a trick I learned as a child.

A thought that popped into my head this day was something this old farmer told me once on one of my mother's trips when I was a child. He said, in a slow country drawl, "Ya' know, boy, sometimes after worrying, thinking and fussing, some things were just meant to happen," as I tried franticly to prevent one of his little pigs from getting out of his barn. From his tone I was never really sure if he was only speaking about the pig or life, but at times like this, I'd repeat it to myself with his same tone and it would allow me to lighten up on myself.

This walk took me an hour, and I almost felt calm by the time I got back. After I got inside Megan looked at me a little strange and said, "Michael, where did you go?"

"I told you, Megan. I'm a big boy. I'd be all right," I joked.

"Megan thought you had gotten mad at her because we decided to hang out here instead of going right out, but I tried to explain to her that you're a little nutty at times."

"Well, thank you for the compliment, honey," I said as I bent over to kiss Patti.

We finally did decide to go out, and we went to a jazz club that I used to walk past when I'd go to visit my mother in prison. When visiting my mother, I'd always walked past the place while it was still early and it wasn't open, so I never had a chance to go inside. It was on the west side over by 26th Street. The thing that originally caught my eye about it was that, through the storefront windows, you could see that everything in the place was flat black and pink. The night we went there, two musicians were playing in a two-man band. While I was listening to the music for a while and tallying up how much the bar was making that night, I started with the observation thing as usual.

This guy sitting at the bar is very relaxed in here, I thought. He looks like an accountant, and he's sipping draft beers, must be a regular. This one's having mixed drinks with a booster shot on the side. He's either pissed off, someone's trying to fuck him over, he's gonna fuck someone over, or he's nervous about getting laid, and he wants to get a jump start on his buzz. He could be a hard worker. That guy with the big mouth has got the look, but I can sense a weakness in him, almost as though he's living on his daddy's money. About halfway through the room, I decided to stop analyzing people and start enjoying myself.

452

Patti, Megan, and I ended up staying there until the bar closed. I'd say that I enjoyed myself, but I knew the enjoyment was similar to throwing a glass of water on a volcano. Above all else, I really hoped that nobody looked or said the wrong thing to me, because unfortunately, due to circumstances, I felt like a bad accident waiting to happen.

After we drove Megan home, Patti and I headed back to Queens. Patti was talking to me as we were driving, but for some reason I was just going through the motions with her and hardly comprehending what she was talking about. Before I dropped her off, we sat outside her house for a little while.

"Listen, Patti, I'm sorry if I didn't seem to be paying attention to you on the ride back. It's just that I've got a lot on my mind, so don't take it personally, okay?"
"No, I won't, Michael. After several months I'm getting used to you having something on your mind."

I gave Patti a kiss, then a long hug, and told her good night. Then I decided to drive around the neighborhood a bit. I ended up driving past the Whitestone house, the College Point house, and then past my mother's house. I sat in front of my mother's house for about 20 minutes and felt pretty depressed by the end of it. It was pretty late by now, and for whatever reason I didn't feel like going home. I started up the car and just started driving. I didn't really know where I was heading, but I knew I didn't feel like being here.

The next day started with the same routine, with Kevin and my phone calls. We got done late, so after I dropped him off, I went straight home to go to bed. The first thing I did when I got in was to turn on my answering machine. "Beep – Hello I'm calling in regards to your mortgage that is now in foreclosure. I am the attorney who is handling it for the bank. It's imperative that you return my call and let me know how you want to rectify this situation. My number is ____- etc, etc."

Great, I thought. Now they've got my new phone number, and I'll have to hear about this aggravating situation every time I come home at night.

"Beep"- "Hello, Michael, it's your mother."

Well, here it comes again, I figured.

"Listen, I can't find your beeper number, and Wally, the old guy who rents a room in the attic, just fell down the stairs, and I think he's dead. Ummmm – do me a favor, and call me okay. Okay, bye."
Oh, man, what the fuck now?
"Beep"- "Michael, its mommy again. Listen, I asked Jim in number 4 to go and check on Wally, and he really didn't want to do it, but he did anyhow. He said that Wally is dead and that it looks like Wally broke his neck when he fell backwards. I'm really scared, and I think it would be better if you called the police about it. Give me a call – okay, bye."

Great... just great... another dead body in that house.

"Beep- Michael, I can't understand why you can't call me. This is the third message I've left you. This is not mommy bullshit. I can't call 911 and tell them there's another dead body here. Would you please give me a fucking call? Okay, bye."

After my answering machine turned off, I called my mother.

"Yeah, Ma?"
"Finally... I can't believe you didn't call me, Michael!"
"Ma, it's not like I was sitting by the phone all day, okay? Now you're sure Wally's dead?"
"Yes, I'm sure he's dead."
"He's still in the house?"
"Yes, he's still in the house."
"Well, Ma, I think it'll look a little suspicious if Wally's body is sitting in the house and you don't call 911."
"Well, yeah, I know that, Michael. That's what I was really worried about. Thank you."
"Ma, don't get on my shit, because I just got your messages. Did you call 911?"
"Well, I made Jim in #4 do it."
"Oh... okay. That poor bastard, he's been through so much shit in that house."
"I know. That's one of the reasons why he didn't want to do it, that poor bastard. He could write a book about the shit he's been through living here."
"So why is Wally's body still there?"
"Well, it's just like the last time. They sent a police car over to check on him first, then some detectives stopped here, then they called the morgue."
"Yeah, that's right. It took all day for them to pick up Frank that time."
"Please, don't remind me about that poor bastard. I swear, I never thought I'd say this, but I hate this fucking house."
"I don't know, Ma. Maybe it's a good thing losing that house. I know it tried to kill me a few times."
"Tell me about it, Michael. Did I ever tell you about the time that my girlfriend Maryann and I saw a ghost in the basement?"
"Oh, come on."
"No, I swear. I don't know why we were down there, but we were over by the boiler room where I used to keep my sewing machine, and we both saw this little old man standing there. It almost looked like Grandpa, so I said 'Daddy, is that you?' Then you know how ballsy Maryann is. She starts walking towards the little old man, saying, 'Who the hell are you?' And I swear, Michael, the little old man stopped smiling, and then the spool of thread that was locked onto my sewing machine flew across the basement and hit the far wall. Well, you know Maryann and me are not small, so we both ran for the door trying to squeeze our fat asses through it at the same time, punching and kicking each other all the way up the stairs and out the side door."
"What the hell do you think it was?"
"I don't know, Michael. But I had found out that Mr. Babcock, the man who used to own this house, was found behind the boiler, standing there naked, laughing to himself. And get this! They sent him to Creedmore State Hospital and into the same section that I went to."
"So what do you think? He's haunting the house?"
"No, I don't really think so. Mr. Babcock had a sister who lived here, also. From what I found out,

after Mr. Babcock's wife died, his sister ruled the roost with an iron fist. People said that she could always be heard yelling and screaming at Mr. Babcock and at his son. Everyone I talked to said that she was just a real nasty bitch."

"Well, maybe you shouldn't talk so loud."

"Yeah, right, tell me about it."

"Don't worry, Ma. If you start yelling and screaming and the phone goes dead, I'll make sure I send someone over there."

"Yeah, well, you better be the one to come over, otherwise I'll find you and haunt you for the rest of your life."

"Okay, okay, just kidding. So Wally's still there, huh?"

"Yeah."

"All right, I'll be there in a little bit. Do you need anything from the store?"

"Yeah, bring me a ticket to Hawaii and ten grand."

It's kinda funny, I thought, after I hung up. But after all the shit my mother and I had been through over the years, we could talk normal and joke through otherwise abnormal situations. I mean, here I am asking my mother if she needs anything before I stop by, and there is a dead body sitting on the third floor landing.

By the time I got there, there was a cop car sitting out front and the meat wagon was there. When I walked in, the morgue guys were already taking Wally down the stairs in a body bag. I walked into the kitchen, and my mother was sitting there drinking a cup of tea.

"Hey, Ma," I said.

"Hi. Let me have a cigarette."

"Don't smoke now; you quit."

"I know, but I need one now."

After I gave her a cigarette, the cop knocked on the kitchen door and told us that they were done.

"Oh, yeah, listen. If for some reason there is any questions about this death, some detectives will stop by again, okay?" the cop said.

With my back towards him I looked at my mother, rolled my eyes towards the ceiling, and answered, "Oh, that will be just fine, Officer. Thanks for waiting."

"That's okay, it s my job. Whenever there's a body, a police officer has to stay on the scene until the morgue comes. Good night."

"Good night," I answered.

After I heard the front door close, I looked at my mother and said, "I'll bet Detective Lizio will volunteer for the job."

"Tell me about it."

"Well, if he does, I found the body, and I'll talk to the asshole."

My mother put her hand to her forehead, looked down towards the table, and said, "I don't know what I'm going to do. I'm losing the house, and another poor bastard dies here. I don't know what the fuck to do."

For once I knew my mother wasn't taking to me like a son. She was just talking in general, and it sank so deep, I just closed my eyes and gritted my teeth with nothing to say.

After all this time working on her house, all this time working on my house, all the running around, all the bullshit, I was still at square one and not in a position to be able to do anything for myself or my mother. It almost made me want to go out and get a baseball bat and smash a few choice heads in the morning. To see my mother sitting there just brought all my frustrations to a boiling point. I felt beyond frustrated, I had been chasing the moon for so long with nothing accomplished that I almost thought I would have felt better if I would have never got involved in real estate. I thought about me and my personal life that I hardly had, and in the middle of all these feelings, I couldn't walk over and put my arm around my mother and tell her not to worry because I was going to fix everything and it would be all right. Instead I talked and joked with my mother and lied that everything would be all right.

After a little while I told her that I was going to leave. I wrote down my pager number for her again, kissed her on top of her head, and walked into the hallway. Man, the house looked good: new rugs, new wallpaper, new paint and for what? Just to lose it all. I went outside and walked around the yard and reminisced about when I was a kid and painted myself red, and then when we had the pool. I had so many memories here that it really bothered me to think about losing this place.

Okay, Mike, now here's something else you have to think about, I thought. You've sunk, and are still sinking money into College Point. For what? Whether or not you want to admit it, you're in deep shit over there, with money tied up, and not being able to get it out. The time zone on your black hole into utopia is shrinking by the minute. So what are you going to do?

I ended up sitting in the backyard for about an hour, and I realized that I had to get away. I had to go to a neutral place in a neutral, relaxed setting. I really had to assess my situation before I made another move. If nothing else, my mind was made up about it. I had to get away; where I went wasn't really an issue. One thing was sure, though, now looked like a perfect time. I drove home, packed a small bag, and left that night.

I got into the car and just started driving. Somehow I ended up on the Van WyckLori Expressway. From there I crossed the Whitestone Bridge and headed towards the George Washington Bridge. By the time I got to the George Washington Bridge, I almost felt the calmness come back to me, but I knew it was similar to drinking a cup of coffee in the morning. It helps you wake up, but you know you're not really up. When I got to the end of the bridge, I saw a little sign that said, "Orange, N.J., turn right." Yep, that's where I want to be- Orange, N.J., I mused, as I turned right.

Then I started to sing up a little song out loud. "Orange N.J. is the place to be, where everything is orange as far as the eye can see."

As I drove there, I imagined that the whole town would be orange and that possibly everybody there dressed in orange. I mean, I know this all might sound a little crazy, but it's okay to let yourself be crazy as long as you are aware of it and you set yourself a little time limit. I got there almost two hours later, and I'll be damned; nothing was orange. I had built myself up for two hours about how everything was going to be orange that it almost depressed me again when it wasn't.

I found a Holiday Inn Motel and got myself a room. While I was in the lobby, I noticed that someone was playing a piano in the lounge area, so I decided to go in and have myself a drink or two. I sat there and drank in the music and alcohol until I felt relaxed. Then I decided to get my things and go to bed, because I had a big day ahead of me.

The next morning I got up and took a bath. I hadn't taken a bath as opposed to a shower since I was eleven-years-old, and that was eighteen years ago. I had forgotten how relaxing they were. Then I got dressed and went into town.

I parked, and then I walked into the little town diner. It was about 9am and even though I never really ate breakfast any more, for some reason I was hungry for it. I bought a newspaper, sat down, and picked up a menu.

"Good morning, would you like coffee, tea or juice?" a cheerful waitress said.

As a matter of fact, she was so cheerful she actually startled me a bit.

"Well, I guess I'd like some coffee please."
"Coming right up," she said in her cheerful voice again.

As I looked at the breakfast menu I noticed that the most expensive thing was only $3.50, so I ordered it. After a few minutes into the paper, the waitress came back with a huge plate of food. She obviously noticed the expression on my face, because she said, "Is everything okay?"

"No, no, everything is fine, just fine. Thank you."
"Okay, if you need anything, just give me a holler," she said as she walked away.

About half a minute after that, she came back and said, "Oh, I'm sorry, here is your grits."
"Grits?"
"You've never had grits?"
"No."
"Oh, don't look so scared. Just put a little butter, sugar, and milk in them, and you'll be fine."
"All right. I'll give them a try," I answered.

Through that whole meal, I don't think my cup of coffee was half full once. If I hadn't noticed her filling up everybody's cup as they ate, I'd almost swear I was getting special treatment, and damn, these grits were good. When I finished eating and reading the paper, I asked the waitress where I could get myself some stationery, and after she told me, I tipped her nicely, paid, and left.

I ended up getting a spiral notebook, and then I drove towards the big lake I had seen. Once I found a nice little rest spot, I parked, got out, and walked closer to the water with my pen and pad in hand. I sat out there for hours, and then I drove to another relaxing location until about suppertime. Just before I got back into my car, I looked at my pad and realized that I hadn't written anything down on it. It's amazing what a whole lot of nothing can do for a person. I drove back to town and found myself another little diner. I went inside and treated myself to a very nice meal and had the pleasure of dealing with another friendly waitress. When I got finished, I treated myself to a nice little walk through this quaint little town.

As strange as it may seem, sometimes, like now, when I took these little walks I'd look for the manicured lawns, the curtains, wind chimes, or a glimpse of the interior of the home. I'd imagine what type of people would live there. I'd wonder what kind of jobs they had, how close they were to their families and their friends. I'd also wonder what type of problems life threw their way and how they would deal with them.

Whenever I would come upon a house that was a little beat up, I'd look at the car they drove and try to assume the ages of the people living there. For instance, if there was a Trans Am with T- tops, I'd assume they were young people. If they were young, I'd wonder why, if they lived in a house, they didn't take care of it. I could probably count on one hand a few people I knew who would like to live in a house instead of an apartment or a room.

After walking for about an hour, I went back to the car and drove over to the motel. When I got there I went to the lounge, ordered a mixed drink, and casually observed the clientele. About an hour after that, I went to my room, watched some TV, and then I fell asleep.

The next day, which was Sunday, I got up early and headed over to the diner. After a pleasant breakfast I went out for another ride in the country. I drove for about another 45 minutes until I found a place that looked nice and secluded. Once I got there I parked, grabbed my book, and took a walk into the woods. I've always enjoyed taking walks in the woods since I lived in the country. I used to walk until I found a nice scenic spot up there, sit down, and kinda mediate. Being that I had learned my way around in the woods back then, I wasn't too worried about getting lost.

After a little while, I found a place with a creek that looked peaceful, so I sat down. I ended up spending most of the day out there, but by the time I was finished, I had written out myself a game plan. The first thing I decided that I had to do was to fully complete the College Point house and then load it with tenants, because there was nothing I could do without a decent cash flow. Then I would explain to John, whom Kirk had left behind, that he had to cover Richard's second Mortgage in Whitestone if he was going to stay there. One of the reasons I decided to do that was that John was comfortable living there, so there wouldn't be a lapse in the income from that place while I looked for another tenant. I also decided that I would move into the small apartment upstairs there to have myself a new fresh visual living scene. I also needed to go back to work and make as many phone calls as I could to find some kind of lending on College Point, and somehow I'd have to find time to have a life.

It was about four o'clock by the time I hit the road back home. Along the way, I stopped and had a nice steak dinner at a restaurant. I joked to myself and hoped that it wasn't a last meal.

When I got to my place, the first thing I did was to start packing my things. Within the course of the next two weeks I moved into Whitestone, and I got a good jump on finishing up my plan with the College Point house. Unfortunately by the end of the second week, I was pretty low on cash, and it was pretty bad timing for Kevin to ask me for a loan one day over at the house.

"Kevin, why didn't you ask me sooner?"

"Well, I knew you had to finish the house and that you were planning on refinancing it, so I figured I'd wait until then."

"Oh, great, Kev. That whole thing fucked up."

"Oh, man, you're shitting me!"

"No, I'm not. As a matter of fact, Kirk fucked up with me, too. He moved out and split."

"No shit. After all you did for him?"

"Tell me about it. Why? How much do you need?"

"Well, a grand."

"Shit, Kev. What do you need it for?"

"My rent. I guess I waited so long now that they're trying to evict me."

"Look, Kev, I ain't got a grand. All I could give you is about $400."

We both looked at each other for a second, and then Kev said, "Well, it's better than nothing. I just don't know if they'll accept it though."

"Well, why not? It's money."

"Yeah, I know, but I kinda made a deal with them already, and I told them I'd have about a grand."

"I'm sorry, Kev but that's all I'd be able to come up with."

"Well, all right. It's better than nothing."

After all the money I put into that shithead Kirk's hand, it killed me not to be able to put more money into Kev's hand. As it turned out, Kev wasn't able to stop his eviction, and he had to move out of the apartment that he had for five years. I know how he felt, but for some reason, I felt worse about it.

Being that I had gotten some work with the union, I wasn't able to help Kev with his entire move, but I did what I could to help. Kevin's father was a maintenance man for a large building over in Que Gardens, Queens, and his father had a large two- bedroom apartment, so Kev moved in there.

I didn't have very much luck trying to find someone to give me any type of financing for my situation in College Point. It was extremely frustrating, because I knew that somewhere, if I could get past the bullshit red tape, someone would give me some type of financing there so I could pull the Whitestone house out of foreclosure. One thing I did learn was that, if I got rid of one of the houses, namely the Whitestone house, then there was a chance that I might be able to do a refinance at College Point. Even if I did decide to do this, I had to prove, on paper, that I could afford College Point because lenders were starting to tighten up on no income verification loans.

Another difficulty I had in making this decision was that, from the way my checks were coming in from work right now, I was living on the rent money till I would get paid. Then there was the grand finale. If I gave the Whitestone house back to the bank, Richard, who was holding a second mortgage there, might put a lien on the College Point House to try and collect his money which would shut down any chance of a refi on College Point. Sal, the attorney who closed on both houses for me, was a personal friend of Richard's, so I knew that it wouldn't take long for that to happen. It was if I had to purposely keep myself in suspended animation until I came up with a solution or made something else happen. It was extremely frustrating.

My old friend John Slocum stopped by one day, and after we got to talking, he told me that he had a friend named Ernie who was looking for a room to rent. After talking to John about him for a little bit, I decided to take Ernie in as a boarder without ever meeting him. I needed the money.

By now I had a couple of tenants, and I noticed a little bit of a cash flow coming in. Collecting rent was a little bit of a hassle. If I didn't get there by Friday evening, I'd get stories and no money by Saturday.

One day when I was dropping Kevin off by his father's apartment, I asked him if he knew anything about this big brick house next to his father's house.

"Why?" he asked.
"Well, I noticed that a couple of windows were knocked out of it, so it must be abandoned or something."
"Oh, shit, you're right," Kev said as he looked over at the house. "I don't know. I'll ask my father if he knows anything about it.
"I'm gonna check the place out," I said as I double parked the car and got out.

As I walked around, I noticed that the grass had overgrown and died, so I figured the place had to be sitting for a while. Then I walked over to the brick two-car garage and noticed that the side door was open a little bit, so I opened it. The garage had a few piles of old plaster and some lumber in it. Obviously someone had started some work on the place at some time. When I walked back up front, Kevin was peeking into one of the windows, and he turned towards me and said, "You're right. The place doesn't have any furniture."
"Yeah, I thought it might've been empty. Well, ask your father if he knows anything," I said as I walked back to the car.

After living over at Whitestone for a couple of weeks, I was finally settled in. One day while I was home, I ran into John, Kirk's nephew. He asked me if a friend of his could move in with him to help him pay the rent. He explained that, because he was only at his job a short time, and was barely clearing $320 per week, he needed someone to help him pay the rent. After paying off Richard's second at $600 he hardly had anything left after his other bills for the month. Of course this time around, I asked him to confirm it by showing me a pay stub, which he did. After seeing it I decided to let his friend Wayne move in with his dog.

I met Wayne, and I could see that he was a kinda happy- go- lucky type of guy. I didn't see any trouble coming from him, so I decided to agree to it. As far as Richard, the lien holder on Whitestone, I had decided to let John pay him directly after having a conversation with Richard earlier in the month. I still wasn't 100 percent sure how I was going to handle the Whitestone house yet, so for now I didn't need another headache with him. But I was sure it was going to happen one day. Being that I was very unsure about which route I was going to take with the Whitestone house, I decided not to raise their rent for the time being, as long as they were taking care of a headache for me, Richard's second mortgage...

By the end of that week, the College Point house was pretty well wrapped up, thanks to Kev giving me a hand. I also got a few more tenants; now I had about 8 of them. At $75 to $90 dollars per week I finally started getting a little juice out of it. I had also gotten some information about the house next to Kev from the County Assessor's office, particularly the owner's name. What I thought was odd about it, was that it showed the owner's name but, it had a different address, and name, for contact. It almost made the information that Kev had gotten from his father about nobody living there for two years, make sense. I would think that a house of this size, in a bustling neighborhood, wouldn't just be left her to rot.

Being that I was the type who thought things were better face to face with someone, I decided to take the time to go and check out the address I had gotten. Who knows? Maybe that place was empty, too. It turned out that the place was a TV repair shop with two apartments above it. The place was open, so I decided to ask someone inside if they knew anything about the owner or the other house. When I went inside, I could see that it was set up like an old time type of shop.

An older man sat at the desk, working on some electrical component, and he fit right in. A woman was sitting a few feet away, drinking tea and watching a television. Being that she seemed very relaxed, I automatically assumed that it was his wife.

I introduced myself and asked him if he knew anything about the other property. He stopped what he was doing, looked over at the female, and then kinda sized me up.

"Yes, I know something about that property," he said in a Middle Eastern accent. "What can I help you with?"
"Well, I was wondering if it was for sale."
"Well, it might be."
"Do you own it?" I asked.
"Well, no, but I'm the caretaker of the property."

I almost needed to bite my tongue when he said this, considering the state of the property. He must've noticed a different look on my face, because then he added:
"You can see that the place is not in good shape. I recently took it over from someone else who did a very bad job."
"I noticed that there was a lot of old plaster in the garage, as if somebody was tearing down some walls."
"Well, there was a big problem over there. The last caretaker forgot to turn the boiler on, and there was a lot of water damage. That was about two years ago."

Hmmm, water damage, I thought. The place must need a lot of work then. That can be good and bad, good because I can probably get it for a good price and bad because the boiler and all the pipes are probably cracked.

"Is there a way that I could take a look at the place and see how much work there would be to repair it?"

"Well, yes, I could meet you there one day and let you in."

I decided that if he had come forth with this much information, then he would probably be in a position to negotiate a sale on the property, so there wasn't much sense in digging any deeper for that information now. Instead I figured that it would be better to inspect the property to see exactly what I was dealing with before I got involved with any type of purchase price, so I set up an appointment and cut it short.

On the day of the selected appointment, I went inside to view the place, and it looked like hell. A lot of the plaster that had fallen down was still piled on the floor in areas; the rest just lay where it fell. After I walked through the entire house, it was obvious that the basement apartment had gotten the worst of it. The only good thing left down there was the marble tile floor.

The first floor also looked like hell, because everything from the second floor leaked down to there. Oddly enough the second floor looked pretty well preserved, aside from some expansion crack in the plaster that happened over the winters. Being that there was no radiator's in the large three-roomed finished attic, it was also in good shape. Aside from the brick exterior, the place needed a considerable amount of work, which was still good and bad in my mind. This place was twice the size of my College Point house, had more rooms, and a finished basement. If I had just gotten a $300,000 appraisal on that one, this one had to be good for $350,000 to $400,000 I figured.

After walking around the outside again, I told the caretaker to call the owner, who lived in Europe I learned. After explaining all the damages to the property caretaker, I told him to tell me what kind of money the owner wanted for the place. After exchanging phone numbers, he agreed to call me as soon as he had some information.

CHAPTER 11

LET IT RIDE

I ended up eventually getting involved in the Briarwood House. The deal I made with the owner was this: If he would give me six months to fix the house up with my money, I would get the financing and close on it. A few days later, I got an answer from the caretaker. He told me that the owner would be willing to do this, but because I would be tying up the property for six months, he wanted me to pay him two hundred thousand for it. That was peanuts for this house in my book.

Unfortunately I started working over there by the beginning of the winter. This meant that, without a boiler, I had to rely on electric heaters to dry the plaster and paint after the proper repairs were done. This also meant that I had a high monthly electric bill to deal with, being that the heaters just about ran day and night. My game plan over there was to fix the water pipes and rehab the place enough so it would pass an appraisal by a bank. Then I would deal with the boiler because it should be warm out by then.

My theory was that, if I managed to get the Briarwood house finished soon enough, once again I could probably bail out everything now that I had come to a crossroads with trying to find financing at College Point. Fortunately I had enough tenants in College Point to support this project. Unfortunately I could no longer support College Point with the bank if I gambled and financed the Briarwood house. Just like the Whitestone house before it, I decided to keep paying Mineo on his second Mortgage, because it was on a more personal level. I had already spoken to Patti, and we decided to put the Briarwood house in her name. My plan was to get financing to buy the place and then re-finance it. After that, I could get the money I needed to cover my other two houses. Then we would split the responsibility for that place 50/50, and she would own half of it.

As I worked through the winter with Kevin's help, for some reason, through mutiny or revolt, it became more and more difficult to collect rents in College Point. It actually got to a point where I would have to do recon patrols over there at different hours of the night. That even became a joke, because it was similar to a bug spray commercial where, when the can of bug spray would walk into a building, the bugs would run out. I had people jumping out of the second floor windows and running down the block. Patti took some notice to my frustrations, and after a couple of weeks she suggested that I let her collect the rent over there so I could get some sleep and concentrate on my work at Briarwood. But I didn't feel comfortable with her idea. Then Patti turned to me and said, "Listen,

Michael, you're barely collecting any money there now. What do you have to lose by letting me try to get the money you're not getting- some extra sleep at night?"

I kinda hated to admit it, but I really didn't have an answer for her. So I begrudgingly agreed with her, and told her I would notify the tenants that she would be collecting rent.

I really didn't think it would work for her, considering that at times I had to go there with a baseball bat for rent. I must say that I was quite surprised that first week she took over that she gave me more rent money from there than I had been collecting for weeks. After I told Kevin about it, he busted my balls and said, "Gee, I don't know, Mike. Maybe you should keep an eye out on Patti when she collects rent. Maybe you could learn a thing or two."

"Yeah, really funny, Kev."

The process of fixing the Briarwood house was very slow due to the weather. Although it would seem that the electric heaters had dried the plaster, once I went to sand it, huge pieces would fall away from the wall because the heat hadn't penetrated through to the cold walls. Then I'd have to start the process all over again.

I worked on that house and took over chasing tenants again for several months until the weather got warm. As far as I could tell, I had spent about 10 grand and countless hours preparing it for an appraisal. My electric bill there had probably amounted to about 25 percent of that figure. After all this time and effort, I finally got to make an appointment for an appraisal just as the weather started to warm up.

The place wasn't really 100 percent complete as of then, but my money and my closing deadline were getting short, especially since I had just recently rotated stock with my tenants in College Point and had less money coming in. This also meant that I didn't have enough money to do two appraisals with two different banks. This didn't make me comfortable. I also didn't have Sal, the attorney on the first deals, there to help on the closings. Nor did I have Kirk to help me with the paperwork, which also limited me as to how many banks I could go with. I still had some work to do in the basement, but I had managed to get all the floors complete. I even had the hardwood floors re-sanded and shellacked. When the appraiser came, he looked at the entire house and then the outside. The whole inspection took about a half hour. Before he left, he told me to call him in about two weeks.

Being that I finally had a little time on my hands, I was able to relax slightly and go out with Patti. She had stuck by me for several months, without hardly seeing me, and it was nice to spend some time with her. One night we went out to dinner with her father and Zena, his girlfriend. As we were all getting ready to sit down, her father turned and started walking towards the kitchen.

"Where is he going?" I asked.
"Oh, He's going to check the kitchen," Patti answered.
"Excuse me?"
"He does it all the time."
"He goes and checks out kitchens at restaurants? What is he looking for?"
"He goes in to see how clean the kitchens are."

"What if they're not up to his standards?"

"Well, then, he'll come out and say, let's go."

"Well, that's cool, I guess. I hope it's clean because I'm hungry."

Fortunately it passed, so we were able to eat.

Being that the Briarwood house had taken me a lot longer than I had expected, my debts, particularly in College Point, ran up. That's another reason why I was pretty devastated after the new appraisal didn't come in high enough. I was about $25,000 short, and it looked like I wasn't going to be able to close on the Briarwood house in time. Twenty-five grand short, I couldn't believe it. It took about two days just to get over the numbness. I had been so confident that the numbers would come in with this bank. Now I had to try and scramble and force something together. The first thing I did was to prepare five sets of applications the next day. Then I sent them all out and called some of the high-interest lenders I was dealing with in College Point.

My mother got in touch with me during this time. It was very difficult listening to the pain in her voice behind our conversations while we spoke. I really disliked the feeling of not being able to help my mother.

This conversation was different. She told me that Citibank had sent a letter addressed to John Garramone. It stated that, if he didn't pay a $375 dollar storage fees on a storage box that the bank was going to repossess it. I asked if the letter was from the Citibank that was down the block from the store, and she told me that the letter didn't say where the box was; there was only a phone number. It was decided that I would make the call about it.

The next day when I called I was told, in an embarrassed tone of voice, that they had no idea where the box was.

"Well, considering that my father died 15 years ago, I'm not too sure where it would be either. If there are any Citibank's out in Upper Saddle River New Jersey, it might be there. Otherwise, I'd say that it might be over in Flushing where we used to own a store," I said.

I was told that they would look into it and get back to me on it.

The thing that really had my interest about this was that my father was supposed to have had about $20,000 on him the night he died. Maybe, instead of the story about how someone in the store ran off with it, maybe it was in the safety deposit box, I hoped.

Man, I thought, wouldn't that be something? Right on time, too. It's just what I would need to close on this house.

When the bank finally did get back in touch with me, they told me that it was the Citibank down the block from the store. Now it was my call, and they asked me what I wanted to do. I think one of the hardest things to think about was that the NY State Lottery was up to 55 million for the first time ever, and $375 dollars in lottery tickets would have certainly gone a long way. I was very concerned that the bank would open the box on their own, take what was in it, and reclose it. But if I never opened the box, it would probably haunt me for the rest of my life, so I decided to go with the box.

Once I got there on the scheduled day, I was told that I would have to pay an additional $35 to have the box drilled open. So now it was $410 in lottery tickets.

When I got into the safety deposit room with the bank manager, a maintenance man was there with a cordless drill. He proceeded to drill out the lock. Then he opened the door, pulled it out, shook it two times, and then looked at me as he handed it in my direction, and said, "Tough luck. It's empty."

I took the box from him with a frown, opened it, and sure enough it was empty. It was a little difficult standing there nonchalantly while it felt like someone had just punched me in the gut. Oh, well. Next time I play the lottery, I guess.

The owners of the Briarwood house were starting to get impatient with the closing date so, like an idiot, I estimated how long it would take to get back replies from the banks and then added on a week or two for good measure for a closing date with them. But sometimes, good measure isn't good enough because, as it turned out, the best deal I had for them after they flew in from Europe was the original $160,000 that I got from the first bank. They got so pissed off about the whole situation that they made a contract with the caretaker and sold it to him. I could have put a lien on the place for the ten grand I invested in the place, but fortunately I'm a man of my word and as I said from the git' go with them, if I didn't get the money in 6 months, I'd walk, which I did.

It was another untimely defeat for me, and I managed to mope around for a month. It was the only energy I had left to use. All my bills now seemed titanic, and I didn't have a clue how to get out from under them.

It actually took me a month until I could even use any type of brain energy just to think about it. But I finally did come up with an idea. As it turned out, John and Wayne, who were still living in Whitestone, told me that they were planning to move out by the end of the month. This spurred me to think about renting out the entire house to, let's say, one family for about $1500 per month. I'd have to move out, but it would allow me to move into College Point where I could be on top of my tenants over there. This way, I figured, I could make close to $1,000 per month in Whitestone, which is what I should have been making this whole time. Then I could save that money, get rent money out of College Point, and try to see if I could get more work out of the Teamsters. With any luck, I might be able to save up enough money to save one of my houses or possibly my mother's.

Aside from it being my only plan, it seemed like a good plan, so I went with it. I moved out, fixed the place up a bit, and then put it up for rent. At first I wanted a month's rent with first and last months on top of it. That would give me a boost of about $4,500, but after a couple of weeks passed without getting a bite from a bunch of real estate agents, I decided to ask only for two months up front. That still took another two weeks, but I finally did get a bite. The only problem was that they wanted me to put a new rug in the living room. Of course, I hated to do it but with the house being empty for about a month now I was a little desperate, so I spent $600 to make $2,400.

The Spanish people who rented it looked like average middle- class people, but what I didn't realize until a month later was that they had about 12 people of all different ages living there. But as long as I was getting paid, I was happy. Besides, what could I do now? Evict them?

I was late on paying Richard on his second mortgage over in Whitestone, and he started ragging on me the next time I saw him. Being that I was a little tired of playing a charade with him, I dropped the bomb on him and broke the news about how Kirk had fucked me. Being that Sal, our attorney, had been Kirk's attorney for a few years and the fact that Sal had helped set up the deal between Kirk and Richard, I'm sure it wasn't news to Richard. He looked at me with a bit of shock, for dramatic effect, on his face and then said, "Mike, what am I supposed to do? I've got a wife and kids to support."
"Well, look, Rich," I said. "Being that I'm either a good guy or a sap, I'll keep paying you instead of the 1st mortgage until this thing is either resolved or collapses okay?"
"Well, if it doesn't work out, then what am I supposed to do?"
"Well, I guess you could always rent me a room at your house, Rich. Listen, I don't mean to seem rude but I've got to go now, okay."

After I left, I kinda thought that he had some balls not even to be slightly concerned about my situations and went directly into his own worries and fears. It kinda made me really wonder about my good guy status with him.

By several months later, I had managed to save up close to 10 grand. I figured that if things kept up this way, I might be able to make some type of move with either my place in College Point or possibly my mother's house once again. But unfortunately things didn't hold out. I found this out after I went to collect rent one day in Whitestone.

After I knocked on the door, two of the older sisters opened it and told me that two people from the bank had come over to the house. After finding out that they were the tenants there, they offered them relocation money to move out so that they could take the house back.

"Really? So what do you plan on doing?" I asked. "Take their offer?"

Their answer really surprised me, because what they told me was that being that their parents had just lost a house, they knew that they didn't have to pay any money until the sheriff evicted them at the end of their lease after it went to auction. So they, as a family, decided not to pay me anymore, and that if I wanted, I could start an eviction process against them, which they knew would take me about two months. At this point they wouldn't care because they would have saved up enough money to move somewhere else anyhow.

I had to admit that I was slightly shocked, and I actually didn't know whether to clap for their genius, or slap them for being smart asses. Feeling that I didn't have too many options to go with, I said, "Well, why don't you take the money the bank offered, and I'll throw in another $1,000 to help you move, so that I can still make some moves here?"

The two sisters looked at each other and whispered into each other's ears. Then the older one said, "Make it 2 thousand, and you've got a deal."

Man, these girls really wanted to get slapped, I thought.

"No, I'll stick with my offer of $1,000."

"Well, in that case, we're going to stay here then," one of them answered with a sneer as they said good night and closed the door.

I don't want to tell you what my first thoughts were, because I'm afraid that you might get a bad opinion of me, so I went with my second thought, which was to step back and laugh.

Man, that's some shit. They've got it all figured out, I thought. Then I drove home empty- handed and quite pissed off, needless to say.

On the ride back, I contemplated my options over there, but I decided that shooting 12 people and getting rid of that many bodies was far too much work, I joked with myself.

It was around this time that I started making a few calls to the attorneys who were handling my mother's foreclosure for the bank. Being that it wasn't public record as of yet I had to make up a little story about how I found out about the foreclosure. The first question I was asked was whether or not I was related to the owner, which almost caught me off guard.

"No, why do you ask?" I questioned.

"Because we don't like to sell to any family members who wouldn't help out during the foreclosure."

"Well, I can understand your point of view on that, I guess," I lied.

Basically I was told that the bank was about to write off the mortgage as a loss and then put it up for sale for $200,000.

Shit, I thought. That's $145,000 they're willing to write off right from the start. If I were to buy it, I could even flip it over for a profit and not even deal with it.

"But," I was warned, "we do have a builder who's also interested in purchasing it. We'd rather sell it to someone who was interested in purchasing it for themselves and not knock it down, such as yourself."

"$200,000, huh?"

"Yes, and personally speaking, that is a great price for that property, especially since we only want a 10 percent down payment," he added.

"Well, how long would I have until I had to give you an answer if I was able to have an option on it?"

"Well, you can speak to me personally, and you'd still have about 2 months to get back to me on it.

"Very well, I said in my businessman tone, you will hear from me, and thank you for your time."

As soon as I hung up, my wheels started spinning. Two hundred thousand with a twenty thousand dollar down payment. Shit, if I didn't get involved in that Briarwood house, I'd have that by now. So let me see. I've got ten, and with closing costs, I'd probably need about another twenty, unless I could assign the loan to someone else and get a couple of bucks on the table. I've got to think about this one a little bit and see what I can come up with.

A few days after this, Danny, an old friend of mine and mutual friend of Kirk's, called me.

"Hey, Danny. How's the insurance business treating you?"

"Good, good, Mike."

"So what's up?"

"Well, I'd like to talk to you about something one day this week. It's about Kirk."

"Kirk...? That's right, that little shithead owes you some money, too, doesn't he?"

"Well, yeah, that's what I want to talk to you about."

"Yeah, sure, when's good for you?"

"How about tomorrow?" Danny asked.

"Tomorrow? Yeah, that's fine. Where? At your office?"

"Well, I'll tell you what. I've got an appointment up on Bell Boulevard, at about noon time, and I should be done by 2:00 pm; let's meet at the pizza parlor down the block from White Castle."

"Yeah, all right, I'll see you at 2:00. Hey, Danny, this isn't a set-up, is it?"

"Huh? What, what do you mean?"

"Well, I don't know. Maybe Kirk hit it big, and now wants me out of the way."

"Mike, if that was the case I think we both know it wouldn't be at a crowded pizza parlor on a busy street like Bell Boulevard."

"Yeah, I know, Danny. But it doesn't hurt to ask. I'll see you at two."

I mean, who's to say that this wasn't a set-up; maybe I just didn't feel like trusting too many people these days. But by the same token, Danny always seemed to have something up his sleeve.

Just as a precaution, the next day I got over to Bell Boulevard a little early. I wanted to make sure I got a parking space on Bell Boulevard as opposed to a quiet side street. Then I walked around to see if anything looked suspicious. I hung around the pizza shop for a good half-hour until I saw Danny walking down the block.

"Hey, Danny, what's up?"

"Hey, Mike, how you doing? Let's go in the Pizzeria and get a bite. I'm starved."

After we sat down and ordered, the conversation soon turned to Kirk.

"Let me ask you something, Mike. Are you planning on killing Kirk?"

"Why do you ask, Danny?"

"Well, you know he still owes me some money"

It's funny, but I knew this day had felt like a set-up of some kind. Now I think the next couple of answers I said were really going to shape the outcome of the situation. That's not to say that I was just going to roll over easily though. I decided to do a little reverse psychology on Danny and see if I could feel him out some way.

"Well, Danny, now that you ask, let me tell you what I've found out so far. I know that Kirk is living in Pennsylvania, and I know that his wife, Linda, is collecting welfare in her name."

As I spoke to Danny our pizza had arrived, and I noticed that Danny was consciously making himself poised, as if he had something uncomfortable to say.

"Now," I continued, "I've also got a connection with someone over at Motor Vehicle, and if Kirk or Linda applied for a new license or any type of I.D. over there, I could probably get his home address, and just wait for him to come home from work one night, and then "Bam," settle our differences."

"So that's what you plan on doing then?"

Being that I knew that Danny was hanging on my every word, at this point, I allowed myself to pause for a second to study his moves. I mean, even if I did feel the need in my heart to kill Kirk, I certainly wouldn't discuss my plans with anybody, especially if something of this nature was involved. Now that I realized that Danny did have something up his sleeve, I decided to play the other side of the coin and peek over to his side of the fence.

"But you see, Danny, I came to a conclusion about my situation with Kirk, and I decided that just because he fucked me over once, that doesn't mean that I'm going to let him fuck me over twice. By that, I mean this. If I was to take the time to drive all the way over to Pennsylvania and kill Kirk, first of all that would be premeditated murder, and I would get more time in jail as opposed to getting a charge like manslaughter. But second of all, and more important than the first, getting the satisfaction of killing this motherfucker is not worth me going to jail and doing big time over, like I said, he fucked me once. He's not going to fuck me again."

After I explained this to Danny, I noticed his act of being poised faded away, and he became more natural. Then he said, "Well, actually, Mike, that's kind of why I wanted to talk to you. You see, my business is getting a little bigger now, and being that Kirk's thing flopped out there, he's got nowhere to go again, and he called me to make amends and to ask for a job."

"Yeah, but the little prick didn't call me up."

"Well, maybe not. But he did tell me that he was trying to do something out there that would make him enough money to fix shit over here," Danny said.

"Yeah, well, that's what he says."

"Believe me, Mike, I know. He's still paying me back, too, remember?"

"Yeah."

"Well, look, here's the thing, Mike. Kirk's broke, and if anything I'd have to lay out the money to move him back here and set him up in an apartment. I really don't want to waste any more money on this prick, especially if you turn around and kill him a week later. You know what I mean?"

"Well..., that would be bad business for you."

"I know, and I just don't want to lose anything else here over him. Look, Mike, Kirk only ran off owing me a couple of thousand, but believe me I still felt fucked over by him. I know it's only a fraction of what he owed you, but he beat me, too, and I also felt like killing him. But that was then and this is now. If he's offering to work off what he owes me, that's fine with me. But I just want you to know that I'm not going behind your back with this, because you and I don't have any problems with each other. Don't forget this. You'll always know what kind of money he's making and what he's up to, so we shake on it then?"

Before I reached over the table to shake Danny's hand, I thought about it for a second. Then I agreed and shook it. Well, what the hell? If nothing else, if I did snap and change my mind about Kirk one day, at least this way he'd be right under my nose. After our "meeting" we agreed to stay in touch, and then we left.

By now my situation with my tenants in College Point resembled a bit of a circus. I could write a book just on the stories and excuses. The best one I got so far though was from a tenant named Brian. Brian had been playing catch-up with me on rent for some time, and on this particular day Brian owed me about $160. I knocked on his door, and when he opened it, the conversation went something like this, "Oh, yeah. Hey, Mike, what's up? Oh, yeah, I know you're probably here for rent money. Well, look," he said as he reached in his pocket, "I know I owe you $160 but this is what I'd like to do, if you can. I've got $140 as a tenant, but I'd like to borrow $30 back as a friend."

With all the shit I had going on, this is one of the things that resembled getting slapped with a wet towel to me. I mean, with all the money I was spending, all the money I had lost, having to deal with a situation over $30 almost made me blow a circuit with him.

"Brian, don't take it personally, but, if you ever say something like that to me again, I'll fucking kill you. Next time just tell me you only have $110."
"Oh, yeah... Okay. Ahh, Mike, I've only got $110.00."
"Thanks," I said as I took the money and walked away.

After dealing with Brian, I went to my room, and no sooner did I lie down for a little nap than I heard a knock at the door downstairs. When I went downstairs and opened the door, a guy from my old neighborhood named Tony was standing there.
"Hey, Tony. What are you doing here?"
"Hey, Mike, what's up? Listen, I had gone to your mother's house to try and rent a room, and she told me she was full. Then she suggested that I come over her to see if you had anything available."
"Well, yeah, I do. I could give you a room for $80 per week. It's one of the smaller ones up on the top floor."
"Cool, I'll take it."
"Yeah, well, that's $160 for one week rent and one week security."
"No problem, man. I'll take it."

Sometimes it was nice renting rooms. I mean, here I am negotiating with Brian twenty minutes ago about $30, and now I'm having $160 handed to me. While I was standing there with Tony, this young guy who had been ducking me for rent for a few weeks pulled up in a car.

"Well, look who it is. You got any money?" I said as he got out of his car.
"Look, Mike, I know I owe you quite a bit of money."

Well, here we go again, I thought.

"So look, instead of giving you cash, I'll give you my car for what I owe you and maybe one week

471

extra?"

The car was easily a $700 dollar car, so after checking my shoe to see if I had stepped in shit, I said yes. Then we all went upstairs, and I showed Tony his new room.

"Hey! Where's my stereo?" the young kid said.
"I've got that in the basement for collateral. I'll let you down there in a minute to get it," I answered.

After all was said and done, I went back to my room and sat at my desk.

Man, I thought, this is how every day should be around here; I'd be on top of my shit in no time. After I let the kid go and get his stereo, he signed the car title over to me, and I went back to my room, a little happier this time.

As I lay down on my bed, I looked over at the calendar that was hanging on the wall, and I really got a good idea of how much time had gone by since I first got involved with all these houses. I could remember when I first went to one of these real estate seminars and got my books with their wealth of information. Boy, I was hot for this, but it was such a nice feeling, and I thought I had problems then. I'd give my left eye for those problems. Fuck, for that matter, I'd give up a foot for the day I made Kirk a partner. Well, I can't dwell on that shit too much. I'm stuck in the here and now, I thought, just before I dozed off.

Danny called me a few days later. He wanted to set up a little meeting between Kirk and me.

"A meeting?" I asked.
"Well, yeah, Mike. Kirk still thinks you're going to kill him. I mean, you did give me your word, right,1 Mike?"
Yeah, that's right. I did, huh?"
"C'mon, Mike, don't start that shit. We had an agreement."
"So he must have a set of balls to want to see me. What is this, some kind of set-up where I come to your office and find myself rolled up in a rug?"
"C'mon, Mike, you've got my word on that."
"So why does he want to see me? Just tell him I'm not going to kill him."
"I did, but he doesn't believe me."
"Danny, c'mon. What if Kirk's holding a gun when I get there?"
"Mike, you gave me your word. I give you mine, Okay?"
"All right, Danny, but people will know I'm going there. That's all."
"I know that. How about tomorrow?"
"Yeah, sure. Afternoon?"
"Yeah, that's good," Danny answered.

After I hung up the phone, I wondered if I should take a gun and blow this little prick's head off, but I guess a deal's a deal.

I went out and had some dinner with Patti that night. Without really explaining why, I talked to her in subliminal messages that night, just in case anything might happen to me tomorrow. Patti wasn't the type you could just talk straight to, without answering a dozen other questions. I also told a few friends from the neighborhood where I would be for good measure.

The next day when I got to Danny's office, I walked in and saw Erica, who was Patti's sister's friend, sitting at a desk.

"Erica, what are you doing here?"
"Michael, how are you? I work here. Why? Did you come here for insurance?"
"Well no. I'm a friend of Danny's."
"Oh, I didn't know that."
"Yeah, we've been friends for a while. Well, I'll talk to you before I leave, Okay?"
"Okay, say hi to Sharron."
"I will," I said.

I kept walking into Danny's office, and I saw Kirk sitting in a small office at a desk with a sheepish smile. I had been harboring a large amount of anger at him for such a long time that it was hard for me not to lunge at him and smash his fucking head in. But fortunately life had taught me to think before I acted, so I decided that it would be better if I didn't. I walked past him and over to Danny's desk.

Danny and I chitchatted for a minute or two, and then he leaned his head towards me as if to say, Mike, be good. I slowly closed my eyes towards him to acknowledge his question and to signal a truce on words.

"Well, I don't think you guys need any introductions," Danny said loud enough for us both to hear.

On that, I got up and walked into Kirk's office and sat down.

"Hi, Mike." Kirk questioned.
"You fucking little prick."
"Mike, I know I fucked up with you but I swear, man, I didn't mean it"
"Oh, it was an accident."
"Mike, I moved my whole family out to Pennsylvania to try and do some work out there with new houses."
"And what happened? Nobody would fall for your bullshit, so you had to come back?"
"Mike, I swear."
"Man fuck you! Don't ever "Mike I swear" to me again!"
"Erica," Danny called, "you can go out and have your cigarette break now."
"Okay." she answered.

"I went out there with a friend of mine; he's a builder. We had someone put up a few acres of property, and we built a model home on one lot. At first we were going to just sell them as homes, but after a while when nobody showed any interest in buying them, we tried to use the model home for vacation time-shares. If that hit, then we were going to build more of them. But we didn't get a bite, and we were paying on a construction loan the whole time."

"Yeah, I think I know the rest of the story. The shit hit the fan so Kirk split, right? So in other words, what you're trying to tell me, Kirk, that if this would have hit for you, that's when you were going to call me to square up with me right? I feel so much better. I'm really glad that you explained this to me then, because God knows what I would have thought. Now let me ask you something. You couldn't make the payments on the Whitestone house because you were waiting for your deals to come in right?"

"Well, yeah," Kirk answered.

"So what happened to the twenty- five grand you got at the closing?"

"Mike, before we got involved together I did a few deals with my brother, Ray, and he fucked some big people on them."

"Well, I heard there was a contract on him."

"There was, and there was one on me, too. That's where the $25,000 went. They were going to kill me."

"So you decided to go from one deal where you're going to be killed into another one where someone is going to kill you. That's pretty smart business, Kirk. Now what about the ten grand that was in the joint account? What the fuck did you do with that money, Kirk? That was supposed to be show money to get the loan for the Whitestone deal."

"Yeah, but that money was to buy me out of our partnership, anyway, so it was my money."

"Partnership...! What fucking partnership!? You got paid 35,000 dollars to live in Whitestone for 9 months free, while you fucked up my credit and didn't say a fucking word about it while I was sinking every dime I had into College Point!! I gave you an extra 10 grand for that???"

I don't really know what was holding me back from slapping the shit out of him, at this point in time. I think I was smart enough to know that, if I did touch him, I wouldn't be able to stop. And like I mentioned, I wasn't going to let myself get double fucked with him.

"Well, look, Kirk. You can say what you like. Maybe it will allow you to believe your bullshit. I'm not here for that okay? Because no matter how you cut it, you fucked up. I came here because Danny asked me to tell you that, because I gave him my word. I'm not going to kill you. Danny's also going to keep me updated on your progress, and once you get done paying him off, you're going to start paying me. Oh, one more thing, Kirk. I suggest that you go to church on Sunday and thank God."

I stood up to leave after I said that, and for a second I wondered if I should just slap him in his face, but I decided not to. I walked inside, said goodbye to Danny, and then I left.

A few weeks after this meeting, I got official word about the Whitestone house from the bank. The house was going to be sold at an auction if I didn't respond within 30 days. Just for the fuck of it, I felt like mailing out a copy to Richard and Sal and maybe one to Kirk.

Instead, I decided to call Sal, the attorney, and let him know that Richard was going to have to start worrying about his own shit now, especially since he wasn't getting a payment this month. Not that he should have gotten one after Kirk left, but live and learn, I guess.

For the last couple of weeks while driving back from Patti's house to College Point, while I was at the stop light by 20th Avenue. I noticed a bunch of black kittens playing close to the street, as they ran back and forth to a house that they must have lived in. There were few things in life that bothered me, and that was that I really didn't want to drive by one day and see one of these little suckers squished in the street if I didn't try to do anything about it. So one day I stopped when there were some kids playing in the yard.

"Are these your kittens?" I asked.
"Yes, they are," two kids said in harmony.
"Well, you know, if you leave them playing out by the street they could get run over."
"Yeah, we know, but our parents don't want us to bring them in the house."
"Well, why don't you try and give them away?"
"We asked, but nobody wants them."
"Well, I'm going to ask some people then okay?" I said as one of the little kittens ran up my pants leg, looked at me, and then jumped off and ran.

The kids started laughing, and one of them said, "Yeah, but nobody is going to want that one. He's the crazy one."
"Well, just because someone's crazy, that doesn't mean that they can't be a good friend, sometimes."

The kids looked at each other, laughed, and then continued playing. I guess I was getting a little too deep in my own philosophy for them.

After I left there, I went home to the College Point house. Within the last two weeks I went back to being a slumlord, by putting up with stories and chasing people for rent. Even Chris, my good tenant, was late. If there is only one lesson I learned from this real estate trip, it's this... Don't ever rely on the tenants to pay your mortgage. Have your mortgage covered by a business or your job, their rent money is just a bonus.

While I was making my rounds, I asked any of the tenants if they or anybody they knew wanted any kittens. None of them did, but they said they'd ask around.

Tony, now my new ex-old friend and new tenant, showed up this day. He was good for the rent for about 2 weeks, and then he got on my shit list. But to my surprise, Tony came over to me and says, "Mike, I've got the money I owe you, and I want to pay you for the whole month, too."

I was a bit shocked, needless to say. So I had to ask him where he got all of his money all of a sudden.

"Well, you remember Anthony Picarelli?"
"Yeah."
"You remember that he got into a little motorcycle accident?"
"I heard something about it," I answered.

"Yeah, well, he got a settlement from it."

"So he's giving you money to pay your bills?"

"No, we went in on a little business venture together."

"Oh, I see, how much did he get?"

"About 50-60 thousand."

"Really? You think he might want to invest in some real estate?"

"Yeah, he might. Here's his phone number; ask him yourself."

Because I wasn't 100 percent sure of my plans, I decided to hold off on calling Tony for now until I was a little more certain. It was good to know, I thought. I mean, I had known Anthony from the neighborhood and, even though he hung out with a younger crowd, we got along well and liked each other.

When I was coming home from Patti's house one day, I happened to be at the intersection where I would always see the black kittens playing, and there they were, playing out by the parked cars in the street. After the light changed, I pulled over and told the kids playing in the yard to get me the real crazy one because I was going to take him home.

Fuck it, I thought. I might not be able to save them all, but at least I can save the crazy one.

I put him in the car and started to drive home. It's a good thing I had the windows closed, because the kitten was screaming so loud I would have sounded like a police car to other motorists. Obviously he didn't like riding in a car.

When I got home, I called Patti and asked her what I should name the little guy. Between the two of us, we couldn't come up with anything that was good.

"I know. I'll call Megan and ask her. She always has good ideas," she said.

About ten minutes after we hung up, Patti called me back and said, "Megan came up with a great name."

Knowing that Megan worked in the cosmetic field I said, "Oh, great. What did she come up with? A name like lipstick?"

"No, I told her he was black, so she said that pepper was black so we should call him Pepper."

"Pepper? Like salt and pepper?"

"Yes."

"Hmmm, okay. Pepper it is. Hey kid, you just became a part of society and got a name, and it's Pepper."

Patti and I talked for a few more minutes, and then we hung up. After that Pepper took a leak on the rug, so I figured it might be a good time to get him some food and a litter box.

A day or two later I got a call from the tenants in Whitestone. They hadn't called me in quite some time, so I didn't have any idea why they were calling now.

"Listen," one of the sisters said. We just wanted to tell you that we were notified that the bank bought back the house here when it was auctioned off, and they gave us a little time to move out, so we're going to move."

"Well, thanks for telling me," I said sarcastically.

"Well, the reason why we're telling you is because we know you still have stuff here, so we'll be out in two weeks, and then you can get what you need."

"Well, thanks for the call then. Bye."

A few days after that I got a call from Sal, the attorney and Richard's friend.

"Mike, what are you going to do about Richard now?"

"Well, to be quite honest, Sal, I shouldn't have done what I did for him this whole time, because believe me, I could have done a lot of other things with that money. But now unfortunately he is on his own, like I've been. The way I look at it, Sal, is that I fulfilled Kirk's obligation to Richard for as long as I could. Now my hands are tied, and I don't know what you expect of me."

"Well, what about your other house? Don't you get money from over there?"

"You know, Sal, I know you're a pretty important attorney and all, but you really got a set of balls asking me about that other house. Because whether or not you want to admit it, you know now that Kirk set me up as a fall guy over there with a bunch of bullshit, and I still covered Rich's ass. And now you want me to take bread from somewhere else and still feed that abortion?"

"Well, first of all, Mike, I had no knowledge of any agreement that you had with Kirk. Bottom line is that you are responsible to Richard for about $65,000, and if he has to, he will put a lien on your other property."

"That's bullshit, but, in that case, let me break the bad news to you now and save you some legwork. I'm losing that house, too, so Rich is going to have to come up with another option for himself."

"Really?"

"Really!"

"Well, I'll tell him what you said."

"Please do. Have a nice day, Sal. Oh, and thanks for the call. Bye."

I called up the bank lawyer who was handling my mother's foreclosure that day, and after speaking with them, I was told that the house was going to be offered up for sale and that they wanted me to put a $22,000 down payment on it. After hanging up the phone I knew that I was about 5 grand short for the down payment money, and I wondered if Patti would lend me the money. The next problem I would have was getting the closing cost money. In order to pay them, I'd have to come up with about another $9,000, which meant that someone would have to work on the paperwork for me. I decided to ask Kirk's old lawyer, Michael Apple, if he could close on the deal, and he said he could.

With Kirk back in town, I didn't really feel 100 percent sure about letting Michael handle it, but I didn't really have too many other alternatives. I spoke with Patti and she agreed to lend me the money to make a profit on her money within 2 months. Then I called Michael again, and he told me he would handle the deal. With all that being said and done, I called up and made an appointment to, put a down payment, and get the ball rolling, to close on my mother's house.

During the course of the month, I called Michael at least 20 times to make sure everything was going all right with the paperwork, and he assured me that everything was fine.

On the day that was set for the closing on my mother's house, I was extremely happy that out of this whole mess I had been through at least I was going to be able to save my mother's house. That feeling lasted for only 40 minutes while I sat and waited for Michael, my attorney, to show up while I was sitting at the closing table with the bank's attorney and their representative. Finally the bank representative suggested that I try to call Michael's office. When I called there, I got his answering machine and told him that I couldn't believe that he hadn't shown up for the closing, and then I hung up. I turned back around to the bank representative and asked her if I could get a postponement. She looked at me and said that I couldn't. When I asked her why, she said that there were 2 reasons why she didn't want to give me a postponement. The first reason was because she had a builder on hold who wanted to buy the house for cash. The second reason was because I hadn't fired Michael, my attorney, when I was on the phone.

"Look," I said, "I'll call him back and fire him."
"I'm sorry. It's too late now."

I walked out of that office with my head hung so low I was scraping my chin on the concrete.

After trying to reach Michael on the phone for a few days, I decided that it wouldn't be a good idea to allow myself to get any more pissed off about him, so I stopped calling.

Within a week my mother got a letter from the Sheriff's office, telling her that she had three weeks to move before he came to evict her. The next couple of weeks were spent packing up 26 years of memories. Fortunately my mother had some good friends who not only helped with the packing, but they also volunteered to drive back and forth to the building upstate, which was a four- hour trip, 4 times. I also paid them some money to help

I knew my mother was very upset about the whole thing, but she tried to pretend that it was all being done on a happy note. She would even stop and reminisce about items that were being packed into the boxes. I would try to amuse her, but it was extremely difficult. I began to wonder if she might have been losing her mind a little bit.

CHAPTER 12

SHERMAN'S MARCH

I would have loved to have some time to be depressed about things, but I was too busy separating and packing my mother's and my things from her house. We lived there for 26 years, but now we had to be out by the end of the month. One day while I was packing, Gerald stopped by. He told me that he and Michael Baxter were going to Florida because a big hurricane named Andrew had hit down there and that there was tons of work to be had. Because I wasn't really in a position just to jump into a van with Gerald and drive down to Florida, I told Gerald to give me a call when he got down there and to tell me what it really looked like. Gerald agreed to do that and told me that he'd call in a few days.

My mother's friend made arrangements with her to drive to the building upstate and help unload their possessions with a friend of mine. The funny thing about this was that even though 4 truck-loads of important stuff were taken upstate, there were still 6 truckloads left in the house. Being that I had found out that the builder had gotten the deal and bought my mothers' house and that I knew that the house would be knocked down, I told friends in the neighborhood to go in and take what they wanted.

I would go to the house some nights after it was empty now and sit in Jim's room that the priest had blessed, the raven's room, staring at the trees, reviewing my life. Poor Jim, he had been here about two months after we bought the house, and he had lived here to the end. He actually had tears in his eyes the day he was moving out. He said to me, "Where am I going to go? This is my home."

It was sad to hear him say this, because, after all, it was his home to. I asked him where he might go, and he just shook his head, while looking at the ground, saying he didn't know.

Oddly, it felt nice to be at home now with nobody there. I think in the whole time that I had lived there, there were maybe a handful of times that nobody else was there. Because I had a specific time limit to enjoy this time at home, I felt the need to absorb as much of it as I could, because now it was priceless time that was definitely going to end. It was like I was paying my respects to an old friend and a dream that had died. What a fucking trip this house had been. I thought about the time that I first came to this house. I was sitting on the grass with my mother, and even though I loved the idea of the big lawn to play on, something about this big house had scared me. Maybe it was a premonition. I went there every night, walked the halls, and remembered all the times that were had in each room. For lack of a better explanation, it saddened me. After all the shit I went through in this house, all the money that went into 'deals' I couldn't save the farm, and I had to say goodbye.

Within two weeks the locks were changed. About week after that, they knocked the old girl down.

Gerald called me from Florida one day; he told me that he had never seen so much construction work in his life. I wasn't too convinced by Gerald's answers, so I asked him exactly how much work he was talking about. Gerald told me, from the miles and miles that he had traveled, there looked like years of work. Gerald finally convinced me to come down by telling me that after all I had been through in the last 2 years, I could probably use a week in the sun and call it a vacation anyhow.

I couldn't really argue with him when he put it that way. Besides, I probably could use a vacation, and it was starting to get cold out anyway. I told Patti that I was going to take a business trip down to Florida, and some of the details, but she was against it. While this was taking place, Mike Viale got out of jail after serving his ten years. I went to go meet him a couple of days after he got home out in Northport L.I. I was glad to see him, even though he was only twenty-nine years old, I could see that surviving in jail for ten years had aged him. I told him to come and live in my house in College Point until I lost it or until he got on his feet, but Mike explained that he was going to stay at his mother's house for a while.

"Mike, I don't think it's a good idea for you to come back to your old stomping ground. I think it would be better for you to come to a neutral setting until you got your cap screwed on tight," I said.
"What are you trying to say? I'm nuts?"
"No, not at all. What I'm trying to say is that I know when I got out, it took a couple of weeks for me to adjust to the outside world, and I was only in for a month. It's almost like the poor bastards that came back from Vietnam and thrown back into society. It's hard to adjust, and let's face it, Mike, you've been at war for ten years."
"Michael, look. You know I love you, man. But I'm gone. My life is over."
Mike... You're a young guy. You still got your whole life in front of you. This is what I mean about getting your cap screwed on tight."

Suddenly Mike's mood changed, and he almost sounded like he was growling while he was talking.

"They put me away for ten fucking years, Mike. Ten fucking years! I was a fucking puppy, and they caged me with full grown dogs. And for what? That fucking asshole who threatened to kick my ass for five blocks. I know, I know. Why did I have to kill him right? Mike, the first time I beat this motherfucker down I turned and walked away. And he jumped up, grabs a bottle, and cracks it across my head. So I turn around and made sure he wasn't getting up again. I didn't think he was going to fucking die. You saw the cuts on my head. I told them, but do you think the fucking cops put that in their report? No. You know why. Because I beat up one of their own when I hit that asshole cop with you that night at the hospital. And do you think in that report anyone said, "Oh, well, Officer Such and Such grabbed Mr. Viale by the hair, which caused him to drop his injured friend onto the floor. No. So they take ten years of my life, then throw me back into the world, and tell me you better be good or else. Well, fuck that. I am what they turned me into now, a fucking animal. I don't need to say this to anyone, Mike, and I won't say it to anyone else, but do you know how many guys I had to kill in jail just to survive...? Four. It was me or them... and it wasn't going to be me.

Mike paused and rubbed his eyebrows for a second as if he had a headache. Then he said, Mike, I know you love me and you're trying to look out for me. But don't worry...I'll be fine."

Even after he said that, I still tried to talk Mike into coming back with me, but he tried to reassure me that he would be fine out there.

Within two months Mike was arrested and charged with another murder. A few weeks after that, the D.A. gave him a deal, fifty years to life. Mike decided to do his own time, so he hanged himself in jail.

A couple of days after Mike died, I spoke to Patti's father about my plans in Florida. Her father told me that a very good friend of his had a son who was already working down there. He went on to explain that this son was working through a contractor, and he had plenty of work lined up.

Based on this information and the need for a vacation, I decided to go to Florida. It looked like an atomic bomb had gone off in some areas. There were some blocks that only had slabs left where the entire house had been blown away. It was eerie.

After seeing for myself the total devastation down there and hooking up with Reza's friend's son, I decided that it was a good idea to come back to Florida. My plan was to maybe get something going on with them, until I could get a Contractor's license, and then, start working for myself. Being that half of my tenants were old friends and most of them owed me back rent, I decided to send four of them down to Florida, along with Freddy Capeeto, and Jimmy Dugid, to start working for me. My idea was to send them down with a truck and some supplies to sell that were badly needed down there. It might pay for the expenses for sending the truck. After buying a truck, I loaded it up with supplies and sent them off. Because I was going to fly and meet them down there in a few days, it was decided that for now Patti would move into my house to collect rent for me while I was gone. A day before the guys got to Florida, I flew down to meet them. Before I left, I made sure to put the word on the street that if anybody messed with my cousin Dawn, I'd come back and cut their ears off.

Once I got down there, I had to set up work through Reza's friend's son. The only problem with that was that the work couldn't be started for two weeks.

I supported everyone until the work started and money started coming in, first with food and hotels. I was spending $100 per day on gas to drive from Ft. Lauderdale to Kendall every day, so I decided to rent a house down there instead. My guys weren't too happy the first week they worked when they were told that they had to pay me back from their pay. I mean it's not like they really had to think about the thousands of dollars I had already laid out.

This went on for two months until the house I was working on was almost completed, and I would be getting my final check which would be most of my profit. By that time I sent two of my friends back to New York. Mainly because I realized that I could hire guys in Florida for a fraction of what I paying my guys from New York. Getting food for my guys at lunch was a huge hassle now because there were only a few places open, and, or, had enough food for all the different trades that were working down there now. The line was so long at 7-11, it would take you a half hour to get food, and get out of there at the very least. That, along with drive time to find a place that had food took at least an hour and a half of my time each day. God forbid, if you had to go to Home Depo.

So, I come back with lunch one day, and everything is extremely quite on the jobsite. Freddy, is standing there, kinda just kicking the dirt, and I said, "What's up?"

"Well... you're not gonna want to hear this, but Jimmy cut his leg real bad with a circular saw."

As it turned out, Jimmy Dugid, had cut his thigh down to the bone with the circular saw. While this was going on, my new, partner is telling me for three weeks that he's not getting paid by the contractor. On that note, I decided to drive over to the contractor's house, and ask him what was going on. As it turned out, my "partner" was also partners with the contractor on jobs that I was getting, so he was double dipping on both ends. This was news to both of us. The contractor also informed me that he gave "my" partner a check, last week, for $3,000. I ended up having to call Rudy, and to make a long story short, my partner's father flew down to Miami, and paid me the $3000 that his son had spent. Shortly after this took place, the contractor showed up at the job and said, "Mike, I've got to tell you, you, and your crew are the fastest, and neatest workers I've ever seen. That's the good news. The bad news is that you're employee is suing me, so, I'm sorry, but you have to leave the job, today," he said as he pulled a check out of his pocket.

I took the check, told him I was sorry, than told my guys to pack up.

Even though all these seemingly bad things were talking place, I had hooked up with another contractor, and I lined up some smaller jobs, so all was not lost in my mind.

I had been visiting Jimmy, in the hospital, but after I heard he was suing the contractor, I stopped visiting him. Then, one day, he called me.

"Hey, Mike. What's up?"
"What's up? You're suing the contractor, so I got thrown off the job. That's what's up, Jimmy."
"Mike, I'm sorry, but this wasn't like a little cut. They had to call in a specialist to sew me back up, and they were telling me that they weren't sure how well I could walk again. Aside from that, there were lawyers here every day asking me if I wanted to sue. I don't even know how they found me, I never called them."
"Okay, so, I should be happy for you then... right," I said sarcastically.
"Mike, look, I didn't mean for you to get thrown off the job. When they started telling me that I might be walking on a cane for the rest of my life, I got scared, and started thinking about it. Look, if I get some money, you know I'm gonna hook you up. You've been taking care of me for months, at the very least, I owe you for that."
"Yeah, well, it's still fucked up Jimmy."
"Well, look. I'm gonna get released in a few days..."
"And?"

"And, I've got nowhere to go. I don't know anybody down here."

"Oh, great. So, what are you saying, I'm gonna be stuck with you again?"

"I got no place to go."

"Great. Fine, Jimmy."

"Thanks, Mike."

I swear, if it was anybody else, I might have told them to go to hell. But I've known Jimmy for like, twenty years, since we were kids.

There was another issue that was troubling me and that was the long-distance relationship I was having with Patti. One night, in the middle of an argument, I told her that I would stop what I was doing and I would come and get her. Within a week I made arrangements for me and Jimmy to fly back to New York, and it was decided that Freddy would stay and hold the fort.

When I got back, I found out that my cousin Dino had gotten out of jail after serving his ten years and was living with his father. We touched base, and I told Dino what I was doing. Even though it bothered me, I decided that after seeing what had happened with Mike V. in a short amount of time, I couldn't afford to take a risk with my cousin in Florida. I was hardly settled in myself.

Within a month I bought another truck, packed all of my stuff, all of Patti's things, and whatever Jimmy had. Because I hadn't lost the house in College Point yet, I did some repairs on it, and rented it out to one family. I had to spend some money, but it put a little more in my pocket then I had spent. Then we set off to Florida with Patti's small dog, Pom Pom, and my cat, Pepper, for the ride. It had taken me about a month to get going, and it wasn't a moment too soon because from the conversations I was having with Freddy, things didn't seem "fine" by the tone of his voice.

By the time I got halfway into Virginia the next morning, I was tired and decided to let Jimmy drive for part of the way while I took a nap. We pulled off at an exit and looked for a place to park. It was weird because usually every exit off I-95 had at least one gas station, but this one didn't. There was only an older abandoned gas station. As we pulled up to it, Jimmy started to sing the theme song from the Burt Reynolds movie "Deliverance." As we stretched ourselves Patti yelled at Pom Pom for drinking out of one of the muddy puddles next to the building. Then we got ready to leave. Before we did, I warned Jimmy to keep his eyes on all the water, oil and temperature gauges. Aside from that I told him he could drive like a nutcase if he wanted to, while I napped, as Pepper ran around the inside of the truck screaming like a police siren.

When I woke up, the first thing I saw was a sign with a weird-sounding Indian river on it. The second thing I did was to take a look at the gauges, and the first words out of my mouth were, "Jimmy, we've got no fucking oil pressure."

"Oh, shit. You're right. What should I do...?

"Well, how about pulling the truck over and turning off the motor...?!

No sooner was that said than the engine started knocking. I knew the engine had blown, and my first thought was to strangle Jimmy. Fortunately for Jimmy, I went with my next thought, which was to have Jimmy drive off the exit and find a gas station.

Once we got off the highway, we pulled into "Bubba's Garage." I had to rub my eyes for a second, because I could hardly believe the name of the place. It almost seemed like someone had put the garage there on purpose, being that it was in the middle of nowhere with only trees around. After Bubba confirmed my worst fear, we went into the office, and the mechanic got on what appeared to be a telephone. As he did this, Patti scolded Pom Pom for drinking out of another muddy puddle.

After ten long minutes, Bubba hung up the phone and told me that I was lucky because he had found a used motor for $2,000. He also told me that he would install it for another $1,000, but he'd waive the delivery charge for me, because the motor was in the next town. The worst part about this motor in my mind was that it was a junkyard motor for two-thousand dollars.

I explained to Bubba that, even though it was a very large truck, I had bought it for under $2,000 at a Post Office truck auction, and for that kind of money, it almost made sense to go back to New York and buy another one, shift loads and keep on going to Florida. Bubba shrugged his shoulders and told me to let him know what I wanted to do. He offered to ride us over to the town motel because he was closing, and he was heading that way anyhow.

After we got settled into the motel, I knew that I was kinda screwed because all I had between cash and credit cards was about $4,000. Aside from that, I knew I was getting screwed on the price of the motor.

The next morning I decided to make a few phone calls myself. To my surprise, after several phone calls, I found out was that Bubba wasn't using a telephone; he was using a type of CB radio, and every junk yard for miles around knew that I was broken down at Bubba's and needed a $2,000 motor. Not one to give up easily, I decided to call a bunch of other places. From the calls I made, nobody had my motor lying around, but I did find out that I could get a rebuilt motor for about $2,400.

A big problem I was facing was that, aside from the numbers I was now juggling for the truck repairs, Frankie had come clean about some things. He told me that, even though I had left him working with a contractor, the rent was past due and the electric had been turned off, which brought the immediate bills down there up to $850, not to mention my traveling expenses to get to Miami.

That night after dinner while, Pepper, was screaming at the door to go out, Patti was very worried because her dog seemed to be sick. The thing that really had Patti upset was that her dog might have drunk some antifreeze that could have been in the dirty puddle of water. Being that she had the dog for 14 years, it wouldn't be a good thing if something bad happened to him in my mind.

Everybody went to bed early that night, and the next morning at 6:30 there was a knock at the door. When I got up and opened it, there was an older colored man standing there. Thinking the guy must've gone to the wrong door, I announced to him which room it was. The colored man asked me if I was the man who was broken down with the truck. After I nodded my head, the colored man told me that I ought to throw some clothes on and shake a leg, because my ride to find a motor wasn't going to be standing outside all morning, waiting for him. On that note, I ran inside, threw my clothes on, kissed Patti goodbye, and thanked God for sending me an angel before I ran outside and jumped into the colored guy's pickup truck. This was the start of a 2-week odyssey.

About a week into this odyssey I found a motor for $250. Then I had found someone to install it for $700, which would take another couple of days. During this time Patti's dog got very sick and was going to the veterinarian in the next town over almost every day for all types of tests. Jimmy had also accidentally let my cat out of the room, and the cat would be seen from time to time running off doing cart-wheels into the woods. During one of the visits to the mechanics shop, that was twenty miles away, Jimmy, possibly out of boredom or possibly to get the mechanic to start moving his ass, told the owner of the shop in private that they were hauling mail for the U.S. Post Office. The truck was an old postal truck, so the guy must have believed Jimmy. At 6:30 the next morning, his cousin- the sheriff- came and knocked on the door.

When I answered the door, the sheriff went on to explain that nobody was under arrest at this time, but that he had personally contacted the postal inspector who handled the eastern seaboard of the United States last night and that he was driving down from Washington, D.C., that morning so that, as he put it, we can get to the bottom of this. I tried to explain to the sheriff that it was all a big mistake and that he should cancel the postal inspector's visit, but the sheriff didn't want to hear any of it. I decided that I would quit trying, because I needed a ride over to check on the progress of the truck anyhow.

After the postal inspector arrived, I pulled him to the side, and told him that this was all a misunderstanding. He put his hand to his head, and said, "Well, I drove all morning, I might as well take a look anyhow."

Everybody drove in the sheriff's car to the auto shop, and the sheriff had the enthusiasm as if he had broken the crime of the century. For the next half hour we had to listen to all the "big" cases he was involved in. He was driving particularly slow, and one part of me wanted to tell him to shut the fuck up, and drive, but I figured that this, outburst, might not help my cause. His deputy arrived shortly after we did.

When we got there, the sheriff asked me to unlock the back door of the truck. The first shock he got was the smell of the full kitty litter box that hadn't been emptied. He looked at all the boxes, and furniture, as the postal inspector placed his hand back on his forehead, and said to me, "Okay, start unloading it."

I looked back at him and said, "Yeah... No. If you need to see what else is in there, you're gonna have ta' do it yourself. And it looks like rain, so please get it back in before it does."

The sheriff started stuttering for a minute, and then he looked at his deputy and said, "Well, go on. Get in there."

"C'mon, sheriff, there no mail in there," the deputy said.
"I don't care what you think- Get!" The sheriff said as he pointed into the truck.

The two of them played around in the back of the truck for about twenty minutes, and I went to talk to the mechanic, then we all left. Along the ride back the sheriff had the pride of a mouse, and didn't let out a squeak the entire ride back.

The day that the truck was finished, I finally caught my cat, and Patti was waiting to be picked up at the vet's. It turned out that her dog was very sick, it was determined that he had drunk some antifreeze, and his liver was failing. Patti decided that we had to drive to Georgia that night where there was a huge animal medical center and have Pom Pom put on a kidney dialysis machine, at two hundred dollars an hour.

I went and picked up the truck. Then I went back to the motel, packed, paid the balance of the bill there, and went to get Patti and Pom Pom. While I was back tracking and driving through the next town to get Patti, the truck broke down and appeared to overheat. Fortunately it was close to an auto parts store, so I drove it over to their lot. The auto parts guys, Jimmy, and I all determined that the thermostat on the truck must have frozen, so it needed to be replaced. I decided to call Patti from the auto parts place and tell her the problem I was now handling. Patti was very upset, and she told me to hurry up because the dog didn't look like he was doing that well. I told her I would and gave her the phone number there just in case.

While I changed the thermostat, one of the bolts snapped, and I went into the auto parts place and asked them for their advice. The owner, who was there, suggested that I use a tap and die set to get the bolt out and re-thread the hole to a 9mm size, even though it was metric, it would be the next size up the chart. The owner even offered to loan me his electric drill to help out, which I thought was very nice.

After everything was done, I went back inside and asked the owner for a 9mm bolt, and the owner told me that they didn't carry a 9mm bolt.

My first thought was to ask him if he was born an idiot, or if he thought it just took some time to become one. Instead, I went with my second thought.

"You're shitting me, right?"
"Nope. I only carry standard size here."
"You suggest that I go with 9mm, sell me the bit I need, loan me your drill, and electric, and I'm screwed now, because I didn't ask you if you carried a 9mm bolt."
"Yep. I thought you might'a had one."

I decided not to jump over the counter and strangle the good ol' boy, I asked him for a phone book instead. The first place I decided to call was a Mercedes auto parts dealer. It was close to 5 pm when I called, and I hoped that the place didn't close early and found myself very happy when someone answered the phone. I asked the Mercedes technician for a 9mm bolt, and the guy asked me for a parts number. After explaining my situation, I was told that, without a part number, he couldn't help me, and he hung up. Instead of running over there and strangling this guy, I got more change for the phone, and called a few more places that might have this size bolt. I kept being put on hold, and it was getting closer and closer to 5 pm.

Not having much luck over the phone, I thought that it would be better if I drove to some of these locations in person. I went back into the auto parts place and asked the owner how far away some of the places were that I had called, and the owner told me that they were all downtown, which was about 8 blocks away. With that information I ran out to my truck and un-buried a ten-speed bicycle I had in the truck. Then I headed for downtown. I rode as fast as I could and stopped into about 8 stores before 5pm, but nobody had a 9mm bolt. The anger and stupidity of my predicament finally overwhelmed me to the point where I had to sit down at a bus stop and just peacefully watch the world flow by. But there had to be something I could do, I thought. There just had to be something.

Then in the stillness of insanity, I came up with the perfect solution. Instead of changing the bolt one size up to a 9mm, I should have gone just one size bigger and turned the threaded hole back into a regular standard bolt size. Now my main concern was that either the auto place was open later than 5, or Jimmy hadn't said or done something dumb enough to make that place close before 5 or worse, I thought, as I peddled my ass off back to the auto parts store.

When I got there, I dropped the bike out front, walked inside, and said while huffing and puffing as nice as possible to the owner, "I could take the tap and die set and thread this thing one size higher and turn it back into a regular bolt – can't I!"
"Well, yeah, I guess," the owner said.
"And you do have that size bolt in stock, don't you?"
"Yeah, we got that bolt," he answered.
"Fine, charge me for what I'll need then," I said through clenched teeth and a big smile.

I got everything I needed and then went outside to start to work. The first thing I needed to do before I started re-threading the hole was to drill out the cast iron cover plate that the bolt had to go through. By the time I got done drilling through the cast iron cover plate, one of the counter guys came out and handed me a bolt.

"What's this?" I asked.
"Well, my boss felt bad about your situation, so he had one of us make you a 9mm bolt," he answered.

While steam was blowing out of my ears I thanked the guy and told him as nicely as possible that they were so nice for helping me. After the guy walked inside, I told Jimmy to go inside and thank the owner, because I felt that if I went in there to thank him I would definitely kill him.

I finally finished the truck, and then I went to go and pick up Patti. The veterinarian had Patti's dog, Pom Pom, hooked up to an I.V. bottle and gave us two needles filled with steroids in case Pom Pom seemed to be getting very weak on the journey, in order to jumpstart his body. After paying the $300 bill, we went outside, and I told Jimmy to drive so that I could hold up the I.V. bottle for Pom Pom.

By now it was getting late in the day, and I knew we would be hitting rush hour traffic, but it didn't matter because I only had one thought on my mind, and that was to get out of Thornsburg, Virginia.

I hadn't realized it but in order to pick Patti up I had to backtrack through 2 towns before I was able to get back onto Interstate 95, which meant I would have to pass next through the town of Thornsburg again.

While we were driving, I noticed the weird sounding river sign again, as I was explaining to Patti and Jimmy that this was the same sign I had seen once I woke up on our first drive two weeks ago, a fire started in the dashboard of the truck. Jimmy looked at me, as the cab of the started to fill with smoke, and screamed, "What should I do, we're on fire!"

I looked at him calmly, and said, "Keep driving until we reach the other side of this town."

Jimmy looked at me for a long second in the smoke-filled cab and asked me if that was really what I wanted him to do. I looked back at him for a long second and said, "Okay, fine. Stop, and we'll put the fire out first."

It was weird, for a split second, I really didn't give a flying fuck about anything while everything was spinning out of control, but then I came to my senses.

As we jumped out of the truck and lifted the cab-over, the first thing to go out was the windshield from a wrench that was laying in the back of the cab. Once the cab was fully turned over, I could see the wire that was burning like a fuse, so without thinking about any harm to myself, I grabbed it and yanked it out while it was burning. While this was going on, a state trooper pulled up to see if he could help out. As Jimmy was running around the truck yelling out loud how he couldn't believe this was happening, Patti was knelt down by the side of the highway with my cat, that had just recently been shoved into a cat carrier, holding an intravenous bottle over her head in one arm while cradling her dog in the other, as she stared into the distance, repeating to herself how she should have never left New York.

While I was explaining to the state trooper about how we had been broken down in this town for a month and just had the motor replaced, Patti yelled out, "Where's Pom Pom's needles?"

On that note the state trooper said, "Are you carrying any illegal drugs in this vehicle?"
"No Officer, it's..." I started.
"Do you mind if I check the vehicle?" he added as he put his hand on his handgun.
"Well, Officer, I could probably save you a lot of trouble if you were to call the man responsible for delivery of all U.S. mail on the eastern seaboard in Washington, D.C. I believe his name was Dave, or you could call the sheriff of Thornsburg and ask him if we were carrying anything illegal in this truck. I'm sure he'd be happy to answer you, and..., quite frankly, I'd love to see you do that," I said dryly.

The state trooper did not understand, nor was he amused by my comments. After he had Jimmy, and I, raise our hands, and place them on the side of the truck, Patti had to actually produce the receipt from the vet's office until he did understand about the needles. The truck eventually did start up, but I decided to drive the truck off at the next exit and park it at Bubba's garage so that he could check it in the morning.

The state trooper offered to drive everybody to the nearest motel, and I explained to him that I knew where there was a good one.

That night, Pom Pom, started to die. I gave Jimmy 20 dollars, and told him to get lost at the truck stop down the road until I came to get him. Everybody in Patti's family always joked about not wanting to be around when he died, and now, I would have to be the strong one to walk her through this with her little boy. Well, that didn't work as planned, cause I was a blubbering wreck. She had him wrapped in a towel, lying on the bed, looking into his eyes, telling him, 'It's okay, Pom Pom. Mommy knows, you can go now. It's okay.' And he's letting out these little cries cause he knows he's dying. It was one of the saddest scenes, and my heart was breaking for both of them. But, Patti, was calm, cool, and loving, through the whole thing. As this sad situation is taking place, Jimmy, is knocking on the door, asking me if he could come in and watch TV now because he's bored. I felt like opening the door and cracking him across his face with a bat because this was the third time I told him to leave. I even got down on one knee, and asked God to either take him, or take a year from me, and give it to him. Pom Pom died shortly after that.

I decided to take a little walk down the road after it was over. As I got out to the front of the motel I crossed the street to take a look at the moonlit historical sign that was there. As a child they would always fascinate me on trips with my mother and cousins. I would always make my mother pull up alongside them so I could read them.

For a second after reading this one, I didn't know whether to laugh or cry because the marker said, "On this spot General Lee camped with his men for several days while he decided to either fight his way up north or to turn around to go home."

It numbed me after reading it, because in the back of my mind, I had a similar thought rolling in my head.

The next day Patti decided that she wanted her dog to be buried at her mother's home. Because she had lost something so precious to her, I knew better than to argue with her. I picked up the truck and paid for it. Then I went and got some dry ice, a plastic cooler, head gasket sealer, a drill, and screws and shipped her dog back to New York in the airtight cooler. Needless to say, Patti was quite upset the next day when the shipping company tried to explain to her that they had lost the package and asked if it was considered perishable.

When we finally did get to the house in Florida, the first thing we saw when we pulled up was my other truck sitting there with 2 flat tires. When we went inside, Freddy was there but all of my stuff wasn't. He told me that, because he was staying with some family members who lived in Florida part-time, he didn't trust the stuff alone in the house. So he took it to his cousins' house and swore that he would get it and bring it all back that night. I knew he was bullshitting me, and it took a lot of energy not to kick the shit out of him, but, it was Freddy, and he was like a brother to me. Aside from that, I never expected to leave him alone down here this long when I left, so, a part of me was to blame. I pretended to take his word for it, and let him leave. It was the last time I would see Freddy.

The first thing I did after that was to call the contractor I had been stalling and, because I no longer had any tools, I told him that I couldn't work for him. Then I paid the two month's rent that was due and had the phone and electric turned back on. That all took about three days.

Patti was not only upset by the house being in a bad neighborhood with no beach in the area, but, being that the shipping company still could not find the lost package, it compounded her feelings about her dog's death. When they told Patti that they were willing to replace the contents, she dropped the phone, placed her face in a pillow, and started to cry. I picked up the phone, and asked them to start a trace on the package, and then I tried to console her.

I had fought so hard, to get to Florida, but now, with the situation I was in, it seemed all for nothing. Needless to say after all this time, and money, I felt like a popped balloon.

Patti was usually a happy-go-lucky type of person, but by now she was on the edge. One of her first demands was that Jimmy get some type of job and help me to support himself, which he eventually did. I think she also took on the persona that she had seen in me for some time, and it was good timing, on her part, because I was a little shell-shocked from the whole experience.

By now my cat, Pepper, was also on edge about being a prisoner on this voyage and would look for any opportunity to get himself outside. After another day of him howling to go out, I decided to let him out at night, and bring him back inside in the morning.

The next day, Pepper came home with another cat that had no tail, and they seemed to act like long lost friends. Being that the cat seemed very tame and friendly, I told Patti that one of the saddest things I had seen in this area that the hurricane had hit was that there were far too many stray animals, and we talked about keeping him.

A few days later while I was sitting outside waiting to drive Jimmy to work in the morning, he walked out and noticed a big black ball of fur out in the street. It was my cat; he had been run over by a car. I didn't have the heart to tell Patti after I had buried him, but, after watching her walk around the neighborhood calling his name for two days, I decided to tell her. It was very heart wrenching, she was very upset, and it rehashed everything in her mind.

"Why? Why did we come here? So my animals could die? There are no fucking stores. No fucking neighbors. No fucking beaches. What the fuck did you bring me here for!?! Because I was to fucking happy with my life in New York? Is that why?"

It made me feel like shit. The only silver lining in it for me was that I was already pretty numb from the last few months.

Sometime during that week Patti got herself a part-time job but I wasn't quite ready to go to work for someone for $10 per hour which is what they wanted to pay experienced people down here. My state of mind was still reeling from going from playing with the Big Boys to practically being a busboy over night. I knew I was going to have to turn up the flame soon, but right now just wasn't the time. Besides that, I had put one of my trucks up for sale and already had a few offers on it, so I knew I could float for a little while.

Jimmy was unfazed by the whole turn of events. I almost envied him, I mean, what the fuck, this was like some big vacation for him, and I had footed the bill. Why should he be depressed about it?

Within the next few weeks, the tailless cat had made my home his home, Patti found a dog roaming the streets that was identical to her dog, and I sold a truck and paid the rent. A few days after paying the rent, the landlord told me that the house had been sold, and I needed to move out by the end of the month. It didn't really matter to me that the landlord had asked me to move because living and being there left a bad taste in my mouth from a dream that had died there anyhow.

I decided that I wanted to move out of Miami altogether, so I drove up to Fort Lauderdale and stopped at a supermarket to see if they had any rental guides like they did in the Miami grocery stores. After I couldn't find any, I asked one of the checkout girls if the store carried any, and she said that they were all out of them. As I was about to leave, a guy standing in line paying for his groceries asked me what type of a place I was looking for. I told him that I needed a two-bedroom apartment that had a pool, would take a small dog and cat, and would allow me to park my 16-foot box truck there overnight, and was close to the beach. The guy told me that everything I had asked for was fine except for the fact that the place was only a one-bedroom. I looked back at him and said I'd take it.

By the end of that week the truck was packed, and we moved to Ft. Lauderdale. When we got there, Jimmy complained that the place was only a one-bedroom apartment, and Patti explained to him that maybe that would inspire him to work on getting his own place so that we could finally live alone. I didn't add anything to what Patti had said because, after supporting Jimmy for too long, I was tired of having him around also. For the next couple of days, Patti got up in the morning and just about threw Jimmy out of the house and warned him not to come home until 5 pm unless he had himself a job.

After two days of searching, Jimmy came home at lunchtime and told Patti that he had gotten a job and that he would be starting it in 2 weeks. Patti told Jimmy to get up off the couch and to go out and find a job that he would start tomorrow, because he wasn't going to sit around the apartment for 2 weeks doing nothing. With that, Jimmy left. Jimmy came back that night and told me that he had gotten in touch with a relative in the area and that he was going to move in with him. After Patti asked Jimmy why he hadn't done it sooner, the two of them began to argue.

Before Jimmy had arrived, I was sitting on the couch drinking a cup of coffee, relaxing, and the last thing I wanted to hear was the guy I had been supporting for months standing there yelling at Patti. So I told Jimmy to leave, and go for a walk. Jimmy stopped arguing with Patti, looked at me, and said, "That's it!" and charged at me with his head down.

One part of me told me to jump up and kick Jimmy in his face to end Jimmy's charge, but after taking into consideration how many years I knew Jimmy, I decided to grab Jimmy in a headlock and then just wrestle him out the door. What I didn't take into consideration was the force and speed that Jimmy was running with. Jimmy tackled me as we both fell backwards over the couch.

I had Jimmy in a real good headlock by the time we both flipped over the couch and landed on the floor. Jimmy wasn't going to be able to go anywhere, so in order for this to end without anyone getting hurt, I told Patti to call the police. Patti calmly reminded me that our phone hadn't been installed yet, and I told her I knew that and suggested that maybe she could go and use one of the neighbor's phones in the building as I wrestled with Jimmy. No sooner did Patti walk out the door when Jimmy started frantically grabbing at the coffee table. By the time I realized that Jimmy was trying to grab the coffee cup off the table, it was too late. Even though Jimmy couldn't see my head he had a good enough idea where his target was and proceeded to pound it against the top of my head.

After the 2nd shot the cup had broken, and now all that Jimmy was doing was smashing the jagged edge against the top of my head. Having bled many times before, I realized that the warm sweat I felt was blood covering my face. By the 6th shot what was left of the cup was gone, and now I was attempting to break Jimmy's neck. About halfway into this, Patti walked back inside, saw all the blood, yelled, and then ran into the kitchen and grabbed a huge knife. When she ran back over to us I was still lying on my back holding Jimmy in a headlock, while Jimmy was on top of me in the position that we had fallen to the floor. Patti put the tip of the knife onto Jimmy's back, placed her other hand on top of the handle, and shouted, "Should I do it? Should I do it, Michael...? I'll stab him right through his heart! Is this where his heart is, or the other side??"

"NO, NO, NO! Patti...! Don't do it, don't do it!" I shouted, as Jimmy gurgled from me strangling him.

While I was lying there, holding Jimmy in a headlock, tasting my own blood, staring into my girlfriend's eyes, while she is holding a knife, asking me if she should kill him, I laughed, I had to. It was so absurd, my entire life journey, led me to this moment in time. It was so fucking sad, and pathetic, I just had to laugh.